FIFTH EDITION

A History of Modern Psychology

Duane P. Schultz
University of South Florida

Sydney Ellen Schultz

Harcourt Brace Jovanovich College Publishers
Fort Worth Philadelphia San Diego New York Orlando Austin
San Antonio Toronto Montreal London Sydney Tokyo

ISBN: 0-15-537467-2

Library of Congress Catalog Card Number: 91-73220

Printed in the United States of America

Photo and Illustration Credits

Cover, The Image Bank West/Chris Alan Wilton © 1991; Figure 2-1,
p. 28, The National Museum of American History, Smithsonian
Institution; p. 50, National Portrait Gallery, London; p. 96. The
Bettmann Archive; p. 115, Department of Manuscripts, University
Archives, Olin Library, Cornell University; p. 147, The Bettmann
Archive/Hulton; p. 170, The Bettmann Archive; p. 218, Ferdinand
Hamburger, Jr. Archives, The Johns Hopkins University; p. 224,
Frontispiece, Poffenberger, A. T. (Ed.), (1947), *James McKeen Cattell,
Man of Science*. Vol. 1, *Psychological Research*. Lancaster, PA: The
Science Press; p. 239, Culver Pictures; p. 253, courtesy Western
Electric; p. 263, Manuscripts and Archives, Yale University Library;
p. 269, Office of Public Information, Columbia University; Figure 9-1,
p. 273, After Thorndike, 1898, as reproduced in J. C. Burnham, 1972,
"Thorndike's puzzle boxes," *Journal of the History of the Behavioral
Sciences*, Brandon, VT: Clinical Psychology Publishing Co.; Figure 9-2,
p. 281, Yerkes, R. M., and Margulis, S. (1909) The method of Pavlov
in animal psychology. *Psychological Bulletin*, 6:257–73; p. 313,
Ferdinand Hamburger, Jr. Archives, The Johns Hopkins University; p.
316, Reproduced by permission, University Archivist, The Bancroft
Library, University of California; p. 350, Nina Leen/Life Magazine ©
Time Warner Inc.; p. 380, The Bettmann Archive; p. 384, Swarthmore
College; p. 397, courtesy Yerkes Photo Lab, Emory University; p. 436,
© Mary Evans/Sigmund Freud Copyrights; p. 492, AP/Wide World; p.
506, The City College of New York/CUNY; p. 510, © Ted Polumbaum;
p. 513, courtesy Center for the Studies of the Person, La Jolla; p. 519,
The Bettmann Archive; p. 522, © Office of Communications, Princeton
University; p. 525, photo by Billy Howard © Emory University. Photos
on the following pages are courtesy of the Archives of the History of
American Psychology, University of Akron; pp. 61, 105, 107, 175, 190,
193, 204, 265, 289, 324, 333, 339, 342, 382, 405, 433, 461, 473, 486,
and 503.

Photos courtesy of the National Library of Medicine: pp. 30, 39, 47, 64,
68, 80, 102, 154, 215, 276, 416, 423, 463, and 480.

Preface

The focus of this book is the history of modern psychology, that period beginning in the late nineteenth century when psychology became a separate and primarily experimental discipline. Although we do not ignore earlier philosophical thought, we concentrate on that which relates directly to the establishment of psychology as a new and distinct field of study. We are presenting a history of modern psychology, not of psychology and all the philosophical work that preceded it.

We have chosen to recount the history of psychology in terms of its great ideas or schools of thought. Since the formal beginning of the field in 1879, psychology has been defined in various ways as new ideas have captured the loyalty of large numbers of adherents and come, for a time, to dominate the field. Our interest, then, is in the developing sequence of ideas put forth to define psychology's subject matter, methods, and goals.

Each of the schools of thought is discussed as a movement growing out of its historical context and not as an independent or isolated entity. Contextual forces, denoted by contemporary historians as the "new" history, include not only the intellectual spirit of the times (the Zeitgeist), but also social, political, and economic factors.

Although this book is organized in terms of the schools of thought — the different definitions that mark the evolution of psychology — we recognize that these ideas and approaches are the work of scholars, researchers, and systematizers. It is, after all, human beings, not abstract forces, who write the articles, conduct the research, present the papers, and teach the next generation of psychologists. In so doing, these men and women have developed and promoted psychology's schools of thought. We, therefore, discuss the lives of these pivotal individuals who shaped the field, noting that their work was influenced not only by the times in which they flourished but also by the personal context of their own experiences.

Finally, we discuss each school of thought in terms of its connection to the great ideas and theories that preceded and followed it. We describe how each school evolved from or revolted against the existing order, and how each in its turn inspired points of view that challenged, opposed, and eventually replaced it. Thus, with the hindsight of history, we can trace a pattern, a continuity of development within the field of psychology.

Preparing the fifth edition of this textbook almost a quarter century after writing the first one, and seeing how much there is to add, delete, revise, and elaborate on, is vivid testimony to the dynamic nature of the history of psychology. It is not fixed or finished but is in a state of change and growth. There is an enormous amount of scholarly work being produced, translated, and published on persons, issues, methods, and theories in the history of psychology. Accordingly, we have added more than 200 new references to this edition.

A significant addition to the fifth edition is the explicit recognition of the new history, that is, the influence on psychology of social, economic, and political contextual forces. A discussion of these factors is included in Chapter 1, and examples have been noted throughout the book. Also, we have cited in virtually every chapter instances of new, refined, or revised data of history that continue to affect our understanding of the field.

Another change here is a greater emphasis on the role and importance of applied psychology within the history of psychology in the United States. Acting on the enthusiastic response to the applied-psychology material in the last edition, and reflecting the impact of contextual forces at the end of the nineteenth and beginning of the twentieth centuries, we have expanded the coverage of applied psychology and placed it where the movement began, as a legacy of the functionalist school of thought. In addition to the applied contributions of Hall and Cattell, we have included the work of Witmer, Scott, and Münsterberg.

The contextual factors of prejudice and discrimination within the academic and professional establishments are given increased coverage as they apply to opportunities for women and African-Americans in the history of psychology.

Other features of this edition include new material on the lives of prominent psychologists to demonstrate how personal experiences may have influenced their work; the reinstatement of John Stuart Mill, along with his notion of mental chemistry and his call for a science of psychology; the role of the unconscious in structuralism, functionalism, and behaviorism; the cognitive challenge within behaviorism and the ideas of Bandura and Rotter. Also included are Freud's suppression of the seduction theory, experimental tests of Freudian concepts, ego psychology, object-relations theory, and the work of Anna Freud; a reevaluation of the influence of humanistic psychology; and the works of Miller and Neisser and the development of the cognitive psychology movement.

We have expanded the introductions to the five original source articles by explaining the purpose of exposing students to this material and listing the major points covered by each theorist. These articles describe in the theorists' own words their unique approach to psychology and show today's readers the kind of material studied by earlier generations of college students.

Illustrative tables, figures, and photographs are presented throughout the book, along with chapter outlines and annotated reading lists. Important terms are highlighted where they are defined, and a reference list is included at the back of the book. A test item file is available for instructors.

We are grateful to the many instructors and students who have contacted us over the years with valuable suggestions. The book has benefited throughout its history from the rigorous and perceptive evaluations of Ludy T. Benjamin, Jr., of Texas A & M University. We also wish to thank the other reviewers of this edition who offered insightful and timely comments: Douglas P. Boer, Concordia College, Alberta, Canada; Gerald S. Clack, Loyola University, New Orleans; D. Brett King, Colorado State University; and Michael Scavio, California State University, Fullerton. At Harcourt Brace Jovanovich, Niamh Foley-Homan proved to be a source of encouragement, enthusiasm, and stability during a difficult transitional period. We appreciate her attention to all facets of this project.

D.P.S.
S.E.S.

Contents

CHAPTER 8
The Legacy of Functionalism: Applied Psychology   210

CHAPTER 13
Psychoanalysis: The Beginnings   412

CHAPTER 14
Psychoanalysis: Dissenters and Descendants   458

CHAPTER 15
Beyond the Schools of Thought: More Recent Developments   497

The Study of the History of Psychology

1

From the most ancient subject we shall produce the newest science.

Hermann Ebbinghaus
On Memory

The Development of Modern Psychology

We begin with a paradox, a seeming contradiction, by noting that psychology is one of the oldest of the scholarly disciplines as well as one of the newest. Interest in psychology can be traced to the earliest inquiring minds. We have always been fascinated by our own behavior, and speculations about human nature and conduct fill many philosophical and theological volumes. As early as the fifth century B.C., Plato, Aristotle, and other Greek scholars grappled with many of the same problems that concern psychologists today: memory, learning, motivation, perception, dreaming, and abnormal behavior. The same kinds of questions currently

1

being asked about human nature were asked centuries ago, which shows a vital continuity in subject matter from the past to the present day.

Although the intellectual precursors of psychology are as ancient as those of any discipline, the modern approach to psychology began little more than one hundred years ago. The centennial of the birth of modern psychology was commemorated in 1979.

The distinction between modern psychology and its antecedents is found less in the kinds of questions asked about human nature than in the methods used to seek the answers to those questions. It is the approach taken and the techniques employed that distinguish the older discipline of philosophy from modern psychology and denote the emergence of psychology as a separate, primarily scientific, field of study.

Until the last quarter of the nineteenth century, philosophers studied human nature through speculation, intuition, and generalization based on their own limited experience. A transformation occurred when philosophers began to apply the tools and methods that had already proved successful in the biological and physical sciences to questions about human nature. Only when researchers came to rely on carefully controlled observation and experimentation to study the human mind did psychology begin to attain an identity separate from its philosophical roots.

The new discipline of psychology needed to develop more precise and objective ways of dealing with its subject matter. Much of the history of psychology, after its separation from philosophy, is the story of the continual refinement of tools, techniques, and methods of study to achieve increased precision and objectivity in both its questions and its answers.

If we are to understand the complex issues that define and divide psychology today, then the proper starting point for the history of the field is the nineteenth century, the time when psychology became an independent discipline with distinctive methods of inquiry and theoretical rationales. We cannot deny that the early philosophers and scholars speculated on problems concerning human nature; certainly they did. "When we examine the topics now filling the literature in professional psychology," wrote Daniel Robinson, a historian of psychology at Georgetown University, "we are hard pressed to find one that was not put forth, often in a form still to be improved on, [in] the nineteenth century" (Robinson, 1981, pp. 390–391). But the influence of those early scholars on the development of psychology as a separate and primarily experimental science is limited.

Only in the last hundred years or so have psychologists defined the subject matter of psychology and established its foundation, thus confirming its independence from philosophy. The early philosophers concerned themselves with problems that are still of general interest, but they approached these problems in ways vastly different from those of today's psychologists. Those early scholars were not *psychologists* in the contemporary usage of the term, and we will discuss their ideas only as they relate directly to the establishment of modern psychology.

The idea that the methods of the physical and biological sciences could be applied to the study of mental phenomena was inherited from both the philosophical thinking and the physiological investigations of the seventeenth to nineteenth centuries. That exciting era forms the immediate background out of which modern psychology emerged. While the nineteenth-century philosophers were clearing the way for an experimental attack on the functioning of the mind, the physiologists were independently approaching some of the same problems from a different direction. Nineteenth-century physiologists were making great strides toward understanding the bodily mechanisms that underlie mental processes. Their methods of study differed from those of the philosophers, but the eventual union of these disparate disciplines — philosophy and physiology — produced a field of study in which, at least in its formative years, an attempt was made to preserve the conflicting traditions and beliefs of each. Fortunately, the new psychology quickly succeeded in attaining an identity and stature of its own.

The first sign of a distinct field of inquiry known as psychology came in the last quarter of the nineteenth century when the scientific method was adopted as the means for attempting to solve psychology's problems. During that period there were several formal indications that psychology was beginning to flourish. In December of 1879, in Leipzig, Germany, Wilhelm Wundt established the world's first psychology laboratory. In 1881 he founded the journal *Philosophische Studien* (*Philosophical Studies*), which is considered to be the first journal of psychology to be largely devoted to experimental reports.

In 1887, G. Stanley Hall founded the *American Journal of Psychology*, the first psychology journal published in the United States. And in 1888, the University of Pennsylvania appointed James McKeen Cattell, an American who had studied with Wundt, to be professor of psychology, the first such professorship in the world. Until then, psychologists had received appointments in philosophy departments. Cattell's position gave psychology recognition in academic circles as an independent discipline.

Between 1880 and 1895, dramatic and sweeping changes occurred in American psychology. During that time, twenty-six psychology laboratories and three psychology journals were established. The American Psychological Association (APA), the first scientific and professional organization of psychologists, was founded in 1892. The association marks its centennial in 1992 with a special issue of the journal *American Psychologist* devoted to the history of psychology.

William McDougall, a British psychologist, defined psychology in 1908 as the "science of behavior," apparently the first use of this phrase. Thus, by the early part of the twentieth century American psychology had succeeded in gaining its independence from philosophy, developing laboratories in which to apply the methods of science, forming its own scientific association, and giving itself a formal definition as a science — the science of behavior.

Once the new discipline had been launched, it grew rapidly, particularly in the United States, which assumed and maintains a position of dominance in the psychological world. Today more than half the world's psychologists work in the United States, and a great many psychologists from other countries have received at least a portion of their training at United States institutions. The major share of the world's psychological literature is published in the United States. The American Psychological Association, established with twenty-six charter members, grew to include eleven hundred psychologists by 1930. By 1991, the membership stood at more than one hundred thousand.

This population explosion of psychologists has been paralleled by an information explosion of research reports, theoretical and review articles, computer data files, books, films, videocassettes, and other forms of publication. It is increasingly difficult for psychologists to remain knowledgeable about developments beyond their own specialty areas.

Psychology has grown not only in terms of its practitioners, researchers, scholars, and published literature, but also in its impact on our daily lives. Whatever your age, occupation, or interests, your life is influenced in some ways by the work of psychologists.

The Relevance of the Past for the Present

You are probably taking this course because you have to, because your psychology department requires it for an undergraduate or graduate degree. If so, you are certainly not alone. Most college departments of psychology in the United States demand such a course, and periodic surveys on how best to prepare both undergraduate and graduate students for a career in psychology continue to urge the study of the history of the field (see Hilgard, Leary, & McGuire, 1991; McGovern, 1990; Moses, 1991).

Of all the sciences, psychology is unique in this regard. Most science departments do not have similar requirements; many do not offer a course that presents the history of the field. Why are psychologists so interested in the historical development of their field? One reason has to do with the point we made earlier, that for centuries the issues and problems psychology deals with have attracted attention and interest. Scholars have been trying to understand human thought and behavior from the beginning of recorded time. Their efforts have produced many respectable insights and conclusions, as well as inaccuracies and myths. As we said, many of the questions asked centuries ago are still relevant today, demonstrating a long continuity of problems if not of methods within psychology, a continuity that is not found in other sciences. This means that psychology has a tangible and vital link with its own past, a connection that many psychologists find satisfying and useful to explore.

The interest of psychologists in the history of their field has led to its formalization as an area of study. Just as there are psychologists who specialize in social problems, psychophysiological issues, abnormal behavior, or adolescent development, so there are those who specialize in the history of psychology.

In 1965, a multidisciplinary journal, the *Journal of the History of the Behavioral Sciences*, was begun under the editorship of a psychologist. That same year the Archives of the History of American Psychology was established at the University of Akron, Ohio, to serve the needs of scholars by collecting and preserving source materials in the history of psychology. The Division of the History of Psychology (Division 26) was formed within the APA in 1966, and in 1969 the International Society for the History of the Behavioral and Social Sciences (the Cheiron Society) was founded. Organizations for the study of the history of psychology have been established in Canada, Britain, Germany, and other countries. Graduate work in the history of psychology is offered at several universities, and a doctoral program is available at the University of New Hampshire. The growth in the number of textbooks, monographs, biographies, journal articles, professional meetings, translated works, and sources for archival research reflects the importance that psychologists attribute to the study of the history of psychology.

"That's mildly interesting," you may be thinking, "but why does it follow that I have to study the history of psychology?" Consider what you have learned from your other psychology courses, namely, that there is no single form, approach, or definition of modern psychology on which all psychologists agree. Instead, there is an enormous diversity, even divisiveness and fragmentation, in both professional and scientific specialization and subject matter.

Some psychologists focus on cognitive processes, others deal with unconscious forces, and still others work only with overt behavior or physiological and biochemical factors. Contemporary psychology encompasses many areas that may appear to have little in common beyond a broadly stated interest in human nature and conduct and an approach that attempts in some way to be scientific.

The framework that binds these differing areas and approaches is the history, the evolution of the discipline of psychology. Only by exploring its origins and studying its development over time can we see clearly and in context the diversity of modern psychology. A knowledge of history can bring order to disorder and meaning out of chaos, putting the past into perspective and explaining the present.

Many psychologists believe in and practice a technique that accepts the influence of the past in shaping the present. Clinical psychologists, for example, attempt to understand the condition of their clients by exploring the past, by examining the forces and events that may have caused their patients to behave or think in certain ways. By compiling case histories, clinicians reconstruct the evolution of their clients' lives and, often, that process leads to explanations of present behaviors. Behavioral psychologists also accept the influence of the past in shaping the present. In general, they believe that behavior is determined by prior conditioning and reinforcing experiences, that the current state of the organism is accounted for by its history.

So it is with the discipline of psychology. Knowledge of the history of psychology will help you integrate the areas and issues that constitute modern psychology. You should come to recognize the relationships among various ideas and theories and research efforts, and to understand how different (and, in some cases, seemingly unrelated) pieces of psychology fit together in the pattern of their historical development. Thus, we might describe the history of psychology as a case history, an exploration of the early events and experiences that have made psychology what it is today.

Finally, the history of psychology is a fascinating tale in its own right, offering drama, tragedy, and revolutionary ideas. The stories of these men and women and their beliefs should give you some appreciation of the substantial progress that has been made in knowledge and methodology in the comparatively short time since psychology became an independent discipline. There were false starts, errors, and misconceptions, but overall there is a continuity that has shaped contemporary psychology and that provides us with an explanation for its richness and diversity today.

The Data of History

The data of history—the materials historians use to reconstruct lives, events, and eras—differ markedly from the data of science. The most distinctive feature of scientific data is the way they are gathered. When psychologists want to discover, for example, the conditions under which some persons will help others who are in apparent distress, or the ways in which different reinforcement schedules influence the behavior of laboratory animals, or whether children will imitate the aggressive behavior they observe in others, the psychologists construct situations or establish conditions out of which data will be generated. They may conduct a laboratory experiment, or observe behavior systematically under controlled conditions in the real world, or take a survey, or determine the correlation between two variables. In using these approaches, scientists shape the situations or events they wish to study; those situations and events can be reconstructed or replicated by other scientists working in other places and at other times. The data of the science of psychology can be verified by establishing conditions similar to those of the original study and repeating the observation.

In contrast, the data of history cannot be reconstructed or replicated. Each event or situation of interest occurred at some time in the past — perhaps centuries ago — and historians of that time may not have recorded all the details of the event as it unfolded. Michael Wertheimer, a historian of psychology at the University of Colorado, wrote that "history is an all-or-nothing affair; something happened once, and that is that — you cannot bring past events back into the present to study them and their determinants and effects at leisure, turning them this way and that, as you can examine some scientific statement in the laboratory" (Wertheimer, 1979, p. 1).

The historical incident itself is lost to view. How, then, can historians deal with it? What data can they use to develop an account of it? And how can anyone possibly tell us all that happened? Just because historians cannot replicate a situation and generate pertinent data does not mean the data do not exist. The data of history are available to us in the form of fragments of past events, such as descriptions recorded by participants or witnesses, letters and diaries, or official accounts. It is from these data-fragments that historians try to recreate the events and persons of the past.

The historical approach to psychology is similar to that taken by archeologists who, working with fragments of past civilizations — such as arrowheads, broken pots, or human bones — try to describe the characteristics of those civilizations. Some archeological excavations yield more complete data (more fragments) than others, allowing for more accurate reconstructions. Similarly, with excavations in history, the amount of data may be so great as to leave little doubt about the accuracy of the reconstruction.

Sometimes, however, historical data are incomplete. They may be lost, deliberately suppressed, distorted by a participant or a scholar motivated by self-interest, or translated inaccurately. The history of psychology contains many incomplete or perhaps inaccurate examples in the generation of historical truth.

Let us describe, first, data that have been lost. It has happened that important personal papers were missing for decades before being discovered. In 1984, an extensive collection of papers of Hermann Ebbinghaus — prominent in the study of learning and memory — was found, some seventy-five years after his death. In 1983, ten large boxes containing the handwritten diaries of Gustav Fechner, the scientist who developed psychophysics, were uncovered. These diaries dealt with the period 1828–1879, a time of great significance in the early history of psychology. Yet for more than one hundred years psychologists had been unaware of the existence of these diaries. Books were written about these scholars and their work by authors who did not have access to these important collections of papers. Uncovering these new fragments of history means that more pieces of the puzzle can be set in place.

Other data may be deliberately hidden from public view or changed in various ways to protect the image or reputation of the person involved. Sigmund Freud's first biographer, Ernest Jones, minimized Freud's use of cocaine, commenting in a letter to a colleague, "I'm afraid that Freud took more cocaine than he should though I'm not mentioning that [in my biography]" (Isbister, 1985, p. 35). As we shall see in Chapter 13, data revealed more recently confirm that Freud used cocaine in his personal life for a longer period than Jones was willing to admit in print.

Another case of suppressed data was discovered during an investigation of the Gestalt psychologist Wolfgang Köhler and his activities during World War I. "Based on the sample of documents I had read," the researcher reported, "my impression was that they had been carefully selected to present a favorable profile of Köhler. The papers revealed nice things that Köhler said and flattering things that were said about him" (Ley, 1990, p. 197). This story illustrates one of the difficulties faced by a researcher who must assess the worth of historical material: Is a document an accurate representation of the life and work of an individual, or has it been chosen to foster a particular image — positive or negative?

For a final example of suppressed data–fragments, let us return to Sigmund Freud. He died in 1939, and in the years since his death many of his papers and letters have been released to scholars and have been published. A large collection of Freud's personal documents is held by the Library of Congress in Washington, D.C.; at the request of the Freud estate, those will not be made available until well into the twenty-first century. The stated reason for this restriction is to protect the privacy of Freud's patients and their families, and perhaps of Freud and his family as well.

Psychologists do not know how these documents will affect our understanding of Freud and his work. Perhaps they will fundamentally alter our perceptions, or perhaps they will not change our knowledge at all. Until the data are available for study, however, the history of one of psychology's pivotal figures remains incomplete and, possibly, inaccurate.

Another problem with the data of history relates to information that has come to the historian in distorted form. In such cases, the data are available, but they have been changed in some way, perhaps through faulty translation or through distortions introduced by a participant in recording his or her own activities.

We may refer to Freud's life and work again for examples of the misleading effects of translations. Only a minority of American psychologists and students are sufficiently fluent in the German language to read Freud in the original. Most of us rely on a translator's choice of the most suitable or equivalent words and phrases, but the correspondence between the translation and the author's intended meaning is not always exact.

Three fundamental concepts in Freud's theory of the structure of personality are the id, the ego, and the superego, terms with which you are familiar. They do not, however, convey Freud's ideas precisely. They are the Latin equivalents of Freud's German words: ego for *Ich* (I), id for *Es* (it), and superego for *Über-Ich* (above-I).

Freud intended to indicate something highly intimate and personal with his use of *Ich* (I) and to distinguish it clearly from *Es* (it), which represents something distinct from or foreign to "I." "The translation of the personal pronouns [from the German] into their Latin equivalents — the 'ego' and the 'id' — rather than their English ones turned them into cold technical terms, which arouse no personal associations" (Bettelheim, 1982, p. 53). The distinction between "I" or "me," on the one hand, and "it," on the other, is not as forceful in the translation as in the original. Indeed, Freud is quoted as saying that he "should not have written *Das Ich und das Es*, for the *Es* cannot be rendered into English" (Paskauskas, 1988, p. 119).

Consider the common Freudian term *free association*. Here the word *association* implies a conscious link or connection between one idea or thought and another, as though each one acts as a stimulus to elicit the next word in a chain. This is not what Freud believed. His term in German was *Einfall*, which does not mean an association. It means, instead, an intrusion or an invasion, and Freud used the word to denote something from the unconscious that is uncontrollably intruding on or invading conscious thought.

These differences in meaning are seen by some psychologists as small and subtle, but they are changes nonetheless. The data — Freud's own words — have not been rendered by historians exactly as they were written but have undergone some distortion in the process of translation.

An Italian proverb — "to translate is to betray" — expresses this idea succinctly (Baars, 1986, p. 73). Historians who rely on translations may be dealing with inaccurate or imprecise data–fragments. In the 1980s, the British Psycho-Analytical Society recommended that the standard translation of Freud's works be revised radically, because it was held to present a distorted view of his ideas (Holder, 1988).

The data of history may also be affected by the actions of the participants in the events recorded. They may, consciously or unconsciously, bias their accounts to protect themselves or to enhance their public images. B. F. Skinner, the prominent behavioral psychologist, described in his autobiography his rigorous self-discipline while he was a graduate student at Harvard University in the late 1920s. The following paragraph has been quoted frequently in biographies of Skinner.

> I would rise at six, study until breakfast, go to classes, laboratories, and libraries with no more than fifteen minutes unscheduled during the day, study until exactly nine o'clock at night and go to bed. I saw no movies or plays, seldom went to concerts, had scarcely any dates and read nothing but psychology and physiology (Skinner, 1967, p. 398).

This description seems to be a useful data–fragment in that it provides an insight into Skinner's character. Twelve years after publishing this recollection of his schedule, and fifty-one years after the period described, Skinner denied that his graduate school days had been as spartan and difficult as he had suggested. Referring to the passage quoted above he wrote, "I was recalling a pose rather than the life I actually led" (Skinner, 1979, p. 5).

Although Skinner's school days are of minor importance in the history of psychology, the two versions in print, both written by the participant, indicate something of the difficulty historians face. Which set of data, which version of this incident, is more accurate? Which characterization comes closer to reality? Which is biased by the vagaries or the self-serving nature of memory? And how are we to know?

In some cases it is possible to find corroborating data from colleagues or observers. If Skinner's graduate school regimen were highly significant for historians of psychology, they could try to locate Skinner's classmates, or at least their diaries or letters, and compare those recollections of Skinner's behavior at Harvard with his own. Some distortions in history can be investigated and resolved by using additional sources. This has occurred with inconsistencies in descriptions of certain aspects of Freud's life and work. Freud liked to present himself as a martyr to his psychoanalytic cause, a visionary who was constantly opposed, scorned, rejected, and vilified. His first biographer, Ernest Jones, echoed these claims. Data uncovered later indicates that both men were wrong. Far from being ignored, Freud's ideas, by 1906, had begun to exert an immense influence on the younger generation of intellectuals in Vienna. Freud's private practice was thriving, and he could even be described, in modern terms, as something of a celebrity.

For years it was believed that Freud's important book, *The Interpretation of Dreams* (1900), was almost totally disregarded and that, on those rare occasions when it was reviewed, it was severely criticized. In truth, the book received wide recognition in professional journals in philosophy, psychology, psychiatry, and medicine, as well as in popular magazines and newspapers in Vienna, Berlin, and other major European cities. Many of these reviews praised the book (Ellenberger, 1970). Freud himself had distorted the record, and these distortions were perpetuated by several biographers. The false impression has now been corrected, but for several decades, until new data–fragments were excavated, that aspect of our understanding of Freud was inaccurate.

What do these problems with the data of history suggest about the study of the history of psychology? They show primarily that history is not static or stagnant but rather is dynamic, changing, growing, that it is being refined and enhanced whenever new data are uncovered and misconceptions are corrected. History can never be considered finished or complete. It is always in progress, a story without an ending. The story told by the historian can only approximate or approach the truth, but it does so more fully with each passing year, with each new finding and each refinement of the fragments that are the data of history.

Contextual Forces in Psychology

Psychology has not developed in a vacuum, subject only to internal influences. It is part of the larger culture in which it functions and is, therefore, subject to external influences that shape its nature and direction in significant ways. A proper understanding of psychology's history must consider the context in which the discipline emerged and evolved — the social, economic, and political forces that characterize different eras and places (see Altman, 1987; Furumoto, 1989).

We shall see examples throughout this book of how these various contextual forces shaped psychology's past and continue to affect its present. Let us mention briefly here the impact of three such forces: economic opportunities, wars, and discrimination.

During the early years of the twentieth century, the nature of American psychology and the type of work many psychologists were doing changed drastically, primarily as a result of economic opportunities. The focus of American psychology shifted from the pure research of the university laboratory to the application of psychological knowledge and techniques to real-world problems. The primary explanation for this shift was practical. As one psychologist put it, "I became an applied psychologist in order to earn a living" (O'Donnell, 1985, p. 225).

Although the number of psychology laboratories in the United States was increasing steadily toward the end of the nineteenth century, so was the number of Ph.D. psychologists competing for jobs in those laboratories. By the turn of the century, there were three times as many psychologists in the United States as there were research laboratories in which they could find employment. Fortunately, more teaching jobs were becoming available at the state institutions being established throughout the Midwest and the West, but in most of those universities, psychology, as the newest science, received the smallest amount of financial support. Compared to other more established disciplines, psychology consistently ranked lowest in annual appropriations; there was little money for research projects, laboratory equipment, and faculty salaries.

Psychologists quickly realized that if their academic departments, budgets, and incomes were ever to grow, they would have to demonstrate to university administrators, and to the state legislators who voted for appropriations, just how useful psychology could be in solving social, educational, and industrial problems. And so, in time, psychology departments came to be judged on the basis of their practical worth.

At the same time, as a result of a major new social force sweeping over the United States, an exciting opportunity to apply psychology to a practical problem presented itself. Because of the influx of immigrants to the United States around the turn of the century, and their high birth rate, public education became a growth industry. Between 1890 and 1918, public school enrollments increased 700 percent, and new high schools were built across the country at the rate of one a day. More money was spent on education than on the military and social welfare programs combined.

Many psychologists took advantage of this situation and sought ways to apply their knowledge and research methods to education. This was the beginning of a rapid change in emphasis in American psychology, from the experimentalism of the academic laboratory to the application of psychology to learning, teaching, and other practical classroom issues.

Wars were another contextual force that helped to shape psychology. The experiences of psychologists in aiding the United States war effort in World Wars I and II accelerated the growth of applied psychology and extended its influence into areas such as personnel selection, testing, and engineering psychology. This work demonstrated to the psychological community at large, as well as to the general public, how useful psychology could be in solving problems of everyday life.

World War II also changed the face and fate of psychology in Europe — particularly in Germany, where experimental psychology began, and in Austria, the birthplace of psychoanalysis. Many noted psychologists fled the Nazi menace in the 1930s, and most of them came to the United States. That abrupt, forced exile and emigration marked the final phase of the shift of dominance in psychology from the old world to the new.

War has influenced the theoretical positions of individual psychologists. After witnessing the carnage of World War I, Sigmund Freud was moved to propose that aggression was as important a motivating force in human life as was sex; this was a major change in his system of psychoanalysis. Erich Fromm attributed his interest in the study of irrational and abnormal behavior to his observation of the frenzy of fanaticism that swept over his native Germany during World War I.

A third contextual factor is discrimination and prejudice, which for many years influenced who could become a psychologist and where he or she could work. For decades, African-Americans were largely excluded from psychology and from most fields requiring advanced academic study. As late as 1940, only four black colleges in the United States offered undergraduate degrees in psychology, and few universities admitted black men and women as graduate students. Between 1920 and 1966, the ten most prestigious psychology departments in the United States granted only eight Ph.D. degrees to African-Americans; nearly four thousand doctorates were awarded to whites during those same years (Guthrie, 1976).

Jews were also victims of discrimination, especially during the first half of psychology's history. The late 1800s saw the founding of Johns Hopkins University in Baltimore, Maryland, and Clark University in Worcester, Massachusetts, both important institutions in the early history of psychology. Their general policy was to exclude Jewish professors from their faculties. And well into the middle of the twentieth century, Jewish men and women faced admissions quotas in most graduate schools. Those who did succeed in earning doctoral degrees found it difficult to obtain academic jobs. When Julian Rotter, today a leading personality theorist, received his Ph.D. in 1941, he said that he "had been warned that Jews simply could not get academic jobs, regardless of their credentials" (Rotter, 1982, p. 346). Like many other Jewish psychologists of that era, Rotter began his professional career as an employee of a state mental hospital instead of a university.

Widespread prejudice against women has existed throughout most of the history of psychology. We shall see examples throughout this book of women who were denied admission to graduate school or were excluded from faculty positions. Even when women were able to obtain such appointments, they were paid lower salaries than men, and they encountered barriers to promotion and tenure. Sandra Scarr, a developmental psychologist and professor at the University of Virginia, recalled her interview for admission to graduate school at Harvard University in 1960. She was told by Gordon Allport, an eminent social psychologist, that "we hate accepting women here. Seventy-five percent of you get married, have kids and never finish your degrees, and the rest of you never amount to anything anyway" (Scarr, 1987, p. 26).

These examples, and others we shall cite in later chapters, show the impact of economic, political, and social forces on the development of modern psychology. The history of psychology has been shaped not only by the ideas, theories, and research of its great leaders, but also by external influences — contextual forces — over which it had little control.

Personalistic and Naturalistic Conceptions of Scientific History

Two approaches can be taken to explain how the science of psychology has developed: the personalistic theory and the naturalistic theory. The **_personalistic theory of scientific history_** focuses on the monumental achievements and contributions of certain individuals. According to this view, progress and change are attributable directly to the will and force of unique persons who charted and changed the course of history. A Napoleon, a Hitler, or a Darwin were — so this theory goes — the prime movers and shapers of great events. The personalistic theory implies that particular events would not have occurred had it not been for these singular figures. The theory says, in effect, that the person makes the times.

At first glance, it seems obvious that science is, indeed, the work of creative, talented, and intelligent men and women who have determined its direction. We often define an era by the name of the person whose discoveries or theories or other contributions marked the period. We talk of physics "after Einstein," sculpture "after Michelangelo," and psychology "after Watson." It is apparent, both in science and in the general culture, that individuals have produced dramatic — and sometimes traumatic — changes that have altered the course of history. We have only to think of Sigmund Freud to realize how true that is.

Therefore, the personalistic theory has merit, but it is not sufficient to explain the development of a science or a society. The work of scientists and philosophers and scholars has too often been ignored or denied in one time period, only to be recognized long afterward. These occurrences imply that the times determine whether an idea will be heeded or scorned, praised or forgotten. The history of science is replete with examples of the rejection of new discoveries and insights. Even the greatest minds (perhaps especially the greatest minds) have been constrained by a contextual factor called the *Zeitgeist*, the spirit or intellectual climate of the times. The acceptance and application of a discovery may be limited by the dominant pattern of thought in a culture, region, or era, but an idea that is too novel to gain acceptance in one period may be readily accepted a generation or a century later. Slow change seems to be the rule for scientific progress.

The notion that the person makes the times, then, is not entirely correct. Perhaps, as the *naturalistic theory of scientific history* would have it, the times make the person, or at least make possible the recognition of what an individual has to say. Unless the Zeitgeist is ready for the new idea, its proponent may not be heard — or may be laughed at or even put to death; this, too, depends on the Zeitgeist.

The naturalistic theory suggests, for example, that if Darwin had died in his youth, a theory of evolution would still have been advanced in the middle of the nineteenth century. Someone else would have proposed it because the Zeitgeist was calling for a new way of looking at the origin of the human species. (We shall see in Chapter 6 that someone else did propose such a theory.)

The inhibiting or delaying capacity of the Zeitgeist operates not only at the level of the culture but also within science itself, where its effects may be even more pronounced. Many scientific discoveries remained dormant for a long time, then were rediscovered and embraced. The concept of the conditioned response was suggested by Robert Whytt, a Scottish scientist, in 1763, but no one was interested in it then. Well over a century later, when researchers in psychology were adopting more objective methods, the Russian physiologist Ivan Pavlov elaborated on Whytt's observations and expanded them into the basis of a new system of psychology. A discovery must often await its time. "There is not much new in this world," observed one psychologist, "and certainly not much new about the psychological nature of human beings. What passes for discovery these days tends to be an individual scientist's rediscovery of some well-established phenomenon" (Gazzaniga, 1988, p. 231).

Instances of independent simultaneous discovery also support the naturalistic theory of history. Similar discoveries have been made by individuals working far apart geographically, often in ignorance of one another's work. In 1900, three investigators unknown to one another coincidentally rediscovered the work of the Austrian botanist Gregor Mendel, whose writings on genetics had been largely ignored for thirty-five years.

Current and popular theoretical positions in a scientific field often obstruct or prohibit consideration of new points of view. One theory may so dominate a discipline that investigation of a new method or line of inquiry is stifled. An established theory can also determine the ways in which phenomena or data are organized and examined, and this may prevent scientists from considering the data in other ways. "It is the theory," Albert Einstein said, "which decides what we can observe" (Broad & Wade, 1982, p. 138).

A dominant theory can also determine the type of research results that are published in the scientific journals. Findings that contradict or oppose prevailing views may be rejected by the journals' editors, who thus, inadvertently or deliberately, function as censors. They are able to enforce conformity by rejecting or trivializing a revolutionary idea or an unusual interpretation.

An example of this occurred in the 1970s, when psychologist John Garcia attempted to publish the results of research that challenged the prevailing S-R (stimulus-response) theory of learning (Lubek & Apfelbaum, 1987). The mainstream journals refused to accept Garcia's articles, even though the work was considered to be well done and had already received professional recognition and prestigious awards. He eventually published his findings in lesser known, smaller circulation journals; this delayed the dissemination of Garcia's ideas to a wider audience.

The Zeitgeist within a science can have an inhibiting effect on methods of investigation, on theoretical formulations, and on the definition of the discipline's subject matter. We shall describe in the chapters that follow the early tendency in scientific psychology to focus on consciousness and the subjective aspects of human nature. Even as its methods became more objective and precise, the focus of study in psychology continued to be subjective. Not until the 1920s could it be said that psychology finally "lost its mind," then it lost consciousness altogether. But a half century later, under the impact of a different Zeitgeist, psychology began to regain consciousness, continually responding to the changing intellectual climate of the times.

We can easily understand this situation in terms of an analogy with the evolution of a living species. Both a science and a living species change or evolve in response to the conditions and demands of the environment. What happens to a species over time? Very little, as long as its environment remains largely constant. When the environment changes, however, the species must adapt to the new conditions or face extinction.

Suppose that the climate grew significantly colder or that coastal waters became barren. To survive, the animals in the affected areas would have to alter their forms. A hairless species, for example, would need to grow fur to cope with colder temperatures; a short-legged species would need to evolve into a long-legged species if the food once available to it in shallow waters was now found only in deeper waters.

Some species did not adapt to environmental changes, and science knows only their historical remains. Others modified their forms somewhat, while retaining basic features. In these cases, the newer forms are recognizably linked with the older forms. Still others change so radically that they become new species, and their relation to their predecessors is not readily apparent. However mild or extreme the alteration, the important point is that living species can adapt to environmental demands. The more the environment changes, the more the species must change.

Consider the parallel with the evolution of a science. It, too, exists in the context of an environment to which it must be responsive. The environment of a science, its Zeitgeist, is not so much physical as it is intellectual. But like the physical environment, the Zeitgeist is subject to changes. The intellectual climate that characterizes one generation or century may be totally different by the next. Such a situation occurred, for example, when the belief in God and the teachings of the established church as the source of all human knowledge was replaced by the belief in reason and science.

This evolutionary process marks the entire history of psychology. When the Zeitgeist favored speculation, meditation, and intuition as paths to truth, psychology also favored those methods. When the spirit of the times dictated an observational and experimental approach to truth, the methods of psychology followed in that direction. When one form of psychology found itself in two different intellectual climates, it became two species of psychology; when the initial German form of psychology emigrated to the United States, it was modified to become a uniquely American psychology, whereas the psychology that remained in Germany evolved in a different way.

Our emphasis on the Zeitgeist does not negate the importance of the great men and women in the history of science, but it does require us to consider them in a different perspective. A Copernicus or a Marie Curie does not single-handedly change the course of history through sheer force of genius. He or she does so only because the way has already been cleared. We shall see that this has been true for every major figure in the history of psychology.

It seems clear, then, that while the evolution of psychology must be considered in terms of both the personalistic and the naturalistic theories of history, the Zeitgeist appears to play the major role. No matter how weighty their contributions are judged today, if the significant figures in history and science had held ideas too far out of phase with the intellectual climate of their times, their insights would have died in obscurity. Individual creative work is more like a prism—diffusing, elaborating, and magnifying the spirit of the times—than like a beacon, although both will shed light on the path ahead.

The Schools of Thought: Landmarks in the Development of Modern Psychology

During the initial years of the evolution of psychology as a separate scientific discipline, in the last quarter of the nineteenth century, the direction of the new psychology was influenced profoundly by Wilhelm Wundt, who had definite ideas about the form this new science—*his* new science—should take. He determined the subject matter, the method of research, the topics to be studied, and the goals of the new science. He was, of course, affected by the spirit of his times and by the current thinking in philosophy and physiology. Nevertheless, it was Wundt, in his role as the agent of the times, who drew together the various lines of thought. Through the force of his personality and his intensive writing and research, he fashioned the new psychology. Because he was a compelling promoter of the inevitable, psychology was, for some time, molded in his image.

Before long, the situation changed. Controversy arose among the growing number of psychologists. The Zeitgeist was changing and new ideas were being advanced in other sciences and in the general culture. Some psychologists, reflecting these new currents of thought, came to disagree with Wundt's version of psychology and proposed their own views. By the turn of the century, several systematic positions or schools of thought coexisted. These were, essentially, different definitions of the nature of psychology.

The term *school of thought* refers to a group of psychologists who become associated ideologically, and sometimes geographically, with the leader of a movement. Usually the members of a school work on common problems and share a theoretical or systematic orientation. The emergence of different and sometimes simultaneous schools of thought and their subsequent decline and replacement by others is one of the more striking characteristics of the history of psychology.

This stage in the development of a science, when it is still divided into schools of thought, has been called the pre-paradigmatic stage. (A *paradigm* — a model or pattern — has been described in this context as a recognized way of thinking within a scientific discipline that provides, for a time, the essential questions and answers for researchers in that field.) The more mature or advanced stage in the development of a science is reached when it is no longer characterized by schools of thought, that is, when the majority of the members of a discipline agree on theoretical and methodological issues. At that stage, a common paradigm or model defines the entire field, and there are no longer competing factions.

In the history of physics we can see paradigms at work. The Galilean-Newtonian concept of mechanism was accepted by physicists for some three hundred years; during that time virtually all work in the field was undertaken within that framework. Paradigms are not inviolate, however. They can and do change, once a majority of those in a discipline accepts a new way of ordering or working with the subject matter. In physics this occurred when the Galilean-Newtonian model was replaced by the Einsteinian model. The eminent historian of science, Thomas Kuhn, called this process of replacing one paradigm with another a *scientific revolution* (Kuhn, 1970).

Psychology has not yet reached the paradigmatic stage. For the more than one hundred years of its history, psychology has been seeking, embracing, and rejecting different definitions, but no single system or point of view has yet succeeded in unifying the various positions. The cognitive psychologist George Miller commented that "no standard method or technique integrates the field. Nor does there seem to be any fundamental scientific principle comparable to Newton's laws of motion or Darwin's theory of evolution" (Miller, 1985, p. 42). The field remains specialized, with each group adhering to its own theoretical and methodological orientation, approaching the study of human nature with different techniques and promoting itself with different jargon, journals, and the other trappings of a school of thought.

Each of the early schools of thought in psychology was a movement of protest, even a revolution, against the prevailing systematic position. Each school pointed out what it saw as the shortcomings and failures of the older system and offered new definitions, concepts, and research strategies to correct the perceived weaknesses. When a new school of thought captured the attention of the scientific community, rejection of the formerly honored viewpoint was the result. These intellectual conflicts between incompatible old and new positions were fought with feverish tenacity on both sides.

Often, the leaders of an older school never became wholly converted to the new school of thought. Usually older in years, these psychologists remained too deeply committed to their position, intellectually and emotionally, to change. Many of the younger and less committed adherents became supporters of the new position, leaving the others to cling to their traditions and to work in increasing isolation.

The physicist Max Planck wrote that "a new scientific truth does not triumph by convincing its opponents and making them see the light, but rather because its opponents eventually die, and a new generation grows up that is familiar with it" (Planck, 1949, p. 33). "What a good thing it would be," Charles Darwin wrote to a friend, "if every scientific man was to die when sixty years old, as afterward he would be sure to oppose all new doctrines" (Boorstin, 1983, p. 468).

Different schools of thought have developed during the course of the history of psychology, each one an effective protest against what had gone before. Each new school used its older opponent as a base against which to push and gain momentum. Each position proclaimed loudly what it was not and how it differed from the older theoretical system. As the new system developed and gained supporters and influence, it inspired opposition, and the whole combative process began anew. What was once a pioneering, aggressive revolution became, with success, the established tradition, which then succumbed to the vigorous force of a youthful new movement. Success destroys vigor. A movement feeds on opposition. When the opposition has been defeated, the passion and ardor of the once new movement die.

Although the dominance of at least some of the schools of thought was only temporary, each played a vital part in the development of psychology. The influence of the schools can still be seen in contemporary psychology, although the factions in the psychology of today bear little similarity to the earlier systems because new doctrines have again replaced the old. Edna Heidbreder, a noted historian of psychology, compared the function of the schools of thought in psychology to that of the scaffolding used in erecting a tall building (Heidbreder, 1933). Without the scaffolding from which to work, the structure could not be built, yet the scaffolding does not remain; it is torn down when it is no longer needed. Likewise, the structure of today's psychology has been built within the framework and guidelines (the scaffolding) established by the earlier schools of thought.

We cannot consider any of the schools of thought as a complete account of scientific fact. The schools are not finished products in any sense. Rather, they provide the tools, methods, and conceptual schemes that psychology has used to accumulate and organize a body of scientific fact. As we noted, modern psychology is not in its final form. New schools have replaced the old, but nothing guarantees their permanence in the evolutionary process of building a science. The schools of thought are temporary but necessary stages in the development of psychology.

It is in terms of the historical development of the schools of thought that the exciting advance of psychology can best be understood. Prominent individuals have made outstanding contributions and inspiring pronouncements, but the significance of their work is most notable when considered within the context of the ideas that preceded theirs, ideas on which they often built, as well as the work that followed.

We describe the beginnings of experimental psychology in Chapters 2 and 3. Subsequent chapters discuss each of the major schools of thought on three levels: (1) the prescientific development of the position, including the work of early scholars who developed their insights without the use of the experimental method; (2) the early attempts to attack particular problems using the methods of science; and (3) the formal establishment of each school and its contemporary derivatives.

The work of Wilhelm Wundt (Chapter 4), and its outgrowth, the school of thought called structuralism (Chapter 5), developed from the early work in philosophy and physiology. This was followed by functionalism (Chapters 6, 7, and 8), behaviorism (Chapters 9, 10, and 11), and Gestalt psychology (Chapter 12), all of which either evolved from or revolted against structuralism. On a roughly parallel course in time, though not in subject matter, methods, or aims, psychoanalysis (Chapters 13 and 14) evolved from philosophical thought on the nature of the unconscious and from psychiatry's attempts to treat the mentally ill.

Both psychoanalysis and behaviorism generated a number of subschools. In the 1950s, the humanistic psychology movement developed in reaction to behaviorism and psychoanalysis, while incorporating principles of Gestalt psychology. Around 1960, the cognitive psychology movement successfully challenged behaviorism, and the definition of psychology changed once again. The major aspect of that change has been a return to consciousness and to the study of mental or cognitive processes. Having "lost its mind" in the behaviorist revolution, psychology has now regained it. These developments are described in Chapter 15. You will see that a progression is apparent in the evolutionary process that distinguishes the history of psychology, a process that continues today.

Suggested Readings

Boorstin, D. (1983). *The Discoverers*. New York: Random House. A lengthy, readable, and dramatic account of the great discoveries in the history of human knowledge. The author describes how the originators and proponents of these ideas often had to fight entrenched myth and dogma to achieve acceptance of their work.

Buxton, C. E. (Ed.). (1985). *Points of View in the Modern History of Psychology*. Orlando FL: Academic Press. A book of readings on issues in historiography (the principles and techniques of historical research); see especially Chapter 14 (pp. 417–436) on the influence of contextual forces such as philosophical, biological, and religious viewpoints.

Cadwallader, T. C. (1975). Unique values of archival research. *Journal of the History of the Behavioral Sciences, 11*, 27–33. Discusses the rewards of archival research with unpublished documents, diaries, correspondence, and notebooks in tracing the development of a theory from its published form back through its earlier versions, and in revealing the impact of a theorist's personal circumstances on his or her ideas.

Furumoto, L. (1989). The new history of psychology. In I. S. Cohen (Ed.), *The G. Stanley Hall Lecture Series* (vol. 9, pp. 5–34). Washington DC: American Psychological Association. Urges a consideration of contextual forces in historical analysis, such as the influence of institutions and cultures, and shows how this approach leads to a different understanding of the role of women psychologists in the development of the field.

Hilgard, E. R., Leary, D. E., & McGuire, G. R. (1991). The history of psychology: A survey and critical assessment. *Annual Review of Psychology, 42*, 79–107. Reviews current issues in historical research, methods used by contemporary historians of psychology, and approaches to teaching the history of psychology.

Sarup, G. (1978). Historical antecedents of psychology: The recurrent issue of old wine in new bottles. *American Psychologist, 33*, 478–485. Distinguishes between "anticipations" (older notions that appear similar to contemporary ideas in psychology) and actual "foundations" (older ideas that can be linked directly to current ideas and theories).

Philosophical Influences on Psychology

2

The Spirit of Mechanism

In the royal gardens of Europe in the seventeenth century there appeared a whimsical form of amusement among the many marvels of a truly exciting age. Water, running through underground pipes, operated mechanical figures that performed a variety of movements, played musical instruments, and even produced wordlike sounds. Hidden pressure plates, activated when people unknowingly stepped on them, sent water flowing through the pipes to the machinery that moved the statues.

These amusements of the aristocracy reflected and reinforced the seventeenth-century fascination with the miracle of the machine. All manner of machines were invented and perfected for use in science, industry, and entertainment. The mechanical clock — called by one historian the "mother of machines" — is the most important example because of its impact on scientific thought (Boorstin, 1983). Clockmakers were the first to apply theories from physics and mechanics to the construction of machines. In addition to clocks, pumps, levers, pulleys, and cranes were developed to serve human needs, and there seemed to be no limit to the kinds of machines that could be devised or the uses to which they could be put.

You may wonder what this has to do with the history of modern psychology. We are referring, after all, to a time two hundred years before the establishment of psychology as a science, and we are focusing on technology and physics, disciplines that may seem far removed from the study of human nature. The relationship, however, is compelling and direct because the principles embodied by those seventeenth-century mechanical clocks and figures influenced the direction the new psychology would take for most of its existence.

We are dealing here with the Zeitgeist of the seventeenth to nineteenth centuries, the intellectual soil that nourished the new psychology. The basic idea or context of the seventeenth century — the philosophy that would nurture the new psychology — was the spirit of *mechanism*, the image of the universe as a great machine. This doctrine held that all natural processes are mechanically determined and are capable of being explained by the laws of physics.

The idea originated in physics — then known as natural philosophy — as a result of the work of Galileo and, later, of Newton (who, perhaps not so incidentally, had been trained as a clockmaker). The nature of everything that existed in the universe was believed to be nothing more than particles of matter in motion. According to Galileo, matter was composed of discrete corpuscles or atoms that affected each other by direct contact, as billiard balls do. Newton later improved on the Galilean version of mechanism by postulating that movement was communicated not by physical contact but by attracting and repelling forces. His idea, although important in physics, did not radically alter the concept and the way it was used in psychology.

If the universe consisted of atoms in motion, then every physical effect (the movement of each atom) would follow from a direct cause (the movement of the atom that had struck it). It would be subject to laws of measurement and calculation and should, therefore, be predictable. This game of billiards, the operation of the physical universe, was orderly and lawful, like a clock or any other good machine. The physical universe had been designed by God with absolute perfection — in the seventeenth century it was still possible for scientists to attribute cause and perfection to God — and once scientists knew the laws by which the universe functioned, it would be possible to determine how it would behave in the future.

The methods and findings of science were growing apace with technology during this period, and the two meshed effectively. Observation and experimentation came to be the hallmarks of science, followed closely by measurement. Scholars were soon attempting to define or describe every phenomenon by a number, a process that was vital to the study of the universe as a machine. Thermometers, barometers, slide rules, micrometers, pendulum clocks, and other measuring devices were developed and perfected in this age of the machine, and they served to reinforce the notion that it was possible to measure all aspects of the mechanical universe.

The Clockwork Universe

The clock was the perfect metaphor for this seventeenth-century spirit of mechanism, and it has justly been called one of the greatest inventions of all time. Clocks were then a technological sensation, not unlike computers in this century. No other machine had had such an impact on human thought at all levels of society. By the seventeenth century, clocks were being produced in large numbers and in many sizes. Some were small enough to fit on a mantelpiece. Larger ones, housed in the towers of churches and civic buildings, could be seen and heard by all the residents of a town. Whereas the mechanical, water-powered figures in the royal gardens were visible only to the elite, clocks were available to everyone, regardless of class or economic circumstances. The concept of the mechanical clock "took possession of the minds and spirits of an entire civilization, in a way no other machine had ever done . . . Rarely in history has a machine so directly expressed, and in turn affected, the intellectual climate of its time" (Maurice & Mayr, 1980, pp. vii, ix).

Because of the visibility, regularity, and precision of clocks, scholars began to consider them as models for the physical universe, asking if the world itself might not be "a vast clock made and set in motion by the Creator." Many scientists—including the British physicist Robert Boyle, the German astronomer Johannes Kepler, and the French philosopher René Descartes—answered this question in the affirmative and came to look upon the universe as a "great piece of clockwork" (Boorstin, 1983, pp. 71, 72). They believed that the harmony and order of the universe could now be explained in terms of the clock's regularity, which is built into the machine by the clockmaker just as the regularity of the universe was thought to be built into it by God.

A German philosopher, Christian von Wolff, described the clock and the universe in simple terms: "The universe behaves no differently than a clockwork." His student, Johann Cristoph Gottsched, elaborated on this principle:

> Insofar as the universe is a machine, it has to that extent a resemblance to a clock; and it is in a clock that we can on a small scale make plainer to one's understanding that which takes place in the universe on a large scale. The wheels of the clock represent the parts of the universe; the motions of the hands [represent] the events and changes taking place in the universe. Just as in the clock all positions of the wheels and the hands ensue from the inward arrangement, shape, size, and linkage of all its parts in accordance with the rules of motion, so everything that takes place in the universe also produces its effect (Maurice & Mayr, 1980, p. 290).

When seen as a clocklike machine, the universe, once constructed and set in motion, will continue to function efficiently without any outside interference. The use of the clock metaphor includes the idea of **_determinism_**, the belief that every act is determined by past events. We can predict the changes that will occur in the clock, as well as in the universe, because of the regularity and order of the operation of its parts. Gottsched added: "He who has perfect insight into [the clock's] structure can see every future thing from its past and its present state of arrangement" (Maurice & Mayr, 1980, p. 290).

It was not difficult to gain perfect insight into the clock's structure. A person could easily disassemble a clock and see exactly how it operated. Hence, **_reductionism_** as a method of analysis was propagated as an article of faith in the new science. The workings of machines such as clocks could be understood by analyzing them, by reducing them to their basic components. Similarly, one could understand the physical universe—which was, after all, just another machine—by analyzing or reducing it to its simplest parts, its molecules and atoms. Reductionism as a method of analysis would come to characterize every science as it developed, including the new psychology.

If the clock metaphor and scientific analysis could be applied to an explanation of the workings of the physical universe, might they also hold for the study of human nature? If the universe was like a machine—orderly, predictable, observable, and measurable—could not human beings be considered in the same way? Were people and animals also a kind of machine?

The intellectual and social aristocracy of the seventeenth century already had the models for such a notion in the mechanical figures in their gardens, and the proliferation of clocks provided similar models for everyone. At all levels of society people had only to look around to see mechanical contraptions called *automata* performing marvelous feats with precision and regularity.

These automata can be seen today in the central squares of many European cities where mechanical figures in the town hall's clock tower march and cavort, play musical instruments, and strike huge bells with hammers on the quarter hour. In France's Strasbourg Cathedral, figures of the Magi bow hourly before a statue of the Virgin Mary, while a rooster opens its beak, sticks out its tongue, flaps its wings, and crows. At England's Wells Cathedral, pairs of knights in armor circle each other in mock combat. As the bell strikes the hour, one knight knocks the other off his horse. The Bavarian National Museum in Munich, Germany, houses a parrot that is only sixteen inches tall. As its clock strikes the hour, the parrot whistles, moves its bill, flaps its wings, rolls its eyes, and drops a steel pellet from its tail!

In Figure 2-1 you can see the inner workings of a sixteen-inch figure of a monk, now in the collection of the National Museum of American History in Washington, D.C. The monk is programmed to move within the space of a two-foot square. Its feet appear to kick out from beneath its robe, but actually the statue is moving on wheels. It beats its chest with one arm and waves with the other, turns its head from side to side, nods, opens and shuts its mouth, and rolls its eyes.

This kind of clockwork technology seemed to the philosophers and scientists of the time to be capable of fulfilling their dream of creating an artificial being. Indeed, many of the early automata clearly gave that appearance. We might consider them to be the Disney-like figures of their day, and it is easy to understand why people reached the conclusion that humans and animals were simply other forms of machines.

Look again at the inner workings of the monk. We can comprehend almost at a glance the functioning of the gears, levers, ratchets, and other devices that account for the figure's movements. René Descartes and other philosophers adopted these automata as, at least to some extent, models for human beings. Not only was the universe a clockwork machine to them, but so also were its people. Descartes wrote that this idea would not "appear at all strange to those who are acquainted with the different automata, or moving machines, fabricated by human industry... such persons will look upon this body as a machine made by the hands of God, which is incomparably better arranged and adequate to movements more admirable than in any machine of human invention" (Descartes, 1637/1912, p. 44). People might be better machines than the ones the clockmakers could build, but they were machines nonetheless.

Thus, clocks paved the way for the idea that humans were mechanical

Figure 2-1
Automaton figure of a monk

and that the same experimental and quantitative methods that were so successful in exploring the secrets of the physical universe could be applied to the exploration of human nature. In 1748, the French physician Julien de La Mettrie (who died of an overdose of pheasant and truffles) said, "Let us then conclude boldly that man is a machine." This became a driving force of the Zeitgeist, not only in philosophy but in all aspects of life, and it drastically altered the prevailing image of human nature.

And so there emerged during the seventeenth to nineteenth centuries the conception of humans as machines, and the method — the ***scientific method*** — by which human nature could be investigated. People became machines, the modern world became dominated by the scientific outlook, and all aspects of life became subject to mechanical laws.

The Beginnings of Modern Science

We noted that the seventeenth century saw far-ranging developments in science. Until that time, philosophers had looked to the past for answers, to the works of Aristotle and other ancient scholars, and to the Bible. The ruling forces of inquiry were dogma and figures of authority. In the seventeenth century a new force became dominant: ***empiricism***, the pursuit of knowledge through the observation of nature. Knowledge handed down from the past became suspect. The golden age of the seventeenth century was illuminated by the discoveries and insights of scholars who successfully created or reflected the changing atmosphere in which scientific inquiry was flourishing. Although those scholars are important in the history of science, their work, for the most part, is not directly related to the evolution of psychology.

One scholar, however, René Descartes, did contribute directly to the history of modern psychology. More than anyone else, he freed inquiry from the rigid theological and traditional dogmas that had controlled it for centuries. He symbolized the transition from the Renaissance to the modern era of science, and he applied the idea of the clockwork mechanism to the human body. Many believe that he thus inaugurated modern psychology.

René Descartes (1596–1650)

Descartes was born in France on March 31, 1596. His father was a councillor in the parliament of Brittany, and from him Descartes inherited enough money to support a life of study and travel. Descartes, unlike others in similar circumstances, did not become a dilettante, a tendency that may be attributable to his genius, curiosity, and hunger for knowledge, his indifference to dogmatic authority, and his desire for evidence and proof.

From 1604 to 1612 he was a student at a Jesuit school, where he was educated in the humanities and mathematics. He also displayed

Among the contributions of French mathematician and philosopher René Descartes to psychology were the doctrine of innate ideas, the notion of reflex action, and a theory of mind-body interaction.

considerable talent in philosophy, physics, and physiology. Because Descartes's health was frail, the rector excused him from morning religious services and permitted him to lie in bed until noon, a habit Descartes retained all his life. It was during these quiet mornings that he studied his lessons and did his most creative thinking.

After completing his formal education, Descartes sampled the delights of life in Paris. Eventually finding this tiresome, he went into seclusion to study mathematics. In 1617 he became a gentleman volunteer in the armies of Holland, Bavaria, and Hungary, a strange act for a person of such a contemplative nature. He loved to dance and to gamble, and he was a successful gambler because of his mathematical talents. He was also an adventurer and a swordsman who reportedly partook of all human vices and pleasures. His only lasting romantic attachment was a three-year love affair with a Dutch woman who, in 1635, gave birth to their child. Descartes adored the infant and was heartbroken when she died at the age of five. He described the loss as the deepest sorrow of his life.

Descartes was keenly interested in applying knowledge to practical concerns. He investigated techniques that might keep his hair from turning gray, and he conducted experiments on the use of wheelchairs by physically handicapped persons.

In November 1619, while serving in the army, Descartes had a series of dreams that changed his life. As he told it, he spent the day of November 10 alone in a stove-heated room, thinking about mathematical and scientific ideas. He fell asleep and in his dreams he was — as he later interpreted it — rebuked for his idleness. He was visited by the Spirit of Truth, who took possession of his mind. This profound experience persuaded him that he should devote his life to the proposition that mathematics could be applied to all the sciences and thus produce certainty of knowledge.

He returned to Paris in 1623 to pursue his work in mathematics, but he again found the life there too distracting. He sold the estates he had inherited from his father and moved to a country house in Holland in 1628. His need for solitude and seclusion was so great that he lived in thirteen towns and twenty-four different houses over the next twenty years, keeping his address secret from all but his closest friends, with whom he corresponded voluminously. His only other apparent requirements were proximity to a Roman Catholic church and to a university.

Most of Descartes's important works were written during his years in Holland, where freedom of thought was upheld. He did, however, encounter some religious persecution. At one time booksellers were forbidden to sell his works, and he was brought before the magistrates to answer charges made by theologians in two Dutch towns that he was an atheist and a profligate, serious charges against a devout Catholic.

Descartes's growing fame brought him to the attention of Queen Christina of Sweden, who invited him to instruct her in philosophy. Although reluctant to give up his freedom and solitude, he nevertheless had great respect for the royal prerogative. A warship was sent to fetch him, and he embarked for Sweden in the fall of 1649. The queen, who has been described as not a very good student, insisted on starting her lessons at five o'clock in the morning in a poorly heated library during an unusually bitter winter. Descartes withstood the early rising and extreme cold for nearly four months before succumbing to pneumonia on February 11, 1650.

An interesting postscript to the death of a man who devoted much of his life to the study of the interaction between the mind and the body is the story of the disposition of his own body. Sixteen years after Descartes's death, his friends decided that his body should be brought back to France. Unfortunately, the coffin they sent to Sweden was too short to contain the remains. The solution reached by the authorities was to cut off the head and reinter it in Stockholm until arrangements could be made for its return to Paris.

While the corpse was being prepared for the journey to France, the French ambassador to Sweden decided that he wanted a souvenir, and he severed the right forefinger. The body, now minus its head and one finger, was reburied in Paris amid much pomp and splendor. Some time later, an army officer dug up the skull as a memento, and, for 150 years, it changed hands from one Swedish collector to another until it finally reached Paris, where it is now on display at Musée de l'Homme.

Mechanism and the Mind-Body Problem

Descartes's most important work for the development of psychology is his attempt to resolve the ***mind-body problem***, an issue that had been controversial for centuries. Throughout the ages scholars had argued about how the mind, or mental qualities, could be distinguished from the body and all other physical qualities. The basic and deceptively simple question is this: Are mind and body—the mental world and the material world—distinct essences or natures? Since the time of Plato, most scholars had taken a dualistic position; it was held that the mind (or soul or spirit) and the body were of different natures. The acceptance of that position, however, raises other questions: If the mind and body are of different natures, what is their relationship? Does one influence the other, or are they independent?

The theory held before Descartes's time was that the interaction was essentially in one direction. The mind could exert an enormous influence on the body, but the body had little impact on the mind. A contemporary historian has suggested that before Descartes, the body and mind were thought to be related to each other in the same way that a puppet and its puppeteer are joined (Lowry, 1982). The mind is like the puppeteer, pulling the strings of the body.

Descartes accepted this dualistic position. In his view, mind and body were indeed different essences, but he deviated from tradition in his definition of the relationship between the two. In his theory of mind–body interaction, Descartes suggested that the mind influences the body and that the body can exert a much greater influence on the mind than previously supposed. The relationship is not one way but rather is a mutual interaction. This idea, radical in the seventeenth century, had important implications.

After Descartes proposed his doctrine, many scholars found that they could no longer support the idea that the mind was the master of the two entities, the puppeteer functioning almost independently of the body. The body, the material essence, came to be seen as more central, and certain functions previously attributed to the mind were now considered to be functions of the body. In the Middle Ages, for example, the mind was held to be responsible not only for thought and reason, but also for reproduction, perception, and locomotion. Descartes argued that the mind had only one function, that of thought. All other processes were functions of the body.

Descartes thus introduced an approach to the mind-body problem that focused attention on a physical/psychological duality. In so doing, he diverted attention from the abstract concept of the soul to the study of the mind and its mental operations. As a result, methods of inquiry changed from metaphysical analysis to objective observation. Whereas one could only speculate on the existence of the soul, one could observe the mind and its processes.

Mind and body, then, are two separate entities. There is no qualitative similarity between the body (the material or physical world) and the mind (the mental world). Matter, the material substance of the body, has extension (it takes up space) and operates in accordance with mechanical principles. The mind, however, is free, unextended, and lacking in substance. But the revolutionary idea is that mind and body, although distinct, are capable of interacting within the human organism. The mind can influence the body, and the body can influence the mind.

Let us look more closely at Descartes's conception of the body. Because the body is composed of physical matter, it must possess those characteristics common to all matter — extension in space and the capacity for movement. If the body is matter, then the laws of physics and mechanics that account for movement and action in the physical world must also apply to the body. When the body is considered apart from the mind — and it can be so considered because the two are distinct entities — the body is like a machine whose operation can be explained by the mechanical laws that govern the movement of objects in space. Following this line of reasoning, Descartes proceeded to explain physiological functioning in terms of physics.

Descartes was strongly influenced by the mechanistic spirit of the age, as reflected in the mechanical clocks and automata we described earlier. While recovering from what his biographers called a "nervous breakdown" at the age of eighteen, he recuperated in a village near Paris, where his only diversion was walking in the recently completed royal gardens. He was fascinated by the mechanical marvels installed there and spent many hours trodding on the pressure plates that caused water jets to activate the figures, making them move and dance and utter sounds.

This experience helped to shape his views of the physical universe, in particular his views of the human body and the animal body. Descartes believed that the body operated exactly like a machine, and he recognized no difference between the body and the hydraulically operated figures in the gardens. He explained every aspect of physical functioning — such as digestion, circulation, sensation, and locomotion — in mechanical terms.

When Descartes described the body, he referred directly to the figures he had seen in the royal gardens. He compared the body's nerves to the pipes through which the water passed, and the muscles and tendons to engines and springs. The movement of the mechanical models was not caused by voluntary action on their part but by external objects; the involuntary nature of this movement was reflected in Descartes's observation that bodily movements frequently occur without a person's conscious intention. From this line of thought he arrived at the idea of the *undulatio reflexa*, a movement not supervised or determined by a will to move. Because of this proposal, he is often called the author of the **theory of reflex action**. The idea of reflex action is a precursor of modern behavioristic stimulus-response (S-R) psychology — in which an external object (a stimulus) brings about an involuntary response — and is a cornerstone of much of twentieth-century American psychology.

Descartes found support for his mechanical interpretation of the workings of the human body in the field of physiology. In 1628, William Harvey, an English physician, had discovered the gross facts about the circulation of the blood, and much was being learned about the process of digestion. It was also known that the muscles of the body worked in opposing pairs, and that sensation and movement depended somehow on the nerves.

Although physiological researchers were making great strides in understanding the human body, their information was far from complete. The nerves, for instance, were thought to be hollow tubes through which animal spirits flowed. Our concern here, however, is not with the accuracy or comprehensiveness of seventeenth-century physiology, but rather with its consistency with a mechanical interpretation of the body.

Because animals did not possess souls, they were believed to be automata. Thus, the difference between humans and animals so important in Christian thought was preserved. Also, animals were believed to be devoid of feelings. How could they have feelings if they did not have souls? Descartes dissected live animals, before anesthesia was available, and seemed "amused at their cries and yelps since these were nothing but the hydraulic hisses and vibrations of machines" (Jaynes, 1970, p. 224).

These ideas were part of an overall trend toward the notion that human behavior was predictable. The mechanical body moves and behaves in expected ways so long as the inputs are known. Animals, being machinelike, belong entirely to the category of physical phenomena. Hence, animals have no immortality, are incapable of thought, and have no freedom of will. Descartes made some minor revisions in his thinking about animals in later years, but he never altered his conviction that animal behavior can be explained totally in mechanistic terms.

Descartes's writings frequently refer to the clocklike nature of animals. "I know quite well that animals do many things better than we, but that does not astonish me; for precisely that serves to prove that they act naturally and by such spring forces as a clock which indicates what time it is far better than our judgment tells us" (Maurice & Mayr, 1980, p. 5).

Although the mind, according to Descartes, is nonmaterial (that is, not composed of physical matter), it is capable of thought and consciousness and, consequently, provides us with knowledge about our external world. The mind has none of the properties of matter. Its most important characteristic is the capacity to think, and this sets it apart from the material world.

Because the mind perceives and wills, it must somehow influence and be influenced by the body. When the mind decides to move from one point to another, for example, this decision is carried out by the body's nerves and muscles. Similarly, when the body is stimulated — by light or heat, for example — it is the mind that recognizes and interprets these sensory data and determines the appropriate response.

Descartes formulated a theory about the interaction of these two entities, but he needed first to find a physical point where the mind and the body engaged in their mutual influence. Descartes conceived of the soul as unitary, which meant that it must interact with only one part of the body. He also believed that the point of interaction was somewhere within the brain, because research had demonstrated that sensations travel to the brain and movement originates within the brain. Clearly, then, the brain had to be the focal point for the mind's functions. The only structure of the brain that is single and unitary (that is, not divided and duplicated in each hemisphere) is the pineal body or conarium, and Descartes considered this the logical choice for the site of interaction.

He described the manner in which interaction between mind and body takes place in mechanistic terms. Descartes suggested that the movement of animal spirits in the nerve tubes produces an impression on the conarium, and from this impression the mind produces a sensation. In other words, a quantity of motion (the flow of animal spirits) produces a purely mental quality (a sensation). The reverse also occurs, in that the mind can somehow make an impression on the conarium (in a manner he never made clear), which, by inclining to one direction or another, influences the direction of the flow of animal spirits to the muscles, resulting in a movement. Thus, a mental quality can influence motion, a property of the body.

Descartes did not maintain that the soul was confined to or contained in the conarium, which he designated only as the site of the interaction. He believed that the soul was united with all parts of the body and that the entire body was the seat of the soul.

Descartes proposed a doctrine of ideas that had a profound influence on the development of modern psychology. He suggested that the mind gives rise to two kinds of ideas: derived ideas and innate ideas. **Derived ideas** are those produced by the direct application of an external stimulus, such as the sound of a bell or the sight of a tree. Derived ideas are thus products of the experiences of the senses. **Innate ideas** are not produced by objects in the external world that impinge on the senses. The label *innate* describes the source of these ideas; they develop out of the mind or consciousness alone. The potential existence of innate ideas is independent of sensory experiences, although innate ideas may be realized or actualized in the presence of appropriate experiences. Some of the innate ideas Descartes identified are the self, God, geometric axioms, perfection, and infinity.

The doctrine of innate ideas is discussed in later chapters. We shall see that it culminates in the nativistic theory of perception — the idea that our ability to perceive is innate rather than learned — and in the Gestalt school of psychology. It also inspired spirited opposition among the early British empiricists and associationists, and among later empiricists such as Helmholtz and Wundt.

The work of Descartes served as a catalyst for many trends that later became prominent in psychology. His most noteworthy systematic contributions are the mechanistic conception of the body, the notion of reflex action, the theory of mind–body interaction, the localization of the mind's functions in the brain, and the doctrine of innate ideas. With Descartes we see the idea of mechanism applied to the human body. So pervasive was the mechanistic philosophy, however, that it was only a matter of time before it would be applied to the human mind. It is to that significant event — the reduction of the mind to a machine — that we now turn.

British Empiricists and Associationists: Acquiring Knowledge through Experience

After Descartes, the development of modern science in general and of psychology in particular was rapid and prolific. By the middle of the nineteenth century, the long period of prescientific psychology had come to an end. During this time, European philosophical thought became infused with a new spirit: positivism. The term and the conception are the work of the French philosopher Auguste Comte, who was undertaking a systematic survey of all knowledge, an ambitious project indeed. To make his task more manageable, Comte decided to limit his work to facts that were beyond question, those facts that had been determined through the methods of science. *Positivism*, then, refers to a system based exclusively on facts that are objectively observable and not debatable. Everything of a speculative, inferential, or metaphysical nature is rejected as illusory.

The acceptance of positivism meant that there were now two types of propositions. "One refers to the objects of sense, and it is a scientific statement. The other is nonsense!" (Robinson, 1981, p. 333). Knowledge derived from metaphysics and theology was to be rejected. Only knowledge derived from science was seen as valid.

Other ideas in philosophy supported antimetaphysical positivism. Those scholars subscribing to *materialism* believed that all things could be described in physical terms and could be understood in the light of the physical properties of matter and energy. They thought that consciousness could also be explained in the terms of physics and chemistry. Materialist considerations of mental processes focused on the physical aspect, that is, the anatomical and physiological structures of the brain.

A third group of philosophers, those who advocated *empiricism*, were concerned with how the mind acquires knowledge. They argued that all knowledge is derived from sensory experience.

The popular conception of human nature and the world was rapidly changing. Positivism, materialism, and empiricism were to become the philosophical foundations of the new psychology. Discussions of psychological processes were beginning to be conducted within a framework of factual, observational, and quantitative evidence based on sensory experience; increasing emphasis was being placed on the physiological processes involved in mental functioning.

Of these three philosophical orientations, empiricism played the major role in shaping the early development of the new science of psychology. Empiricism related to the growth of the mind, to how the mind acquires knowledge. According to the empiricist view, the mind grows through the progressive accumulation of sensory experiences. This idea contrasts with the nativistic viewpoint exemplified by Descartes, which states that some ideas are innate. We will consider some of the major British empiricists: John Locke, George Berkeley, David Hume, David Hartley, James Mill, and John Stuart Mill.

John Locke (1632–1704)

John Locke, the son of an attorney, studied at universities in London and Oxford in England and received his bachelor's degree in 1656 and his master's degree shortly thereafter. He remained at Oxford for several years, tutoring in Greek, writing, and philosophy, then took up the practice of medicine. He developed an interest in politics and in 1667 went to London to become secretary to the Earl of Shaftesbury and, in time, the confidant and friend of this controversial statesman. Shaftesbury's influence in the government declined, and in 1681, after participating in a plot against King Charles II, Shaftesbury fled to Holland. Although Locke was not involved in the plot, his relationship with the earl brought him under suspicion, and so he too left for Holland. Several years later he was able to return to England, where he became commissioner of appeals and wrote treatises on education, religion, and economics. He was particularly concerned with religious freedom and the right of people to govern themselves. His writings brought him much fame and influence, and he was heralded throughout Europe as a champion of liberalism in government.

Locke's major work of importance to psychology is *An Essay Concerning Human Understanding* (1690), which was the culmination of some twenty years of study and thought. This book, which had appeared in four editions by 1700 and had been translated into French and Latin, marked the formal beginning of British empiricism.

Locke was concerned primarily with cognitive functioning, that is, the ways in which the mind acquires knowledge. In attacking this issue he denied the existence of innate ideas, as proposed by Descartes, arguing that humans are not equipped at birth with any knowledge whatsoever. Locke admitted that certain concepts, such as the idea of God, may seem

English empirical philosopher John Locke argued that at birth the mind is a blank slate that acquires knowledge through sensory experience.

to us as adults to be innate, but that is only because we were taught those ideas in childhood and cannot remember any time when we were unaware of them. Thus Locke explained the seeming innateness of some ideas in terms of learning and habit.

How, then, does the mind acquire knowledge? To Locke, knowledge was acquired through experience. All knowledge was empirically derived. He wrote:

> Let us then suppose the mind to be, as we say, white paper, void of all characters, without any ideas. How comes it to be furnished? Whence comes it by that vast store which the busy and boundless fancy of man has painted on it with an almost endless variety? Whence has it all the materials of reason and knowledge? To this I answer, in one word, from *experience*. In that all our knowledge is founded; and from that it ultimately derives itself (Locke, 1690/1959).

Aristotle held a similar notion, that the mind at birth was a *tabula rasa*, a blank or clean slate on which experience would write.

Locke recognized two different kinds of experiences, one deriving from sensation and the other from reflection. The ideas that derive from sensation, from direct sensory input from physical objects in the environment, are simple sense impressions. In addition to the operation of these sensations on the mind, the mind itself operates on these sensations, reflecting on them and thus giving rise to ideas. The mental or cognitive function of reflection as a source of ideas depends on sensory experience, however, because the ideas produced by the reflection of the mind are based on those already experienced through the senses.

In the development of the individual, sensation occurs first. It is a necessary precursor to reflection because there must first be a reservoir of sense impressions for the mind to be able to reflect. In reflection, the person remembers past sensory impressions and combines them in various ways to form abstractions and other higher-level ideas. All ideas, no matter how complex, arise from these two sources, but the ultimate source remains sense impressions or experience.

Locke also distinguished between simple ideas and complex ideas. *Simple ideas* can arise from both sensation and reflection and are received passively by the mind. They are elemental and thus cannot be analyzed or reduced to simpler ideas. As we noted, however, the mind, through the process of reflection, actively creates new ideas by combining other ideas. These derived ideas are what Locke called *complex ideas*, and they are formed from simple ideas arising from both sensation and reflection. Complex ideas are compounded of simple ideas, and hence they are capable of being analyzed or resolved into their simpler component ideas.

This notion of combining or compounding ideas and analyzing them marks the beginning of the mental-chemistry approach that characterizes the theory of *association*, in which simple ideas may be linked to form complex ideas. Association is an early name for the process that came to be called learning. The reduction or analysis of mental life into elements or simple ideas, and the association of these elements to form complex ideas, formed the core of the new scientific psychology. Just as clocks and other machines could be reduced to their component parts and those parts reassembled to form the complex machine, so could ideas.

In essence, Locke treated the mind as though it behaved in accordance with the laws of the physical universe. The basic particles or atoms of the mental world are the simple ideas, which are conceptually analogous to the material atoms in the mechanistic Galilean–Newtonian scheme. The basic elements of the mind are indivisible. They cannot be broken down into anything simpler, and, like their counterparts in the material world, they can join in various ways to form more complex structures. This was a significant step in the direction of considering the mind, like the body, to be a machine.

Another doctrine Locke proposed that is of importance to psychology is the notion of primary and secondary qualities as they apply to simple ideas of sense. *Primary qualities* exist in an object whether or not we perceive them. The size and shape of a building are primary qualities, whereas the color of the building is a secondary quality. Color is not inherent in the object but is dependent on the experiencing person. These *secondary qualities*, such as color, odor, sound, and taste, exist not in the object but in a person's perception of the object. The tickle of a feather is not in the feather itself but in our reaction to the feather. The pain inflicted by a knife is not in the knife itself but in our experience in relation to the knife.

A simple experiment will illustrate this doctrine. Prepare three containers of water: one cold, one lukewarm, and one hot. Place one hand in the cold water and the other in the hot water, then place both hands in the pan of warm water. One hand will perceive this water as warm and the other will perceive it as cool. The lukewarm water is, of course, one temperature; it is not both warm and cool at the same time. The secondary quality or experience of heat or cold exists only in our perception and not in the object (in this case, the water). To reiterate, secondary qualities exist only in the act of perception. If we did not bite into a peach, its taste would not exist. Primary qualities, such as the size and shape of the peach, exist in it whether or not we perceive them.

Locke was not the first scholar to make a distinction between primary and secondary qualities. Galileo had proposed essentially the same notion: "I think that if ears, tongues, and noses were removed, shapes and numbers and motions [primary qualities] would remain, but not odors nor tastes nor sounds [secondary qualities]. The latter, I believe, are nothing more than names when separated from living beings" (Boas, 1961, p. 262). This position is necessarily congruent with the spirit of mechanism, and Locke admitted as much when he noted that the distinction resulted from a "little excursion into natural philosophy."

The mechanistic view of the universe held that matter in motion constituted the only objective reality. If matter were all that existed objectively, it would follow that perception of anything else — such as colors, odors, and tastes — would be subjective. Therefore, the primary qualities are all that can exist independently of the perceiver.

In making this distinction, Locke was recognizing the subjectivity of much of our perception of the world, an idea that intrigued him and enhanced his need to understand the mind and conscious experience. He introduced the secondary qualities in an attempt to explain the lack of a precise correspondence between the physical world and our perception of it.

Once scholars accepted the distinction in theory between primary and secondary qualities — that some existed in reality and others existed only in our perception — it was inevitable that someone would ask whether there was, after all, any real difference between primary and secondary qualities. Perhaps all perception is in terms of secondary qualities, subjective and dependent on the observer. The person who did ask, and answer, this question was George Berkeley.

George Berkeley (1685–1753)

George Berkeley was born and educated in Ireland. A deeply religious man, he was ordained a deacon in the Anglican Church at the age of twenty-four. Shortly after, he published two philosophical works that were to exert an influence on psychology: *An Essay Towards a New Theory of Vision* (1709) and *A Treatise Concerning the Principles of Human Knowledge* (1710). With these two books, his contribution to psychology ended.

He traveled extensively throughout Europe and held a number of posts in Ireland, including a teaching position at Trinity College in Dublin. He became financially independent when he received a sizable gift of money from a woman he met once at a dinner party. He visited the United States, spending three years at Newport, Rhode Island, and donated his house and library to Yale University when he departed. The last years of his life were spent as Bishop of Cloyne. When he died, his body was left untended in his bed, in accordance with his instructions, until it began to decompose. Berkeley believed that putrefaction was the only sure sign of death, and he did not wish to be buried before his time.

Berkeley's fame — or at least his name — lingers in the United States today. In 1855, a clergyman from Yale, the Reverend Henry Durant, established an academy in California. He named it Berkeley in honor of the good bishop, perhaps in recognition of Berkeley's poem, "On the Prospect of Planting Arts and Learning in America," which includes the famous line: "Westward the course of empire takes its way."

Berkeley agreed with Locke that all knowledge of the external world comes from experience, but he disagreed with Locke's distinction between primary and secondary qualities. Berkeley argued that there are no primary qualities; there are only what Locke called secondary qualities. To Berkeley, all knowledge was a function of the experiencing or perceiving person. Some years later his position was given the name *mentalism*, to denote the emphasis on purely mental phenomena.

He stated that perception is the only reality of which we can be sure. We cannot know with certainty the nature of physical objects in the experiential world. All we can know is how we perceive those objects. Because perception is within ourselves and thus is subjective, it does not mirror the external world. A physical object is nothing more than an accumulation of sensations experienced concurrently, so that force of habit renders them associated in the mind. The experiential world — the world derived from or based on our own experience — is, in Berkeley's view, the summation of our sensations.

There is, then, no material substance of which we can be certain, because if we take away the perception, the quality disappears. There can be no color without the perception of color, no shape or motion without the perception of shape or motion.

Berkeley was not saying, however, that real objects exist in the material world only when they are perceived. His thesis was that because all experience is within ourselves, relative to our own perception, we can never know with certainty the physical nature of objects. We can depend only on our perception of them.

He recognized that there was a degree of independence, consistency, and stability in the objects of the material world, and he had to find some way to account for this. He did so by invoking God; Berkeley was, after all, a bishop. God functioned as a kind of "permanent perceiver" of all the objects in the universe. A tree in the forest could be said to exist and to possess certain characteristics, even if no one was there to perceive it, because God would always be perceiving it.

Berkeley applied the theory of association to explain our knowledge of objects in the real world. This knowledge is essentially a construction or composition of simple ideas or mental elements bound by the mortar of association. Complex ideas are formed by the joining of simple ideas received through the various senses, as he explained in *An Essay Towards a New Theory of Vision*.

> Sitting in my study I hear a coach drive along the street; I look through the [window] and see it; I walk out and enter into it. Thus, common speech would incline one to think I heard, saw, and touched the same thing, to wit, the coach. It is nevertheless certain the ideas intromitted by each sense are widely different, and distinct from each other; but, having been observed constantly to go together, they are spoken of as one and the same thing. (Berkeley, 1709/1957)

To Berkeley, the idea of the coach is fashioned from the sound of its wheels, the feel of its frame, the smell of its leather, and the sight of its boxy shape. The mind constructs the complex ideas by fitting together the simple ideas, the basic building blocks of the mind. The mechanical analogy in the use of the words *construct* and *building blocks* is not coincidental.

Berkeley also used association to explain depth perception. He examined the problem of perceiving the third dimension — depth — given that the human eye has a retina of only two dimensions. His answer was that we perceive depth as a result of our experience, that is, through the recurring association of visual impressions with the sensations of touch and movement that occur in the adjustments and accommodations the eyes make when we look at objects at different distances, or in the bodily movements we make in approaching or retreating from the objects that we see. In other words, the continuous sensory experiences of walking toward or reaching for objects, plus the sensations from the eye muscles, become associated or linked to produce the perception of depth. When an object is brought closer to the eyes, the pupils will converge. This convergence diminishes when the object is moved away. Thus, depth perception is not a simple sensory experience but rather an association of ideas that must be learned.

Here, perhaps for the first time, a purely psychological process was explained in terms of the association of sensations, and therefore Berkeley was continuing the growing associationist trend within empiricism. His explanation accurately anticipated the modern view of depth perception in its consideration of the influences of the physiological cues of accommodation and convergence.

David Hume (1711–1776)

David Hume, a philosopher and historian, studied law at the University of Edinburgh, Scotland, but did not graduate. He embarked on a career in business but found this not to his liking, so he lived on his small income during three years of self-study in philosophy in France. He moved to England and wrote *A Treatise of Human Nature* (1739), his most important work for psychology. Other books followed, and he achieved considerable fame as a writer while working as a secretary, a librarian, a judge advocate on a military expedition, and a tutor to a lunatic of noble birth. He also held several government posts and was well received throughout Europe.

Hume supported Locke's notion of the compounding of simple ideas into complex ideas, developing and making more explicit the theory of association. He agreed with Berkeley that the material world did not exist for the individual until it was perceived, and he took this idea a step further: He abolished mind as a substance and said that it was a secondary quality, like matter. The mind is observable only through perception, and it is nothing more than the flow of ideas, sensations, and memories.

He drew a distinction between two kinds of mental contents: impressions and ideas. *Impressions* are the basic elements of mental life and are akin to sensation and perception in today's terminology. *Ideas* are the mental experiences we have in the absence of any stimulating object; the modern equivalent is image.

Hume did not define impressions and ideas in physiological terms or in reference to any external stimulus. He was careful not to assign any ultimate causes to impressions. These mental contents differ from ideas not in their source or point of origin but in their relative strength. Impressions are strong and vivid whereas ideas are weak copies of impressions. Both of these mental contents may be simple or complex, and a simple idea resembles its simple impression. Complex ideas do not necessarily resemble any simple ideas because complex ideas evolve from a combination of several simple ideas in some new pattern, and they are compounded from these simple ideas by association.

Two laws of association were proposed: *resemblance* or *similarity*, and *contiguity* in time or place. The more similar and contiguous are two ideas, the more readily they will be associated.

Hume's work fits within the mechanistic framework and continues the development of empiricism and associationism. He argued that just as astronomers determined the laws and forces of the physical universe by which the planets function, so it is possible to determine the laws of the mental universe. He believed that the laws of the association of ideas were the mental counterpart of the law of gravity in physics, that they were universal principles for the operation of the mind. Once again we see the notion that complex ideas are constructed mechanically by an amalgamation of simple ideas.

David Hartley (1705–1757)

David Hartley, the son of a minister, was preparing for a career in the church, but because of doctrinal difficulties, he turned to medicine instead. He led a quiet and uneventful life as a doctor and pursued the study of philosophy on his own. In 1749 he published *Observations on Man, His Frame, His Duty, and His Expectations*. This was Hartley's most important work and is considered by many to be the first systematic discourse on association.

Hartley is noteworthy not so much for the originality of his ideas on association as for the clarity and precision with which he organized and presented the earlier work of others. The concept of the association of ideas is not new with Hartley, as we have seen, but he served the significant purpose of bringing together the earlier threads of thought and is often acknowledged as the formal founder of associationism as a doctrine.

Hartley's fundamental law of association is contiguity, by which he attempted to explain the processes of memory, reasoning, emotion, and voluntary and involuntary action. Those ideas or sensations that occur together, simultaneously or successively, become associated, so that the occurrence of one results in the occurrence of the other. Hartley also believed that repetition as well as contiguity is necessary for the formation of associations.

He agreed with Locke that all ideas and knowledge are derived from sensory experience; there are no innate associations, no knowledge present at birth. As the child grows and accumulates a variety of sensory experiences, connections or trains of association of increasing complexity are established. In this way, higher systems of thought develop by the time the person reaches adulthood. Higher-order mental life may be analyzed or reduced to the elements or atoms from which it was formed through the mental compounding of associations. Hartley was the first to apply the doctrine of association to explain all types of mental activity.

Like others before him, Hartley viewed the mental world in mechanistic terms. In one respect he exceeded the aims of the other empiricists and associationists. Not only did he explain psychological processes in mechanical terms, but he also tried to explain their underlying physiological processes within that framework. It seems a natural thing for him to

David Hartley formalized the doctrine of association, which he used to explain all types of mental activity.

have attempted because of his training in medicine, which few of his predecessors or colleagues in philosophy shared.

Newton had stated that impulses in the physical world are vibratory in nature. Hartley used this principle to explain the operation of the brain and nervous system, and his ideas have been said to "prefigure some aspects of contemporary neurophysiology" (Smith, 1987, p. 123). Vibrations in the nerves — which Hartley believed were solid, not hollow as Descartes had thought — transmit impulses from one part of the body to another. These vibrations initiate smaller vibrations in the brain, which Hartley considered to be the physiological counterparts of ideas. The importance of this notion for psychology is that it was yet another attempt to use knowledge of the mechanical universe as a model for understanding human nature.

James Mill (1773–1836)

James Mill was educated at the University of Edinburgh in Scotland and served for a short time as a clergyman. When he discovered that no one could understand his sermons, he left the Church of Scotland to earn his living as a writer. His books were many and varied, and his most famous literary work is the *History of British India*, which took eleven years to complete. His most important contribution to psychology is *Analysis of the Phenomena of the Human Mind* (1829).

Mill applied the doctrine of mechanism to the human mind with a rare directness and comprehensiveness. His goal was to destroy the idea of subjective or psychic activities and demonstrate that the mind is nothing more than a machine. Mill believed that other empiricists, in arguing that the mind is similar to a machine in its operations, had not gone far enough. The mind *is* a machine — it functions in the same mechanical way as a clock — and it is set in operation by external physical forces and run by internal physical forces.

In James Mill's view, the mind is a passive entity that is acted on by external stimuli. The person responds to these stimuli automatically and is incapable of acting spontaneously. Obviously, then, Mill allowed for no freedom of the will. This point of view persists today in the forms of psychology that have derived from the mechanistic tradition, most notably in the behaviorism of B. F. Skinner.

As the title of his major work suggests, Mill believed that the mind should be studied by reducing or analyzing it into elementary components. This is, as we have seen, a tenet of mechanism. To understand complex phenomena in the mental or the physical world, whether ideas or clocks, it is necessary to break them down into their smallest parts. Mill wrote that a "distinct knowledge of the elements is indispensable to an accurate conception of that which is compounded of them" (Mill, 1829, Vol. 1, p. 1).

He suggested that sensations and ideas are the only kinds of mental elements that exist. In the familiar empiricist-associationist tradition, all knowledge begins with sensations, from which are derived the higher-level complexes of ideas through the process of association. To Mill, association is a matter of contiguity or concurrence alone and may be either simultaneous or successive.

Mill believed that the mind has no creative function, because association is a passive process. In other words, sensations that have occurred together in a certain order will be reproduced mechanically as ideas, and these ideas occur in the same order as their corresponding sensations. Association is treated in mechanical terms, and the resulting ideas are merely the accumulation or sum of the individual elements.

John Stuart Mill (1806–1873)

James Mill subscribed to Locke's argument that the human mind, at birth, is like white paper, a blank slate on which experience will write. When his son John was born, Mill vowed that he would determine the experiences that would fill the boy's mind, and he embarked on what may be the most rigorous example of private tutoring on record. Every day, for up to five hours, he drilled the child in Greek, Latin, algebra, geometry, logic, history, and political economy, repeatedly questioning the boy until he gave the correct answers.

At the age of three, John Stuart Mill was reading Plato in the original Greek. At eleven he wrote his first scholarly paper, and by twelve he had mastered the standard university curriculum of the day. By eighteen he described himself as a "logical machine," and at twenty-one he suffered a severe mental breakdown with intense feelings of depression. It took several years for him to recover a sense of self-worth.

He held a job with the East India Company for many years, handling routine correspondence concerning England's governance of India. At the age of twenty-four he fell in love with a beautiful and intelligent married woman, Harriet Taylor, who was to have a profound influence on his work. When Mrs. Taylor's husband died, nearly twenty years later, Mill married her, and he later wrote an essay entitled *The Subjection of Women*, which was inspired by her marital experiences with her first husband.

Mill was appalled that women had no financial or property rights, and he compared the plight of women to that of other disadvantaged groups. He condemned the idea that a wife was expected to submit to sex with her husband on demand, even against her will, and that divorce on the grounds of incompatibility was not permitted. He suggested that marriage should be more of a partnership between equals than a master–slave relationship (Rose, 1983).

Sigmund Freud later translated this essay into German, and in letters to his fiancée disparaged Mill's notion of the equality of the sexes. Freud wrote: "The position of woman cannot be other than what it is: to be an adored sweetheart in youth, and a beloved wife in maturity" (Freud, 1964, pp. 75–76).

Through his writings on a variety of topics, John Stuart Mill became a well-known figure and an influential contributor to what would soon become the new science of psychology. He argued against the mechanistic and atomistic position of his father, James Mill, who had viewed the mind as entirely passive, as something acted on by external stimuli. To John Stuart Mill the mind played an active role in the association of ideas. Complex ideas, he suggested, do not simply summate through the association of simple ideas. Complex ideas generated from simple ideas are

John Stuart Mill believed that the mind played an active role in the association of ideas.

more than the sum of the individual parts (the simple ideas), because they take on new qualities that were not present in the simpler elements. For example, mixing blue, red, and green pigments in the proper proportion yields white, which is an entirely new quality. In this creative synthesis point of view, the combination of mental elements always produces something new.

John Stuart Mill was influenced in his thinking by the findings from the science of chemistry, which provided him with a model or context that was different from the physics that had so strongly shaped the ideas of his father and the earlier empiricists and associationists. Researchers in chemistry were demonstrating the concept of synthesis, in which chemical compounds exhibited attributes not found in their component parts or elements. The proper combination of hydrogen and oxygen produces water, which has properties not found in either of the elements. Similarly, complex ideas emerge from combinations of simple ideas and possess characteristics not found in those elements. Mill called his approach to association *mental chemistry*.

Mill's second important contribution to psychology is his persuasive argument that it is possible to have a *science* of psychology. Mill made this assertion at a time when other philosophers, notably Auguste Comte, were denying that the mind could ever be studied scientifically. John Stuart Mill also proposed a field of study, which he called ethology, devoted to the consideration of factors that influence the development of the human personality.

Contributions of Empiricism to Psychology

With the development of empiricism, philosophers turned away from the earlier approaches to knowledge. Although they remained concerned with many of the same problems, their approach to these problems had become atomistic, mechanistic, and positivistic.

Reconsider the emphases of empiricism: the primary role of the processes of sensation, the analysis of conscious experience into elements, the synthesis of elements to form more complex mental experiences through the process of association, and the focus on conscious processes. The major role empiricism played in shaping the new scientific psychology was about to become evident, and we will see that the concerns of the empiricists form psychology's basic subject matter.

By the middle of the nineteenth century philosophy had done all it could. The theoretical rationale for a natural science of human nature had been established. What was needed to translate theory into actuality was an experimental attack on the subject matter. And that was soon to develop under the influence of experimental physiology, which provided the kinds of experimentation that completed the foundation for the new psychology.

Suggested Readings

Mechanism and the Clockwork Universe

Landes, D. S. (1983). *Revolution in Time: Clocks and the Making of the Modern World*. Cambridge MA: Belknap Press of Harvard University Press. Calls the invention of the mechanical clock one of the most significant events in human history and assesses the impact of clocks on the development of science and of society.

Lowry, R. (1982). *The Evolution of Psychological Theory: A Critical History of Concepts and Presuppositions* (2nd ed.). New York: Aldine. An analysis of the major assumptions and viewpoints from which modern psychology developed, beginning with seventeenth-century ideas of mental and physiological mechanism.

Descartes and the Mind-Body Problem

Watson, R. I. (1971). A prescriptive analysis of Descartes's psychological views. *Journal of the History of the Behavioral Sciences, 7*, 223–248. An overview and critical discussion of Descartes's views on the structure of the mind and his distinction between mind and body.

British Empiricism and Associationism

Drever, J. (1965). The historical background for national trends in psychology: On the nonexistence of English associationism. *Journal of the History of the Behavioral Sciences, 1*, 123–130. Describes the contributions to associationist thought of Locke, Berkeley, Hume, Hartley, and others.

Miller, E. F. (1971). Hume's contribution to behavioral science. *Journal of the History of the Behavioral Sciences, 7*, 154–168. Discusses the ideas in Hume's writings that provide a foundation for an empirical science of behavior.

Moore-Russell, M. E. (1978). The philosopher and society: John Locke and the English revolution. *Journal of the History of the Behavioral Sciences, 14*, 65–73. Notes the impact of the Zeitgeist and other social and political forces on the development of Locke's theories.

Smith, C. U. M. (1987). David Hartley's Newtonian neuropsychology. *Journal of the History of the Behavioral Sciences, 23*, 123–136. Describes Hartley's vibration theory of the functioning of the brain and nervous system, relating it to Newton's earlier work and to ideas in contemporary neuropsychology.

Warren, H. C. (1916). Mental association from Plato to Hume. *Psychological Review, 23*, 208–230. Covers ideas in associationism advanced by Locke, Berkeley, Hume, and others, and notes their roots in the work of earlier scholars such as Plato, Aristotle, and St. Augustine.

Physiological Influences on Psychology

3

The Role of the Human Observer

It all started with a difference of five-tenths of a second in the observations made by two astronomers. The year was 1795. The royal astronomer of England, Nevil Maskelyne, noticed that his assistant's observations of the time it took for a star to pass from one point to another were always slower than his own. Maskelyne admonished the man for repeatedly making mistakes and warned him to be more careful. The assistant tried, but the differences persisted. In time they increased, and five months later his observations were eight-tenths of a second slower than Maskelyne's. As a result, the assistant was fired, and he passed into that crowded place known as obscurity.

For the next twenty years the incident was ignored, until the phenomenon was investigated by Friedrich Wilhelm Bessel, a German astronomer who had long been interested in errors of measurement. He suspected that the mistakes made by Maskelyne's assistant were attributable to individual differences, personal differences over which people have no control. If this supposition was correct, Bessel reasoned, then such differences in observation would be found among all astronomers. He tested this hypothesis and found it to be correct. Disagreements were common, even among the most experienced astronomers.

This finding is important because it pointed to two inexorable conclusions. First, it meant that astronomy would have to take into account the nature of the human observer, because his or her personal characteristics could influence the reported observations. Second, if the role of the human observer had to be considered in astronomy, then surely it would need to be considered in every other science that relied on observation.

Philosophers such as Locke and Berkeley discussed the subjective nature of perception, arguing that there is not always — or even often — an exact correspondence between the nature of an object and a person's perception of it. With Bessel's work we have data from a hard science, astronomy, to illustrate the same point.

This event, then, forced the scientific community to focus on the role of the human observer and the nature of observation to account fully for the results of their experiments and the conclusions they drew about the nature of the physical world. Scientists proceeded to investigate the psychological processes of sensing and perceiving by studying the sense organs, those physiological mechanisms through which we receive our information about the world. Once the early physiologists began to study sensation, psychology was but a short and inevitable step away.

Developments in Early Physiology

The physiological research that directly stimulated and guided the new psychology was a product of the late nineteenth century. As with all endeavors, it had its antecedents, and it is instructive to consider that early work.

Physiology became an experimentally oriented discipline during the 1830s, primarily under the influence of the German physiologist Johannes Müller (1801–1858), who advocated the application of the experimental method to physiology. Müller held the prestigious position of professor of anatomy and physiology at the University of Berlin and was a phenomenally productive scientist, publishing, on the average, one scholarly paper every seven weeks. He maintained this pace for thirty-eight years. One of his most influential publications is the *Handbuch der Physiologie des Menschen* (*Handbook of Physiology of Mankind*), which summarized the physiological research of the period and systematized a large body of knowledge. Volumes of the *Handbuch* published between 1833 and 1840 cited much new work, indicating how widespread research in experimental physiology had become. The need for such a book was reflected in the rapid translation into English of the first volume in 1838 and the second in 1842.

Müller is also of importance to physiology and psychology for his theory of the ***specific energies of nerves***. He proposed that the arousal or stimulation of a given nerve always gives rise to a characteristic sensation, because each sensory nerve has its own specific energy. This idea stimulated a great deal of research that sought to localize functions within the nervous system and to delimit sensory receptor mechanisms on the periphery of the organism.

Several early physiologists made substantial contributions to the study of brain functions. Their work is significant for psychology because of their discoveries of specialized areas of the brain and their development of research methods that later were widely used in physiological psychology.

A pioneer in the investigation of reflex behavior was Marshall Hall (1790–1857), a Scots physician working in London. Hall observed that decapitated animals continued to move for some time when subjected to appropriate forms of stimulation. He concluded that various levels of behavior depended on different parts of the brain and nervous system. Specifically, he postulated that voluntary movement depends on the cerebrum, reflex movement on the spinal cord, involuntary movement on direct stimulation of the musculature, and respiratory movement on the medulla.

Pierre Flourens (1794–1867), a professor of natural history at the Collège de France in Paris, systematically destroyed various parts of the brain and spinal cord and observed the consequences. He concluded that the cerebrum controls the higher mental processes, parts of the midbrain control visual and auditory reflexes, the cerebellum controls coordination, and the medulla governs heartbeat, respiration, and other vital functions.

The findings of Hall and Flourens, although still generally valid, are for our purposes second in importance to their introduction of the method of *extirpation*. In this technique, the investigator attempts to determine the function of a given part of the brain by removing or destroying it and observing the resulting changes in the animal's behavior.

The mid-nineteenth century brought two additional experimental approaches to the study of the brain: the clinical method and the use of electrical stimulation. The clinical method was developed in 1861 by Paul Broca (1824–1880), a surgeon at a hospital for the insane near Paris. He performed an autopsy on a man who had been unable to speak intelligibly for many years. The examination revealed a lesion in the third frontal convolution of the cerebral cortex. Broca labeled this section of the brain the speech center; later it came to be called, appropriately, Broca's area. The clinical method is a useful supplement to extirpation because it is difficult to secure human subjects who will agree to removal of parts of their brains. As a sort of posthumous extirpation, the clinical method provides the opportunity to examine the damaged area of the brain — the area that is assumed to be responsible for a behavioral condition that existed before the patient died.

The use of electrical stimulation to study the brain was introduced by Gustav Fritsch and Eduard Hitzig in 1870. It involves the exploration of the cerebral cortex with weak electric currents. Fritsch and Hitzig found that stimulation of certain cortical areas resulted in motor responses. With the development of more sophisticated and precise electronic equipment, electrical stimulation became what is probably the single most productive technique for studying brain functions.

Much was being learned by physiologists about the structure and functioning of the human brain. Considerable research on the structure of the nervous system and the nature of neural activity was also being conducted. As we noted, there were two earlier theories about how nervous activity was transmitted in the body: the nerve tube theory embraced by Descartes, and Hartley's theory of vibrations.

Toward the end of the eighteenth century, the Italian researcher Luigi Galvani (1737–1798) had suggested that the nature of nerve impulses was electrical. His research was continued by his nephew, Giovanni Aldini, who "mixed serious research with showmanship. One of the more gruesome of Aldini's displays, designed to emphasize the effectiveness of electrical stimulation for obtaining spasmodic movements from muscles, involved using the recently severed heads of two criminals" (Boakes, 1984, p. 96). Research proceeded so rapidly and the results were so convincing that by the middle of the nineteenth century the electrical nature of nerve impulses was accepted as fact. It was believed that the nervous system was essentially a conductor of electrical impulses and that the central nervous system functioned much like a switching station, shunting the impulses onto either sensory or motor nerve fibers.

Although this position was a great advance over Descartes's nerve tube theory and Hartley's theory of vibrations, it was conceptually similar. Both the newer and older viewpoints were reflexive. Both suggested that something from the external world (a stimulus) impinged on a sense organ and excited a nerve impulse that traveled to the appropriate place in the brain or central nervous system. There, in response to the impulse, a new impulse was generated and transmitted via the motor nerves to effect some response by the organism.

The anatomical structure of the nervous system was also being defined during the nineteenth century. It came to be understood that the nerve fibers were actually composed of separate structures called neurons, which were somehow joined or linked at points called synapses. Such findings were congruent with a mechanistic and materialistic image of human beings. It was believed that the nervous system, like the mind, was composed of atomistic structures that combined to produce the more complex product.

The spirit of mechanism, therefore, was just as dominant in nineteenth-century physiology as it was in the philosophy of the time. Nowhere was this more pronounced than in Germany. In the 1840s, a group of scientists, many of them former students of Johannes Müller, formed the Berlin Physical Society. These scientists, all in their twenties, committed themselves to one proposition — that all phenomena, including those that pertained to living matter, could be accounted for in physical terms. What they hoped to do was to relate or connect physiology with physics. A physiology consonant with the spirit of mechanism was their goal. In a dramatic gesture, four of the young scientists (including Hermann von Helmholtz, whom we will meet shortly) took a solemn oath, signing it in their own blood, according to legend. The oath stated that the only forces active within an organism are the common physicochemical ones. And so the threads came together to form the core of nineteenth-century physiology: materialism, mechanism, empiricism, experimentation, and measurement.

The developments in early physiology indicate the kinds of research techniques and the discoveries that supported a scientific approach to the psychological investigation of the mind. We have suggested how the direction of physiological research influenced the newly emerging psychology. The major point is that while philosophers were paving the way for an experimental attack on the mind, physiologists were experimentally investigating the mechanisms underlying mental phenomena. The next step was to apply the experimental method to the mind itself.

The British empiricists had argued that sensation was the only source of all knowledge. The astronomer Bessel had demonstrated the importance of sensation and perception in science. Physiologists were defining the structure and function of the senses. It was time to experiment with and to quantify this doorway to the mind, the subjective, mentalistic experience of sensation. Techniques were available to investigate the body; now they were being developed to explore the mind. Experimental psychology was ready to begin.

The Beginnings of Experimental Psychology

Four scientists are directly responsible for the initial applications of the experimental method to the subject matter of psychology: Hermann von Helmholtz, Ernst Weber, Gustav Theodor Fechner, and Wilhelm Wundt. All four were German, trained in physiology, and aware of the impressive developments in physiology and in science in the middle of the nineteenth century.

Why Germany?

Scientific thought was developing in most of the countries of western Europe in the nineteenth century, particularly in England, France, and Germany. No one country had a monopoly on the enthusiasm, conscientiousness, or optimism with which the tools of science were viewed and used. Why, then, did experimental psychology begin in Germany and not in England or France? Were there some unique characteristics that made German science a more fertile breeding ground for the new psychology?

Although generalizations may be suspect and exceptions to the rule are frequently found, it can nonetheless be suggested that the times favored Germany as the place of origin for the new psychology. For a century, German intellectual history had paved the way for an experimental science of psychology. Experimental physiology was firmly established and was recognized to a degree not yet achieved in France and England. The so-called German temperament was well suited to the conscientious and minute taxonomic description and classification needed for work in biology, zoology, and physiology. The deductive and mathematical approach to science was favored in France and England whereas Germany, with its emphasis on the careful and thorough collection of observable facts, had adopted a classificatory or inductive approach.

Because biological and physiological science does not lend itself to grand generalizations from which facts can be deduced, biology was only slowly accepted into the scientific communities of England and France.

Germany, however, with its interest and faith in description and categorization, welcomed biology to its family of sciences.

Further, the Germans construed science broadly. Science in France and England was limited to physics and chemistry, which could be approached quantitatively; science in Germany included such areas as phonetics, linguistics, history, archeology, esthetics, logic, and literary criticism. French and English scholars were skeptical about applying science to something as complex as the human mind. Not so the Germans, and they plunged ahead, unconstrained by that prejudgment, using the tools of science to explore and measure the facets of mental life.

Germany also provided greater opportunities to learn and practice the new scientific techniques, and in this we see the influence of the contextual factor of the prevailing economic conditions. Because of its political situation, Germany had a great many universities. Prior to 1870, the year Germany became a unified nation with a central government, it consisted of a loose confederation of autonomous kingdoms, duchies, and city-states. Each of these separate districts or provinces had established its own well-financed university. Each had a highly paid faculty and the most advanced scientific laboratory equipment.

In contrast, England at that time had only two universities, Oxford and Cambridge, and neither facilitated, encouraged, or supported scientific research in any discipline. Indeed, they opposed adding new fields of study to the curriculum. In 1877, Cambridge vetoed a request to teach experimental psychology because it would "insult religion by putting the human soul on a pair of scales" (Hearnshaw, 1987, p. 125). Experimental psychology would not be taught at Cambridge for another twenty years and was not offered at Oxford until 1936. The only way to practice science in England was in the private manner of the gentleman-scientist, living on an independent income, the way of Charles Darwin or Francis Galton (see Chapter 6). The situation was similar in France, and in the United States there were no universities devoted to research until 1876, when Johns Hopkins University was founded in Baltimore, Maryland.

Thus, there were more opportunities for scientific research in Germany than elsewhere. Stated in pragmatic terms, a person could make a living as a research scientist in Germany but not in France, England, or the United States.

In the early nineteenth century, a wave of educational reform swept through the German universities. A new kind of institution, unknown elsewhere, was developing. It was devoted to the principles of academic freedom and to research for professors and students alike. Faculty members were free to teach whatever they wished without outside interference, and to conduct research on topics of their own choosing. Students were free to take whatever courses they preferred and were not bound by a rigid curriculum. This freedom also extended to the consideration of new sciences such as psychology.

This style of university provided the ideal environment for the flourishing of scientific inquiry. Professors could not only lecture, but they could also direct students in experimental research in well-equipped laboratories. In no other country was such an approach to science fostered at that time.

The climate of reform in German universities also encouraged their growth, and this meant that there were more positions for those interested in academic careers in science. The chances of becoming a well-paid and respected professor were much higher in Germany, although it remained difficult to attain the top positions. The promising university scientist was required to produce research judged by experts in the field to be a major contribution, research that went beyond the typical doctoral dissertation. This meant that most of those admitted to a university career were of extremely high caliber. Once these scientists joined the university community, the pressure on them to make ever greater contributions was keen.

Although the competition was intense and the demands were great, the rewards were more than worth the effort. Only the best succeeded in German science of the nineteenth century, and the result was a series of breakthroughs in all the sciences, including the new psychology. It is no coincidence that the persons directly responsible for the emergence of scientific psychology were German university professors.

Hermann von Helmholtz (1821–1894)

Helmholtz, a prolific researcher in physics and physiology, was one of the greatest scientists of the nineteenth century. Psychology ranked third among his areas of scientific contribution, yet his work, together with that of Fechner and Wundt, was instrumental in beginning the new psychology.

The Life of Helmholtz

Born in Potsdam, Germany, where his father taught at the *Gymnasium* (in. Europe, a high school–junior college preparatory for the university), Helmholtz was initially tutored at home because of his delicate health. At the age of seventeen he enrolled in a Berlin medical institute where no tuition was charged to those who agreed to serve as army surgeons after

The work of physicist-physiologist Hermann von Helmholtz on nerve conduction, color vision, and audition had a major impact on sensory psychology.

graduation. Helmholtz served for seven years, during which time he continued his studies in mathematics and physics and published several articles. He presented a paper on the indestructibility of energy, in which he mathematically formulated the law of the conservation of energy. After leaving the army, Helmholtz accepted a position as associate professor of physiology at the University of Königsberg. Over the next thirty years he held academic appointments in physiology at universities in Bonn and Heidelberg, and in physics at Berlin.

The tremendously energetic Helmholtz wrote in several different areas. In the course of his work on physiological optics he invented the ophthalmoscope, a device for examining the retina of the eye. His three-volume work on physiological optics (*Handbuch der Physiologischen Optik*) (1856–1866) proved to be so influential and enduring that it was translated into the English language sixty years later. He published his research on acoustical problems in 1863 in *On the Sensations of Tone*, which summarized his own findings and all the rest of the available literature. He also wrote on such diverse subjects as afterimages, color blindness, the Arabian-Persian musical scale, human eye movements, the formation of glaciers, geometrical axioms, and hay fever. In later years he contributed indirectly to the invention of wireless telegraphy and radio.

In the fall of 1893, while returning from a trip to the United States that included a visit to the Chicago World's Fair, Helmholtz suffered a severe fall aboard ship. Less than a year later he had a stroke that left him semiconscious and delirious. "His thoughts ramble on confusedly," his wife wrote, "real life and dream life, time and scene, all float mistily by in his brain — for the most part he does not know where he is . . . It is as if his soul were far, far away, in a beautiful ideal world, swayed only by science and the eternal laws" (Koenigsberger, 1965, p. 429).

Problems in Sensory Psychology

Of interest to psychology are Helmholtz's investigations of the speed of the neural impulse and his research on vision and audition. Before his time, it was thought that the neural impulse was instantaneous, or at least that it traveled too fast to be measured. Helmholtz provided the first empirical measurement of the rate of conduction by stimulating a motor nerve and the attached muscle in the leg of a frog, arranged so that the precise moment of stimulation as well as the resulting movement could be recorded. Working with different nerve lengths, he recorded the delay between stimulation of the nerve near the muscle and the muscle's response, and did the same for stimulation farther from the muscle. These measurements yielded the time required for conduction, the modest rate of ninety feet per second.

Helmholtz also experimented on the reaction times for sensory nerves in human subjects, studying the complete circuit from stimulation of a sense organ to the resulting motor response. The findings showed such enormous individual differences, as well as differences for the same person from one trial to the next, that Helmholtz abandoned the research.

Helmholtz's demonstration that the speed of conduction was not instantaneous suggested that thought and movement follow each other at a measurable interval and do not occur simultaneously, as had previously been thought. Helmholtz, however, was interested only in the measurement and not in its psychological significance. Later, the psychological implications of his research were recognized by others, who went on to make reaction-time experiments a fruitful line of research in the new psychology. Helmholtz's research was one of the first indications that it was possible to experiment on and measure a psychophysiological process.

His work on vision also had an influence on psychology. He investigated the external eye muscles and the mechanism by which the internal eye muscles focus the lens. In addition, he extended a theory of color vision that had been published in 1802 by Thomas Young; this is now known as the Young–Helmholtz theory.

No less important is Helmholtz's research on audition, namely the perception of combination tones and individual tones, and the nature of harmony and discord. He also formulated a resonance theory of hearing. The enduring influence of his work on vision and audition is evident from its inclusion in modern textbooks of psychology.

Helmholtz was not a psychologist, nor was psychology his main interest, but he contributed a large and important body of knowledge to sensory psychology and helped to strengthen the experimental approach to the study of psychological problems. He considered psychology to be a separate discipline, allied to metaphysics. The psychology of the senses was an exception, to Helmholtz, because of its connection with physiology. He was not concerned with the establishment of psychology as an independent science, but his influence was of such magnitude that he must be included among its direct contributors.

Ernst Weber (1795–1878)

Ernst Weber, the son of a theology professor, was born in Wittenberg, Germany. He earned his doctorate at the University of Leipzig in 1815 and taught anatomy and physiology there from 1817 until his retirement in

The experimental research on the two-point threshold by physiologist Ernst Weber provided a way of measuring a stimulus and a subject's perception of it.

1871. His primary research interest was the physiology of the sense organs, an area in which he made outstanding and lasting contributions.

Previous research on the sense organs had been limited almost exclusively to the higher senses of vision and hearing. Weber's work consisted largely of exploring new fields, notably cutaneous and muscular sensations. He is particularly noteworthy for his application of the experimental methods of physiology to problems of a psychological nature. His major contributions to psychology are his work on the two-point threshold of discrimination of the skin, and the just noticeable difference detected by the muscles. His experiments on the sense of touch mark a fundamental shift in the status of the subject matter of psychology. The ties with philosophy were, if not severed, at least severely weakened. Weber allied psychology with the natural sciences and helped to pave the way for the use of experimental investigation in the study of the mind.

The Two-Point Threshold

One of Weber's two major contributions to the new psychology involved his experimental determination of the accuracy of the two-point discrimination of the skin — the distance between two points that is necessary before subjects report feeling two distinct sensations. Without looking at the apparatus, which resembles a drawing compass, subjects are asked to report whether they feel one or two points touching the skin. When the two points of stimulation are close together, subjects report a clear sensation of being touched at only one point. As the distance between the two sources of stimulation is increased, subjects report uncertainty about whether they feel one or two sensations. Finally, a distance is reached where subjects report two distinct points of stimulation.

This procedure demonstrates the ***two-point threshold***, the threshold at which the two points of stimulation can be distinguished as such. Weber's research marks the first systematic, experimental demonstration of the concept of threshold — the point at which a psychological effect begins to be produced — and it is an idea that has been widely used in psychology from its beginnings to the present day.*

In additional research Weber demonstrated that this two-point threshold varies in different parts of the body of the same subject, and from one subject to another for the same part of the body. Although his attempt to account for these findings by hypothesizing sensory circles (areas in which doubleness is not perceived) is no longer of much importance, his experimental technique remains significant.

---

*Earlier in the nineteenth century the German philosopher and educator Johann Friedrich Herbart discussed the concept of threshold and applied it to consciousness, proposing a point at which unconscious ideas become conscious ideas (see Chapter 13).

The Just Noticeable Difference

Weber's second major contribution eventually led to the formulation of the first quantitative law of psychology. Weber wanted to determine the *just noticeable difference*, that is, the smallest difference between weights that could be detected. To do so, he asked his subjects to lift two weights, a standard weight and a comparison weight, and report whether one felt heavier than the other. Small differences between the weights resulted in judgments of sameness; large differences resulted in judgments of disparity between the weights. As the research progressed, Weber found that the just noticeable difference between two weights was a constant ratio, 1:40, of the standard weight. In other words, a weight of 41 grams was reported to be just noticeably different from a standard weight of 40 grams, and an 82-gram weight was just noticeably different from a standard weight of 80 grams.

Weber then undertook to investigate the contributions of muscular sensations in discriminating between weights. He found that subjects could discriminate much more accurately when the weights to be judged were lifted by the subjects themselves rather than placed in their hands by the experimenter. Lifting the weights involved both tactile and muscular sensations, whereas when the weights were placed in the hands, only tactile sensations were experienced. Because smaller differences in weights could be discriminated when the weights were lifted (a ratio of 1:40, as noted) than when the weights were placed in the hand (a ratio of 1:30), Weber concluded that the internal muscular sensations in the first instance influenced the ability to discriminate.

From these experiments Weber found that discrimination seemed to depend not on the absolute difference between two weights but on their relative difference or ratio. He conducted experiments involving visual discrimination and found that the ratio was smaller than for the muscle sense experiments. From this he suggested that there is a constant fraction or ratio for the just noticeable difference between two stimuli that is constant for each of the senses.

Weber's research showed that there is not a direct correspondence between a physical stimulus and our perception of it. Like Helmholtz, however, Weber was concerned with physiological processes and did not appreciate the significance of his work for psychology. What his research revealed was a way of investigating the relationship between body and mind, between the stimulus and the resulting sensation. This was indeed a major breakthrough; all that was necessary was for someone to realize its importance.

The work of Weber was experimental in the strictest sense of the term. Under well-controlled conditions, he systematically varied the stimuli and recorded the differential effects on the reported experience of each subject. His experiments stimulated a great deal of subsequent research and served to focus the attention of later physiologists on the validity and importance of the experiment as a means of studying psychological phenomena. Weber's research on threshold measurement was to be of paramount importance to the new psychology, and his demonstration that sensations can be measured has influenced virtually every aspect of psychology to the present day.

Gustav Theodor Fechner (1801–1887)

Fechner was a scholar who followed remarkably diverse intellectual pursuits during an active career of more than seventy years. He was a physiologist for seven years, a physicist for fifteen, a psychophysicist for fourteen, an experimental estheticist for eleven, a philosopher for forty—and an invalid for twelve. Of these endeavors, it is the work on psychophysics that brought his greatest fame, although he did not wish to be so remembered by posterity.

The Life of Fechner

Fechner was born in a village in southeastern Germany, where his father was the minister. He began medical studies at the University of Leipzig in 1817, and while there he attended Weber's lectures on physiology. Fechner remained at Leipzig for the rest of his life.

Even before he graduated from medical school, Fechner's humanistic side showed signs of rebelling against the prevailing materialism of his scientific training. Under the pen name "Dr. Mises" he wrote satirical essays lampooning medicine and science, a practice he continued for twenty-five years. This suggests a persistent conflict between the two sides of his personality—a love of science and an interest in metaphysics. His first such essay, "Proof that the Moon Is Made of Iodine," attacked the medical fad of using iodine as a panacea. Fechner was obviously troubled by the materialistic approach and strove to establish what he called his "day view"—that the universe can be regarded from the point of view of consciousness—in opposition to the "night view"—that the universe, including consciousness, consists of inert matter.

After completing his medical studies, Fechner began a second career in physics and mathematics at Leipzig, during which time he translated handbooks of physics and chemistry from French into German. By 1830

By demonstrating that the amount of sensation depends on the amount of stimulation, Gustav Theodor Fechner showed that the mental and material worlds could be related quantitatively.

he had translated more than a dozen volumes, and this activity brought him some recognition as a physicist. In 1824 he began lecturing in physics at the university and conducting research of his own. By the late 1830s he had developed an interest in sensation, and in undertaking research on visual afterimages he seriously injured his eyes by looking at the sun through colored glasses.

In 1833, after many years of hard work, Fechner obtained the prestigious appointment of professor at Leipzig, whereupon he fell into a depression that lasted for several years. He had difficulty sleeping, could not digest food (yet he felt no hunger and his body approached a state of starvation), and was unusually sensitive to light. He spent most of his time in a darkened room whose walls were painted black, listening while his mother read to him through a narrow opening in the door. He complained of chronic exhaustion and, for a time, lost all interest in living.

He tried walking — at first only at night, when it was dark, and then in daylight with his eyes bandaged — hoping to counter his boredom and depression. As a form of catharsis he composed a number of riddles and poems, including one he called "Mouse Heaven." He also tried a variety of medical therapies, including laxatives, electric shock, steam treatments, and a form of shock therapy that involved the application of burning substances to the skin, but none of them provided a cure.

Fechner's illness may have been neurotic in nature, a suggestion that is supported by the bizarre way in which he was eventually cured. His recovery began when a friend dreamed that she had made him a meal of spiced raw ham soaked in Rhine wine and lemon juice. The next day she prepared the dish and brought it to Fechner, insisting that he eat it. He did, albeit reluctantly, and began to eat more and more of the meat every day, which led him to feel somewhat better.

His improvement was short-lived, however, and after about six months, the symptoms worsened to the point where he feared for his sanity. "I had the distinct feeling," he wrote, "that my mind was hopelessly lost unless I could stem the flood of disturbing thoughts. Often the least important matters bothered me in this manner and it took me often hours, even days, to rid myself of these worries" (Kuntze, 1892, quoted in Balance & Bringmann, 1987, p. 42).

Fechner forced himself to keep busy at routine, mechanical chores, as a form of occupational therapy, but he was limited to tasks that did not make demands on his mind or his eyes. "I made strings and bandages," he wrote, "dipped candles . . . rolled yarn and helped in the kitchen sorting [and] cleaning lentils, making bread crumbs, and grinding a sugarloaf into powdered sugar. I also peeled and chopped carrots and turnips . . . a thousand times I wished to be dead" (Kuntze, 1892, quoted in Balance & Bringmann, 1987, p. 43).

Slowly, gradually, Fechner redeveloped an interest in the world around him, and he continued the diet of spiced raw ham soaked in wine and lemon juice. Then he had a dream in which the number 77 appeared. This persuaded him that he would be cured in seventy-seven days. And of course he was. He felt so well that his depression turned to euphoria and delusions of grandeur, and he claimed that God had chosen him to solve all the riddles of the world. Out of this experience he developed the notion of the pleasure principle, which many years later would influence the work of Sigmund Freud.

In 1844 Fechner was given a small pension from the university and officially established as an invalid. Yet not one of the next forty-three years of his life passed without a serious scholarly contribution from him, and his health remained excellent until his death at the age of eighty-six.

The Quantitative Relationship Between Mind and Body

October 22, 1850 is an important date in the history of psychology. While lying in bed that morning, Fechner had an insight that the law governing the connection between mind and body could be found in a quantitative relationship between a mental sensation and a material stimulus. An increase in the intensity of a stimulus, Fechner said, does not produce a one-to-one increase in the intensity of the sensation. Rather, a geometric series characterizes the stimulus, whereas an arithmetic series characterizes the sensation. For example, adding the sound of one bell to that of an already ringing bell produces a greater increase in sensation than adding one bell to ten others already ringing. The effects of stimulus intensities, therefore, are not absolute but are relative to the amount of sensation that already exists.

What this simple yet brilliant revelation showed was that the amount of sensation (the mental quality) depended on the amount of stimulation (the physical or material quality). To measure the change in sensation, we must measure the change in stimulation. Thus, it is possible to relate the mental and material worlds quantitatively. Fechner crossed the barrier between body and mind by relating one to the other empirically.

Although the concept was clear, how was it to be translated into actuality? One would have to measure precisely both intensities, the subjective and the objective, the mental sensation and the physical stimulus. To measure the physical intensity of the stimulus was not difficult — one could record the level of brightness or the weight of various stimulus objects, for example — but how was one to measure sensation, the conscious experience that the subjects reported when they responded to the stimulus?

Fechner noted two ways to measure sensations. First, we can determine whether a stimulus is present or absent, sensed or not sensed. Second, we can measure the stimulus intensity at which subjects report that sensation first occurs; this is the *absolute threshold* of sensitivity, that point in stimulus intensity below which no sensation is reported and above which subjects do experience a sensation.

The absolute threshold, although useful, is limited because only one value of a sensation — its lowest level — is determined. To relate both intensities, we must be able to specify the full range of stimulus values and their resulting sensation values. To accomplish this, Fechner proposed the ***differential threshold*** of sensitivity, the least amount of change in a stimulus that will give rise to a change in sensation. For example, by how much must a weight be decreased before subjects will sense the change, before they will report a just noticeable difference in sensation?

To measure how heavy a particular weight feels (how heavy the subjects sense it to be), we cannot use the physical measurement of the object's weight. We can, however, use that physical measurement as a basis for measuring the psychological intensity of the sensation. First, we measure how much the weight must be decreased in intensity before subjects are barely able to discriminate the difference. Second, we change the weight of the object to this lower value and then measure the size of the difference threshold again. Because both weight changes are just barely noticeable, Fechner assumed that they were subjectively equal. This process can be repeated until the object is barely felt by the subjects. If every decrease in weight is subjectively equal to every other decrease, the number of times the weight has to be decreased — the number of just noticeable differences — can be used as an objective measure of the subjective magnitude of the sensation. In this way we are measuring the stimulus values necessary to give rise to a difference between two sensations.

Fechner suggested that for each sense modality there is a certain relative increase in the stimulus that always produces an observable change in the intensity of the sensation. Thus, the sensation (the mind or mental quality), as well as the excitatory stimulus (the body or material quality), can be measured, and the relationship between the two can be stated as an equation:

$$S = K \log R$$

in which S is the magnitude of the sensation, K is a constant, and R is the magnitude of the stimulus. The relationship is logarithmic; one series increases arithmetically and the other geometrically.

Fechner said that this notion had not been suggested to him by Weber's work, even though Weber was also at the University of Leipzig, where the two saw each other frequently, and Weber had written on this topic only a few years earlier. Fechner wrote that he did not discover Weber's work until after he had begun the series of experiments designed to test his hypothesis. He later realized that the principle to which he gave mathematical form was essentially what Weber's work had demonstrated.

The Methods of Psychophysics

The immediate result of Fechner's insight was the development of a research program on what he later called psychophysics. (The word *psychophysics* defines itself—the relationship between the mental and material worlds.) In the course of this research, with its experiments on lifted weights, visual brightness, and tactile and visual distances, Fechner developed one and systematized two of the three fundamental methods of psychophysics that are still used today: the method of average error, the method of constant stimuli, and the method of limits.

Fechner developed the *method of average error* (also called the *method of adjustment*) in collaboration with A. W. Volkmann, a professor of physiology at the University of Halle in Germany. The method consists in having subjects adjust a variable stimulus until they perceive it to be equal to a constant standard stimulus.

Over a number of trials, the mean value of the differences between the standard stimulus and the subjects' setting of the variable stimulus represents the error of observation. The method assumes that our sense organs are subject to variability, which prevents us from obtaining a true measure. Accordingly, we obtain a large number of approximate measures, the mean or average of which represents the best single approximation of the true value. The technique is useful for measuring reaction time, visual and auditory discriminations, and the extent of illusions. In an extended form, it is fundamental to much current psychological research. Every time we calculate a mean we are, in essence, using the method of average error.

The *method of constant stimuli*, first called the method of right and wrong cases, was originated by Karl von Vierordt, a physiologist, but was developed as a tool by Fechner. He used it for his elaborate work with lifted weights, studies that consisted of more than 67,000 comparisons. The technique involves two constant stimuli, and the aim is to measure the stimulus difference that is required to produce a given proportion of correct judgments. For example, subjects first lift the standard weight of 100 grams and then lift a comparison weight of, say, 88, 92, 96, 104, or 108 grams. They must judge whether the second weight is heavier, lighter, or equal to the first. The process is continued until a certain number of judgments have been made for each comparison.

For the heavier weights, subjects almost always report a judgment of "heavier," and the lightest weights almost always are reported as "lighter." From these data, the stimulus difference (standard versus comparison weights) is determined for that point at which subjects correctly report "heavier" 75 percent of the time. A number of variations of the basic procedure have rendered it useful for a range of measurement problems in determining sensory thresholds.

The third of Fechner's psychophysical methods was originally known as the method of just noticeable differences and later came to be called the *method of limits*. The technique has been traced to 1700 and was formalized by Charles Delezenne in 1827. Weber also investigated just noticeable differences, as we noted, but the method was developed formally by Fechner in connection with his work on vision and temperature sensations.

In the method of limits, two stimuli are presented to the subjects. One stimulus is increased or decreased until subjects report that they detect a difference. Fechner recommended starting the variable stimulus at an intensity clearly higher than the standard stimulus at one time, and clearly lower than the standard stimulus the next time. Data are obtained from a number of trials, and the just noticeable differences are averaged to determine the differential threshold. A variation using a single stimulus is used to determine the absolute threshold.

Fechner carried on his research in psychophysics for seven years, publishing part of it for the first time in two short papers in 1858 and 1859. In 1860 the formal and complete exposition of his work appeared in the *Elemente der Psychophysik* (*Elements of Psychophysics*), a textbook of the exact science of the "functionally dependent relations . . . of the material and the mental, of the physical and psychological worlds" (Fechner, 1860/1966, p. 7). The book is one of the outstanding original contributions to the development of the science of psychology. Fechner's statement of the quantitative relationship between stimulus intensity and sensation was considered, at the time, to be comparable to Galileo's discovery of the laws of the lever and of falling bodies.

At the beginning of the nineteenth century, the German philosopher Immanuel Kant insisted that psychology could never become a science because it was impossible to experiment on or measure psychological phenomena and processes. Because of Fechner's work, which did indeed make it possible to measure the mind, Kant's assertion could no longer be regarded seriously.

It was largely because of Fechner's psychophysical research that Wilhelm Wundt conceived the plan of his experimental psychology. Fechner's methods have proved applicable to a wider range of psychological problems than he ever imagined, and with only minor modifications these methods are still applied in psychological research today. Fechner gave psychology what every discipline that hopes to be a science must possess — precise, elegant techniques of measurement.

Although Weber's work preceded his, the accolades have been heaped upon Fechner. He seems to have used and built on Weber's work, but he did much more than extend it. Weber's aims were limited; he was a physiologist working on just noticeable differences, and the larger significance of this work escaped him. Fechner sought a mathematical statement of the relationship between the physical and mental worlds. His brilliant and independent insights about measuring sensations and relating them to their stimulus measures were necessary before the implications and consequences of Weber's earlier work could be recognized and applied to make psychology an exact science.

The Formal Founding of the New Science of Psychology

By the middle of the nineteenth century, the methods of natural science were being used to investigate purely mental phenomena. Techniques had been developed, apparatus devised, important books written, and widespread interest aroused. British empiricism and the work in astronomy emphasized the importance of the senses, and the German scientists were describing how the senses functioned. The positivistic spirit of the times encouraged the convergence of these two lines of thought. Still lacking, however, was someone to bring them together, someone, in a word, to *found* the new science. This final touch was provided by Wilhelm Wundt.

Wundt is the founder of psychology as a formal academic discipline, the first person in the history of psychology to be designated properly and unreservedly a psychologist. As the first psychologist, Wundt founded the first laboratory, edited the first journal, and began experimental psychology as a science. The areas he investigated — including sensation and perception, attention, feeling, reaction, and association — became basic chapters in textbooks that were yet to be written. That so much of the history of psychology after Wundt consists of opposition to his view of psychology does not detract from his achievements and contributions as the founder.

Why have the honors for founding the new psychology fallen to Wundt and not to Fechner? Fechner's *Elements of Psychophysics* was published in 1860, at least fifteen years before Wundt is said to have begun psychology. Wundt himself wrote that Fechner's work represented the "first conquest" in experimental psychology (Wundt, 1888, p. 471). Historians agree on Fechner's importance; some even question whether psychology could have begun when it did were it not for Fechner's work. Why, then, does history not credit Fechner with founding psychology? The answer lies in the nature of the process of founding.

Founding is a deliberate and intentional act involving abilities and characteristics that differ from those necessary for brilliant scientific achievement. Founding requires the integration and consideration of previous work and the publication and promotion of the newly organized material. "When the central ideas are all born, some promoter takes them in hand, organizes them, adding whatever else seems to him essential, publishes and advertises them, insists upon them, and in short 'founds' a school" (Boring, 1950, p. 194). Wundt's contribution to the founding of modern psychology stems not so much from any unique scientific discovery as from his "heroic propagandizing for experimentalism" (O'Donnell, 1985, p. 16).

Founding is thus quite different from originating, although the distinction is not meant to be a disparaging one. Originators and founders are both essential to the formation of a science, as indispensable as are the designer and the builder in the construction of a house.

With this distinction in mind, we can understand why Fechner is not called the founder of psychology. Stated simply, he was not trying to found a new science. His quest was to understand the nature of the relationship between the mental and material worlds. He sought to demonstrate a unified conception of mind and body that proceeded from mystical speculation but had a scientific basis. "One cannot say that his innovation of psychophysics would have been developed into a discipline of experimental psychology if an institutionally-based movement had not been founded subsequently" (Ben-David & Collins, 1966, p. 455).

Wundt, however, set out deliberately to found a new science. In the preface to the first edition of his *Principles of Physiological Psychology* (1873–1874) he wrote: "The work I here present to the public is an attempt to mark out a new domain of science." Wundt was interested in promoting psychology as an independent science. Nevertheless, it bears repeating that although Wundt is considered to have founded psychology, he did not originate it. Psychology emerged, as we have seen, from a long line of creative efforts.

During the last half of the nineteenth century, the Zeitgeist was ready for the application of the experimental approach to problems of the mind. Wundt was a vigorous agent of what was already developing, a gifted promoter of the inevitable.

Suggested Readings

Why Germany?
Dobson, V., & Bruce, D. (1972). The German university and the development of experimental psychology. *Journal of the History of the Behavioral Sciences, 8,*

204–207. Cites the freedom of teaching and learning in German universities as a precondition for the growth of the new discipline of psychology.

Early Experimental Physiology

Fearing, F. (1970). *Reflex Action: A Study in the History of Physiological Psychology*. Cambridge MA: MIT Press. Covers discoveries and advances in neurophysiology of the seventeenth to nineteenth centuries; originally published in 1930.

Kirsch, I. (1976). The impetus to scientific psychology: A recurrent pattern. *Journal of the History of the Behavioral Sciences, 12*, 120–129. Describes the rise of experimental psychology and notes the parallels between its history and the history of the physical sciences.

Ladd, G. T., & Woodworth, R. S. (1911). *Elements of Physiological Psychology* (rev. ed.). New York: Scribner's. A classic textbook summarizing the major findings in early physiological psychology; covers research on the anatomy of the nervous system and the senses, the localization of cerebral functioning, psychophysics, and sensations and feelings.

Helmholtz

Pastore, N. (1973). Helmholtz's "Popular Lectures on Vision." *Journal of the History of the Behavioral Sciences, 9*, 190–202. Describes Helmholtz's work on vision, especially the problems of constancy and illusions.

Stumpf, C. (1895). Hermann von Helmholtz and the new psychology. *Psychological Review, 2*, 1–12. A review of Helmholtz's research as it relates to the focus and goals of the new psychology; written by an important early psychologist working at the University of Berlin.

Turner, R. S. (1977). Hermann von Helmholtz and the empiricist vision. *Journal of the History of the Behavioral Sciences, 13*, 48–58. Describes the influence of Helmholtz's philosophical ideas on his program of research.

Fechner

Boring, E. G. (1961). Fechner: Inadvertent founder of psychophysics. *Psychometrika, 26*, 3–8. Presents an overview of Fechner's life and assesses the importance of his work for the founding and development of experimental psychology.

Fechner, G. (1966). *Elements of Psychophysics* (vol. 1). New York: Holt, Rinehart and Winston. A reprint of Fechner's classic work, originally published in 1860; describes the methods of psychophysics that gave psychology its scientific techniques of measurement and discusses the relationship between physical or material stimuli and mental sensations.

Marshall, M. E. (1969). Gustav Fechner, Dr. Mises, and the comparative anatomy of angels. *Journal of the History of the Behavioral Sciences, 5*, 39–58. Explores the topics of Fechner's essays written under the pseudonym "Dr. Mises" and offers insights on his day view and night view of the universe.

The New Psychology

4

A Case of Distorted Data

Wilhelm Wundt, as the founder of the new science of psychology, is one of the field's most important figures. A knowledge of his approach to psychology is vital to an understanding of the history of the discipline. Yet more than a century after Wundt founded psychology, new data (or refinements of known data) led some psychologists to conclude that the accepted view of Wundt's system was wrong. Wundt, who had "a horror of being misunderstood and misrepresented," suffered just that fate (Baldwin, 1980, p. 301).

Many articles published in the 1970s and 1980s echoed this theme — that the Wundt depicted in psychology's textbooks and classrooms had little in common with the actual person and his views (see, for example, Blumenthal, 1975, 1979; Leahey, 1981). Descriptions of Wundtian psychology had portrayed his positions inaccurately, sometimes ascribing to him beliefs that were the opposite of his own intentions.

How could such mistakes be made with the work of such a prominent person? Wundt wrote many books and articles presenting his views of the nature of psychology. His system was there for all to see — for all, that is, who were fluent in the German language and were willing to devote the time needed to study Wundt's phenomenal output of published material.

But why go to all that trouble? Most psychologists did not think it was necessary to read Wundt in the original German, because his most important works had been translated into English by his student E. B. Titchener, an English psychologist, who spent most of his career at Cornell University in Ithaca, New York (Chapter 5). Titchener pronounced himself to be Wundt's loyal follower and true interpreter. He proclaimed that Wundt was the "source of his psychology and the precursor who validated his credentials" (Anderson, 1980, p. 95). Therefore, it came to be believed that Titchener's approach to psychology, which he called structuralism, was essentially a mirror-image of the work of his mentor Wundt. If one knew Titchener's system, then one knew Wundt's as well.

Later research on Wundt's writings cast doubt on that conclusion. Titchener did not represent Wundt. Evidence suggested that he altered Wundt's positions to make them appear compatible with his own, to lend credibility to his own views by asserting that they were consistent with those of psychology's great founder.

Titchener apparently elected to translate only those portions of Wundt's publications that supported his own approach to psychology. We do not know whether he made a deliberate decision to do this, but the result — the distorted presentation of Wundt's system of psychology — was the same, whether or not Titchener was consciously aware of his actions.

Titchener's inaccurate and incomplete version of Wundt's system influenced several generations of psychologists, not only because of the status Titchener achieved within American psychology, but also because of the visibility attained by his student E. G. Boring, who became, for a time, the leading historian of psychology. Boring claimed that Titchener was a Wundtian in the Leipzig tradition. Although Boring also stated that Titchener's work was "distinct from the [school] of Wundt" (Boring, 1950, p. 419), many psychologists who learned their history from Boring's *A History of Experimental Psychology* (1929, 1950) came to identify Titchener's system with Wundt's.

Thus, generations of students were offered a portrait of Wundtian psychology that turned out to be more myth than fact, more legend than truth. For one hundred years, teachers and textbooks in the history of psychology (including earlier editions of this text) compounded and reinforced the error under the imprimatur of their alleged expertise. This experience provides another example of how the changing data of history can influence our understanding of past events. As we noted in Chapter 1, history is not static or stagnant but is subject to revision as new data or refinements of existing data are revealed.

Wilhelm Wundt (1832–1920)

After reviewing Wundt's life, we shall consider his definition of psychology and how it influenced the subsequent development of the field.

The Life of Wundt

Wilhelm Wundt spent his early years in small towns near Mannheim, Germany, and his childhood was marked by intense loneliness. He earned poor grades in school and lived the life of an only child; his older brother was at boarding school. His only friend his own age was a mentally retarded boy who was good natured but could barely speak. Wundt's father was a pastor, and although both parents seem to have been sociable, Wundt's early memories of his father were unpleasant. He recalled that his father visited his school one day and hit him across the face for not paying attention to the teacher.

Beginning in the second grade, Wundt's education was undertaken by his father's assistant, a young vicar for whom the boy developed a strong emotional attachment. When the vicar was transferred to a neighboring town, Wundt became so upset that he was allowed to live with the vicar until the age of thirteen.

There was a strong tradition of scholarship in the Wundt family, with ancestors of intellectual renown in virtually every discipline. It appeared, nonetheless, that this impressive line would not be continued by the young Wundt. He spent much more time daydreaming than studying, and he failed in his first year at the *Gymnasium*. He did not get along well with his classmates and was ridiculed by his teachers.

Gradually, however, Wundt learned to control his daydreaming, and he even became relatively popular. He always disliked school, but he

Wilhelm Wundt founded the experimental science of psychology and established its first laboratory at the University of Leipzig, Germany.

nevertheless developed his intellectual interests and abilities. By the time he graduated at the age of nineteen, he was ready for the university.

To earn a living and study science at the same time, Wundt decided to become a physician. His medical studies took him to the University of Tübingen and then to the University of Heidelberg, where he studied anatomy, physiology, physics, medicine, and chemistry. (In his work in chemistry he came under the influence of the famous Robert Bunsen.) Wundt slowly came to realize that the practice of medicine was not for him, and he changed his major field to physiology.

After a semester of study at the University of Berlin with the great physiologist Johannes Müller, Wundt returned to Heidelberg to take his doctorate in 1855. He held an appointment as lecturer in physiology at Heidelberg from 1857 to 1864, and in 1858 was appointed laboratory assistant to Hermann von Helmholtz. He found the work of drilling new students in their laboratory fundamentals to be dreary, so he resigned the post after a few years. In 1864 he was promoted to associate professor and remained at the University of Heidelberg for another ten years.

In the course of his physiological research at Heidelberg, Wundt began to conceive of a psychology that would be an independent and experimental science. He presented his initial proposal for a new science of psychology in a book entitled *Beiträge zur Theorie der Sinneswahrnehmung* (*Contributions to the Theory of Sensory Perception*), which was published in sections between 1858 and 1862. In addition to describing his own original experiments, which he conducted in a crude laboratory built in his home, he offered his views on the methods of the new psychology. In this book Wundt also used the term *experimental psychology* for the first time. Along with Fechner's *Elements of Psychophysics* (1860), the *Beiträge* is often considered to mark the literary birth of the new science.

The *Beiträge* was followed in 1863 by *Vorlesungen über die Menschen- und Thierseele* (*Lectures on the Minds of Men and Animals*). An indication of the importance of this publication was its revision almost thirty years later, with an English translation and repeated reprintings until after Wundt's death in 1920. In it Wundt discussed many problems, such as reaction time and psychophysics, that were to occupy the attention of experimental psychologists for years.

Beginning in 1867, Wundt offered a course at Heidelberg on physiological psychology, the first formal offering of such a course anywhere in the world. Out of his lectures came a highly significant book, *Grundzüge der physiologischen Psychologie* (*Principles of Physiological Psychology*), published in two parts in 1873 and 1874. Six editions appeared over thirty-seven years, with the last published in 1911. Undoubtedly Wundt's masterpiece, this book firmly established psychology as a laboratory science with its own problems and methods of experimentation.

For many years, the successive editions of the *Grundzüge* served experimental psychologists as a storehouse of information and a record of the progress of the new psychology. It was in the preface to this book that Wundt stated his goal of attempting "to mark out a new domain of science." The term *physiological psychology* in the title may be misleading. At the time, the word *physiological* was used as a synonym for the word for *experimental* in German. Thus, Wundt was teaching and writing about experimental psychology, not physiological psychology as we know it today.

Wundt began the longest and most important phase of his career in 1875 when he accepted a position as professor of philosophy at the University of Leipzig, where he worked prodigiously for forty-five years. He established a laboratory at Leipzig shortly after he arrived, and in 1881 began the journal *Philosophische Studien* (*Philosophical Studies*), the official organ of the new laboratory and the new science. He had intended to call the journal *Psychological Studies*, but he changed his mind, apparently because there already was such a journal (although it dealt with spiritualism and the occult). In 1906, however, Wundt retitled his journal *Psychological Studies*. With a handbook, a laboratory, and a scholarly journal, psychology was well under way.

Wundt's spreading fame and his laboratory drew a large number of students to Leipzig to work with him. Among these were many subsequent contributors to psychology, including several Americans, most of whom returned to the United States to begin laboratories of their own. Through these students, the Leipzig laboratory exerted an immense influence on the development of modern psychology, serving as the model for the many new laboratories that were being developed. In addition to those begun in the United States, laboratories were established in Italy, Russia, and Japan by students from those countries who had journeyed to Leipzig to study with Wundt. More of Wundt's books were translated into Russian than into any other language, and Russian adulation of Wundt led psychologists in Moscow to build a duplicate of Wundt's own lab in 1912. Another replica was built by Japanese students at Tokyo University in 1920, the year Wundt died, but it was burned in a student riot in the 1960s (Blumenthal, 1985). The students who flocked to Leipzig were united in point of view and purpose — at least initially — and constituted the first formal school of thought within psychology.

Wundt's lectures at Leipzig were popular and well attended. At one time he had more than six hundred students in a class. His classroom manner has been described by his student E. B. Titchener in a letter Titchener wrote in 1890, just after attending Wundt's lectures for the first time:

The [attendant] swung the door open, and Wundt came in. All in black, of course, from boots to necktie; a spare, narrow-shouldered figure, stooping a little from the hips; he gave the impression of height, though I doubt if in fact he stands more than 5 ft. 9.

He clattered—there is no other word for it—up the side-aisle and up the steps of the platform; slam bang, slam bang, as if his soles were made of wood. There was something positively undignified to me about this stamping clatter, but nobody seemed to notice it.

He came to the platform, and I could get a good view of him. Hair iron-grey, and a fair amount of it, except on the top of his head— which was carefully covered by long wisps drawn up from the side. . . .

The platform has a long desk, I suppose for demonstrations, and on that an adjustable bookrest. Wundt made a couple of mannered movements—snatched his forefinger across his forehead, arranged his chalk—and then faced his audience with both elbows set on this rest. A curious attitude, which favors the impression of height. He began his lecture in a high-pitched, weak, almost apologetic voice; but after a sentence or two, during which the room settled down to silence, his full lecturing voice came out, and was maintained to the end of the hour. It is an easy and abundant bass, somewhat toneless, at times a little barking; but it carries well, and there is a certain persuasiveness, a sort of fervor, in the delivery that holds your inter-est and prevents any feeling of monotony. . . . The lecture was given without reference to notes: Wundt, so far as I could tell, never looked down once at the bookrest, though he had some little shuffle of papers there between his elbows. . . .

Wundt did not keep his arms lying on the rest: the elbows were fixed, but the arms and hands were perpetually coming up, pointing and waving. . . . the movements were subdued, and seemed in some mysterious way to be illustrative. . . .

He stopped punctually at the stroke of the clock, and clattered out, stooping a little, as he had clattered in. If it wasn't for this absurd clatter I should have nothing but admiration for the whole proceed-ing. (Baldwin, 1980, pp. 287–289)

At the first conference with each new group of graduate students, Wundt appeared with a list of research topics. An American student from Pennsylvania, James McKeen Cattell (Chapter 8), recalled the manner in which Wundt's students received their assignments (Baldwin, 1980, p. 283): "He had in his hand a memorandum containing a list of subjects for research, and taking us in the order in which we stood—there was no question of our being seated — assigned the topics and hours to us." Wundt closely supervised the doctoral research and held absolute power of acceptance or rejection on completion of the dissertation. The spirit of German scientific dogmatism flourished openly at the Leipzig laboratory.

In his personal life, Wundt was quiet and unassuming, and his days followed a carefully regulated pattern. (The diaries of Mrs. Wundt were found in the 1970s, revealing much new material about Wundt's personal life; this is another instance of newly discovered data of history.) In the morning Wundt worked on a book or article, read student theses, and edited his journal. In the afternoon he attended examinations or visited the laboratory. Cattell recalled that Wundt's laboratory visits were limited to five or ten minutes. Apparently, despite his great faith in laboratory research, "he was not himself a laboratory worker" (Cattell, 1928, p. 545). Later in the day Wundt would take a walk while thinking about his afternoon lecture, which he habitually delivered at 4:00 P.M. Many of his evenings were devoted to music, politics, and, at least in his younger years, concern with student and worker rights. The Wundt family enjoyed a sizable income, employed servants, and entertained frequently.

With the laboratory and journal established, and an immense amount of research under his direction, Wundt turned his energy to philosophy. During the years from 1880 to 1891, he wrote on ethics, logic, and systematic philosophy. He published the second edition of *Principles of Physiological Psychology* in 1880 and the third edition in 1887, and continued to contribute articles to the *Studien*.

Another field on which Wundt focused his considerable talent had been outlined in the *Beiträge* in 1862, the creation of a social psychology. Toward the end of the century he returned to this project, which culminated in the ten volumes of his *Völkerpsychologie* (*Cultural Psychology*), published between 1900 and 1920; the title is often translated inaccurately as "folk psychology."

Cultural psychology was concerned with the investigation of the various stages of mental development as manifested in language, art, myths, social customs, law, and morals. The implications of this work for psychology are of greater significance than its content; it served to divide the new science of psychology into two parts, the experimental and the social. The simpler mental functions, such as sensation and perception, can and must be studied by laboratory investigation, Wundt believed. But he argued that scientific experimentation is impossible for the study of the higher mental processes, such as learning and memory, because they are conditioned by linguistic habits and other aspects of cultural training. To Wundt, the higher thought processes could be studied effectively only by the nonexperimental approaches of sociology, anthropology, and social psychology. The contention that social forces play a major role in the development of the higher mental processes is important, but Wundt's conclusion that these processes cannot be studied experimentally was refuted not long after he stated it, as we shall see later in this chapter.

Wundt devoted ten years to the development of his cultural psychology and considered it a central part of psychology, but it has had little impact on American psychology. A survey covering ninety years of articles published in the *American Journal of Psychology* showed that, of all the citations to Wundt's publications, less than 4 percent were to *Cultural Psychology*. In contrast, Wundt's *Principles of Physiological Psychology* accounted for more than 61 percent of the references to his works (Brožek, 1980).

Why was a work of such scope so widely recognized in Germany but virtually ignored in the United States? One possibility is that Titchener, who brought his version of Wundtian psychology to America, dismissed it as unimportant because it was not congruent with his own structural psychology.

Wundt's productivity continued without a break until his death in 1920. The historian E. G. Boring (1950) noted that Wundt wrote 53,735 pages between 1853 and 1920, an output of 2.2 pages every day.

Wundt's System of Psychology

Wundt's psychology drew on the experimental methods of the natural sciences, particularly the techniques used by the physiologists. Wundt adapted these scientific methods of investigation for the new psychology and proceeded to study its subject matter in the same way the physical scientists were studying theirs. Thus, the spirit of the times in physiology and philosophy helped to shape both the subject matter of the new psychology and its methods of investigation.

The subject matter of Wundt's psychology was, in a word, consciousness. In a broad sense, the impact of nineteenth-century empiricism and associationism was at least partly reflected in Wundt's system. His view of consciousness was that it included many different parts or features and could be studied by the method of analysis or reduction. Wundt wrote: "The first step in the investigation of a fact must therefore be a description of the individual elements . . . of which it consists" (Diamond, 1980, p. 85).

With that point, however, the similarity ends between Wundt's approach and that of the majority of the empiricists and associationists. Wundt did not agree with the thesis that the elements of consciousness were static entities, atoms of the mind, passively linked by some mechanical process of association. Instead, Wundt agreed with John Stuart Mill that consciousness was more active in organizing its own content. Hence, the study of the elements, the content, or the structure of consciousness alone would provide only a beginning to the understanding of psychological processes.

Because of Wundt's focus on the self-organizing capacity of the mind or consciousness, he referred to his system as ***voluntarism***, which derives from the word *volition*, defined as the act or power of willing. Voluntarism refers to the power of the will to organize the contents of the mind into higher-level thought processes. Wundt emphasized not the elements themselves, as had the British empiricists and associationists (and as Titchener would later do), but rather the process of actively organizing or synthesizing those elements.

It is important to reiterate, however, that although Wundt stressed the power of the mind to synthesize elements into higher-level cognitive processes, he nevertheless recognized that the elements of consciousness were basic. Without the elements, there would be nothing for the mind to organize.

The Nature of Conscious Experience

According to Wundt, psychologists should be concerned with the study of immediate experience rather than mediate experience. ***Mediate experience*** provides us with information or knowledge about something other than the elements of the experience itself. This is the usual form in which we use experience to acquire knowledge about our world. For example, when we look at a flower and say, "The flower is red," this statement implies that our primary interest is in the flower and not in the fact that we are experiencing redness.

The ***immediate experience*** of looking at the flower, however, is not in the object itself but rather in the experience of something that is red. Thus, for Wundt, immediate experience is unbiased by interpretations, such as describing the experience of the flower's red color in terms of the object — the flower — itself. Similarly, when we describe our feelings of discomfort when we have a toothache, we are reporting our immediate experience. If we were simply to say, however, "I have a toothache," we would be concerned with mediate experience.

In Wundt's view, it was the basic experiences (such as the experience of redness) that formed the states of consciousness or mental elements that the mind would then actively organize or synthesize. He intended to analyze the mind or consciousness into its elements or component parts, just as the natural scientists were breaking down their subject matter, the material universe. The work of the Russian chemist Dimitri Mendeleev in developing the periodic table of chemical elements supported Wundt's aim. Some historians have suggested that Wundt may have been striving to develop a "periodic table of the mind" (Marx & Hillix, 1979, p. 67).

The Method of Study: Introspection

Because Wundt's psychology is the science of conscious experience, the method of psychology must involve observation of that experience. Only the person having such an experience can observe it, so the method must involve *introspection* — the examination of one's own mental state. Wundt referred to this as internal perception. The use of introspection was not new with Wundt; its use can be traced to Socrates. Wundt's innovation was the application of precise experimental control over the conditions of introspection. Some critics, however, worried that continued exposure to this kind of self-observation would drive students insane (Titchener, 1921).

The use of introspection in psychology was derived from physics, in which the method had been used to study light and sound, and from physiology, in which it had been applied to the study of the sense organs. To obtain information about the operation of the sense organs, for example, an investigator applied a stimulus to a sense organ and asked the subject to report on the sensation produced; this is similar to Fechner's psychophysical research methods. When subjects compared two weights and reported whether one was heavier, lighter, or equal in weight to the other, they were introspecting, reporting on their conscious experiences. If you said "I am hungry," you would be introspecting, reporting on an observation you have made of your own internal condition.

Introspection, or internal perception, as practiced in Wundt's Leipzig laboratory was conducted under stringent experimental conditions. Wundt set forth explicit rules: (1) Observers must be able to determine when the process is to be introduced. (2) They must be in a state of readiness or strained attention. (3) It must be possible to repeat the observation several times. (4) The experimental conditions must be capable of variation in terms of the controlled manipulation of the stimuli. The last condition invokes the essence of the experimental method, varying the conditions of the stimulus situation and observing the resulting changes in the subjects' experiences.

Wundt rarely used the kind of qualitative introspection in which subjects simply described their inner experiences, although that approach was adopted by some of his students, notably Titchener and Oswald Külpe. The type of introspective report Wundt sought in his own laboratory dealt primarily with the subjects' conscious judgments about the size, intensity, and duration of various physical stimuli—the kinds of quantitative judgments made in psychophysical research. Only a small number of studies involved reports of a subjective or qualitative nature, such as the pleasantness of different stimuli, the intensity of images, or the quality of certain sensations. The majority of Wundt's studies relied on objective measurements that involved sophisticated laboratory equipment, and many of these measurements concerned reaction times, which can be recorded quantitatively. Wundt then inferred information about conscious elements and processes from these objective measures.

The Elements of Conscious Experience

Having defined psychology's subject matter and method, Wundt proceeded to psychology's goal. As he saw it, the problem of psychology was threefold: (1) to analyze conscious processes into their basic elements, (2) to discover how these elements are synthesized or organized, and (3) to determine the laws of connection governing their organization.

Wundt considered sensations to be one of two elementary forms of experience. Sensations are aroused whenever a sense organ is stimulated and the resulting impulses reach the brain. He classified sensations according to sense modality (vision, hearing, and so on), intensity, and duration. Wundt recognized no fundamental difference between sensations and images, because images are also associated with cortical excitation. In keeping with his physiological orientation, he assumed the existence of a direct correspondence between the excitation of the cerebral cortex and the corresponding sensory experience. He regarded the mind and the body as parallel but not interacting systems. Because the mind did not depend on the body, it could be studied effectively by itself.

Feelings are the other elementary form of experience. Wundt stated that sensations and feelings are simultaneous aspects of immediate experience. Feelings are the subjective complements of sensations, but they do not arise directly from a sense organ. Sensations are accompanied by certain feeling qualities, and when sensations combine to form a more complex state, a feeling quality will result.

Wundt developed a *tridimensional theory of feeling* from his introspective observations. Working with a metronome (a device that produces audible clicks at regular intervals), Wundt reported that after he experienced a series of clicks, some rhythmic patterns seemed to him to be more pleasant or agreeable than others. He concluded that part of the experience of any such pattern is a subjective feeling of pleasure or displeasure.

(Note that this subjective feeling is a simultaneous aspect of the sensation of the clicks.) He then suggested that this feeling state can be placed at a point along a continuum ranging from agreeable to disagreeable.

Wundt detected a second kind of feeling while listening to the pattern of clicks, reporting a slight tension while waiting for each successive sound, followed by relief after the anticipated click occurred. From this he concluded that in addition to a pleasure–displeasure continuum, his feelings had a tension–relief dimension. Moreover, he reported a mildly excited feeling when the rate of clicks was increased, and a calmer feeling when the rate was reduced.

Through a laborious procedure of patiently varying the speed of the metronome and meticulously introspecting and reporting on his immediate conscious experiences (his sensations and feelings), Wundt arrived at three independent dimensions of feeling: pleasure–displeasure, tension–relaxation, and excitement–depression. Every feeling, he stated, can be located somewhere within this three-dimensional space.

Wundt believed that emotions are complex compounds of these elementary feelings, and that elementary feelings could be effectively described by defining their position on each of the three dimensions. Thus, he reduced emotions to conscious contents of the mind. His theory of feelings stimulated a great deal of research in the Leipzig and other laboratories, but it has not withstood the test of time.

Apperception: Organizing the Elements of Conscious Experience

Despite his emphasis on the elements of conscious experience, Wundt recognized that when we look at objects in the real world, we see a unity or synthesis of perceptions. We see a tree as a unity, for example; we do not actually see each of the many and varied sensations of brightness, hue, or shape that observers in a laboratory might report as a result of their introspections. Our visual experience comprehends the tree as a whole and not as each of the numerous elementary sensations and feelings that may constitute our perception of the tree.

How is this totality of conscious experience compounded or built up from elementary component parts? Wundt postulated the ***doctrine of apperception*** to account for our unified conscious experiences. He designated the actual process of organizing the various elements into a unity as the principle of ***creative synthesis*** or the ***law of psychic resultants***. The many elementary experiences are organized into a whole by this process of creative synthesis, which asserts, in essence, that the combination of elements creates new properties. "Every psychic compound has characteristics which are by no means the mere sum of the characteristics of the elements" (Wundt, 1896, p. 375). Something new is created out of the synthesis of the elemental parts of experience. We might say, as the Gestalt psychologists have said since 1912, that the whole is different from the sum of its parts.

The notion of creative synthesis has its counterpart in chemistry. The combining of chemical elements produces resultants that contain properties that were not properties of the original elements. Apperception, therefore, is an active process. The mind is not merely acted upon by the experienced elements; rather, the mind acts on the elements in the creative synthesis of the parts to make up the whole. Thus, Wundt did not treat the process of association in the passive and mechanical fashion favored by the majority of the British empiricists and associationists.

The Research Topics of the Leipzig Laboratory

Wundt determined the problems for experimental psychology during the early years of the Leipzig laboratory, and for a number of years, the issues with which the new experimental psychology was concerned were defined primarily by the work done at Leipzig. More important, the extensive research performed there demonstrated that an experimentally based science of psychology was possible, and the work of Wundt and his students formed the foundation of the new science. Wundt believed that psychology should deal initially with research problems that had already been investigated and reduced to some kind of empirical and quantitative form. For the most part, he did not occupy himself with new areas of research but rather with the extension and formal development of current topics.

Almost all of the work emerging from his laboratory was published in the *Studien*. Indeed, this journal contained little research that had not been undertaken either at Leipzig or by Wundt's students so soon after leaving Leipzig that their work still bore the imprint of the master. More than one hundred studies were performed in the first twenty years of the laboratory's existence.

The first series of studies involved the psychological and physiological aspects of vision and hearing, and, to some extent, of the so-called minor senses. Typical problems investigated in the area of visual sensation and perception included the psychophysics of color, color contrast, peripheral vision, negative afterimages, visual contrast, color blindness, visual size, and optical illusions. Psychophysical methods were used to investigate auditory sensations. Tactile sensations were studied, as was time sense (the perception or estimation of intervals of varying lengths of time).

A topic that claimed a great deal of attention in the laboratory was reaction time, a subject that arose from the work of Bessel on the speed of reaction among astronomers. The speed of a reaction had been a topic of investigation since the end of the eighteenth century and had been studied by Helmholtz and by F. C. Donders, a Dutch physiologist. Wundt believed that he could demonstrate experimentally three stages in a person's response to a stimulus: perception, apperception, and will.

After a stimulus is presented, subjects first perceive it, then they apperceive it, and finally they will to react; from the will to react, muscular movement results. Wundt hoped to develop a chronometry of the mind by measuring the times for the various mental processes, such as cognition, discrimination, and will. The promise of the method was not to be realized, however, because in practiced subjects the three stages were not clearly apparent, and the times for the separate processes were not constant from person to person or from study to study.

Studies on reaction time were supplemented by research on attention and feeling. Wundt considered attention to be the most vivid perception of only a small portion of the entire content of consciousness at any one time. The reference is to what is commonly called the focus of attention. Those stimuli in the focus are the most clearly perceived and are distinct from the rest of the visual field. A simple example is your focus on the words you are now reading relative to the rest of the page and the other objects on your desk, which are perceived less clearly. Research was undertaken on the range and fluctuation of attention as well as on attention span. Wundt's student Cattell investigated attention span and found that four, five, or six units of material, such as numbers or words, could be perceived in one short exposure.

Studies of feeling were undertaken to attempt to support the tridimensional theory. Wundt used the method of paired comparisons, which requires the comparison of stimuli in terms of the subjective feeling aroused. Other studies attempted to relate bodily changes, such as in pulse and breathing rate, to corresponding feeling states.

Another area of investigation was the analysis of verbal associations, which had been begun by Francis Galton (Chapter 6). Subjects were asked to respond with a single word when presented with a stimulus word. Wundt proceeded to classify the types of associations discovered when single-word stimuli were presented, to determine the nature of all verbal association.

The experimental areas of the psychophysiology of the senses, reaction time, psychophysics, and association constituted more than half of all the work published in the first few years of the *Studien*. Wundt showed some slight concern with child psychology and animal psychology but apparently did no experiments in these areas, believing that the conditions of study could not be adequately controlled.

Comment

The act of establishing the first psychology laboratory required a person well versed in contemporary physiology and philosophy and capable of combining these disciplines effectively. To accomplish his goal of establishing a new science, Wundt had to reject the nonscientific past and cut the intellectual ties between the new scientific psychology and the old mental philosophy. By postulating that the subject matter of psychology was conscious experience, and that psychology was a science based on experience, Wundt was able to avoid discussions about the nature of the immortal soul and its relationship to the mortal body. He said simply and emphatically that psychology did not deal with that issue. This assertion was a great step forward.

We cannot help but marvel at Wundt's outstanding energy and endurance over a period of more than sixty years. His creation of a scientific experimental psychology commands immense respect and is the source of his greatest influence. He began a new domain of science, as he had announced he would, and conducted research in a laboratory he designed exclusively for that purpose. He published the results in his own journal and tried to develop a systematic theory of the human mind. Some of his students founded additional laboratories and continued experimenting on the problems and with the techniques he set forth. Thus, Wundt provided psychology with all the trappings of a modern science.

The times, of course, were ready for the Wundtian movement, which was the natural outcome of the development of the physiological sciences, particularly in the German universities. That Wundt was the culmination of this movement and not its originator does not diminish his stature. It did, after all, require a kind of genius and a firm sense of dedication and courage to bring such a movement to fulfillment. The results of his efforts represent an achievement of such overwhelming importance that Wundt is accorded a position unique among psychologists of the modern period.

It is important to note that although Wundtian psychology spread rapidly, it did not immediately or completely transform the nature of academic psychology in Germany. In Wundt's lifetime — and, indeed, as late as 1941 — psychology in German universities remained primarily a subfield of philosophy. In part, this was because some psychologists and philosophers, including Wundt late in his career, argued against the split of psychology and philosophy. But also it was attributable to a more practical contextual factor: the government officials in charge of funding German universities did not see sufficient practical value in the new field of psychology to warrant supplying money to establish independent academic departments and separate laboratories (Ash, 1987).

Nor was the new psychology, with its focus on the elementary contents of consciousness and their synthesis, amenable to solving real-world problems. Perhaps that was a reason why Wundt's psychology did not gain popularity in the pragmatic climate of the United States. His psychology was a pure academic science, and intended to be only that; Wundt had no interest in attempting to apply his psychology to practical concerns.

Despite its acceptance in universities throughout the world, then, Wundtian psychology at home in Germany was slow to develop as a separate science. By 1910, ten years before Wundt's death, German psychology had three journals and several textbooks and research laboratories, but there were only four scholars who listed themselves in official records as psychologists instead of as philosophers. By 1925 in Germany, only twenty-five people called themselves psychologists, and only fourteen of twenty-three universities had institutes or departments of psychology (Turner, 1982). At the same time, there were a great many more psychologists and psychology departments in the United States, as well as diverse applications of psychological knowledge and techniques to practical issues. But these developments, too, owe their origins to Wundt's psychology.

Wundt's position, like that of any innovator, was subject to criticism of many points of his system and of his experimental technique of introspection. When introspection by different persons gives different results, for example, how do we decide who is correct? Experiments using introspection do not ensure agreement among experimenters, because introspective observation is a private experience. As such, disagreements cannot be settled by repeated observations. It was thought, however, that observers with greater training and experience could improve the method.

It was difficult to criticize Wundt's system during his lifetime, primarily because he wrote so much and so fast. By the time a critic had prepared an attack on a specific point, Wundt had changed his argument in a new edition of a book or was writing on an entirely different topic. Opponents were outwritten and buried under volumes of detailed and complex research findings. Further, because Wundt's theories were like classificatory schemes, they tended to be loosely knit and almost impossible to verify.

There was no vital center to his program, no point at which a critic might damage his credibility or undermine his system with a single blow.

The Wundtian position is not an active subject for discussion in contemporary psychology and has not been for many years. As one historian noted, "the precipitous decline of Wundtian psychology between the world wars [1918–1939] was breathtaking. The massive body of Wundtian research and writings all but disappeared in the English-speaking world" (Blumenthal, 1985, p. 44). Nor did it fare well in the German-speaking world. In Wundt's lifetime, two other schools of thought arose in Europe to overshadow his views: Gestalt psychology in Germany and psychoanalysis in Austria. In the United States, two additional viewpoints, functionalism and behaviorism, eclipsed the Wundtian approach.

It has also been suggested that economic and political factors — contextual forces again — contributed to the disappearance of the Wundtian system in Germany (Blumenthal, 1985). The collapse of the economy, following Germany's defeat in World War I, left its universities in financial ruin. The University of Leipzig could not even afford to purchase copies of Wundt's last books for its library. Wundt's laboratory, at which he trained the first generation of psychologists, was destroyed in a British and American bombing raid on December 4, 1943, during World War II. Thus, the nature, content, form — and even the home — of Wundtian psychology were lost forever.

Wundt's monumental achievements are not diminished by that loss or by the fact that much of the history of psychology after Wundt consists of rebellion against some of the limitations he placed on the field. Indeed, that rebellion may enhance his greatness. Forward movement must have something to push against, and as such, Wilhelm Wundt provided a compelling and magnificent beginning to modern experimental psychology.

Other Early European Psychologists

Wundt had a monopoly on the new psychology for only a short time. The science was also beginning to flourish at other laboratories in Germany. Although Wundt was obviously the most important organizer and systematizer in the early days of psychology, others were also influential in the development of psychology. These early non-Wundtian psychologists proposed different points of view, but all were engaged in the common enterprise of expanding psychology as a science. Their endeavors, along with Wundt's, made Germany the undisputed center of the movement.

There were, however, developments in England that were to give psychology an entirely different theme and direction. Charles Darwin proposed his theory of evolution and Francis Galton began work on the psychology of individual differences. These ideas would influence the development of psychology in the United States, even more than did the work of Wundt. In addition, early American psychologists, most of whom had studied under Wundt at Leipzig, returned home and made of Wundtian psychology something uniquely American in form and temperament. We will discuss these developments later; the important point now is that very shortly after Wundt founded psychology, it became divided into factions. Although Wundt had founded the field, his approach to psychology was soon only one of several. Let us turn to a discussion of Wundt's contemporaries in Germany.

Hermann Ebbinghaus (1850–1909)

Only a few years after Wundt had stated that it was not possible to conduct experiments on the higher mental processes, a then-unknown psychologist working alone, isolated from any center of psychology, began to experiment successfully on those processes. Hermann Ebbinghaus became the first psychologist to investigate learning and memory experimentally. In doing so, he not only challenged Wundt but also changed the way in which association or learning could be examined.

Before Ebbinghaus, most notably in the work of the British empiricists and associationists, the customary way to study association was to deal with associations that were already formed. The investigator would, in a sense, work backward, attempting to determine how the connections had been established. Ebbinghaus began at a different starting point: the development of the associations. In this way it was possible to control the conditions under which the associations were formed and thus to make the study of learning more objective.

Accepted as one of the great manifestations of original genius in experimental psychology, Ebbinghaus's investigation of learning and forgetting was the first venture into a truly psychological problem area, one that was not a part of physiology, as was the case with so much of Wundt's research. As a result, the work of Ebbinghaus considerably broadened the scope of experimental psychology.

Born near Bonn, Germany, in 1850, Ebbinghaus undertook his college studies first at the University of Bonn and then at universities in Halle and Berlin. In the course of his academic training, his interests shifted

Through his studies of
learning and memory,
Hermann Ebbinghaus
broadened the scope of
experimental psychology.

from history and literature to philosophy, in which he received his degree
in 1873, following military service during the Franco–Prussian War. He
devoted seven years to independent study in England and France, where
his interests changed again, inclined this time toward science. About 1876,
three years before Wundt established his laboratory, Ebbinghaus bought a
secondhand copy of Fechner's *Elements of Psychophysics* at a bookstall in
London. This chance encounter influenced him—and the new psychology—profoundly.

Fechner's mathematical approach to psychological phenomena was
an exciting revelation to the young Ebbinghaus, and he resolved to do for
the study of memory what Fechner had done for psychophysics, using
rigid and systematic measurement. He wanted to apply the experimental

method to the higher mental processes and decided, probably as a result of the influence of the British associationists, to make the attempt in the field of memory.

Consider Ebbinghaus's daring course of action in light of the problem he chose and his own situation. Learning and memory had never been studied experimentally. Indeed, the eminent psychologist Wilhelm Wundt said that could not be done. Further, Ebbinghaus had no academic appointment, no university setting in which to conduct his work, no teacher, and no laboratory. Nevertheless, he carried out alone, over a period of five years, a series of carefully controlled and thorough studies using himself as the only subject.

For the basic measure of learning he adapted a technique from the associationists, who emphasized the principle of frequency of associations as a condition of recall. Ebbinghaus reasoned that the difficulty of learning material could be measured by counting the number of repetitions needed for one perfect reproduction of the material. (This is another example of the influence of Fechner. Fechner measured sensations indirectly by measuring the stimulus intensity necessary to produce a just noticeable difference in sensation. Ebbinghaus approached the problem of measuring memory in a similarly indirect way, by counting the number of trials or repetitions required to learn the material.)

Ebbinghaus used similar, but not identical, lists of syllables as the material to be learned, and he repeated the task frequently to be confident of the accuracy of his results. In this way he could cancel out variable errors from trial to trial and take an average measure. So systematic was Ebbinghaus in his experimentation that he even regulated his personal habits, keeping them as constant as possible and following a rigid routine, always learning the material at the same time each day.

For the subject matter of his research — the material to be learned — Ebbinghaus invented the series of syllables known today as ***nonsense syllables***, which revolutionized the study of learning. E. B. Titchener later commented that the use of nonsense syllables marked the first significant advance in the area since Aristotle.

Ebbinghaus recognized an inherent difficulty in using prose or poetry as stimulus materials. Meanings or associations are already attached to words by those who know the language. These existing associations can facilitate the learning of material and, because these connections are already present at the time of the experiment, they cannot be controlled by the experimenter. Ebbinghaus sought material that would be uniformly unassociated, completely homogeneous, and equally unfamiliar, material with which there could be few past associations. His nonsense syllables, typically formed of two consonants with a vowel in between (as in lef, bok, or yat), satisfied these criteria. He wrote all possible combinations of consonants and vowels on cards, yielding a supply of 2,300 syllables from which to draw at random those to be learned.

New data of history, supplied by a German psychologist who carefully read the footnotes in Ebbinghaus's published works and the workbook for one set of his experiments, and who compared the English translation with Ebbinghaus's words in German, lend a new interpretation to our understanding of nonsense syllables (Gundlach, 1986). They were found to be not necessarily nonsense at all, nor were they limited to only three letters.

This meticulous investigation of the data of history — in this case, Ebbinghaus's own writings — revealed that some of the syllables he constructed were four, five, or six letters long. More important, what Ebbinghaus called a "meaningless series of syllables" as the subject matter of his research was incorrectly translated into the English language as a "series of nonsense syllables." To Ebbinghaus, it was not the individual syllables that were designed to be meaningless (although many of them were), but rather the entire series of syllables. That is, the list of syllables itself was constructed to have no meaning or interconnections.

This new look at Ebbinghaus's writings also revealed that he was fluent in English, French, and German, and had studied Latin and Greek. "He would have had a very hard time, indeed, to construct any syllable at all that would be nonsense to him. The vain struggle for the definitively nonsensical, association-free syllable is the endeavor of some of his followers" (Gundlach, 1986, pp. 469–470).

Ebbinghaus designed a number of experiments using his meaningless series of syllables to determine the influence of various conditions on learning and retention. One of these studies investigated the difference between his speed in memorizing his lists of syllables versus his speed in memorizing more meaningful materials. To determine the difference, he memorized stanzas of Byron's "Don Juan." Each stanza has eighty syllables, and Ebbinghaus found that it required about nine readings to memorize one stanza. He then memorized a list of eighty of his nonsense syllables and discovered that the task required almost eighty repetitions. He concluded that meaningless or unassociated material is approximately nine times harder to learn than meaningful material.

He also studied the effect of the length of the material to be learned on the number of repetitions necessary for a perfect reproduction. He concluded that longer material requires more repetitions and, consequently, more time to learn. He found that the average time to memorize one syllable increased when he increased the number of syllables to be learned. These results are predictable in a general way: the more we have to learn, the longer it will take us. The significance of Ebbinghaus's work, however, is in his careful control of the experimental conditions, the quantitative analysis of the data, and the finding that both total learning time and time per syllable increase with longer lists of syllables.

Ebbinghaus studied other variables thought to influence learning and memory, such as the effect of overlearning (repeating the lists more times than necessary for one perfect reproduction), near and remote associations within lists, repeated learning or review, and the influence of time between learning and recall. His research on the effect of time yielded the famous Ebbinghaus curve of forgetting. This curve, as every psychology student knows, demonstrates that material is forgotten very rapidly in the first few hours after learning and more slowly thereafter.

In 1880 Ebbinghaus received an academic appointment at the University of Berlin, where he continued his research, replicating and verifying his earlier studies. He published the results of his work in a book entitled *Über das Gedächtnis* (*On Memory*) in 1885, which represents what is perhaps the most brilliant single investigation in the history of experimental psychology. In addition to beginning a new field of study, which is still vital today, it provides an example of technical skill, perseverance, and ingenuity. It is not possible to find in the history of psychology any other investigator working alone who subjected himself to such a painstaking regimen of experimentation. The research was so exacting, thorough, and systematic that it is cited, more than one hundred years later, in contemporary textbooks.

Ebbinghaus was content to let others develop the field of learning and memory, and extend and refine the methodology. He published relatively little after 1885, and a year later he was promoted to assistant professor at Berlin. He established a laboratory, and in 1890 he founded a journal, with the physicist Arthur König, the *Zeitschrift für Psychologie und Physiologie der Sinnesorgane* (*Journal of Psychology and Physiology of the Sense Organs*). A new journal was needed in Germany, because Wundt's *Studien*, the primary organ of the Leipzig laboratory, could not publish reports of all the psychological research being conducted at the time. The need for another journal, just nine years after Wundt had begun his, is significant testimony to the phenomenal growth of the new psychology, in both size and diversity.

In the first issue of their journal, Ebbinghaus and König made a bold claim for the two disciplines named in their title: psychology and physiology. These fields, they wrote, have "consequently grown together . . . to form one whole; they promote and presuppose one another, and so constitute two coequal members of one great double science" (Turner, 1982, p. 151). Such a declaration, only eleven years after Wundt opened his experimental laboratory, shows how far Wundt's idea of psychology as a science had come.

Ebbinghaus was not promoted again at the University of Berlin, apparently because of his lack of publications, and in 1894 he accepted a position at the University of Breslau, where he remained until 1905. In 1897 he developed a sentence completion test, probably the first successful test of the higher mental processes; a modified form of that test is included today in tests of general intelligence or cognitive ability.

In 1902 Ebbinghaus published a highly successful general textbook, *Die Grundzüge der Psychologie* (*The Principles of Psychology*), dedicated to Fechner's memory, and in 1908 a more popular text, *Abriss der Psychologie* (*A Summary of Psychology*). Both books appeared in several editions and were revised by others after Ebbinghaus's death. Ebbinghaus went to the University of Halle in 1905 and died suddenly of pneumonia in 1909.

Ebbinghaus did not make any theoretical contributions to psychology; he created no formal system and had no disciples of importance to psychology. He did not found a school, nor did he seem to want to do so. Yet he is of great importance not only to the study of learning and memory, which he began, but also to experimental psychology as a whole.

One measure of the overall historical worth of a scientist is how well his or her position and conclusions stand the test of time. By that standard, it can be suggested that Ebbinghaus is more important than Wundt. Ebbinghaus's research brought objectivity, quantification, and experimentation to the study of learning, a topic that is central to modern psychology. It is because of Ebbinghaus that work on the concept of association changed from speculation about its attributes to formal scientific investigation. Many of his conclusions about the nature of learning and memory remain valid, a century after he published them.

Georg Elias Müller (1850–1934)

A physiologist and philosopher by training, a man who never went to bed before midnight, Georg Müller had a strong interest in psychology, which he manifested during a forty-year career at the University of Göttingen in Germany. From 1881 to 1921, his well-equipped laboratory rivaled Wundt's at Leipzig and attracted many students from Europe and the United States.

Müller did considerable work on color vision, and extensively criticized and elaborated on Fechner's work in psychophysics. Müller's research contributions were so substantial that E. B. Titchener delayed for two years the second volume of his textbook on experimental psychology, so that he could incorporate material from Müller's latest book.

Müller was one of the first to work in the area begun by Ebbinghaus, the experimental study of learning and memory, and his research verified and extended many of Ebbinghaus's findings. Ebbinghaus's approach had been strictly objective; he had not recorded introspections about his mental processes while engaged in his learning tasks. Müller, however, believed that Ebbinghaus's approach tended to make the learning process appear too mechanical or automatic. He believed that the mind was more actively involved in learning. He used Ebbinghaus's objective methods, but he added introspective report. His results confirmed that learning did not proceed mechanically. His subjects were actively involved in consciously grouping and organizing the material, and they even found meanings in the lists of nonsense syllables.

On the basis of his research, Müller concluded that association by contiguity alone cannot adequately account for learning, because the subjects seemed to actively seek relationships among the stimuli to be learned. He suggested that a set of mental phenomena, such as readiness, hesitation, and doubt (the so-called conscious attitudes), actively influence learning. Similar findings soon followed, as we shall see, from the work of Oswald Külpe at the University of Würzburg.

Müller was the first to propose and to demonstrate in the laboratory the *interference theory of forgetting*. In his view, forgetting was less a function of memory decay over time than of new material interfering with the recall of material that had been learned earlier.

One final contribution to the study of learning deserves mention. Along with Friedrich Schumann, his laboratory assistant, Müller developed the memory drum, a revolving drum that makes possible the uniform presentation of material to be learned. Now a familiar piece of laboratory equipment, this apparatus is significant because it increased the precision and objectivity of research on learning and memory.

Franz Brentano (1838–1917)

At about the age of sixteen, Franz Brentano began training for the priesthood, studying at universities in Berlin, Munich, and Tübingen, Germany, and receiving his degree in philosophy at Tübingen in 1864. He was ordained the same year, and two years later began teaching philosophy at the University of Würzburg and writing and lecturing on Aristotle. In 1870 the Vatican Council in Rome accepted the doctrine of papal infallibility, with which Brentano could not agree. He resigned his professorship, to which he had been appointed as a priest, and left the church.

Brentano's most famous book, *Psychologie vom empirischen Standpunkte* (*Psychology from an Empirical Standpoint*), was published in

Franz Brentano argued that psychology should be empirical, studying mental activity rather than mental content.

1874, the year in which the second part of the first edition of Wundt's *Principles of Physiological Psychology* appeared. Brentano's book stood in direct opposition to the Wundtian view, attesting to the dissent already apparent in the new psychology. Also in 1874, Brentano was appointed professor of philosophy at the University of Vienna, Austria. He remained there for twenty years, and during that time his influence grew considerably. He was a popular lecturer, and among his students were several who achieved prominence in the history of psychology: Carl Stumpf, Christian von Ehrenfels, and Sigmund Freud. In 1894 Brentano retired and spent his remaining years in Italy and Switzerland engaged in study and writing.

Brentano was one of the more important non-Wundtians because of his diverse influences within psychology. (We will see later that he was an intellectual precursor of Gestalt psychology and humanistic psychology.) He shared with Wundt the goal of making psychology a science. Whereas Wundt's psychology was experimental, however, Brentano's was empirical. The primary method of psychology for Brentano was observation, not experimentation, although he did not reject the experimental method. An empirical approach generally is broader in scope, in that it obtains its data from observation and individual experience as well as from experimentation.

Brentano opposed Wundt's fundamental idea that psychology should study the content of conscious experience. He argued that the proper subject matter for psychology is mental activity—the mental act of seeing, for example, rather than the mental content of that which is seen. Thus, Brentano's so-called *act psychology* countered the Wundtian view that the mental processes involve contents. Brentano argued that a distinction must be drawn between experience as a structure and experience as an activity. The sensory content of redness, for example, is different from the activity of sensing redness. Brentano urged that this act of experiencing is the true subject matter of psychology. He stated that a color is not a mental quality but strictly a physical quality. The act of seeing the color, however, is mental. Of course, an act always involves an object; a content is always present because the act of seeing is meaningless unless there is something to be seen.

This redefined subject matter necessitated a different method of study, because acts, unlike sensory contents, are not accessible through the method practiced at Wundt's Leipzig laboratory. The study of mental acts required observation on a larger scale than that used by Wundt. For this reason, act psychology was more empirical than experimental in its methodology. This does not imply that Brentano's psychology was a return to speculative philosophy; although not experimental, it did rely on systematic observation.

Brentano's position had its adherents, but Wundtian psychology maintained prominence in the new psychology. Because Wundt published more than Brentano, his position became better known. Also, it was easier to study sensations or conscious contents with the methods of psycho-physics than it was to study the more elusive acts.

Carl Stumpf (1848–1936)

Born into a medical family, Carl Stumpf came in contact with science at an early age but developed a greater interest in music. At the age of seven he began studying the violin and by age ten was composing music. As a student at the University of Würzburg, he became interested in Brentano's work and turned his attention to philosophy and science. At Brentano's suggestion, Stumpf went to the University of Göttingen, where he received his doctoral degree in 1868. Stumpf held a number of academic appoint-ments over the following years while he began his work in psychology.

In 1894 Stumpf was awarded an appointment at the University of Berlin, the most prized professorship in German psychology. Wundt, who at that time was considered the dean of German psychologists, had seemed the logical choice for the position. It has been suggested that the influential Helmholtz opposed Wundt's appointment.

The years Stumpf spent at Berlin were extremely productive, and his original laboratory of three small rooms grew into a large and important institute. Although the laboratory never rivaled Wundt's in scope or inten-sity of research, Stumpf is often considered Wundt's major competitor. Stumpf trained the psychologists who later founded Gestalt psychology, a school of thought that opposed Wundt's views.

Stumpf's early writings in psychology were concerned with the per-ception of space, but his most influential work is *Tonpsychologie* (*Psy-chology of Tone*), which appeared in two volumes in 1883 and 1890. This work, and his later studies of music, earned him a place second only to Helmholtz in the field of acoustics, and were considered a pioneering effort in the psychological study of music.

The influence of Brentano may explain Stumpf's acceptance of a less rigorous approach to psychology than that considered necessary by Wundt. Stumpf argued that the primary data of psychology are phenom-ena. ***Phenomenology***, the kind of introspection Stumpf favored, refers to the examination of unbiased experience, that is, experience just as it oc-curs. He did not agree with Wundt about breaking experience down into elements. To do so, Stumpf argued, is to render the experience artificial and abstract, and thus no longer natural. A student of Stumpf's, Edmund Husserl, later proposed a philosophy of phenomenology; this movement was a precursor of other forms of psychology, notably Gestalt psychology.

His studies of acoustics led Carl Stumpf into a bitter debate with Wundt over the proper use of introspection in psychology.

In a series of publications, Stumpf and Wundt waged a bitter controversy about the introspection of tones. The debate was initiated by Stumpf on a theoretical level, but Wundt made it personal. Essentially, the issue involved the question of whose introspectionists' reports were the more credible. When dealing with tones, should one accept the results of highly trained laboratory observers, as required by Wundt, or of expert musicians, as used by Stumpf? Stumpf would not accept the results obtained at Wundt's Leipzig laboratory on this problem.

While continuing to write on music and acoustics, Stumpf established a center for the collection of recordings of primitive music from all over the world. He founded the Berlin Association for Child Psychology and published a theory of feeling in which he attempted to reduce feeling to sensation. Stumpf was one of a number of German psychologists who maintained their independence from Wundt and so strove to expand the boundaries of psychology.

Oswald Külpe (1862–1915) and the Würzburg School

Initially a student, disciple, and follower of Wundt, Oswald Külpe in the course of his career led a group of students in a movement to break away from what he considered the limitations of the founder's work. Although Külpe's movement was not a revolution, it was a declaration of freedom from the narrowness of some of Wundt's views. Külpe worked on several problems that Wundt's psychology disregarded.

At the age of nineteen Külpe began his studies at the University of Leipzig. His intention was to study history, but under the influence of Wundt he switched to philosophy and to experimental psychology, which, in 1881, was still in its infancy. Külpe continued to be strongly attracted to history, however, and after a year with Wundt he resumed its study at Berlin. Two further academic forays into psychology and history followed before he returned to Wundt in 1886; he remained at Leipzig for eight years.

After receiving his degree at Leipzig, Külpe stayed on as assistant professor and assistant to Wundt, carrying on research in the laboratory. He wrote a textbook, *Grundriss der Psychologie* (*Outline of Psychology*), which was published in 1893 and dedicated to Wundt. In it Külpe defined psychology as the science of the facts of experience as dependent on the experiencing individual.

In 1894 Külpe became a professor at the University of Würzburg, and two years later he established a laboratory that soon threatened to rival Wundt's in importance. Among the students attracted to Würzburg were several Americans; one, James Rowland Angell, became a pivotal figure in the development of functionalism (Chapter 7).

In the *Outline of Psychology*, Külpe did not discuss the higher mental process of thought. At that time, his position was still compatible with

Trained at Leipzig, Oswald Külpe and his Würzburg school extended psychology's subject matter to include the higher mental processes.

Wundt's. Only a few years later, however, Külpe was convinced that the thought processes could be studied experimentally. Memory, another of the higher mental processes, had been studied experimentally by Ebbinghaus. If memory could be studied in the laboratory, why not thought? Posing this question put Külpe in direct opposition to his former teacher, because Wundt had emphasized that the higher mental processes could not be studied experimentally.

A second point of difference between the Würzburg school, as it came to be called, and the Wundtian system relates to introspection. Külpe developed a method he called *systematic experimental introspection*. This involved the performance of a complex task (such as establishing logical connections between concepts), after which subjects were required to render a retrospective report of their cognitive processes during the task. In other words, subjects were required to perform some mental process, such as thinking or judging, and then examine how they had thought or judged. Wundt had rejected the use of retrospective report in his laboratory. He believed in studying conscious experience as it occurred, not the memory of it after it had occurred.

Külpe's introspective method was systematic, in that the whole experience was described in a precise way by fractionating it into time periods. Similar tasks were repeated many times, so that the introspective accounts could be corrected, corroborated, and amplified. These reports were often supplemented by questions that directed a subject's attention to particular points.

There were several other differences between the introspective approaches of Külpe and Wundt. Wundt did not favor having subjects describe their conscious experiences in detail. Most of his research focused on objective, quantitative measurements, such as reaction times and the kinds of judgments required in psychophysical research.

In contrast, Külpe's systematic experimental introspection emphasized subjective, qualitative, and detailed reports from subjects on the nature of their thought processes. Subjects were not just to make simple judgments about the intensity of a stimulus, for example. Rather, they were to describe the complex mental processes they underwent during their exposure to some experimental task. Külpe's approach was aimed directly at investigating what was going on in a subject's mind during a conscious experience.

Külpe did not reject Wundt's focus on conscious experience, the research tool of introspection, or the fundamental task of analyzing consciousness into its elements. The goal of his work was to expand Wundt's conception of psychology's subject matter to include the higher mental processes, and to refine the method of introspection.

What were the results of this attempted expansion and refinement? Wundt's point of view emphasized that conscious experience could be reduced to its component sensory or imaginal elements. All experience, Wundt said, is composed of sensations or images. Külpe's direct introspection of thought processes found evidence to support the opposite viewpoint, that thought can occur without any sensory or imaginal content.

This finding came to be identified as ***imageless thought***, to represent the notion of meanings in thought that do not seem to involve any specific images. Thus, Külpe's research identified a nonsensory form or aspect of consciousness.

The research topics of the Würzburg school were varied. An important contribution was a study by Karl Marbe on the comparative judgment of weights. Marbe found that, although sensations and images were present during the task, they seemed to play no part in the process of judgment. Subjects could not report on how the judgments of lighter or heavier weights came into their minds. This finding contradicted the long-held belief about the thought processes — that in making a judgment of this kind, subjects retained a mental image of the first object (the weight) and compared it with a sensory impression of the second object. Marbe's experiment demonstrated that there is no such comparison of image and sensory impression and that the process of judgment is more elusive than had been supposed.

Külpe's Würzburg group also dealt with association and will. A study by Henry Watt demonstrated that in a word association task (asking subjects to respond to a stimulus word), subjects have little relevant information to report about their conscious process of judgment. This finding provided a further demonstration of conscious experience that could not be reduced to sensations and images. Watt found that his subjects were able to respond correctly without being consciously aware of intending to do so at the time of response. He concluded that the conscious work was done before the task was performed, at the time when the instructions were given and understood.

According to Watt, the subjects received these instructions and somehow decided to react in the manner required. When presented with the stimulus word, they carried out the instructions without any further conscious effort. As a result of understanding the instructions, Watt explained, the subjects apparently established an unconscious ***set*** or ***determining tendency*** to respond in the desired way. Once the task had been understood and the determining tendency adopted, the actual task was performed with little, if any, conscious effort. This research suggested that predispositions outside of consciousness are somehow able to control conscious activities.

A new period in the Würzburg school began in 1907, with the work of Karl Bühler. His research method involved presenting to subjects a question that required some thought before it could be answered. Subjects were asked to give as complete an account as possible of the steps involved in reaching the answer, while the experimenter interjected questions about the process. Bühler's results reinforced the notion of nonsensory elements of experience. He asserted that these new types of structural elements are vital to the process of thought.

Not unexpectedly, Külpe's modification of Wundt's introspective method and his attempt to add to the list of elements evoked strong criticism from the orthodox Wundtians and scathing attacks from Wundt. Wundt called the Würzburg form of introspection "mock" experiments and claimed that their method did not really involve introspection or experimentation.

In one sense, it is strange that the Wundtians so strongly opposed Külpe's suggestion of nonsensory mental life. After all, Külpe was proceeding along paths that Wundt had cleared. Had not Wundt moved along not too dissimilar lines? Was not his notion of feelings a recognition of nonsensory elements of conscious experience? It was certainly no accident that Külpe, a product of Wundtian training, had instigated this movement.

The Würzburg interest in the area of motivation is a major contribution to today's psychology. The concept of a set or determining tendency bears directly on current work in the field. Also, the demonstration that experience depends not only on conscious elements but also on unconscious determining tendencies suggests the role of unconscious determinants of behavior, an idea that forms an important part of the system developed by Sigmund Freud.

Comment

We can see, then, that division and controversy enveloped psychology almost as soon as it was founded. It must be emphasized, however, that for all their differences, these early psychologists were united in theme and purpose.

Wundt, Ebbinghaus, Brentano, Stumpf, and others irrevocably changed the study of human nature. Because of their efforts, psychology was no longer

> a study of the soul [but] a study, by observation and experiment, of certain reactions of the human organism not included in the subject matter of any other science. The German psychologists, in spite of their many differences, were to this extent engaged in a common enterprise; and their ability, their industry, and the common direction of their labors all made the developments in the German universities the center of the new movement in psychology. (Heidbreder, 1933, p. 105)

Germany did not remain the center of the new movement for long. A version of Wundt's psychology was soon brought to the United States by his student E. B. Titchener.

Suggested Readings

Wundt and Early Experimental Psychology

Anderson, R. J. (1975). The untranslated content of Wundt's *Grundzüge der Physiologischen Psychologie. Journal of the History of the Behavioral Sciences, 21*, 381–386. Suggests that Titchener translated only that portion of Wundt's work that supported his own position.

Baldwin, B. T. (1921). In memory of Wilhelm Wundt by his American students. *Psychological Review, 28*, 153–158. Contains reminiscences of Wundt's American students including such notable psychologists as Angell, Cattell, Hall, and Titchener.

Benjamin, L. T., Jr. (1991). *Harry Kirke Wolfe: Pioneer in Psychology*. Lincoln: University of Nebraska Press. A fascinating and poignant biography of an early student of Wundt and Ebbinghaus, and one of the first two Americans to earn a doctorate from the University of Leipzig; Wolfe established at the University of Nebraska one of the first American laboratories for research in psychology and was a distinguished teacher, training a generation of psychologists who later became prominent in the field.

Blumenthal, A. L. (1975). A reappraisal of Wilhelm Wundt. *American Psychologist, 30*, 1081–1088. Reevaluates Wundt's contributions and relates his ideas to trends in cognitive psychology; illustrates the importance of studying Wundt in the original German to form an accurate picture of his work.

Bringmann, W. G., Balance, W., & Evans, R. B. (1975). Wilhelm Wundt, 1832–1920: A brief biographical sketch. *Journal of the History of the Behavioral Sciences, 11*, 287–297. Describes Wundt's early years, education, research, and professional activities.

Danziger, K. (1990). *Constructing the Subject: Historical Origins of Psychological Research*. Cambridge, England: Cambridge University Press. Traces the changes in psychological research methodology from Wundt's nineteenth-century introspection to the mid-twentieth-century emphasis on quantification and statistical analysis; explores the impact of social contextual factors on American and German research practices.

Haeberlin, H. K. (1916). The theoretical foundations of Wundt's folk psychology. *Psychological Review, 23*, 279–302. An exposition and analysis of Wundt's cultural psychology.

Leahey, T. H. (1979). Something old, something new: Attention in Wundt and modern cognitive psychology. *Journal of the History of the Behavioral Sciences, 15*, 242–252. Describes and compares the work of Wundt and contemporary researchers on problems of apperception.

Sokal, M. M. (Ed.). (1981). *An Education in Psychology: James McKeen Cattell's*

Journal and Letters from Germany and England, 1880–1888. Cambridge MA: MIT Press. Reprints and annotates more than 450 documents covering Cattell's university education and professional career; see especially the material covering his years as a researcher in Wundt's Leipzig laboratory.

Ebbinghaus

Ebbinghaus, H. (1964). *Memory: A Contribution to Experimental Psychology.* New York: Dover. A reprint of Ebbinghaus's classic work, originally published in 1885, describing his research methodology, his lists of syllables, and his findings on learning, retention, and forgetting.

Kintsch, W. (1985). Reflections on Ebbinghaus. *Journal of Experimental Psychology: Learning, Memory, and Cognition, 11,* 461–463. Brief remarks on the contributions of Ebbinghaus and criticisms of his experimental methodology and theorizing.

Postman, L. (1968). Hermann Ebbinghaus. *American Psychologist, 23,* 149–157. Describes Ebbinghaus's contributions to the experimental study of memory.

Young, R. K. (1985). Ebbinghaus: Some consequences. *Journal of Experimental Psychology: Learning, Memory, and Cognition, 11,* 491–495. Argues that Ebbinghaus's work was so impressive that for nearly 80 years psychologists were reluctant to suggest other ways of approaching problems of learning and memory.

Müller

Boring, E. G. (1941). An operational restatement of G. E. Müller's psychophysical axioms. *Psychological Review, 48,* 457–464. Discusses Müller's views on the relationship between mental processes and brain processes.

Brentano

Rancurello, A. C. (1968). *A Study of Franz Brentano: His Psychological Standpoint and His Significance in the History of Psychology.* New York: Academic Press. A biography of Brentano and an assessment of his historical significance.

Sussman, E. J. (1962). Franz Brentano: Much alive, though dead. *American Psychologist, 17,* 504–506. A note on the continuing influence of Brentano's ideas.

Stumpf

Langfeld, H. S. (1937). Stumpf's "Introduction to Psychology." *American Journal of Psychology, 50,* 33–56. Describes the beginning psychology course taught by Stumpf at the University of Berlin in 1906–1907.

Külpe and the Würzburg School

Lindenfeld, D. (1978). Oswald Külpe and the Würzburg School. *Journal of the History of the Behavioral Sciences, 14,* 132–141. Assesses Külpe's importance and relates his conception of psychology to his philosophical views.

Ogden, R. M. (1951). Oswald Külpe and the Würzburg School. *American Journal of Psychology, 64,* 4–19. Describes the experimental research at Külpe's psychology laboratory at the University of Würzburg.

Structuralism  5

Introduction

E. B. Titchener altered Wundt's system dramatically, while professing to be a loyal follower. He offered his own approach, which he called ***structuralism***, and claimed that it represented the form of psychology espoused by Wundt. Yet the two systems were radically different, and the label, structuralism, cannot be applied to Wundt's psychology, only to Titchener's work.

Structural psychology attained a prominence in the United States that lasted for some years, until it was challenged and overthrown by newer movements. Although Titchener was undoubtedly an influential figure in the history of American psychology, his contemporaries were developing different definitions of psychology, as we shall see in the following chapters.

Wilhelm Wundt recognized elements or contents of consciousness, but his overriding concern was with their organization or synthesis into higher-level cognitive processes through the principle of apperception. He viewed the mind as having the power to synthesize the elements voluntarily, a position that contrasted with the mechanical and passive notion of association favored by most of the British empiricists and associationists.

Titchener accepted the empiricist and associationist focus on the elements or contents of the mind and their mechanical linkage through the process of association. He discarded Wundt's emphasis on apperception, however, and concentrated instead on the elements that form the structure of consciousness. In Titchener's view, the fundamental task of psychology was to discover the nature of these elementary conscious experiences—that is, to analyze consciousness into its separate parts and thus determine its structure. To accomplish this, Titchener modified Wundt's introspective method so that it more resembled Külpe's method.

Edward Bradford Titchener (1867–1927)

Titchener spent his most productive years at Cornell University in New York. For Titchener, who is often pictured clad in the academic gown he invariably wore to class, every lecture was a dramatic production. The staging was carefully prepared by assistants under his watchful eye. The junior faculty, who attended all his lectures, entered through one door to take front-row seats, and Professor Titchener came through another door that led directly onto the lecture platform. Titchener asserted that his Oxford gown gave him the right to be dogmatic. Although he studied with Wundt for only two years, he resembled his mentor in many respects, including his autocratic nature, his formal lectures, and even his bearded appearance.

The Life of Titchener

Born in Chichester, England, into an old family that had little money, Titchener relied on his considerable intellectual abilities to win scholar-

Structuralism was established as the first American school of thought in psychology by Edward Bradford Titchener.

ships to advance his education. He attended Malvern College and then Oxford University, where he studied philosophy and the classics for four years and became a research assistant in physiology for the fifth year.

While at Oxford, Titchener became interested in Wundt's new psychology, an interest that was not shared or encouraged by anyone at the university. It was natural, then, that he should journey to Leipzig, the mecca for scientific pilgrims, to study under Wundt, earning his doctoral degree in 1892. There seems no doubt that Wundt made a lifelong impression on the young student, although Titchener apparently saw little of him. The years at Leipzig determined Titchener's future in psychology and that of his many students. He had an impact on American psychology, but before long psychology in America was to follow a course of its own, one that diverged from Titchener's approach.

After receiving his degree, Titchener planned to become the pioneer in England of the new experimental psychology. English scholars, however, were skeptical of a scientific approach to one of their favorite philosophical subjects. Therefore, after only a few months as an extension lecturer in biology at Oxford, Titchener left England for the United States to teach psychology and direct the laboratory at Cornell University. He was twenty-five years old, and he remained at Cornell for the rest of his life.

Titchener spent the years from 1893 to 1900 developing his laboratory, acquiring equipment, conducting research, and writing sixty-two articles. As his reputation attracted more and more students to Cornell, he relinquished the time-consuming task of participating personally in every research study, and in later years the research was conducted almost entirely by his students. Overall, he "published very little experimental work under his own name. . . . Like Wundt, he placed himself at the head of his research enterprise, defending it, relating it to other enterprises, promulgating it to students, professionals, and laypersons" (Tweney, 1987, p. 40).

It was through the direction of his students' research, then, that Titchener's systematic position reached fruition. He supervised more than fifty doctoral candidates in psychology in thirty-five years, and most of their dissertations bear the imprint of his personal thought. He exercised his authority in the selection of their research problems, assigning topics that were related to the issues with which he was concerned. The graduate students were expected to work collectively on his ideas, and in this way he built a unified systematic position, which he called "the only scientific psychology worthy of the name" (Roback, 1952, p. 184).

Titchener translated some of Wundt's books from German into English. When he had completed his work on Wundt's third edition of the *Principles of Physiological Psychology*, he found that Wundt had already finished the fourth edition. Titchener then translated the fourth edition, only to learn that the tireless Wundt had published a fifth edition.

Titchener's own books include *An Outline of Psychology* (1896), *Primer of Psychology* (1898), and the four-volume *Experimental Psychology* (1901–1905). Külpe is said to have described the last as "the most erudite psychological work in the English language" (Boring, 1950, p. 413). Even today, Titchener's *Experimental Psychology* is considered "among the most important books in the history of psychology" (Benjamin, 1988a, p. 210). These Manuals, as the individual volumes of that work came to be called, enhanced the growth of laboratory work in psychology in the United States and influenced a generation of experimental psychologists, including those who later differed with structural psychology. Among them was John B. Watson, the founder of the behaviorist school of thought (Chapter 10). Titchener's textbooks enjoyed wide popularity and were translated into Russian, Italian, German, Spanish, and French.

Titchener had several hobbies that diverted time and energy from psychology. He conducted a small musical ensemble at his home every Sunday evening and for many years was "professor in charge of music" at Cornell, before a music department was established. His interest in coin collecting led him, with typical thoroughness, to learn Chinese and Arabic so that he could master the characters on the coins. He was also conversant in a half dozen modern languages. He maintained a voluminous correspondence with colleagues, and the majority of those letters were typewritten with additional material written by hand.

As he grew older, Titchener withdrew from social and university life. He was considered a living legend at Cornell, although a growing number of faculty members had never met him or even seen him. He did a great deal of his work in his study at home and spent relatively little time at the university. After 1909, he lectured only on Monday evenings during the spring semester of each academic year. His wife screened all callers and protected him from intrusions from the outside world; it was understood that no student would telephone him except in an extreme emergency.

Although he was autocratic in the manner of the German professor, he was also kind and helpful to students and colleagues, so long as they accorded him the deference and respect he felt were his due. Stories are told of how junior faculty members and graduate students washed his car and installed window screens at his house in the summer, not on command but out of respect and admiration.

One former student, Karl Dallenbach, quotes Titchener as saying that "a man could not hope to become a psychologist until after he had learned to smoke" (Dallenbach, 1967, p. 91). Accordingly, many of his students took to smoking cigars, at least in Titchener's presence. Another doctoral student, Cora Friedline,

> was discussing her research in Titchener's office when his ever-present cigar caught his beard on fire. He was talking at the time and his imposing manner made her reluctant to interrupt. Finally she said, "I beg your pardon, Dr. Titchener, but your whiskers are on fire." By

the time he extinguished the flames, the fire had burned through his shirt and his underwear.*

Titchener's concern for his students did not end when they left Cornell, nor did his impact on their lives. Dallenbach, on receiving his Ph.D., intended to go to medical school, but Titchener obtained a teaching position for him at the University of Oregon. Dallenbach had thought that Titchener would approve of medical school, but he was wrong. "I had to go to Oregon, as [Titchener] did not intend to have his training and work with me wasted" (Dallenbach, 1967, p. 91).

Titchener's relations with psychologists outside his own group were sometimes strained. Elected to the American Psychological Association by the charter members in 1892, he resigned shortly thereafter because the association declined to expel a member he had accused of plagiarism. The story is told that a friend paid Titchener's dues for a number of years so that his name would be listed as a member.

In 1904, a group of psychologists called the "Titchener Experimentalists" was formed, and they met regularly to compare research notes. Titchener selected the topics and the guests and generally dominated the meetings. One of his rules for the gatherings was that no women were allowed to attend. His student E. G. Boring commented that Titchener "wanted oral reports that could be interrupted, dissented from, and criticized in a smoke-filled room with no women present—for in 1904, when the Experimentalists were formed, women were considered too pure to smoke" (Boring, 1967, p. 315).

Several women students from Bryn Mawr College in Pennsylvania attempted to attend the meetings but were told to leave. On one occasion, they hid under a table throughout the session. Boring's fiancée and another woman waited in the room next door "with the door ajar to hear what unexpurgated male psychology was like. They came through unscathed" (Boring, 1967, p. 322).

It has been argued that Titchener was not so much deliberately discriminating against women as he was reflecting the patriarchal attitudes of the day. Of the fifty-six doctoral degrees he awarded, more than one-third were to women, a very high proportion for that time (Furumoto, 1988). The first woman to receive a Ph.D. in psychology, and Titchener's first doctoral student, was Margaret Floy Washburn. "He did not quite know what to do with me," she recalled (Washburn, 1932, p. 340). She had chosen Columbia University, but they would not admit women graduate students.

*From Ludy T. Benjamin, Jr., based on material in the Cora Friedline papers, Archives of the History of American Psychology, University of Akron, Ohio.

Titchener accepted her, and after she received her degree at Cornell, she undertook a successful career in psychology. Her professional contributions include a major book on animal psychology and the presidency of the American Psychological Association.

Around 1910 Titchener began work on what he envisioned as a complete exposition of his system. Unfortunately, he died of a brain tumor at the age of sixty, before he had finished the work. A few sections of it were published in a journal and later reprinted in a book after his death. Titchener's pickled brain is reported to be on display at Cornell.

Titchener's System of Psychology

According to Titchener, the subject matter of psychology is conscious experience. All sciences, he noted, share this subject matter — some portion of the world of human experience — but each deals with a different aspect. The subject matter of psychology is experience as it is dependent on experiencing persons. This kind of experience is different from that studied by scientists in other disciplines. For instance, light and sound are studied by both physicists and psychologists. The physicists look at the phenomena from the standpoint of the physical processes involved; psychologists view them in terms of how they are experienced by human observers.

Other sciences, Titchener said, are independent of experiencing persons, and he offered the example of temperature. The temperature in a room may be, say, 85° whether or not anyone experiences it. When observers stand in that room, however, and report that they feel uncomfortably warm, that feeling is experienced by and dependent on those experiencing individuals. Such experience alone is the subject matter for psychology.

Titchener cautioned that in the study of conscious experience one must not commit what he called the ***stimulus error***, that is, confusing the mental process with the stimulus or with the object being observed. For example, observers who see an apple and describe it as an apple, instead of reporting the hues, brightnesses, and spatial characteristics they are experiencing, are committing the stimulus error. The object of observation is not to be described in everyday language but rather in terms of the conscious content of the experience.

When observers focus on the stimulus object instead of the conscious process, they fail to distinguish what they know about the object (that it is called an apple) from their own immediate experience. All observers really know about an object such as an apple are its color, brightness, and spatial pattern (that it is red, shiny, and round). When they describe anything other than these characteristics, they are interpreting the object, not observing it, and thus they are dealing with mediate—not immediate—experience.

Titchener defined *consciousness* as the sum of our experiences as they exist at a given time, and *mind* as the sum of our experiences accumulated over a lifetime. Mind and consciousness are similar, except that consciousness involves mental processes occurring at the moment whereas mind involves the total accumulation of these processes.

The structural psychology of Titchener was a pure science. He argued that psychology must study and come to understand the generalized human mind, not individual minds, and certainly not individual differences among minds. His psychology would, therefore, have no applied or utilitarian concerns. Psychology was not in the business of curing "sick minds," he said, or of reforming individuals or society. Its only legitimate purpose was to discover the facts or the structure of the mind. He believed that scientists had to remain free of concerns about the practical worth of their work, and he expressed his opposition to child psychology, animal psychology, and other areas that did not fit with his introspective experimental psychology of the content of consciousness.

The Method of Study: Introspection

Psychology, like all sciences, depends on observation, but it depends on the observation of conscious experience. Titchener's form of self-observation, or introspection, relied on well-trained observers who were required to relearn how to perceive so that they could describe their conscious state and not the stimulus. Titchener realized that everyone learns to describe experience in terms of the stimulus—such as calling a red shiny round object an apple—and that in everyday life this is beneficial and necessary. In the laboratory, however, this practice had to be unlearned through intensive training.

Titchener adopted Külpe's label, systematic experimental introspection, to describe his approach. Like Külpe, he used detailed, qualitative, subjective reports of his subjects' mental activities during the act of introspecting. He opposed the Wundtian approach, with its equipment and its focus on objective measurements, and in 1912, he publicly criticized the kind of research performed in the Leipzig laboratory.

> Those who remember the psychological laboratories of twenty years ago can hardly escape an occasional shock of contrast which, for the moment, throws into vivid relief the difference between the old order and the new. The experimenter of the early [1890s] trusted, first of all, in his instruments; chronoscope and kymograph and tachistoscope were—it is hardly an exaggeration to say—of more im-

portance than the observer. . . . There were still vast reaches of the mental life which experiment had not touched. (Titchener, 1912a, p. 427)

Those vast reaches of mental life to which Titchener referred were the elementary sensations and images that, in his view, composed the structure of consciousness. These were the core of his psychology—not the synthesis of the elements through apperception that was of concern to Wundt, but rather the analysis of complex conscious experience into its component parts. Titchener emphasized the parts, whereas Wundt emphasized the whole. It was a view Titchener may have acquired from James Mill's *Analysis of the Phenomena of the Human Mind*. In line with most of the British empiricists and associationists, Titchener's goal was to discover the atoms of the mind.

Titchener was also influenced by the doctrine of mechanism, and the mechanistic spirit is evident in the structuralist image of the observers who supplied his data. In the published research reports of the day, subjects were sometimes called ***reagents***, a term used by scientists to denote substances that, because of their capacity for certain reactions, are used to detect, examine, or measure other substances. A reagent is generally a passive agent, one that is applied to something to elicit certain responses. The parallel with chemistry is obvious.

Transposing this concept to the human observers in Titchener's laboratory, we see that his subjects were considered to be recording instruments, objectively noting the characteristics of the stimulus they were observing. The subjects were nothing more than impartial and detached machines. Titchener wrote that trained observation would become mechanized or habitual and thus would no longer be a conscious process.

If human subjects are considered to be machines, then it is easy to think that all human beings are machines. This view shows the continuing impact of the Galilean-Newtonian mechanical view of the universe, an influence that did not disappear with the eventual demise of structuralism. We shall see as the history of psychology unfolds that this image of human-as-machine characterized much of experimental psychology through the first half of the twentieth century.

Titchener believed that observation in psychology must be not only introspective but also experimental. He diligently observed the rules of scientific experimentation, noting that

an experiment is an observation that can be repeated, isolated, and varied. The more frequently you can repeat an observation, the more likely are you to see clearly what is there and to describe accurately what you have seen. The more strictly you can isolate an observation, the easier does your task of observation become, and the less danger is there of your being led astray by irrelevant circumstances, or of placing emphasis on the wrong point. The more widely you can vary an observation, the more clearly will the uniformity of experience stand out, and the better is your chance of discovering laws. All experimental appliances, all laboratories and instruments, are provided and devised with this one end in view: that the student shall be able to repeat, isolate and vary his observations. (Titchener, 1909, p. 20)

The reagents or subjects in Titchener's laboratory introspected on a variety of stimuli, providing their lengthy and detailed observations of the elements of their experiences. Introspection was a serious endeavor, and the graduate student subjects had to be highly dedicated to pursue what Titchener called the "hard introspective labor."

Titchener's doctoral student Cora Friedline recalled the time when the Cornell laboratory was studying organic sensitivity. The observers were asked to swallow a stomach tube in the morning and to keep it in place throughout the day. Many of them vomited at first (being unable to stomach the task), but they gradually got used to it. In between their lectures and other activities they reported to the laboratory. There hot water was poured down the tube, and they introspected on the sensations they were experiencing. The process was later repeated with iced water.

Introspection sometimes carried over into the graduate students' private lives. For a time, the students were required to carry notebooks when they used the toilet and to record their sensations and feelings during urination and defecation.

Another bit of introspective research provides an example of data lost to history. Married graduate students were asked to make notes of their elementary sensations and feelings during sexual intercourse and to attach measuring instruments to their bodies to record physiological changes. This research went generally unpublicized at the time and was revealed by Cora Friedline in 1960. It did become known around the Cornell University campus, however, giving the psychology laboratory a reputation as an immoral place. The housemother in the women's dormitory would not allow her students to visit the laboratory after dark. When word spread that condoms had been attached to the stomach tubes the graduate students were swallowing, the talk in the dormitory was that "the lab was full of condoms and that it wasn't a safe place for anyone to go."*

---

*Friedline's recollections were offered on April 11, 1960, at Randolph-Macon College in Lynchburg, Virginia. We are grateful to Frederick B. Rowe for providing a copy of her remarks.

The more routine research conducted in Titchener's laboratory is described in the original source material reprinted later in this chapter.

The Elements of Consciousness

To Titchener, the three problems or aims of psychology were: (1) to reduce conscious processes to their simplest or most basic components, (2) to determine the laws by which these elements are associated, and (3) to bring the elements into connection with their physiological conditions. Thus, the aims of psychology coincide with those of the natural sciences. After scientists decide which part of the natural world they wish to study, they proceed to discover its elements, to demonstrate how those elements are compounded into more complex phenomena, and to formulate the laws governing those phenomena. The bulk of Titchener's efforts were devoted to the first problem — discovering the elements of consciousness.

Titchener proposed three elementary states of consciousness: sensations, images, and affective states. *Sensations* are the basic elements of perception and occur in the sounds, sights, smells, and other experiences evoked by physical objects present in the environment. *Images* are the elements of ideas and are found in the process that pictures or reflects experiences not actually present at the moment, such as a memory of a past experience. It is not clear from Titchener's writings whether he thought sensations and images were mutually exclusive. He emphasized the similarity between the two while arguing that they could be distinguished. *Affective states* (affections or feelings) are the elements of emotion and are found in experiences such as love, hate, or sadness.

In *An Outline of Psychology* (1896), Titchener presented a list of tne elements of sensation uncovered through his research; it included more than 44,000 sensation qualities; 32,820 were visual, and 11,600 were auditory. Each element was believed to be conscious and distinct from all others, and each could be combined with others to form perceptions and ideas.

Although basic and irreducible, these elements could be categorized, just as chemical elements are grouped into various classes. Despite their simplicity, elements have characteristics that enable us to distinguish among them. To the Wundtian attributes of quality and intensity, Titchener added duration and clearness. He considered these four attributes to be basic characteristics of all sensations that are present, to some degree, in all experience.

Quality is the characteristic — such as "cold" or "red" — that clearly distinguishes each element from every other. Intensity refers to the strength or weakness, loudness or brightness of a sensation. Duration refers to the course of a sensation over time. Clearness refers to the role of attention in conscious experience; that which is the focus of our attention is clearer than that toward which attention is not directed.

Sensations and images possess all four of these attributes, but affective states have only quality, intensity, and duration; they lack clearness. Titchener believed that it was not possible to focus attention directly on an element of emotion. When we try to do so, the affective quality — the sadness or the pleasantness, for example — disappears. Some sensory processes, particularly vision and touch, also possess the attribute of extensity, in that they spread out in space.

All conscious processes are reducible to one of these categories. The findings of the Würzburg school did not cause Titchener to modify his position. He recognized that obscure and ill-defined qualities may occur during thought, but he held that these were still sensory or imaginal elements. The subjects in Külpe's laboratory had, Titchener said, succumbed to the stimulus error because they paid more attention to the stimulus object than to their conscious processes.

Titchener's graduate students in the Cornell laboratory carried out a great deal of research on affective or feeling states, and their findings resulted in the rejection of Wundt's tridimensional theory of feeling. Titchener suggested that affections had only one of the dimensions in Wundt's theory, that of pleasure-displeasure, and he denied the dimensions of tension-relaxation and excitement-depression.

Toward the end of his life, Titchener began to alter his system in major ways. As early as 1918, he dropped the concept of mental elements from his lectures and began to argue that psychology should study not elements but the larger dimensions or processes of mental life. These he listed as quality, intensity, duration (protensity), clearness (attensity), and extensity. Seven years later he wrote to a graduate student that "You must give up thinking in terms of sensations and affections. That was all right ten years ago; but now, as I have told you, it is wholly out of date. . . . You must learn to think in terms of dimensions rather than in terms of systematic constructs like sensation" (Evans, 1972, p. 174).

Even the term *structural psychology* had fallen out of favor with Titchener by the early 1920s, and he began to refer to his approach as existential psychology. He also reconsidered the controlled form of introspection he had been practicing for so long and came to favor a more open, phenomenological approach.

These are dramatic shifts, and had Titchener lived long enough to implement them, they would have radically altered the face — and the fate — of structural psychology. They also suggest the flexibility and openness that scientists like to think they possess, but which not all can demonstrate. The evidence for these changes was pieced together from meticulous examination of Titchener's letters and lectures (Evans, 1972; Henle, 1974). Although the ideas were never formally incorporated into Titchener's system, they indicate a direction and a goal toward which he was moving, but which death prevented him from reaching.

Original Source Material on Structuralism: From *A Text-Book of Psychology* by E. B. Titchener

The following material, drawn from Titchener's popular *A Text-Book of Psychology* (1909),* describes the orthodox structuralist conception of the subject matter and methodology of the new science of psychology.

You may be wondering why we are asking you to read something Titchener wrote more than eighty years ago. After all, you have just read about Titchener's system, and your instructor has elaborated on it in class. This should have given you a broad overview of Titchener's approach to psychology. It must be remembered, however, that both textbook authors and teachers provide their own versions, visions, and perceptions of the material under study. They must reduce, abstract, and synthesize the original data, to distill them to manageable proportions. In that process something of the unique form and style, if not content, of the original may be lost.

To understand a system of thought more thoroughly, one should, ideally, read the original data of history on which writers base their books and instructors base their lectures. In practice, however, this is impossible in the space of one semester. That is why we are providing a sample of the original data, the theorists' own words, for each of the major schools of thought. These excerpts will show you how the theorists described their unique approaches to psychology and will acquaint you with the style of exposition studied by previous generations of psychology students.

With each of the five original articles included in this book, we indicate the salient points, to give you a preview and a framework for a better understanding of what each theorist is saying.

In Titchener's description of his structural psychology, reprinted below, he discusses: (1) the difference between experience that is independent of the experiencing person and experience that is dependent on the

*Reprinted with permission of Macmillan Publishing Co., Inc., from *A Text-Book of Psychology* by E. B. Titchener (pp. 6–9, 15–25, 36–41). Copyright 1909 by Macmillan Publishing Co., Inc. Revised 1937 by Sophia K. Titchener. (Footnotes omitted.)

person, with examples of each; (2) the distinction between mental process, consciousness, and mind, and the relationship between mental life and the nervous system; (3) the nature of introspection as Titchener practiced it, and its relationship to the kind of introspection or observation used in other sciences; and (4) the problem or goal of structural psychology and the similarity between psychology and the natural sciences, including the basic questions of "what," "how," and "why," which he believed were posed by all the sciences.

All human knowledge is derived from human experience; there is no other source of knowledge. But human experience, as we have seen, may be considered from different points of view. Suppose that we take two points of view, as far as possible apart, and discover for ourselves what experience looks like in the two cases. First, we will regard experience as altogether independent of any particular person; we will assume that it goes on whether or not anyone is there to have it. Secondly, we will regard experience as altogether dependent upon the particular person; we will assume that it goes on only when someone is there to have it. We shall hardly find standpoints more diverse. What are the differences in experience, as viewed from them?

Take, to begin with, the three things that you first learn about in physics: space, time and mass. Physical space, which is the space of geometry and astronomy and geology, is constant, always and everywhere the same. Its unit is 1 cm., and the cm. has precisely the same value wherever and whenever it is applied. Physical time is similarly constant, and its constant unit is the 1 sec. Physical mass is constant; its unit, the 1 gr., is always and everywhere the same. Here we have experience of space, time and mass considered as independent of the person who experiences them. Change, then, to the point of view which brings the experiencing person into account. The two vertical lines in Fig. 1 [*Figure 5-1*, this volume] are physically equal; they measure alike in units of 1 cm. To you, who see them, they are not equal. The hour that you spend in the waiting-room of a village station and the hour that you spend in watching an amusing play are physically equal; they measure alike in units of 1 sec. To you, the one hour goes slowly, the other quickly; they are not equal. Take two circular cardboard boxes of different diameter (say, 2 cm. and 8 cm.), and pour sand into them until they both weigh, say, 50 gr. The two masses are physically equal; placed on the pans of a balance, they will hold the beam level. To you, as you lift them in your two hands, or raise them in turn by the same hand, the box of smaller diameter is considerably the heavier. Here we have experience of space, time

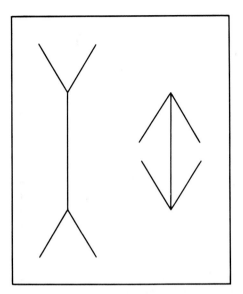

Figure 5-1 ▬▬▬▬▬▬▬▬▬▬▬▬

and mass considered as dependent upon the experiencing person. It is the same experience that we were discussing just now. But our first point of view gives us facts and laws of physics; our second gives us facts and laws of psychology.

Now take three other topics that are discussed in the physical textbooks: heat, sound and light. Heat proper, the physicists tell us, is the energy of molecular motion; that is to say, heat is a form of energy due to a movement of the particles of a body among themselves. Radiant heat belongs, with light, to what is called radiant energy — energy that is propagated by wave-movements of the luminiferous ether with which space is filled. Sound is a form of energy due to the vibratory movements of bodies, and is propagated by wave-movements of some elastic medium, solid, liquid or gaseous. In brief, heat is a dance of molecules; light is a wave-motion of the ether; sound is a wave-motion of the air. The world of physics, in which these types of experience are considered as independent of the experiencing person, is neither warm nor cold, neither dark nor light, neither silent nor noisy. It is only when the experiences are considered as dependent upon some person that we have warmth and cold, blacks and whites and colours and greys, tones and hisses and thuds. And these things are the subject-matter of psychology. . . .

MENTAL PROCESS, CONSCIOUSNESS AND MIND. The most striking fact about the world of human experience is the fact of change. Nothing stands still; everything goes on. The sun will someday lose its heat; the eternal hills are, little by little, breaking up and wearing away. Whatever we observe, and from whatever standpoint we observe it, we find process, occurrence; nowhere is there permanence or stability. Mankind, it is true, has sought to arrest this flux, and to give stability to the world of experience, by assuming two permanent substances, matter and mind: the occurrences of the physical world are then supposed to be manifestations of matter, and the occurrences of the mental world to be manifestations of mind. Such an hypothesis may be of value at a certain stage of human thought; but every hypothesis that does not accord with the facts must, sooner or later, be given up. Physicists are therefore giving up the hypothesis of an unchanging, substantial matter, and psychologists are giving up the hypothesis of an unchanging, substantial mind. Stable objects and substantial things belong, not to the world of science, physical or psychological, but only to the world of common sense.

We have defined mind as the sum-total of human experience considered as dependent upon the experiencing person. We have said, further, that the phrase "experiencing person" means the living body, the organized individual; and we have hinted that, for psychological purposes, the living body may be reduced to the nervous system and its attachments. Mind thus becomes the sum-total of human experience considered as dependent upon a nervous system. And since human experience is always process, occurrence, and the dependent aspect of human experience is its mental aspect, we may say, more shortly, that mind is the sum-total of mental processes. All these words are significant. "Sum-total" implies that we are concerned with the whole world of experience, not with a limited portion of it; "mental" implies that we are concerned with experience under its dependent aspect, as conditioned by a nervous system; and "processes" implies that our subject-matter is a stream, a perpetual flux, and not a collection of unchanging objects.

It is not easy, even with the best will possible, to shift from the common-sense to the scientific view of mind; the change cannot be made all in a moment. We are to regard mind as a stream of processes? But mind is personal, my mind; and my personality continues throughout my life. The experiencing person is only the bodily organism? But, again, experience is personal, the experience of a permanent self. Mind is spatial, just as matter is? But mind is invisible, intangible; it is not here or there, square or round.

These objections cannot be finally met until we have gone some distance into psychology, and can see how the scientific view of mind works out. Even now, however, they will weaken as you look at them.

Face that question of personality. Is your life, as a matter of fact, always personal? Do you not, time and again, forget yourself, lose yourself, disregard yourself, neglect yourself, contradict yourself, in a very literal sense? Surely, the mental life is only intermittently personal. And is your personality, when it is realised, unchanging? Are you the same self in childhood and manhood, in your working and in your playing moods, when you are on your best behaviour and when you are freed from restraint? Surely, the self-experience is not only intermittent, but also composed, at different times, of very different factors. As to the other question: mind is, of course, invisible, because sight is mind; and mind is intangible, because touch is mind. Sight-experience and touch-experience are dependent upon the experiencing person. But common sense itself bears witness, against its own belief, to the fact that mind is spatial: we speak, and speak correctly, of an idea in our head, a pain in our foot. And if the idea is the idea of a circle seen in the mind's eye, it is round; and if it is the visual idea of a square, it is square.

Consciousness, as reference to any dictionary will show, is a term that has many meanings. Here it is, perhaps, enough to distinguish two principal uses of the word.

In its first sense, consciousness means the mind's awareness of its own processes. Just as, from the common-sense point of view, mind is that inner self which thinks, remembers, chooses, reasons, directs the movements of the body, so is consciousness the inner knowledge of this thought and government. You are conscious of the correctness of your answer to an examination question, of the awkwardness of your movements, of the purity of your motives. Consciousness is thus something more than mind; it is "the perception of what passes in a man's own mind"; it is "the immediate knowledge which the mind has of its sensations and thoughts."

In its second sense, consciousness is identified with mind, and "conscious" with "mental." So long as mental processes are going on, consciousness is present; as soon as mental processes are in abeyance, unconsciousness sets in. "To say I am conscious of a feeling, is merely to say that I feel it. To have a feeling is to be conscious; and to be conscious is to have a feeling. To be conscious of the prick of the pin, is merely to have the sensation. And though I have these various modes of naming my sensation, by saying, I feel the prick of a pin, I feel the pain of a prick, I have the sensation of a prick, I have the feeling of a prick, I am conscious of the feeling; the thing named in all these various ways is one and the same."

The first of these definitions we must reject. It is not only unnecessary, but it is also misleading, to speak of consciousness as the mind's awareness of itself. The usage is unnecessary, because, as we shall see later, this awareness is a matter of observation of the same general kind as observation of the external world; it is misleading, because it suggests that mind is a personal being, instead of a stream of processes. We shall therefore take mind and consciousness to mean the same thing. But as we have the two different words, and it is convenient to make some distinction between them, we shall speak of mind when we mean the sum-total of mental processes occurring in the life-time of an individual, and we shall speak of consciousness when we mean the sum-total of mental processes occurring *now*, at any given "present" time. Consciousness will thus be a section, a division, of the mind-stream. This distinction is, indeed, already made in common speech: when we say that a man has "lost con-sciousness," we mean that the lapse is temporary, that the mental life will shortly be resumed; when we say that a man has "lost his mind," we mean — not, it is true, that the mind has altogether disappeared, but certainly that the derangement is permanent and chronic.

While, therefore, the subject-matter of psychology is mind, the direct object of psychological study is always a consciousness. In strictness, we can never observe the same consciousness twice over; the stream of mind flows on, never to return. Practically, we can observe a particular consciousness as often as we wish, since mental processes group themselves in the same way, show the same pattern of arrangement, whenever the organism is placed under the same circumstances. Yesterday's high tide will never recur, and yesterday's consciousnesses will never recur; but we have a science of psychol-ogy, as we have a science of oceanography.

THE METHOD OF PSYCHOLOGY. Scientific method may be summed up in the single word "observation"; the only way to work in science is to observe those phenomena which form the subject-matter of science. And observation implies two things: attention to the phenomena, and record of the phenomena; that is, clear and vivid experience, and an account of the experience in words or formulas. . . . The method of psychology, then, is observation. To distinguish it from the observa-tion of physical science, which is inspection, a looking-at, psycholog-ical observation has been termed introspection, a looking-within. But this difference of name must not blind us to the essential likeness of the methods. Let us take some typical instances.

We may begin with two very simple cases. (1) Suppose that you are shown two paper discs: the one of a uniform violet, the other composed half of red and half of blue. If this second disc is rapidly rotated, the red and blue will mix, as we say, and you will see a certain blue-red, that is, a kind of violet. Your problem is, so to adjust the proportions of red and blue in the second disc that the resulting violet exactly matches the violet of the first disc. You may repeat this set of observations as often as you like; you may isolate the observations by working in a room that is free from other, possibly disturbing colours; you may vary the observations by working to equality of the violets first from a two-colour disc that is distinctly too blue, and secondly from a disc that is distinctly too red. (2) Suppose, again, that the chord *c-e-g* is struck, and that you are asked to say how many tones it contains. You may repeat this observation; you may isolate it, by working in a quiet room; you may vary it, by having the chord struck at different parts of the scale, in different octaves.

It is clear that, in these instances, there is practically no difference between introspection and inspection. You are using the same method that you would use for counting the swings of a pendulum, or taking readings from a galvanometer scale, in the physical laboratory. There is a difference in subject-matter: the colours and the tones are dependent, not independent experiences: but the method is essentially the same.

Now let us take some cases in which the material of introspection is more complex. (1) Suppose that a word is called out to you, and that you are asked to observe the effect which this stimulus produces upon consciousness: how the word affects you, what ideas it calls up, and so forth. The observation may be repeated; it may be isolated — you may be seated in a dark and silent room, free from disturbances; and it may be varied — different words may be called out, the word may be flashed upon a screen instead of spoken, etc. Here, however, there seems to be a difference between introspection and inspection. The observer who is watching the course of a chemical reaction, or the movements of some microscopical creature, can jot down from moment to moment the different phases of the observed phenomenon. But if you try to report the changes in consciousness, while these changes are in progress, you interfere with consciousness; your translation of the mental experience into words introduces new factors into that experience itself. (2) Suppose, again, that you are observing a feeling or an emotion: a feeling of disappointment or annoyance, an emotion of anger or chagrin. Experimental control is still possible; situations may be arranged, in the psychological laboratory, such that these feelings may be repeated, isolated and varied. But your observation of them interferes, even more seriously than before, with the course of consciousness. Cool consideration of an emotion is fatal to its very existence; your anger disappears, your disappointment evaporates, as you examine it.

To overcome this difficulty of the introspective method, students of psychology are usually recommended to delay their observation until the process to be described has run its course, and then to call it back and describe it from memory. Introspection thus becomes retrospection; introspective examination becomes *post mortem* examination. The rule is, no doubt, a good one for the beginner; and there are cases in which even the experienced psychologist will be wise to follow it. But it is by no means universal. For we must remember (*a*) that the observations in question may be repeated. There is, then, no reason why the observer to whom the word is called out, or in whom the emotion is set up, should not report at once upon the first stage of his experience: upon the immediate effect of the word, upon the beginnings of the emotive process. It is true that this report interrupts the observation. But, after the first stage has been accurately described, further observations may be taken, and the second, third and following stages similarly described; so that presently a complete report upon the whole experience is obtained. There is, in theory, some danger that the stages become artificially separated; consciousness is a flow, a process, and if we divide it up we run the risk of missing certain intermediate links. In practice, however, this danger has proved to be very small; and we may always have recourse to retrospection, and compare our partial results with our memory of the unbroken experience. Moreover, (*b*) the practised observer gets into an introspective habit, has the introspective attitude ingrained in his system; so that it is possible for him, not only to take mental notes while the observation is in progress, without interfering with consciousness, but even to jot down written notes, as the histologist does while his eye is still held to the ocular of the microscope.

In principle, then, introspection is very like inspection. The objects of observation are different; they are objects of dependent, not of independent experience; they are likely to be transient, elusive, slippery. Sometimes they refuse to be observed while they are in passage; they must be preserved in memory, as a delicate tissue is preserved in hardening fluid, before they can be examined. And the standpoint of the observer is different; it is the standpoint of human life and of human interest, not of detachment and aloofness. But, in general, the method of psychology is much the same as the method of physics.

It must not be forgotten that, while the method of the physical and the psychological sciences is substantially the same, the subject-matter of these sciences is as different as it can well be. Ultimately, as we have seen, the subject-matter of all the sciences is the world of human experience; but we have also seen that the aspect of experience treated by physics is radically different from the aspect treated by psychology. The likeness of method may tempt us to slip from the one aspect to the other, as when a text-book of physics contains a chapter on vision and the sense of colour, or a text-book of physiology contains paragraphs on delusions of judgment; but this confusion of subject-matter must inevitably lead to confusion of thought. Since all the sciences are concerned with the one world of human experience, it is natural that scientific method, to whatever aspect of experience it is applied, should be in principle the same. On the other hand, when we have decided to examine some particular aspect of experience, it is necessary that we hold fast to that aspect, and do not shift our point of view as the enquiry proceeds. Hence it is a great advantage that we have the two terms, introspection and inspection, to denote observation taken from the different standpoints of psychology and of physics. The use of the word introspection is a constant reminder that we are working in psychology, that we are observing the dependent aspect of the world of experience.

Observation, as we said above, implies two things: attention to the phenomena, and record of the phenomena. The attention must be held at the highest possible degree of concentration; the record must be photographically accurate. Observation is, therefore, both difficult and fatiguing; and introspection is, on the whole, more difficult and more fatiguing than inspection. To secure reliable results, we must be strictly impartial and unprejudiced, facing the facts as they come, ready to accept them as they are, not trying to fit them to any preconceived theory; and we must work only when our general disposition is favourable, when we are fresh and in good health, at ease in our surroundings, free from outside worry and anxiety. If these rules are not followed, no amount of experimenting will help us. The observer in the psychological laboratory is placed under the best possible external conditions; the room in which he works is fitted up and arranged in such a way that the observation may be repeated, that the process to be observed may stand out clearly upon the background of consciousness, and that the factors in the process may be separately varied. But all this care is of no avail, unless the observer himself comes to the work in an even frame of mind, gives it his full attention, and is able adequately to translate his experience into words. . . .

THE PROBLEM OF PSYCHOLOGY. Science seeks always to answer three questions in regard to its subject-matter, the questions of what, how, and why. What precisely, stripped of all complications and reduced to its lowest terms, is this subject-matter? How, then, does it come to appear as it does; how are its elements combined and arranged? And, finally, why does it appear now in just this particular combination or arrangement? All three questions must be answered, if we are to have a science. . . .

To answer the question "what" is the task of analysis. Physical science, for example, tries by analysis to reduce the world of independent experience to its lowest terms, and so arrives at the various chemical elements. To answer the question "how" is the task of synthesis. Physical science traces the behaviour of the elements in their various combinations, and presently succeeds in formulating the laws of nature. When these two questions have been answered, we have a description of physical phenomena. But science enquires, further, why a given set of phenomena occurs in just this given way, and not otherwise; and it answers the question "why" by laying bare the cause of which the observed phenomena are the effect. There was dew on the ground last night because the surface of the earth was colder than the layer of air above it; dew forms on glass and not on metal because the radiating power of the one is great and of the other is small. When the cause of a physical phenomenon has thus been assigned, the phenomenon is said to be explained.

So far, now, as description is concerned, the problem of psychology closely resembles the problem of physics. The psychologist seeks, first of all, to analyse mental experience into its simplest components. He takes a particular consciousness and works over it again and again, phase by phase and process by process, until his analysis can go no further. He is left with certain mental processes which resist analysis, which are absolutely simple in nature, which cannot be reduced, even in part, to other processes. This work is continued, with other consciousnesses, until he is able to pronounce with some confidence upon the nature and number of the elementary mental processes. Then he proceeds to the task of synthesis. He puts the elements together, under experimental conditions: first, perhaps, two elements of the same kind, then more of that kind, then elementary processes of diverse kinds: and he presently discerns that regularity and uniformity of occurrence which we have seen to be characteristic of all human experience. He thus learns to formulate the laws of connection of the elementary mental processes.* If sensations of tone occur together, they blend or fuse; if sensations of

---

*By using the phrase "connection of the elementary mental processes," Titchener reveals the influence of the empiricists and associationists and their mechanical view of association. In Wundt's view, the elements were synthesized or organized by the active power of the mind, not connected passively and mechanically.

colour occur side by side, they enhance one another: and all this takes place in a perfectly regular way, so that we can write out laws of tonal fusion and laws of colour contrast.

If, however, we attempted to work out a merely descriptive psychology, we should find that there was no hope in it of a true science of mind. A descriptive psychology would stand to scientific psychology very much as the old-fashioned natural histories stand to modern text-books of biology, or as the view of the world which a boy gets from his cabinet of physical experiments stands to the trained physicist's view. It would tell us a good deal about mind; it would include a large body of observed facts, which we might classify and, in large measure, bring under general laws. But there would be no unity or coherence in it; it would lack that single guiding principle which biology has, for instance, in the law of evolution, or physics in the law of the conservation of energy. In order to make psychology scientific we must not only describe, we must also explain mind. We must answer the question "why."

But here is a difficulty. It is clear that we cannot regard one mental process as the cause of another mental process, if only for the reason that, with change of our surroundings, entirely new consciousnesses may be set up. When I visit Athens or Rome for the first time, I have experiences which are due, not to past consciousnesses, but to present stimuli. Nor can we, on the other hand, regard nervous processes as the cause of mental processes. The principle of psychophysical parallelism lays it down that the two sets of events, processes in the nervous system and mental processes, run their course side by side, in exact correspondence but without interference: they are, in ultimate fact, two different aspects of the same experience. The one cannot be the cause of the other.

Nevertheless, it is by reference to the body, to the nervous system and the organs attached to it, that we explain mental phenomena. The nervous system does not cause, but it does explain mind. It explains mind as the map of a country explains the fragmentary glimpses of hills and rivers and towns that we catch on our journey through it. In a word, reference to the nervous system introduces into psychology just that unity and coherence which a strictly descriptive psychology cannot achieve. . . .

Physical science, then, explains by assigning a cause; mental science explains by reference to those nervous processes which correspond with the mental processes that are under observation. We may bring these two modes of explanation together, if we define explanation itself as the statement of the proximate circumstances or conditions under which the described phenomenon occurs. Dew is formed under the condition of a difference of temperature between the air and the ground; ideas are formed under the condition of certain processes in the nervous system. Fundamentally, the object and the manner of explanation, in the two cases, are one and the same.

In [conclusion], just as the method of psychology is, on all essential points, the method of the natural sciences, so is the problem of psychology essentially of the same sort as the problem of physics. The psychologist answers the question "what" by analysing mental experience into its elements. He answers the question "how" by formulating the laws of connection of these elements. And he answers the question "why" by explaining mental processes in terms of their parallel processes in the nervous system. His programme need not be carried out in this order: he may get the hint of a law before his analysis is completed, and the discovery of a sense-organ may suggest the occurrence of certain elementary processes before he has found these processes by introspection. The three questions are intimately related, and an answer to any one helps toward the answers to the other two. The measure of our progress in scientific psychology is our ability to return satisfactory answers to all three.

The Fate of Structuralism

People often gain prominence in history because they oppose an older thought or position, but the situation may be reversed with Titchener, who stood firm when everyone else appeared to oppose him. The climate of thought in American and European psychology was changing by the second decade of the twentieth century, but the formal statement of Titchener's system was not. Some psychologists came to regard his work as a futile attempt to cling to antiquated principles and methods.

Titchener believed he was establishing the basic pattern for psychology, but his efforts proved to be only one phase in its history. The era of structuralism collapsed when he died. That it was sustained for so long is an effective tribute to his commanding personality.

Criticisms of Structuralism

The most severe criticisms of structuralism have been directed at the method of introspection. These criticisms are much more relevant to introspection as practiced at Titchener's and Külpe's laboratories, which dealt with subjective reports of the elements of consciousness, than to Wundt's method of internal perception, which dealt with more objective responses to external stimuli.

Introspection, broadly defined, had been in use for a long time, and attacks on the method were not new. The German philosopher Immanuel Kant had written, a century before Titchener's work, that any attempt at introspection necessarily alters the conscious experience being studied, because it introduces an observing element into the content of the conscious experience. The positivist philosopher Auguste Comte also attacked the introspective method. Several decades before Titchener proposed his structural psychology, Comte wrote:

> The mind may observe all phenomena but its own. . . . The observing and observed organ are here the same, and its action cannot be pure and natural. In order to observe, your intellect must pause from activity; yet it is this very activity that you want to observe. If you cannot effect that pause, you cannot observe; if you do effect it, there is nothing to observe. The results of such method are in proportion to its absurdity. (Comte, 1830/1896, Vol. I, p. 9)

Additional criticisms were leveled against introspection in 1867 by the English physician Henry Maudsley, who wrote extensively on psychopathology:

> There is little agreement among introspectionists. Where agreement does occur, it can be attributed to the fact that introspectionists must be meticulously trained, and thereby have a bias built into their observations. A body of knowledge based on introspection cannot be inductive; no discovery is possible from those who are trained specifically on what to observe. Due to the extent of the pathology of mind, self-report is hardly to be trusted. Introspective knowledge cannot have the generality we expect of science. It must be restricted to the class of sophisticated, trained adult subjects. Much of behavior (habit and performance) occurs without conscious correlates. (Turner, 1967, p. 11)

There were, then, substantial doubts about introspection before Titchener sharpened and modified it to bring it in line with the requirements of the experimental method. His modifications did not reduce the criticism. As the method was made more specific, so were the attacks.

One point relates to the definition of introspection. Titchener apparently had difficulty defining introspection with the necessary degree of rigor, and he attempted to do so by relating it to particular experimental conditions. "The course that an observer follows," he wrote, "will vary in detail with the nature of the consciousness observed, with the purpose of the experiment, with the instruction given by the experimenter. Introspection is thus a generic term, and covers an indefinitely large group of specific methodical procedures" (Titchener, 1912b, p. 485). With so much variation, it is difficult to find commonalities among his uses of the term.

A point we mentioned earlier relates to the question of what, precisely, the structuralist introspectors were trained to do. Titchener's graduate student observers learning to introspect were instructed to ignore certain classes of words (so-called meaning words) that had become a fixed part of their vocabulary. The phrase, "I see a table," for example, has no scientific meaning to a structuralist; the word *table* is a meaning word, based on previously established and generally agreed-upon knowledge about the specific combination of sensations we have learned to identify and label as a table. Thus, the observation "I see a table" told the structuralist nothing about the observers' conscious experience. The structuralist was interested not in the aggregate of sensations summarized in a meaning word but in the specific elementary forms of the experience. Observers who said "table" were committing the stimulus error.

If these ordinary words were stricken from the vocabulary, how was the experience to be described? An introspective language would have to be developed. Because Titchener (and Wundt, as well) emphasized that the external conditions of the experiment must be carefully controlled, so that the conscious experience could be precisely determined, two observers should have identical experiences and their results should corroborate one another. Because of these highly similar experiences under controlled conditions, then, it seemed theoretically possible to develop a working vocabulary devoid of meaning words. It is, after all, because of commonalities of experience in everyday life that we are able to agree on conventional meanings for familiar words.

Although the development of such an introspective vocabulary may be possible in principle, it was never realized. There was frequent disagreement among the observers, even under the most rigidly controlled experimental conditions. Introspectors at different laboratories obtained different results. Even subjects at the same laboratory often failed to agree. Titchener nevertheless maintained that agreement would be reached eventually. And had there been sufficient agreement on introspective findings, structuralism might have lasted longer than it did.

There were additional criticisms of introspection. It was charged that introspection, in reality, was retrospection, because some time elapsed between the experience and the reporting of it. Because forgetting, as Ebbinghaus demonstrated, is most rapid immediately after an experience, it seemed likely that some of the experience was lost before introspection occurred. The structuralist answer to this charge was to specify that observers work with brief time intervals, and to postulate the existence of a primary mental image that was alleged to maintain the experience for the observers until it could be reported.

Another difficulty we noted is that the act of minutely examining an experience in introspective fashion may radically change it. Consider the difficulty in introspecting the conscious state of anger. In the process of rationally attending to and trying to dissect the experience into its elementary components, the anger may subside or disappear. Titchener believed, however, that experienced and well-trained introspectors became unconscious of their observational task with continued practice.

The method of introspection was not the only target of criticism. The structuralist movement was accused of artificiality and sterility because of its attempt to analyze conscious processes into elements. Critics charged that the whole of an experience cannot be recovered by any connection or association of the elemental parts. Experience, they argued, does not come to us in sensations, images, or affective states, but rather in unified wholes. Something of the conscious experience must inevitably be lost in any artificial effort to analyze it. We shall see that the Gestalt school of psychology made effective use of this criticism in launching their new movement, their revolt against structuralism.

The structuralists' narrow definition of psychology came under attack. The scope of modern psychology was growing in a number of areas that the structuralists chose to exclude, because those areas were not congruent with their definition and method. Titchener regarded animal psychology and child psychology as not psychology at all. His conception of the field was too limited to embrace all the new work being carried out by the rapidly increasing number of psychologists in the United States. Psychology was moving beyond Titchener, and moving very quickly.

Contributions of Structuralism

There is no denying that Titchener and the structuralists made important contributions to psychology. Their subject matter—conscious experience—was clearly defined. Their research methods were in the best tradition of science, involving observation, experimentation, and measurement. Because consciousness was best perceived by the person having the conscious experience, the best method for that subject matter was self-observation.

Although the subject matter and aims of the structuralists are no longer vital, introspection — defined as the giving of a verbal report based on experience — is still used in many areas of psychology. Researchers in psychophysics, for example, ask subjects to report whether a second tone sounds louder or softer than the first. Verbal reports are rendered by persons describing their experiences in unusual experimental environments, such as sensory deprivation cubicles. Clinical reports from patients, and responses on personality tests and attitude scales, are also introspective in nature.

Introspective reports involving cognitive processes such as reasoning can also be obtained from subjects. For example, industrial/organizational psychologists consider introspective reports from employees about how they interact with computer terminals in the development and refinement of such equipment. These and other instances involve verbal reports based on experience and are legitimate forms of data collecting. We shall see in Chapter 15 that the cognitive movement in psychology, with its renewed interest in conscious processes, has conferred even greater legitimacy on introspection.

Another contribution of structuralism is essentially negative, that is, its service as a target of criticism. Structuralism provided a strong orthodoxy against which newly developing movements could array their forces. These newer schools of thought owed their existence in no small measure to their progressive reformulation of the structuralist position. We noted that advances in science require something to oppose. With the help of Titchener and the structuralists, psychology moved far beyond his initial boundaries.

Suggested Readings

Angell, F. (1928). Titchener at Leipzig. *Journal of General Psychology, 1*, 195–198. A fellow student describes the time at Leipzig and discusses Titchener's research and personality characteristics.

Boring, E. G. (1953). A history of introspection. *Psychological Bulletin, 50*, 169–189. Discusses introspection as practiced in Titchener's structural psychology and describes the use of introspective methods (though often under different names) in later schools of psychological thought.

Dunlap, K. (1912). The case against introspection. *Psychological Review, 19*, 404–413. Notes inconsistencies among various definitions and applications of introspection.

Evans, R. B. (1972). E. B. Titchener and his lost system. *Journal of the History of the Behavioral Sciences, 8*, 168–180. Describes the development of Titchener's structuralist approach to psychology and speculates on the changes in his thinking toward the end of his life.

Henle, M. (1971). Did Titchener commit the stimulus error? The problem of meaning in structural psychology. *Journal of the History of the Behavioral Sciences, 7*, 279–282. Describes inconsistencies in Titchener's approach to introspection and suggests ways in which he revised his view of psychology in his later years.

Hindeland, M. J. (1971). Edward Bradford Titchener: A pioneer in perception. *Journal of the History of the Behavioral Sciences, 7*, 23–28. Describes Titchener's experimental approach to problems in sensation and perception.

Radford, J. (1974). Reflections on introspection. *American Psychologist, 29*, 245–250. Reviews historical views of introspection and compares Titchener's approach with the work of the behaviorist John B. Watson.

Titchener, E. B. (1912). *A Primer of Psychology* (rev. ed.). New York: Macmillan. A basic textbook on the structuralist approach to psychology covering research methodology and specific topics such as attention, feeling, emotion, memory, and thought.

Washburn, M. F. (1922). Introspection as an objective method. *Psychological Review, 29*, 89–112. An analysis of similarities in methods between structuralism and behaviorism.

Functionalism: Antecedent Influences

6

The Functionalist Protest

Functional psychology, as the name suggests, is concerned with the mind as it functions or is used in an organism's adaptation to its environment. The functionalist movement focused on a practical question: What do mental processes accomplish? Functionalists studied the mind not from the standpoint of its composition (a structure of mental elements) but rather as a conglomerate of functions or processes that lead to practical consequences in the real world.

    The studies of the mind undertaken by Wundt and by Titchener revealed nothing of the outcomes or accomplishments of mental activity.

Nor did they aspire to; such a utilitarian goal was not consistent with their pure science approach to psychology. Functionalism, as the first uniquely American system of psychology, was a deliberate protest against Wundt's psychology and Titchener's structuralism, both of which were viewed as too narrow and restrictive. They could not answer the questions the functionalists were asking: What does the mind do? How does it do it?

Functionalism was not a protest against the methods and topics of research at Leipzig and Cornell. Indeed, the functionalists adopted many of the findings from those laboratories. They did not object to introspection, nor did they argue against the experimental study of consciousness. What the functionalists did oppose were the earlier definitions of psychology that ruled out any consideration of the useful and practical functions of the mind, the ongoing activities or operations of consciousness.

Although functionalism was a protest against the current school of thought, its proponents did not intend to become a full-fledged school. The primary reason for this seems to have been personal rather than ideological. None of the supporters of the functionalist position had the ambition to found and lead a formal movement. In time, functionalism did gain many of the characteristics of a school of thought, but that was not its aim. Its leaders appeared content to challenge the positions of Wundt and Titchener and to broaden the base and scope of the new psychology, and they did so with considerable success. They modified the existing orthodoxy without striving to replace it.

As a result, functionalism was never as rigid or as formally differentiated a systematic position as was Titchener's structuralism. It cannot, therefore, be described as neatly or as precisely. There was not a single functional psychology, as there was a single structural psychology. Several functional psychologies existed, and although they differed somewhat, they all shared an interest in the functions of consciousness. And as an outgrowth of this emphasis on the functioning of an organism in its environment, functionalists became interested in the possible applications of psychology. Thus, applied psychology developed rapidly in the United States, where today it is the most important legacy of the functionalist movement.

An Overview of Functionalism

Functionalism has a long history, dating from the mid-1850s. Its historical development, unlike that of structuralism, was advanced by intellectual leaders with various interests and backgrounds. It may be partly attributable to this diversified base that functionalism, unlike structuralism, did not stagnate and decline.

We will consider in this chapter the antecedent influences on the functional psychology movement, including the works of Charles Darwin, Francis Galton, and early students of animal behavior. Although these initial sources of influence were British, functionalism formally began and flourished in the United States. It is important to note the time when the precursors of functionalism were developing their ideas — the period before and during the years in which the new psychology was developing. Darwin's *On the Origin of Species* (1859) was published one year before Fechner's *Elements of Psychophysics* (1860) and twenty years before Wundt established his laboratory at Leipzig. Galton began work on individual differences in 1869, before Wundt wrote his *Principles of Physiological Psychology* (1873–1874). Animal psychology experiments were conducted in the 1880s, before Titchener had journeyed to Germany and come under Wundt's influence. Thus, major work on the functions of consciousness, individual differences, and animal behavior was being done at the time Wundt and Titchener were excluding these areas from the province of psychology. It remained for the new American psychologists, with their different temperament, to bring function, individual differences, and the white rat to positions of prominence in psychology.

American psychology today is functionalist in orientation and attitude. This is evident in the emphasis placed on testing, and on learning, perception, and other functional processes that aid our adaptation and adjustment to our environment.

The Evolution Revolution: Charles Darwin (1809–1882)

Charles Darwin's *On the Origin of Species by Means of Natural Selection*, published in 1859, is one of the most important books in the history of Western civilization. The ***theory of evolution*** presented in this work freed scholars from constraining traditions and superstitions and ushered in the era of maturity and respectability for the life sciences. The theory of evolution was also to have a tremendous impact on contemporary American psychology, which owes its form and substance as much to the influence of Darwin's work as to any other idea or individual. In addition, evolutionary theory exerted an enormous influence on the work of Sigmund Freud, as we shall see in Chapter 13.

The suggestion that living things change with time, which is the fundamental notion of evolution, did not originate with Darwin. Although intellectual anticipations of this general idea can be traced to the fifth century B.C., it was not until the late eighteenth century that the theory was first investigated systematically. Erasmus Darwin (the 340-pound grandfather of Charles Darwin and Francis Galton) expressed the belief that all warm-blooded animals had evolved from a single living filament, given animation by God. In 1809 the French naturalist Jean Baptiste Lamarck formulated a behavioral theory of evolution that emphasized the modification of an animal's bodily form through its efforts to adapt to its environment; these modifications, Lamarck suggested, were inherited by succeeding generations. According to this theory, to give one example, the giraffe developed its long neck over generations of having to reach for higher and higher branches to find food. In the mid-1800s, the British geologist Charles Lyell introduced the notion of evolution into geological theory, arguing that the earth had passed through various stages of development in evolving to its present structure.

Why, after so many centuries of acceptance of the biblical account of creation, were scholars driven to seek an alternative explanation? One reason is that more was being learned about the other species that inhabited the earth. Explorers were discovering and studying intriguing kinds of animal life found on several continents. It was inevitable, therefore, that some thinkers should begin to ask how Noah could possibly have put a pair of each of these animals into the Ark. There were simply too many species to allow for continued belief in that biblical story.

Explorers and scientists had uncovered fossils and bones of creatures that did not match those of existing species — bones that apparently belonged to animals that had once roamed the earth and then disappeared. Thus, living forms could no longer be seen as constant, unchanged since the beginning of time, but were subject to modification. Old species became extinct and new species appeared, some of them alterations of current forms. Perhaps, some scientists speculated, all of nature results from change and is still in the process of evolving.

The impact of continuing change was being observed not only in the intellectual and scientific realm but also in everyday life. Society was being transformed by the forces of the Industrial Revolution. Values, social relationships, and cultural norms that had been constant for generations were being disrupted as great numbers of people migrated from rural areas and small towns to huge urban manufacturing centers.

Above all was the growing influence of science. People were less content to base their knowledge of human nature and society on what the Bible and ancient authorities asserted to be true. Instead, they were ready to put their faith in science.

Change was the Zeitgeist of the day. It affected the peasant farmer, whose life now pulsed to the rhythm of the machine instead of the seasons, as much as the scientist whose time was spent puzzling over a newly found set of bones. The intellectual and social climate rendered the idea of an evolutionary theory scientifically respectable. There was a great deal of speculating and theorizing but, for a long time, little in the way of supporting evidence. Then *On the Origin of Species* provided so much well-organized data that the idea of evolution could not be ignored. The times demanded such a theory, and Charles Darwin became its agent.

The Life of Darwin

As a boy, Charles Darwin gave little indication of becoming the keen, hard-working scientist the world would later know. Indeed, he was expected to become nothing other than an idler and a gentleman-sportsman. In his early years he showed so little promise that his father, a wealthy physician, worried that young Charles would end up a disgrace to the family. Although he never liked school and never did well at his studies, Charles displayed an early interest in natural history and in collecting coins, shells, and minerals. Sent by his father to the University of Edinburgh to study medicine, he found it dull. Aware that Charles was doing poorly, his father decided that the young man should become a clergyman instead.

Darwin spent three years at Cambridge University and described the experience as wasted, at least from an academic standpoint. Socially, he had a wonderful time and described it as the happiest period of his life. He collected beetles, went hunting, and spent much time drinking, singing, and playing cards with a group of fellow students he referred to as dissipated and low minded.

One of Darwin's instructors, the noted botanist John Stevens Henslow, promoted Darwin's appointment as a naturalist aboard the ship *H.M.S. Beagle*, which the British government was preparing for a scientific voyage around the world. This famous excursion, which lasted from 1831 to 1836, began in South American waters, proceeded to Tahiti and New Zealand, and returned to England by way of Ascension Island and the Azores. The trip afforded Darwin a unique opportunity to observe a variety of plant and animal life, and he was able to collect an immense amount of data. The trip changed Darwin's character. No longer the pleasure-loving dilettante, he returned to England a serious, dedicated scientist with one passion and aim in life — to promulgate his theory of evolution.

In 1839 Darwin married, and three years later he and his wife moved to Down, a village sixteen miles from London, where he could concentrate on his work without the distractions of city life. Never robust, he continued to be plagued by physical ailments, complaining of vomiting, flatulence,

The theory of evolution proposed by Charles Darwin set the stage for functional psychology, which studied the adaptive role rather than the content of consciousness.

boils, eczema, dizziness, trembling, and bouts of depression. The symptoms were apparently neurotic, triggered by any change in his daily routine. Whenever the outside world intruded, preventing him from working, he would suffer another attack. Illness became a useful device, protecting him from mundane affairs and allowing him the solitude and concentration he needed to create his theory. One writer has termed Darwin's condition a "creative malady" (Pickering, 1974).

From the time of his return with the *Beagle*, Darwin was convinced of the validity of the theory of the evolution of species. Why, then, did he wait twenty-two years before presenting his work to the world? The answer seems to lie in his extremely conservative attitude, a temperamental requisite for a good scientist. Darwin knew that his theory was revolutionary, and he wanted to be certain that when he published, it would be backed by sufficient supporting evidence. And so he proceeded with painstaking caution.

Not until 1842 did Darwin feel prepared to write a brief thirty-five-page summary of the development of his theory. Two years later he expanded this into a two-hundred-page essay, but still he was not satisfied. He continued to keep his ideas to himself, sharing them only with Charles Lyell and the botanist Joseph Hooker. For fifteen more years Darwin pored over his data, checking, elaborating, revising, to be sure that when he finally did publish, the theory would be unassailable.

No one knows how much longer Darwin might have delayed if he had not received in June of 1858, a shattering letter from one Alfred Russel Wallace, a young naturalist. Wallace, while staying in the East Indies to recover from an illness, had developed the outline of a theory of evolution that was amazingly similar to Darwin's, although it did not rest on the wealth of data Darwin had accumulated. Wallace said that his work had taken three days! In his letter, Wallace asked for Darwin's opinion of the theory and for his help in getting it published. We can imagine Darwin's feelings, after more than two decades of laborious and painstaking work.

Darwin possessed another characteristic — personal ambition — that is not uncommon among scientists. Even before his journey on the *Beagle* he had written in his diary that he was "ambitious to take a fair place among scientific men." And later he wrote, "I wish I could set less value on the bauble fame" and "I rather hate the idea of writing for priority, yet I certainly should be vexed if anyone were to publish my doctrines before me" (Merton, 1957, pp. 647–648).

With an enviable sense of fair play, however, Darwin thought about Wallace's letter and decided that "It seems hard on me that I should lose my priority of many years' standing, but I cannot feel at all sure that this alters the justice of the case. . . . It would be dishonorable in me now to publish" (Merton, 1957, p. 648).

Darwin's friends Lyell and Hooker suggested that he read Wallace's paper and portions of his own forthcoming book at a meeting of the Linnean Society on July 1, 1858. The rest is history. Every one of the 1,250 copies of the first printing of *On the Origin of Species* was sold on the day of publication. The book generated immediate excitement and controversy, and Darwin, although subjected to considerable abuse and criticism, nevertheless won "the bauble fame."

The Works of Darwin

The Darwinian theory of evolution is so well known that only an overview of the fundamental points is necessary here. Starting with the obvious fact of variation among individual members of a species, Darwin reasoned that this spontaneous variability was inheritable. In nature, a process of natural selection results in the survival of those organisms best suited for their environment and the elimination of those not fit. A continuing struggle for survival takes place, Darwin wrote, and those forms that survive are the ones that have made successful adaptations or adjustments to the environmental circumstances to which they are exposed. Species that cannot adapt do not survive.

Darwin formulated the idea of a struggle for survival after reading *Essay on the Principle of Population*, written by the economist Thomas Malthus in 1789. Malthus had noted that the world's food supply increases arithmetically, whereas the human population tends to increase geometrically. The inevitable result, which Malthus described as having a "melancholy hue," is that many human beings will live under near-starvation conditions. Only the most forceful and cunning will survive.

Darwin extended this principle to all living organisms and developed the concept of natural selection. Those forms of organisms that survive the struggle and reach maturity tend to transmit to their offspring the skills or advantages that enabled them to thrive. Further, because variation is another general law of heredity, offspring will show variation among themselves; some will possess the advantageous qualities developed to a higher degree than their parents. The qualities tend to survive, and in the course of many generations great changes in form may occur. These changes can be so extensive as to account for the differences among species that are found today.

Natural selection was not the only mechanism of evolution Darwin recognized. He also believed in Lamarck's doctrine that changes in form brought about by experience during an animal's lifetime can be passed to subsequent generations.

Although many of the clergy were receptive to the idea of evolutionary theory, others saw it as a threat because they believed it to be inconsistent with a literal interpretation of the biblical account of creation. One distinguished minister called it "an attempt to dethrone God," adding that "If the Darwinian theory is true, Genesis is a lie . . . and the revelation of God to man, as we Christians know it, is a delusion" (White, 1896/1965, p. 93). The controversy was intense and long lasting.

Within a year of the publication of *On the Origin of Species*, a debate took place at Oxford University, at a meeting of the British Association for the Advancement of Science. The speakers were the biologist Thomas

Henry Huxley, who defended Darwin and evolution, and Bishop Samuel Wilberforce, who defended the Book of Genesis. "Referring to the ideas of Darwin, [Wilberforce] congratulated himself... that he was not descended from a monkey. The reply came from Huxley: 'If I had to choose, I would prefer to be a descendant of a humble monkey rather than of a man who employs his knowledge and eloquence in misrepresenting those who are wearing out their lives in the search for truth" (White, 1896/1965, p. 92).

During the debate, a man walked about the hall holding a Bible over his head. "The book, the book," he kept shouting. It was Robert Fitzroy, captain of the *Beagle* during Darwin's voyage. A religious fundamentalist, Fitzroy blamed himself for his part in the development of the theory of evolution. Five years later he committed suicide (Gould, 1976, p. 34).

Newly discovered data of history have led to a reevaluation of the story of this famous confrontation (Richards, 1987). Apparently the account of the Oxford debate stems from Huxley's anticlerical attitude and his attempt (perhaps unwitting) to bolster his stature as a scientist. It was actually less a debate than a series of speeches. Captain Fitzroy merely took his turn at the podium, and it was Joseph Hooker, not Huxley, who offered the more effective rebuttal to Wilberforce. Darwin remained on good terms with Wilberforce; he found the bishop's remarks "uncommonly clever, not worth anything scientifically, but [he] quizzes me in splendid style" (Gould, 1986, p. 31).

The battle is not yet finished. In 1925, at the famous Scopes "monkey trial" in Dayton, Tennessee, a high school teacher, John T. Scopes, was prosecuted for teaching the theory of evolution. Almost a half century later, in 1972, a Tennessee clergyman charged that Darwin's theory "breeds corruption, lust, immorality, greed, and such acts of criminal depravity as drug addiction, war, and atrocious acts of genocide" (*New York Times*, October 1, 1972). The United States Supreme Court in 1968 struck down the final law that banned the teaching of evolution in the public schools, but a 1985 survey showed that half of a national sample of American adults rejected evolutionary theory (*Washington Post*, June 3, 1986). In 1987 the Supreme Court ruled against a bill in the state of Louisiana requiring that if evolution were taught in the public schools, then "creation science," the biblical view of the origin of species, had to be given equal time. And in 1990, the Texas state board of education approved science textbooks that cover the theory of evolution, but one-third of its members objected.

Darwin remained aloof from the disputes of his time and wrote other books of importance for psychology. His second major report on evolution, *The Descent of Man* (1871), marshaled the evidence for human evolution from lower forms of life, emphasizing the similarity between animal and human mental processes. The book quickly became popular. A writer in a prominent magazine, the *Edinburgh Review*, said that "In the drawing room it is competing with the latest novel, and in the study it is troubling alike the man of science, the moralist, and the theologian. On every side it is raising a storm of mingled wrath, wonder, and admiration" (Richards, 1987, p. 219). Wonder, admiration, and acceptance soon won out.

Darwin made an intensive study of emotional expressions in humans and animals, suggesting that the changes in gestures and postures that characterized the major emotions could be interpreted in evolutionary terms. In his book, *The Expression of the Emotions in Man and Animals* (1872), he argued that emotional expressions were remnants of movements that once had served some practical function.

Beginning in 1840, Darwin kept a diary about his infant son, recording the child's development. He published it as "A Biographical Sketch of an Infant" in the journal *Mind* in 1877. It is considered to be one of the early sources for modern child psychology.

The importance of mental factors in the evolution of species was apparent in Darwin's theory, and he frequently cited conscious reactions in humans and animals. Because of the role accorded consciousness in evolutionary theory, then, psychology was compelled to accept an evolutionary point of view.

The Influence of Darwin on Psychology

Darwin's work in the last part of the nineteenth century was a major force in shaping modern psychology. The theory of evolution raised the intriguing possibility of a continuity in mental functioning between humans and the lower animals. The evidence was largely anatomical, but it strongly suggested continuities in the development of behavior and mental processes. If the human mind had evolved from more primitive minds, then it would follow that similarities in mental functioning might exist between animals and humans. The gap between animals and humans posited two centuries earlier by Descartes was thus open to serious question, and the study of animal behavior could now be seen as vital to an understanding of human behavior. Scientists turned to investigations of animal mental functioning, introducing a new subject into the psychology laboratory. This new field of animal psychology was to have far-reaching implications.

Evolutionary theory also brought about a change in the subject matter and goal of psychology. The focus of the structuralists was the analysis of conscious content. Darwin's work inspired some psychologists, particularly those in the United States, to consider the functions that consciousness might serve. This seemed to many researchers to be more important than determining the elements of consciousness. And so as psychology came to be more concerned with how the organism functioned in adapting to its environment, the detailed investigation of mental elements began to lose its appeal.

Darwin's theory also influenced psychology by broadening the methodology the new science could legitimately use. The methods employed in Wundt's laboratory at Leipzig were derived primarily from physiology, notably the psychophysical methods of Fechner. Darwin's methods, which produced results applicable to both humans and animals, bore no resemblance to physiologically based techniques. Darwin's data came from a variety of sources including geology, archeology, demography, observations of wild and domesticated animals, and research on breeding. Information from all these fields provided support for his theory.

Here was tangible and impressive evidence that scientists could study human nature by techniques other than experimental introspection. Following Darwin's example, the psychologists who were influenced by evolutionary theory and its emphasis on the functions of consciousness became more eclectic with regard to their research methods. As a result, the kinds of data psychologists collected were broadened.

Another effect of evolution on psychology was seen in the growing focus on individual differences. The fact of variation among members of the same species was obvious to Darwin as a result of his observation, during the *Beagle* voyage, of so many species and forms. Evolution could not occur if each generation was identical to its forebears. Variation, therefore, was an important tenet of evolutionary theory.

While the structural psychologists continued their search for general laws to encompass all minds, the psychologists influenced by Darwin's ideas began to search for the ways in which individual minds differed, and for techniques to measure those differences. The psychology of the structuralists had little room for the consideration of animal minds or individual differences. It remained for scientists of a functionalist persuasion to pursue those problems. As a result, the form and nature of the new psychology began to change.

Individual Differences: Francis Galton (1822–1911)

Galton effectively brought the spirit of evolution to bear on psychology with his work on the problems of mental inheritance and individual differences in human capacity. Before Galton's efforts, the phenomenon of individual differences had not been considered a necessary subject for study in psychology; this was a serious omission. Only a few isolated attempts had been made, notably by Weber, Fechner, and Helmholtz, who had reported individual differences in their experimental results but had not investigated them systematically. Wundt and Titchener did not consider individual differences to be a part of psychology.

The Life of Galton

Francis Galton possessed an extraordinary intelligence (an estimated IQ of 200) and a wealth of novel ideas. He is perhaps without equal in the history of modern psychology. His creative curiosity and genius attracted him to a variety of problems, the details of which he left to be filled in by others. A few of the areas he investigated are fingerprints (which the police force soon adopted for identification purposes), fashions, the geographical distribution of beauty, weight lifting, and the efficacy of prayer. There was little that did not interest this versatile and inventive man.

Galton was born in 1822 near Birmingham, England, the youngest of nine children. His father was a prosperous banker whose wealthy and socially prominent family included important persons in major spheres of influence: the government, the church, and the military. From an early age Galton was acquainted with influential persons through his family connections. At the age of sixteen, at his father's insistence, Galton began the study of medicine as a house pupil at Birmingham General Hospital. He worked as an apprentice to the physicians, dispensed pills, studied medical books, set broken bones, amputated fingers, pulled teeth, vaccinated children, and provided his own diversion by reading the classics, notably Horace and Homer. Overall, it was not a pleasant experience, and only continued pressure from his father kept him there.

One incident during this medical apprenticeship illustrates Galton's ever-present curiosity. Wanting to learn for himself the effects of the various medications in the pharmacy, Galton began taking small doses of each, beginning in systematic fashion with those under the letter "A." This scientific venture ended at the letter "C" when he took a dose of croton oil, a powerful laxative.

After serving a year at the hospital Galton continued his medical education at King's College, London. A year later he changed his plans and enrolled at Trinity College of Cambridge University where, with a bust of Isaac Newton opposite his fireplace, he pursued his interest in mathematics. Although his work was interrupted by a severe mental breakdown, he did manage to earn his degree. He returned to the study of medicine, which by now he disliked intensely, but his father's death released him from that profession.

Evolution left its first imprint on psychology in the work of Francis Galton on mental inheritance and individual differences.

Travel and exploration claimed Galton's attention. He journeyed to the Sudan in 1845 and to Southwest Africa in 1850, the year he invented a teletype printer. He published accounts of his travels and was awarded a medal from the Royal Geographic Society. In the 1850s he stopped traveling, because of marriage and poor health, he said, but maintained his interest in exploration and wrote a guidebook called *The Art of Travel*. He organized expeditions for other explorers and gave lectures on camp life to soldiers training for duty in the Crimea. His spirited restlessness led him next to meteorology and the design of instruments to plot weather data. He summarized his findings in a book considered to be the first attempt to chart large-scale weather patterns.

When his cousin Charles Darwin published *On the Origin of Species*, Galton immediately turned his attention to the new theory. The biological aspect of evolution captivated him first, and he undertook an investigation of the effects of blood transfusions between rabbits, to determine whether acquired characteristics could be inherited. Although the genetic side of evolutionary theory did not hold his interest for long, the social implications guided Galton's subsequent work and determined his influence on modern psychology.

Mental Inheritance

Galton's first important book for psychology was *Hereditary Genius*, published in 1869. In it he sought to demonstrate that individual greatness or genius occurred within families far too often to be explained by environmental influences. His thesis, briefly, was that eminent men have eminent sons. For the most part, the biographical studies Galton reported in this book were investigations into the ancestries of influential persons such as scientists and physicians. His data showed that each famous person inherited not only genius but a specific form of genius. A great scientist, for example, was born into a family that had attained eminence in science.

Galton's ultimate aim was to encourage the birth of the more eminent or fit individuals and to discourage the birth of the unfit. To help achieve this end, he founded the science of *eugenics* (the science that deals with the factors that may improve the hereditary qualities of the human race), and he argued that humans, not unlike livestock, could be improved by artificial selection. He believed that if men and women of considerable talent were selected and mated generation after generation, a highly gifted race of people would result. He proposed that intelligence tests be developed for use in choosing the brightest men and women for selective breeding, and he recommended that those who earned the highest scores on the tests be offered financial inducements for marrying and having children. (It is interesting that Galton, who founded eugenics and believed that only the very intelligent should reproduce, had no children. The problem was apparently genetic; neither of his brothers fathered children either.)

In attempting to verify his eugenic thesis, Galton became involved in problems of measurement and statistics. In *Hereditary Genius* he applied statistical concepts to the problems of heredity and sorted the celebrated men in his sample into categories according to the frequency with which their level of ability occurred in the population. He found that eminent men have a higher probability of fathering eminent sons than do average men. His sample consisted of 977 famous men, each so outstanding as to be one in 4000. On a chance basis, this group would be expected to have only one prominent relative; instead it had 332. The probability of eminence in certain families was high, but not high enough for Galton to consider seriously any possible influence of a superior environment, education, or opportunity open to the sons of the outstanding families he studied. Eminence, or the lack of it, was a function of heredity, he argued, not of opportunity.

Galton wrote *English Men of Science* (1874), *Natural Inheritance* (1889), and more than thirty papers on the problems of inheritance. His interest in heredity grew from the individual and the family to encompass the human race as a whole. He started the journal *Biometrika* in 1901, established the Eugenics Laboratory at University College, London, in 1904, and founded an organization for promoting the idea of racial improvement; all of these still exist today.

Statistical Methods

We noted Galton's interest in measurement and statistics. Throughout his career he seemed never fully satisfied with a problem until he had found some way to quantify the data and analyze them statistically. He not only applied statistical methods, he also developed them.

A Belgian statistician, Adolph Quetelet, had been the first to apply statistical methods and the normal curve of probability to biological and social data. The normal curve had been used in work on the distribution of measurements and errors in scientific observation, but the principle of the normal distribution had not been applied to human variability until Quetelet demonstrated that anthropometric measurements of unselected samples of persons typically yielded a normal curve. He demonstrated that measures of physical stature of ten thousand subjects approximated the normal curve of distribution, and he used the phrase *l'homme moyen* (the average man) to express the finding that most individuals cluster around the average or center of the distribution, and fewer and fewer are found toward either extreme.

Galton was impressed by Quetelet's data and assumed that similar results would be found for mental characteristics. He found, for example, that the grades given on university examinations followed the same normal curve distribution as Quetelet's physical measurement data. Because of the simplicity of the normal curve and its consistency over a number of traits, Galton proposed that a large set of measurements or values on human traits could be meaningfully defined and summarized by two numbers: the average value of the distribution (the mean), and the dispersion or range of variation around this average value (the standard deviation).

Galton's work in statistics yielded one of science's most important measures, the ***correlation***. The first report of what he called "co-relations" appeared in 1888. Modern techniques for determining the validity and reliability of tests, as well as factor analytic methods, are direct outgrowths of Galton's discovery of correlation, which resulted from his observation that inherited characteristics tend to regress toward the mean. For example, he noted that tall men are, on the average, not as tall as their fathers, whereas the sons of very short men are, on the average, taller than their fathers. He devised the graphic means to represent the basic properties of the correlation coefficient and developed a formula for its calculation, although the formula is no longer in use.

Galton applied the correlational method to variations in physical measurements, demonstrating, for example, a correlation between body height and head length. With Galton's encouragement, his student Karl Pearson developed the mathematical formula that is still in use today for the calculation of the correlation coefficient, called the Pearson product–moment coefficient of correlation. The symbol for the correlation coefficient, r, is taken from the first letter of the word *regression*, in recognition of Galton's discovery of the tendency of inherited human traits to regress toward the average or mean. Correlation is a fundamental tool in the social and behavioral sciences, and in engineering and the natural sciences. Many other statistical techniques have been developed on the basis of Galton's pioneering work.

Mental Tests

With the development of specific mental tests, Galton may properly be called the first practitioner of psychology. It has been said that he originated ***mental tests***, although the term came from James McKeen Cattell, an American disciple of Galton and a former student of Wilhelm Wundt. Galton began by assuming that intelligence could be measured in terms of a person's sensory capacities — that is, the higher the intelligence, the higher the level of sensory discrimination. He derived this assumption from John Locke's empiricist view that all knowledge comes through the senses. If that is true, Galton concluded, then it follows that "the most

In his laboratory at London's South Kensington Museum, Galton used a variety of novel devices to conduct the first large-scale mental testing program.

capable individuals have the most acute senses. The fact that the lowest grade of idiots often have sensory deficits seemed to confirm this line of thinking" (Loevinger, 1987, p. 98).

Galton needed to invent the apparatus with which sensory measurements could be made quickly and accurately for large numbers of people. With typical ingenuity and enthusiasm, he devised several instruments. To determine the highest frequency of sound that could be heard, he invented a whistle, which he tested on animals as well as people. (He liked to walk through London's zoo with the whistle fixed in the lower end of a hollow walking stick; he would squeeze a rubber bulb at the upper end and observe the reactions of the animals.) This Galton whistle, in improved form, was a standard piece of psychology laboratory equipment until it was replaced by a more sophisticated electronic device in the 1930s.

Other instruments included a photometer to measure the precision with which a subject could match two spots of color, a calibrated pendulum to measure reaction time to sounds and lights, a series of weights to be arranged in order of heaviness to measure kinesthetic sensitivity, a bar with a variable distance scale to test estimation of visual extension, and sets of bottles containing different substances to test olfactory discrimination. Most of Galton's tests served as prototypes for the standard equipment found in laboratories today.

Armed with his new tests, Galton proceeded to collect a mass of data. He established his Anthropometric Laboratory in 1884 at the International Health Exhibition, and later moved it to London's South Kensington Museum. The laboratory remained active for six years, during which time Galton collected data from more than nine thousand people. Instruments for the anthropometric and psychometric measurements were arranged on a long table at one end of a narrow room. For a threepence admission fee, a person could pass along the table and be measured by an attendant who recorded the data on a card. In addition to the measurements noted above, information was obtained on height, weight, breathing power, strength of pull and squeeze, quickness of blow, hearing, vision, and color sense. The aim of this large-scale testing program was to define the range of human capacities. Galton hoped to test the entire British population to determine the precise level of its collective mental resources.

A century later a group of psychologists in the United States analyzed Galton's data (Johnson et al., 1985). They found substantial test-retest correlations, indicating that the data were statistically reliable. In addition, Galton's data provided useful information on developmental trends during childhood, adolescence, and maturity within the population tested. Measures such as weight, armspan, breathing power, and strength of squeeze were shown to be similar to development in these capacities as reported in more recent psychology literature, except that the rate of development in Galton's time appears to have been slightly slower. Thus, the psychologists concluded that Galton's data continue to be instructive today.

Association

Galton worked on two problems in the area of association: the diversity of the associations of ideas, and the time required to produce associations. One of his methods for studying the diversity of associations was to walk 450 yards along Pall Mall, the London street that runs between Trafalgar Square and St. James Palace, focusing his attention on an object until it suggested one or two associated ideas to him. The first time he tried this he was amazed at the number of associations that developed from the nearly three hundred objects he had seen. He found that many of these associations were recollections of past experiences, including incidents long forgotten. Repeating the walk a few days later he found considerable repetition of the associations that had occurred during the first walk. This greatly diminished his interest in the problem, and he turned instead to reaction-time experiments, which produced more useful results.

For these reaction-time experiments Galton prepared a list of seventy-five words, writing each one on a separate slip of paper. After a week he viewed them one at a time and used a chronometer to record the time necessary to produce two associations for each word. Many of the associations were single words, but several appeared to him as images or mental pictures that required several words to describe. His next task was to determine the origin of these associations. He discovered that about 40 percent of them could be traced to events in his childhood and adolescence; this can be seen as an early demonstration of the influence of childhood experiences on the adult personality.

Of perhaps greater importance than Galton's results was his experimental method in studying associations. His invention of the *word association test* marked the first attempt to subject association to laboratory experimentation. Wilhelm Wundt adapted the technique, limiting the response to a single word, and used it for research in his Leipzig laboratory. The analyst Carl Jung elaborated on it for his own word association studies.

Mental Imagery

Galton's investigation of mental imagery marks the first extensive use of the psychological questionnaire. Subjects were asked to recall a scene, such as their breakfast table that morning, and to try to elicit images of it. They were instructed to indicate whether the images were dim or clear, bright or dark, colored or not colored, and so on. To Galton's amazement, his first group of subjects, scientific acquaintances, reported no clear imagery at all! Some were not even sure what Galton was talking about when he asked them about images. Turning to subjects of more average ability, Galton obtained reports of clear and distinct images that were often full of color and detail. He found that the imagery of women and children was particularly concrete and detailed. As he questioned more and more people, he determined that imagery is generally distributed normally in the population.

This work spurred a long line of research on imagery, and those studies have largely supported Galton's results. As with much of Galton's research, the work on imagery was rooted in his attempt to demonstrate hereditary similarities. He found that similarity in imagery is greater between siblings than between persons who are unrelated.

Other Studies

The richness of Galton's talent is evident in the variety of his research studies. In addition to the important programs discussed above, he once tried to put himself into the state of mind of the insane by imagining that everyone or everything he saw while he was taking a walk was spying on him. "By the end of the morning stroll, every horse seemed to be watching him either directly or, just as suspicious, disguising their espionage by elaborately paying no attention" (Watson, 1978, pp. 328–329).

Galton lived at a time when the controversy between evolutionary theory and fundamentalist theology was acute. With characteristic objectivity he investigated the problem and concluded that although large numbers of people held intense religious beliefs, this was not sufficient evidence that those beliefs were valid. He discussed the power of prayer to produce results and found that it was of no use to physicians in curing patients or to meteorologists in invoking changes in the weather, or even to clergy in conducting their everyday affairs. He believed that there was little difference between persons who professed a religious belief and those who did not in terms of their dealings with other people or in their own emotional lives. He hoped to give the world a new set of beliefs structured in terms of science, as a substitute for religious dogma. He thought that the evolutionary development of a finer and nobler human race through eugenics should be the goal, rather than a place in heaven.

Galton always seemed to be counting something. He occupied himself at lectures and the theater by counting the yawns and fidgets of the audience, describing the results as a measure of boredom. While he was having his portrait painted he counted the artist's brushstrokes, some twenty thousand. At one time he decided to count by odors instead of numbers; training himself to forget what numbers meant, he assigned numerical values to smells such as camphor and peppermint and learned to add and subtract by thinking of them. Out of this intellectual exercise came a paper entitled "Arithmetic by Smell," published in the first issue of the American journal *Psychological Review*.

Comment

Galton spent only fifteen years investigating issues of a psychological nature, but his efforts during that relatively short period influenced the direction the new psychology would take. He was not truly a psychologist any more than he was a eugenicist or an anthropologist. He was an extremely gifted individual whose talent and temperament could not be bound by the confines of a single discipline. Consider his research areas in which psychologists later became interested: adaptation, heredity versus environment, comparison of species, child development, the questionnaire method, statistical techniques, individual differences, mental tests. In the scope of his interests and his methods, then, Galton influenced American psychology far more than the founder Wilhelm Wundt.

The Influence of Animal Psychology on Functionalism

The evolutionary theory of Charles Darwin provided the impetus for animal psychology. Before Darwin published his theory, there was no reason for scientists to be concerned with the animal mind, because animals were considered to be mindless or soulless automata. After all, Descartes had emphasized that animals possessed no similarity with humans.

On the Origin of Species altered this notion. Darwin's evidence led to the suggestion that there was no sharp distinction between human and animal minds. A continuity could be postulated between all mental and physical aspects of humans and animals, because humans were believed to be derived from animals by the continuous evolutionary process of change and development. "There is no fundamental difference between man and the higher mammals in their mental faculties," Darwin stated (1871, p. 66). If mind could be demonstrated to exist in animals, and if continuity between animal minds and human minds could be shown, such evidence would serve as a refutation of the human–animal dichotomy espoused by Descartes. Thus, a quest was begun for evidence of mind or intelligence in animals.

Darwin presented the defense of his theory in his book, *The Expression of the Emotions in Man and Animals* (1872), in which he argued that human emotional behavior results from the inheritance of behavior that was once useful to animals but was no longer relevant for humans. One of many examples he described to demonstrate this idea was the way people curl their lips when they sneer. He held this gesture to be a remnant of the way animals bare their canine teeth in rage.

In the years following the publication of *On the Origin of Species*, the topic of animal intelligence grew in popularity, not only among scientists but also with the general public. In the 1860s and 1870s many people wrote to both scientific and popular magazines to report instances of animal behavior that were taken to suggest hitherto unsuspected mental abilities. Thousands of stories circulated about the unusually intelligent feats of pet cats and dogs, horses and pigs, snails and birds.

Even Wilhelm Wundt was not immune to this trend. In 1863, before he became the world's first psychologist, he wrote about the intellectual abilities of a wide range of living forms, from polyps to beetles to beavers. He argued that animals that displayed even minimal sensory capacities must also possess powers of judgment and conscious inference. The so-called inferior animals differed from humans not so much in their abilities as in the fact that they had not received as much education and training. Thirty years later Wundt became much less generous in attributing intelligence to animals, but for a time his voice was added to the many suggesting that animals might be as intelligent as humans.

The person who formalized and systematized the study of animal intelligence was the British physiologist George John Romanes (1848–1894) who, as a child, was considered by his parents to be "a shocking dunce" (Richards, 1987, p. 334). As a young man, Romanes had been impressed by Darwin's writings. Later, after he and Darwin had become friends, Darwin gave Romanes his notebooks on animal behavior. Darwin thus chose Romanes to carry on that portion of his work, to apply the theory of evolution to the mind as Darwin had applied it to the body. Romanes became a worthy successor. He was quite wealthy and did not have to be concerned about earning a living. The only job he held was that of part-time lecturer at the University of Edinburgh, which required his presence only two weeks a year. He spent winters in London and Oxford and summers on the seacoast, where he built a private laboratory that was as well equipped as that of any university.

In 1883 Romanes published *Animal Intelligence*, generally considered to be the first book on comparative psychology. He collected data on the behavior of protozoa, ants, spiders, reptiles, fish, birds, elephants, monkeys, and domestic animals. His purpose was to demonstrate the high level of animal intelligence as well as its similarity to human intellectual functioning, thus illustrating a continuity in mental development. As he put it, he wanted to show that "there is no difference in kind between the acts of reason performed by the crab and any act of reason performed by a man" (Richards, 1987, p. 347).

Romanes's methodology is referred to in somewhat contemptuous terms as the ***anecdotal method***, that is, the use of observational, often casual, reports about animal behavior. Many of the reports he accepted came from uncritical and untrained observers and were, therefore, vulnerable to criticisms that they were incorrect observations, careless descriptions, and biased interpretations.

How did Romanes derive his findings on animal intelligence from these anecdotal observations? He worked through a curious and eventually discarded technique known as ***introspection by analogy***. In this approach, investigators assume that the same mental processes that occur in their own minds also occur in the minds of the animals being observed. The existence of mind and of specific mental functions is inferred by observing animal behavior and then drawing an analogy—a correspondence or a relationship—between human mental processes and those assumed to be taking place in the animals.

Romanes described the process of introspection by analogy in these terms:

> Starting from what I know subjectively of the operations of my own individual mind, and of the activities which in my own organism these operations seem to prompt, I proceed by analogy to infer from the observable activities displayed by other organisms the fact that certain mental operations underlie or accompany these activities. (Mackenzie, 1977, pp. 56–57)

Through the use of this technique, Romanes concluded that animals are capable of the same kinds of rationalization, ideation, complex reasoning, and problem-solving ability as humans. Some of his followers even credited animals with a level of intelligence far superior to that of the average person.

In a study of cats, which Romanes considered to be more intelligent than all other animals except monkeys and elephants, he wrote about the behavior of the cat that belonged to his coachman. Through a series of intricate movements, the cat was able to open a door leading to the stables. Introspecting by analogy, Romanes reached the following conclusion:

> Cats in such cases have a very definite idea as to the mechanical properties of a door; they know that to make it open, even when unlatched, it requires to be pushed. . . . First the animal must have observed that the door is opened by the hand grasping the handle and moving the latch. Next she must reason, by "the logic of feelings," if a hand can do it, why not a paw? . . . The pushing with the hind feet after depressing the latch must be due to adaptive reasoning. (Romanes, 1883, pp. 421–422)

Although Romanes's work fell far short of modern scientific rigor, he did adhere to certain criteria for judging the reliability of the reports he used. Despite this precaution, the line between fact and subjective interpretation in his data is unclear. While the deficiencies in his data and method are recognized, he is respected for his pioneering efforts in stimulating the development of comparative psychology and preparing the way for the experimental approach that followed. We have seen that in many areas of science, reliance on observational data precedes the development of refined experimental methodology, and it was Romanes who launched the observational stage of comparative psychology.

The weaknesses inherent in the anecdotal method and in introspection by analogy were recognized by Conwy Lloyd Morgan (1852–1936), whom Romanes designated as his successor. Morgan, a professor of psychology and education at the University of Bristol, England, and one of the first men ever to ride a bicycle within the city limits, was also a geologist and zoologist. He proposed a *law of parsimony* (also called *Lloyd Morgan's Canon*), in an effort to counter the tendency to anthropomorphize and attribute too much intelligence to animals. The principle states that an animal's behavior must not be interpreted as the outcome of a higher mental process when it can be explained in terms of a lower mental process. Morgan advanced this idea in 1894 and may have derived it from a law of parsimony published by Wundt two years earlier. Wundt had stated that "complex explanatory principles can be used only when the simpler have proved insufficient" (Richards, 1980, p. 57).

Morgan followed essentially the same methodological approach as Romanes, observing an animal's behavior and trying to explain it through an introspective examination of his own mental processes. Applying his law of parsimony, however, Morgan refrained from ascribing complex higher-level mental processes to animals when their behavior could be explained more simply in terms of lower-level processes. He believed that most animal behavior could be seen as the result of learning or association based on sensory experience, learning being a lower-level process than rational thought or ideation. With Morgan's canon, the use of introspection by analogy became more restricted but was eventually superseded by more objective methods.

Morgan was the first to conduct large-scale experimental studies in animal psychology. Although his early experiments were not performed under rigid scientific conditions, they did involve careful and detailed observations of animal behavior, mostly in natural environments but with some artificially induced modifications. These studies did not permit the same degree of control as laboratory experiments, but they were an important advance over Romanes's anecdotal method.

This initial work in comparative psychology was British in origin, but leadership in the field rapidly passed to the United States. Reasons for this shift include Romanes's early death from a brain tumor, and Morgan's decision to change from a career in research to one in university administration.

Comparative psychology was an outgrowth of the excitement and controversy engendered by Darwin's notion of the continuity of species.

Perhaps comparative psychology would have begun without the theory of evolution, but most likely it would not have had such a sound or early start. Basic to Darwin's theory are the notion of function and the assertion that as a species evolves, its physical structure is determined by its requirements for survival. This premise led biologists to regard each anatomical structure as a functioning element in a total living, adapting system. When psychologists began to examine mental processes in the same way, they created a new movement: functional psychology. Chapters 7 and 8 consider the development of the new functionalism in the United States. We continue the story of the development of animal psychology in Chapter 9.

Suggested Readings

Darwin

Angell, J. R. (1909). The influence of Darwin on psychology. *Psychological Review, 16*, 152–169. Discusses Darwin's ideas on evolution and the expression of the emotions and assesses the impact of this work on functional psychology.

Boring, E. G. (1950). The influence of evolutionary theory upon American psychological thought. In S. Persons (Ed.), *Evolutionary Thought in America* (pp. 268–298). New Haven CT: Yale University Press. Notes the influence of Darwin's theory of evolution on the ideas of Baldwin, Dewey, Hall, James, and Watson, all contributors to the development of psychology in the United States.

Darwin, C. (1958). *The Autobiography of Charles Darwin and Selected Letters.* New York: Dover. A reprint of Darwin's autobiography, originally published in 1887, with supplementary material contributed by Darwin's son.

Gould, S. J. (1986). Knight takes bishop? *Natural History, 95*(5), 18–33. Compares the facts with the legend about the 1860 debate on evolution between Wilberforce, Bishop of Oxford, and the scientist Thomas Henry Huxley.

Richards, R. J. (1983). Why Darwin delayed, or interesting problems and models in the history of science. *Journal of the History of the Behavioral Sciences, 19*, 45–53. Discusses contextual factors that may explain Darwin's reluctance to publish his theory of evolution and the findings from his voyage on the *Beagle*.

Richards, R. J. (1987). *Darwin and the Emergence of Evolutionary Theories of Mind and Behavior.* Chicago: University of Chicago Press. A well-written and carefully researched account of the evolution of Darwin's ideas and their impact on the scientific study of the mind. Considers social and psychological contextual factors including the personalities of the great scientists of the time.

Shields, S. A. (1975). Functionalism, Darwinism, and the psychology of women: A study in social myth. *American Psychologist, 30*, 739–754. Discusses the psychology of women, biological bases of sex differences, and ideas on women's education in terms of their roots in the functionalist movement.

Galton

Burt, C. (1962). Francis Galton and his contributions to psychology. *British Journal of Statistical Psychology, 15*, 1–49. A biographical sketch and a review and assessment of Galton's work.

Buss, A. R. (1976). Galton and sex differences: A historical note. *Journal of the History of the Behavioral Sciences, 12*, 283–285. Suggests that the social context of the Victorian society in which Galton worked affected his interpretation of his research on sex differences.

Diamond, S. (1977). Francis Galton and American psychology. *Annals of the New York Academy of Sciences, 291*, 47–55. Describes the influence of Galton's ideas, especially quantification and statistical analysis, and their impact on pioneers in American psychology such as James McKeen Cattell at the University of Pennsylvania and Joseph Jastrow at the University of Wisconsin.

Forrest, D. W. (1974). *Francis Galton: The Life and Work of a Victorian Genius*. New York: Taplinger. A biography of Galton, emphasizing his work on heredity and eugenics. Includes a list of his inventions.

Pearson, K. (1914, 1924, 1930). *The Life, Letters and Labors of Francis Galton*. Cambridge, England: Cambridge University Press. The massive, now classic, 3-volume biography of Galton, covering his life, his research interests, and his application of statistics to problems in heredity and eugenics.

Animal Psychology

Boakes, R. (1984). *From Darwin to Behaviourism: Psychology and the Minds of Animals*. Cambridge, England: Cambridge University Press. Surveys the ideas about the relationship between human and animal behavior from 1870 to 1930 and their impact on the development of psychology.

Carr, H. (1927). The interpretation of the animal mind. *Psychological Review, 34*, 87–106. Discusses the problem of anthropomorphism in the early research on animal psychology.

Domjan, M. (1987). Animal learning comes of age. *American Psychologist, 42*, 556–564. Evaluates the field of animal learning in terms of its historical context, beginning with Darwin, Romanes, Morgan, and Thorndike, and relates it to contemporary learning theory.

Lockard, R. B. (1971). Reflections on the fall of comparative psychology: Is there a message for us all? *American Psychologist, 26*, 168–179. Traces the development of comparative psychology, from the work of Darwin through the 1950s, and the challenges presented by research in behavioral biology.

Richards, R. J. (1977). Lloyd Morgan's theory of instinct: From Darwinism to neo-Darwinism. *Journal of the History of the Behavioral Sciences, 13*, 12–32. Reviews the work of Darwin, Romanes, Morgan, and McDougall.

Waters, R. H. (1939). Morgan's canon and anthropomorphism. *Psychological Review, 46*, 534–540. Discusses the impact of Morgan's canon on psychological research and on the interpretation of findings on animal behavior.

Functionalism: Development and Founding

7

Only in America

By the turn of the century, psychology in the United States had assumed a character all its own, distinct from Wundt's psychology and Titchener's structuralism, neither of which was concerned with the purpose or function of consciousness. We have seen that the functionalist movement was evolving from the works of Darwin and Galton, and that its focus was on the operation of conscious processes rather than their structure or content. The major interest of functional psychologists was the utility or purpose of mental processes to the living organism in its continuing attempts to adapt to its environment. Mental processes were considered to be activities leading to practical consequences, not elements in some kind of pattern.

Functionalism's practical orientation inevitably led psychologists to an interest in applying psychology to real-world problems. Disdained by Wundt and Titchener, applied psychology was embraced enthusiastically by the functionalists and became their most important legacy, one that characterizes American psychology today. We consider the growth and impact of applied psychology in Chapter 8. In this chapter we deal with the development and formalization of functional psychology in the United States at the end of the nineteenth and beginning of the twentieth century.

Why did functional psychology develop and thrive in the United States and not in England, where the functional spirit originated? The answer lies in the American temperament—its unique social, economic, and political characteristics. The American Zeitgeist was ready for evolution and the functionalist attitude that derived from it.

Herbert Spencer (1820–1903) and Synthetic Philosophy

In 1882 a sixty-two-year-old self-taught English philosopher, who had invented a collapsible fishing rod, arrived in the United States where he was hailed as a national hero. He was met at the ship in New York by Andrew Carnegie, the multimillionaire patriarch of the American steel industry. Carnegie praised the philosopher as a messiah. In the eyes of many leaders of American business, science, politics, and religion, the man was indeed a savior, and he was wined and dined; honors and appreciation were lavished upon him.

His name was Herbert Spencer, the scholar Darwin called "our philosopher," and his impact on the American scene was monumental. Spencer's mind was prolific, and he produced a large number of books, many of which he dictated to a secretary between sets of tennis or while lounging in a rowboat. His works were serialized in popular magazines, his books sold hundreds of thousands of copies, and his system of philosophy was taught in universities by scholars in almost every discipline. His ideas, read by people at all levels of society, influenced a generation of Americans. Had there been television then, Spencer would undoubtedly have appeared on talk shows and received even greater adulation.

Herbert Spencer was acclaimed for his philosophy of social Darwinism — the utopian view that human character and society, without aid or regulation, would naturally evolve toward perfection.

The philosophy that brought Spencer so much recognition and acclaim was, briefly stated, Darwinism — the notion of evolution and survival of the fittest — carried beyond Darwin's own work.

In the United States, interest in Darwin's theory of evolution was intense, and Darwin's ideas had been accepted more rapidly and fully than in England, its birthplace. Evolutionary theory was discussed and embraced not only in universities and learned societies but also in popular magazines and even some religious publications.

Spencer wrote about the implications of evolution for human knowledge and experience. He argued that the development of all aspects of the universe, including human character and social institutions, is evolutionary, operating in accordance with the principle of *survival of the fittest*, a phrase he coined. It was this emphasis on what came to be called *social Darwinism*, the application of evolution to human nature and society, that met with such enthusiasm in America. Spencer's utopian view held that through the survival of the fittest, obviously only the best would survive. Human perfection, therefore, was inevitable as long as nothing was done to interfere with the natural order of things. He emphasized individualism and a laissez-faire economic system and opposed any governmental attempts to regulate its citizens' lives, even subsidies for education and housing.

People and organizations were to be left to develop themselves and their society in their own ways, just as other living species were left to develop and adapt in the world of nature. Any help from the state would interfere with the natural evolutionary process. Those individuals or businesses or institutions that could not adapt to the environment were unfit for survival and should be allowed to perish or become extinct, for the betterment of society as a whole. If governments continued to support the poor and the weak, then they would endure, ultimately weakening the entire society and violating the primary law that only the strongest and most fit shall survive. Spencer pointed out that by ensuring that only the best survive, societies can improve themselves and eventually reach perfection.

This message was compatible with America's individualistic creed and spirit at the time, and the phrases "survival of the fittest" and "the struggle for existence" quickly became part of the national consciousness. They well reflect the American society of the late nineteenth century, a time when the United States was a living example of Spencer's ideas.

This pioneer nation was being settled by hard-working people who believed in free enterprise, self-sufficiency, and independence from government regulation. And they knew all about the survival of the fittest from their own daily experiences. Land was still freely available to those with the courage, cunning, and ability to take it and wrest a living from it. The principles of natural selection were vividly demonstrated in everyday life, particularly on the Western frontier, where survival and success depended on one's ability to adapt to the demands of a hostile environment; those who could not adapt did not survive. The American historian Frederick Jackson Turner described the survivors in these terms: "That coarseness and strength combined with acuteness and inquisitiveness; that practical, inventive turn of mind, quick to find expedients; that masterful grasp of material things... powerful to effect great ends; that restless, nervous energy; that dominant individualism" (Turner, 1947, p. 235).

The people of the United States were oriented toward the practical, the useful, and the functional, and American psychology in its pioneering stages mirrored these qualities. For this reason, America was more amenable to evolutionary theory than Germany or even England. American psychology became a functional psychology, because evolution and its functional spirit were in keeping with the basic temperament of the United States. And because Spencer's views were congruent with the American ethos in general, his philosophical system influenced every field of learning, including the new psychology.

Spencer had written about evolution as early as 1850, but his publications had attracted relatively little attention. After Darwin's *On the Origin of Species* was published in 1859, Spencer associated himself with the movement, and his own brand of more speculative evolutionism gained strength from Darwin's well-documented position. Their work was complementary; whereas Darwin was cautious about generalizing beyond his detailed data, Spencer was prone to discussing the implications of the theory and to applying the evolutionary doctrine universally.

To accomplish this, Spencer formulated what he called ***synthetic philosophy***. (He used the word *synthetic* in the sense of synthesizing or combining, not to mean something artificial or unnatural.) He based this all-encompassing system on the application of evolutionary principles to all human knowledge and experience. Specifically, he argued that the development of all aspects of the universe involves two processes: differentiation followed by integration. Any developing or growing thing is initially homogeneous and simple. Recognizably distinct parts emerge (differentiation), and at a later stage these unique parts are joined or combined (integration) in a new functioning whole.

Spencer saw the sequence of differentiation followed by integration, in which all things proceed from homogeneity to heterogeneity, as evolutionary. The implication of this idea for psychology is that as the nervous system evolves in ever more complex species, there is a corresponding increase in the richness and variety of experience to which the organism is exposed, and thus there are ever higher levels of functioning.

Spencer's system of synthetic philosophy was published in ten volumes between 1860 and 1897. These books were hailed by many of the leading scholars of the time as works of genius. C. Lloyd Morgan wrote to Spencer that "to none of my intellectual masters do I owe a larger debt of gratitude than to you." Alfred Russel Wallace named his first son after Spencer. Darwin said after reading one of Spencer's books that he was "a dozen times my superior" (Richards, 1987, p. 245).

Two of the volumes on synthetic philosophy constitute *The Principles of Psychology*, published first in 1855, and later used by William James as a textbook for the psychology course he taught at Harvard University. In these two volumes Spencer discussed the notion that the mind exists in its present form because of past and continuing efforts to adapt to various environments. He emphasized the adaptive nature of nervous and mental processes and wrote that an increasing complexity of experiences, and hence behavior, is part of the evolutionary process of an organism's need to adapt to its environment in order to survive.

William James (1842–1910):
Anticipator of Functional Psychology

There is much that is paradoxical about William James and his role in American psychology. On the one hand, he was certainly the leading American precursor of functional psychology. He was the pioneer of the new scientific psychology in the United States and its senior psychologist, and he is still considered by many to be the greatest American psychologist who ever lived. On the other hand, James at times denied that he was a psychologist or that there was a new psychology.

In addition, James was viewed by some psychologists of his day as a negative force in the development of a scientific psychology because of his highly publicized interest in mental telepathy, clairvoyance, spiritualism, communication with the dead at séances, and other mystical experiences. Titchener, Cattell, and other leading American psychologists criticized James for his enthusiastic espousal of mentalistic and psychical phenomena which they, as experimental psychologists, were trying to dissociate from the field.

James founded no formal system of psychology and had no disciples. Although the psychology with which he was associated was attempting to be scientific and experimental, James was not an experimentalist in attitude or deed. Psychology, which he once called that "nasty little science," was not his lifelong passion, as it was for Wundt and Titchener. James worked in psychology for a while and then moved on.

Even when he was active in psychology he remained independent, refusing to be absorbed by any ideology, system, or school. James was neither a follower nor a founder, neither a disciple nor a leader. He was aware of current developments and changes in psychology and was very much involved in them, but he was able to select from among the various positions those parts that were congenial with his view of psychology, and he rejected the rest.

This fascinating man who contributed so much to psychology turned his back on it later in life. (Prior to delivering a talk at Princeton University, he asked that he not be introduced as a psychologist.) He said that the field consisted of an "elaboration of the obvious," and he allowed it to fumble on without his commanding presence. Still, his place in the history of psychology is both assured and significant.

Although James did not found functional psychology, he wrote and thought clearly and effectively in the functionalist atmosphere that permeated American psychology at the time. In doing so, he influenced the functionalist movement through the inspiration he provided to subsequent generations of psychologists.

The Life of James

William James was born in the Astor House, a New York City hotel, into a well-known and wealthy family. His father devoted himself with enthusiasm to the education of his five children, alternating between Europe (because of his belief that American schools were too restrictive) and the United States (because of an equally strong belief that his children should be educated among their compatriots). Thus, James's early formal education, often interrupted by travel, took place in England, France, Germany, Italy, Switzerland, and the United States. The father also encouraged intellectual independence among his children.

These stimulating experiences exposed James to the intellectual and cultural advantages of England and Europe, and he frequently journeyed abroad throughout his life. Further, his father's favorite method for dealing with illness was to send the ailing family member to Europe rather than to a hospital. And his mother provided her children with significant love and attention only when they were sick. Perhaps as a result, James's health for many years was seldom good.

Although his father seemed to believe that none of the James children need be concerned with learning a vocation or earning a living, he did try to encourage William's early interest in science. At age fifteen, William received a microscope as a Christmas gift. He already had a chemistry

The essence of functional psychology — the adaptation of living persons to their environment, assisted by an active consciousness — is expressed in the writings of William James, considered by many to be the greatest American psychologist.

set—a "Bunsen burner and vials of mysterious liquids which he mixed, heated, and transfused, staining his fingers and clothes, to his father's annoyance, and sometimes even causing alarming explosions" (Allen, 1967, p. 47).

James decided at the age of eighteen to become an artist. Six months at the studio of the painter William Hunt, in Newport, Rhode Island, persuaded him that he lacked promise, and in 1861 he entered the Lawrence Scientific School at Harvard. He switched from his first choice, chemistry, apparently because he disdained the painstaking demands of laboratory work, and enrolled in medical school. He had little enthusiasm for the practice of medicine, however, noting that "there is much humbug therein. . . . With the exception of surgery, in which something positive is sometimes accomplished, a doctor does more by the moral effect of his presence on the patient and family, than by anything else. He also extracts money from them" (Allen, 1967, p. 98).

James interrupted his medical studies for a year to assist the zoologist Louis Agassiz on an expedition to Brazil to collect specimens of marine animals in the Amazon River basin. The trip gave him the opportunity to sample another possible career, that of biologist, but he found that he could not tolerate the precise and orderly collecting and categorizing that this field required. His reaction to chemistry and biology was prophetic of his subsequent distaste for experimentation in psychology.

Although medicine was no more attractive to him after the 1865 expedition than it had been before, James reluctantly resumed his studies because nothing else appealed to him. He interrupted the work because of illness, complaining of depression, digestive disorders, insomnia, visual disturbances, and a weak back. "It was obvious to everyone," a historian wrote, "that he was suffering from America; Europe was the only cure" (Miller & Buckhout, 1973, p. 84).

He journeyed to a spa in Germany, dabbled in literature, and wrote long letters to his friends. But overall James seemed just as unhappy as he had been at home. He attended some lectures in physiology at the University of Berlin and remarked that it was time for "psychology to begin to be a science" (Allen, 1967, p. 140). He also expressed the wish that if he survived his illness and lived through the winter, he could learn something about psychology from the great Helmholtz and "a man named Wundt" at Heidelberg. James did live through the winter, but he did not meet Wundt at that time. The fact that he had heard of Wundt, however, shows his awareness of current intellectual trends some ten years before Wundt started his laboratory.

James obtained his medical degree from Harvard in 1869, but his depression worsened and he had frequent thoughts of suicide. He experienced nameless and horrible dreads and reported a feeling of insecurity the likes of which he had never before known. For months he was unable to go out at night alone, so intense was his fear and despair. In those dark months he began to build a philosophy of life, compelled not so much by intellectual curiosity as by his desperation.

After reading the essays on freedom of the will by the philosopher Charles Renouvier, James became persuaded of its existence and resolved that his first act of free will would be to believe in free will, and then to believe that he could cure himself through this belief in the power of the will. He apparently succeeded to some extent, because in 1872 he felt well enough to accept a teaching position at Harvard in physiology, commenting that "it is a noble thing for one's spirits to have some responsible work to do" (James, 1902, p. 167). After a year he took time off to travel in Italy, but then he returned to teaching.

In the 1875–1876 academic year James taught his first course in psychology, which he called "The Relations Between Physiology and Psychology." Thus, Harvard became the first university in the United States to offer the new experimental psychology. James had never received formal classroom instruction in psychology; the first psychology lecture he attended was his own. He secured $300 from the college to purchase laboratory and demonstration equipment for his course.

In 1878 two important events occurred. The first was James's marriage, which would produce five children and a certain amount of much needed order in his life. The second event was the signing of a contract with the publishing house of Henry Holt, which resulted in one of the classic books in psychology. James believed that it would take him two years to write the book; it took twelve, and he began the work, to the amusement of his friends, on his honeymoon.

One reason it took James so long to write the book was that he was an almost compulsive traveler. If he was not off in Europe, then he could be found wandering in the Adirondack Mountains of New York or in New Hampshire. One biographer wrote that:

> His letters give the impression that he periodically needed to be alone, that any intimate relationship was fatiguing for him over time, and that he saw travel as a crucial means of coping with restlessness. It was well known to James's friends that he arranged a journey in the aftermath of each child's birth, and then wrote to [his wife] about his guilt for having done so. He was often absent, if only as far away as Newport, on holidays such as Christmas, New Year's Day, and birthdays. Although he must have appreciated the difficulties his absence caused for his family, he seems to have been powerless to alter the

habit. . . . James's flights from his family were escapes from human entanglements to nature, solitude, and mystical relief. (Myers, 1986, pp. 36–37)

James continued to teach at Harvard between trips and in 1880 was made assistant professor of philosophy. He was promoted to professor of philosophy in 1885, and the title was changed to professor of psychology in 1889. On his travels abroad he met many European psychologists, including Wundt, who, he wrote, "made a pleasant and personal impression on me, with his agreeable voice and ready, tooth-showing smile." A few years later James noted that Wundt "isn't a genius, he is a professor — a being whose duty is to know everything, and have his own opinion about everything" (Allen, 1967, pp. 251, 304).

James's book, *The Principles of Psychology*, was finally published in two volumes in 1890 and was a tremendous success. It is still considered a major contribution to the field. Almost eighty years after its publication one psychologist wrote: "James's *Principles* is without question the most literate, the most provocative, and at the same time the most intelligible book on psychology that has ever appeared in English or in any other language" (MacLeod, 1969, p. iii). One indication of its continuing popularity is that it is often read by people who are not required to do so. Not everyone reacted favorably to the book, however. Wundt and Titchener, whose views James attacked, did not like it. "It is literature," Wundt wrote, "it is beautiful, but it is not psychology" (Bjork, 1983, p. 12).

James's reaction to the book on its completion was not favorable either. In a letter to his publisher he described the manuscript as a "loathsome, distended, tumefied, bloated, dropsical mass, testifying to nothing but two facts: 1st, that there is no such thing as a science of psychology, and 2nd, that W. J. is an incapable" (Allen, 1967, pp. 314–315).

With the publication of *The Principles*, James decided that he had said all he wanted to about the science of psychology and that he was no longer interested in directing the psychology laboratory. He arranged for Hugo Münsterberg, then teaching at the University of Freiburg, Germany, to become director of the Harvard laboratory and teach the psychology courses, freeing James for work in philosophy. Münsterberg had been criticized by Wundt, which was high praise in James's eyes, but he never fulfilled the role James had intended for him, of providing leadership in experimental research for Harvard. Münsterberg pursued his work in a variety of applied fields and paid little attention to the laboratory after the first few years. He is important for helping to popularize psychology and make it a more applied discipline, as we shall see in Chapter 8.

Although James began and equipped the laboratory at Harvard, he was not an experimentalist. He was never fully convinced of the value of laboratory work in psychology and did not like it personally. "I naturally hate experimental work," he commented to Münsterberg. In 1894 he said that the United States had too many laboratories, and in *The Principles* he stated that the results of laboratory work were not in proportion to the amount of painstaking effort involved. It is not surprising, then, that James contributed little of importance in the way of experimental work.

Although he trained no graduate students or disciples to carry on his point of view, several of his students — notably Angell, Woodworth, and Thorndike — made noteworthy contributions to the development of psychology. We shall discuss their work later.

James was also instrumental in facilitating the graduate education of Mary Whiton Calkins, who developed the paired-associate technique used in the study of memory and became the first woman president of the American Psychological Association. She had never been allowed to enroll formally at the university, but James welcomed her into his seminars and urged the university to grant her the degree. Despite James's high opinion of Calkins's abilities, Harvard refused to award the Ph.D. degree to a woman. She later succeeded James as APA president.

For the last twenty years of his life, James worked to refine his philosophical system, and in the 1890s he was recognized as America's leading philosopher. In 1899 he published *Talks to Teachers*, developed from lectures he had given to teachers, which showed how psychology could be applied to the classroom learning situation. *The Varieties of Religious Experience* appeared in 1902, and three additional works in philosophy were published in 1907 and 1909.

James's health remained poor throughout his life, and he retired from Harvard in 1907. Several years before, while mountain climbing, he had become lost for thirteen hours, and the ordeal apparently aggravated a heart lesion. The condition worsened and he died in 1910, two days after returning from a final trip to Europe.

The Principles of Psychology

Since James was neither an experimentalist nor a founder — nor even a psychologist for the last several years of his life — how did he come to exert such a profound influence on psychology? Why is he considered by many to be the greatest American psychologist? Three reasons have been suggested for his overwhelming stature and influence. First, James wrote with a brilliance and clarity rare in science, then as well as now. His writing style has magnetism, spontaneity, and charm. The second reason for his influence is negative, in the sense in which all movements are negative, because they oppose the existing order. James opposed the Wundtian position that the goal of psychology was the analysis of consciousness into elements. Third, James offered an alternative way of looking at the mind, an approach congruent with the new American functional approach to psychology. The times were ready for what James had to say.

The concept of functionalism is explicit in James's psychology, and in *The Principles of Psychology* he presents what subsequently became the central tenet of American functionalism: the goal of psychology is not the discovery of the elements of experience but rather the study of living persons as they adapt to their environment. The function of consciousness, James wrote, is to guide us to those ends required for survival. Consciousness is vital to the needs of complex beings in a complex environment; without it, the process of human evolution could not have occurred.

When *The Principles of Psychology* was published in 1890, it was

> hailed both at home and abroad as an event of the first magnitude in the psychological world. Not only was it a comprehensive survey of a new field of learning, not only was it a new synthesis of the facts of psychology; it was itself a contribution to psychology. . . . Because of its freshness and power, because of its definite attitudes and stimulating suggestions, it was itself an event in the history of psychology. (Heidbreder, 1933, p. 197)

James's book treats psychology as a natural science, specifically a biological science. This was not new in 1890, but in James's hands the science of psychology took a different direction from Wundtian psychology. James was concerned with conscious processes as activities of an organism that produced some change in that organism's life. Mental processes were believed to be useful, functional activities of living organisms as they attempted to maintain themselves and adapt to their world.

A related attitude is James's emphasis on the nonrational aspects of human nature. People, he noted, are creatures of action and passion as well as of thought and reason. Even when discussing purely intellectual processes, James stressed the nonrational. He noted that intellect operates under the physiological influences of the body, that beliefs are determined by emotional factors, and that reason and concept formation are affected by human wants and needs. James did not consider human beings to be wholly rational creatures.

In the following sections, we describe several of the major areas James wrote about in *The Principles*.

The Subject Matter of Psychology: A New Look at Consciousness

James stated at the beginning of *The Principles* that "Psychology is the Science of Mental Life, both of its phenomena and their conditions" (James, 1890, Vol. 1, p. 1). In terms of subject matter, the key words are *phenomena* and *conditions*. "Phenomena" is used to indicate that the subject matter is to be found in immediate experience; "conditions" refers to the importance of the body, particularly the brain, in mental life. According to James, the physical substructures of consciousness form a basic part of psychology. He recognized the importance of considering consciousness, the focal point of his interest, in its natural setting, which is the physical human being. This awareness of biology, of the action of the brain on consciousness, is a unique feature of James's approach to psychology.

James rebelled against what he considered to be the artificiality and narrowness of the Wundtian position, a revolt that anticipated the more general protest subsequently made by the functional and Gestalt psychologists. Experiences are simply what they are, James said, not groups or amalgamations of elements. The discovery of discrete elements through introspective analysis does not demonstrate that these elements exist independently of the observer. James argued that psychologists may read into an experience what their systematic position in psychology tells them should be there.

A trained tea-taster learns to discriminate individual elements in a flavor that may not be perceived by the untrained individual. The latter, sipping tea, experiences a fusion of the alleged flavor elements, a total blend not capable of analysis. Similarly, James argued, the fact that some people can analyze their conscious experiences does not mean that the discrete elements they report are present in the consciousness of anyone else exposed to the same experience. James considered such an assumption to be the *psychologists' fallacy*.

Striking at the heart of the Wundtian approach, James declared that simple sensations do not exist in conscious experience but exist only as a result of a rather tortuous process of inference or abstraction. In a blunt and characteristically eloquent statement, James wrote: "No one ever had a simple sensation by itself. Consciousness, from our natal day, is of a teeming multiplicity of objects and relations, and what we call simple sensations are results of discriminative attention, pushed often to a very high degree" (James, 1890, Vol. 1, p. 224).

In place of the artificial analysis and reduction of conscious experience to alleged elements, James called for a new program for psychology. Mental life is a unity, he said, a total experience that changes. The basic point of his conception of consciousness is that it flows like a stream, and he coined the phrase *stream of consciousness* to express this property. Because consciousness is a continuous flow, any attempt to subdivide it into temporally distinct elements or phases can only distort it.

Another characteristic of consciousness is that it is always changing; we can never have exactly the same state or thought more than once. Objects in the environment may recur, but not the identical sensations or thoughts they stimulate. We may think of an object on more than one occasion, but each time we think of it we do so in a different fashion because of the effect of intervening experiences. Consciousness, then, is cumulative and not recurrent.

The mind is also sensibly continuous, that is, there are no sharp breaks in the stream of consciousness. There may be gaps in time, such as during sleep, but upon awakening we have no difficulty making connection with the stream of consciousness that was going on before the interruption. The mind is also selective. It chooses from among the many stimuli to which it is exposed, filtering out some, combining or separating others, selecting or rejecting still others. We can attend to only a small part of our experiential world, and the criterion of selection, according to James, is relevance. The mind selects relevant stimuli so that consciousness may operate in a logical manner, and a series of ideas may arrive at a rational end.

Above all, James stressed the purpose of consciousness. He believed that consciousness must have some biological utility or it would not have survived. The purpose or function of consciousness is to enable us to adapt to our environment by allowing us to choose. James distinguished between conscious choice and habit; he believed habit to be involuntary and nonconscious. When the organism faces a new problem and needs a new mode of adjustment, consciousness comes into play. This emphasis on purposiveness clearly reflects the influence of evolutionary theory.

Always interested in increasing his own knowledge of conscious experience, James tried to expand his consciousness by inhaling nitrous oxide, a gas used as an anesthetic. While under its influence, he believed that he was experiencing mystical revelations of great cosmic truths that resolved some of the riddles of the universe. Unfortunately, he could never remember in the morning what those great truths were, but one night he managed to write one of them down. When he awoke, he rushed to his desk and found that he had written the following: "Hogamous, higamous, man is polygamous. Higamous, hogamous, woman is monogamous." James did not continue with these experiments.

The Methods of Psychology

The discussion of James's subject matter for psychology provides clues to his methods of study. Because psychology deals with a highly personal and immediate consciousness, introspection must be a basic tool. James believed that it was possible to investigate states of consciousness by examining one's own mind through introspection, and he considered introspection to be the exercise of a natural gift. "Introspective Observation is what we have to rely on first and foremost and always. . . . it means, of course, the looking into our own minds and reporting what we there discover. Everyone agrees that we there discover states of consciousness" (James, 1890, Vol. 1, p. 185).

James was aware of the difficulties and limitations of introspection, and he accepted it as a less than perfect form of observation. He thought, however, that introspective results could be verified by appropriate checks and by comparing the findings obtained from several observers.

Although he did not himself make widespread use of the experimental method, James believed in its use as another possible means to psychological knowledge — especially for psychophysics, for the analysis of space perception, and for research on memory.

To supplement introspective and experimental methods, James noted the use of the comparative method in psychology. By inquiring into the psychological functioning of different populations, such as animals, infants, preliterate peoples, and the mentally disturbed, James believed that the psychologist could discover meaningful and useful variations in mental life.

The methods James cited in his book point up a major difference between structuralism and the newly developing functionalism. The American movement was not to be restricted to a single technique, such as introspection. It would apply other methods as well, and this eclecticism broadened the scope of psychology. This diversity in methodology was another of Darwin's legacies.

James emphasized the value for psychology of *pragmatism*, the basic tenet of which is that the validity of an idea or conception is to be tested by its practical consequences. The popular expression of the pragmatic viewpoint is that "anything is true if it works." The notion of pragmatism had been advanced in the 1870s by Charles Sanders Peirce, a mathematician and philosopher and a lifelong friend of James. Peirce's work remained largely unrecognized until James wrote *Pragmatism* (1907), which formalized the doctrine as a philosophical movement and is one of James's major contributions as a philosopher.

The Theory of Emotions

One of James's most famous theoretical contributions deals with emotions. His theory, published in an article in 1884 and later in *The Principles*, contradicted current thinking about emotions. The subjective experience of an emotional state had been assumed to precede the physical or bodily expression or action. The traditional example — we meet a bear, we are frightened, and we run away — exemplifies the idea that the emotion (fear) precedes the bodily expression (running away).

James reversed this notion and stated that the arousal of the physical response precedes the appearance of the emotion, especially for what he termed the "coarser" emotions such as fear, rage, grief, and love. For example, we see the bear, we run, and then we are afraid. In essence, "our feeling of the [bodily] changes as they occur IS the emotion" (James, 1890, Vol. 2, p. 449). For supporting evidence James turned to the introspective observation that if these bodily changes, such as increased heart rate, rapid breathing, and muscle tension, did not occur, then there would be no emotion. In a case of simultaneous discovery, the Danish physiologist Carl Lange published an analogous theory in 1885. The similarity between the two led to the designation *James–Lange theory*. James's view of emotion has led to a great deal of controversy and has stimulated considerable research.

Habit

The chapter in *The Principles* dealing with habit is in keeping with James's awareness of physiological influences. He described all living creatures as being "bundles of habits" (James, 1890, Vol. 1, p. 104), and he considered habit to involve the functioning of the nervous system. He postulated that repeated or habitual actions serve to increase the plasticity of neural matter. As a result, the actions become easier to perform on subsequent repetitions and require less attention from the individual.

James also believed that habits have enormous social implications, as noted in this frequently quoted passage:

> Habit is thus the enormous flywheel of society, its most precious conservative agent. It alone is what keeps us all within the bounds of ordinance. . . . It dooms us all to fight out the battle of life upon the lines of our nurture or our early choice, and to make the best of a pursuit that disagrees, because there is no other for which we are fitted, and it is too late to begin again. It keeps different social strata from mixing. Already at the age of twenty-five you see the professional mannerism settling down on the young commercial traveler, on the young doctor, on the young minister, on the young counselor-at-law. You see the little lines of cleavage running through the character, the tricks of thought, the prejudices, the ways of the "shop," in a word, from which the man can by-and-by no more escape than his coatsleeve can suddenly fall into a new set of folds. On the whole, it is best he should not escape. It is well for the world that in most of us, by the age of thirty, the character has set like plaster, and will never soften again. (James, 1890, Vol. 1, p. 121)

Comment

There is no denying that James is one of the most important psychologists the United States has ever produced. *The Principles* was a major influence, and its publication has legitimately been acclaimed as a great event in the history of psychology. The book affected the views of thousands of students, and James's position inspired John Dewey and other functional psychologists to shift the new science of psychology away from the structuralist view and toward the formal founding of the functionalist school of thought.

The Founding of Functionalism

As we noted at the beginning of Chapter 6, the scholars associated with the founding of functionalism were not ambitious to start a new school of psychology. They protested against the strictures of Wundtian psychology and Titchenerian structuralism, but they did not want to replace these with another "ism" characterized by the rigidity and narrowness that formalization usually entails. A graduate student at the University of Chicago, the major center of functional psychology, recalled that the psychology department there was clearly functional in orientation but "without self-consciousness and certainly without promoting functional psychology as a school" (McKinney, 1978, p. 145). The formalization of this movement of protest was partly imposed on its leaders by E. B. Titchener.

Paradoxically, it was Titchener who may have "founded" functional psychology when he adopted the word *structural* as opposed to *functional* in an article, "The Postulates of a Structural Psychology," published in the *Philosophical Review* in 1898. In this article Titchener pointed out the differences between structural and functional psychology and argued that structuralism was the only proper study for psychology. But by establishing functionalism as an opponent, Titchener unwittingly served to bring it into clearer focus. "What Titchener was attacking was in fact nameless until he named it; hence he thrust the movement into high relief and did more than anyone else to get the term *functionalism* into psychological currency" (Harrison, 1963, p. 395).

Not all the credit for founding functionalism can go to Titchener, of course, but those whom history has labeled the founders of functional psychology were reluctant founders, at best.

The Chicago School

In 1894, John Dewey and James Rowland Angell, each of whom appeared on the cover of *Time* magazine, came to the newly established University of Chicago. Their combined influence was largely responsible for that institution becoming a leading center of functionalism, but the university itself played a role in the founding of this new school of psychology. As one historian wrote,

> It is appropriate, surely, that the first distinctively American school of psychology arose at the new university that was itself an expression of so much that is characteristically American. The almost incredible feat of creating a great university outright — of actualizing a plan, of assembling a distinguished faculty, of bringing into being the whole complex organization, body and soul — gave the place an air of great things accomplished and about to be accomplished; and it is not

surprising that a school of thought, starting in such circumstances, should thrive and grow. (Heidbreder, 1933, p. 204)

John Dewey (1859–1952)

When functionalism is considered as a distinct school of psychology rather than as an orientation or attitude, John Dewey is usually credited with sparking its development. An article Dewey published in 1896 is cited as a landmark in the formal establishment of functionalism, and he exerted a great influence on this school of thought, although his years of active contribution to psychology were few.

Dewey had an undistinguished early life and showed no great intellectual promise until his junior year at the University of Vermont. After graduation he taught high school for a few years and studied philosophy on his own, publishing several scholarly articles. He enrolled in graduate school at Johns Hopkins University, received his Ph.D. in 1884, and taught at the universities of Michigan and Minnesota. In 1886 he published the first American textbook in the new psychology (called, appropriately, *Psychology*), which was popular until it was eclipsed by William James's *The Principles of Psychology* in 1890.

In 1894 Dewey was invited to the University of Chicago, where he remained for ten years, during which time he became a vital force in psychology. He began an experimental or laboratory school, then considered a radical innovation in education, and it served as the cornerstone for the modern progressive education movement. He spent the years 1904–1930 at Columbia University in New York, working on the application of psychology to educational and philosophical problems, providing another example of the practical orientation of many functional psychologists.

Dewey was a brilliant man but not a good teacher. One of his students recalled that Dewey "always wore a little green cap — a beret. . . . He would come [to class], sit down at a desk, and he'd lay the green cap down in front of him, and then he would lecture to the green cap — in a monotone. . . . If there was anything that would put students to sleep, it was that. But if you could pay attention to what that guy had to say, it was well worth it" (May, 1978, p. 655).

Dewey's 1896 article, "The Reflex Arc Concept in Psychology," published in the *Psychological Review*, was the point of departure for functional psychology. In this work — his most important and, unfortunately, last contribution to psychology proper — Dewey attacked the psychological molecularism, elementism, and reductionism of the reflex arc, with its distinction between stimulus and response, an idea that had been promoted by some physiologists.

The proponents of the reflex arc argued that a behavior unit ends with the response to a stimulus, such as when a child withdraws his or her hand from a flame. Dewey countered by saying that the reflex forms more of a circle or circuit than an arc, because the child's perception of the flame has now been changed and thus serves a different function. Whereas initially the flame attracted the child, now it will repel the child. The response has altered the child's perception of the stimulus (the flame) and so perception and movement (stimulus and response) must be considered as a unit and not as individual sensations and responses. Thus, Dewey argued that the behavior involved in a reflex response cannot be meaningfully reduced to its basic sensory-motor elements any more than consciousness can be meaningfully analyzed into its elementary components.

When this form of artificial analysis and reduction of behavior is undertaken, Dewey believed, behavior loses all meaning. Only abstractions in the minds of the psychologists performing the exercise are left. Dewey wrote that behavior should be treated not as an artificial scientific construct but in terms of its significance to the organism in adapting to the environment. He argued that the proper subject matter for psychology is the study of the total organism as it functions in its environment.

Dewey was strongly influenced by the theory of evolution, and his philosophy was based on the notion of social change. He opposed the idea of a static world and favored progress achieved through the struggle of the human intellect with reality. In this struggle for survival, both consciousness and behavior function for the organism, with consciousness bringing about the appropriate behavior that enables the organism to survive and to progress. A function is a total coordination of an organism toward the accomplishment of the goal of survival. Thus, to Dewey, as to other psychologists of the day, functional psychology was the study of the organism in use.

The time Dewey spent in psychology was brief. In keeping with his functional orientation, he devoted most of his efforts to applying psychology to problems in education. His program for the progressive education movement is spelled out in "Psychology and Social Practice," a lecture given on his retirement as president of the American Psychological Association (Dewey, 1900). More than anyone else, Dewey is responsible for the pragmatic spirit of American education, and he believed that teaching should be oriented toward the student rather than the subject matter.

Dewey's significance for psychology lies in his influence on psychologists and other scholars and his development of the philosophical framework for functionalism. When he left the University of Chicago, the leadership of the new school passed to James Rowland Angell.

James Rowland Angell (1869–1949)

James Rowland Angell molded the functionalist movement into a working school of thought. He made the psychology department at the University of Chicago the most influential of the day, the major training ground for functional psychologists.

Angell was born into an academic family in Vermont. His grandfather had been president of Brown University in Providence, Rhode Island, and his father was president of the University of Vermont and, later, of the University of Michigan. Angell did his undergraduate work at Michigan, where he studied under Dewey and was introduced to James's *The Principles of Psychology*, which, Angell reported, influenced his thinking more than any other book he ever read. He worked with James for a year at Harvard and received his master's degree in 1892.

He continued his graduate studies at the University of Halle, Germany, after learning to his disappointment that Wilhelm Wundt could not accept any more students at Leipzig that year. Angell did not obtain his Ph.D. His dissertation was accepted subject to revision (rendering it into better German), but to undertake this task he would have had to remain at Halle without remuneration. He chose, instead, to accept an appointment at the University of Minnesota, where the salary, although low, was better than nothing, particularly for a young man eager to get married. Although he never earned a doctoral degree, Angell was instrumental in granting doctorates to many others, and in the course of his career he received twenty-three honorary degrees.

After a year at Minnesota, Angell went to the University of Chicago, where he remained for twenty-five years. Following in the family tradition, he became president of Yale University, where he helped to develop the Institute of Human Relations. In 1906 he was elected fifteenth president of the American Psychological Association. After retiring from academic life, he served as an officer of the National Broadcasting Company (NBC).

In 1904 Angell published a textbook, *Psychology*, that embodied the functionalist approach. The book was so successful that it appeared in four editions by 1908, indicating the appeal of the functionalist position. In it

By articulating function-
alism's utilitarian aims,
James Rowland Angell
transformed that view-
point into a school of
thought that flourished
under his leadership
at the University
of Chicago.

he maintained that the function of consciousness is to improve the organ-ism's adaptive abilities. The goal of psychology was to study how the mind aids in this adjustment of the organism to its environment.

A more important contribution to functional psychology is Angell's 1906 presidential address to the American Psychological Association, published in the *Psychological Review*. In this paper, entitled "The Province of Functional Psychology," he spells out clearly the functionalist view:

Functional psychology is at the present moment little more than a point of view, a program, an ambition. It gains its vitality primarily perhaps as a protest against the exclusive excellence of another starting point for the study of the mind, and it enjoys for the time being at least the peculiar vigor which commonly attaches to Protestantism of any sort in its early stages before it has become respectable and orthodox. (Angell, 1907, p. 61)

We have seen that new movements gain vitality and momentum only with reference to, or in opposition to, an established position. Angell drew the battle lines from the beginning, but in this paper he concluded his introductory remarks modestly: "I formally renounce any intention to strike out new plans; I am engaged in what is meant as a dispassionate summary of actual conditions."

Functional psychology, he went on, was not at all new but had been a significant part of psychology from the earliest times. It was structural psychology that had set itself apart from the older and more truly pervasive functional form of psychology. He brought together three ideas that he considered to be the major themes of the functionalist movement.

1. Functional psychology is the psychology of mental operations in contrast to the psychology of mental elements (structuralism). Titchenerian elementism was still strong, and Angell promoted functionalism in opposition to it. The task of functionalism is to discover how a mental process operates, what it accomplishes, and under what conditions it occurs. Angell argued that a mental function, unlike a moment of consciousness as studied by the structuralists, is not a perishable thing. It persists and endures in the same manner as biological functions persist and endure. Just as a physiological function may operate through different structures, so, too, a mental function may operate through ideas that are different in content.

2. Functional psychology is the psychology of the fundamental utilities of consciousness. Consciousness, viewed in this utilitarian spirit, serves to mediate between the needs of the organism and the demands of its environment. Functionalism studies mental processes not as isolated and independent events but as an active, ongoing part of biological activity and as part of the larger movement of organic evolution. Structures and functions of the organism exist because, by allowing the organism to adapt to its environment, they have enabled it to survive. Angell believed that because consciousness has survived, it, too, must perform an essential service for the organism. Functionalism had to discover precisely what this service was, not only for consciousness, but also for specific mental processes, such as judging and willing.

3. Functional psychology is the psychology of psychophysical relations, concerned with the total relationship of the organism to its environment. Functionalism encompasses all mind-body functions and leaves open the study of nonconscious or habitual behavior. It assumes a relationship between mental and physical, an interplay of the same sort that occurs between forces in the physical world. Functionalism holds that there is no real distinction between mind and body. It considers them not as different entities but as belonging to the same order and assumes an easy transfer from one to the other.

Angell's presidential address to the APA in 1906 was given at a time when the spirit of functionalism was already firmly established and influential. He shaped it into an active, prominent enterprise with a laboratory, a body of research data, an enthusiastic staff of teachers, and a dedicated core of graduate students. In guiding functionalism to the status of a formal school, he gave it the focus and stature necessary to make it effective. He continued to insist, however, that functionalism did not really constitute a school and should not be identified exclusively with the psychology taught at Chicago. He believed that the movement was too broad to be encompassed within the framework of a single institution. The formal school of functionalism flourished despite Angell's protestations and was permanently associated with the psychology taught and practiced at Chicago.

Harvey A. Carr (1873–1954)

Harvey Carr, who majored in mathematics at DePauw University in Indiana and at the University of Colorado, switched to psychology because of the friendliness and interest of a professor who was a disciple of G. Stanley Hall (Chapter 8). Because there was no psychology laboratory at Colorado, Carr transferred to the University of Chicago, where his first course in experimental psychology was taught by the young assistant professor Angell. In Carr's second year at Chicago, in which he served as a laboratory assistant, he worked with John B. Watson, then an instructor and later the founder of the behaviorist school of psychology. Watson introduced Carr to animal psychology.

Carr received his Ph.D. in 1905, and after much difficulty obtained a job at a high school in Texas, then an appointment at a state teachers college in Michigan. In 1908 he returned to Chicago to replace Watson, who had left for Johns Hopkins University. Carr succeeded Angell as head of the psychology department at Chicago and went on to extend Angell's theoretical position on functionalism. During Carr's tenure as chair (1919–1938), the psychology department awarded 150 doctoral degrees.

Under Harvey A. Carr, Angell's successor at Chicago, functionalism ceased to be a protest against structuralism and assumed its final systematic form.

The work of Carr represents functionalism when it no longer needed to crusade against structuralism. It had become a recognized position in its own right. Under Carr, functionalism at Chicago reached its peak as a formally defined system. He held the view that functional psychology was *the* American psychology. The work being done at Chicago was the psychology of the time, and as such it did not require a highly refined systematic formulation to distinguish it from any other approach. Other versions of psychology, such as behaviorism, Gestalt psychology, and psychoanalysis, were regarded as needlessly exaggerated developments operating on more limited aspects of psychology. It was thought that these schools had little to add to the all-encompassing functionalist psychology.

Because Carr's book, *Psychology* (1925), is an expression of the finished form of functionalism, it is instructive to consider two of its major points. First, Carr defined the subject matter of psychology as mental activity—processes such as memory, perception, feeling, imagination, judgment, and will. Second, the function of mental activity is to acquire, fixate, retain, organize, and evaluate experiences and to use these experiences in the determination of action. Carr called the specific form of action in which mental activities appear adaptive or adjustive behavior.

We see here functional psychology's familiar emphasis on mental processes rather than on the elements and content of consciousness. And we see also a description of mental activity in terms of what it accomplishes in enabling the organism to adapt or adjust to its environment. It is significant that by 1925 these points were discussed dispassionately as fact, no longer as matters for argument.

In discussing the methods for studying mental activity, Carr recognized the validity of both introspective and objective observation. He noted that the experimental method is the more desirable but admitted that adequate experimental investigation of the mind is difficult, if not impossible. Carr believed, as did Wundt, that the study of cultural products such as literature, art, language, and social and political institutions could provide information on the kinds of mental activities that produced them. He also recognized the value of learning about the physiological processes that are involved in mental activity.

Although functionalism did not adhere to any one method of study, as did structuralism, in practice there was an emphasis on objectivity. A great deal of the research undertaken at the University of Chicago did not use introspection, and where it was used, it was checked as much as possible by objective controls. It is important to note that both animals and humans served as subjects in the research at Chicago.

The Chicago school of functionalism started the shift away from the exclusive study of the subjective mind or consciousness toward the study of objective, overt behavior. Functionalism helped to move American psychology to the opposite extreme from structuralism, eventually to the point where it focused only on behavior, dropping the study of the mind altogether. In this way the functionalists provided a bridge between structuralism and the revolutionary movement of behaviorism.

Original Source Material on Functionalism: From *Psychology* by Harvey A. Carr

The following discussion is reprinted from Chapter 1 of Carr's *Psychology*, published in 1925.* It indicates the finished form of functionalism we have described and covers these topics: (1) the subject matter of functional psychology, with illustrations of the kinds of adaptive acts in which the mind engages; (2) the psychophysical nature of mental activity, showing the relationship between mental activities and their physiological or bodily underpinnings; (3) the research methods of functional psychology, indicating the variety of methods of data collection in addition to the structuralists' technique of introspection; and (4) the relationship between functional psychology and the other sciences, noting that psychology is a biological science that can be applied to other disciplines and to problems of everyday life.

THE SUBJECT MATTER OF PSYCHOLOGY. Psychology is primarily concerned with the study of mental activity. This term is the generic name for such activities as perception, memory, imagination, reasoning, feeling, judgment, and will. The essential features of these various activities can hardly be characterized by a single term, for the mind does various things from time to time. Stated in comprehensive terms, we may say that mental activity is concerned with the acquisition, fixation, retention, organization, and evaluation of experiences, and their subsequent utilization in the guidance of conduct. The type of conduct that reflects mental activity may be termed adaptive or adjustive behavior. . . . An adaptive act is a response on the part of an organism in reference to its physical or social environment of such a character as to satisfy its motivating conditions. Illustrations of these mental operations may be drawn from the professional education of a physician. At times his mind is mainly engaged in the task of acquisition from lectures, books, and clinics, or from his experiences as a practitioner. At other moments his mind is primarily engaged in the attempt to memorize certain important data. Again, the reflective activities may predominate, and his mind is concerned with the task of analyzing, comparing, classifying, and relating the data in hand to other aspects of his medical knowledge. Finally comes the aspect of adaptive conduct — the use of this knowledge and skill in diagnosis, treatment, or surgical operation.

*From Harvey A. Carr, *Psychology* (New York: Longmans, Green, 1925), pp. 1–14.

Every mental act is thus more or less directly concerned with the manipulation of experience as a means of attaining a more effective adjustment to the world. Every mental act can thus be studied from three aspects — its adaptive significance, its dependence upon previous experience, and its potential influence upon the future activity of the organism. For example, perception is a constituent part of a larger act; it is a process of cognizing objects on the basis of what we are doing, or in terms of their relation to some contemplated mode of behavior. Perception also involves the use of past experience, for the significance of any object can be appreciated only in terms of our previous experiences connected with that object. Likewise every experience with an object is likely to exert some effect upon the way in which that object is apprehended on subsequent occasions.

The importance of these various aspects of mental activity is apparent on a moment's reflection. Retention is essential to all learning, mental development, and social progress. The acquisition of an act of skill involves a series of successive trials or practice periods during which the act is gradually perfected and established. Each step of progress is a result of the preceding trials. The effects of each practice period are retained and it is these accumulated effects that render the succeeding attempts more facile. Without retention there could be no mind. If any individual should suddenly lose all his past experiences, he would become almost as helpless as an infant.

Our experiences must be properly organized and systematized in order to be utilized effectively. In popular speech, we often say that an insane person has lost his mind. As a matter of fact these people do have minds. They accumulate, organize, and evaluate their experiences in some sort of fashion, and they react to the world on the basis of these experiences. These people have disordered minds. Their experiences are improperly organized and evaluated. Theoretically, any group of experiences can be organized in various ways. An individual's manner of thinking and the character of his conduct are functions to a large extent of his previous organization. Certain types of organization are conducive to irrational modes of thought and to anti-social forms of behavior. Experiences must not only be organized, but they must be properly organized in order to be utilized effectively in reacting to the world in an intelligent and rational fashion.

The mind is also continuously evaluating the various aspects of experience. The mind not only labels things as good, bad, and indifferent, but it also arranges the good things of life in a crude scale of relative worth. Aesthetic appreciation in the realms of literature, music, and the graphic arts illustrates this function. Ethical values may also be cited. We label social conduct as right and wrong and develop concepts of such virtues as charity, chastity, honesty, sobriety, and punctuality. An individual's system of values constitutes perhaps the most important aspect of his personality. Some students over-emphasize the relative value of study and become bookworms and grinds. Some boys attach too great an importance to the value of financial independence, and leave school to seek a job. Some people under-estimate the importance of neatness of dress, correct habits of speech, courtesy, kindliness, and many other traits that make for an effective personality in social relations. Some individuals take their politics, their religion, or their science too seriously, and overesti-mate the relative importance of those aspects of life. . . . The mind does evaluate its experiences, and . . . an individual's conduct is to a large extent a function of his ideals and system of values.

All experiences of an individual during life are thus organized into a complex but unitary system of reaction tendencies that deter-mine to a large extent the nature of his subsequent activity. The reactive disposition of an individual, i.e., what he does and what he can and can not do, is a function of his native equipment, of the nature of his previous experiences, and of the way in which these have been organized and evaluated. The term "self" is generally employed to characterize an individual from the standpoint of his reactive disposition. We also speak of an individual's personality when we wish to refer to all those traits and characteristics of his self that make or mar his efficiency in dealing with other individuals, while the term "mind" is used when we wish to characterize an individual from the standpoint of his intellectual characteristics and potentialities. . . . Psychology is thus concerned with the study of per-sonality, mind, and the self, but these are conceptual objects that can be studied only indirectly through their manifestations — only inso-far as they express themselves in the reactions of the individual. The various concrete activities involved in an act of adjustment are the observable data and the subject matter of psychology.

THE PSYCHO-PHYSICAL NATURE OF MENTAL ACTIVITY. These various mental operations that are involved in the performance of an adjustive re-sponse are usually termed psycho-physical processes. By their phys-ical character, we mean that they are acts of which the individual has some knowledge. For example, an individual not only perceives and reacts to an object, but he is at least aware of the fact and he may have some knowledge of the nature and significance of those acts. Individ-uals are not accustomed to reason, make decisions and react on the basis of those decisions and be wholly oblivious of the fact. The performance of any mental act on the part of an individual implies some sort of experiential contact with that act. For this reason we shall refer to these mental acts from time to time as experiences or as experiential activities. These acts are not only experienced, but they are also the reactions of a physical organism. They are acts that directly involve such structures as the sense organs, muscles, and nerves. The participation of sense organs and muscles in such activities as perception and voluntary acts is obvious. The nervous system is also concerned in every mental act. While this fact is not one of the obvious sort, yet the truth of the doctrine has been thoroughly established. The integrity of these structures is essential to normal mental activity. An excision or lesion in any part of the brain is usually correlated with some sort of a mental disturbance. All conditions that affect the metabolism of these structures also influence the character of the mental operations. We shall make no attempt to explain the nature of this psycho-physical relationship. We merely note the fact that these mental acts are psycho-physical events and insist that they must be studied as such. . . .

According to our conception, psychology can not be differentiated from physiology in terms of the metaphysical character of its subject matter. Both psychology and physiology are concerned with the study of the functional activities of organisms. Psychology is concerned with all those processes that are directly involved in the adjustment of the organism to its environment, while physiology is engaged in the study of the vital activities such as circulation, digestion, and metabolism that are primarily concerned with the maintenance of the structural integrity of the organism. Psychology and physiology are thus concerned with two mutually related and interactive groups of organic processes. . . .

METHODS OF APPROACH. Mental acts can be studied from several avenues of approach. Mental acts can be directly observed, they can be studied indirectly through their creations and products, and finally they can be studied in terms of their relation to the structure of the organism.

Mental acts may be subjectively or objectively observed. Objective observation refers to the apprehension of the mental operations of another individual insofar as these are reflected in his behavior. Subjective observation refers to the apprehension of one's own mental operations. Subjective observation is often termed introspection, and in times past it was regarded as a unique mode of apprehension different in kind from that involved in perceiving an external event. As a matter of fact, the two processes are essentially alike in nature and they can be differentiated only in terms of the objects cognized. Each mode of observation possesses certain advantages and limitations.

1. Introspection gives us a more intimate and comprehensive knowledge of mental events. Some mental events can not be objectively apprehended. For example, we might know from an individual's behavior that he is engaged in thought without being able to tell what he is thinking about. The individual himself not only knows that he is thinking but is keenly aware of the topic under consideration. Neither will objective observation give us any clue as to whether these thoughts are mediated in terms of words or visual imagery. Introspection often reveals the motives and considerations derived from past experience that influence us in any particular act. It would be very difficult to obtain knowledge of this character by the exclusive use of the objective method.

2. Subjective observations are rather difficult. Many mental operations consist of a series of complex and rapidly shifting events that are difficult to analyze and apprehend in a comprehensive manner. Inasmuch as our minds are usually engaged in dealing with objective situations, many people encounter a considerable amount of difficulty in the attempt to break this habit and become introspective.

3. The validity of a subjective observation can not always be tested. Given a report by a subject that he thinks by means of visual imagery, any verification or disproof of this statement is practically impossible inasmuch as this particular mental event can be observed only by that individual. Neither can we decide that the statement is untrue because other people assert that they think in verbal terms, for it is possible that individuals may differ in their manner of thinking. On the other hand, any objective act can be observed by several people and their reports compared.

4. Naturally the use of the subjective method must be confined to subjects of training and ability. Psychology must thus rely upon the objective method in the study of animals, children, primitive peoples, and many cases of insanity.

5. Instruments may be used to record and measure any of the objective manifestations of mind. These records can then be analyzed at leisure. Acts can be detected in this manner that would otherwise escape our notice. For example, photography has been utilized as a means of studying the finer eye movements that are involved in an act of perception. This method has been extensively employed in the study of the perceptual activities involved in reading and in certain visual illusions.

Subsidiary to observation is the method of experimentation. In an experiment, the mental operations are observed under certain prescribed and defined conditions. An experiment is often called a controlled observation. An experiment may be relatively simple or quite complex according to the degree of control that is exercised. As an illustration of a simple type of experiment, we may cite the case of memorizing a list of words for the purpose of analyzing this process and discovering some of the conditions that influence our ability to recall this material on some subsequent occasion. In general, the performance of any mental act for the purpose of studying that act may be termed an experiment. A psychological experiment does not necessarily involve the employment of an elaborate technique and complicated forms of apparatus. The character of the apparatus is a function of the problem. Instruments are employed as a means of controlling the experimental conditions, or as a means of measuring and recording any feature of the experimental situation. The primary value of an experiment depends upon the fact that the observations are made under certain prescribed and specified conditions. An experiment is thus a means of discovering facts and relations that would escape detection during the ordinary course of experience. Furthermore the results of any experiment can be tested by other investigators. The experimental method has its limitations in the field of psychology. Not all aspects of the human mind are subject to control. An individual's mental reactions are to a very large extent a function of his previous experiences. A complete experimental control of a human mind implies a freedom in manipulating its development throughout life in ways that are both impossible and socially undesirable.

The nature of mind may also be studied indirectly through its creations and products — industrial inventions, literature, art, religious customs and beliefs, ethical systems, political institutions, etc. This method might well be termed the social avenue of approach. Naturally this method will not be used when the mental operations themselves can be studied. Consequently the method is mainly utilized in the study of primitive races or of past civilizations. The method in practice is essentially historical or anthropological. Obviously our knowledge of the human mind would be exceedingly limited if we were forced to rely exclusively upon such data. Facts of this character, however, are significant for an understanding of the developmental aspects of mind.

Mental acts can also be studied from the standpoint of anatomy and physiology. The structure of any organ and its functional possibilities are intimately related. The neurologist attempts to conceive of the structural arrangements of the nervous system in terms of their relation to the various activities in which they are involved. A study of the mutual relations between mental acts and the architectural features of the nervous system will obviously clarify the conceptions of both psychology and neurology. We know that the character of mental acts is influenced by the metabolic conditions of the nervous system. Neural defects are frequently correlated with disturbances of perception, memory, recall, and voluntary activity. A considerable portion of our accurate and detailed knowledge of the relation of mental operations to the nervous structures has been gained in this way. Certain parts of the nervous structures are excised in animals and the effect of this loss of nerve tissue upon the subsequent ability of the organism is noted. Many features of mind must be explained in terms of the physiological peculiarities of the nervous system. The fact of retention, certain temperamental peculiarities of mind, and some aspects of the process of forgetting must be explained in this manner.

It is thus apparent that any fact is a psychological datum whenever it can be utilized in comprehending the nature and significance of the mental operations. The same fact may be significant to several sciences such as neurology, psychology, and physiology, and such a fact will constitute a part of the data of each of these branches of knowledge. Psychology like the other sciences utilizes any fact that is significant for its purposes irrespective of how or where or by whom it was obtained. No single avenue of approach can give a complete knowledge of a mental act. The various sources of knowledge supplement each other and psychology is concerned with the task of systematizing and harmonizing the various data in order to form an adequate conception of all that is involved in the operations of mind.

Facts of common observation constitute perhaps the major portion of the factual data upon which the present conceptions of psychology are based. Psychology differs from most of the natural sciences in that it deals to a considerable extent with the obvious facts of everyday life. Mental acts are experienced events, and naturally everyone must acquire a certain amount of knowledge concerning his own mental operations during the course of life. A considerable portion of our time and energy is also devoted to the task of dealing with other minds. Everyone thus acquires a certain amount of psychological knowledge of a practical sort. Psychology as a science differs from the common-sense variety in several respects. It observes and analyzes mental operations more carefully and systematically, it employs the experimental method whenever possible, it gathers its factual data from a greater variety of sources, and it attempts to construct a more adequate system of conceptions for comprehending these data. Any such system of conceptions is valuable only insofar as the student utilizes them in comprehending his own mental operations or in understanding the actions of others. To a large extent a student must regard a textbook of psychology merely as a guide to the study of his own mind. . . .

RELATION TO OTHER SCIENCES. So far as its systematic relations are concerned, psychology must be classed with the biological group of sciences which deal with the phenomena of living organisms. Psychology finds its closest kinship with physiology in that both are engaged in studying the reactions of animal organisms. There are no fixed lines of demarcation between the two fields. Psychology is interested in the adaptive reactions of organisms in reference to their environmental conditions insofar as those reactions are dependent upon their previous experiences. Physiologists have evinced but little systematic interest in this topic. They have been concerned for the most part with the study of the vital activities. If physiology be arbitrarily defined as the study of organic functions, psychology must naturally be regarded as a special branch of physiology. However, it is wholly immaterial whether psychology be regarded as subordinate to or coördinate with physiology. As a matter of fact, the two sciences do study different aspects of organic activity.

Psychology gathers materials from a great many fields of human endeavor. Psychology appropriates any facts that are significant for an understanding of mind. A professional psychologist naturally encounters a very limited range of mental phenomena and hence must gather his materials from a great variety of sources. Psychology takes facts from sociology, education, neurology, physiology, biology, and anthropology, and hopes in time to be able to borrow from biochemistry. Most of our factual knowledge concerning the great variety of mental disorders has been contributed by physicians and psychiatrists. Peculiar facts of mind and personality are frequently contributed by the legal profession. The various practices of business and industry contribute many suggestive data. In fact, psychological materials can be gathered from any line of human endeavor.

Psychology in turn is interested in making whatever contributions it can to all allied fields of thought and endeavor such as philosophy, sociology, education, medicine, law, business, and industry.

Naturally, any knowledge of human nature will be extremely service-able to any field of endeavor that is in any way concerned with human thought and action. While psychology has exerted a considerable amount of influence upon certain of these fields, yet this practical program must be regarded as somewhat of an ideal, for psychology has not as yet attained any very adequate or complete knowledge of human nature.

Functionalism at Columbia University

We noted in Chapter 6 that there is not a single approach to, or form of, functional psychology, as there is a single structural psychology. Although the primary development and founding of functionalism took place at the University of Chicago, another approach was shaped at Columbia University by Robert Woodworth. We shall see in Chapters 8 and 9 that Columbia was also the academic base for two other psychologists with a functionalist orientation: James McKeen Cattell, whose work on mental tests embodied the American functionalist spirit, and E. L. Thorndike, whose research on problems of animal learning reinforced the functionalist trend toward greater objectivity.

Robert Sessions Woodworth (1869–1962)

Robert Woodworth did not belong formally to the functionalist school in the tradition of Angell and Carr. Indeed, he expressed dislike for the constraints imposed by membership in any school of thought. He wrote in 1930 that the kind of psychology he was developing "does not aspire to be a school. That is the very thing it does not wish to be. Personally, I have always balked on being told, as we have been told at intervals for as long as I can remember, what our marching orders are — what as psychologists we ought to be doing, and what in the divine order of the sciences psychology must be doing" (Woodworth, 1930, p. 327). Although we cannot label Woodworth a strict functionalist, his work is nevertheless appropriate in a chapter on American functionalism because he expressed and reflected a free form of functionalism that still characterizes American psychology. Much of what Woodworth said about psychology is in the functionalist spirit of the Chicago school, but he added an important new ingredient.

Woodworth was active in psychology for more than seventy years as a researcher, beloved teacher, writer, and editor. After receiving his B.A.

Robert Sessions Woodworth championed an eclectic approach to psychology with an emphasis on motivation.

from Amherst College in Massachusetts, he taught high school science and then mathematics at a small college. During that period he reported two experiences that changed his life. First, he heard the noted psychologist G. Stanley Hall give a talk, and second, he read William James's *The Principles of Psychology*. He knew then that he had to become a psychologist.

He enrolled at Harvard University, where he earned his M.A., and he received his Ph.D. in 1899 from Cattell at Columbia. Woodworth taught physiology in New York City hospitals for three years and spent another year working with the physiologist Charles Scott Sherrington in England. In 1903 he returned to Columbia, where he remained until his first retirement in 1945. He was so popular, however, that he continued to lecture to large classes until 1958, when he retired from Columbia, at the age of eighty-nine, for a second time.

Woodworth's list of publications is lengthy, and his work has influenced several generations of students. His position is described in a number of journal articles and in *Dynamic Psychology* (1918) and *Dynamics of Behavior* (1958). He wrote an introductory text, *Psychology*, published in 1921, which had appeared in five editions by 1947 and is said to have outsold every other psychology text for twenty-five years. His *Experimental Psychology* (1938, 1954) also became a classic. In 1956 Woodworth received the first Gold Medal Award of the American Psychological Foundation for having made "unequaled contributions to shaping the destiny of scientific psychology" as an "integrator and organizer of psychological knowledge."

Woodworth maintained that his approach was not really new but was the one followed by "good" psychologists even in the days before psychology became a science. Psychological knowledge must begin, he said, with an investigation of the nature of the stimulus and the response, that is, with objective, external events. But when psychology considers only the stimulus and the response in attempting to explain behavior, it misses perhaps the most important part — the living organism itself. The stimulus is not the complete cause of a particular response. The organism, with its varying levels of energy and its current and past experiences, also acts to determine the response.

Thus, according to Woodworth, psychology must consider the organism itself as interpolated between the stimulus and the response. It follows that the subject matter for psychology must be both consciousness and behavior, a position later adopted by the humanistic psychologists. The external stimulus as well as the overt response may be discovered by the objective observation of behavior, but what occurs inside the organism can be known only through introspection. Woodworth therefore accepted introspection as a useful tool for psychology, along with the observational and experimental methods.

Woodworth introduced into functionalism a ***dynamic psychology*** that seemed to be an extension or elaboration of the teachings of Dewey and James. (The word *dynamic* had been used as early as 1884 by Dewey and in 1908 by James.) A dynamic psychology is one concerned with change and with the interpretation of the causal factors in change. As such, it represents an interest in motivation. Indeed, Woodworth said in 1897 that he wanted to develop a *motivology*.

The first expression of Woodworth's systematic position is *Dynamic Psychology* (1918), which is a plea for a functional psychology that includes the topic of motivation. Although there are similarities between Woodworth's position and that of the Chicago functionalists, Woodworth emphasized more heavily the physiological events underlying behavior. His dynamic psychology, or motivology, is concerned with cause-and-effect relationships. He believed that psychology's goal should be to determine why people behave as they do, why they feel and act in certain ways. Thus his primary interest was in the forces that drive or activate the human organism.

In discussing causal sequences in behavior, Woodworth distinguished two kinds of events: mechanisms and drives. A mechanism is concerned with how a task is performed, such as the mechanical aspects of a physical movement. A drive is concerned with why the task is performed. Mechanisms and drives are similar in that both are responses of the organism; mechanisms may become drives, and drives may become mechanisms.

In another example of distorted data in the history of psychology, Woodworth is usually credited with introducing the term *drive*. Some eight months before Woodworth used the term in print, however, John B. Watson used it in an article in the *American Journal of Psychology* (Watson & Morgan, 1917), giving it the same meaning.

Woodworth's position was essentially eclectic. He did not wish to adhere to a single system, nor did he want to develop a school of his own. His viewpoint was built not from protest but from growth, elaboration, and synthesis, and he sought the best features of each system of thought.

Criticisms of Functionalism

Attacks on the functionalist movement came quickly and vehemently from the structuralists. And for the first time, at least in the United States, the new psychology was divided into warring factions. Cornell and Chicago became the respective headquarters of the structuralist and functionalist enemy camps. Accusations, charges, and countercharges were flung back and forth between the universities with all the righteousness characteristic of those who are convinced they possess the truth.

One criticism directed against functionalism was that the term itself was not clearly defined. In 1913, C. A. Ruckmick, a student of Titchener's, examined fifteen general psychology textbooks to determine how function was defined by the various writers. The two most common usages were "an activity or process," and "a service to other processes or to the whole organism." In the first usage, function is essentially the same as activity; for example, remembering and perceiving are functions. In the second usage, function is defined in reference to the usefulness of some activity to the organism, such as the function of digestion or breathing. Ruckmick charged that the functionalists sometimes used the word *function* to describe an activity and sometimes to refer to its utility.

It was some seventeen years before this charge of inconsistent and ambiguous usage was answered. Writing in 1930, Harvey Carr argued that the two definitions were not inconsistent because both referred to the same processes. Functionalism was interested in a particular activity both for its own sake (the first definition) and for its relationship to other conditions or activities (the second definition). A similar practice was followed in biology, he noted. One historian has suggested, however, that "Functionalism used the concept first and defined it later; and this sequence of events is characteristic of the movement. . . . Functionalism has never been disposed to place definition and systematization in the foreground" (Heidbreder, 1933, p. 228).

Another criticism, particularly from E. B. Titchener, related to the definition of psychology. The structuralists claimed that functionalism was not psychology at all because it was not restricted to the subject matter and methodology of structuralism. In Titchener's view, any approach other than the introspective analysis of the mind into elements was not psychology. Of course, it was his definition of psychology that the functionalists were questioning and working to replace.

Other critics found fault with the functional psychologists' interest in activities of a practical or applied nature, a manifestation of the long-standing controversy between pure and applied science. The structuralists did not look favorably on applied psychology. The functionalists, however, were unconcerned with maintaining psychology as a pure science and never apologized for their practical interests. Carr suggested that rigorous scientific procedures can be adhered to in both pure and applied psychology and that valid research can be performed in a factory, office, or classroom, as well as in a university laboratory. It is the method and not the subject matter, Carr noted, that determines how scientific a field of inquiry is. This controversy between pure and applied science is no longer as extreme in American psychology today, largely because applied psychology is so widespread. This can be seen as a contribution of functionalism, not a defect.

Contributions of Functionalism

As an attitude or general viewpoint, functionalism became part of the mainstream of American psychology. Its early and vigorous opposition to structuralism was of immense value to the development of psychology in the United States. The long-range consequences of the shift in emphasis from structure to function were also significant. One result was that research on animal behavior, which was not a part of the structuralist approach, became an important part of psychology.

The functionalists' broadly defined psychology also incorporated studies of infants, children, and the mentally impaired. In addition, functionalism allowed psychologists to supplement the method of introspection with other ways of securing data, such as physiological research, mental tests, questionnaires, and objective descriptions of behavior. All these methods, which were anathema to the structuralists, became, to the functionalists, respectable sources of information for psychology.

By the time of Wundt's death in 1920 and Titchener's in 1927, their approaches to psychology had been overshadowed in the United States by the more pervasive and practical approach of the functionalists. The functionalist victory was complete by 1930, and in the United States today psychology is, to some extent, functional in its orientation. Functionalism does not exist today as a separate school of thought, however. Because of its success, there is no longer any need for it to retain the characteristics of a school. It has left its imprint on contemporary American psychology primarily through its emphasis on applying the methods and findings of psychology to real-world problems.

Suggested Readings

Allen, G. W. (1967). *William James: A Biography*. New York: Viking Press. A colorful, absorbing biography of James, drawing on unpublished papers of the James family.

Angell, J. R. (1913). Behavior as a category of psychology. *Psychological Review, 20*, 255–270. Discusses problems associated with the use of the term "consciousness," and comments on the value for psychology of consciousness and introspection.

Century of the birth of William James. (1943). *Psychological Review, 50,* 81–139. Contains articles by Angell, Thorndike, Allport, Dewey, and others, on the life and work of William James.

Crissman, P. (1942). The psychology of John Dewey. *Psychological Review, 49,* 441–462. Reviews and evaluates important concepts in Dewey's approach to psychological issues.

Dewey, J. (1917). The need for social psychology. *Psychological Review, 24,* 266–277. Discusses the importance of research in social psychology for reaching a complete understanding of human behavior.

James, W. (1962). *Psychology: Briefer Course.* New York: Collier Books. The abridged version of James's 2-volume *The Principles of Psychology,* adapted by James for classroom use.

McKinney, F. (1978). Functionalism at Chicago — memories of a graduate student: 1929–1931. *Journal of the History of the Behavioral Sciences, 14,* 142–148. Describes the faculty, students, course work, and intellectual Zeitgeist of the psychology department at the University of Chicago.

Myers, G. E. (1986). *William James: His Life and Thought.* New Haven CT: Yale University Press. A biographical sketch of James and the James family and an exposition of James's ideas in psychology and philosophy, showing how his thinking changed over time.

O'Donnell, J. M. (1985). *The Origins of Behaviorism: American Psychology, 1870–1920.* New York: New York University Press. Describes how contextual forces such as social pressures, economic competition, and the rise of the modern university transformed American psychology from the study of conscious processes to the science of conditioned behavior; relates nineteenth-century trends in philosophy and science to American formulations of structuralism, functionalism, and behaviorism.

Raphelson, A. C. (1973). The pre-Chicago association of the early functionalists. *Journal of the History of the Behavioral Sciences, 9,* 115–122. An overview of the work of John Dewey and its impact on the development of functional psychology at the University of Chicago.

Thorne, F. C. (1976). Reflections on the Golden Age of Columbia's psychology. *Journal of the History of the Behavioral Sciences, 12,* 159–165. Describes the faculty and the research orientation of the psychology department at Columbia University from 1920 to 1940.

The Legacy of Functionalism: Applied Psychology

8

The Growth of Psychology in the United States

We have seen that evolutionary doctrine and the functional psychology that derived from it rapidly took hold in the United States toward the end of the nineteenth century, and that American psychology was guided much more by the ideas of Darwin and Galton than by the work of Wundt. This was a curious, even paradoxical, historical phenomenon. Wundt trained many of the first generation of American psychologists in his form of psychology, including Hall, Cattell, Witmer, Scott, and Münsterberg. Yet "little of Wundt's actual system of psychology ever survived the return passage across the Atlantic with the young Americans who traveled abroad" (Blumenthal, 1977, p. 13). When these students of Wundt's, these new psychologists, returned to the United States, they set about establishing a psychology that bore little resemblance to what Wundt had taught them. The new science, not unlike a living species, was adapting to its new environment.

Wundt's psychology and Titchener's structuralism could not long survive in their original form in the American intellectual climate, the American Zeitgeist, and so they evolved into functionalism. They were not practical kinds of psychology; they did not deal with the mind in use and could not be applied to the everyday demands and problems of life. American culture was oriented toward the practical, the pragmatic. People valued what worked. A utilitarian, shirtsleeves form of psychology was demanded. "We need a psychology that is usable," wrote G. Stanley Hall, America's premier applied psychologist. "Wundtian thoughts can never be acclimated here, as they are antipathetic to the American spirit and temper" (Hall, 1912, p. 414).

The newly trained American psychologists returned from Germany and in typically direct and aggressive American fashion transformed the uniquely German species of psychology. They began to study not what the mind is but what it does. While some American psychologists — notably James, Angell, and Carr — were developing the functionalist approach in academic laboratories, others were applying it in settings outside the universities. Thus, the move toward a practical kind of psychology was occurring at the same time that functionalism was being founded as a separate, formal school of thought.

The applied psychologists took their psychology into the real world, into the schools, factories, advertising agencies, courthouses, child guidance clinics, and mental health centers, and made of it something functional in both subject matter and use. In doing so, they changed the nature of American psychology as radically as did the academic founders of functionalism. The professional literature of the day reflects their impact. At the turn of the century 25 percent of the research articles published in American psychology journals dealt with applied psychology, and less than 3 percent involved introspection (O'Donnell, 1985). The approaches of Wundt and Titchener, themselves so recently the new psychology, were rapidly being overtaken by a newer psychology.

Psychology grew and prospered in the United States, as did the country as a whole. The vibrant and dynamic development of American psychology during the period 1880–1900 is a striking event in the history of science. In 1880 there were no laboratories in the United States; by 1895 there were twenty-six, and they were better equipped than laboratories in Germany. In 1880 there were no American psychology journals; by 1895 there were three. In 1880, Americans had to go to Germany to study psychology; by 1900, they could enter graduate programs at home. By 1903, more Ph.D.s were awarded by American universities in psychology than in any other science except chemistry, zoology, and physics. The British publication *Who's Who in Science* (1913) stated that the United States was predominant in psychology, having more of the world's leading psychologists — numbering eighty-four — than Germany, England, and France combined (Jonçich, 1968).

In little more than twenty years after psychology began in Europe, American psychologists had assumed undisputed leadership in the field. James McKeen Cattell reported in his presidential address to the American Psychological Association in 1895 that "the academic growth of psychology in America during the past five years is almost without precedent. . . . Psychology is a required subject in the undergraduate curriculum . . . and among university courses psychology now rivals the other leading sciences in the number of students attracted and in the amount of original work accomplished" (Cattell, 1896, p. 134).

Psychology made its American debut before an eager public at the Chicago World's Fair of 1893. In a program reminiscent of Francis Galton's Anthropometric Laboratory in England, psychologists organized exhibits of research apparatus and a testing laboratory in which, for a fee, visitors could have their capacities measured. A more extensive exhibition was mounted at the 1904 Louisiana Purchase Exposition in St. Louis, Missouri. This "star-studded event" featured lectures by the leading psychologists of the day — E. B. Titchener from Cornell, C. Lloyd Morgan, Pierre Janet, G. Stanley Hall, and a new Ph.D. by the name of John B. Watson (Benjamin, 1986). Such a popular display of psychology would not have found favor with Wundt, and nothing like it ever took place in Germany. The popularizing of psychology reflected the American temperament that so substantially remade Wundt's brand of psychology into functional psychology and extended it far beyond the laboratory.

Thus, America embraced psychology with enthusiasm, and the field quickly became established in college classrooms and in people's daily lives. Its scope today is far broader than its founders ever thought possible, or even desirable.

Contextual Influences on Applied Psychology

While the American Zeitgeist, the intellectual spirit and temper of the times, helped to foster the emergence of applied psychology, other more practical contextual forces were also responsible for its development. In Chapter 1 we discussed the role of economic factors in shifting the focus of American psychology from pure research to application. We saw that while the number of psychology laboratories was increasing toward the end of the nineteenth century, the number of Americans with doctoral degrees in psychology was growing three times as fast. Many of these new Ph.D.s, particularly those without an independent source of income, had to look beyond the university for economic survival.

The psychologist Harry Hollingworth (1880–1956), for example, could not afford to live on his annual salary of $1000 for teaching at Barnard College in New York City, and he supplemented it by teaching courses at other universities and proctoring examinations for fifty cents an hour. He offered workshops on psychology to advertising executives and tried everything he could think of to support his goal of a life devoted to research and scholarly activities. He found, however, that he had no choice but to turn to applied psychology to make a living (Benjamin, Rogers, & Rosenbaum, 1991).

Hollingworth was not alone. Other pioneers in applied psychology acted out of economic necessity. This does not mean that they did not find this practical work to be stimulating and challenging. Most did, and they also came to recognize that human behavior and mental life could be studied in real-world settings just as effectively as in the academic laboratory. It should also be noted that some of these psychologists entered applied fields out of a genuine interest and desire to work in that capacity. Yet the fact remains that many of the first generation of applied psychologists in the United States were compelled to abandon their dreams of pure experimental research as the only way to escape a life of poverty.

The situation was even more dire for psychologists who taught at the less well endowed state universities in the Midwest and West at the turn of the century. By 1910, one-third of all American psychologists held such positions, and as their numbers grew, so did the pressure on them to deal with practical problems and thus prove psychology's financial worth.

In 1912, Christian A. Ruckmick surveyed his fellow psychologists and concluded that psychology was held in low esteem in American colleges and universities, despite its popularity with students. It was poorly funded and equipped, and there was only a little hope for improvement in the future (Leary, 1987). The best possible way to improve the situation—to increase departmental budgets and salaries — was to demonstrate to university administrators and state legislators that the science of psychology could help cure many of society's ills.

G. Stanley Hall advised a colleague in the Midwest to make psychology's influence felt "outside the university, lest some irresponsible, sensational man or party criticize it in the legislature." Cattell urged his colleagues to "make practical applications and develop a profession of applied psychology" (O'Donnell, 1985, pp. 215, 221).

The solution, then, was obvious: make psychology more valuable by applying it. But to what? Fortunately, the answer soon became clear. Public school enrollments were increasing dramatically; between 1870 and 1915 they rose from seven to twenty million. The amount of money spent on public education during that period grew from $63 million to $605 million (Siegel & White, 1982). Education was suddenly big business, and it got the psychologists' attention.

Hall proclaimed in 1894 that the "one chief and immediate field of application for [psychology] was its application to education" (Leary, 1987, p. 323). Even William James, who could not be considered an applied psychologist, wrote a book on the uses of psychology in classroom situations (James, 1899). By 1910 more than one-third of all American psychologists expressed interest in applying psychology to problems in education. Three-fourths of those calling themselves applied psychologists were already working in that area. Psychology had found its place in the real world.

We will discuss in this chapter the careers and contributions of five pioneering applied psychologists who extended the new science not only into education but also into business and industry, testing centers, courtrooms, and mental health clinics. All of these men were trained at Leipzig by Wilhelm Wundt to become pure academic psychologists, but all moved away from Wundt's teachings when they began their careers in American universities. They provide striking examples of how American psychology came to be influenced more by Darwin and Galton than by Wundt, and how the Wundtian approach was refashioned when it was transplanted to American soil.

After considering the work of these leading practitioners, we describe how three major areas of applied psychology began: psychological testing, industrial/organizational psychology, and clinical psychology.

Granville Stanley Hall (1844–1924)

Although William James was the first great American psychologist, the explosive growth of psychology in the United States between 1880 and

A man of diverse professional interests, American Psychological Association founder Granville Stanley Hall made notable contributions to educational psychology, applying a belief in evolution to problems of human development.

1900 was not the result of his work alone. Another remarkable figure in the history of American psychology was Granville Stanley Hall.

Hall's career was one of the most interesting and varied of any psychologist. He worked in bursts of energy and enthusiasm in a number of areas and moved on, leaving the details to be investigated by others. He was not a founder of functionalism, but his contributions to new applied fields and activities had a pronounced functional flavor.

American psychology owes Hall a debt because of his outstanding record of firsts. He received the first American doctoral degree in psychology, and he claimed to be the first American student in the first year of the first psychology laboratory. (New data of history reveal that he was actually the second; see Benjamin, Acord, Durkin, Link, & Vestal, 1992.) He began what is considered by many to be the first psychology laboratory in the United States, and he started the first American journal of psychology. He was the first president of Clark University, the organizer and first president of the American Psychological Association, and one of the first applied psychologists.

The Life of Hall

G. Stanley Hall was born on a farm in Massachusetts and at an early age developed a succession of interests that characterized his later life. Also characteristic was his great ambition. At the age of fourteen, "he vowed to leave the farm and 'do and be something in the world.' . . . His most intense adolescent fear was the fear of mediocrity" (Ross, 1972, p. 12). In 1863 he entered Williams College. By the time he graduated, Hall had won a number of honors and had developed an enthusiasm for philosophy, especially evolutionary theory, which was to influence his career in psychology.

In 1867 he enrolled in the Union Theological Seminary in New York City, although without a strong commitment to the ministry. His interest in evolution was no advantage in this situation, and he was not noted for his religious orthodoxy. The story has been told that when Hall gave his trial sermon to the faculty and students, the seminary president knelt and prayed for his soul.

On the advice of the preacher Henry Ward Beecher, Hall went to the University of Bonn, Germany, to study philosophy and theology. From there he traveled to Berlin, where he added studies in physiology and physics. This phase of his education was supplemented by romantic interludes and the frequenting of beer gardens and theaters, all daring experiences for a young man of pious upbringing. He wrote of his amazement and delight at seeing one of his theology professors drinking beer on a Sunday. Hall's European sojourn became a time of liberation.

He returned home in 1871, twenty-seven years old, with no degree and heavily in debt. He completed his divinity studies and preached in a country church in Cowdersport, Pennsylvania, for all of ten weeks. After working as a private tutor for more than a year, Hall secured a teaching job at Antioch College in Ohio. He taught English literature, French and German languages and literature, and philosophy, served as librarian, led the choir, and preached in the chapel. In 1874 he read Wundt's *Physiological Psychology*, and his interest in the new science was aroused, causing him some uncertainty about his career. He took a leave of absence from Antioch, settled in Cambridge, Massachusetts, and became a tutor in English at Harvard.

In addition to the monotonous and time-consuming work of teaching sophomore English, Hall undertook graduate studies and conducted research at the medical school. In 1878 he presented his dissertation on the muscular perception of space and was awarded the first degree in psychology in the United States. He also came to know William James quite well, but the two men, although close in age, were far apart in background and temperament.

Immediately after receiving his doctoral degree, Hall left for Europe, first to study physiology at Berlin and then to become Wundt's student at Leipzig. The anticipation of working with Wundt was apparently greater than the reality. Although Hall attended Wundt's lectures and dutifully served as a subject in the laboratory, his own research was conducted along more physiological lines, and his subsequent career demonstrates that Wundt ultimately had little influence on him. When Hall returned to America in 1880 he had no prospect of a job, yet within a span of ten years he had become a figure of national renown.

Hall recognized, when he returned from Germany, that the best chance to satisfy his ambition lay in the application of psychology to education. In 1882 he gave a talk to a meeting of the National Education Association (NEA), urging that the psychological study of the child be made a core component of the teaching profession. He repeated this message at every opportunity, and it soon led to the first step of his rapid rise from obscurity. The president of Harvard invited Hall to deliver a series of Saturday morning talks on education. These well-received speeches brought Hall much favorable publicity and an invitation to lecture part time at Johns Hopkins University, which had been established six years earlier as the first graduate school in the United States.

Hall's lectures were a great success, and he was given a professorship at Hopkins in 1884. During his time there he began what is usually considered to be the first American psychology laboratory (formally established in 1883), which he called his "laboratory of psychophysiology" (Pauly, 1986, p. 30). He taught a number of students who later became prominent psychologists, among them John Dewey and James McKeen Cattell. In 1887 Hall founded the *American Journal of Psychology*, the first psychology journal in the United States and still an important publication. It provided

Hall's psychology laboratory at Johns Hopkins University is considered to be the first in the United States.

a platform for theoretical and experimental ideas and a sense of solidarity and independence for American psychologists. In a burst of enthusiasm Hall had printed an excessive number of copies of the first issue; it took five years for the journal and Hall to pay back those initial costs.

In 1888 Hall became the first president of Clark University in Worcester, Massachusetts. Before taking up his new position, he embarked on an extended tour abroad to study European universities and hire faculty for his new school. The trip served another purpose as well. "Hall seems to have regarded the trip as a combination Grand Tour and paid vacation for labors not yet commenced. . . . it included a number of stops wholly irrelevant to the task ahead, such as Russian military academies, ancient Greek historical sites, and [the] standard run of brothels, circuses, and curiosities" (Koelsch, 1987, p. 21).

Hall aspired to make Clark a graduate university along the lines of Johns Hopkins and the German universities, with the primary emphasis on research rather than teaching. Unfortunately, the founder — the wealthy merchant Jonas Gilman Clark — had different ideas and did not provide as much money as Hall had been led to expect. After Clark died in 1900, the endowment was devoted to the founding of an undergraduate college, which had been opposed by Hall but long advocated by Clark.

Hall made Clark University more receptive to women and minority students than were most other schools in the United States at that time. Although he shared the nationwide opposition to coeducation for undergraduates, he did admit women as graduate students. He also took the unusual step of encouraging Asian (especially Japanese) students to enroll at Clark, and the unprecedented step of encouraging African-Americans to become graduate students. The first black American to earn a Ph.D. in psychology, Francis Sumner, studied with Hall. Hall refused to place restrictions on hiring Jews as faculty members at a time when most universities would not hire them (Guthrie, 1976; Sokal, 1990).

He was professor of psychology as well as university president, and he taught in the graduate school for several years. He also found time in 1891 to establish, at his own expense, another journal, the *Pedagogical Seminary* (now the *Journal of Genetic Psychology*), to serve as an outlet for research in child study and educational psychology. In 1915 he founded the *Journal of Applied Psychology*, bringing the number of American psychology journals to sixteen.

The American Psychological Association (APA) was founded in 1892, largely through Hall's efforts. At his invitation, approximately a dozen psychologists met in the study of his home to plan the organization, and they elected him the first president. By 1900 the group had 127 members.

Hall's interest in religion persisted. He began the *Journal of Religious Psychology* (1904), which ceased publication after a decade. In 1917 he published a book entitled *Jesus, the Christ, in the Light of Psychology*. His portrayal of Jesus as a kind of "adolescent superman" was not well received by organized religion (Ross, 1972, p. 418).

Psychology at Clark prospered under Hall. During his thirty-six years there, eighty-one doctorates were awarded in psychology. His students remember the exhausting but exhilarating Monday evening seminars at Hall's home, when doctoral candidates were quizzed by the faculty and other graduate students. After the meetings, which lasted up to four hours, a household servant would bring in a gigantic tub of ice cream.

Hall's comments on his students' papers were often devastating. "Hall would sum things up," Lewis Terman recalled, "with an erudition and fertility of imagination that always amazed us and made us feel that his offhand insight into the problem went immeasurably beyond that of the student who had devoted months of slavish drudgery to it." And when the evening sessions ended, Terman "always went home dazed and intoxicated, took a hot bath to quiet my nerves, then lay awake for hours rehearsing the drama and formulating the clever things I should have said and did not" (Sokal, 1990, p. 119).

The graduate students were somewhat in awe of Hall. One recently recalled his impression of Hall from seventy years past. "Hall was a man of powerful build, standing taller than six feet. He was frequently seen operating his hand lawn mower along the three-foot bank that sloped from his front yard down to the sidewalk. . . . Striding easily along the top edge of the slope, his left hand in his pocket, he manipulated the mower up and down with his right, in successively brisk push and pull from one end of the bank to the other, a good one hundred feet away. Sometimes as he moved he carried on a conversation with a student pacing the sidewalk beside him" (Averill, 1990, p. 125).

Adept at nurturing bright students, as long as they were properly deferential, Hall could be generous and supportive. At one time it could be claimed that the majority of American psychologists had been associated with Hall either at Clark or at Johns Hopkins, although he was not the primary source of inspiration for all of them. Perhaps his personal influence is reflected best in the fact that one-third of his doctoral students eventually went into administration, as he had done.

Hall was one of the first Americans to become interested in psychoanalysis and was largely responsible for the early attention it received in the United States. In 1909, to celebrate the twentieth anniversary of the founding of Clark University, he invited Sigmund Freud and Carl Jung to participate in a series of conferences, an invitation that was courageous because of the suspicion with which psychoanalysis was viewed. Hall also invited his former teacher, Wilhelm Wundt, who declined because of age and because he was scheduled to be the featured speaker at the five-hundredth anniversary of his own university.

Hall continued to write after his retirement from Clark in 1920. He died four years later, a few months after his election to a second term as president of the APA. After his death a survey was taken of APA members to evaluate Hall's contributions to psychology. Of the 120 people who responded, 99 ranked Hall among the world's top ten psychologists. Many of them praised his teaching ability, his efforts in promoting psychology, and his defiance of orthodoxy, but they, and others who knew him, were critical of his personal qualities. He was described as difficult to get along with, untrustworthy, unscrupulous, devious, and aggressively self-promoting. William James once called him the "queerest mixture of bigness and pettiness I ever knew" (Myers, 1986, p. 18). Even his critics, however, would have agreed with the judgment of the APA survey: "[Hall] has been the cause of more writing and research than any other three men in the field" (Koelsch, 1987, p. 52).

Evolution as a Framework for Human Development

Although Hall was interested in many areas, his intellectual wanderings had a single guiding theme: evolutionary theory. His work on a variety of psychological topics was governed by the conviction that the normal growth of the mind involves a series of evolutionary stages. Thus, Hall used the theory of evolution as a framework for broad theoretical and applied speculations. He contributed more to educational psychology than to experimental psychology. Only in the early phases of his career did he focus on experimental psychology. He agreed that the experimental method was important for psychology, but he became impatient with its limitations. Laboratory work in the new psychology proved too narrow for Hall's more general goals and efforts.

Hall is often called a genetic psychologist because of his concern with human and animal development and with the related problems of adaptation. At Clark, Hall's geneticism led him to the psychological study of childhood, which he made the core of his psychology. In a speech at the 1893 Chicago World's Fair he said, "Hitherto we have gone to Europe for our psychology. Let us now take a child and place him in our midst and let America make her own psychology" (Siegel & White, 1982, p. 253). Hall intended to apply his psychology to the functioning of the child in the real world. As a former student aptly remarked, "The child became, as it were, his laboratory" (Averill, 1990, p. 127).

In his child studies Hall made extensive use of questionnaires, a procedure he had learned in Germany. By 1915 Hall and his students had developed and used 194 questionnaires covering many topics (White, 1990). So extensive was his use of questionnaires that for a time the method came to be associated in the United States with Hall's name, even though the technique had been developed earlier by Francis Galton.

These early studies of children generated great public enthusiasm and led to the formalization of the so-called child study movement. Although it disappeared in a few years because of poorly executed research, the movement served to establish the importance of both the empirical study of the child and the concept of psychological development.

Hall's most influential work is the lengthy (some thirteen hundred pages), two-volume *Adolescence: Its Psychology, and Its Relations to Physiology, Anthropology, Sociology, Sex, Crime, Religion, and Education,* published in 1904. This encyclopedia contains the most complete statement of Hall's recapitulation theory of psychological development. He believed that children in their personal development repeat the life history of the human race. When children play cowboys-and-Indians games, for example, they are repeating or summarizing the history of preliterate human beings. The book included much material of interest to child psychologists and educators and went through several printings, one done twenty years after its initial publication.

Adolescence also became controversial because of what some considered an excessive focus on sex. Hall was accused of having prurient interests. In a book review, the psychologist E. L. Thorndike wrote that "the acts and feelings, normal and morbid, resulting from sex are discussed in a way without precedent in English science." Thorndike was even more critical in a letter to a colleague, saying that Hall's book was "chock full of errors, masturbation and Jesus. He is a mad man" (Ross, 1972, p. 385). At the time, Hall was giving a series of weekly lectures at Clark on sex. This was a scandalous act, even though he did not allow women to attend. He eventually stopped the talks because "too many outsiders got in and even listened surreptitiously at the door" (Koelsch, 1970, p. 119).

Many psychologists were uneasy about Hall's enthusiasm for sex. "Is there no turning Hall away from this d----d sexual rut?" wrote Angell to Titchener. "I really think it is a bad thing morally and intellectually to harp so much on the sexual string" (Boakes, 1984, p. 163). They need not have worried. The productive and energetic Hall soon moved on to other interests.

As Hall grew older he naturally became curious about a later stage of development: old age. At the age of seventy-eight he published the two-volume work *Senescence* (1922), which was the first large-scale survey of geriatric issues of a psychological nature. In the last few years of his life he also wrote two autobiographies, *Recreations of a Psychologist* (1920) and *The Life and Confessions of a Psychologist* (1923).

G. Stanley Hall was once introduced to an audience as "the Darwin of the mind." It was a characterization that evidently pleased him and vividly expressed his aspirations and the basic attitude that permeated his work. He was introduced to another audience as "the greatest authority in the world on the study of the child." He reportedly said that the praise was correct (Koelsch, 1987, p. 58). Throughout his career he remained versatile and agile. His seemingly limitless enthusiasm was bold, diverse, and nontechnical, and it is perhaps this characteristic that made him so stimulating and influential.

In his second autobiography he wrote, "All my active conscious life has been made up of a series of fads or crazes, some strong, some weak; some lasting long . . . and others ephemeral" (Hall, 1923, pp. 367–368). It was a perceptive observation. Hall was mercurial, aggressive, quixotic, often at odds with colleagues, but never dull. He once noted that Wilhelm Wundt would rather have been commonplace than brilliantly wrong. Perhaps Hall would rather have been brilliantly wrong than commonplace.

James McKeen Cattell (1860–1944)

The functionalist spirit of American psychology was also well represented in the life and work of James McKeen Cattell, who influenced the movement toward a practical, test-oriented approach to the study of mental processes. Cattell's psychology was concerned with human abilities rather than conscious content, and in this respect he comes close to being a functionalist. Like Hall and William James, however, he was never formally associated with the movement, but he typified the American functionalist spirit in his emphasis on mental processes in terms of their usefulness to the organism and in his development of mental tests, now a major area of applied psychology.

The Life of Cattell

Cattell was born in Easton, Pennsylvania. He earned his bachelor's degree in 1880 at Lafayette College, where his father was the president. Following the custom of going to Europe for graduate study, Cattell went first to the University of Göttingen and then to Leipzig and Wilhelm Wundt.

A paper in philosophy won him a fellowship to Johns Hopkins University in 1882. At the time, his major interest was philosophy, and during his first semester at Hopkins no psychology courses were offered. It appears that Cattell became interested in psychology as a result of his own experiments with drugs. He tried a variety of substances ranging from hashish, morphine, and opium to caffeine, tobacco, and chocolate. He found the results to be of both personal and professional interest. Some drugs, notably hashish, cheered him considerably and reduced the depression he had been experiencing. He also took note of the effects of the drugs on his mental functioning.

"I felt myself making brilliant discoveries in science and philosophy," he confided to his journal, "my only fear being that I could not remember them until morning." A month later he wrote, "Reading has become uninteresting. I keep reading without paying much attention. It takes a long time to write a word. I'm rather confused" (Sokal, 1981a, pp. 51, 52). Cattell was not so confused, however, that he failed to recognize the psychological importance of the drugs, and he observed his own behavior and mental state with increasing fascination. "I seemed to be two persons," he wrote, "one of whom could observe and even experiment on the other" (Sokal, 1987, p. 25).

The practical, test-oriented methods of James McKeen Cattell reflected the spirit of American functional psychology.

During Cattell's second semester at Johns Hopkins, G. Stanley Hall began to teach classes in psychology, and Cattell (along with John Dewey) enrolled in Hall's laboratory course. Shortly thereafter Cattell began research on reaction time, the time required for different mental activities; this work reinforced his desire to become a psychologist.

Cattell's return to Wundt in Germany in 1883 is the subject of some well-known anecdotes in the history of psychology, which provide additional examples of how historical data can be distorted. Cattell allegedly appeared at the University of Leipzig laboratory and boldly announced to Wundt, "Herr Professor, you need an assistant, and I shall be your assistant" (Cattell, 1928, p. 545). He made it clear to Wundt that he would choose his own research project, on the psychology of individual differences, a topic that was not central to Wundtian psychology. Wundt is said to have characterized Cattell and his project as *ganz Amerikanisch* ("typically American"), which was a prophetic remark. The interest in individual differences, a natural outcome of an evolutionary point of view, has since been a feature of American and not of German psychology.

Cattell supposedly gave Wundt his first typewriter, on which most of Wundt's books were written. For this gift Cattell was criticized in jest for having "done a serious disservice . . . for it had enabled Wundt to write twice as many books as would otherwise have been possible" (Cattell, 1928, p. 545).

Careful and thorough archival research by historian Michael M. Sokal of Worcester Polytechnic Institute on Cattell's letters and journals indicates that these stories are questionable. Cattell's account of these events, written many years later, is not supported by his own correspondence and journal entries written at the time the events occurred. For example, Sokal (1981a) points out that Wundt thought highly of Cattell and appointed him as his laboratory assistant in 1886. Also, there is no evidence that Cattell wanted to study individual differences at that time. Third, Cattell introduced Wundt to the use of the typewriter, but he did not give him one.

Cattell found that he was unable to perform Wundtian introspection satisfactorily. He was incapable of fractionating reaction time into various activities, such as perception or choice, and he questioned whether anyone was equal to the task. This attitude did not ingratiate him with Wundt; consequently, Cattell conducted some of his research in his own room.

In spite of their differences, Wundt and Cattell agreed on the value of studying reaction time. Cattell believed it to be useful for the study of various mental operations and for research on individual differences. Many of the now classic reaction-time studies were carried out by Cattell during his three years at Leipzig, and he published several articles on his work before leaving there.

After obtaining his doctorate in 1886, Cattell returned to the United States to lecture on psychology at Bryn Mawr College and the University of Pennsylvania. He then became a lecturer at Cambridge University in England, where he met Francis Galton. The two had similar interests and views on individual differences, and Galton, then at the peak of his fame, broadened Cattell's horizons. "Galton provided [Cattell] with a scientific goal — the measurement of the psychological differences between people" (Sokal, 1987, p. 27). Cattell admired Galton's versatility and his emphasis on measurement and statistics. As a result, Cattell later became one of the first American psychologists to stress quantification, ranking, and ratings, even though personally he was "mathematically illiterate—his addition and subtraction were often inaccurate" (Sokal, 1987, p. 37). Cattell developed the order of merit method (also called the ranking method), which is widely used in psychology, and was the first psychologist to teach the statistical analysis of experimental results.

Wundt did not favor the use of statistical techniques, so it was the influence of Galton on Cattell that resulted in the new American psychology coming to resemble Galton's work more than Wundt's. This also explains why American psychologists began to focus on studies of large groups of subjects, for which statistical comparisons could be made, rather than on individual subjects (the approach favored by Wundt). The initial impact of this shift was felt in educational psychology; the majority of research studies published in this field between 1900 and 1910 dealt with statistical data collected from large groups of subjects (Danziger, 1987).

Cattell was also influenced by Galton's work in eugenics. Cattell argued for the sterilization of delinquents and "defectives," and for giving incentives to the most intelligent and healthiest people if they would intermarry. He offered his seven children $1,000 each if they would marry the sons or daughters of college professors (Sokal, 1971).

In 1888 Cattell became professor of psychology at the University of Pennsylvania, an appointment that was arranged for him by his father. Learning that an endowed chair in philosophy was to be established at the university, the elder Cattell lobbied the school's provost, an old friend, to secure the post for his son. The elder Cattell urged his son to publish more articles to enhance his professional reputation, and he even traveled to Leipzig to obtain Wundt's personal letter of recommendation. He told the provost that because the family was wealthy, salary was not a consideration, and thus Cattell was hired for an extremely low rate of pay (O'Donnell, 1985). Cattell would later claim, inaccurately, that his was the first psychology professorship in the world, but his appointment was actually in philosophy. He stayed at Pennsylvania only three years, then left to become professor of psychology and head of the department at Columbia University, where he remained for twenty-six years.

Because of his dissatisfaction with Hall's *American Journal of Psychology*, he began the *Psychological Review* in 1894 with J. Mark Baldwin. That same year Cattell acquired from Alexander Graham Bell the weekly journal *Science*, which was about to cease publication for lack of funds. Five years later it became the official journal of the American Association for the Advancement of Science (AAAS). In 1906 Cattell began a series of reference works, including *American Men of Science* and *Leaders in Ed-*

ucation. He bought *Popular Science Monthly* in 1900; after selling the name in 1915, he continued to publish it as *Scientific Monthly*. Another weekly, *School and Society*, was established in 1915. The phenomenal organizing and editing work required a great deal of his time and, not surprisingly, his research productivity in psychology declined.

During his career at Columbia, more doctorates in psychology were awarded there than at any other graduate school in the United States. Cattell emphasized the importance of independent work and gave his students considerable freedom to conduct research on their own. He believed that a professor should be independent of both the university and the students, and to make this point he lived forty miles from the campus, opposite the military academy at West Point. He established a laboratory and editorial office at his home and visited the university only certain days each week. Thus he was able to avoid the frequent distractions common to academic life.

This aloofness was only one of several factors that strained relations between Cattell and the university administration. He urged increased faculty participation in university affairs, arguing that many decisions should be made by faculty and not by administrators. To this end, he helped to found the American Association of University Professors (AAUP).

He was not tactful in his dealings with the Columbia University administration. He has been described as difficult to get along with, "un-gentlemanly, irretrievably nasty, and lacking in decency" (Gruber, 1972, p. 300). He did not play by the accepted rules of social conduct, preferring slashing satire to polite persuasion in his attacks on the administration.

On three occasions between 1910 and 1917 the trustees considered retiring Cattell. The deciding blow fell during World War I, when Cattell wrote two letters to United States congressmen protesting the practice of sending draftees into combat. This was an unpopular position to take, but Cattell, characteristically, remained adamant. He was dismissed from Columbia in 1917 on the grounds that he had been disloyal to his country. He sued the university for libel, and although he was awarded $40,000, he was not reinstated. He isolated himself from his colleagues and wrote caustic pamphlets about the university administration. He made many enemies and remained embittered by the experience for the rest of his life.

Cattell never returned to academics. He devoted himself to his publications and to the AAAS and other learned societies. His promotional efforts as a spokesman for psychology to the other sciences elevated psychology to a higher standing in the scientific community.

In 1921 Cattell realized one of his greatest ambitions, the promotion of applied psychology as a business. He organized the Psychological

Corporation, with stock purchased by members of the APA, to provide psychological services to industry, the psychological community, and the public. This organization has grown considerably and is today an international enterprise.

Cattell remained active as an editor and a champion of psychology until his death in 1944. His extremely rapid rise in American psychology deserves mention. He was a professor at the University of Pennsylvania at the age of twenty-eight, chair of the department at Columbia at thirty-one, president of the American Psychological Association at thirty-five, and at forty the first psychologist elected to the National Academy of Sciences.

Mental Testing

We mentioned Cattell's early work on reaction time and his interest in the study of individual differences. The scope of his other work was illustrated in 1914 when a group of his students collected his research papers. They found that, in addition to reaction time and individual differences, his studies dealt with reading and perception, association, psychophysics, and the order of merit method. Although the importance of these areas cannot be denied, Cattell influenced psychology most through his applied work on individual differences and the development and use of mental tests to measure those differences.

In an article published in 1890 he coined the term ***mental tests***, and while at the University of Pennsylvania he had administered a series of such tests to his students. "Psychology," Cattell wrote, "cannot attain the certainty and exactness of the physical sciences unless it rests on a foundation of experiment and measurement. A step in this direction could be made by applying a series of mental tests and measurements to a large number of individuals" (Cattell, 1890, p. 373). This is precisely what he was attempting to do. He continued the testing program at Columbia and collected data from several classes of entering students.

The kinds of tests Cattell used in trying to measure the range and variability of human capacities differed from the intelligence or cognitive ability tests developed later. Intelligence tests used more complex tasks of mental ability. Cattell's tests, like Galton's, dealt primarily with such elementary bodily or sensory-motor measures as dynamometer pressure, rate of movement (how quickly the hand can be moved fifty centimeters), sensation (using the two-point threshold), pressure causing pain (amount of pressure on the forehead necessary to cause pain), just noticeable differences in judging weights, reaction time for sound, time for naming colors, bisection of a fifty-centimeter line, judgment of a ten-second time period, and the number of letters remembered after a single presentation.

By 1901 he had amassed enough data to correlate the test scores with measures of the students' academic performance. The correlations proved disappointingly low, as did intercorrelations among the individual tests. Since similar results had been obtained in E. B. Titchener's laboratory, Cattell concluded that tests of this type were not valid predictors of college achievement, or, by assumption, of intellectual ability.

In 1905 the French psychologist Alfred Binet, together with Victor Henri and Théodore Simon, developed an intelligence test using more complex measures of higher mental abilities. This approach provided what was considered to be an effective measure of intelligence and marked the beginning of the phenomenal growth of intelligence testing.

Despite his failure to measure mental abilities, Cattell's influence on the mental testing movement was strong. His student E. L. Thorndike became a leader in the psychology of mental tests, and for years Columbia University was the center of the testing movement.

Building on Galton's work, Cattell undertook a series of studies to investigate the nature and origin of scientific ability, using his order of merit ranking technique. Stimuli ranked by a number of judges were arranged in a final rank order by calculating the average rating given to each stimulus item. The method was applied to eminent American scientists by having competent persons in each scientific field rank in order a number of their outstanding colleagues. The source book *American Men of Science* emerged from this work. Despite the book's title, it also covered American women of science. The 1910 edition lists nineteen women psychologists, about 10 percent of the total number of psychologists included (O'Donnell, 1985).

Cattell's impact on American psychology was made not through the development of a system of psychology — he had little patience with theory — or through an impressive list of research publications. Rather, his influence was exerted most strongly through his work as an organizer, executive, and administrator of psychological science and practice, and as a vocal link between psychology and the larger scientific community. Cattell became an ambassador of psychology, delivering lectures, editing journals, and promoting the practical applications of the field.

He also contributed to the development of psychology through his students. During his years at Columbia he trained, as we noted, more graduate students in psychology than anyone else in the United States, and several — Robert Woodworth and E. L. Thorndike among them — became prominent in the field. Through his work on mental testing, the measurement of individual differences, and the promotion of applied psychology, Cattell energetically reinforced the functionalist movement in American psychology. When Cattell died, the historian E. G. Boring wrote to one of Cattell's children: "In my opinion your father did more than William

James even to give American psychology its peculiar slant, to make it different from the German psychology from which it stemmed" (Bjork, 1983, p. 105).

Lightner Witmer (1867–1956)

While Hall was changing forever the nature of American psychology by applying it to the child and the schoolroom, and Cattell was applying psychology to the measurement of mental abilities, a student of Cattell's and Wundt's was applying it to the assessment and treatment of certain types of abnormal behavior. Only seventeen years after Wundt founded the new science of psychology, another of his former students was using psychology in a practical manner that was inconsistent with Wundt's intentions. In 1896 Lightner Witmer, who replaced Cattell at the University of Pennsylvania and insisted that his lecture room be kept at sixty-eight degrees, opened the world's first psychology clinic, and thereby began the field he called clinical psychology.

Witmer went on to offer the first college course on clinical psychology and started the first journal, called *Psychological Clinic*, which he edited for twenty-nine years. He was one of those pioneers of the functionalist approach to psychology who believed that the new science should be used to help people solve problems rather than to study the contents of their minds.

It is important to note that what Witmer practiced in his psychology clinic was not clinical psychology as it is known today. We shall see that Witmer's work was devoted to the assessment and treatment of behavioral and learning problems in school children, an applied specialty area now called *school psychology*. Modern *clinical psychology* deals with a wider range of psychological disorders, from mild to severe, in people of all ages. Although Witmer was instrumental in the development of clinical psychology, and used that label freely, the field has broadened far beyond what he envisioned.

The Life of Witmer

Born in 1867 in Philadelphia, Pennsylvania, Lightner Witmer was the son of a prosperous pharmacist who stressed to his three children the importance of education. Witmer's brother and sister became medical doctors, and Witmer received his Ph.D. from Wilhelm Wundt at Leipzig. Always an excellent student, Witmer first attended a private school, then entered the University of Pennsylvania in 1884. After graduation he taught history and English at a private school in Philadelphia before enrolling in law courses at the University of Pennsylvania.

He apparently had no thought of a career in psychology but, for reasons that remain obscure, he took courses in experimental psychology from Cattell and was given a graduate assistantship in the psychology department. Witmer began research studies on individual differences in reaction time under Cattell's guidance and expected to earn his Ph.D. at Pennsylvania. Cattell had other plans. He thought so highly of Witmer that he chose him to be his successor when he departed for Columbia University. It was a remarkable opportunity for the young man, but Cattell placed one condition on the appointment: Witmer would have to go to Leipzig to earn his doctorate from Wundt. The prestige of a German Ph.D. was still paramount, and so Witmer agreed to go.

He studied with Wundt, and also with Oswald Külpe; one of his classmates, recently arrived from England, was E. B. Titchener. Witmer was not impressed with Wundt's approach to research, and he later commented that he got nothing out of his Leipzig experience except his degree. Wundt refused to allow Witmer to continue the reaction-time work he had begun with Cattell and forced him to pursue traditional introspective research on conscious contents.

Witmer was critical of what he called Wundt's "slovenly research methods," describing how Wundt had made Titchener "do over again an investigation . . . because the results obtained by Titchener were not such as he, Wundt, had anticipated. Also, he excluded me as a subject . . . because in his opinion my sensory reaction to sound and touch was too short to be a true sensory reaction" (O'Donnell, 1985, p. 35).

Nevertheless, Witmer received his degree and returned to his new position at the University of Pennsylvania in the summer of 1892, the same time Titchener got his degree and went to Cornell, and that another student of Wundt's, Hugo Münsterberg, was brought to Harvard by William James. Also in that year Hall started the American Psychological Association, with Witmer as one of its charter members. It was the time when the functionalist and applied spirits had begun to take hold of American psychology.

For the next two years Witmer worked as an experimental psychologist, conducting research and presenting papers on individual differences and on the psychology of pain. All the while, however, he was searching for ways to apply psychology to abnormal behavior. The impetus to do that came one day in March of 1896, as a result of an incident that had its origins in the economic circumstances mentioned earlier — the money available in the expanding field of public education.

Many state boards of education were establishing departments of pedagogy (instruction in the principles and methods of teaching) in their colleges and universities, and psychologists were being called on to offer courses to the growing numbers of education majors as well as public school teachers working for advanced degrees. Psychologists were also urged to shift the focus of their laboratory research, to find ways to train students to become educational psychologists. Psychology departments profited handsomely from this sudden influx of students, because then, as now, departmental budgets were contingent on enrollments.

The University of Pennsylvania established courses for public school teachers in 1894, and Witmer taught some of them. Two years later a student, Margaret Maguire, consulted Witmer about the problems she was having with one of her pupils, a fourteen-year-old boy who was having difficulty learning to spell, although he did well in some other subjects. Could psychologists help solve this problem? "It appeared to me," Witmer wrote, "that if psychology was worth anything to me or to others, it should be able to assist in a retarded case of this kind" (McReynolds, 1987, p. 853). He organized a primitive clinic and thus began his lifelong work.

Within a few months Witmer was preparing courses on methods of treating mentally defective, blind, and disturbed children, and he published an article on that theme, called "Practical Work in Psychology," in the journal *Pediatrics*. He presented a paper on the topic at the annual meeting of the APA, and it was there that he used the term *clinical psychology* for the first time. In 1907 he founded the journal *Psychological Clinic*, which became the first, and for many years the only, journal in the field. In its first issue Witmer proposed a new application of psychology — indeed a new profession — to be called clinical psychology. The following year he established a boarding school for retarded and disturbed children, and in 1909 his university clinic expanded and was established as a separate administrative unit.

Witmer remained at the University of Pennsylvania throughout his working life, teaching, promoting, and practicing his clinical psychology. He retired from the university in 1937 and died in 1956 at the age of 89, the last of the small group of psychologists who had met in G. Stanley Hall's study in 1892 to found the American Psychological Association.

Psychology Clinics

As the world's first clinical psychologist, Witmer had no examples or precedents on which to base his actions, and he developed his own methods of diagnosis and treatment as he went along. With his first case, the boy who had trouble spelling, Witmer examined the child's level of intelligence, reasoning, and reading ability and concluded that the last was deficient. After exhaustive analyses over many hours Witmer concluded that the boy was suffering from what Witmer called visual verbal amnesia. Although the child could recall geometric figures, he had trouble remembering words. Witmer developed an intensive remedial program that produced some improvement, but the boy never became proficient at reading or spelling.

Teachers sent to Witmer's new clinic many other children with a broad spectrum of deficiencies and problems, including hyperactivity, various learning disabilities, and inadequate speech or motor development. As Witmer's experience became broader, he developed standard programs of assessment and treatment, and he added physicians, social workers, and more psychologists to his staff.

Witmer recognized that medical problems could interfere with psychological functioning, and so he had a physician examine the children to determine if malnutrition or visual and hearing defects were contributing to any child's difficulties. The patients were tested and interviewed extensively by psychologists, while social workers prepared case histories on their family backgrounds.

At first, Witmer believed that genetic factors were largely responsible for many of the behavioral disturbances and cognitive deficits he saw, but he later realized, as his clinical experience grew, that environmental factors were more important. He emphasized the need to provide a variety of sensory experiences early in a child's life, anticipating the Head Start enrichment programs of more recent times. He also believed in direct intervention in the lives of his patients and their families, arguing that if home and school conditions were changed for the better, so too might a child's behavior.

The growth in public education offered the new psychology ample opportunities — and ample rewards — for those who took its methods and findings out of the academic laboratory. Witmer's example was followed and built on by many other psychologists. By 1914 nearly twenty psychological clinics were in operation in the United States, the majority of them patterned on Witmer's clinic. In addition, the students he trained spread his approach, teaching the next generation of students about clinical work.

Witmer was also influential in the area of special education, training many of the early workers in these fields. One of his students, Morris Viteles, extended Witmer's work by establishing a clinic in 1920 that was devoted to vocational guidance, the first such facility in the United States. Others expanded clinical work to include adults. In addition, newer approaches to psychotherapy developed by Sigmund Freud and his followers moved the field considerably beyond its origins. This growth, which occurs naturally in every field, in no way detracts from the importance of Lightner Witmer in the development of clinical psychology.

Walter Dill Scott (1869–1955)

Another student of Wundt, Walter Dill Scott, left the world of pure introspective psychology he had learned at Leipzig to apply the new science to advertising and business. A college football player and would-be missionary, Scott dedicated much of his adult life to making the marketplace and the workplace more efficient, and to determining how business leaders could motivate both employees and consumers.

Scott's work reflects functional psychology's growing concern with the practical. "Upon returning from Wundt's Leipzig to turn-of-the-century Chicago, Scott's publications shifted from Germanic theorizing to American usefulness. Instead of explaining motives and impulses in general, Scott described how to influence people, including consumers, lecture audiences, and workers" (Von Mayrhauser, 1989, p. 61).

Scott compiled an impressive list of firsts. He was the first person to apply psychology to advertising and to personnel selection and management, the first to hold the title of professor of applied psychology, founder of the first psychological consulting company, and the first psychologist to receive the Distinguished Service Medal from the United States Army.

The Life of Scott

Walter Dill Scott was born on a farm in Illinois in 1869 and became dedicated to the idea of increased efficiency at the age of twelve while plowing a field. Because his father was often ill, the boy essentially ran the small family farm. One day he paused at the end of a furrow he had plowed to give his two horses a rest. Staring at the buildings of Illinois State Normal University in the distance, he suddenly realized that if he was ever going to achieve anything, he would have to stop wasting time. Here he was losing ten minutes out of every hour of plowing to rest the horses! That added up to about an hour and a half every day, time he could put to use reading and studying. From that day on, Scott always carried at least one book with him and read every spare moment.

To earn his college tuition, he picked and canned blackberries, salvaged scrap metal to sell, and took on odd jobs. He saved some of the money and bought books with the rest. At the age of nineteen he enrolled at Illinois State Normal University and began his long journey away from the farm. Two years later he won a scholarship to Northwestern University in Evanston, Illinois, where he took tutoring jobs to make extra money, played varsity football, met the woman he would marry, and decided to become a missionary to China.

That career meant three additional years of education, however, and by the time Scott graduated from a Chicago theological seminary and was prepared to leave for China, he found there were no vacancies. China was full. It was then that he thought of a career in psychology. He had taken one course in the field and enjoyed it. And he had read magazine articles about the new science and the laboratory Wundt had established at Leipzig. Through his scholarships, tutoring, and frugal living, Scott had saved several thousand dollars, enough not only to go to Germany but also to get married.

On July 21, 1898, Scott and his bride departed. While he studied under Wundt at Leipzig, Mrs. Scott worked on her Ph.D. in literature at the University of Halle, twenty miles away. They saw each other on weekends. Both received their doctoral degrees two years later and returned home, where Scott joined the faculty at Northwestern University as an instructor of psychology and pedagogy. Scott was, therefore, already under the influence of the trend toward applying psychology to problems of education.

His switch to a new and different field of application came in 1902 when a leader in the field of advertising sought out Scott, who had been recommended by a former professor, and asked him to apply psychological principles to advertising to make it more effective. Scott was intrigued by the idea. In keeping with the spirit of American functionalism, he had already moved away from Wundtian psychology and had been looking for a way to make psychology more applicable to real-world concerns. Now he had his chance.

He wrote *The Theory and Practice of Advertising*, the first book on the topic, and followed it with a torrent of magazine articles and books as his expertise, reputation, and contacts in the business community widened. He then turned his attention to problems of personnel selection and management. In 1905 he was promoted to professor at Northwestern, and in 1909 became professor of advertising in the university's school of commerce. In 1916 he was appointed professor of applied psychology and director of the bureau of salesmanship research at Carnegie Technical University in Pittsburgh.

In 1917, when the United States entered World War I, Scott offered his skills to the army to help select military personnel. At first, he and his proposals were not well received; not everyone was convinced of the practical value of psychology. The army general to whom Scott spoke was also suspicious of professors, almost exploding with rage. "He said it was his function to see that college professors did not get in the way of progress, that we were at war with Germany and that we had no time to fool with experiments; that many people felt that the army was a great dog on which to try experiments, and that he would see that no college professor did that" (Von Mayrhauser, 1989, p. 65). Scott calmed the irate man, took him to lunch, and persuaded him of the value of his selection techniques. By the end of the war he had proved his point, and the army awarded him the Distinguished Service Medal, the highest honor bestowed on civilians.

In 1919 Scott formed his own company (called, imaginatively, The Scott Company), which provided consulting services to more than forty major corporations that sought help with personnel selection and methods for increasing worker efficiency. A year later he became president of Northwestern University, and retired in 1939.

Advertising and Personnel Selection

The imprint of Scott's training in Wundtian experimental psychology and his attempt to extend it into the realm of the practical are both evident in Scott's early writings on advertising. He wrote, for example, that the sense organs were the

> windows of the soul. The more sensations we receive from an object, the better we know it. The function of the nervous system is to make us aware of the sights, sounds, feelings, tastes, et cetera, of the objects in our environment. The nervous system which does not respond to sound or to any other sensible quality is defective.
>
> Advertisements are sometimes spoken of as the nervous system of the business world. The advertisement of musical instruments which contains nothing to awaken images of sounds is a defective advertisement.... As our nervous system is arranged to give us all the possible sensations from every object, so the advertisement which is comparable to the nervous system must awaken in the reader as many different kinds of images as the object itself can excite. (Jacobson, 1951, p. 75)

Scott argued that consumers are nonrational and easily influenced, and he focused on emotion and sympathy as important factors in heightening this suggestibility. He also believed, as was common then, that women were more easily influenced than men by ads that played on their emotions and sentimentality. Applying what he called the law of suggestibility to advertising, he recommended that companies use direct commands — such as "Use Pears Soap" — to sell their products. He also promoted return coupons because they required specific and direct action on the part of consumers, who had to tear the coupon out of the magazine or newspaper, fill it in, and mail it to receive a free sample. Both techniques — direct commands and coupon returns — were quickly adopted by advertisers and were in widespread use by 1910 (Kuna, 1976).

For his work on employee selection, especially for salespersons, executives, and military personnel, Scott developed rating scales and group tests to measure the characteristics shown by those who were already successful in those occupations. Like Witmer in clinical psychology, Scott had no prior work on which to base his approach, so he had to develop his own. He questioned superior officers in the army and supervisors in business, asking them to construct lists of their subordinates and to place them in categories signifying appearance, demeanor, sincerity, productivity, character, and value to the organization. Job applicants were then ranked on the qualities found to be necessary for successful performance of the job in question, a procedure not so different from that in use today.

Scott developed psychological tests to measure intelligence and other abilities, but instead of assessing each applicant individually, as was standard, he constructed tests that could be administered to groups. Business and the military demanded that large numbers of candidates be assessed and evaluated rapidly, and it was more efficient and less expensive to test them in groups.

Scott's tests differed in another way from those being developed by Cattell and others. Scott was not attempting to measure the nature of a person's general intelligence as a content or faculty, but rather how that person used his or her intelligence. In other words, he wanted to measure how intelligence functioned in a real-world setting. He defined intelligence not in terms of specific cognitive abilities but in practical terms such as judgment, quickness, and accuracy — the characteristics needed to perform well on a job. He was interested only in how the applicants' test scores compared with the scores of employees already successful on the job, not in what those scores might represent in terms of mental content. This practical approach to testing typified the man and all of his work.

Scott, like Witmer, has received only passing attention in the history of psychology. There are several reasons for this relative neglect. Like most applied psychologists, Scott formulated no theories, founded no school of thought, trained no loyal core of students to continue his work, conducted little pure research, and published rarely in the mainstream journals of the day. His work for private corporations and the military was strictly practical, designed to satisfy their needs. In addition, many academic psychologists, particularly those in tenured positions with major universities and well-funded laboratories, tended to discount the work of applied psychologists, believing that it did not contribute to the advancement of psychology as a science.

Scott and other applied psychologists disputed this position. They saw no conflict between useful applications and the advancement of the science. Indeed, they believed that "psychology's empirical progress depended greatly upon the results of extra-academic experience" (Von Mayrhauser, 1989, p. 63). Applied psychologists argued that bringing psychology before the public demonstrated its worth, which, in turn, increased the recognition of the importance of psychological research in the universities. Thus, the early applied psychologists were reflecting the legacy and impact of the functionalist spirit in American psychology, to make that psychology useful.

Hugo Münsterberg (1863–1916)

Hugo Münsterberg, the stereotypical German professor, was for a time a phenomenal success in American psychology and the psychologist best known to the public. He wrote hundreds of popular magazine articles and almost two dozen books. He was a frequent visitor to the White House as the guest of two American presidents, Theodore Roosevelt and William Howard Taft. Münsterberg was sought as a consultant by business and government leaders and counted among his acquaintances the rich and famous and powerful, including Germany's Kaiser Wilhelm, steel magnate Andrew Carnegie, philosopher Bertrand Russell, as well as movie stars and intellectuals.

He was — for a time — an honored professor at Harvard University who was elected to the presidency of both the American Psychological Association and the American Philosophical Association. He was considered to be a founder of applied psychology and was one of only two psychologists accused of being a spy. He has been described as the "most prolific propagandizer for applied psychology," one who "published volumes on educational, legal, industrial, medical, and cultural psychology" (O'Donnell, 1985, p. 225). And according to his biographer, Münsterberg was also a highly successful publicist, "blessed with an uncanny flair for the sensational, and his life can be read as a series of promotions — of himself, his science, and his [German] fatherland" (Hale, 1980, p. 3).

Hugo Münsterberg was influential in promoting several applied specialties including forensic psychology, clinical psychology, and industrial psychology.

Toward the end of his life, Münsterberg became a figure of scorn and ridicule, the subject of newspaper cartoons and caricatures, and an embarrassment to the university he had served for so many years. When he died in 1916 there were no eulogies for the man who had once been called a giant of American psychology.

The Life of Münsterberg

In 1882, at the age of nineteen, Münsterberg left his birthplace in Danzig, Germany, and traveled south to Leipzig, intending to study medicine. But once he had taken a course with Wilhelm Wundt, his career plans changed abruptly. The new psychology excited him and offered opportunities that medical research and practice could not. He received his Ph.D. from Wundt in 1885 and earned an M.D. at the University of Heidelberg two years later, to be better equipped for a career in academic research. He took a teaching job at the University of Freiburg and set up a laboratory in his home, at his own expense, because there were no facilities at the university.

Münsterberg published a book and several articles on his experimental research in psychophysics, which Wundt criticized because they dealt with cognitive contents of the mind, to the exclusion of feeling states. At the same time, Münsterberg's work attracted a loyal band of followers, and students from Germany and beyond flocked to his laboratory. He seemed to be well on his way to securing a professorship at a major university and a reputation as a respected scholar.

William James lured him from this path in 1892 by offering him the chance to become the highly paid director of the psychology laboratory at Harvard University. James used flattery in his appeal, writing to Münsterberg that Harvard was the greatest university in all of the United States and needed a genius to run the laboratory in such a way that it would retain its position of primacy in psychology. Münsterberg would have preferred to stay in Germany, but ambition led him to accept James's offer.

Münsterberg did not make the transition from Germany to the United States and from pure experimental psychology to applied psychology quickly or easily. At first he disapproved of the spread of applied psychology and chided university administrators for paying scholars so little that they were forced to make a living by turning to more practical pursuits. He criticized those American psychologists who wrote popular books for lay audiences, gave lectures to business leaders, and offered, for a fee, their services as experts. Before long, however, Münsterberg would be doing all of these things.

After ten years in the United States, and perhaps realizing by then that no German university was going to offer him a professorship, he wrote his first book in English. Called *American Traits* (1902), it was a psychological, social, and cultural analysis of American society. Münsterberg was a fast and gifted writer, able to dictate to a secretary a highly readable four-hundred-page book in no more than a month. William James commented that Münsterberg's brain never got tired. E. B. Titchener observed that Münsterberg had the "fatal gift of writing easily — fatal especially in science, and most of all in a young science, where accuracy is the one thing needful" (Hale, 1980, p. 23).

The enthusiastic response to Münsterberg's book encouraged him to write more for general audiences than for his colleagues, and he soon was publishing in popular magazines rather than professional journals. He turned away from psychophysical research and the contents of the mind, writing instead about the everyday activities to which psychologists could contribute. His books and articles dealt with courtroom trials and the criminal justice system, advertising of consumer products, vocational counseling, mental health and psychotherapy, education, industrial psychology, and the psychology of motion pictures. He produced correspondence courses on learning and business, and even made a series of films of mental tests that were shown in movie theaters.

Münsterberg never hesitated to involve himself in controversial issues. During the course of a sensational murder trial, he administered almost one hundred mental tests to the confessed killer of eighteen people who had accused a labor union leader of paying for the murders. On the basis of the results of those tests, which included a word association test (dubbed by the press a "lying machine"), Münsterberg announced publicly — before the jury had reached its verdict in the labor leader's trial — that the murderer's statement implicating the labor leader was true. The jury, however, acquitted the labor leader, which was awkward for Münsterberg; one newspaper took to calling him "Professor Monsterwork."

In 1908 Münsterberg became involved in the nationwide fight over the movement to prohibit the sale of alcoholic beverages. He argued against prohibition, citing his expertise as a psychologist, and took the position that alcohol in moderation was beneficial. German-American beer brewers, including Adolphus Busch and Gustave Pabst, were delighted to have Münsterberg's support, and they made sizable financial contributions to Münsterberg's efforts to bolster Germany's image in the United States. In an unfortunate and suspicious bit of timing, Busch donated $50,000 for Münsterberg's proposed Germanic Museum only a few weeks after Münsterberg published an article in *McClure's Magazine* denouncing the idea of prohibition. The coincidence received a great deal of attention in the newspapers and popular magazines.

Münsterberg's beliefs about women were also hard to ignore. Although he was supportive of several women graduate students at Harvard, including Mary Whiton Calkins, he believed that graduate work was too rigorous for most women. His view was that women should not be trained for careers, because that would take them away from the home. He also argued that women should not teach in the public schools, because they could not teach as well as men and were poor role models for boys. And he believed that women should not be allowed to serve on juries because they were incapable of rational deliberation; that remark garnered international headlines.

The president of Harvard University, and most of Münsterberg's colleagues, were not pleased with this sensationalism, nor did they approve of his interest in applying psychology to practical problems. Strained relations reached the breaking point over Münsterberg's continuing and strident defense of his German homeland during World War I; war had broken out in Europe in 1914, although the U.S. did not enter the conflict directly until 1917. American public opinion was decidedly anti-German. Germany was the aggressor in a war that had already cost millions of lives, and Münsterberg was taking an increasingly unpopular position.

He wrote numerous articles defending Germany, and he openly maintained contact with the German ambassador in Washington, D.C., and the German foreign office in Berlin. Newspapers reported that Münsterberg was a secret agent, a spy, and a high-ranking military officer. The Boston newspapers called for his resignation from Harvard. His neighbors suspected that the pigeons his daughter was seen feeding in the back yard were being used to carry messages to other spies. A Harvard alumnus living in London offered the university $10 million if it would fire Münsterberg.

Münsterberg received death threats in the mail and was snubbed by his colleagues. The ostracism and increasingly virulent attacks broke his spirit. But on December 16, 1916, the morning newspapers brought speculations about peace talks in Europe. "By spring we shall have peace," he announced to his wife (Münsterberg, 1922, p. 302). He set off on foot through deep snows on that cold, blustery day to teach his morning class. By the time he reached the lecture hall he felt exhausted. Münsterberg entered the classroom and fell to the floor without saying a word. He died instantly of a massive stroke.

Forensic Psychology and Other Applied Pursuits

The extremes of Münsterberg's behavior and beliefs do not diminish the importance of his work in applied psychology. No one else contributed so much to the advancement of applied psychology in general and to its development in the areas of forensic psychology, clinical psychology, and industrial psychology. For all his faults, Münsterberg remains one of the most influential figures in the development of the uniquely American functional approach to psychology.

The first applied area in which Münsterberg worked, forensic psychology, deals with psychology and the law. He wrote a series of magazine articles on such topics as the use of hypnosis in the questioning of suspects, ways to prevent crime, detection of guilty persons through the use of mental tests, and the untrustworthiness of eyewitness testimony. He was particularly interested in the latter, that is, in the fallibility of human perception of an event such as a crime and the subsequent recollection of the event. He described research on simulated crimes in which witnesses were asked, immediately after seeing the crime, to describe what had occurred. The subjects could not agree on the details of what they had witnessed, even though the scene was still fresh in their memories. How accurate can such testimony be in a courtroom, Münsterberg asked, since the event under discussion would have taken place many months earlier?

In 1908 he published *On the Witness Stand*, which described the problems with eyewitness testimony. It also considered other psychological factors that can affect the outcome of a trial, such as false confessions, the power of suggestion in the questioning of witnesses, and the use of physiological measurements (heart rate, blood pressure, skin resistance) to detect heightened emotional states in a suspect or defendant. The book was reprinted many times, as recently as 1976, almost seventy years after its publication.

The late 1970s brought a resurgence of interest in the issues Münsterberg raised (see Loftus, 1979; Loftus & Monahan, 1980), and the American Psychology–Law Society was established as a division of the American Psychological Association to foster basic and applied research on forensic psychology.

Münsterberg published a book entitled *Psychotherapy* in 1909, beginning work in an entirely different applied area. He treated patients in his laboratory rather than in a clinic, and he never charged a fee. He relied heavily on the authority of his position as a therapist and did not hesitate to make direct suggestions to his patients about how they could be cured. Mental illness, he believed, was a problem of behavioral maladjustment, not something that was attributable to some deep underlying unconscious conflict as Sigmund Freud claimed. Münsterberg opposed Freud's views on mental health, particularly the emphasis on sexual disturbances as the primary cause of emotional problems. Münsterberg did agree, however, that in some cases sexual matters might be at the root of a problem.

Münsterberg's therapeutic approach was to force the patient's disturbing ideas out of awareness, to suppress those behaviors that were undesirable or troubling, and to urge the patient to forget — to put aside — the emotional difficulty. He treated a variety of problems, including alcoholism, drug abuse, hallucinations, obsessive thoughts, phobias, and sexual disorders. He did not take as patients psychotic individuals or those with neurologically based disorders, believing that his form of psychotherapy was ineffective with such cases. For a time he used hypnosis as a method of treatment but stopped the practice after a woman he was treating threatened him with a gun. The story made the newspapers, and Harvard's president demanded that Münsterberg refrain from hypnotizing women.

His book on psychotherapy did much to bring the field of clinical psychology to public attention, but it was not well received by Lightner Witmer, who had opened his clinic at the University of Pennsylvania several years before. Witmer had never achieved — nor had he sought — the kind of popular acclaim Münsterberg thrived on. In an article published in his journal, *Psychological Clinic*, Witmer complained that Münsterberg had "cheapened" the profession by hawking claims of cures "in the marketplace." He called Münsterberg little better than a faith healer because of the "jaunty way in which the professor of psychology at [Harvard] goes about the country, claiming to have treated in his psychological laboratory hundreds and hundreds of cases of this or that form of nervous disorder" (Hale, 1980, p. 110).

At the same time, Münsterberg was systematizing, developing, and promoting yet another field, that of industrial psychology. He embarked on this work in 1909 with an article entitled "Psychology and the Market." It covered several areas to which he believed psychology could contribute, namely vocational guidance, advertising, personnel management, mental testing, employee motivation, and the effects on job performance of fatigue and monotony. His viewpoint was characteristically a broad one, dealing with all aspects and problems of business, from selecting the right workers to performing the job efficiently to marketing the finished product.

Münsterberg was hired as a consultant by several companies, and for them he undertook considerable research. He published his findings in *Psychology and Industrial Efficiency* (1913), another book written for the general public. It became so successful that it made the best-seller lists. He argued that the best way to increase efficiency on the job and assure harmony in the workplace was to select workers for positions that fit their mental and emotional abilities. How could employers best accomplish this? Through the development of psychological selection techniques, such as mental tests and job simulations in which the applicants' various skills and abilities could be assessed.

Münsterberg conducted research on such diverse occupations as ship's captain, streetcar driver, telephone operator, and salesperson, showing how his selection methods brought about improvements in job performance. With regard to problems of efficiency, he described the results of studies that showed, for example, that talking while working decreased efficiency. His solution was not to ban conversation among workers (that, he recognized, would engender hostility), but to design the workplace so that it would be difficult for workers to talk to one another. That goal could be achieved by increasing the distance between machines or separating the work spaces with partitions.

Largely because of Münsterberg's promotional efforts, the field of industrial psychology exerted an ever-widening impact on the world of work. Münsterberg proposed to America's President Woodrow Wilson and to the German Kaiser that their governments establish departments to sponsor research on the applications of psychology to industry. Both leaders indicated interest in the idea, but the onset of war prevented its implementation.

Like other pioneers in the field, Münsterberg formulated no theories, started no new school of thought, and—once he began work in applied psychology—conducted no pure academic research. He insisted that his research serve a definite purpose, that it be functional and oriented toward helping people in some way. Although he had been trained by Wilhelm Wundt in the technique of introspection, he criticized those psychologists who clung to that technique and chastised colleagues who were unwilling to use the findings and methods of psychology for the betterment of humanity.

Münsterberg was not a formal adherent of the functionalist definition of psychology, and he consistently refused to define his own approach to psychology, believing that to do so would limit its usefulness. If there was one theme that characterized Münsterberg's colorful, bombastic, and controversial career, it was that psychology must be useful. In that sense he was, for all his Germanic temperament, the quintessential American psychologist, reflecting and demonstrating the spirit of the times. It is to Münsterberg's credit that applied psychology, which he did so much to found at the beginning of the twentieth century, has grown to become a dominant force in American psychology as the twenty-first century draws near.

Specialties in Applied Psychology

We have reviewed how psychology, under the influence of functionalism, began to be applied to real-world problems early in the twentieth century.

In Chapter 10 we will see that John B. Watson's behaviorism also contributed to the growth of this applied trend. Watson, after leaving the academic world, became a popular applied psychologist. By then, psychology could no longer be restricted to the laboratory world of pure science where Wundt and Titchener had tried valiantly to keep it.

Although the applied movement in psychology dates its beginnings to the years from the turn of the century to World War I, its initial progress was relatively slow. But after America's entry into the war in 1917, applied psychologists were called upon to deal with immediate and practical problems. Psychology was thrust visibly into the public eye. Both psychologists and non-psychologists recognized that the principles and methods of the field could be used to improve human welfare. Cattell commented that the war put psychology "on the map and on the front page" (O'Donnell, 1985, p. 239). Hall wrote that the war had "given applied psychology a tremendous impulse. This will, on the whole, do good for psychology... [we] must not try to be too pure" (Hall, 1919, p. 48). Some journals, such as the *Journal of Experimental Psychology*, ceased publication during the war years, but the *Journal of Applied Psychology* thrived.

In the 1920s, after the war, psychology became a "national mania" (Dennis, 1984, p. 23). People throughout the United States came to believe that psychologists were capable of fixing everything from marital disharmony and job dissatisfaction to marketing deodorant and mouthwash. This increasing clamor for solutions drew more psychologists away from pure research and into applied areas. In the 1921 edition of Cattell's *American Men of Science*, more than 75 percent of the psychologists listed said they were engaged in work of an applied nature; in 1910 the figure had been 50 percent (O'Donnell, 1985). The meetings of the New York branch of the APA in the early 1920s showed a substantial increase from prewar days in the number of papers dealing with applied research (Benjamin, 1991).

By the late 1920s, however, and during the decade of the worldwide economic depression in the 1930s, applied psychology was being attacked for its failure to live up to its promise. Business leaders, for example, complained that industrial psychology, although useful, was not curing all their ills. Bad experiences with poorly designed selection tests had led them to hire some unproductive workers.

Perhaps the expectations of psychologists and their clients had been too high, but whatever the reason, a disenchantment with applied psychology set in. One of the most vocal critics was Grace Adams, who had been one of Titchener's students. In "The Decline of Psychology in America," an article published in a popular magazine, Adams argued that psychology had "forsaken its scientific roots so that individual psychologists might achieve popularity and prosperity." She accused psychologists of "masquerading as scientists" and failing to address the economic and social problems brought on by the economic depression (Benjamin, 1986, p. 944). The *New York Times* and other influential newspapers criticized psychologists for promising more than could be delivered and for failing to ameliorate the malaise created by the depression. The number of popular articles about psychological issues declined after 1929, and psychology's image and promise were not restored until 1941, after the United States entered World War II. Thus we see another example of war as a contextual influence on the development of psychology.

World War II provided another set of pressing problems for psychology to solve, and it revived and extended psychology's general influence. Fully 25 percent of all American psychologists were directly involved in the war effort, and many others made indirect contributions through research and writing. Ironically, the war also revived a flagging psychology in Germany, where the field had fallen into decline after the Nazis expelled all Jewish psychologists from their jobs. The needs of the German military created a fresh demand for psychologists to assist in the selection of officers, pilots, submariners, and other specialists (Geuter, 1987).

In the years since the end of the war in 1945, American psychology as a whole has experienced the most dramatic period of growth in its history. Within the field the most significant growth occurred in the applied areas. Applied psychology outstripped the academic, research-oriented side of psychology that for many years was predominant. No longer was it true that the majority of psychologists belonged to college or university faculties or worked as experimental psychologists. Before World War II almost 70 percent of the doctorates awarded in psychology were in experimental psychology; by 1960 that figure was 25 percent, and by 1984 it had dropped to 8 percent (Goodstein, 1988).

In 1940, just before the United States entered the war, 75 percent of all psychologists worked in academic settings. By 1962 the number had fallen to 47 percent and by 1980 to 42 percent (Gilgen, 1982). One result has been a shift of power within the American Psychological Association, where applied psychologists (particularly clinical psychologists) have assumed a commanding position. A number of the academic and scientific, research-oriented members, chafing under the dominance of the clinicians, formed their own organization, the American Psychological Society (APS), in 1988. As of 1991 it had a membership of more than 12,000.

We complete our coverage of the legacy of functionalism by discussing briefly three areas of applied psychology with the deepest historical

Alfred Binet (shown here with his daughters) developed the first truly psychological test of mental ability, which has evolved into the widely used Stanford–Binet Intelligence Scale.

roots: psychological testing, industrial/organizational psychology, and clinical psychology. Testing is covered first because much of the development of the other two areas derived from it.

The Psychological Testing Movement

In our coverage of the work of Francis Galton and James McKeen Cattell, we discussed the origins of the mental testing movement. It was Cattell who coined the term *mental tests*, but it remained for Alfred Binet, an independently wealthy and self-taught French psychologist, to develop the first truly psychological test of mental ability.

Binet disagreed with the approach taken by Galton and Cattell, which relied on tests of sensory-motor processes to measure intelligence. He believed that assessment of such cognitive functions as memory, attention, imagination, and comprehension would provide a better measure of intelligence. The opportunity to prove his point came in response to a practical need. In 1904 the French ministry of public instruction appointed a commission to study the learning abilities of children who were having difficulties in school. Binet and a psychiatrist, Théodore Simon, were appointed to the commission, and together they investigated the kinds of intellectual tasks that could be mastered by most children at different ages.

From their delineation of these tasks they constructed the first test of intelligence. It consisted of thirty problems arranged in ascending order of difficulty, and it focused on three cognitive functions: judgment, comprehension, and reasoning. Three years later, in 1908, the test was revised and expanded, and the concept of mental age was introduced. ***Mental age*** was described as the age at which children of average ability could perform certain tasks. For example, if a child with a chronological age of four passed all the tests that the sample of average five-year-olds had passed, that four-year-old child was assigned a mental age of five. A third revision of the test was prepared in 1911, but after Binet's death the development of the test and of intelligence testing in general shifted to the United States.

The test was introduced in the United States by Henry Goddard, a student of G. Stanley Hall and a psychologist at a school for mentally retarded children in Vineland, New Jersey. Goddard called his translation of the test the *Binet–Simon Measuring Scale for Intelligence*.

In 1916 Lewis M. Terman, who had also studied with Hall, developed a version of the test that has since become a standard. He named it the *Stanford–Binet*, after the university with which he was affiliated, and adopted the concept of the ***intelligence quotient (IQ)***. The IQ measure, defined as the ratio between mental age and chronological age, had originally been proposed by the German psychologist William Stern. The *Stanford–Binet* has undergone several revisions and continues to be widely used.

On the day the United States entered World War I, a meeting of Titchener's Society of Experimental Psychologists was being held at Harvard University. The president of the APA, Robert Yerkes, was in attendance. Yerkes urged the psychologists present to consider how psychology could aid in the war effort. Titchener demurred, explaining that he was a British subject; perhaps it is more likely that Titchener declined to involve himself in war work because of his dislike of applying psychology to practical problems. He may have feared that the efforts of psychologists to help win the war would cause them to "trade a science for a technology" (O'Donnell, 1979, p. 289).

The army was faced with the problem of assessing the intelligence of great numbers of recruits, in order to screen and classify them and assign them to suitable tasks. The *Stanford–Binet* is an individual test of intelligence, and a highly trained person is required to administer it properly. Such a test cannot be used for any large-scale testing program where many persons must be tested in a short span of time. For that purpose, a group test that is simple to administer is necessary.

Yerkes, given an army commission as a major, assembled a staff of forty psychologists to develop a group intelligence test. They examined a number of tests, none of which was in general use, and selected as a model one developed by Arthur S. Otis, who had studied with Terman. Otis had introduced the multiple-choice question. The Yerkes group prepared the *Army Alpha* and *Army Beta* tests, based on Otis's test. The *Beta* was a version of the *Alpha* specifically for use with non-English-speaking and illiterate persons. Instructions to those taking the *Beta* were given by demonstration or pantomime, rather than orally or in writing.

The establishment of the testing program proceeded slowly, and the formal order to initiate testing was not given until three months before the war ended. More than one million men were tested, but the results were no longer needed by the military. Although the program had little effect on the war effort, it had a major impact on psychology. The attendant publicity did a great deal to enhance the stature of psychology and the tests became the prototypes for many that were devised later.

Development and use of group personality testing was also spurred by the war effort. Prior to that time only limited attempts had been made to assess personality. In the closing years of the nineteenth century the German psychiatrist Emil Kraepelin had used what he called a free association test, in which a patient responded to a stimulus word with the first word that came to mind. The technique had been originated by Galton. In 1910 Carl Jung had developed a similar device, the word-association test, which he used to measure complexes in his patients. Both of these were individual personality tests. When the army expressed interest in separating out recruits who were highly neurotic, Robert Woodworth constructed the *Personal Data Sheet*, a self-report inventory on which respondents indicated the neurotic symptoms that applied to them. Like the *Army Alpha* and *Army Beta*, the *Personal Data Sheet* saw little actual use during the war years, but it too served as a prototype for the development of group personality tests.

Applied psychology won its own victory in the war, the victory that came with public acceptance. Before long, thousands of employees, school children, and college applicants found themselves facing batteries of tests, the results of which could determine the course of their lives. An epidemic of testing swept the United States, but in the haste to answer the call of business and education, it was inevitable that some poorly designed and inadequately researched tests would appear, leading to disappointing results. As a consequence, many companies abandoned the use of psychological tests during the mid-1920s. This was one of the reasons for the general disenchantment with psychology that set in during that period. In time, better tests were developed that enabled business and industry to select better people for jobs, and better jobs for people, and today personnel selection and placement testing have become essential parts of the employment process.

Testing also became part of an important social controversy in the 1920s. The results obtained from testing army recruits during World War I were made public in 1921. The data showed that the mental age of the draftees, and by extension of the white population as a whole, was only thirteen. The results also indicated that almost half of all white Americans could be categorized as morons or as feeble-minded. Further, the data showed that blacks had a lower measured IQ than whites, as did immigrants from Mediterranean and Latin American countries. Only northern European immigrants had IQs equal to white Americans.

These findings raised many questions among scientists, politicians, and journalists. How could a democratic form of government survive if the populace was so stupid? Should groups with low IQs be allowed to vote? Should the government refuse entry to immigrants from low-IQ countries? How could the notion that people were created equal continue to be meaningful?

The concept of racial differences in intelligence had been advanced in the United States as early as the 1880s, and there had been many calls for restrictions on immigrants from Mediterranean and Latin American countries. The allegedly inferior intelligence level of African-Americans had also been generally accepted, even before the development of tests to measure intelligence. One of the most vocal and articulate critics of that view was Horace Mann Bond (1904–1972), a noted African-American scholar and president of Lincoln University in Pennsylvania.

Bond, who had earned a doctorate in education from the University of Chicago, published a number of books and articles in which he argued that any differences in the IQ scores of blacks and whites were attributable to environmental rather than genetic factors. He conducted research that demonstrated that blacks from northern states scored higher on intelligence tests than did whites from southern states, a finding that severely damaged the charge that blacks were genetically inferior in intelligence (Urban, 1989).

Many psychologists responded to the suggestion of racial differences in intelligence by charging that the tests were biased. In time the controversy faded, only to be revived in the 1970s. Since that time psychologists have worked to develop tests that are free of cultural and educational biases and that more accurately assess human abilities. There remains a great practical need for tests, and testing for selection, counseling, and diagnostic purposes continues to be a major focus of applied psychology.

Industrial/Organizational Psychology

We have described the founding of industrial psychology by Walter Dill Scott and the early efforts of Scott and Hugo Münsterberg to promote the application of psychology to the world of work. As it did with other areas of applied psychology, World War I brought about a monumental increase in the scope, popularity, and growth of this field.

Scott volunteered his services to the United States Army during World War I and developed a rating scale for selecting captains, based on scales he had developed for rating business leaders. By the end of the war he had evaluated the job qualifications of three million soldiers, and his work provided another highly publicized example of the practical worth of psychology.

After the war, business, industry, and government vied for the services of industrial psychologists to revamp their personnel procedures and to introduce psychological tests as employee selection devices. In 1919, as we noted, Scott formed his own consulting company, and two years later Cattell established the Psychological Corporation, which also successfully promoted the application of psychology to the business world.

The primary focus of industrial psychology during the 1920s was the selection and placement of job applicants—matching the right person with the right job. The scope of the field was broadened in 1927 by the Hawthorne studies, conducted at the Hawthorne, Illinois, plant of the Western Electric Company (Roethlisberger & Dickson, 1939). This research took the field beyond selection and placement to more complex problems of human relations, motivation, and morale.

The research began as a straightforward investigation of the effects of the physical work environment—lighting and temperature, for example—on employee efficiency. The results astonished both the psychologists and the plant managers. It was found that the social and psychological conditions of the work environment were much more important than the physical conditions under which a job was performed. The Hawthorne studies opened up new areas of exploration into such factors as the quality and nature of leadership, the informal groups workers form among themselves, employees' attitudes toward their jobs, communication between

Studies conducted during the 1920s and 1930s at the Hawthorne, Illinois, plant of the Western Electric Company led applied psychologists into the complex areas of human relations, leadership styles, and employee motivation and morale.

employees and managers, and a host of other social and psychological forces capable of influencing motivation, productivity, and satisfaction.

World War II brought a great many psychologists directly into the war effort. As in World War I, their major contribution was the testing, screening, and classifying of recruits, and by the 1940s far more sophisticated tests had been devised. Operation of the increasingly complex weapons of war, such as high-speed aircraft, required more complex skills. The need to identify persons who possessed the ability to learn those skills led to the refinement of selection and training procedures. These weapons spawned a specialty within industrial psychology variously called engineering psychology, human engineering, human factors engineering, and ergonomics. Working closely with systems engineers, engineering psychologists supplied information about human capabilities and limitations. Their work directly influenced the design of military equipment, to make it more compatible with the skills and abilities of the people who had to use it. Engineering psychologists today work not only on military hardware but also on consumer products such as computer keyboards, office furniture, and automobile dashboard displays.

Since the 1950s business leaders have accepted the influence of motivation, leadership, and other psychological factors on job performance.

These aspects of the work environment have assumed increased importance, as has the impact of the entire social psychological climate in which work takes place. Psychologists today study the nature of different organizational structures, their patterns and styles of communication, and the formal and informal social structures they produce. Recognizing this emphasis on organizational variables, the Division of Industrial Psychology of the American Psychological Association has become the Society for Industrial and Organizational Psychology.

Clinical Psychology

The application of psychology to the assessment and treatment of abnormal behavior was first undertaken by Lightner Witmer at his clinic at the University of Pennsylvania. In addition, two books provided an early impetus to the field. *A Mind That Found Itself* (1908), written by a former mental patient, Clifford Beers, became immensely popular and focused public attention on the need to deal more humanely with the mentally ill. Hugo Münsterberg's *Psychotherapy* (1909), also widely read, detailed techniques for treating a variety of mental disorders. It promoted clinical psychology by showing specific ways in which disturbed persons could be helped.

The first child guidance clinic was established in 1909 by William Healey, a Chicago psychiatrist. Many more such clinics soon followed. Their purpose was to treat childhood disorders early, so that those problems would not develop into more serious disturbances in adulthood. The clinics used the team approach, introduced by Witmer, in which all aspects of a patient's problems were dealt with by psychologists, psychiatrists, and social workers.

The ideas of Sigmund Freud were, of course, crucial to the development of clinical psychology. His work on psychoanalysis fascinated and outraged segments of the psychology establishment and the American public. His ideas provided clinical psychologists with their first psychological techniques of therapy.

Despite these events, clinical psychology advanced slowly, and as late as 1940 it was still a minor part of psychology. There were few treatment facilities for disturbed adults and, consequently, few job opportunities for clinical psychologists. There were no educational programs to train clinical psychologists, and they were limited, in general, to administering tests.

The situation changed abruptly in 1941, when the United States entered World War II. It was that event, more than any other, that made clinical psychology the large and dynamic applied specialty area it has since become. The army established training programs for several hundred clinical psychologists who were needed to treat emotional disturbances among military personnel.

After the war the need for clinical psychologists was even greater. The Veterans Administration (VA) found itself responsible for more than 40,000 veterans with psychiatric problems. Over three million others needed vocational and personal counseling to facilitate their reentry into civilian life, and some 315,000 veterans needed counseling to help them adjust to physical disabilities resulting from war wounds. The demand for mental health professionals was staggering and far exceeded the supply.

To help meet this crushing need, the VA funded graduate programs at universities and paid the tuition of graduate students in return for work at VA hospitals and clinics. A large number of the clinical psychologists trained in the 1950s received much of that instruction under VA auspices. The programs also changed the kind of patient treated by clinical psychologists. Prior to the war, most of their work had been with children with delinquency and adjustment problems, but the postwar needs of the veterans meant that most of those treated were adults with more severe emotional problems. The VA (now the Department of Veterans Affairs) remains the largest single employer of psychologists in the United States, and its impact on the field of clinical psychology has been enormous.

Clinical psychologists are also employed in mental health centers, schools, businesses, and private practice. We will discuss in later chapters the changes that have occurred since the 1950s in treatment methods, notably the behavior therapies, which are an outgrowth of the behaviorist school of thought. Clinical psychology today is the largest of the applied areas, with more than one-third of all graduate students enrolled in clinical programs and some 40 percent of all APA members practicing clinical psychology.

Comment

The nature of American psychology has altered immensely in the years since Hall, Cattell, Witmer, Scott, and Münsterberg studied under Wundt in Germany and brought that psychology back to the United States. As a result of their efforts, psychology is no longer restricted to the lecture halls, libraries, and laboratories but extends into many areas of everyday life. In addition to testing, educational and school psychology, clinical psychology, industrial/organizational psychology, and forensic psychology, psychologists are working in counseling psychology, community psychology, consumer psychology, population and environmental psychology, health and rehabilitation psychology, exercise and sport psychology, public policy and military psychology, and media psychology. None of these areas of applied focus would have been possible had psychology remained concerned with the contents of conscious experience. The people, ideas, and events we have discussed in these chapters on functionalism compelled American psychology to move far beyond the confines of the Leipzig laboratory.

Consider these factors: Darwin's notion of adaptation and function; Galton's recognition of individual differences and his attempts to measure them; the American Zeitgeist with its focus on the practical and the useful; the shift within the academic research laboratories from content to function brought about by James, Angell, Carr, and Woodworth; the economic and social factors and the forces of war. All these intertwined to bring forth a psychology designed to change our lives — an active, assertive, engaging, influential science.

This overall movement in American psychology toward the practical was reinforced by behaviorism, the next school of thought in psychology's own evolution.

Suggested Readings

Averill, L. A. (1990). Recollections of Clark's G. Stanley Hall. *Journal of the History of the Behavioral Sciences, 26*, 125–130. Recounts the author's three years as a graduate student at Clark University and his memories of Hall as a teacher.

Benjamin, L. T., Jr. (1986). Why don't they understand us? A history of psychology's public image. *American Psychologist, 41*, 941–946. Traces the development of psychology's image from its beginnings at a public exhibition at a Chicago World's Fair, through its applications in the field of education, to the writings of psychologists in popular magazines and books.

Diehl, L. A. (1986). The paradox of G. Stanley Hall: Foe of coeducation and educator of women. *American Psychologist, 41*, 868–878. Examines Hall's theory on sex differences in human development — especially his view that a woman's proper role was that of mother — and contrasts this with his efforts on behalf of women graduate students at Clark University.

Hale, M., Jr. (1980). *Human Science and Social Order: Hugo Münsterberg and the Origins of Applied Psychology*. Philadelphia: Temple University Press. The life and work of Münsterberg, a founder of applied psychology, considering especially his view of the nature of society and psychology's role in solving social problems.

Hulse, S. H., & Green, B. F., Jr. (Eds.). (1986). *One Hundred Years of Psychological Research in America: G. Stanley Hall and the Johns Hopkins Tradition*. Baltimore: Johns Hopkins University Press. Presents papers from a symposium held to commemorate the centennial of Hall's founding of the psychology laboratory at Johns Hopkins University. See especially Part I, "Historical Perspective," on Hall's life and his shaping of the graduate psychology department.

McReynolds, P. (1987). Lightner Witmer: Little-known founder of clinical psychology. *American Psychologist, 42*, 849–858. Sketches Witmer's life and career, describes the beginnings of his clinic at the University of Pennsylvania, and assesses his importance in the history of applied psychology.

Sokal, M. M. (Ed.). (1987). *Psychological Testing and American Society: 1890–1930*. New Brunswick NJ: Rutgers University Press. An account of the pioneering ideas, programs, and practices in the mental testing movement in the United States, covering the work of Cattell, Scott, Goddard, Terman, and Otis, among others.

Sokal, M. M. (1990). G. Stanley Hall and the institutional character of psychology at Clark, 1889–1920. *Journal of the History of the Behavioral Sciences, 26*, 114–124. Describes the psychology taught and promoted at Clark University and traces its origins to aspects of Hall's own temperament.

Von Mayrhauser, R. T. (1989). Making intelligence functional: Walter Dill Scott and applied psychological testing in World War I. *Journal of the History of the Behavioral Sciences, 25*, 60–72. Describes the efforts of Scott, Thorndike, and others in constructing the first group tests of intelligence.

Behaviorism: Antecedent Influences

9

A Science of Behavior

By the second decade of the twentieth century, fewer than forty years after Wilhelm Wundt formally launched psychology, the science had undergone drastic revisions. No longer did psychologists agree on the value of introspection, on the existence of elements of the mind, or on the need for psychology to remain a pure science. The functionalists were rewriting the rules of psychology, experimenting with and applying psychology in ways that could not be admitted into Leipzig or Cornell.

The movement to functionalism was less revolutionary than evolutionary. The functionalists did not deliberately set out to destroy the establishment of Wundt and Titchener. Instead, they modified it, adding a bit here, changing something there, so that slowly, over the years, a new form of psychology emerged. It was more a chipping away from within than a deliberate attack from outside. The leaders of the functionalist movement did not feel a great urge to solidify or formalize their position. It was, as they saw it, not so much a break with the past as a building upon it. The change from structuralism to functionalism was, therefore, not so noticeable at the time it was taking place.

There is no particular day or year that we can point to as the start of functionalism, a time when psychology seemed to change overnight. Indeed, it is difficult, as we noted, to point to a particular individual as the founder of functionalism. This was the situation in the second decade of the twentieth century in the United States. Functionalism was maturing and structuralism still held a strong but no longer exclusive position.

In 1913 a protest erupted against both of these positions. This was intended by its author to be an abrupt and open break, a total war designed to shatter both points of view. There was to be no modification of the past, no compromise with it.

This new movement was called behaviorism, and its leader was the thirty-five-year-old psychologist John B. Watson. Just ten years earlier Watson had received his Ph.D. under Angell at the University of Chicago. At that time — 1903 — Chicago was the center of functional psychology, one of the two movements Watson was out to smash.

The basic tenets of Watson's behaviorism were simple, direct, and bold. He called for an objective psychology, a science of behavior that dealt only with observable behavioral acts that could be described objectively in terms such as stimulus and response. He wanted to apply to human beings the experimental procedures and principles of animal psychology, a field in which he had worked.

Watson's interests shed light on what he planned to discard. To be an objective science, a behavioral psychology had to reject all mentalistic concepts and terms. Such words as *image, mind*, and *consciousness* — which had been carried over from the days of mental philosophy — were meaningless for a science of behavior. Watson was particularly vehement in his rejection of the concept of consciousness. He said that consciousness has "never been seen, touched, smelled, tasted, or moved. It is a plain assumption just as unprovable as the old concept of soul" (Watson &

McDougall, 1929, p. 14). The technique of introspection, which assumed the existence of conscious processes, was, therefore, irrelevant.

As the founder of behaviorism, Watson promoted these points forcefully. Of course, as we have seen, founding is different from originating. The ideas of the behaviorist movement that was about to overtake psychology were not original with Watson but had been developing in psychology and in biology for several years.

It is no criticism of Watson to note that he, like all founders, organized, integrated, and advanced ideas and issues already in existence. From this amalgamation he constructed his new system of psychology. The point is worth reiterating: "Creations absolutely [new or fresh] are very rare, if they occur at all; most novelties are only novel combinations of old elements, and the degree of novelty is thus a matter of interpretation" (Sarton, 1936, p. 36).

This chapter examines behaviorism's antecedent influences, the old elements Watson so effectively brought together to form his new psychology. At least three major trends affected his work: (1) the philosophical tradition of objectivism and mechanism; (2) animal psychology; and (3) functional psychology. Animal psychology and functional psychology exerted the most direct and obvious impact. The philosophical traditions of objectivism and mechanism had been developing for some time, and they favored and reinforced the growth of animal psychology and of functionalism.

Watson's insistence on the need for increased objectivity in psychology was not unusual by 1913. That notion has a long history, beginning perhaps with Descartes, whose attempts at mechanistic explanations of the body were among the first steps in the direction of greater objectivity. More important in the history of objectivism is the French philosopher Auguste Comte (1798–1857), founder of the movement called *positivism*, which emphasized positive knowledge (facts), the truth of which was not debatable (see Chapter 2). According to Comte, the only valid knowledge is that which is social in nature and is objectively observable. These criteria rule out introspection, which depends on a private individual consciousness and cannot be objectively observed. Comte vigorously protested against mentalism and subjective methodology.

In the early years of the twentieth century, positivism was part of the Zeitgeist in science. Watson rarely discussed positivism, nor did most American psychologists of the day, but they "acted like positivists, even if they did not assume the label" (Logue, 1985a, p. 149). Thus, by the time Watson set to work on behaviorism, objectivism, mechanism, and materialism were strong. Their influence was so pervasive that they led inexorably to a new kind of psychology, one without consciousness or mind or soul, one that focused on only what could be seen and heard and touched. The science of behavior, which viewed the human being as a machine, was the inescapable result.

The Influence of Animal Psychology on Behaviorism

Watson offered a succinct statement of the relationship between animal psychology and behaviorism: "Behaviorism is a direct outgrowth of studies in animal behavior during the first decade of the twentieth century" (Watson, 1929, p. 327). Clearly, then, the most important single antecedent of Watson's program was animal psychology, which grew out of evolutionary theory. It led to attempts to demonstrate the existence of mind in lower organisms and the continuity between animal and human minds.

We described in Chapter 6 the work of two pioneers in animal psychology — George John Romanes and Conwy Lloyd Morgan. With Morgan's law of parsimony and his greater reliance on experimental instead of anecdotal techniques, the field of animal psychology was becoming more objective. Consciousness was still its focus, however, and information about an animal's level of consciousness was being inferred from observations of its behavior. Thus, while the methodology was becoming more objective, the subject matter was not.

In 1889, Alfred Binet published *The Psychic Life of Micro-Organisms*, in which he proposed that single-celled protozoa possess the ability to perceive and discriminate between objects and to display behavior that has some purpose. In 1908, Francis Darwin (son of Charles Darwin) discussed the role of consciousness in plants. In the early years of animal psychology in the United States, we find, not surprisingly, a continuing interest in animal consciousness. The influence of Romanes and Morgan persisted for quite some time.

A significant step toward greater objectivity in animal psychology was taken by Jacques Loeb (1859–1924), a German physiologist and zoologist who worked at several institutions in the United States, including the University of Chicago. Reacting against the anthropomorphic tradition of Romanes and the method of introspection by analogy, Loeb developed a theory of animal behavior based on the concept of *tropism*, an involuntary forced movement. In this view, an animal's response is a direct and automatic function of or reaction to a stimulus. The behavior is said to be forced by the stimulus, and thus it does not require any explanation in terms of the animal's consciousness. Loeb's theory was influential for a time in the biological sciences, and it represented a change from the work of Romanes and Morgan.

Although Loeb's work represented perhaps the most objective and mechanistic approach to animal psychology then proposed, he had not completely cast off the past. He did not reject consciousness, particularly in animals high on the evolutionary scale, such as humans. Loeb argued that consciousness among animals was revealed by *associative memory*, that is, the animals had learned to react to certain stimuli in a desired way. For example, when an animal responds to the calling of its name, or when it reacts to a specific sound by going repeatedly to the place where it is fed, this is evidence of associative memory. Thus, even in Loeb's otherwise mechanistic system, the mind or consciousness, through the association of ideas, was still being invoked (Loeb, 1918).

Watson took several courses with Loeb at the University of Chicago and expressed the desire to do research under his direction, indicating that he was then in sympathy with (or at least curious about) Loeb's mechanistic views. Angell and another faculty member, the neurologist H. H. Donaldson, talked Watson out of this plan. They argued that Loeb was "unsafe," a word open to interpretation but perhaps indicating their disapproval of Loeb's objectivism.

By the beginning of the twentieth century the study of animal behavior within a biological framework had become popular in the United States. At the same time, experimental animal psychology, notably the work of E. L. Thorndike at Columbia University, was developing rapidly. Robert Yerkes began animal studies in 1900, and his work, using a range of animals, strengthened the position and influence of comparative psychology.

Also in 1900, the rat maze was introduced by W. S. Small at Clark University, and the white rat and maze became a standard method for the study of learning. Yet consciousness continued to intrude in animal psychology, even with the white rat in the maze. In interpreting the rat's behavior, Small wrote, in mentalistic terms, "It is also clear . . . that what properly may be called ideas find slight place in the associative process. Crass images — visual, olfactory, motor — organic conditions, and instinctive activities are assuredly the main elements. That these elements may bleach out and attenuate into ideas is not impossible. Analogy with human experience would indeed point to that conclusion" (Mackenzie, 1977, p. 85).

Although this comment of Small's is more restricted than Romanes's brand of anthropomorphizing, it nevertheless represents a concern with mental processes, even with mental elements. Watson, in the early years

Robert M. Yerkes studied a range of animals — from turtles and frogs to pigs and chimps — and promoted an objective, biological approach to comparative psychology.

of his career, fell under the same influence. His doctoral dissertation, completed in 1903, was entitled "Animal Education: The Psychical Development of the White Rat." As late as 1907 he was discussing the conscious experience of sensation in his rats.

In 1906, Charles Henry Turner, one of the first African-American psychologists and a prolific researcher in comparative psychology, published an article entitled "A Preliminary Note on Ant Behavior." Watson reviewed the article in the prestigious journal *Psychological Bulletin* and had high praise for it. In his review Watson used the word *behavior* from Turner's title. That may have been the first time Watson used the word in print, although he had used it earlier in a grant application (Cadwallader, 1984, 1987).

By 1910, some eight laboratories of comparative psychology had been established (the earliest were at Clark, Harvard, and the University of Chicago), and many universities had added courses in the field. Margaret Floy Washburn, who had been Titchener's first doctoral student, taught animal psychology at Cornell. She wrote a textbook on comparative psychology entitled *The Animal Mind* (1908), which went through three editions. Note the title of Washburn's book: *The Animal Mind*. The imputation of consciousness to animals persisted, as did the method of introspecting the animal mind by analogy with the human mind. Washburn noted that "we are obliged to acknowledge that all psychic interpretation of animal behavior must be on the analogy of human experience.... We must be anthropomorphic in the notions we form of what takes place in the mind of an animal" (Washburn, 1908, p. 88).

Although Washburn's book was called the "most comprehensive review of the animal psychology literature of the time," it also marked the end of an era in animal psychology.

> After it, no other text would use the approach of inferring mental states from behavior. The questions that had interested [Herbert] Spencer, Lloyd Morgan, and Yerkes went out of fashion and mostly disappeared from the literature. Almost all subsequent textbooks in the field were behaviorist in orientation, and primarily concerned with the issues and problems of learning. (Demarest, 1987, pp. 134, 144)

Whether one dealt with mind or with behavior, it was not easy to be an animal psychologist. The field was not considered by state legislators and university administrators to have any practical value. The president of Harvard University "saw no future in Yerkes's brand of comparative psychology. It was smelly and expensive and seemed to have no relation to practical public service. Word came to Yerkes that the way to promotion might lie through educational psychology [instead]" (Reed, 1987b, p. 94).

The students Yerkes trained in his laboratory entered applied fields, unable to find jobs in comparative psychology. Those with university po-

Margaret Floy Washburn was Titchener's first doctoral student at Cornell and wrote a textbook on comparative psychology.

sitions found that they were the most expendable members of their psychology departments. In times of financial hardship, animal psychologists were generally the first to be fired. Watson himself had difficulties early in his career. "I am very hampered in my research at present," he wrote to Yerkes in 1904. "We have absolutely no place to keep animals and no funds to run the 'menagerie' if we had the place" (O'Donnell, 1985, p. 190).

In 1908 only six animal studies were published, representing 4 percent of all the psychological research for the year. In 1909, when Watson suggested to Yerkes that all the animal psychologists arrange to dine together during the APA meeting, he knew they could be seated at one table—all 9 of them. In the 1910 edition of Cattell's *American Men of Science*, only 6 out of 218 psychologists listed said they were active in animal research. Career prospects were obviously poor, yet the field expanded because of the intense dedication of the few who stayed with it.

The *Journal of Animal Behavior*, later the *Journal of Comparative Psychology*, was begun in 1911. In 1909 the work of the Russian physiologist Ivan Pavlov became known in the United States through an article written by Yerkes and a Russian student, Sergius Morgulis. Pavlov's work supported an objective psychology and Watson's behaviorism in particular.

Animal psychology became established and grew increasingly objective in its methods and subject matter. The kinds of conscious experiences being invoked by animal researchers narrowed and eventually disappeared altogether.

Before we consider more specific influences on the development of Watson's behaviorism, let us tell the tale of the most famous horse in the history of psychology.

Clever Hans, the Clever Horse

In the early 1900s virtually every literate person in the Western world had read about Hans the Wonder Horse, surely the most intelligent four-legged creature who ever lived. The horse was a celebrity throughout Europe and the United States. Plays and songs were written about him, as were books and magazine articles, and advertisers used the horse's name to sell their products. Hans was a sensation.

The horse could add and subtract, use fractions and decimals, read, spell, tell time, discriminate among colors, identify objects, and give demonstrations of phenomenal memory. Hans replied to the questions put to him by tapping his hoof a specified number of times or by nodding his head in the direction of the correct object.

"How many of the gentlemen present are wearing straw hats?" the horse was asked.

Clever Hans tapped the answer with his right foot, being careful to omit the straw hats worn by the ladies.

"What is the lady holding in her hand?"

The horse tapped out "Schirm," meaning parasol, indicating each of the letters by means of a special chart. He was invariably successful at distinguishing between canes and parasols and also between straw and felt hats.

More important, Hans could think for himself. When asked a completely novel question, such as how many corners in a circle, he shook his head from side to side to say there were none. (Fernald, 1984, p. 19)

No wonder people were dazzled and amazed. No wonder Hans's owner, Wilhelm von Osten, a retired mathematics teacher in Berlin, Germany, was pleased with what he had accomplished. He had spent several years teaching Hans what he considered to be the fundamentals of human intelligence. The motivation for his painstaking efforts was purely scientific. His goal was to prove that Darwin was correct in suggesting that humans and animals have similar mental processes and abilities. Von Osten believed that the only reason horses and other animals appear to be less intelligent than they are is that they have not been given sufficient education. He was convinced that with the right kind of drill and training, the horse could show that it was an intelligent being.

We should note that von Osten did not profit financially from Hans's performances. He never charged admission fees for the demonstrations he put on in the courtyard of his apartment building, and he never benefited from the resulting publicity.

A government committee was established to examine the phenomenon and to determine if any deception or trickery was involved. The group included a circus manager, a veterinarian, horse trainers, an aristocrat, the director of the Berlin Zoo, and the psychologist Carl Stumpf from the University of Berlin (Chapter 4).

In September 1904, after a lengthy investigation, the committee concluded that Hans was not receiving any intentional signs or cues from his owner. No fraud, no deceit. But Stumpf was not completely satisfied. He was curious about how the horse was able to respond correctly to so many different kinds of questions, and he assigned the problem to one of his graduate students, Oskar Pfungst, who approached the task in the careful manner of an experimental psychologist.

One of Pfungst's first experiments followed a demonstration that Hans could answer questions correctly even when his owner, von Osten, was not present. Pfungst formed two groups of questioners, one composed of persons who knew the answers to the questions put to the horse, and the second composed of persons who did not know the answers. This led to a crucial finding, namely that Hans could only answer correctly when the questioners knew the answers. Obviously Hans was somehow receiving information from the person questioning him, even when that person was a stranger.

After a series of well-controlled experiments, Pfungst concluded that Hans had been unintentionally conditioned to begin tapping his hoof whenever he perceived the slightest downward movement of von Osten's head. When the correct number of taps had been reached, von Osten would move his head slightly upward and the horse would stop. Pfungst demonstrated that virtually everyone, even persons who had never been around a horse before, made the same barely perceptible head movements when speaking to a horse.

Thus, it was shown that Hans did not have a storehouse of knowledge. He had simply been trained to start tapping his hoof, or to incline his head toward an object, whenever his questioner made a certain kind of movement. Further, the horse had been conditioned to stop tapping in response to another kind of movement. During the training period von Osten had reinforced Hans by giving him pieces of carrot or sugar lumps every time he made a correct response. As the training progressed, von Osten no longer had to reinforce Hans's behavior for every correct reply, but rewarded him instead on a partial or intermittent basis. The behavioral psychologist B. F. Skinner would later demonstrate the effectiveness of this kind of partial reinforcement in the conditioning process.

The case of Clever Hans demonstrated the value (indeed, the necessity) of an experimental approach to the study of animal behavior. It made psychologists all the more skeptical of claims of high levels of intelligence in animals. It was clear, however, that animals were capable of learning and could be conditioned to change their behavior. Therefore, the study of animal learning came to be seen as much more profitable than continued speculation about what might be going on in an animal's mind in terms of some alleged level of intelligence. Pfungst's report about his experiments with Clever Hans was reviewed by Watson, and its conclusions influenced Watson's growing inclination to promote a psychology that would deal only with behavior, not with consciousness (Watson, 1908).

Edward Lee Thorndike (1874–1949)

Thorndike, who was never able to learn how to drive a car, is one of the most important researchers in the development of animal psychology. He fashioned an objective and mechanistic theory of learning that focuses on overt behavior. He believed that psychology must study behavior, not mental elements or conscious experience in any form, and he reinforced the trend toward greater objectivity begun by the functionalists. He interpreted learning not in subjective terms but rather in terms of concrete connections between stimuli and responses. However, as we shall see, he permitted some reference to consciousness and mental processes.

Edward Lee Thorndike, a pioneer in the study of learning, advanced his theory of connectionism to explain how organisms associate situations and responses.

The works of Thorndike and Ivan Pavlov provide another example of independent simultaneous discovery. Thorndike developed his law of effect in 1898, and Pavlov proposed a similar law of reinforcement in 1902, but it was many years before the resemblance between the two was recognized.

The Life of Thorndike

E. L. Thorndike was one of the first American psychologists to receive all of his education in the United States. It is significant that this was possible just two decades after psychology was founded. His interest in psychology was awakened, as it was for so many others, when he read William James's *The Principles of Psychology* while an undergraduate at Wesleyan University in Middletown, Connecticut. He later studied under James at Harvard, where he began his investigation of learning.

He had planned to conduct his research using children as subjects, but he was forbidden to do so by the university administration, which was still sensitive about a scandal that had erupted a few years before, when an anthropologist had "loosened" children's clothing to take their body measurements. When Thorndike learned that he could not use children, he chose chickens instead, apparently inspired by lectures given at Harvard by Morgan, who described his own research with chickens.

Thorndike trained his chicks to run through mazes that he improvised by standing books on end. The story is told of Thorndike's difficulties in finding room for his chicks. Since his landlady took a dim view of chickens in Thorndike's bedroom, he turned to William James for advice. James was unsuccessful in finding space in the laboratory or the university museum, so he took Thorndike and the chickens into the basement of his home, apparently to the delight of the James children.

Thorndike did not complete his education at Harvard. Believing that a certain young lady did not return his interest, he applied to Cattell at Columbia, so that he could get away from the Boston area. When Cattell offered him a fellowship, Thorndike went to New York, taking his two best-trained chicks with him. He continued his animal research at Columbia, working with cats and dogs in puzzle boxes of his own design. In 1898 he was awarded his doctorate. His dissertation, "Animal Intelligence: An Experimental Study of the Associative Processes in Animals," was published, along with subsequent research on associative learning in chicks, fish, and monkeys.

Fiercely ambitious and competitive, Thorndike wrote to his fiancée, "I've decided to get to the top of the psychology heap in five years, teach ten more, and then quit" (Boakes, 1984, p. 72). He did not remain an animal psychologist for long, freely admitting that he had no real interest in it. He had stuck with it only to complete his degree requirements and establish a reputation. And it was not the field for someone with such a drive to succeed.

Thorndike became an instructor in psychology at Teachers College of Columbia University in 1899. There he turned to human subjects, applying his animal research techniques to children and young people. The remainder of his long career was spent largely in the areas of human learning, educational psychology, and mental testing. He wrote several textbooks and got to the top of the heap; in 1912 he was elected president of the American Psychological Association. He became quite wealthy from royalties from his mental tests and textbooks and by 1924 enjoyed an income of nearly $70,000 a year, a tremendous sum at that time (Boakes, 1984).

Thorndike's fifty years at Columbia are among the most productive ever recorded. His bibliography lists 507 items, many of which are lengthy books and monographs. He retired in 1939 but continued to work until his death ten years later.

Connectionism

Thorndike created an experimental approach to association that he called *connectionism*. It encompassed several important departures from traditional views of learning. He wrote that if he were to analyze the human mind he would

> find connections of varying strength between (a) situations, elements of situations, and compounds of situations, and (b) responses, readinesses to respond, facilitations, inhibitions, and directions of responses. If all these could be completely inventoried, telling what the man would think and do and what would satisfy and annoy him, in every conceivable situation, it seems to me that nothing would be left out. . . . Learning is connecting. The mind is man's connection-system. (Thorndike, 1931, p. 122)

This position was a direct descendant of the older philosophical notion of association (see Chapter 2), with one significant difference. Instead of talking about associations or connections between ideas, Thorndike proposed connections between situations and responses. He thus incorporated a more objective frame of reference into his psychological theory. His study of learning also differed from classical associationism in that the subjects were animals rather than humans. This method had become acceptable as an outgrowth of Darwin's notion of the continuity of the species.

Although Thorndike focused on connections between situations and responses and argued that learning does not involve conscious reflection, he nevertheless was concerned with mental or subjective processes. He spoke about "satisfaction," "annoyance," and "discomfort" when discussing the behavior of his experimental animals, terms that are more mentalistic than behavioristic. Thorndike thus showed the influence of the framework established by Romanes and Morgan. "For Thorndike . . . detailed analysis of an animal's mental operations on the basis of objective inference was followed by descriptions of the animal's private experience on the basis of subjective inference" (Mackenzie, 1977, p. 70).

It must be noted that Thorndike, like Jacques Loeb, was not granting high levels of consciousness and intelligence to animals as freely and extravagantly as Romanes had. We can see a steady diminution in the role of consciousness in animal psychology from its beginnings to the time of Thorndike, along with a greater focus on the use of the experimental method to study more objective behavior.

In spite of the mentalistic tinge to Thorndike's work, we must not lose sight of the mechanistic nature of his approach. He argued that to study behavior, it must be broken down or reduced to its simplest elements: the stimulus-response units. He thus shared with the structuralists an analytic and atomistic point of view. The stimulus-response units are the elements of behavior (not of consciousness), the building blocks from which more complex behaviors are compounded.

Thorndike's conclusions were derived from research using a piece of equipment of his own design, the *puzzle box* (see Figure 9-1). An animal placed in the box was required to learn how to operate a latch in order to escape. Thorndike's studies of cats involved placing a cat that had been deprived of food in the slatted puzzle box. Food was put outside the box as a reward for escaping. The door of the box was fastened by several latches. The cat had to pull on a lever or a chain, and sometimes engage in several acts in succession, to open the door.

At first the cat displayed random behaviors as it poked and sniffed and clawed to get to the food. Eventually the cat hit on the correct behavior and the door opened. During the first trial the correct behavior occurred by accident. On subsequent trials the random behaviors were displayed less and less frequently, until learning was complete. Then the cat would exhibit the correct behavior as soon as it was placed in the box.

Thorndike adopted quantitative measures of learning. One technique was to record the number of wrong behaviors, acts that did not lead to escape. Over a series of trials these became less frequent. Another technique was to record the time that elapsed from the moment the cat was placed in the box until it succeeded in escaping. As learning took place, this time period became shorter.

Thorndike wrote of the stamping in or stamping out of a response tendency by its favorable or unfavorable results. Unsuccessful response

Figure 9-1
Thorndike's puzzle box.

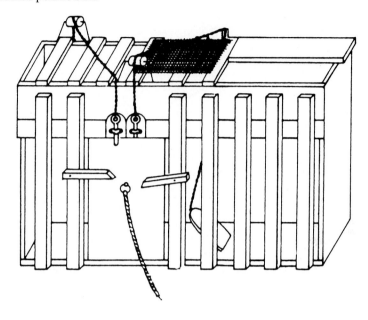

tendencies (those that did nothing to get the cat out of the box) are stamped out over a number of trials. Response tendencies that lead to success are stamped in after a number of trials. This kind of learning has been called ***trial and error learning***; Thorndike preferred to call it "trial and accidental success" (Jonçich, 1968, p. 266).

The stamping in or stamping out of a response tendency was formalized as Thorndike's ***law of effect***: "Any act which in a given situation produces satisfaction becomes associated with that situation, so that when the situation recurs the act is more likely than before to recur also. Conversely, any act which in a given situation produces discomfort becomes disassociated from that situation, so that when the situation recurs the act is less likely than before to recur" (Thorndike, 1905, p. 203).

A companion law — the ***law of exercise*** or the ***law of use and disuse*** — states that any response made in a particular situation becomes associated with that situation. The more the response is used in the situation, the more strongly it becomes associated with it. Conversely, prolonged disuse of the response tends to weaken the association. In other words, simply repeating a response in a situation tends to strengthen that response. Thorndike's later research convinced him that repetition of a response is relatively ineffective compared to the reward consequences of the response.

In the early 1930s Thorndike reexamined the law of effect in an extensive program of research using human subjects. The results revealed that rewarding a response did indeed strengthen it, but punishing a response did not produce a comparable negative effect. He revised the law of effect to place greater emphasis on reward than on punishment.

Comment

Thorndike's investigations of human and animal learning are among the most influential in the history of psychology. His theories were widely applied to education, thus increasing psychology's involvement in that specialty area. In addition, his work heralded the rise of learning theory to its later prominence in American psychology. Although newer learning theories and models have appeared since Thorndike's work, the significance of his contributions remains secure. His work is a cornerstone of associationism, and the objective spirit in which he conducted his research is an important contribution to behaviorism. Indeed, John B. Watson wrote that Thorndike's research laid the foundation for behaviorism.

Ivan Pavlov also paid tribute to Thorndike:

Some years after the beginning of the work with our new method I learned that somewhat similar experiments had been performed in America, and indeed not by physiologists but by psychologists. Thereupon I studied in more detail the American publications, and now I must acknowledge that the honor of having made the first steps along this path belongs to E. L. Thorndike. By two or three years his experiments preceded ours and his book must be considered a classic, both for its bold outlook on an immense task and for the accuracy of its results. (Pavlov, 1928, in Jonçich, 1968, pp. 415–416)

Ivan Petrovitch Pavlov (1849–1936)

The influence of Pavlov is felt keenly in many areas of contemporary psychology. His work on learning helped to shift associationism from its traditional emphasis on subjective ideas to objective and quantifiable glandular secretions and muscular movements. As a result, Pavlov's work provided Watson with a new method for studying behavior and a way of attempting to control and modify it.

The Life of Pavlov

Ivan Pavlov was born in the town of Ryazan in central Russia, the eldest of eleven children of a village priest. His position in such a large family brought him responsibility and hard work at an early age, characteristics he retained all his life. He was unable to attend school for several years because of an accident involving a severe blow to his head when he was seven. His father tutored him at home, and in 1860 he entered the theological seminary, intending to prepare for the priesthood. Later, after reading Darwin, he changed his mind. In 1870, Pavlov walked several hundred miles to St. Petersburg to attend the university, where he chose to specialize in animal physiology.

With this university training, Pavlov joined the emerging third class in Russian society, the intelligentsia. (The other classes were the aristocracy and the peasantry.) Pavlov was

> too well-educated and too intelligent for the peasantry from which he came, but too common and too poor for the aristocracy into which he could never rise. These social conditions often produced an especially dedicated intellectual, one whose entire life was centered on the intellectual pursuits that justified his existence. And so it was with Pavlov, whose almost fanatic devotion to pure science and to experimental research was supported by the energy and simplicity of a Russian peasant. (Miller, 1962, p. 177)

Pavlov obtained his degree in 1875 and began medical training, not to practice medicine but in the hope of pursuing a career in physiological research. He studied in Germany for two years, then returned to St. Petersburg for several years as a laboratory research assistant.

Pavlov's dedication to research was of paramount importance. His single-mindedness was not distracted by practical issues such as salary, clothing, or living conditions. His wife, Sara, whom he married in 1881, devoted herself to protecting him from mundane matters. They made a pact early in their marriage, agreeing that she would allow nothing to distract him from his work. He promised, in return, never to drink or play cards and to socialize only on Saturday and Sunday evenings. Pavlov adhered to a rigorous schedule, working seven days a week from September to May; summers were spent in the country.

Awarded the Nobel Prize in 1904 for his work on the digestive glands, Ivan Petrovitch Pavlov advanced the cause of objectivity in psychology through research on the formation of the conditional reflex.

Characteristic of his indifference to everyday affairs is the story that Sara often had to remind him when it was time to collect his pay. She said that he "shouldn't be trusted to buy a suit of clothes by himself." Nothing mattered to him except his research. When he was seventy-three and riding the streetcar to his laboratory, he jumped off before it stopped, fell, and broke his leg. "He was impetuous. He wouldn't wait for it to stop. A woman standing near saw it and said, 'My, here is a man of genius, but he doesn't know how to get off a streetcar without breaking his leg'" (Gantt, 1979, p. 28).

The family lived in poverty until 1890 when, at the age of forty-one, Pavlov finally obtained the post of professor of pharmacology at the Military Medical Academy in St. Petersburg. In 1883, while Pavlov was preparing his doctoral dissertation, their first child was born. Frail and sickly, the infant would not survive, the doctor said, unless mother and child could rest in the country. After a great struggle Pavlov was able to borrow enough money for the journey but it was too late and the child died. For a time Pavlov had to sleep on a cot in his laboratory while his wife and second child lived with relatives, because they could not afford an apartment. A group of Pavlov's students, knowing of his financial difficulties, gave him money on the pretext of covering the expenses of lectures they had asked him to give. Pavlov spent the money on laboratory animals, keeping nothing for himself. So strong were his dedication and commitment to his work that he did not seem bothered by the hardship. He said that it never caused him "any undue worry."

In 1923, Pavlov visited the United States to attend a conference in New York City and was robbed of $2000, a substantial sum, at Grand Central Station. He had sat down on a bench to rest for a moment and placed his satchel on the seat beside him. He became so absorbed in the crowds and the sights around him that he failed to watch the bag, and when he got up to leave it was gone. "Ah well," he said, "one must not put temptation in the way of the needy" (Gerow, 1986, p. 42).

Pavlov was given to explosive emotional tirades at work, often directed at his research assistants. The story is told that during the Bolshevik Revolution of 1917 he berated one of his assistants for being ten minutes late; gunfire in the streets was not to interfere with research. "What the hell difference does the revolution make," he shouted, "when you've got work to do in the laboratory" (Gantt, 1979, p. 28). Usually these outbursts were quickly forgotten. His students knew what was expected of them, because Pavlov never hesitated to tell them. He was honest and direct, if not always considerate, in his dealings with other people.

He was aware of his own bad temper. When one laboratory worker could no longer tolerate the insults, he asked to be relieved of his duties. "Pavlov replied that his abusive behavior was just a habit and that the co-worker should treat it like the smell of dogs, meaning that it was not of itself a sufficient reason to quit the laboratory" (Windholz, 1990, p. 68). Research failures caused Pavlov to feel depressed, but successes were met with such happiness that he congratulated not only his co-workers but the experimental animals as well.

Known as an excellent teacher, Pavlov was capable of enthralling an audience of students and colleagues. Merciless in an argument, he was nevertheless willing to admit he was wrong, although this was a rare occurrence. He was popular with his students and was one of the few professors who encouraged them to interrupt his lectures with questions. "There was clear jealousy among Pavlov's pupils about who was the closest to him," wrote a colleague. "People boasted when Pavlov spoke to them at some length, and . . . the attitude of Pavlov toward an individual was the main factor determining the hierarchy within the group" (Konorski, 1974, p. 193). Many students began to imitate Pavlov's gestures and manner of speaking.

Pavlov was one of the few Russian scientists to allow women students and Jewish students to work in his laboratory, and he grew irate when anyone expressed even a hint of anti-Semitism. He had a good sense of humor and knew how to enjoy a joke. During the ceremony at which he received an honorary degree from Cambridge University in England, some students lowered a stuffed toy dog into his lap by a rope from the balcony. Pavlov kept the dog by his desk in his apartment.

His relations with the Soviet regime were complicated and difficult; he was openly critical of the revolution and the Soviet government. He wrote dangerously strong, angry letters of protest to Joseph Stalin, the tyrannical leader who killed and exiled millions, and he boycotted Russian scientific meetings to demonstrate his disapproval. Not until 1933 did he finally accept the government and acknowledge that it had achieved some success in uniting the Soviet peoples. For the last three years of his life he lived in peace with the authorities of whom he had been critical for sixteen years. Despite his attitude, Pavlov received generous support for his research from the Soviet bureaucracy and operated largely free of government interference.

A passage from Pavlov's autobiography sums up his overall attitude:

> Looking back on my life I would describe it as being happy and successful. I have received all that can be demanded of life: the complete realization of the principles with which I began life. I dreamed of finding happiness in intellectual work, in science — and I found it. I wanted to have a kind person as a companion in life and I found this companion in my wife . . . who patiently endured all the hardships of our existence before my professorship, always encouraged my scientific aspirations, and who devoted herself to our family just as I devoted myself to the laboratory. I have renounced practicality in life with its cunning and not always irreproachable ways, and I see no reason for regretting this; on the contrary, precisely in this I find now certain consolation. (Pavlov, 1955, p. 46)

Pavlov remained a scientist to the last. He had the habit of self-observation whenever he was ill, and the day of his death was no exception. He called in a physician, a neuropathologist, and described his symptoms. Although extremely weak from pneumonia, Pavlov was able to report, "My brain is not working well, obsessive feelings and involuntary movements appear; mortification may be setting in" (Gantt, 1941, p. 35). He discussed the meaning of the symptoms with the doctor for a while and then fell asleep. When he awoke, Pavlov raised himself up in bed and began to search for his clothes, with the same impatient energy he had shown all his life. "It is time to get up," he cried. "Help me, I must dress!" And with that, he fell back on the pillows and died.

Conditioned Reflexes

During his distinguished and productive career Pavlov worked on three research problems. The first concerned the function of the nerves of the heart, and the second was on the primary digestive glands. This brilliant research on digestion won him worldwide recognition and, in 1904, the Nobel Prize. His third research area, for which he occupies a prominent place in the history of psychology, was the study of the higher nervous centers in the brain. He pursued this work with his typical energy and determination from 1902 until his death in 1936. In his attack on this problem he made use of the conditioning technique, his greatest scientific achievement (Pavlov, 1927).

The notion of ***conditioned reflexes*** originated, like so many scientific breakthroughs, in an accidental discovery. In his work on the digestive glands in dogs, Pavlov used the method of surgical exposure to permit the collection of the digestive secretions outside the body where they could be observed, measured, and recorded. The surgical operations necessary to divert the secretions of a particular gland through a tube to the outside of the body, without damaging the nerves and blood supply, required considerable ingenuity and technical skill.

One aspect of this work dealt with the function of saliva, which would be involuntarily secreted whenever food was placed in the dog's mouth. Pavlov observed that sometimes saliva would flow before the food was given, that is, an anticipatory saliva flow would occur. The dogs salivated when they saw the food or the man who regularly fed them, and even when they heard his footsteps. The reflex of secretion, with its unlearned response of salivation, had somehow become connected or conditioned to stimuli that had, on previous occasions, been associated with feeding. These psychic reflexes (as Pavlov originally called them) were aroused in the animal by stimuli other than the original one (the food). Pavlov realized that this occurred because these other stimuli (such as the sight and sounds of the attendant) had so often been associated with the ingestion of food. The associationists had referred to this phenomenon as association by frequency of occurrence. After a long period of doubting whether to pursue this observation because of its psychical nature, Pavlov decided in 1902 to proceed, and he quickly became absorbed in the new research.

Pavlov, in accordance with the prevailing Zeitgeist in animal psychology (and like Thorndike, Loeb, and others before him), initially focused on the mentalistic experiences of his laboratory animals; this can be seen in his original term for conditioned reflexes—psychic reflexes. He wrote about the animals' desires, judgment, and will, interpreting animal psychic events in subjective, human terms. After a while, however, Pavlov dropped all mentalistic references in favor of a straightforward, objective approach. He described it as follows: "At first in our psychical experiments with the psychical glands . . . we conscientiously endeavored to explain our results by imagining the subjective state of the animal. But nothing came of this except sterile controversy and individual views that could not be reconciled. And so we could do nothing but conduct the research on a purely objective basis" (Cuny, 1965, p. 65).

Pavlov's subsequent research was a model of objectivity and precision. His first experiments were simple. He showed a dog a piece of bread in his hand before giving it to the dog to eat. In time, salivation began as soon as the dog saw the bread. The dog's response of salivating when the bread was placed in its mouth is a natural reflexive response of the digestive system; no learning is necessary for it to occur. Pavlov called this an innate or ***unconditioned reflex***. Salivating at the sight of food, however, is not reflexive but must be learned. This response Pavlov now called a ***conditional reflex*** (instead of the mentalistic *psychic reflex*) because it was conditional or dependent on the formation of an association or connection between the sight of the food and the subsequent eating of it.

Pavlov discovered that any stimulus could produce the conditional salivary response so long as it was capable of attracting the animal's attention without arousing fear or anger. He tested such stimuli as a bell, a buzzer, a light, and a ticking metronome.

His thoroughness and precision are evident in the elaborate and sophisticated technique he used to collect the saliva. A rubber tube was connected to an opening made in the dog's cheek through which saliva flowed. When each drop of saliva fell onto a platform that rested on a sensitive spring, it activated a marker on a revolving drum (see Figure 9-2). This arrangement, which made possible the recording of the precise number of drops and the moment at which each fell, is but one example of Pavlov's painstaking efforts to standardize experimental conditions, apply rigorous controls, and eliminate sources of error.

Figure 9-2 ▬▬▬▬▬▬▬▬▬▬▬▬▬▬▬▬▬▬▬▬▬▬▬▬▬
Pavlov's apparatus for studying the conditional salivary response
in dogs.

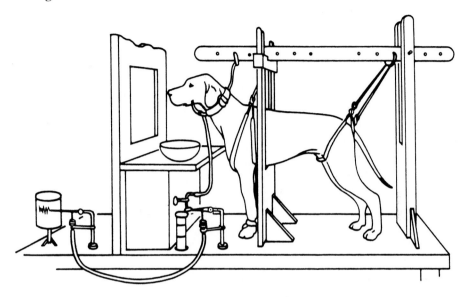

He was so concerned about preventing outside intrusions that he
designed special cubicles for his research. The experimental animal was
placed in a harness in one cubicle and the experimenter occupied another.
The experimenter could operate the various conditioning stimuli, collect
the saliva, and present the food without being seen by the animal.

These precautions did not completely satisfy Pavlov, however. He
believed that extraneous environmental stimuli could still affect the animals. Using funds supplied by a Moscow businessman, Pavlov designed a
three-story research building, later dubbed the "Tower of Silence," in
which the windows were covered with extra-thick glass. The rooms had
double steel doors that formed an airtight seal when closed, and the steel
girders that supported the floors were embedded in sand. A moat filled
with straw encircled the building. Vibration, noise, temperature extremes,
odors, and drafts were eliminated. Pavlov hoped that nothing would influence the experimental animals but the conditioning stimuli to which they
were exposed.

A typical conditioning experiment runs as follows. The ***conditioned
stimulus*** (a light, let us say) is presented (in this case, switched on).
Immediately, the ***unconditioned stimulus*** (the food) is presented. After
a number of pairings of the light and the food, the animal salivates at the
sight of the light. The animal has become conditioned to respond to the

conditioned stimulus. An association or bond has been formed between the light and the food. Learning or conditioning will not occur unless the light is followed by the food a number of times. Thus, *reinforcement* (being fed) is necessary for learning to take place.

In addition to studying the formation of these conditioned responses, Pavlov and his associates investigated related phenomena such as reinforcement, extinction of responses, spontaneous recovery, generalization, discrimination, and higher-order conditioning — all well-known words in the language of psychology today. Some two hundred collaborators came to work with Pavlov, and his experimental program extended over a longer time period and involved more people than any research effort since Wundt's.

A Note on Twitmyer

An interesting historical sidelight involved the independent discovery of the same phenomenon at the same time. In 1904 a young American named Edwin Burket Twitmyer (1873–1943), a former student of Lightner Witmer at the University of Pennsylvania, presented a paper at the APA meeting based on his doctoral dissertation, completed two years earlier. His work concerned the familiar knee jerk reflex. In the course of his study Twitmyer noticed that subjects began to respond to stimuli other than the original stimulus, which was the tap of the hammer just below the knee. He described the subjects' reactions as a new and unusual kind of reflex arc and suggested that it be studied further (Twitmyer, 1905).

No one was interested in Twitmyer's report. There were no questions from the audience after he finished his presentation. His research was ignored. Growing discouraged, he did not pursue the issue.

Several reasons have been advanced to explain Twitmyer's continued residence in obscurity. Perhaps the American Zeitgeist was not yet ready to accept such a notion as a conditioned reflex. Perhaps Twitmyer was too young and inexperienced or lacked the skills and economic resources necessary to persevere and promote his new finding. Or perhaps it was simply a matter of bad timing.

Twitmyer delivered his talk just before lunch in a series of papers chaired by William James. The session was running late, and James (perhaps hungry, maybe bored as well) peremptorily adjourned the meeting without allowing much time for any discussion of Twitmyer's paper. Although the story of Twitmyer is revived periodically as another example of simultaneous discovery (see Coon, 1982; Misceo & Samelson, 1983; Windholz, 1986), it is also a tragic tale of a scientist who might have become famous for making one of the most important discoveries in all of psychology. "Surely Twitmyer must have wrestled with that realization most of his life—an awareness of what his legacy to psychology might have been" (Benjamin, 1987, p. 1119).

Comment

With Pavlov's work, more precise and objective measures and terminology were introduced into the study of learning. Also, Pavlov demonstrated that higher mental processes could be studied in physiological terms with the use of animal subjects and without any reference to consciousness. Further, conditioning has had broad practical applications in areas such as behavior therapy. Thus, Pavlov's work influenced psychology's shift toward greater objectivity in subject matter and methodology and reinforced the trend toward the functional and practical.

Pavlov's conditioning techniques provided the science of psychology with a basic element or atom of behavior, a workable concrete unit to which complex human behavior could be reduced and experimented on under laboratory conditions. As we shall see, John B. Watson seized on this unit of behavior and made it the core of his program. Pavlov was pleased with Watson's work, believing that the growth of behaviorism in the United States represented a confirmation of his ideas and methods.

It is ironic that Pavlov's greatest influence has been in psychology, a field toward which he was not altogether favorable. He was familiar with the structural and functional psychologies, and he agreed with William James that psychology had not yet reached the status of a science. Consequently, Pavlov excluded it from his own work. He levied fines on laboratory assistants who used psychological rather than physiological terminology, and in his lectures he frequently made such remarks as "we must count it an uncontested fact that the physiology of the highest part of the nervous system of higher animals cannot be successfully studied unless we utterly renounce the untenable pretensions of psychology" (Woodworth, 1948, p. 60).

Toward the end of his life Pavlov changed his attitude and even referred to himself as an experimental psychologist. His initially negative view of the field did not, however, prevent psychologists from making effective use of his work. At first they used the conditional response to measure sensory discrimination in animals, and it is still used for that purpose today. During the 1920s they began to use it as the foundation for theories of learning, and it has generated considerable research, application, and controversy.

Vladimir M. Bekhterev (1857–1927)

Vladimir Bekhterev is another important figure in the movement of animal psychology and the study of learning from subjective ideas toward objectively observed overt behavior. Although less well known than Pavlov, this Russian physiologist, neurologist, and psychiatrist was a pioneer in several research areas. He was a contemporary and rival of Pavlov's in the early years of the twentieth century and independently became interested in conditioning.

Bekhterev received his degree from the Military Medical Academy in St. Petersburg in 1881. He studied at the University of Leipzig with Wilhelm Wundt, took additional courses in Berlin and Paris, and returned to Russia to accept the chair of mental diseases at the University of Kazan. In 1893, he was appointed chair of mental and nervous diseases at the Military Medical Academy, where he also organized a mental hospital. In 1907, he founded the Psychoneurological Institute (now called the Bekhterev Psychoneurological Research Institute) and began a program of neurological research.

Pavlov's conditioning research had been conducted almost exclusively on glandular secretions. Bekhterev was interested in the motor conditioning response, extending the Pavlovian conditioning principle to the striped muscles. Bekhterev's basic discovery was the ***associated reflex*** as revealed through the study of motor responses. He found that reflexive movements—such as withdrawing one's finger from the source of an electric shock—could be elicited not only by the unconditioned stimulus (the electric shock), but also by stimuli that had become associated with the original stimulus. For example, sounding a buzzer at the time of the shock soon elicited the withdrawal of the finger.

The associationists explained such connections in terms of the operation of some sort of mental process. Bekhterev, however, considered the reactions to be totally reflexive. He believed that higher-level behaviors of greater complexity could be explained in the same way, that is, as a compounding of the low-level motor reflexes. Thought processes were of similar character, in that they depended on inner activities of the speech musculature. This idea was later adopted by Watson. Bekhterev argued for a completely objective approach to psychological phenomena and against the use of mentalistic terms and concepts.

He presented his views in the book *Objective Psychology*, published in 1907. It was translated into German and French in 1913, when it was read by Watson. A third edition was published in English in 1932 as *General Principles of Human Reflexology*.

Comment

From the beginnings of animal psychology in the work of Romanes and Morgan we can see a steady movement toward increased objectivity in both subject matter and methodology. The initial work in the field invoked the concepts of consciousness and mental processes and relied on research methods that were also subjective. By the early twentieth century, however, animal psychology was completely objective in subject matter and methodology. Glandular secretions, conditional responses, acts, behaviors—such terms left no doubt that animal psychology had finally discarded its subjective past.

Animal psychology was shortly to serve as a model for behaviorism, whose leader much preferred animal to human subjects for his psychological research. Watson adopted the findings and methods of the animal psychologists as a foundation for the development of a science of behavior that was applicable to animals and humans alike.

The Influence of Functionalism on Behaviorism

Another direct antecedent of behaviorism was functionalism. Although not totally objective, functional psychology in Watson's day did represent greater objectivity than its predecessors. Cattell and other functionalists, who were emphasizing behavior and objectivity, had expressed dissatisfaction with introspection. We noted in Chapter 8 that by the turn of the century less than 3 percent of the experimental articles published in American psychology journals involved the use of introspection. Applied psychologists had little use for consciousness and introspection, and their various specialty areas essentially constituted an objective functional psychology. Thus the functional psychologists had moved away from the pure psychology of conscious experience of Wundt and Titchener before Watson came on the scene. In their writings and lectures, some functional psychologists were quite specific in calling for an objective psychology, a psychology that would focus on behavior instead of consciousness.

Cattell, speaking at the 1904 World's Fair in St. Louis, Missouri, said:

I am not convinced that psychology should be limited to the study of consciousness as such. . . . The rather widespread notion that there is no psychology apart from introspection is refuted by the brute argument of accomplished fact. It seems to me that most of the research work that has been done by me or in my laboratory is nearly as independent of introspection as work in physics or in zoology. . . . I see no reason why the application of systematized knowledge to the control of human nature may not in the course of the present century accomplish results commensurate with the nineteenth-century applications of physical science to the material world. (Cattell, 1904, pp. 179–180, 186)

Watson was present at Cattell's talk. The similarity between his later public position and Cattell's statement is so striking that one historian has suggested that Cattell should be called the "grandfather" of Watson's behaviorism (Burnham, 1968, p. 149).

In the decade before Watson formally founded behaviorism, the intellectual climate in the United States favored and reinforced the idea of an objective psychology, and the overall movement of American psychology was in a behavioristic direction. Robert Woodworth at Columbia University noted that American psychologists were "slowly coming down with behaviorism . . . as more and more of them, from 1904 on, expressed a preference for defining psychology as the science of behavior rather than as an attempt to describe consciousness" (Woodworth, 1943, p. 28).

In 1911, Walter Pillsbury, who had studied with Titchener, defined psychology in his textbook as the "science of behavior." He argued that it was possible to treat human beings as objectively as any other aspect of the physical universe. That same year Max Meyer published *The Fundamental Laws of Human Behavior*. In 1912 William McDougall wrote *Psychology: The Study of Behavior*, and Knight Dunlap, a psychologist at Johns Hopkins University, where Watson was teaching, proposed that introspection be banned from psychology.

Angell, perhaps the most forward-looking of the functionalists, predicted that American psychology was ready to move toward greater objectivity. In 1910 he commented that it seemed possible that the term *consciousness* would disappear from psychology, much as had the term *soul*. In 1913, shortly before Watson's behaviorist manifesto appeared, Angell elaborated on this point, suggesting that it would be profitable if consciousness were forgotten and if animal and human behavior were described objectively instead. Thus, the notion that psychology should be the science of behavior was already gaining adherents. Watson's greatness was not in being the first to propose the idea but in seeing, perhaps more clearly than anyone else, what the times were calling for. He responded vigorously and articulately as the agent of a revolution whose inevitability and success were assured, because it was already underway.

Suggested Readings

Bitterman, M. E. (1969). Thorndike and the problem of animal intelligence. *American Psychologist, 24,* 444–453. Discusses Thorndike's career at Columbia University and his puzzle-box experiments on animal learning.

Coon, D. J. (1982). Eponymy, obscurity, Twitmyer, and Pavlov. *Journal of the History of the Behavioral Sciences, 18,* 255–262. Discusses the work of Twitmyer on conditioned responses and suggests that social, economic, intellectual, and personal factors combined to promote Pavlov's discoveries rather than Twitmyer's.

Fernald, D. (1984). *The Hans Legacy: A Story of Science.* Hillsdale NJ: Lawrence Erlbaum. An engaging account of the Clever Hans story and its implications for scientific inquiry.

Jonçich, G. (1968). *The Sane Positivist: A Biography of Edward L. Thorndike.* Middletown CT: Wesleyan University Press. An account of Thorndike's life, times, and contributions to psychology.

Ljunggren, B. (1990). *Great Men with Sick Brains and Other Essays.* Park Ridge IL: American Association of Neurological Surgeons. Includes an essay on Vladimir Bekhterev that offers new information on his life and his work on reflexology.

Mackenzie, B. D. (1977). *Behaviourism and the Limits of Scientific Method.* Atlantic Highlands NJ: Humanities Press. Suggests that behaviorism failed to live up to its early promise because it applied the scientific method too rigorously to psychological issues.

Pauly, P. J. (1981). The Loeb–Jennings debate and the science of animal behavior. *Journal of the History of the Behavioral Sciences, 17,* 504–515. Describes the controversy about animal tropisms between the biologists Jacques Loeb and Herbert Spencer Jennings, an exchange of views carried out in books and articles and at scientific meetings. Notes Loeb's influence on John B. Watson and his development of behaviorism.

Windholz, G. (1990). Pavlov and the Pavlovians in the laboratory. *Journal of the History of the Behavioral Sciences, 26,* 64–74. Describes the daily routine in Pavlov's laboratories at Leningrad between 1897 and 1936, and his personal influence on his associates and students.

Yerkes, R. M., & Morgulis, S. (1909). The method of Pavlov in animal psychology. *Psychological Bulletin, 6,* 257–273. The article that brought Pavlov's work to the attention of American psychologists. Describes Pavlov's experimental procedure for investigating the salivary reflex in dogs, and presents subsequent research on the effects of various auditory stimuli on the dogs' responses.

Behaviorism: The Beginning

10

John B. Watson (1878–1958)

We have discussed several antecedents of the behaviorist movement that influenced Watson in his attempt to construct a new school of thought for psychology. He recognized that founding is not the same as originating, and he described his efforts as a crystallization of current trends in psychology. Like Wilhelm Wundt, psychology's first promoter-founder, Watson set out deliberately to found a new school. This intention distinguishes him from others whom history now labels as precursors of behaviorism.

Although his academic career was brief, John B. Watson, the founder of behaviorism, was influential in conceiving an objective psychology free of mentalism and as scientific as physics.

The Life of Watson

John B. Watson was born on a farm near Greenville, South Carolina, where his early education was conducted in a one-room schoolhouse. His mother was intensely religious, his father just the opposite. The elder Watson drank heavily, was prone to violence, and had several extramarital affairs.

Because Watson's father rarely held any job for long, the family lived on the edge of poverty, barely subsisting on the output of their farm. Their neighbors looked on them with pity and contempt. When Watson was thirteen, his father ran off with another woman, never to return, and Watson resented him all his life. Many years later, when Watson was rich and famous, his father came to New York and tried to see him, but Watson refused to meet with him.

In Watson's youth and teenage years, he was described as a delinquent. He spoke of himself as lazy and insubordinate, and he never earned better than passing grades in school. His teachers remembered him as indolent, argumentative, and sometimes uncontrollable. He got into fistfights and was twice arrested, once for shooting a gun within the city limits. Nevertheless, he enrolled at Baptist-affiliated Furman University in Greenville at the age of sixteen, determined to become a minister. He had promised his mother, many years earlier, that he would embrace the life of a clergyman. He studied philosophy, mathematics, Latin, and Greek, and expected to graduate in 1899 and enter Princeton Theological Seminary the following fall.

A curious thing happened during Watson's senior year at Furman. One of his professors warned the students that anyone who handed in the final examination with the pages in reverse order would receive a failing grade for the course. Watson took the professor up on the challenge, turned in his exam backward, and failed; at least that is how Watson reported the story. A more recent examination of the pertinent data of history—in this case, Watson's grades—shows that he did not fail that particular course. His biographer suggests that the story Watson chose to tell reveals something of his own nature, that is, "his ambivalence toward success. Watson's constant striving for achievement and approval was often sabotaged by acts of sheer obstinacy and impulsiveness more characteristic of a flight from respectability" (Buckley, 1989, p. 11).

Watson remained at Furman for another year and received a master's degree in 1900, but during that year his mother died, freeing him from his vow to become a minister. Instead of Princeton Theological Seminary, Watson went to the University of Chicago. He was at that time "an ambitious, extremely status-conscious young man, anxious to make his mark upon the world but wholly unsettled as to his choice of profession and desperately insecure about his lack of means and social sophistication. He arrived on campus with fifty dollars to his name" (Buckley, 1989, p. 39). He had chosen Chicago to pursue graduate work in philosophy under John Dewey but after a while found Dewey incomprehensible. "I never knew what he was talking about then," Watson recalled, "and, unfortunately for me, I still don't know" (Watson, 1936, p. 274). His enthusiasm for philosophy quickly diminished.

He became attracted to psychology through the work of James Rowland Angell, and he also studied neurology as well as biology and physiology with Jacques Loeb, who introduced him to the concept of mechanism. He worked at several jobs—as a waiter in a fraternity house, a rat caretaker, and an assistant janitor (his duties included dusting Angell's desk). Toward the end of his graduate studies he suffered acute anxiety attacks and was unable to sleep without a light on.

In 1903 Watson received his Ph.D., the youngest person ever to earn a doctorate from the University of Chicago. Although he graduated with high honors, he reported feeling a deep sense of inferiority when Angell and Dewey told him that his doctoral examination was not as good as that of Helen Thompson Woolley, who had graduated two years earlier. (Woolley, despite her competence, faced considerable sex discrimination and was denied an academic career.)

That same year Watson married one of his students, nineteen-year-old Mary Ickes, who was from a socially and politically prominent family. The story is told that the young and impressionable Mary wrote a long love poem to Watson on one of her examination papers, instead of answering the questions. It is not known what grade she got, but she did get Watson. Her family opposed the marriage; her brother called Watson, who had had several affairs with students, a "selfish, conceited cad" (Buckley, 1989, p. 50).

Watson stayed on as an instructor at the University of Chicago until 1908. He published his dissertation on the neurological and psychological maturation of the white rat and demonstrated early his preference for animal subjects.

> I never wanted to use human subjects. I hated to serve as a subject. I didn't like the stuffy, artificial instructions given to subjects. I always was uncomfortable and acted unnaturally. With animals I was at home. I felt that, in studying them, I was keeping close to biology with my feet on the ground. More and more the thought presented itself: Can't I find out by watching their behavior everything that the other students are finding out by using [human observers]? (Watson, 1936, p. 276)

Some of Watson's professors and fellow students recalled that he was not a good introspector. Whatever special talent or temperament was needed for introspection, Watson did not have it. This may have provided some of the impetus that drove him toward an objective behavioral psychology. After all, if he was no good at practicing the primary technique in his field, then his career prospects were dim—unless he could develop another approach. Also, if psychology was a science that studied only behavior, which, of course, could be done with animals as well as humans, then the professional interests of animal psychologists could be advanced and brought into the mainstream of the field.

In 1908, when Watson became eligible for an assistant professorship at Chicago, he was offered a full professorship at Johns Hopkins University in Baltimore. Although he was reluctant to leave Chicago, the promotion, the opportunity to direct the laboratory, and the substantial salary increase offered by Johns Hopkins left him little choice. Watson spent twelve years there, his most productive years for psychology.

The person who offered Watson the job at Johns Hopkins was James Mark Baldwin (1861–1934), who, with Cattell, had started the journal *Psychological Review*. Baldwin's major area of interest was the importance of evolutionary theory in the study of the child. A year after Watson arrived, Baldwin was forced to resign because of a scandal; he had been caught in a police raid on a brothel. Baldwin's explanation for his presence in the house of ill repute was not accepted by the university's president. "I foolishly yielded," Baldwin said, "to a suggestion, made after a dinner, to visit [the brothel] and see what was done there. I did not know before going that immoral women were harbored there" (Evans & Scott, 1978, p. 713). Baldwin became an outcast from American psychology and spent the remainder of his life in Europe. Eleven years later history repeated itself, when the same university president asked for Watson's resignation because of a scandal.

At the time of Baldwin's resignation, however, Watson stood to gain. He became the head of the psychology department and replaced Baldwin as editor of the influential *Psychological Review*. Thus, at the age of thirty-one Watson was a pivotal figure in American psychology, in the right place at the right time.

Watson was extremely popular with the students at Johns Hopkins. The year after his arrival they dedicated their yearbook to him, and in 1919 the senior class voted him the handsomest professor, surely a unique accolade in the history of psychology. Personally he remained driven, ambitious, and intense, often on the edge of exhaustion. Many times he felt "on the verge of a breakdown," struggling with "the fear of losing control, and he usually reacted by working even harder" (Buckley, 1989, p. 67).

He began to think seriously about a more objective approach to psychology around 1903, and he first expressed these ideas publicly in 1908, in a lecture at Yale University. In 1912, at the invitation of Cattell, he spoke again on the subject in a series of lectures at Columbia University. The following year he published his now famous position paper in the *Psychological Review* (Watson, 1913), and behaviorism was officially launched.

Behavior: An Introduction to Comparative Psychology appeared in 1914. In this book Watson argued for the acceptance of animal psychology, and he described the advantages of using animals as subjects in psychological research. Many younger psychologists and students found his behaviorism appealing, believing that Watson was cleansing the muddled atmosphere of psychology by casting off long-standing mysteries and uncertainties carried over from philosophy. Mary Cover Jones (1896–1987), then a student and later president of the APA's Division of Developmental Psychology, recalled, more than a half-century later, the excitement that greeted the publication of each of Watson's books. "It shook the foundations of traditional European-bred psychology, and we welcomed it. . . . It pointed the way from armchair psychology to action and reform and was therefore hailed as a panacea" (Jones, 1974, p. 582). Older psychologists were not universally captivated by Watson's program. Indeed, most rejected his approach. We will discuss their reactions later in the chapter.

Only two years after the publication of the *Psychological Review* article, Watson was elected president of the American Psychological Association, at the age of thirty-seven. This may not have represented an endorsement of his position as much as a recognition of his visibility within the field and his personal connection with many prominent psychologists.

Watson wanted both psychologists and the public at large to see that his new behaviorism had practical value. His approach was not only for the laboratory but for the real world as well, and he worked hard to promote its practical applications in many areas. In 1916, he became a personnel consultant for a large insurance company, and he offered a course at Johns Hopkins for business students on the psychology of advertising.

Watson's professional activities were interrupted by World War I, when he served as a major in the Army Aviation Service. After the war, in 1918, he began his research on children, one of the earliest attempts at experimental work on human infants.

His next book, *Psychology from the Standpoint of a Behaviorist*, was published in 1919. It presented a more complete statement of his behavioral psychology and argued that the methods and principles he recommended earlier for animal psychology were equally applicable and legitimate for the study of humans.

In 1920 Watson fell in love with Rosalie Rayner, his graduate assistant. She was half his age and the daughter of a wealthy and influential Baltimore family that had donated a considerable sum of money to the university. Watson had written her a number of torrid love letters, fifteen of which were found by his wife. Excerpts of the letters were printed in *The Baltimore Sun* during the widely publicized divorce proceedings that followed. "Every cell I have is yours, individually and collectively," Watson had written. "My total reactions are positive and toward you. So likewise each and every heart reaction. I can't be more yours than I am, even if a surgical operation made us one" (Pauly, 1979, p. 40). Thus ended Watson's promising university career. He was forced to resign from Johns Hopkins. He married Rosalie Rayner but was never permitted to return to a full-time academic position.

No university would have him because of the notoriety attached to his name, and he soon realized that he would have to make a new life. "I can find a commercial job," he wrote to a friend. "It will not be as bad as raising chickens or cabbages. But I frankly love my work. I feel that my work is important for psychology and that the tiny flame which I have tried to keep burning for the future of psychology will be snuffed out if I go" (Pauly, 1986, p. 39).

Many academic colleagues, including his mentor Angell at the University of Chicago, publicly criticized Watson on personal grounds during this difficult time. It is understandable that Watson became embittered toward them. Ironically, considering their radically different temperaments and theoretical positions, E. B. Titchener at Cornell was of great help to Watson during this crisis. "You have done more for me than all the rest of my colleagues put together," Watson wrote to Titchener in 1922 (Larson & Sullivan, 1965, p. 346).

Unemployed and ordered to pay two-thirds of his former salary in alimony and child support, Watson began a second professional career as an applied psychologist in the field of advertising. "I shall go into commercial work wholeheartedly and burn all bridges" (Buckley, 1982, p. 211). He joined the J. Walter Thompson advertising agency in 1921, worked in every department, made house-to-house surveys, sold coffee, and clerked in Macy's department store to learn about the business world. Exercising his characteristic ingenuity and drive, within three years he was a vice president. In 1936 he joined another agency, where he remained as vice president until his retirement in 1945.

Watson exerted a major impact on advertising in the United States through the application of the principles of his behaviorist psychology. We can still see the effects of his work in commercials and ads. Watson believed that people were like machines. Their buying behavior could be predicted and controlled, just like the behavior of other machines. To control a consumer "it is only necessary to confront him with either fundamental or conditional emotional stimuli. . . . tell him something that will tie up with fear, something that will stir up a mild rage, that will call out an affectionate or love response, or strike at a deep psychological or habit need" (Buckley, 1982, p. 212).

He proposed that consumer behavior be studied scientifically under laboratory conditions, with careful attention given to surveys. He emphasized that advertising messages should focus on style rather than substance and should convey the impression of new designs and new images. The purpose was to make consumers dissatisfied with the products they had and to engender the desire for new goods. He pioneered the use of celebrity endorsements of products; the manipulation of human motives, emotions, and needs; and the appeal to basic wants and fears to sell everything from automobiles to deodorant soap. In the process Watson achieved a position of prominence and wealth, and he claimed to be very happy.

After 1920 Watson's contact with academic psychology was, of course, only indirect. Instead, he spent a great deal of time presenting his case for behaviorism to the public. He gave lectures and radio addresses and wrote articles for popular magazines such as *Harper's, Cosmopolitan, McCall's, Collier's*, and *The Nation*. The fact that the editors of these publications urged him to write for them attests to the nationwide interest in behaviorism.

In his articles Watson embarked on a crusade to sell the message of behaviorism to a wide audience. He wrote in a clear, readable, if somewhat simplistic style and was well paid for his efforts. In his autobiography Watson pointed out that as long as he could no longer publish in the professional psychology journals, he saw no reason why he should not go public and, in the language of his new field of advertising, "sell his wares" (Watson, 1936).

Watson lectured at the New School for Social Research in New York City, and out of these talks came the book *Behaviorism* (1925, 1930), which described his program for the improvement of society.

In 1928 he published a book on child care, *Psychological Care of the Infant and Child*, in which he presented a regulatory rather than a permissive system of child rearing, in keeping with his strong environmentalist position. The book was full of stern advice on the behaviorist way to bring up children. Parents should never

> hug and kiss them, never let them sit on your lap. If you must, kiss them once on the forehead when they say goodnight. Shake hands with them in the morning. Give them a pat on the head if they have made an extraordinarily good job of a difficult task. Try it out. In a week's time you will find how easy it is to be perfectly objective with your child and at the same time kindly. You will be utterly ashamed at the mawkish, sentimental way you have been handling it. (Watson, 1928, pp. 81–82)

The book transformed American child-rearing practices and had a greater popular impact than anything else Watson wrote. A generation of children, including his own, was brought up in line with these prescriptions.

Watson's son James, a California businessman, recalled in 1987 that his father was unable to show affection to the children and never kissed or held them. He described his father as

> unresponsive, emotionally uncommunicative, unable to express and cope with any feelings or emotions of his own, and determined unwittingly to deprive, I think, my brother and me of any kind of emotional foundation. He deeply believed that any expression of tenderness or affection would have a harmful effect on us. He was very rigid in carrying out his fundamental philosophies as a behaviorist. (Hannush, 1987, pp. 137–138)

James Watson spent six years in psychoanalysis following a suicide attempt. His brother William became a psychiatrist and later took his own life.

The mother of James and William, Rosalie Rayner Watson, wrote an article for *Parents Magazine* entitled "I Am the Mother of a Behaviorist's Sons," in which she admitted to some disagreement with her husband's child-rearing practices. She found it difficult, she said, to restrain completely her affection for her children and occasionally wanted to break all the behaviorist's rules; her son James could not recall that ever happening (Duke, Fried, Pliley, & Walker, 1989).

To the public, Watson displayed an attractive combination of personal characteristics and abilities. He was intelligent and articulate, and his handsome appearance and legendary charm would have made him a star, a charismatic figure, in today's media-oriented culture. He was a celebrity, much in the public eye, throughout most of his life, and he courted and relished the attention. He dressed well, raced speedboats, mingled with the cream of New York society, and "prided himself on being able to take on all challengers in extensive drinking bouts. . . . He had few friends but was obsessed with the pursuit of women" (Buckley, 1989, pp. 177–178). He built a mansion in Connecticut, staffed it with servants, yet delighted in donning old clothes and doing much of the yard work himself.

Watson's life changed dramatically in 1935 when Rosalie died of a tropical fever contracted on a trip to the West Indies. "The light seemed to go out of Watson's life" (Larson, 1979, p. 5). His son James recalled that this was the only time he saw his father cry, and for a brief moment Watson put his arms around both sons' shoulders.

Myrtle McGraw, a psychologist doing research on infant behavior at Columbia-Presbyterian Medical Center in New York, remembered meeting Watson not long afterward. He told her how utterly unprepared he was to deal with his wife's death; because he was twenty years older, he had always expected to die first. He talked to her at some length and "wondered how he could ever recover from this grief" (McGraw, 1990, p. 936).

Watson never did recover. He became a recluse, drinking heavily, shutting himself off from virtually all social contact, and plunging compulsively into his work. He sold the estate and moved to a simple wooden farmhouse that resembled his boyhood home.

In 1957, when he was seventy-nine, the American Psychological Association voted to award him a citation, praising his work as "one of the vital determinants of the form and substance of modern psychology . . . the point of departure for continuing lines of fruitful research." A companion drove Watson to the New York hotel where the presentation ceremony was to be held, "but at the last minute Watson refused to go inside and insisted that his eldest son attend in his stead. . . . Watson was afraid that in that moment his emotions would overwhelm him, that the apostle of behavior control would break down and weep" (Buckley, 1989, p. 182).

Watson died the following year, but first he burned all of his letters, manuscripts, and notes, feeding them into the fireplace one by one, refusing to leave them to history.

Original Source Material on Behaviorism: From *Psychology as the Behaviorist Views It* by John B. Watson

There is no better starting point for a discussion of Watson's behaviorism than the article that began the movement: "Psychology as the Behaviorist Views It" from the *Psychological Review* of 1913.* In his clear and readable style Watson discussed the following ideas: (1) the definition and goal of his new psychology; (2) his criticisms of structuralism and functionalism, the earlier psychologies of consciousness; (3) the role of "hereditary and habit equipments" in enabling organisms to adapt and adjust to their environment; (4) the view that the areas of applied psychology are truly scientific because they seek general laws that can be used to control behavior; and (5) the importance of maintaining uniform experimental procedures in both human and animal research.

---

*From J. B. Watson, "Psychology as the behaviorist views it." *Psychological Review*, 1913, 20, 158–177. Copyright 1913 by the American Psychological Association. Reprinted by permission.

Psychology as the behaviorist views it is a purely objective experimental branch of natural science. Its theoretical goal is the prediction and control of behavior. Introspection forms no essential part of its methods, nor is the scientific value of its data dependent upon the readiness with which they lend themselves to interpretation in terms of consciousness. The behaviorist, in his efforts to get a unitary scheme of animal response, recognizes no dividing line between man and brute. The behavior of man, with all of its refinement and complexity, forms only a part of the behaviorist's total scheme of investigation.

It has been maintained by its followers generally that psychology is a study of the science of the phenomena of consciousness. It has taken as its problem, on the one hand, the analysis of complex mental states (or processes) into simple elementary constituents, and on the other the construction of complex states when the elementary constituents are given. The world of the physical objects (stimuli, including here anything which may excite activity in a receptor), which forms the total phenomena of the natural scientist, is looked upon merely as means to an end. That end is the production of mental states that may be "inspected" or "observed." The psychological object of observation in the case of an emotion, for example, is the mental state itself. The problem in emotion is the determination of the number and kind of elementary constituents present, their loci, intensity, order of appearance, etc. It is agreed that introspection is the method *par excellence* by means of which mental states may be manipulated for purposes of psychology. On this assumption, behavior data (including under this term everything which goes under the name of comparative psychology) have no value *per se*. They possess significance only in so far as they may throw light upon conscious states. Such data must have at least an analogical or indirect reference to belong to the realm of psychology. . . .

I do not wish unduly to criticize psychology. It has failed signally, I believe, during the fifty-odd years of its existence as an experimental discipline to make its place in the world as an undisputed natural science. Psychology, as it is generally thought of, has something esoteric in its methods. If you fail to reproduce my findings, it is not due to some fault in your apparatus or in the control of your stimulus, but it is due to the fact that your introspection is untrained. The attack is made upon the observer and not upon the experimental setting. In physics and in chemistry the attack is made upon the experimental conditions. The apparatus was not sensitive enough, impure chemicals were used, etc. In these sciences a better technique will give reproducible results. Psychology is otherwise. If you can't observe 3–9 states of clearness in attention, your introspection is poor. If, on the other hand, a feeling seems reasonably clear to you, your introspection is again faulty. You are seeing too much. Feelings are never clear.

The time seems to have come when psychology must discard all reference to consciousness; when it need no longer delude itself into thinking that it is making mental states the object of observation. We have become so enmeshed in speculative questions concerning the elements of mind, the nature of conscious content (for example, imageless thought, attitudes, . . . etc.) that I, as an experimental student, feel that something is wrong with our premises and the types of problems which develop from them. There is no longer any guarantee that we all mean the same thing when we use the terms now current in psychology. Take the case of sensation. A sensation is defined in terms of its attributes. One psychologist will state with readiness that the attributes of a visual sensation are *quality, extension, duration*, and *intensity*. Another will add *clearness*. Still another that of *order*. I doubt if any one psychologist can draw up a set of statements describing what he means by sensation which will be agreed to by three other psychologists of different training. Turn for a moment to the question of the number of isolable sensations. Is there an extremely large number of color sensations — or only four, red, green, yellow and blue? Again, yellow, while psychologically simple, can be obtained by superimposing red and green spectral rays upon the same diffusing surface! If, on the other hand, we say that every just noticeable difference in the spectrum is a simple sensation, and that every just noticeable increase in the white value of a given color gives simple sensations, we are forced to admit that the number is so large and the conditions for obtaining them so complex that the concept of sensation is unusable, either for the purpose of analysis or that of synthesis. Titchener, who has fought the most valiant fight in this country for a psychology based upon introspection, feels that these differences of opinion as to the number of sensations and their attributes; as to whether there are relations (in the sense of elements) and on the many others which seem to be fundamental in every attempt at analysis, are perfectly natural in the present undeveloped state of psychology. While it is admitted that every growing science is full of unanswered questions, surely only those who are wedded to the system as we now have it, who have fought and suffered for it, can confidently believe that there will ever be any greater uniformity than there is now in the answers we have to such questions. I firmly believe that two hundred years from now, unless the introspective method is discarded, psychology will still be divided on the question as to whether auditory sensations have the quality of "extension," whether intensity is an attribute which can be applied to color, whether there is a difference in "texture" between image and sensation and upon many hundreds of others of like character. . . .

My psychological quarrel is not with the systematic and structural psychologist alone. The last fifteen years have seen the growth of what is called functional psychology. This type of psychology decries the use of elements in the static sense of the structuralists. It throws emphasis upon the biological significance of conscious processes instead of upon the analysis of conscious states into introspectively isolable elements. I have done my best to understand the difference between functional psychology and structural psychology. Instead of clarity, confusion grows upon me. The terms sensation, perception, affection, emotion, volition are used as much by the functionalist as by the structuralist. The addition of the word "process" ("mental act as a whole," and like terms are frequently met) after each serves in some way to remove the corpse of "content" and to leave "function" in its stead. Surely if these concepts are elusive when looked at from a content standpoint, they are still more deceptive when viewed from the angle of function, and especially so when function is obtained by the introspection method. It is rather interesting that no functional psychologist has carefully distinguished between "perception" (and this is true of the other psychological terms as well) as employed by the systematist, and "perceptual process" as used in functional psychology. It seems illogical and hardly fair to criticize the psychology which the systematist gives us, and then to utilize his terms without carefully showing the changes in meaning which are to be attached to them. I was greatly surprised some time ago when I opened Pillsbury's book and saw psychology defined as the "science of behavior." A still more recent text states that psychology is the "science of mental behavior." When I saw these promising statements I thought, now surely we will have texts based upon different lines. After a few pages the science of behavior is dropped and one finds the conventional treatment of sensation, perception, imagery, etc., along with certain shifts in emphasis and additional facts which serve to give the author's personal imprint.

I believe we can write a psychology, define it as Pillsbury, and never go back upon our definition: never use the terms consciousness, mental states, mind, content, introspectively verifiable, imagery, and the like. . . . It can be done in terms of stimulus and response, in terms of habit formation, habit integrations and the like. Furthermore, I believe that it is really worth while to make this attempt now.

The psychology which I should attempt to build up would take as a starting point, first, the observable fact that organisms, man and animal alike, do adjust themselves to their environment by means of hereditary and habit equipments. These adjustments may be very adequate or they may be so inadequate that the organism barely maintains its existence; secondly, that certain stimuli lead the organisms to make the responses. In a system of psychology completely worked out, given the response the stimuli can be predicted; given the stimuli the response can be predicted. Such a set of statements is crass and raw in the extreme, as all such generalizations must be. Yet they are hardly more raw and less realizable than the ones which appear in the psychology texts of the day. I possibly might illustrate my point better by choosing an everyday problem which anyone is likely to meet in the course of his work. Some time ago I was called upon to make a study of certain species of birds. Until I went to Tortugas I had never seen these birds alive. When I reached there I found the animals doing certain things: some of the acts seemed to work peculiarly well in such an environment, while others seemed to be unsuited to their type of life. I first studied the responses of the group as a whole and later those of individuals. In order to understand more thoroughly the relation between what was habit and what was hereditary in these responses, I took the young birds and reared them. In this way I was able to study the order of appearance of hereditary adjustments and their complexity, and later the beginnings of habit formation. My efforts in determining the stimuli which called forth such adjustments were crude indeed. Consequently my attempts to control behavior and to produce responses at will did not meet with much success. Their food and water, sex and other social relations, light and temperature conditions were all beyond control in a field study. I did find it possible to control their reactions in a measure by using the nest and egg (or young) as stimuli. It is not necessary in this paper to develop further how such a study should be carried out and how work of this kind must be supplemented by carefully controlled laboratory experiments. Had I been called upon to examine the natives of some of the Australian tribes, I should have gone about my task in the same way. I should have found the problem more difficult: the types of responses called forth by physical stimuli would have been more varied, and the number of effective stimuli larger. I should have had to determine the social setting of their lives in a far more careful way. These savages would be more influenced by the responses of each other than was the case with the birds. Furthermore, habits would have been more complex and the influences of past habits upon the present responses would have appeared more clearly. Finally, if I had been called upon to work out the psychology of the educated European, my problem would have required several lifetimes. But in the one I have at my disposal I should have followed the same general line of attack. In the main, my desire in all such work is to gain an accurate knowledge of adjustments and the stimuli calling them forth. My final reason for this is to learn general and particular methods by which I may control behavior. My goal is not "the description and explanation of states of consciousness as such," nor that of obtaining such proficiency in mental gymnastics that I can immediately lay hold of a state of consciousness and say, "this, as a whole, consists of gray sensation number 350, of such and such extent, occurring in conjunction with the sensation of cold of a certain intensity; one of pressure of a certain intensity and extent," and so on *ad infinitum*. If psychology would follow the plan I suggest, the educator, the physician, the jurist and the business man could utilize our data in a practical way, as soon as we are able, experimentally, to obtain them. Those who have occasion to apply psychological principles practically would find no need to complain as they do at the present time. Ask any physician or jurist today whether scientific psychology plays a practical part in his daily routine and you will hear him deny that the psychology of the laboratories finds a place in his scheme of work. I think the criticism is extremely just. One of the earliest conditions which made me dissatisfied with psychology was the feeling that there was no realm of application for the principles which were being worked out in content terms.

What gives me hope that the behaviorist's position is a defensible one is the fact that those branches of psychology which have already partially withdrawn from the parent, experimental psychology, and which are consequently less dependent upon introspection are today in a most flourishing condition. Experimental pedagogy, the psychology of drugs, the psychology of advertising, legal psychology, the psychology of tests, and psychopathology are all vigorous growths. These are sometimes wrongly called "practical" or "applied" psychology. Surely there was never a worse misnomer. In the future there may grow up vocational bureaus which really apply psychology. At present these fields are truly scientific and are in search of broad generalizations which will lead to the control of human behavior. For example, we find out by experimentation whether a series of stanzas may be acquired more readily if the whole is learned at once, or whether it is more advantageous to learn each stanza separately and then pass to the succeeding. We do not attempt to apply our findings. The application of this principle is purely voluntary on the part of the teacher. In the psychology of drugs we may show the effect upon behavior of certain doses of caffeine. We may reach the conclusion that caffeine has a good effect upon the speed and accuracy of work. But these are general principles. We leave it to the individual as to whether the results of our tests shall be applied or not. Again, in legal testimony, we test the effects of recency upon the reliability of a witness's report. We test the accuracy of the report with respect to moving objects, stationary objects, color, etc. It depends upon the judicial machinery of the country to decide whether these facts are ever to be applied. For a "pure" psychologist to say that he is not interested in the questions raised in these divisions of the science because they relate indirectly to the application of psychology shows, in the first place, that he fails to understand the scientific aim in such problems, and secondly, that he is not interested in a psychology which concerns itself with human life. The only fault I have to find with these disciplines is that much of their material is stated in terms of introspection, whereas a statement in terms of objective results would be far more valuable. There is no reason why appeal should ever be made to consciousness in any of them. Or why introspective data should ever be sought during the experimentation, or published in the results. In experimental pedagogy especially one can see the desirability of keeping all of the results on a purely objective plane. If this is done, work there on the human being will be comparable directly with the work upon animals. For example, at Hopkins, Mr. Ulrich has obtained certain results upon the distribution of effort in learning — using rats as subjects. He is prepared to give comparative results upon the effect of having an animal work at the problem once per day, three times per day, and five times per day. Whether it is advisable to have the animal learn only one problem at a time or to learn three abreast. We need to have similar experiments made upon man, but we care as little about his "conscious processes" during the conduct of the experiment as we care about such processes in the rats.

I am more interested at the present moment in trying to show the necessity for maintaining uniformity in experimental procedure and in the method of stating results in both human and animal work, than in developing any ideas I may have upon the changes which are certain to come in the scope of human psychology. Let us consider for a moment the subject of the range of stimuli to which animals respond. I shall speak first of the work upon vision in animals. We put our animal in a situation where he will respond (or learn to respond) to one of two monochromatic lights. We feed him at the one (positive) and punish him at the other (negative). In a short time the animal learns to go to the light at which he is fed. At this point questions arise which I may phrase in two ways: I may choose the psychological way and say "does the animal see these two lights as I do, i.e., as two distinct colors, or does he see them as two grays differing in brightness, as does the totally color blind?" Phrased by the behaviorist, it would read as follows: "Is my animal responding upon the basis of the difference in intensity between the two stimuli, or upon the difference in wave-lengths?" He nowhere thinks of the animal's response in terms of his own experiences of colors and grays. He wishes to establish the fact whether wave-length is a factor in that animal's adjustment. If so, what wave-lengths are effective and what differences in wave-length must be maintained in the different regions to afford bases for differential responses? If wave-length is not a factor in adjustment he wishes to know what difference in intensity will serve as a basis for response, and whether that same difference will suffice throughout the spectrum. Furthermore, he wishes to test whether the animal can respond to wave-lengths which do not affect the human eye. He is as much interested in comparing the rat's spectrum with that of the chick as in comparing it with man's. The point of view when the various sets of comparisons are made does not change in the slightest.

However we phrase the question to ourselves, we take our animal after the association has been formed and then introduce certain control experiments which enable us to return answers to the questions just raised. But there is just as keen a desire on our part to test man under the same conditions, and to state the results in both cases in common terms.

The man and the animal should be placed as nearly as possible under the same experimental conditions. Instead of feeding or punishing the human subject, we should ask him to respond by setting a second apparatus until standard and control offered no basis for a differential response. Do I lay myself open to the charge here that I am using introspection? My reply is not at all; that while I might very well feed my human subject for a right choice and punish him for a wrong one and thus produce the response if the subject could give it, there is no need of going to extremes even on the platform I suggest. But be it understood that I am merely using this second method as an abridged behavior method. We can go just as far and reach just as dependable results by the longer method as by the abridged. In many cases the direct and typically human method cannot be safely used. Suppose, for example, that I doubt the accuracy of the setting of the control instrument, in the above experiment, as I am very likely to do if I suspect a defect in vision? It is hopeless for me to get his introspective report. He will say: "There is no difference in sensation, both are reds, identical in quality." But suppose I confront him with the standard and the control and so arrange conditions that he is punished if he responds to the "control" but not with the standard. I interchange the positions of the standard and the control at will and force him to attempt to differentiate the one from the other. If he can learn to make the adjustment even after a large number of trials it is evident that the two stimuli do afford the basis for a differential response. Such a method may sound nonsensical, but I firmly believe we will have to resort increasingly to just such a method where we have reason to distrust the language method.

There is hardly a problem in human vision which is not also a problem in animal vision: I mention the limits of the spectrum, threshold values, absolute and relative, flicker, Talbot's law, Weber's law, field of vision, the Purkinje phenomenon, etc. Every one is capable of being worked out by behavior methods. Many of them are being worked out at the present time.

I feel that all the work upon the senses can be consistently carried forward along the lines I have suggested here for vision. Our results will, in the end, give an excellent picture of what each organ stands for in the way of function. The anatomist and the physiologist may take our data and show, on the one hand, the structures which are responsible for these responses, and, on the other, the physico-chemical relations which are necessarily involved (physiological chemistry of nerve and muscle) in these and other reactions.

The situation in regard to the study of memory is hardly different. Nearly all of the memory methods in actual use in the laboratory today yield the type of results I am arguing for. A certain series of nonsense syllables or other material is presented to the human subject. What should receive the emphasis are the rapidity of the habit formation, the errors, peculiarities in the form of the curve, the persistence of the habit so formed, the relation of such habits to those formed when more complex material is used, etc. Now such results are taken down with the subject's introspection. The experiments are made for the purpose of discussing the mental machinery involved in learning, in recall, recollection and forgetting, and not for the purpose of seeking the human being's way of shaping his responses to meet the problems in the terribly complex environment into which he is thrown, nor for that of showing the similarities and differences between man's methods and those of other animals.

The situation is somewhat different when we come to a study of the more complex forms of behavior, such as imagination, judgment, reasoning, and conception. At present the only statements we have of them are in content terms. Our minds have been so warped by the fifty-odd years which have been devoted to the study of states of consciousness that we can envisage these problems only in one way. We should meet the situation squarely and say that we are not able to carry forward investigations along all of these lines by the behavior methods which are in use at the present time. In extenuation I should like to call attention to the paragraph above where I made the point that the introspective method itself has reached a *cul-de-sac* with respect to them. The topics have become so threadbare from much handling that they may well be put away for a time. As our methods become better developed it will be possible to undertake investigations of more and more complex forms of behavior. Problems which are now laid aside will again become imperative, but they can be viewed as they arise from a new angle and in more concrete settings.

Will there be left over in psychology a world of pure psychics, to use Yerkes' term? I confess I do not know. The plans which I most favor for psychology lead practically to the ignoring of consciousness in the sense that that term is used by psychologists today. I have virtually denied that this realm of psychics is open to experimental investigation. I don't wish to go further into the problem at present because it leads inevitably over into metaphysics. If you will grant the behaviorist the right to use consciousness in the same way that other natural scientists employ it — that is, without making consciousness a special object of observation — you have granted all that my thesis requires.

In concluding, I suppose I must confess to a deep bias on these questions. I have devoted nearly twelve years to experimentation on animals. It is natural that such a one should drift into a theoretical position which is in harmony with his experimental work. Possibly I have put up a straw man and have been fighting that. There may be no absolute lack of harmony between the position outlined here and that of functional psychology. I am inclined to think, however, that the two positions cannot be easily harmonized. Certainly the position I advocate is weak enough at present and can be attacked from many standpoints. Yet when all this is admitted I still feel that the considerations which I have urged should have a wide influence upon the type of psychology which is to be developed in the future. What we need to do is to start work upon psychology, making *behavior*, not *consciousness*, the objective point of our attack. Certainly there are enough problems in the control of behavior to keep us all working many lifetimes without ever allowing us time to think of consciousness *an sich*. Once launched in the undertaking, we will find ourselves in a short time as far divorced from an introspective psychology as the psychology of the present time is divorced from faculty psychology.

The Reaction to Watson's Program

Watson's vigorous attack on the old psychology and his call for a new approach made a stirring appeal. Consider the major points. Psychology was to be the science of behavior — not the introspective study of consciousness — and a purely objective experimental branch of natural science. Both human and animal behavior would be investigated. The new psychology would discard all mentalistic concepts and use only behavior concepts such as stimulus and response. The goal of psychology would be the prediction and control of behavior.

As we discussed, these points did not originate with Watson. Objective experimental methods had been used for some time, and functional concepts had been influential, indeed dominant, in the United States. Research on animal learning had begun to yield data that was applicable to human learning, and objective tests had been developed and used with some success to predict and control behavior. Even Watson's definition of psychology as the science of behavior had been anticipated. Thus, Watson's basic issues were not new. What was unique and provocative about his program was what he proposed to eliminate from psychology: the mind and consciousness, mentalistic concepts, speculation about what might be occurring in the brain, and the use of introspection.

Watson's program was not embraced immediately or universally. The first published response to his 1913 article came from Mary Whiton Calkins, who disagreed with his rejection of introspection. She reflected the opinion of many psychologists who believed that certain kinds of psychological processes could be studied only by introspection. The argument persisted for several years, into the 1920s, and the debate was often heated.

Margaret Floy Washburn went so far as to call Watson an enemy of psychology (Samelson, 1981).

This is not to suggest that there was a sudden outpouring of attacks on Watson's views. At first behaviorism received relatively little attention in the professional journals. Support was growing quietly, however, particularly among younger psychologists, and by the 1920s, universities were offering courses in behaviorism and the word *behaviorist* was appearing in the journals. William McDougall, an opponent of behaviorism, became sufficiently worried about these developments to issue a warning about the flourishing of behaviorism. In 1924, E. B. Titchener complained that behaviorism had engulfed the country like a great wave. And by 1930 Watson proudly proclaimed that behaviorism had become so popular that no university could avoid teaching it.

Behaviorism succeeded, of course, but it did so slowly. The changes Watson called for were a long time in coming. When they finally arrived, his was not the only form of behavioral psychology being promoted.

The Methods of Behaviorism

We have seen that when scientific psychology began, it was eager to ally itself with the older, well-established natural science of physics. The new psychology consistently tried to adapt the methods of the natural sciences to its own needs. In no previous form of psychology was this tendency as strong, however, as in Watsonian behaviorism.

Watson argued that psychology must restrict itself to the data of the natural sciences, to what could be observed — in other words, to behavior. Therefore, only the most truly objective methods of investigation were admissible in the behaviorist's laboratory. Watson stated explicitly that his methods would encompass the following: (1) observation, with and without the use of instruments; (2) testing methods; (3) the verbal report method; and (4) the conditioned reflex method.

The method of observation, self-explanatory and fundamental, is a necessary basis for the other methods. Objective testing methods were already in use, but Watson proposed that the test results were to be treated as samples of behavior, not as measures of mental qualities. To Watson, a test did not measure intelligence or personality; it measured, instead, the responses the subject made to the stimulus situation of taking the test, and nothing more.

The verbal report method is unique to Watson's system and deserves comment, perhaps justification. Because Watson was so strongly opposed to introspection, his use of verbal reporting in the laboratory has been questioned. Some psychologists considered it a compromise whereby he let introspection in the back door after vigorously throwing it out the front.

Let us consider first why Watson opposed introspection. In addition to the suggestion, noted above, that he was not very good at it, there is the fact that introspection could not be used for animal research unless one accepted Romanes's technique of introspection by analogy. Obviously, a behaviorist could not accept such a method. Also, Watson distrusted the accuracy of introspection. If highly trained introspectors could not agree on what they had observed, how was psychology to make any progress? More fundamental was the argument that a behaviorist could not tolerate in the laboratory anything that could not be objectively observed. Watson would deal only with tangibles, and he disagreed with the pretensions of introspective reports about occurrences within an organism that could not be verified by independent observation.

Despite these reasons for opposing introspection, Watson could not ignore the work in psychophysics, which had made use of introspection. He suggested, therefore, that speech reactions, because they are objectively observable, are as meaningful to the behaviorist as any other type of motor reaction. Watson wrote: "Saying is doing — that is, behaving. Speaking overtly or to ourselves (thinking) is just as objective a type of behavior as baseball" (Watson, 1930, p. 6).

The use of the verbal report method in behaviorism was a concession widely debated by Watson's critics, who contended that Watson was proposing merely a semantic change and not a genuine alteration of research procedures. He admitted that verbal report was an inexact method and not a satisfactory substitute for more objective methods of observation, and he limited the use of verbal report to those situations in which it was capable of verification, for example, observing differences between tones (Watson, 1914). Unverifiable verbal reports, such as imageless thoughts or comments about feeling states, were ruled out.

The most important research method of the behaviorists, the conditioned reflex method, was not adopted until 1915, two years after behaviorism's formal beginning. Conditioning methods were being used before the advent of behaviorism, but their adoption by American psychologists had been limited. Watson was largely responsible for their widespread application in American psychological research, and in later writings, he acknowledged his debt to Pavlov and Bekhterev for the conditioning method.

Watson wrote of conditioning in terms of stimulus substitution. A response, he said, is conditioned when it becomes attached or connected to a stimulus other than the one that originally aroused it. (The salivating of Pavlov's dogs to the sound of a bell instead of to the sight of food is a conditioned response.) Watson seized upon this approach because it provided an objective method of analyzing behavior, that is, of reducing behavior to its elementary units, the stimulus-response (S-R) bonds. All behavior, he argued, could be reduced to these elements, providing a method for laboratory investigation of complex human behavior.

We see that Watson was continuing in the atomistic and mechanistic tradition established by the British empiricists and used by the structuralists. Psychologists would study human behavior in the same way physical scientists study the universe, by breaking it down into the component parts, the atoms or elements.

The exclusive focus on the use of objective methods and the elimination of introspection meant a change in the nature and role of the human subject in the psychology laboratory. In the approaches of Wundt and Titchener, subjects were both observer and observed; they observed their own conscious experience. As such, their role was much more important than that of the experimenter.

In behaviorism, subjects assumed a less important role; they no longer observed but instead were observed by the experimenter. It was with this change in status that subjects came to be called *subjects* rather than observers (see Danziger, 1988; Scheibe, 1988). The true observers were the experimenters, who set up the conditions of the experiment and observed how the subjects responded to them. Thus, humans were demoted in status; they no longer observed, they merely behaved. And almost anyone can behave — children, the mentally ill, animals. This point of view reinforced psychology's image of humans as machines: "you put a stimulus in one of the slots and out comes a packet of reactions" (Burt, 1962, p. 232).

Initially, Watson's arguments for the use of only objective methods seemed to be a major advance for psychology. Retrospective analysis reminds us, however, that objective methods have characterized the field since its beginnings as a science. Studies in psychophysics, memory, and conditioning all applied objective methods. The behaviorists' contributions, therefore, consisted more of extending and refining established methods than of developing new ones.

The Subject Matter of Behaviorism

The primary subject matter or data for psychology must be items of behavior: muscular movements or glandular secretions. Psychology, as the science of behavior, must deal only with acts that can be described objectively in terms such as stimulus and response, habit formation, or habit integration. All human and animal behavior can be reported in this way without resorting to mentalistic concepts and terminology. Through the objective study of behavior, behavioral psychology can fulfill its aim of predicting the response given the stimulus, and predicting the antecedent stimulus given the response. Human and animal behavior can be effectively predicted, and controlled, by reducing it to the level of stimulus and response.

Despite the goal of reducing behavior to S-R units, Watson argued that ultimately behaviorism deals with the overall behavior of the total organism. Although a response can be something as simple as a knee jerk or some other reflex, it can also be more complex; in this case the term act is applied. Watson considered response acts to include such things as taking food, writing a book, playing baseball, or building a house. Thus, an act involves the organism's response through movement in space, such as talking, reaching, or walking. Watson appears to have conceived of a response as accomplishing some result in one's environment, rather than as an assemblage of muscular elements. In other words, he thought of response in more molar than molecular terms. Nevertheless, behavioral acts, no matter how complex, are capable of being reduced to lower-level motor or glandular responses.

Responses are classified in two ways: (1) learned or unlearned, and (2) explicit or implicit. Watson considered it important for behaviorism to distinguish between innate or unlearned responses and those that are learned, and to discover for the latter the laws of learning. Explicit responses are overt and therefore directly observable. Implicit responses, such as visceral movements, glandular secretions, and nerve impulses, occur within the organism. Although such internal movements are not overt, they are nonetheless items of behavior. In introducing the notion of implicit responses, Watson modified his initial requirement that psychology's subject matter be actually observable, and accepted, instead, that it must be potentially observable. The movements or responses occurring within the organism are observable through the use of instrumentation.

The stimuli, like the responses with which the behaviorist deals, may be simple or complex. Light waves striking the retina of the eye may be considered relatively simple stimuli, but stimuli can also be physical objects in the environment or a larger situation (a constellation of specific stimuli). Just as the constellation of responses involved in an act can be reduced to particular responses, so the stimulus situation can be resolved into its specific component stimuli.

Thus, behaviorism deals with the behavior of the whole organism in relation to its environment. Specific laws of behavior can be worked out through the analysis of the total stimulus-response complexes into their more elemental stimulus and response segments. This analysis was not to be as detailed as that of the physiologist determining the structure and organization of the central nervous system. Because of the inaccessibility of the brain, which Watson called the "mystery box," he had little interest in cortical functioning. He believed that behavior concerned the total organism and could not be restricted to the nervous system alone. Watson focused on larger units of behavior, the whole response of the organism to a given situation.

In both methodology and subject matter, Watson's new psychology was an attempt to construct a science that was free of mentalistic notions and subjective methods, a science as objective as physics. We will consider here his treatment of some of the traditional topics in psychology: instinct, learning, emotion, and thought. Like all systematic theorists, Watson developed his psychology in accordance with his fundamental theses. All areas of behavior were to be treated in objective stimulus-response terms.

Instinct

Initially Watson accepted the role of instincts in behavior. In his book *Behavior: An Introduction to Comparative Psychology* (1914), he described eleven instincts, including one dealing with random behaviors. He had studied the instinctive behaviors of the tern, an aquatic bird, in the Dry Tortugas Islands off the coast of Florida, with Karl Lashley, a student at Johns Hopkins University. (Lashley said that the expedition had been cut short when he and Watson ran out of cigarettes and whiskey.)

By 1925 Watson changed his position and ruled out the concept of instinct. All those aspects of human behavior that seem instinctive, he argued, are in reality socially conditioned responses. With the view that learning is the key to understanding the development of human behavior, Watson became an extreme environmentalist. He then went beyond denying instincts in his system and refused to admit that there were inherited capacities, temperaments, or talents of any kind. Things that seemed inherited could be traced to early training. Children were not born with the ability to be great athletes or musicians, for example, but were slanted in that direction by their parents, who encouraged and reinforced the appropriate behaviors. This emphasis on the overwhelming nurturing effect of the parental and social environment, with its corollary that children can be trained to be whatever one wants them to be, was one reason for Watson's large public following.

Watson was not alone in espousing the primacy of environmental influences over instincts; a trend was already evident in psychology toward

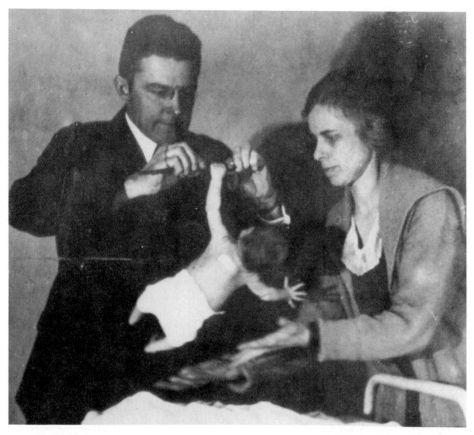

Watson tests the grasping reflex of an infant (a still photo made from a 1919 film).

discounting the role of instincts in determining behavior. Thus Watson's position reflected a movement toward environmentalism that was already in progress. In addition, his stand may have been influenced by the practical, applied orientation that characterized early twentieth-century American psychology. Psychology could not be applied to the modification of behavior unless behavior were capable of being changed. If behavior was governed by instincts, then it could not be changed, but if it depended on learning or training, then, indeed, it could be modified or changed. Watson's insistent support of the environmentalist position may have been a way to show the "applicability and universality of his behavioristic theories" (Logue, 1978, p. 74).

Learning

The adult, according to Watson, is solely a product of childhood conditioning. Watson's views on learning changed over time to incorporate conditioning. In his 1913 article there is no mention of conditioning, and his 1914 book, *Behavior*, gives but slight emphasis to Pavlov's conditioning experiments. Indeed, Watson expressed doubt that the method could be used with primates. In his 1915 APA presidential address, however, Watson suggested that the conditioned reflex method should displace introspection (Watson, 1916).

From that time, conditioning became an important research method of the behaviorists. It is surprising that, in spite of his enthusiasm for the method, Watson failed to recognize the importance of Pavlov's law of reinforcement and its similarity to Thorndike's law of effect. Watson never developed a satisfactory theory of learning, and his views seemed to have much in common with the outdated pre-Thorndikian associationists. Although he accepted conditioning principles and used them in his research, he continued to emphasize repetition, frequency, and recency as primary factors in learning, ignoring reinforcement or reward.

Emotion

Watson suggested that emotions were simply bodily responses to specific stimuli. A stimulus, such as the presence of danger, produces internal bodily changes and the appropriate learned overt responses. This notion implies no conscious perception of the emotion or mass of sensations from the internal organs. Each emotion involves its particular pattern of changes in the general body mechanism particularly in the visceral and glandular systems. Although Watson recognized that all emotional responses involve overt movements, he believed that the internal responses are predominant. Emotion, then, is a form of implicit behavior in which the internal responses are evident, to some extent, as physical manifestations such as blushing or increases in pulse rate and breathing.

Watson's theory of emotion is less complex than that of William James (Chapter 7). In James's theory, the bodily changes followed immediately the perception of the stimulus; the feeling of those bodily changes was the emotion. Watson criticized James's position, noting that "James gave to the psychology of the emotions a setback, from which it has only recently begun to recover" (Watson, 1930, p. 140). Discarding the conscious process of the perception of the situation and the feeling state, Watson claimed that emotions can be understood solely in terms of the objective stimulus situation, the overt bodily response, and the internal physiological changes.

In a now classic study, Watson investigated the stimuli that produce emotional responses in infants. He posited three fundamental emotions in infants: fear, rage, and love. Fear is produced by loud noises and sudden loss of support; rage is produced by the hampering of bodily movement; and love is produced by stroking the skin and by rocking and patting. He also found characteristic reaction patterns to these stimuli. He believed that fear, rage, and love are the only unlearned emotional responses. Other human emotional responses are compounded of these three emotions through the process of conditioning, that is, they may become attached to other stimuli that were not originally capable of eliciting them.

Watson demonstrated his theory of conditioned emotional responses in his experimental study of eleven-month-old Albert, who was conditioned to fear a white rat, something he had not feared before the conditioning trials (Watson & Rayner, 1920). The fear was established by making a loud noise (striking a steel bar with a hammer) behind Albert's head whenever the rat was presented to him. Within a short time, the mere sight of the rat produced signs of fear in the child. Watson showed that this conditioned fear could be generalized to similar stimuli such as a rabbit, a white fur coat, and a set of Santa Claus whiskers. Watson believed that adult fears, aversions, and anxieties are likewise conditioned in early childhood.

The Albert study has never been successfully replicated. Watson described the research as preliminary, only a pilot study, and psychologists have since noted serious flaws in his methodology. Nevertheless, the results of the Albert study have been accepted as scientific evidence and are cited in virtually every introductory textbook, usually incorrectly (see Harris, 1979; Samelson, 1980).

Although Albert may have been conditioned to fear the objects mentioned, he was no longer available as a subject when Watson wanted to attempt to remove or eliminate those fears. Not long after this experiment Watson left academics, and he did not pursue the problem. Some time later, when he was working in advertising in New York City, he gave a talk about his research with Albert. In the audience was Mary Cover Jones, a classmate of Rosalie Rayner Watson's at Vassar and a former student of Washburn. Watson's remarks sparked her interest, and she wondered whether the conditioning technique could be used to remove children's fears. She asked Rosalie to introduce her to Watson and then undertook a study that has become another classic in the history of psychology (Jones, 1924).

The subject was named Peter, and he already showed a fear of rabbits, although his fear had not been conditioned in the laboratory. While Peter

Mary Cover Jones anticipated modern behavior therapy with her experiments on reconditioning techniques.

was eating, a rabbit was brought into the room but kept at a distance great enough so as not to elicit the fear response. Over several trials, the rabbit was brought progressively closer, always while the child was eating. Eventually Peter could handle the rabbit without demonstrating any fear. Generalized fear responses to similar objects were also eliminated by this procedure. The study has been described as a precursor of behavior therapy (the application of learning principles to change maladaptive behavior), almost fifty years before the technique became popular. Mary Cover Jones, associated with the Institute of Child Welfare at the University of California, Berkeley, received the G. Stanley Hall award in 1968 for her outstanding contributions to developmental psychology.

Watson's behaviorist approach to the emotions and his interest in the physiological changes that accompany emotional behavior stimulated considerable research on the emotional development of children and on the reaction patterns for the specific emotions.

Thought

Before Watson's behaviorism, the traditional view of the thought processes was that they occurred in the brain "so faintly that no neural impulse passes out over the motor nerve to the muscle, hence no response takes place in the muscles and glands" (Watson, 1930, p. 239). According to this thesis, because thought processes occur in the absence of muscular movements, they are not accessible to observation and experimentation. Thought was regarded as intangible, something that was exclusively mental and that had no physical referents. The structuralists' concept of image is an example of this point of view.

Watson proposed a theory of thinking, which opposes the older notion and attempts to reduce thinking to nothing more than implicit motor behavior. He argued that thinking, like all other aspects of human functioning, must be sensory-motor behavior of some sort. He reasoned that the behavior of thinking involves implicit speech reactions or movements. Thus, verbal thinking can be reduced to subvocal talking that involves the same muscular habits learned for overt speech. As children grow up, these muscular habits become inaudible and invisible because parents and teachers admonish children to stop talking aloud to themselves. In this way, thinking becomes simply talking silently to ourselves.

Watson suggested that the focal points for much of this implicit behavior are the muscles of the larynx (the so-called voice box) and the tongue. Initially he considered the larynx to be the organ of thought, and he suggested that thought is mediated by gestures, such as frowns and shrugs, which are overt reactions to situations.

An obvious source of corroboration for Watson's theory of thinking is that most of us are aware that we talk to ourselves while we are thinking. This evidence is inadmissible to the behaviorists, however, because it is introspective, and Watson could hardly call on introspection to support his behavioral theory. Behaviorism required objective evidence of these implicit speech movements, so attempts were made to record tongue and laryngeal movements during thought. These measurements revealed slight movements some of the time that the subjects were thinking. Measurements taken from the hands and fingers of hearing-impaired persons using sign language also revealed movements some of the time during thought. Despite his inability to secure more supportive results, Watson remained convinced of the existence of implicit speech movements. He believed that their demonstration awaited only the development of more sophisticated laboratory equipment.

The Popular Appeal of Behaviorism

Why did Watson's bold pronouncements win him such a large public following? Surely people were not interested because some psychologists practiced introspection and others refuted its use, or because some psychologists pretended to be conscious while others proclaimed that psychology had finally lost its mind, or because there was dispute about whether thinking took place in the head or in the neck. These issues aroused comment among psychologists, but they hardly concerned others.

What stirred the public was Watson's call for a society based on scientifically shaped and controlled behavior, free of myths, customs, and conventional ways. His ideas offered hope to people who had become disenchanted with older guiding creeds, such as those based on religious dogma. In fervor and in faith, behaviorism attracted many people and took on some of the aspects of a religion. Among the many articles and books written about behaviorism was one entitled *The Religion Called Behaviorism* (Berman, 1927). It was read by a young man of twenty-three by the name of B. F. Skinner, who wrote a review of the book and sent it to a popular literary magazine. "They did not publish [my review]," he wrote later, "but in writing it I was more or less defining myself for the first time as a behaviorist" (Skinner, 1976, p. 299).

Some of the ferment generated by Watson's ideas can be appreciated from the newspaper reviews of his book *Behaviorism* (Watson, 1925). The *New York Times* said dramatically, "It marks an epoch in the intellectual history of man" (August 2, 1925). The *New York Herald Tribune* called it "the most important book ever written. One stands for an instant blinded with a great hope" (June 21, 1925).

The hope stemmed in part from Watson's emphasis on the nurturing effect of one's environment in determining behavior and his denial of the influence of instinctual or inherited tendencies. The following passage from *Behaviorism* is frequently quoted:

> Give me a dozen healthy infants, well-formed, and my own specified world to bring them up in, and I'll guarantee to take any one at random and train him to become any type of specialist I might select—doctor, lawyer, artist, merchant-chief, and, yes, even beggar-

man and thief, regardless of his talents, penchants, tendencies, abilities, vocations, and race of his ancestors. (Watson, 1930, p. 104)

Watson's conditioning experiments, such as the Albert study, persuaded him that emotional disturbances in adulthood cannot be traced to sexual factors alone, as Sigmund Freud believed. Watson argued that adult problems are linked to conditioned and transferred responses established in infancy, childhood, and adolescence. And if adult disturbances are a function of faulty childhood conditioning, then a proper program of conditioning in childhood should prevent the emergence of adult disorders. Watson believed that this type of practical control over childhood behavior (and hence over the later adult behavior) was not only possible but was absolutely necessary. He developed a plan for the improvement of society—a program of experimental ethics—based on the principles of behaviorism.

No one gave him a dozen healthy infants so that he might test his claim, and he later admitted that in making it he was going beyond the facts. He noted, however, that the people who disagreed with him—the ones who believed that heredity was predominant over environment—had been stating their case for thousands of years and still had no real supporting evidence.

The following paragraph from *Behaviorism* reveals the vitality with which Watson described his program for life under behaviorism's banner. It may help explain why so many people flocked to behaviorism as a new faith.

Behaviorism ought to be a science that prepares men and women for understanding the principles of their own behavior. It ought to make men and women eager to rearrange their own lives, and especially eager to prepare themselves to bring up their own children in a healthy way. I wish I could picture for you what a rich and wonderful individual we should make of every healthy child if only we could let it shape itself properly and then provide for it a universe in which it could exercise that organization—a universe unshackled by legendary folklore of happenings thousands of years ago; unhampered by disgraceful political history; free of foolish customs and conventions which have no significance in themselves, yet which hem the individual in like taut steel bands.

I am not asking here for revolution; I am not asking people to go out to some Godforsaken place, form a colony, go naked and live a communal life, nor am I asking for a change to a diet of roots and herbs. I am not asking for "free love." I am trying to dangle a stimulus in front of you, a verbal stimulus which, if acted upon, will gradually change this universe. For the universe will change if you bring up your children, not in the freedom of the libertine, but in behavioristic freedom—a freedom which we cannot even picture in words, so little do we know of it. Will not these children in turn, with their better ways of living and thinking, replace us as society and in turn bring up their children in a still more scientific way, until the world finally becomes a place fit for human habitation? (Watson, 1930, pp. 303–304)

Watson's program of experimental ethics to replace the older speculative ethics based on religion remained only a hope; it was never carried out. He outlined his program only briefly and left it as a framework for future research. A later behaviorist, B. F. Skinner, formulated a more detailed program for a scientifically shaped utopia in the spirit of the one Watson espoused; we describe it in Chapter 11.

An Outbreak of Psychology

Psychology had already become popular by the 1920s, as we discussed in Chapter 7. Under Watson's influence, given his charm, charisma, persuasiveness, and message of hope, Americans were almost overcome with what one wag called an "outbreak" of psychology. Much of the American public was convinced that the path to health, happiness, and prosperity was through psychology, and psychological advice columns sprouted in the daily newspapers. Psychologist Joseph Jastrow's column, "Keeping Mentally Fit," was syndicated in more than 150 papers. One Albert Wiggam, who was not a psychologist, wrote a column in 1928 called "Exploring Your Mind." Many people agreed with his views:

Men and women never needed psychology so much as they need it today. Young men and women need it in order to measure their own mental traits and capacities with a view to choosing their careers early and wisely. . . . businessmen need it to help them select employees; parents and educators need it as an aid in rearing and educating children; all need it in order to secure the highest effectiveness and happiness. You cannot achieve these things in the fullest measure without the new knowledge of your own mind and personality that the psychologists have given us. (Benjamin, 1986, p. 943)

The Canadian humorist Stephen Butler Leacock noted that psychology used to be confined to college campuses, where it had no connection with reality and did no visible harm to anyone who studied it. By 1924, however, psychology could be seen everywhere. "For almost every juncture of life," wrote Leacock, "we now call in the services of an expert psychologist as naturally as we send for an emergency plumber. In all our great cities there are already, or soon will be, signs that read 'Psychologist — Open Day and Night'" (Benjamin, 1986, p. 944).

Thus was psychology epidemic in the United States, and Watson may have done more than any other individual to help it spread.

Other Early Behaviorists:
Holt, Weiss, and Lashley

By the 1920s, as we noted, behaviorism had captured the attention of many American psychologists. Not all of them adopted Watson's form of behaviorism, however. Some developed their own behavioral psychologies, taking the school of thought in different directions. Three of these early behaviorists are Edwin Holt, Albert Weiss, and Karl Lashley.

Edwin B. Holt (1873–1946) received his Ph.D. from Harvard University and spent his academic career there and at Princeton. He disagreed with Watson's rejection of consciousness and mental phenomena, and he thought that it was possible to relate conscious experience to physical referents. Like Watson, Holt believed in the determining influence of the environment. However, he suggested that learning also occurs in response to what he called inner motivation (internal needs and drives such as hunger and thirst) as well as outer motivation (external stimuli). Holt was one of the first theorists to postulate such internal drives, thus anticipating the important work of Clark Hull on motivation (Chapter 11).

Holt dealt with behavior on a larger scale than did Watson. He did not subscribe to attempts to reduce behavior to stimulus-response units but preferred to deal with behaviors that had purpose, that accomplished some goal. (The term and concept of purpose was, of course, alien to Watson's system.) Holt's emphasis on purpose served as a stimulus for the work of the neobehaviorist E. C. Tolman (Chapter 11).

Albert P. Weiss (1879–1931), born in Germany, earned his Ph.D. from the University of Missouri and taught at Ohio State University. A more radical behaviorist than Watson, he agreed that all reference to consciousness and mental phenomena had to be eliminated. Anything that was not accessible to a natural-science approach had no place in psychology.

Where he differed from Watson was in his extreme position on reduction-ism. Weiss wanted to reduce all behavior to physical-chemical entities, and in that respect he was more a physiologist than a psychologist.

However, Weiss also held that humans are social as well as biological beings, and he coined the term *biosocial* to indicate that our behavior is shaped by both biological and social forces. We are solely biological enti-ties during infancy, but as we mature and develop, we interact with other people, and these social experiences modify our behavior. Weiss argued that psychology must study both physiological and social processes to understand how infants develop into social adults.

Karl Lashley (1890–1958), a student of Watson, received his Ph.D. from Johns Hopkins University. His career as a physiological psychologist took him to the universities of Minnesota and Chicago, to Harvard, and finally to the Yerkes Laboratory of Primate Biology. He was an ardent supporter of Watson's behaviorism, even though his research on brain mechanisms in rats challenged a basic point in Watson's system. He sum-marized his findings in *Brain Mechanisms and Intelligence* (1929) and postulated two now famous principles: (1) the *law of mass action*, which states that the efficiency of learning is a function of the total mass of the cortex left intact — that is, the more cortical tissue available, the better the learning; and (2) the *principle of equipotentiality*, which states that one part of the cortex is essentially equal to another in its contribution to learning.

Lashley had expected to find specific sensory and motor centers in the cortex, as well as corresponding specific pathways and connections between sensory and motor apparatus. Those findings would have sup-ported the primacy and simplicity of the reflex arc as an elemental unit of behavior. His results, however, disputed Watson's notion of a simple point-to-point connection in reflexes, according to which the brain serves merely to switch incoming sensory nerve impulses into outgoing motor impulses. Lashley's findings suggested that the brain plays a more active role in learning than Watson could accept, and he took issue with Watson's assumption that behavior is compounded bit by bit through conditioned reflexes.

Although Lashley's work thus discredited a fundamental point in Wat-son's system, it did not weaken the behaviorists' contention that only com-pletely objective research methods should be used. Indeed, Lashley's work confirmed the value of objective methods in psychological research.

The work of these early behaviorists — Holt, Weiss, and Lashley — was undertaken only shortly after Watson introduced his system. Although differing in certain respects from Watson's approach, their research con-tributed to the overall growth of behaviorism and reinforced the call for an objective natural science of behavior.

Criticisms of Watson's Behaviorism

Any systematic program that proposes sweeping revisions and so blatantly attacks the existing order — indeed, suggests that the earlier version of the truth should be discarded — is bound to receive criticism. We know that American psychology was already moving toward greater objectivity when Watson founded behaviorism, but not all psychologists were ready to accept the extreme form of objectivity Watson proposed. Many, including some who supported objectivity, believed that Watson's system omitted important components of psychology, such as sensory and perceptual processes.

One of Watson's outstanding opponents was William McDougall (1871–1938), an English psychologist who came to the United States in 1920 and was affiliated first with Harvard and later with Duke University. Mc-Dougall is recognized for his *instinct theory of behavior* and for the impetus his book on social psychology gave to that field (McDougall, 1908). He was also a supporter of a number of unpopular causes, including freedom of the will, Nordic superiority, and psychic research, and was regularly denounced in the American press for his views.

McDougall was also vilified in the American psychological community because of his vocal criticism of behaviorism in the 1920s, when most psychologists had, to some degree, come under the behaviorist influence. By 1928 McDougall was so "ostracized by America's psychological mainstream that he believed himself to be an object of contempt" (Jones, 1987, p. 931). Ten years later, when McDougall was dying of cancer, the psychologist Knight Dunlap, Watson's successor at Johns Hopkins, said that "the sooner he died, the better it would be for psychology" (Smith, 1989, p. 446).

McDougall's instinct theory states that all human action results from innate tendencies to thought and action. His ideas were initially well received but rapidly lost ground to behaviorism. Watson had rejected the notion of instincts, and on this issue, and many others, the two men clashed.

They met to debate their differences on February 5, 1924, at the Psychology Club in Washington, D.C. The fact that Washington had a psychology club that was not affiliated with a university attests to the widespread popularity of the field. One thousand people attended the debate. Only a few were psychologists; there were only 464 members of the APA nationwide at that time. Thus, the size of the crowd also reflects the popularity of Watson's behaviorism. The judges of the debate, however, voted in McDougall's favor. Watson and McDougall published their arguments jointly in *The Battle of Behaviorism* (1929).

McDougall began the debate on a falsely optimistic note: "I have an initial advantage over Dr. Watson," he said, "an advantage which I feel to

In a debate with Watson, William McDougall argued that psychology must study not only behavior but also consciousness.

be so great as to be unfair; namely, all persons of common sense will of necessity be on my side from the outset" (Watson & McDougall, 1929, p. 40).

McDougall said that he agreed with Watson that the data of behavior are necessary to the science of psychology, but he argued that the data of consciousness are also indispensable. His position was later upheld by humanistic psychologists, and more recently by the social learning theorists.

If psychologists do not use introspection, McDougall asked, how can they determine the meaning of a subject's response or the accuracy of speech behavior (what Watson called verbal report)? How can we know anything of the world of daydreams and fantasies? How can we understand or appreciate aesthetic experiences? He challenged Watson to explain how a behaviorist would account for the experience of enjoying a violin concert. McDougall said,

> I come into this hall and see a man on this platform scraping the guts of a cat with hairs from the tail of a horse, and, sitting silently in attitudes of rapt attention, are a thousand persons, who presently break into wild applause. How will the Behaviorist explain these strange incidents? How explain the fact that the vibrations emitted by the catgut stimulate all the thousands into absolute silence and quiescence, and the further fact that the cessation of the stimulus seems to be a stimulus to the most frantic activity?
>
> Common sense and psychology agree in accepting the explanation that the audience heard the music with keen pleasure, and vented their gratitude and admiration for the artist in shouts and hand clappings. But the Behaviorist knows nothing of pleasure and pain, of admiration and gratitude. He has relegated all such "metaphysical entities" to the dust heap, and must seek some other explanation. Let us leave him seeking it. The search will keep him harmlessly occupied for some centuries to come. (Watson & McDougall, 1929, pp. 62–63)

Then McDougall questioned Watson's assumption that human behavior is fully determined, that everything we do is the direct result of past experience and can be predicted once the past events are known. Such a psychology, McDougall stated, leaves no room for free will or freedom of choice.

The issue of whether behavior is predetermined did not, of course, begin with Watson and McDougall. The opposition between advocates of determinism and advocates of free will is long standing. Science accepts a determined natural world, whereas some theologies and philosophies accept freedom of the will. Watson belongs in the determinist camp. If all behavior can be interpreted in physical terms, then all acts of behavior must be physically predetermined. Watson believed that we are not personally responsible for our actions, and this belief has important social consequences, particularly for the treatment of abnormal and socially deviant behavior. According to Watson, such persons should not be punished for their actions; they should be "reconditioned."

McDougall and other critics of behaviorism argued that if the determinist position were true—that humans have no free will and therefore cannot be held responsible for their actions—then there would be no human striving, no exertion, no desire to improve ourselves or our society. No one would make any effort to prevent war, alleviate injustice, or achieve any personal or social ideal.

Additional criticism was directed, as we mentioned, against Watson's admission of the verbal report method in his research. He was charged with being inconsistent, with using it only when it could be verified and rejecting it when it could not. Of course, that was Watson's point, and the goal of the entire behaviorist movement—to use only data that could be verified.

The Watson–McDougall debate came eleven years after the formal founding of behaviorism. McDougall predicted that in a few more years Watson's position would disappear without a trace. In a postscript to the published version of the debate, McDougall wrote that his forecast had been too optimistic: "It was founded upon a too generous estimate of the intelligence of the American public. . . . Dr. Watson continues, as a prophet of much honor in his own country, to issue his pronouncements" (Watson & McDougall, 1929, pp. 86, 87).

Contributions of Watson's Behaviorism

Watson's productive career in psychology lasted less than twenty years, but he profoundly affected the course of psychology's development. He was an effective agent of the Zeitgeist, and the times were changing not only in psychology but in general scientific attitudes as well. The nineteenth century had witnessed magnificent advances in every branch of science; the twentieth century promised even more marvels. It was thought that scientists, if given enough time, were capable of finding solutions to every problem, answers to every question. It was an era in which idealism was rapidly yielding to tough-minded realism. Watson's behaviorist crusade helped American psychology in its transition from a focus on consciousness and subjectivism to materialism and objectivism in the study of behavior.

Watson's primary contribution was his advocacy of a completely objective science of behavior. He exerted an enormous influence in rendering psychology more objective in both methods and terminology. Although his positions on specific topics stimulated a great deal of research, his original formulations are no longer useful. Watsonian behaviorism as a separate school of thought has been replaced by the newer forms of psychological objectivism that built on it. The historian E. G. Boring said in 1929 that behaviorism was already past its prime as a movement. Because movements depend on protest for their existence and strength, it is an effective tribute to Watson's behaviorism that only sixteen years after its introduction, it no longer needed to protest.

Watsonian behaviorism had certainly overcome the earlier positions. A graduate student at the University of Wisconsin in 1926 reported that few students had ever heard of Wundt and Titchener (Gengerelli, 1976). Objective methodology and terminology were incorporated in American psychology, and so Watsonian behaviorism died, as have other successful movements, by being absorbed into the main body of thought where it provided a strong conceptual base for modern psychology.

Although Watson's program did not realize its ambitious goals, Watson himself is widely recognized for his founding role. The centennial of his birth was celebrated in April of 1979, the same year as the centennial of the birth of psychology as a science. A symposium at Furman University in Greenville, South Carolina (where the psychology laboratory is named for Watson) drew psychologists and other scholars from all over the United States. The speakers included B. F. Skinner, whose talk was entitled "What J. B. Watson Meant to Me." Apparently, however, Watson is remembered less favorably by his hometown residents, many of whom "regarded him as an upstart and an atheist who had turned his back on his Southern heritage and Baptist upbringing" (*Greenville News*, April 5, 1979).

To some degree, the acceptance of Watsonian behaviorism was a function of the abilities and force of Watson himself. He was charming and attractive, and he expressed his ideas with enthusiasm, optimism, self-confidence, and clarity. He was a bold and appealing figure who scorned tradition and rejected the current version of psychology. These personal qualities, interacting with the spirit of the times that he so ably reflected, define John B. Watson as one of psychology's pioneers.

Suggested Readings

Buckley, K. W. (1989). *Mechanical Man: John Broadus Watson and the Beginnings of Behaviorism*. New York: Guilford Press. Presents the life and work of the founder of the behaviorist school of thought, drawing on published and unpublished sources including correspondence and interviews; assesses Watson's academic and business careers, his role as a popularizer of psychology, and his status within the context of the development of modern psychology.

Duke, C., Fried, S., Pliley, W., & Walker, D. (1989). Rosalie Rayner Watson: The mother of a behaviorist's sons. *Psychological Reports, 65*, 163–169. A biographical sketch of Watson's second wife, who co-authored the work on conditioned emotional reactions and assisted in the preparation of his popular book on child care.

Hannush, M. J. (1987). John B. Watson remembered: An interview with James B.

Watson. *Journal of the History of the Behavioral Sciences, 23,* 137–152. An attempt to explore the personality of John B. Watson, the founder of behaviorism, through an interview with Watson's son.

Harris, B. (1979). Whatever happened to little Albert? *American Psychologist, 34,* 151–160. Questions the design, interpretation, and popular understanding of Watson's classic study of conditioned fear.

Jones, R. A. (1987). Psychology, history, and the press: The case of William McDougall and *The New York Times. American Psychologist, 42,* 931–940. Suggests that the decline in McDougall's influence and credibility after his arrival at Harvard University in 1920 was partially due to the negative image of him conveyed in *The New York Times.*

McGraw, M. B. (1990). Memories, deliberate recall, and speculations. *American Psychologist, 45,* 934–937. Excerpts from a manuscript written by child psychologist Myrtle McGraw, covering her career and marriage and her recollections of John B. Watson.

Samelson, F. (1981). Struggle for scientific authority: The reception of Watson's behaviorism, 1913–1920. *Journal of the History of the Behavioral Sciences, 17,* 399–425. A report of research on books, articles, and papers in psychology to trace the impact of Watson's ideas after the publication of his behaviorist manifesto.

Behaviorism: After the Founding

11

Neobehaviorism

Watson's intended revolution did not transform psychology overnight, as he had hoped. It took time. Yet by 1924, little more than a decade after

Watson launched behaviorism, even his greatest opponent, E. B. Titchener, conceded that it had engulfed the entire nation. By 1930 Watson was able to proclaim, with considerable justification, that his victory was complete. Although other varieties of behaviorism had been proposed—such as those of Holt, Weiss, and Lashley—they served to reinforce Watson's movement toward defining psychology as a totally objective natural science. Thus, by 1930, behaviorism in several forms had vanquished all earlier approaches to the field.

The first stage in the evolution of behaviorism, Watsonian behaviorism, lasted from 1913 to about 1930. The second stage, *neobehaviorism*, can be dated from 1930 to about 1960, and it included the work of Edward Tolman, Edwin Guthrie, Clark Hull, and B. F. Skinner. During that thirty-year period, they, along with many other American experimental psychologists, worked to advance and solidify the behaviorist approach to psychology.

One point of consensus was their use of a common data base derived exclusively from studies of animal learning. Through a large number of conditioning and discrimination learning experiments, the neobehaviorists amassed enormous amounts of data and, in general, they agreed on what the important data or facts were for psychology.

The neobehaviorists also agreed on several points about the systems they designed to explain their data. Watsonian behaviorism encompassed many facts and findings but little in the way of useful explanatory or predictive principles, and no theories comparable to those in the physical sciences. Although the neobehaviorists advanced explanatory systems that differed in their specifics, as we shall see, they agreed on the following: (1) the core of psychology is the study of learning; (2) association is the key concept in learning; (3) all behavior, no matter how complex, can be accounted for by the laws of conditioning; and (4) psychology must adopt the principle of operationism.

After we discuss operationism, we will consider the work of four leading neobehaviorists—Tolman, Guthrie, Hull, and Skinner. Then we will note the third stage in behaviorism's evolution, *neo-neobehaviorism*, which dates from about 1960.

The Influence of Operationism

Operationism is an attitude or general principle, the purpose of which is to render the language and terminology of science more objective and precise, and to rid science of problems that are not actually observable or physically demonstrable (the so-called *pseudo-problems*). Briefly, operationism holds that the validity of a given scientific finding or theoretical construct is dependent on the validity of the operations used in arriving at that finding.

The operationist viewpoint was championed by the Harvard University physicist Percy W. Bridgman in his book, *The Logic of Modern Physics* (1927), which captured the attention of many psychologists. Bridgman proposed that physical concepts be defined in precise and rigid terms and that all concepts lacking physical referents be discarded. He wrote:

> We may illustrate by considering the concept of length. What do we mean by the length of an object? We evidently know what we mean by length if we can tell what the length of any and every object is, and for the physicist nothing more is required. To find the length of an object, we have to perform certain physical operations. The concept of length is therefore fixed when the operations by which length is measured are fixed; that is, the concept of length involves as much as and nothing more than a set of operations; *the concept is synonymous with the corresponding set of operations.* (Bridgman, 1927, p. 5)

Thus, a physical concept is the same as the set of operations or procedures by which it is determined. Many psychologists found this principle to be of use in the science of psychology and were eager to apply it.

Bridgman's concern with discarding pseudo-problems, those questions that defy answer by any known objective test, is particularly important. Notions or propositions that cannot be put to experimental test — such as the issue of the existence and nature of the soul — are meaningless for science. What is this thing "soul"? Can it be observed in the laboratory? Can it be measured and manipulated under controlled conditions to determine its effects on behavior? If not, it has no use or meaning or relevance for science. It follows that the concept of individual or private conscious experience is a pseudo-problem for psychology. Neither the existence of consciousness nor its characteristics can be determined or even investigated through objective methods. Therefore, according to the operationist viewpoint, consciousness has no place in a scientific psychology.

It can be argued that operationism is little more than a formal statement of principles already used by psychologists when defining words and concepts in terms of their physical referents. There is little in operationism that cannot be traced to the works of the British empiricists. We have noted the long-term trend in American psychology toward increasing objectivity in methods and subject matter, so it can be said that operationism, as an attitude and a framework within which to conduct research and formulate theories, had already been accepted by many American psychologists before the publication of Bridgman's 1927 book. Since the days of Wundt, however, physics had been the paragon of scientific respectability for the newer psychology, and when physicists proclaimed their acceptance of operationism as a formal doctrine, psychologists followed suit. Indeed, psychology favored and used operationism to a much greater extent than did physics.

Operationism did not win universal acceptance in psychology, however. Controversy arose about the relative utility or futility of limiting psychology's subject matter to only that which has empirical reference. Also, as historian E. G. Boring noted, "the reduction of concepts to their operations turned out to be dull business. No one wants to trouble with it when there is no special need" (Boring, 1950, p. 658). Even Bridgman had doubts about the use psychologists made of the concept. Writing twenty-seven years after proposing the operationist viewpoint he said, "I feel that I have created a Frankenstein which has certainly gotten away from me. I abhor the word *operationalism* or *operationism*. . . . The thing I have envisaged is too simple to be so dignified by so pretentious a name" (Bridgman, 1954, p. 224).

This appears to be another case of the disciples becoming more fanatical than their leader. Nevertheless, the important point about operationism, for our purpose, is that the generation of neobehaviorists that came of age in the late 1920s and 1930s included operationism in their approach to psychology.

Edward Chace Tolman (1886–1959)

One of the early adherents of behaviorism, Edward Tolman originally studied engineering at the Massachusetts Institute of Technology. He switched to psychology and worked under Edwin Holt at Harvard, where he received his Ph.D. in 1915. In the summer of 1912, Tolman studied with the Gestalt psychologist Kurt Koffka in Germany, and in Tolman's final year of graduate school, while being trained in the Titchener tradition, he became acquainted with Watsonian behaviorism. As a graduate student Tolman had already questioned the scientific usefulness of introspection. In his *Autobiography* (1952), he wrote that Watson's behaviorism came to him as a "tremendous stimulus and relief."

Edward Chace Tolman invoked purposive behaviorism to give empirical form to the unobservable processes that direct an organism's behavior toward some goal.

After completing his degree, Tolman became an instructor at Northwestern University in Evanston, Illinois, and in 1918 went to the University of California at Berkeley. It was at Berkeley, where he taught comparative psychology and conducted research on learning in rats, that he became dissatisfied with Watson's behaviorism and began to develop his own. His career at Berkeley was interrupted by World War II, when he served in the Office of Strategic Services, and again from 1950 to 1953, when he helped lead the spirited and commendable faculty opposition to the California state loyalty oath. During the latter period he taught at Harvard and the University of Chicago.

Purposive Behaviorism

The definitive statement of Tolman's position is presented in his first and most important book, *Purposive Behavior in Animals and Men* (1932). His system may appear at first glance to be a curious blend of two contradictory terms: *purpose* and *behavior*. Attributing purpose to an organism seems to imply consciousness, a mentalistic concept that surely had no place in a behavioral psychology. Tolman made it clear, however, both in this book and in his research, that he was very much the behaviorist in subject matter and methodology. He was not urging psychology to return to consciousness. Like Watson, he vigorously rejected introspection and had no interest in any presumed internal experiences of the organism that were not accessible to objective observation. Any reference to conscious processes in Tolman's system was phrased in terms of cautious inference from observed behavior.

It is equally clear that Tolman was not a Watsonian behaviorist. First, Tolman was not interested in studying behavior at the molecular level, in terms of stimulus-response connections. Unlike Watson, he was not concerned with elemental units of behavior, the activities of the nerves, muscles, and glands. His focus was molar behavior, the total response actions of the whole organism. In this respect his system combines behaviorist and Gestalt concepts.

A second difference between Tolman and Watson, and the major tenet of Tolman's system, is the notion of purposive behavior. Purposiveness in behavior, Tolman said, can be defined in objective behavioral terms without resorting to introspection or to reports about how the organism might "feel" about an experience. It seemed obvious to him that all behavior is directed toward some goal. The cat, for example, tries to get out of the puzzle box, the rat tries to master a difficult maze, the human tries to learn to play the piano. Behavior, Tolman said, "reeks of purpose." All behavior is oriented toward the achievement of some goal object, learning the means to an end. The rat persistently runs the maze, making fewer errors, reaching the goal faster each time. In other words, the rat is learning, and the fact of learning — in rat or human — is highly objective behavioral evidence of purpose. Note that Tolman is dealing with the organism's response and that his measures are of the changes in response behavior as a function of learning. These yield objective data.

Watsonian behaviorists were quick to criticize the attribution of purpose to behavior because, they said, it had to rest on the assumption of consciousness. Tolman replied that it made no difference to him whether the organism was conscious or not. The conscious experience — if there was any — associated with purposive behavior did not in any way influence the animal's behavioral responses. Tolman was concerned only with the overt response behavior.

If organisms did have any conscious awareness of the goal, Tolman believed, this would be a private matter within each organism and thus not available to the objective tools of science. And anything that is internal and cannot be observed from outside the organism is not within the realm of science.

Intervening Variables

As a behaviorist, Tolman believed that the initiating causes of behavior and the final resulting behavior must be capable of objective observation and operational definition. He suggested that the initiating causes of behavior consist of five independent variables: the environmental stimuli (S), physiological drives (P), heredity (H), previous training (T), and age (A). With animal subjects, the experimenter can control these variables, but with humans there is obviously less opportunity for control. Tolman expressed the relationship between the causes of behavior and the final resulting behavior (B) in terms of an equation: Behavior is a function (f) of the five independent variables.

$$B = f_x (S, P, H, T, A)$$

Between these observable independent variables and the final response behavior (the observable dependent variable), Tolman postulated a set of inferred and unobserved factors, the *intervening variables*. These intervening variables are the actual determinants of behavior. They are the internal processes that connect the stimulus situation with the observed response. The statement S-R (stimulus-response) must now read S-O-R. The intervening variable is what is going on within O (the organism) that brings about a given behavioral response to a given stimulus.

Because this intervening variable cannot be objectively observed, it is of no use to psychology unless it can be clearly related to both the experimental (independent) variables and the behavior (dependent) variable. The classic example of an intervening variable is hunger, which cannot be seen in a person or a laboratory animal. However, hunger can be precisely and objectively related to an experimental variable, such as the length of time since the organism was last given food. It can also be related to an objective response or behavior variable, such as the amount of food eaten or the speed with which it was consumed. Thus, the unobservable, inferred variable of hunger can be given precise empirical referents and is, therefore, amenable to quantification and experimental manipulation.

Tolman introduced the concept of the intervening variable so that psychology would have a way to make precise and objective statements about internal states and processes that cannot be observed. He believed that intervening variables were a way of rendering these states and processes useful to psychology. By specifying the independent and dependent variables, which are observable events, Tolman was, in effect, able to provide operational definitions of unobservable states. Before he chose the term intervening variable, he called his approach operational behaviorism.

Tolman originally proposed two kinds of intervening variables: demand variables and cognitive variables. The demand variables are essentially motives and include sex, hunger, and safety in the face of danger. The cognitive, or know-how, variables are abilities such as motor skills and the perception of objects. Tolman later revised the concept and established three categories: (1) *need systems*, the physiological deprivation or drive situation at a given time; (2) *belief-value motives*, the intensity of the preference for certain goal objects and the relative strength of these objects in satisfying needs; and (3) *behavior spaces*, the situation within which the organism's behavior takes place. In the behavior space, some objects are attractive to the individual (said to have a positive valence), whereas others are repellent (have a negative valence).

The concept of intervening variables has not gone uncriticized. Intervening variables appear to be useful in developing a theory of behavior, as long as they are empirically related to experimental and behavior variables. To do this comprehensively and completely, however, turned out to be such a monumental task that Tolman later came to "repudiate the hope of ever making a complete definition of any intervening variables and declared that, if they were not to be abandoned altogether, then at best all they could be considered was 'an aid to thinking'" (Mackenzie, 1977, p. 146).

Learning Theory

Tolman believed that all animal and human behavior (with the exception of simple reflexes and the tropisms or forced movements proposed by Jacques Loeb) is capable of being modified through experience. Thus, learning plays a major role in his purposive behaviorism. He rejected Thorndike's law of effect, saying that reward or reinforcement has little influence on learning. In its place Tolman proposed a cognitive theory of learning, suggesting that the repeated performance of a task strengthens the learned relationship between cues in the environment and the organism's expectations. In this way the organism gets to know its environment. Tolman called these learned relationships *sign Gestalts*, and they are built up by the continued performance of a task.

Let us follow Tolman's system as we watch a hungry rat in a maze. The rat moves about in the maze, sometimes exploring correct alleys and sometimes blind alleys. Eventually it discovers food. In subsequent trials in the maze, the goal (finding the food) gives purpose and direction to the rat's behavior. At each choice point in the maze, expectations are established. The rat comes to expect that certain cues associated with the choice point will or will not lead to the food. When the rat's expectancy is confirmed and it gets food, the sign Gestalt (the cue expectancy associated with a particular choice point) is strengthened. Over all the choice points in the maze, the animal thus establishes a pattern of sign Gestalts, which Tolman called a *cognitive map*. This pattern is what the animal learns — a cognitive map of the maze, not a set of motor habits. In a sense, then, the rat establishes a comprehensive knowledge of the maze, or of any familiar environment. Something like a field map is developed in its brain, enabling it to go from one spot in the environment to another, without being restricted to a fixed series of bodily movements.

A classic experiment that supports Tolman's theory of learning investigated this issue of whether the rat in the maze learns a cognitive map or a set of motor responses. A cross-shaped maze was used. One set of rats always found food at the same place, even though, using different starting points, the rats sometimes had to turn to the right and other times to the left to reach the food. The motor responses differed, but the food remained in the same place.

The second group of rats always made the same response regardless of the starting point, but the food was found in different places. For example, starting from one end of the cross-shaped maze, the rats would find food only by turning to the right at the choice point; when starting from the other end of the cross, they also found food only by turning to the right.

The results showed that the first group, the place learners, performed significantly better than the second group, the response learners. Tolman concluded that the same phenomenon occurs with persons who are familiar with their neighborhood or town. They can go from one point to another by a number of different routes because of the cognitive map that they have developed of the area.

Another experiment involved *latent learning*, which is learning that cannot be observed at the time it is taking place. A hungry rat was placed in a maze and allowed to wander about freely. There was no food for it to find. Was the rat learning anything in the absence of reinforcement? After a number of no-reinforcement trials, the rat did find food. The improvement thereafter in the time required by the rat to run the maze was extremely rapid, indicating that some learning had taken place during the period of no reinforcement. Its performance quickly equaled that of a control group that had been reinforced with food on every trial.

Tolman's work had a great influence on psychology, particularly in the area of learning, and its impact is recognized today in the cognitive movement in psychology. He has been criticized, however, for failing to develop a fully integrated theoretical system, and many psychologists believe that he never adequately related behavior to more covert functioning, such as cognitive states. A more obvious point of attack is Tolman's language, which many find subjective and mentalistic.

On the positive side, Tolman initiated many important research topics in learning and introduced the concept of the intervening variable. Because intervening variables are a way of operationally defining unobservable states such as hunger, they have made these states scientifically respectable to some behaviorists. Intervening variables have become a necessary format for dealing with hypothetical constructs and have been widely used by other neobehaviorists such as Guthrie, Hull, and, for a time, Skinner.

Another significant contribution is Tolman's support for the rat as an appropriate subject for psychological study. An essay written in 1945 clearly and colorfully states his position.

> Let it be noted that rats live in cages; they do not go on binges the night before one has planned an experiment; they do not kill each other off in wars; they do not invent engines of destruction, and, if they did, they would not be so inept about controlling such engines; they do not go in for either class conflicts or race conflicts; they avoid politics, economics, and papers on psychology. They are marvelous, pure, and delightful. (Tolman, 1945, p. 166)

Edwin Ray Guthrie (1886–1959)

Edwin Guthrie received his Ph.D. in 1912 from the University of Pennsylvania and spent his academic career at the University of Washington in Seattle, where he remained until his retirement in 1956. While in graduate school he became an ardent convert to a behavioral approach to psychology, although he cannot be described as a Watsonian behaviorist.

Edwin Ray Guthrie proposed a simple learning theory, maintaining that movements are learned during a single pairing of stimulus and response.

One-Trial Learning

Guthrie's most important contribution to psychology is his formulation of a simple learning theory, set forth in his book *The Psychology of Learning* (1935). It is based on a single principle, that of contiguity. In accounting for the strengthening of learned responses, Guthrie rejected Thorndike's laws of effect and frequency as well as Pavlovian reinforcement, and relied instead on what he called simultaneous conditioning, which he considered to be psychology's most general law.

To Guthrie, all learning depends on the contiguity of stimulus and response. When a stimulus elicits a response just once, the S-R association is formed. It is, in essence, a ***one-trial learning*** situation. Repetition and reinforcement are not required to establish a connection between stimulus and response. One pairing of the stimulus and the resulting movement or response serves to establish the association, and thus the behavior is learned. Guthrie's only formal law of learning states: "A combination of stimuli which has accompanied a movement will on its recurrence tend to be followed by that movement" (Guthrie, 1935, p. 26). Note again that there is no mention of internal drive states, repetition of the S-R pairing, or any form of reward or reinforcement.

Guthrie's law refers to movements, which he was careful to distinguish from acts. He defined a movement as a pattern of motor and glandular responses or actions. An act, on the other hand, is a movement or series of movements that brings about results. Although an act is a movement, a movement is not an act; an act is on a larger scale. Hitting a nail with a hammer, for example, is an act composed of a number of separate movements, and it brings about a certain result. Guthrie believed that when psychologists measure learning, the performance of the complete act is usually taken as the criterion of learning, whereas it is the movements that are actually conditioned or learned as responses.

He considered this focus on movements to be a distinguishing feature of his theory. He argued that Thorndike was concerned with the total act, such as the acquisition of a skill (as in a cat trying to escape from a puzzle box), which is actually a function of a number of individual muscular movements. These individual movements, Guthrie argued, are developed or acquired in single trials (one-trial learning), but learning the total act calls for repeated practice. The movements (the individual parts of the learned act) are the raw data in Guthrie's system. Because they are smaller than acts, these movements are more difficult to observe in a learning situation and are often overlooked.

Just as an organism's response is made up of separate components, so too is the stimulation to which the organism is exposed. Because stimulus and response are each composed of many parts, it is necessary to have a large number of pairings of the total stimulus and response situations to achieve any consistency in behavior. Therefore, practice is necessary to bring about improvement in learning the combination of movements (that is, the act), but each component movement is learned after a single pairing with the stimulus.

Guthrie preferred writing and observation to experimentation. He believed in the importance of theory for the development of psychology, and he said that theories, not facts, endure. His several books contain anecdotal observations and comparatively little experimental evidence.

Much of the appeal of Guthrie's system rests on its simplicity and its consistency over the years. It is easy to understand, especially when compared with more complex and mathematically based learning theories, such as Hull's.

The inherent simplicity of Guthrie's system draws praise from some psychologists and criticism from others. It has been suggested that Guthrie maintained this simplicity by failing to deal with problems in learning that might defy explanation within his framework: "Many reviews of Guthrie in the literature have mistaken incompleteness for simplicity" (Mueller & Schoenfeld, 1954, p. 368). These critics suggest that additional principles and assumptions are necessary to encompass the major issues in learning.

Nevertheless, Guthrie maintained his position and his stature as a leading learning theorist. His contributions received formal recognition in 1958, when the American Psychological Foundation presented him with its Gold Medal Award.

Clark Leonard Hull (1884–1952)

First and foremost a behaviorist, Clark Hull achieved a highly respected position in American psychology during the 1940s and 1950s. Perhaps no other psychologist was so consistently and keenly devoted to the problems inherent in the scientific method. He had a prodigious command of mathematics and formal logic and applied them to psychological theory in a way no one had done before.

The Life of Hull

For most of his life, Hull was plagued by poor health and poor eyesight. At the age of twenty-four he contracted polio, which left him disabled in one leg and forced to wear a heavy iron brace of his own design. His family had little money, and he interrupted his education several times to take teaching jobs to earn a living. Hull's greatest asset was an intense aspiration to greatness, and he persevered in the face of many obstacles.

In 1918, at the relatively advanced age of thirty-four, Hull received his Ph.D. from the University of Wisconsin, where he had studied mining engineering before switching to psychology. He remained on the faculty at Wisconsin for ten years. His early research presaged his lifelong emphasis on objective methods and functional laws. He investigated concept formation and the effects of tobacco on behavioral efficiency, surveyed the literature on tests and measurements, and published an important text in

The radical behavior-
ism of Clark Leonard
Hull saw all behavior
as mechanistic and
quantifiable.

the applied area of aptitude testing (Hull, 1928). He worked to develop
practical methods of statistical analysis and invented a machine for calculating correlations. This was one of the first machines designed to perform
mathematical computations by having the data coded by punching holes

in a tape. It is now on display at the Smithsonian Institution in Washington, D.C. He devoted ten years to the study of hypnosis and suggestibility, publishing thirty-two papers and a book that summarized the research (Hull, 1933).

In 1929 he became a research professor at Yale University, where he pursued his final major research interest: a theory of behavior based on Pavlov's laws of conditioning. He first read Pavlov in 1927 and became interested in the problem of conditioned reflexes and learning. He referred to Pavlov's book, *Conditioned Reflexes*, as "that great book," and he turned to animal subjects to carry out his research program. He had not used rats before, because he did not like the odors associated with a rat lab, but at Yale he encountered the rat colony established by E. R. Hilgard, which was kept meticulously clean. Hull looked at the rats, Hilgard recalled, and "sniffed them and said that he guessed he could use rats after all" (Hilgard, 1987, p. 201).

In the 1930s Hull wrote articles about conditioning, arguing that complex, higher-order behaviors could be explained in terms of basic conditioning principles. In 1940 he published, with five colleagues, *Mathematico-Deductive Theory of Rote Learning: A Study in Scientific Methodology*. Although the book was recognized as a notable achievement in the development of scientific psychology, it was difficult to understand and was read by few people.

Hull's next major publication, *Principles of Behavior* (1943), outlined in detail and with characteristic precision a theoretical framework so comprehensive as to include all behavior. This book assured the prominence of Hull's ideas in the area of learning in the United States and stimulated considerable research. Hull soon became the most frequently cited psychologist in the field; in the 1940s, up to 40 percent of all experimental articles and 70 percent of all articles dealing with learning and motivation published in the two leading American psychology journals cited Hull's work (Spence, 1952). Hull revised his system in a number of articles, and its final statement appeared in *A Behavior System* (1952). Hull had been ill for years, and he died before reading the proofs of this book.

The Frame of Reference

Hull believed that behavior involves a continuing interaction between the organism and the environment. The objective stimuli provided by the environment and the objective behavioral responses provided by the organism are observable facts. The interaction, however, takes place within a larger context that cannot be totally defined in observable stimulus-response terms.

This broader context, or *frame of reference*, is the biological adaptation of the organism to its unique environment. The organism's survival is aided by this biological adaptation. When survival is in jeopardy, the organism is said to be in a state of need. Hull asserted that need involves a situation in which the biological requirements for survival are not being met. When in a state of need, the organism behaves in a manner designed to reduce that need. Its behavior serves to reinstate the optimal biological conditions necessary for survival. Hull's concern with biological survival grew out of his interest in evolutionary theory and is consistent with the functionalist emphasis on adaptation to the environment.

Hull was committed to an objective, behaviorist psychology. There was no place in his program for consciousness, purpose, or any other mentalistic notion. His system was an uncompromising, radical behaviorism, in which he attempted to reduce every concept to physical terms. Although his behaviorism was perhaps more rigid than Watson's, he did allow for the notion of intervening variables. However, these variables were closely and concretely tied to objective stimulus and response conditions, which could be quantified and measured with precision.

Hull's system and his image of human nature were couched in mechanistic terms. He regarded human behavior as automatic and cyclical, capable of being reduced to the terminology of physics. He warned against the intrusion of anthropomorphic subjectivism, that is, giving subjective interpretations to the behavior being observed, as the early animal psychologists had done. The observation and interpretation of behavior must be uncompromisingly objective. One way of attaining this, Hull initially suggested, was to think in terms of animal behavior, although even this had its dangers: "[It] all too often breaks down when the theorist begins thinking what he would do if he were a rat, a cat, or a chimpanzee; when that happens, all his knowledge of his own behavior, born of years of self-observation, at once begins to function in place of the objectively stated general rules or principles which are the proper substance of science" (Hull, 1943, p. 27). Hull searched for a greater safeguard against subjectivism and found it in an attitude that considers the organism to be "a completely self-maintaining robot, constructed of materials as unlike ourselves as may be" (Hull, 1943, p. 27).

Thus, to Hull, behaviorists needed to view their subject matter as robotlike. He was far ahead of his time in considering the possibility that machines could be constructed that would think and display other human cognitive functions, an enterprise now being attempted with computers. "It has struck me many times," Hull wrote in 1926, "that the human organism is one of the most extraordinary machines — and yet a machine. And it has struck me more than once that so far as the thinking processes go, a machine could be built which would do every essential thing that the body does" (Amsel & Rashotte, 1984, pp. 2–3).

The spirit of mechanism represented by the mechanical figures of the seventeenth-century European gardens and clocks was faithfully incorporated into Hull's work. One advantage of the robot approach, according to Hull, is that it precludes any attribution of behavior to causes other than strictly mechanical ones. Hull saw little difference between psychology and physics; any such difference was only in degree, not in kind.

Objective Methodology and Quantification

Hull's mechanistic, reductionistic, and objective behaviorism provides a clear view of what his methods of study had to be. Obviously, they were characterized by as much objectivity as possible. In addition, Hull's approach to psychology is distinguished by quantification. The laws of behavior must be stated or expressed in the precise language of mathematics, and thus quantification became the second cornerstone on which Hull erected his behaviorism.

Psychologists, he wrote, must not only develop a thorough understanding of mathematics, they must think in terms of mathematics. In *Principles of Behavior* (1943), Hull explained how a mathematically defined psychology would proceed:

> Progress will consist in the laborious writing, one by one, of hundreds of equations; in the experimental determination, one by one, of hundreds of the empirical constants contained in the equations; in the devising of practically usable units in which to measure the quantities expressed by the equations; in the objective definition of hundreds of symbols appearing in the equations; in the rigorous deduction, one by one, of thousands of theorems and corollaries from the primary definitions and equations; in the meticulous performance of thousands of critical quantitative experiments. (Hull, 1943, pp. 400–401)

This statement provides a good indication of the rigor, and the patience, required of a follower of Hull's system.

Hull described four methods he considered to be useful to science. Three were already in use: (1) simple observation, (2) systematic controlled observation, and (3) the experimental testing of hypotheses. In addition, Hull argued for strict adherence to a fourth method, the **hypothetico-deductive method**, which uses deduction from a set of formulations that are determined *a priori*. The method involves establishing postulates from which experimentally testable conclusions can be deduced. These conclusions are then submitted to experimental test. If the propositions are not supported by experimental evidence, they must be revised. If they are supported and verified, they may be incorporated into the body of science. Hull believed that if psychology were to become an objective science on the order of other natural sciences, in accordance with the behaviorist program, the only appropriate approach would be the hypothetico-deductive one.

Drives

Hull considered bodily need arising from a deviation from optimal biological conditions to be the basis of motivation. However, rather than introducing the concept of biological need directly into his system, he postulated the intervening variable of drive, a term that had already come into use in psychology. Drive was posited as a stimulus arising from a state of tissue need that arouses or activates behavior. The strength of the drive can be empirically determined by the length of deprivation, or by the intensity, strength, and energy expenditure of the resulting behavior. Hull considered the duration of deprivation to be an imperfect measurement and placed greater emphasis on the strength of the response.

Drive was also considered to be nonspecific. In other words, any kind of deprivation — of food, water, or sex, for example — contributed in the same way (though in differing degrees) to the drive. This nonspecificity means that drive does not direct behavior but only energizes it. The steering or guiding of behavior is accomplished by environmental stimuli. Further, drive reduction is the sole basis for reinforcement.

Hull postulated two kinds of drive: primary and secondary. *Primary drives* are associated with biological need states and are directly involved with the organism's survival. These drives, which arise from a state of tissue need, include food, water, air, temperature regulation, defecation, urination, sleep, activity, sexual intercourse, and relief from pain. These are basic innate processes that are vital to the organism's survival.

He recognized that humans and animals are also motivated by forces other than primary drives. Accordingly, Hull postulated the *secondary* or *learned drives*, which refer to situations or stimuli in the environment that are associated with the reduction of primary drives, and which, as a result, may become drives themselves. This means that previously neutral stimuli may assume the characteristics of a drive because they are capable of eliciting responses that are similar to those aroused by the primary drive or original state of need.

A simple example involves touching a hot stove and getting burned. The painful burn, caused by tissue damage, produces a primary drive, the desire for relief from the pain. Other environmental stimuli associated with this primary drive, such as the sight of the stove, may lead to the withdrawal of the hand when this visual stimulus is perceived. In this way, the sight of the stove may become the stimulus for the learned drive of fear. These secondary or learned drives that serve to motivate behavior develop on the basis of the primary drives. Because of this focus on learned drives, then, learning played a key role in Hull's system.

Learning

Hull attempted to integrate, or at least reconcile, Thorndike's law of effect with Pavlovian conditioning. He believed that learning could not adequately be explained by the principles of recency and frequency. His learning theory focuses mainly on the principle of reinforcement, which is essentially Thorndike's law of effect. Hull's law of primary reinforcement states that when a stimulus-response relationship is followed by a reduction in need, the probability increases that on subsequent occasions the same stimulus will evoke the same response. Note that reward or reinforcement is defined not in terms of Thorndike's notion of satisfaction but rather in terms of the reduction of a primary need. Thus, *primary reinforcement* — the reduction of a primary drive — is the basis of Hull's theory of learning.

Just as his system contains secondary or learned drives, it also deals with *secondary reinforcement*. If the intensity of the stimulus is reduced as the result of a secondary or learned drive, it will act as a secondary reinforcement.

> It follows that any stimulus consistently associated with a reinforcement situation will through that association acquire the power of evoking the conditioned inhibition, i.e., reduction in stimulus intensity, and so of itself producing the resulting reinforcement. Since this indirect power of reinforcement is acquired through learning, it is called *secondary reinforcement*. (Hull, 1951, pp. 27–28)

Hull believed that the stimulus-response connection is strengthened by the number of reinforcements that have taken place. He called the strength of the S-R connection *habit strength*, which refers to the persistence of the conditioning and is a function of reinforcement.

Learning cannot take place in the absence of reinforcement, which is necessary to bring about a reduction of the drive. Because of this emphasis on reinforcement, Hull's system is called a need-reduction theory, as opposed to Guthrie's contiguity theory and Tolman's cognitive theory.

Hull's system is presented in verbal and mathematical form in specific and detailed postulates and corollaries. In its last publication (Hull, 1952) there are eighteen postulates and twelve corollaries. Although the system is based on conditioning principles, Hull believed that his fundamental position could be expanded to include complex processes such as problem solving, social behavior, and forms of learning other than conditioning. He lived to see only a portion of this ambition realized.

His system achieved such visibility that it inevitably generated a great deal of criticism. As a leading exponent of neobehaviorism, Hull is subject to the same attacks aimed at Watson and others who followed in the behaviorist tradition. Those who oppose a behavioral approach to psychology on methodological and theoretical grounds will, of course, include Hull in the enemy camp.

Hull's program can be faulted for its lack of generalizability. It has been asserted that, in his attempt to define his variables so precisely in quantitative terms, he necessarily operated on too narrow a base. His approach is extremely particularistic, in that he often formulated postulates from results obtained in a single experimental situation. Opponents argue that it is questionable whether one can generalize to all behavior on the basis of such specific experimental demonstrations as "the most favorable interval for human eyelid conditioning (Postulate 2)," or "the weight in grams of food needed to condition a rat (Postulate 7)" (Hilgard, 1956, p. 181). Although precise quantification is necessary and commendable, Hull's extreme approach does tend to reduce the range of applicability of the findings.

Thus, Hull's adherence to a mathematical and formal system of theory building is open to both praise and criticism. He may have become a victim of his enthusiasm for mathematics, quantifying his propositions so thoroughly and minutely that incomplete or inaccurate formulations are relatively easy to spot. Gaps and inconsistencies in a theory expressed in writing can be more easily filled in with appropriate illustrative examples. Critics have found such gaps in Hull's system and argue that at least some of his formulations are not as tightly constructed as was originally thought.

Hull's influence on psychology cannot be minimized, however. We have already mentioned the great amount of research occasioned by his work, perhaps more than by any other theory, and this alone assures his stature in the history of psychology. He provided an objective terminology that was well accepted and represented a new approach to psychological data, rather than merely a relabeling of old concepts. It is also a tribute to Hull's greatness to note a few of the psychologists who were his disciples and followers: John Dollard, Carl Hovland, Neal Miller, Robert Sears, Hobart Mowrer, and Kenneth Spence. Few psychologists have had such a pronounced and extensive effect on the professional motivation of so many other psychologists.

Hull defended, extended, and expounded the objective behaviorist approach to psychology as had never been done before. Although psychologists question parts or all of Hull's theory, there is general respect and admiration for the rigorous methods he used to develop it. "It is not often in any field that a true theoretical genius comes along; of the very few to whom psychology can lay claim, Hull must surely rank among the foremost" (Lowry, 1982, p. 211).

Burrhus Frederick Skinner (1904–1990)

B. F. Skinner was for decades, beginning in the 1950s, the most influential individual in psychology. His areas of interest over his long career, and their implications for modern society, are diverse. In 1982, a historian of psychology called him "without question the most famous American psychologist in the world" (Gilgen, 1982, p. 97). And when he died in 1990, the editor of the journal *American Psychologist* lauded him as the "greatest contemporary psychologist . . . one of the giants of our discipline," who has "made a permanent mark on psychology" (Fowler, 1990, p. 1203).

For many years Skinner was America's leading behaviorist, and he attracted a large, loyal, and enthusiastic band of followers. He developed a program for behavioral control of society, invented an automatic crib for the care of infants, and was largely responsible for the introduction of behavior modification techniques and teaching machines. He wrote a novel, *Walden Two*, that continues to be popular more than forty years after publication. In 1971 his book *Beyond Freedom and Dignity* became a national best-seller. He published many professional articles and books and has been compared to Francis Galton in the diversity and scope of his interests.

The Life of Skinner

Skinner was born in Susquehanna, Pennsylvania, where he lived until he went away to college. By his own report, his childhood environment was

All behavior is subject to re-inforcement contingencies, according to B. F. Skinner, for many years America's leading behaviorist, who applied his laboratory data to problems of childrearing and education.

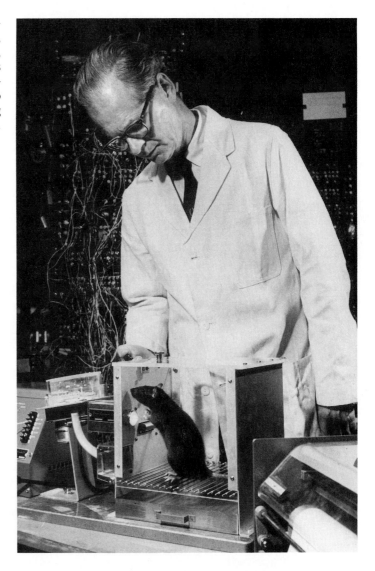

warm and stable. He attended the same high school from which his parents had graduated; there were only seven other students in his graduating class. He liked school and was the first to arrive each morning. As a child and adolescent he was interested in building things: sleds, wagons, rafts, merry-go-rounds, slingshots, model airplanes, and a steam cannon with which he shot potato and carrot plugs over the roofs of his neighbors' houses. He spent years trying to develop a perpetual motion machine. He was also interested in the behavior of animals. He read a great deal about them and kept an assortment of turtles, snakes, lizards, toads, and chipmunks. At a county fair he observed a flock of performing pigeons; years later he trained pigeons to perform a variety of feats.

Skinner's system of psychology is in many ways a reflection of his early life experiences. He viewed life as a product of past reinforcements, and claimed that his own life was just as predetermined, lawful, and orderly as his system dictates all human lives will be. He believed that all aspects of his own experience could be traced to environmental sources alone.

On the advice of a family friend, Skinner enrolled in Hamilton College in New York. He wrote:

> I never fitted into student life. I joined a fraternity without knowing what it was all about. I was not good at sports and suffered acutely as my shins were cracked in ice hockey or better players bounced basketballs off my cranium. . . . In a paper I wrote at the end of my freshman year, I complained that the college was pushing me around with unnecessary requirements (one of them daily chapel) and that almost no intellectual interest was shown by most of the students. By my senior year I was in open revolt. (Skinner, 1967, p. 392)

As part of his revolt Skinner instigated hoaxes that disrupted the college community, and he indulged in verbal attacks on the faculty and administration. His disobedience continued up to graduation day when, at commencement ceremonies, the college president warned Skinner and his friends that if they did not settle down they would not graduate.

Skinner did graduate, with a degree in English, a Phi Beta Kappa key, and a desire to become a writer. As a child he had written poems and stories, and in 1925, at a summer writing school, the poet Robert Frost had commented favorably on his work. For two years after graduation Skinner worked at writing, then decided that he had "nothing important to say." His lack of success as a writer filled him with so much despair that he thought of consulting a psychiatrist. He considered himself a failure, and his sense of self-worth was shattered. He was also disappointed in love; at least a half dozen young women spurned his advances, leaving him in what he described as intense physical pain. He was so distraught that he branded the first letter of one woman's name on his arm, where it remained for years.

After reading about John B. Watson and Ivan Pavlov, Skinner decided to turn from a literary interest in people to a more scientific one. In 1928, he enrolled as a graduate student in psychology at Harvard University, though he had never before taken a psychology course. He went to graduate school, he said, "not because I was a fully committed convert to psychology, but because I was escaping from an intolerable alternative" (Skinner, 1979, p. 37). Committed or not, he received his Ph.D. three years later. His dissertation topic provides an early glimpse of the position to which he consistently adhered throughout his career. His major proposition was that a reflex is the correlation between a stimulus and a response — and nothing more.

After completing several postdoctoral fellowships, Skinner taught at the University of Minnesota (1936–1945) and Indiana University (1945–1947). In 1947 he returned to Harvard. His 1938 book, *The Behavior of Organisms*, describes the basic points of his system. Fifty years later that book was judged to be "one of the handful of books that changed the face of modern psychology" (Thompson, 1988, p. 397), and it is still widely read. His 1953 book, *Science and Human Behavior*, is the basic textbook for his behavioral psychology.

Skinner continued to be productive until his death at the age of eighty-six, working until the end with as much enthusiasm as when he began some sixty years before. In his final years he built, in the basement of his home, his own personal "Skinner box" — a controlled environment that provided positive reinforcement. He slept there in a yellow plastic tank, just large enough to contain a mattress, a few shelves for books, and a small television set. He went to bed each night at 10:00, slept for three hours, worked for an hour, slept for three more hours, and arose at 5:00 in the morning to work for three more hours. Then he walked to his office at the university for more work and administered self-reinforcement every afternoon by listening to music.

At the age of seventy-eight he wrote a paper entitled "Intellectual Self-Management in Old Age," citing his own experiences as a case study (Skinner, 1983a). He described how it is necessary for the brain to work fewer hours each day, with rest periods between spurts of effort, in order to cope with failing memory and the diminished intellectual abilities of age. Terminally ill with leukemia, he presented a paper at the 1990 American Psychological Association convention in Boston just eight days before he died, in which he mounted an attack on cognitive psychology. The evening before his death, he was working on his final article, "Can Psychology Be a Science of Mind?" (Skinner, 1990), another indictment of the cognitive movement that was supplanting his definition of psychology.

Skinner's Behaviorism

In a number of important respects Skinner's position represents a renewal of Watsonian behaviorism. Indeed, one psychologist wrote that "Watson's spirit is indestructible. Cleaned and purified, it breathes through the writings of B. F. Skinner" (MacLeod, 1959, p. 34).

Although Clark Hull is also considered a rigorous behaviorist, there are marked differences between Hull's and Skinner's approaches to psychology. Whereas Hull emphasized the importance of theory, Skinner advocated a strictly empirical system with no theoretical framework within which to conduct research. Where Hull's work consisted of proposing a theory and then checking the deduced conclusions against experimental evidence, Skinner avoided theory and practiced a stringent brand of positivism. Skinner began with empirical data and proceeded carefully and slowly toward tentative generalizations. Hull represents the deductive method; Skinner represents the inductive method.

Skinner summarized his viewpoint this way: "I never attacked a problem by constructing a hypothesis. I never deduced theorems or submitted them to experimental check. So far as I can see I had no preconceived model of behavior — certainly not a physiological or mentalistic one, and I believe not a conceptual one" (Skinner, 1956, p. 227).

Skinner's exclusively descriptive kind of radical behaviorism is devoted to the study of responses. He was concerned with describing behavior rather than explaining it. He dealt only with observable behavior and believed that the task of scientific inquiry is to establish functional relationships between the experimenter-controlled stimulus conditions and the organism's subsequent response.

In *Science and Human Behavior* (1953), Skinner wrote about the mechanical figures in the royal gardens of seventeenth-century Europe and the mechanical image of human beings that those figures portrayed. Under the heading "Man a Machine" he described how his ideas are compatible with that earlier mechanical image. The human organism, Skinner said, is a machine, and like any other machine, a human being behaves in lawful and predictable ways in response to the external forces, the stimuli, that impinge on it.

Skinner was not at all concerned with theorizing or speculating about what might be going on inside the organism. His program includes no presumptions about internal entities, whether they are described as intervening variables or physiological processes. Whatever might occur between the stimulus and the response does not represent objective data for a Skinnerian behaviorist. This purely descriptive behaviorism has been called, with good reason, the ***empty organism approach***. We are operated by forces in the environment, the external world, and not by forces within ourselves.

It is important to note that although Skinner's system is atheoretical, he was not completely opposed to all theorizing. Rather, he stood against premature theorizing in the absence of adequate supporting data. In a 1968 interview, Skinner said that he hoped for "an overall theory of human behavior which will bring together a lot of facts and express them in a general way. That kind of theory I would be very much interested in prompting" (Evans, 1968, p. 88).

In contrast to many contemporary psychologists, Skinner did not subscribe to the use of large numbers of subjects or of statistical comparisons between the mean or average responses of groups. He focused instead on the intense and thorough investigation of a single subject.

> A prediction of what the *average* individual will do is often of little or no value in dealing with a particular individual. . . . A science is helpful in dealing with the individual only insofar as its laws refer to individuals. A science of behavior which concerns only the behavior of groups is not likely to be of help in our understanding of the particular case. (Skinner, 1953, p. 19)

Skinner believed that valid and replicable results could be obtained from a single subject without the use of statistical analysis, as long as sufficient data were collected under well-controlled experimental conditions. He argued that the use of a large group of subjects forced the experimenter to attend to average behavior and, as a result, individual response behavior and individual differences in behavior would be lost. In 1958 Skinnerian behaviorists established their own *Journal for the Experimental Analysis of Behavior*, largely because of the unwritten requirements of the current psychology journals concerning the use of statistical analysis and the size of the subject sample. Ten years later the *Journal of Applied Behavior Analysis* was begun to serve as an outlet for the expanding body of research on behavior modification, an applied outgrowth of Skinner's behaviorism.

Operant Conditioning

All psychology students are aware of Skinner's emphasis on operant as opposed to respondent behavior. In the Pavlovian conditioning situation, a known stimulus is paired with a response under conditions of reinforcement. The behavioral response is elicited by a specific observable stimulus; Skinner called this behavioral response a ***respondent behavior***.

Operant behavior occurs without any observable external stimulus. The organism's response is seemingly spontaneous in that it is not related to any known observable stimulus. This is not to say that there is definitely no stimulus eliciting the response, but rather that no stimulus is detected when the response occurs. As far as the experimenters are concerned, there is no stimulus because they have not applied any and cannot see any.

Another difference between respondent and operant behavior is that operant behavior operates on the organism's environment whereas respondent behavior does not. The harnessed dog in Pavlov's laboratory can do nothing but respond when the experimenter presents the stimulus. The dog cannot act on its own to secure the stimulus. The operant behavior of the rat in the Skinner box, however, is instrumental in securing the stimulus (the food). When the rat presses the bar, it receives food, and it does not get any food until it does press the bar and thus operate on the environment. (Skinner deplored the term ***Skinner box***, which was first used by Hull in 1933, as a label for his operant conditioning apparatus. The term has become so popular, however, that it is listed in most dictionaries and is accepted usage in psychology.)

Skinner believed that operant behavior is much more representative of the real-life human learning situation. Because behavior is mostly of the operant type, the most effective approach to a science of behavior, he argued, is to study the conditioning and extinguishing of operant behaviors. His classic experimental demonstration involved bar pressing in a Skinner box constructed to eliminate extraneous stimuli. In this experiment a rat that had been deprived of food was placed in the apparatus and allowed to explore. In the course of this general exploration the rat sooner or later accidentally depressed a lever that activated a mechanism that released a food pellet into a tray. After receiving a few of these food pellets, the reinforcers, conditioning was usually rapid. Note that the rat's behavior (pressing the bar or lever) operated on the environment and was instrumental in securing food. The dependent variable in this kind of experiment is simple and direct: the rate of response. A cumulative recorder attached to the Skinner box keeps a moment-by-moment record of the rate of bar pressing.

From this basic experiment Skinner derived his law of acquisition, which states that the strength of an operant behavior is increased when it is followed by the presentation of a reinforcing stimulus. Although practice is important in the establishment of high rates of bar pressing, the key variable is reinforcement. Practice by itself will not increase the rate; all it does is provide the opportunity for additional reinforcement to occur.

Skinner's law of acquisition differs from the positions of Thorndike and Hull on learning. Skinner did not speak in terms of pleasure–pain consequences of reinforcement, as did Thorndike, nor did Skinner make any attempt to interpret reinforcement in terms of drive reduction, as did Hull. The systems of Thorndike and Hull are explanatory, whereas Skinner's is descriptive. Skinner considered drive to be simply a set of operations that influence response behavior in a certain way; he did not view drive as a stimulus or a physiological state. He defined drive objectively in terms of the number of hours of deprivation.

Skinner and his followers conducted a great deal of research on problems of learning, such as the role of punishment in the acquisition of responses, the effect of different schedules of reinforcement, the extinction of operant responses, secondary reinforcement, and generalization. Skinner also worked with other animals and with human subjects, using the same basic approach as the Skinner box. With pigeons the operant behavior involves pecking at a key or a spot; the reinforcer is food. The operant behavior for human subjects involves problem solving, reinforced by verbal approval or by the knowledge of having given the correct answer.

He once reported an attempt to use back-rubbing as a reinforcer for his three-year-old daughter, but the experiment backfired. He was talking to her at bedtime while rubbing her back and decided to test this as a reinforcer. "I waited," he wrote, "until she lifted her foot slightly and then rubbed briefly. Almost immediately she lifted her foot again, and again I rubbed. Then she laughed. 'What are you laughing at?' I said. 'Every time I raise my foot you rub my back!'" (Skinner, 1987a, p. 179).

Schedules of Reinforcement

To many psychologists, Skinner's most notable research is that devoted to the effects of different schedules of reinforcement. The initial research on bar pressing in the Skinner box demonstrated the necessary role of reinforcement in operant behavior. In that situation the rat's behavior was reinforced for every bar press, that is, it received food every time it made the correct response. However, as Skinner pointed out, reinforcement in the real world is not always consistent or continuous, yet learning occurs and behaviors persist even when reinforced only intermittently.

> We do not always find good ice or snow when we go skating or skiing. . . . We do not always get a good meal in a particular restaurant

because cooks are not always predictable. We do not always get an answer when we telephone a friend because the friend is not always at home. . . . The reinforcements characteristic of industry and education are almost always intermittent because it is not feasible to control behavior by reinforcing every response. (Skinner, 1953, p. 99)

Even if you study consistently, you may not get an A on every exam or term paper. On the job, you do not receive praise or a pay increase every day. In a football pool or at a slot machine you do not win every time. How is behavior affected by such intermittent reinforcement? Is one schedule of reinforcement optimal in terms of influencing behavior? Skinner and his colleagues devoted years of research to these questions (Ferster & Skinner, 1957; Skinner, 1969).

The impetus for this research came not from intellectual curiosity but from expediency, and it demonstrates that science sometimes operates in a manner quite different from the idealized picture presented in some textbooks. One Saturday afternoon Skinner found that his supply of food pellets was running low. At that time (the 1930s), food pellets could not be purchased from a laboratory supply company. The experimenter had to make them by hand—a laborious and time-consuming process. Rather than spend his weekend concocting food pellets, Skinner asked himself what would happen if he reinforced his rats only once a minute regardless of the number of responses they were making. That way, he would need many fewer food pellets. Skinner designed a lengthy series of experiments to test different rates and times of reinforcement.

In one set of studies, Skinner compared the response rates of animals reinforced for every response with those reinforced only after a certain time interval. The latter condition is known as the *fixed interval schedule of reinforcement*. A reinforcer could be given, for example, once per minute or once every four minutes. The important point is that the animal will be reinforced only after the passage of a fixed period of time. A job in which a salary is paid once a week or once a month provides reinforcement on a fixed interval schedule. Employees in such systems are paid not for the number of items they produce (the number of responses they make) but for the number of days or weeks that elapse. Skinner's research showed that the shorter the interval between reinforcers, the more rapidly the animal responded. Conversely, as the interval between reinforcers lengthened, the rate of responding declined.

The frequency of reinforcement also affects the extinction of a response. Behaviors are extinguished more quickly when they have been reinforced continuously, and the reinforcers are then stopped, than when they have been reinforced intermittently. Some pigeons responded as many as ten thousand times in the absence of reinforcement when they had been conditioned on an intermittent reinforcement schedule.

Skinner also investigated a *fixed ratio schedule of reinforcement*. In this case, reinforcement is presented not after a certain time interval but rather after a predetermined number of responses. The animal's behavior determines how often it will be reinforced. It is required to respond, for example, ten times or twenty times after receiving one reinforcer before it gets another one. Animals on a fixed ratio schedule respond much faster than those on a fixed interval schedule. More rapid responding on fixed interval reinforcement will not bring about additional reinforcement; the animal on a fixed interval schedule may press the bar five times or fifty times, and it will still be reinforced only when the predetermined time interval has elapsed.

The higher rate of responding on the fixed ratio schedule has been found to hold for rats, pigeons, and humans. A fixed ratio schedule of payment is used in business and industry where an employee's pay depends on the number of units produced, or a sales commission depends on the number of items sold. This reinforcement schedule is effective as long as the ratio is not set too high (that is, an impossible amount of work required for each unit of pay), and the reinforcer is worth the effort.

Other reinforcement schedules include variable ratios, variable intervals, and mixed schedules.

Verbal Behavior

Verbal behavior is the only area in which Skinner admitted any difference between rat and human. The sounds the human organism makes in speech, Skinner said, are responses that can be reinforced by other speech sounds or gestures in the same way a rat's bar-pressing behavior can be reinforced by food. For the infant, the specific sounds that will be reinforced depend on the culture, but the mechanics of verbal behavior are independent of culture.

Verbal behavior requires two people in interaction — one speaking and one listening. The speaker makes a response, that is, he or she utters a sound. The listener, by his or her behavior in reinforcing, not reinforcing, or punishing the speaker for what has been said, can control the speaker's subsequent behavior. For instance, if every time the speaker uses a certain word, the listener smiles, the listener is increasing the likelihood that the speaker will use that word again. If the listener responds by frowning, making hostile gestures, or uttering a nasty comment, the listener increases the possibility that the speaker will avoid that word in the future.

We can see examples of this process in the behavior of parents when their children are learning to speak. Unacceptable words, incorrect usage, or poor pronunciation elicit different reactions from polite phrases, correct usage, and clear pronunciation. In this way the child is taught the proper use of speech, at least as the parents understand it.

To Skinner, speech is behavior and is thus subject to contingencies of reinforcement and prediction and control, just like any other behavior. His work is summarized in the book *Verbal Behavior* (Skinner, 1957).

The Machines of Skinner's Behaviorism

We have discussed the Skinner box and its use in operant conditioning experiments, but that is not the only device Skinner developed. The Skinner box brought him prominence in psychology, and the aircrib — a device to mechanize infant care — brought him public notoriety. He described its development in an article in *Ladies Home Journal* in 1945. When he and his wife decided to have a second child, she remarked that baby care through the first two years required too much attention and menial labor, so Skinner invented an automated device to relieve parents of those tasks. His apparatus was made available commercially but was never a big success.

The aircrib has been described as "a large, air-conditioned, temperature controlled, germ free, soundproof compartment in which a baby can sleep and play without blankets or clothing other than a diaper. It allows complete freedom of movement, and relative safety from the usual colds and heat rashes" (Rice, 1968, p. 98). Skinner and his wife reared their second child in the aircrib. Except for a broken leg suffered in a skiing accident while out of the box, she apparently bore no ill effects and learned to beat her father at chess.

Another piece of equipment Skinner promoted is the teaching machine, invented by psychologist Sidney Pressey in the 1920s. Unfortunately for Pressey, the machine was far ahead of its time, and no one expressed any interest in it. Contextual factors may have been responsible for the lack of interest then, and also for the enthusiastic acceptance of the device some thirty years later (Benjamin, 1988b). In the 1920s, when Pressey introduced his teaching machine, it promised to teach students at a faster pace with fewer classroom teachers. At the time, however, there was a surplus of teachers and there was no public pressure to improve the learning process. In the 1950s, when Skinner introduced a similar device, there was a shortage of teachers, an unusually large number of students, and public pressure to improve the quality of education so that Americans could compete with the Russians in space exploration. Skinner reported that he had not known about Pressey's invention when he developed his own teaching machine, but he gave due credit to his predecessor.

Skinner popularized his machine after a visit to his daughter's fourth-grade class, when he decided that something had to be done to improve the teaching process. He summarized his work in this field in *The Technology of Teaching* (1968). Teaching machines were widely used throughout the late 1950s and early 1960s, until they were superseded by computer-assisted instructional methods.

Walden Two — A Behaviorist Society

Skinner mapped out a program of behavioral control, a technology of behavior, in which he attempted to transpose his laboratory findings to society at large. Whereas John B. Watson talked in general terms about a foundation for saner living through the principles of conditioning, Skinner outlined the operation of such a society in detail.

In 1948 he published a novel, *Walden Two*, that describes a one-thousand-member rural community in which every aspect of life is controlled by positive reinforcement. The book was the outgrowth of a period of depression that Skinner suffered at the age of forty-one. He resolved it by returning temporarily to his earlier identity as a writer. He was in turmoil about many aspects of his life, personal and professional, and he poured out his despair in the book, speaking through the story's main character, T. E. Frazier. "Much of the life in *Walden Two* was my own at the time," Skinner admitted. "I let Frazier say things that I myself was not yet ready to say to anyone" (Skinner, 1979, pp. 297, 298). In the novel, the fictional Skinner speaks openly about his emotional problems.

The book was hailed and reviled in reviews and only a few thousand copies a year were sold until the early 1960s. Then sales increased sharply and now number in the millions. The book continues to be popular and is required reading in many college courses.

The long line of thought from Galileo and Newton through the British empiricists to Watson reaches its culmination in Skinner's Walden Two society and his basic assumption about the nature of the human being as a machine. "If we are to use the methods of science in the field of human affairs, we must assume that behavior is lawful and determined. . . . that what a man does is the result of specifiable conditions and that once these conditions have been discovered, we can anticipate and to some extent determine his actions" (Skinner, 1953, p. 6). The mechanistic, analytic, and deterministic approach of natural science, reinforced by Skinner's conditioning experiments, persuaded behaviorists that human behavior could be controlled, guided, modified, and shaped by the proper use of positive reinforcement.

In the free will/determinism controversy, it is easy to see on which side of the fence the Skinnerians sit. Skinner repeatedly made the point that "the issue of personal freedom must not be allowed to interfere with a scientific analysis of human behavior. . . . We cannot expect to profit from applying the methods of science to human behavior if for some extraneous reason we refuse to admit that our subject matter can be controlled" (Skinner, 1953, p. 322).

This position is discussed in *Beyond Freedom and Dignity* (Skinner, 1971), a book that generated a great deal of publicity, brought about Skinner's appearance on television talk shows, and became a best-seller. As with *Walden Two*, the work was praised by some and derided by others. The fact that it was read by so many people demonstrates the public curiosity about Skinner's views.

Behavior Modification

Skinner's program for a society based on positive reinforcement exists only in fictional terms, but the control or modification of the behavior of individuals and small groups is widespread. ***Behavior modification*** through positive reinforcement is a popular technique in mental hospitals, factories, prisons, and schools where it is used to change abnormal or undesirable behaviors to more acceptable and desirable ones. The behavior modification technique works with people in the same way the operant conditioning apparatus works to change the behavior of rats, through reinforcing the desired behavior and not reinforcing undesired behavior.

Consider the child who throws temper tantrums to get food or attention. When parents give in to the child's demands, they reinforce the undesirable behavior. In behavior modification, such behavior as kicking and screaming would never be reinforced. Only more desirable and pleasant behaviors would be reinforced. After a time the child's behavior will be modified, because the temperamental displays will no longer work to bring rewards, whereas more pleasant behaviors will.

Operant conditioning and reinforcement have been applied in the business world, where behavior modification programs have been used successfully to reduce absenteeism and the abuse of sick-leave time and have improved job performance and safety. Behavior modification techniques have also been used to teach job skills, especially to disadvantaged workers, and have often succeeded where more traditional training methods have failed.

Behavior modification has also been used with mental patients. By rewarding patients with tokens, which can be exchanged for possessions or privileges, when they behave in the desired ways, and by not reinforcing negative or disruptive behavior, positive behavioral changes can be induced. Unlike traditional clinical techniques, there is no concern in behavior modification with what might be going on in a patient's mind, any more than there is concern about what might be going on inside the rat in the Skinner box. The focus is exclusively on overt behavior and positive reinforcement.

Punishment is not used; people are not punished for failing to behave in desirable ways. Instead, they are reinforced or rewarded when their behavior changes in positive ways. Skinner believed, as did Thorndike, that positive reinforcement is much more effective than punishment in altering behavior, a position supported by considerable human and animal research. (Skinner wrote that as a child he was never physically punished by his father and only once by his mother; she washed out his mouth with soap and water for saying a naughty word (Skinner, 1976). He did not say whether the punishment was effective in changing his behavior.)

However you view Skinner's intentions—whether you consider him a savior or an enslaver of human beings—there is no denying the extent of his influence on contemporary psychology. He has received much criticism, however, both from inside and outside the psychological establishment. Perhaps the most frequently voiced objection is directed at his extreme positivism and its opposition to theory. Opponents argue that it is impossible to eliminate all theorizing, as Skinner would have had it. The details of an experiment must be planned in advance of its execution, and this planning is evidence of theorizing, however simple. It has also been noted that Skinner's acceptance of the basic principles of conditioning as the framework for his research constitutes some degree of theorizing.

Further, Skinner made confident assertions about economic, social, political, and religious affairs that he apparently derived from his system. In 1986, for example, he wrote an article with the all-embracing title, "What Is Wrong with Daily Life in the Western World?" In it he asserted that "human behavior in the West has grown weak, but it can be strengthened through the application of principles derived from an experimental analysis of behavior" (Skinner, 1986, p. 568). This willingness to extrapolate beyond the data, particularly with regard to proposals about complex human problems, is inconsistent with an atheoretical stand and shows that Skinner went beyond the observable data in presenting a blueprint for the redesign of society.

The narrow range of behavior studied in Skinnerian laboratories (such as bar pressing and key pecking) has also been attacked. Critics argue that such studies ignore many aspects of behavior. For example, Skinner's position that all behavior is learned has been challenged by one of his former students, who conditioned more than six thousand animals of thirty-eight species to perform in television commercials, tourist attractions, and state fairs (Breland & Breland, 1961). Pigs, chickens, hamsters, porpoises, whales, cows, and other animals all demonstrated a tendency toward instinctive drift, that is, they substituted instinctive behaviors for those that had been reinforced, even when these behaviors interfered with obtaining sufficient food.

Skinner's position on verbal behavior, particularly on how infants learn to speak, has been challenged on the grounds that some behavior must be inherited. Critics argue that an infant does not learn a language on a word-by-word basis because of reinforcement received for the correct usage or pronunciation of each word. Instead, the infant masters the grammatical rules necessary to produce sentences, and it is the potential to construct those rules, so this argument goes, that is inherited, not learned (Chomsky, 1959, 1972).

Whether criticism or praise prevails in the long run, it can be said with certainty that Skinner was the uncontested leader and champion of behaviorist psychology. Most of his opponents would be forced to agree that American psychology for at least three decades was molded more by his work than by the work of any other psychologist.

The American Psychological Association granted Skinner the Distinguished Scientific Contribution Award in 1958, noting that "few American psychologists have had so profound an impact on the development of psychology and on promising younger psychologists." In 1968, Skinner received the National Medal of Science, the highest accolade bestowed by the United States government for distinguished contributions to science. In 1971, the American Psychological Foundation presented him with its Gold Medal Award, and he appeared on the cover of *Time* magazine. And in 1990, Skinner was awarded the APA's Presidential Citation for Lifetime Contribution to Psychology.

It is important to note that Skinner's goal was the betterment of people's lives and of society. Despite the mechanistic nature of his system, Skinner was a humanitarian, a quality that was apparent in his efforts to modify behavior in the real-world settings of homes, schools, factories, and mental institutions. He hoped that his technology of behavior would relieve human suffering, and he felt increasingly frustrated that his system, though popular and influential, had not been applied more widely.

There is no question that Skinner's radical behaviorism achieved and maintained a strong position within psychology. The *Journal for the Experimental Analysis of Behavior* and the *Journal of Applied Behavior Analysis* continue to flourish, as does the Division for the Experimental Analysis of Behavior of the APA. The application of Skinnerian principles in the form of behavior modification techniques remains popular, and the results of this work provide additional support for his approach. By any standards of professional and public acclaim, Skinnerian behaviorism has clearly overshadowed all other varieties of behaviorism.

Social Learning Theories: The Cognitive Challenge within Behaviorism

We have seen that behaviorism, like other systematic positions, has a long history. John B. Watson gave voice to the changing climate of the times in American psychology, rebelled against its mentalistic background, and formally established an objective science of behavior. This vigorous movement marked the beginning of the positivist era in American psychology. There followed enthusiastic formulations of different kinds of behaviorism. Fifty years after the publication of Watson's article that launched behaviorism, Skinner marked the anniversary with a paper entitled "Behaviorism at Fifty" (Skinner, 1963), in which he noted that the tremendous progress in experimental psychology in the United States was due primarily to the influence of behaviorism.

For all its popularity and influence, behaviorism has come under attack from many psychologists, including some who identify themselves as behaviorists. They have questioned behaviorism's total denial of mental or cognitive processes and have formed a new movement, the social learning or sociobehaviorist approach, which reflects the broader cognitive revolution in psychology. This movement marks the third stage — the neo-neobehaviorist stage — in the development of behaviorism.

Since about 1960 there has been a movement within psychology away from the "restrictive shackles of behaviorism toward a more flexible emphasis on cognitive processes" (Bruner, 1982, p. 42). Today, consciousness has returned to psychology in full measure. As you might expect, Skinner decried this trend, noting that "mentalism returned in a flood. . . . It became fashionable to insert the word 'cognitive' wherever possible" (Skinner, 1983b, p. 194).

We discuss the larger-scale cognitive movement—its origins and impact on contemporary psychology—in Chapter 15. Let us describe here two examples of how the return to consciousness changed the nature of behaviorism. We will consider briefly the works of the neo-neobehaviorists Albert Bandura and Julian Rotter.

Albert Bandura (1925–   )

Born in Canada, Albert Bandura received his Ph.D. from the University of Iowa in 1952 and joined the faculty of Stanford University. Beginning in the early 1960s he proposed a version of behaviorism that he initially defined as a sociobehavioristic approach but later called a social cognitive theory (Bandura, 1986).

Social Cognitive Theory

Bandura's social cognitive theory is a less extreme form of behaviorism than Skinner's, and it reflects and reinforces the impact of the renewed interest in cognitive factors. Bandura's approach remains behavioristic, however. His research focuses on the observation of the behavior of human subjects in interaction. He does not use introspection, and he stresses the role of reinforcement in acquiring and modifying behaviors.

In addition to being behavioral, Bandura's system is cognitive. He considers the influence on external reinforcement schedules of such thought processes as beliefs, expectations, and instructions. In Bandura's view, behavioral responses are not automatically triggered by external stimuli in the manner of a robot or a machine. Instead, reactions to stimuli are self-activated. When an external reinforcer alters behavior, it does so because the individual is consciously aware of what is being reinforced and anticipates the same reinforcement for behaving in the same way again.

Although Bandura agrees with Skinner that human behavior can change as a result of reinforcement, he also believes, and has empirically demonstrated, that virtually all kinds of behavior can be learned in the absence of directly experienced reinforcement. We do not always have to experience reinforcement ourselves; we can learn through *vicarious reinforcement*, by observing the behaviors of other people and the consequences of those behaviors. This ability to learn by example and vicarious reinforcement assumes the human capacity to anticipate and appreciate consequences that we have only observed in others and have not yet experienced ourselves. We can regulate and guide our own behavior by visualizing or imagining as yet unexperienced consequences of that behavior and by making a conscious decision to behave or not behave in the same way. There is not, then, a direct link between a stimulus and a response, or between behavior and reinforcement, as is the case in Skinner's system. Instead, there is a mediating mechanism interposed between the two, and that mechanism is the person's cognitive processes.

We can see how powerful cognitive processes are in Bandura's approach, and how his views differ from Skinner's. To Bandura, for example, it is not the actual schedule of reinforcement that is effective in changing behavior but rather what the person thinks that schedule is. Rather than learning by experiencing reinforcement directly, we learn through *modeling*, by observing other people and patterning our behavior on theirs. In Skinner's view, whoever controls the reinforcers controls behavior. In Bandura's view, whoever controls the models in a society controls behavior. Bandura has conducted extensive research on the characteristics of the models that can influence our behavior.

Bandura's approach is also a social kind of learning theory, because it studies behavior as it is formed and modified in social situations, that is, in interaction with other people. Bandura has criticized Skinner's emphasis on studying only individual subjects, and mostly rats and pigeons, instead of human subjects interacting with one another. Bandura believes that psychology cannot expect research findings that involve no social interaction to be relevant to the modern world. Few people operate in social isolation or escape the presence of others.

Self-Efficacy

Bandura has conducted considerable research on *self-efficacy*, which he described as our sense of self-esteem or self-worth, our feeling of adequacy and efficiency in dealing with the problems of life. His work has shown that people who are high in self-efficacy believe themselves to be capable of coping with all the events in their lives. They expect to overcome obstacles and, as a result, they seek challenges, persevere, and maintain a high level of confidence in their ability to succeed. In contrast, persons who are low in self-efficacy feel helpless and hopeless in coping with life events and believe that they have little or no ability to influence the conditions or situations that affect them. When they encounter problems, they are likely to give up trying to solve those problems if their initial efforts fail. They believe that nothing they can do will make a difference.

Research has shown that such beliefs can affect many aspects of human functioning, including our choice of career, our persistence in looking for the right job, how well we perform our work, and many aspects of our physical and mental health.

Behavior Modification

Bandura's goal in developing his social cognitive approach to behaviorism has been a practical and applied one: to change or modify behavior that society considers to be abnormal or undesirable. He reasoned that if all behavior, including the abnormal, is learned through observing others and modeling, then behavior can be relearned or changed in the same way. Like Skinner, Bandura focuses on the external aspects of abnormality—the behavior—and not on any presumed internal conscious or unconscious conflicts. Treating the symptom, then, is considered to be treating the disorder, because symptom and disorder are the same.

Modeling is used to change behavior by having subjects observe a model in a situation they find to be frightening or anxiety provoking. For example, children who are afraid of dogs will observe another child of their age approaching and playing with a dog. Watching from a safe distance, the subjects observe the model make progressively closer and bolder movements toward the dog. The model may pet the dog through the bars of a playpen, then enter the pen to play happily with the dog. As a result of this observational learning, the children's fear of dogs will be markedly reduced.

In a variation of this technique, subjects first watch models play with the feared object, such as a snake, then the subjects themselves make progressively closer movements toward the object, eventually touching and manipulating it.

Bandura's form of behavior therapy is immensely popular and has been supported by hundreds of experimental studies. It has proved to be effective in eliminating phobias about snakes, closed spaces, open spaces, and heights, and in dealing with obsessive-compulsive disorders, sexual dysfunctions, and some forms of anxiety. Modeling has also been found to be useful for enhancing self-efficacy, and it is widely applied in industry and in classroom situations.

Radical behaviorists have been critical of Bandura's social cognitive approach to behaviorism, arguing that cognitive processes such as belief and anticipation have no causal effect on behavior. "It is amusing," Bandura commented, "to see radical behaviorists, who contend that thoughts have no causal influence, devoting considerable time to speeches, articles, and books in an effort to convert people's beliefs to their way of thinking" (Evans, 1989, p. 83).

For the most part, Bandura's social cognitive approach has gained a high degree of acceptance in psychology as an effective way of studying behavior in the laboratory and changing it in the clinic. Bandura's contributions to contemporary psychology have been recognized by his peers. He was president of the American Psychological Association in 1974 and received the APA's Distinguished Scientific Contribution Award in 1980. His theory and the modeling therapy that derives from it are congruent with the functional, practical cast of so much of twentieth-century American psychology. His work is highly objective, amenable to precise laboratory methods, responsive to the current intellectual climate of psychology in its recognition of internal cognitive variables, and applicable to real-world issues. To many psychologists it represents one of the most exciting and productive innovations in behaviorism's long history.

Julian Rotter (1916–   )

Julian Rotter grew up in Brooklyn, New York, and discovered the works of Sigmund Freud and Alfred Adler while in high school. He decided then that he wanted to be a psychologist. There were few jobs for psychologists at that time, during the Great Depression, and he chose to major instead in chemistry at Brooklyn College. While there he met Adler, and on the advice of two professors, Rotter switched to psychology after all, even though it did not seem practical. He received his Ph.D. from Indiana University in 1941, and found a job at a state mental hospital in Connecticut. He served as a psychologist with the U.S. Army during World War II, taught at Ohio State University until 1963, then went to the University of Connecticut.

Cognitive Processes and the Locus of Control

Rotter was the first to use the term *social learning theory*. He developed a cognitive approach to behaviorism, which, like Bandura's, invokes the existence of internal subjective experiences. Thus, his behaviorism (again, like Bandura's) is less extreme than Skinner's. He criticized Skinner for studying individual subjects in isolation, arguing that we learn our behavior primarily through social experiences and interactions. Rotter's approach depends on rigorous, well-controlled laboratory research of the kind that is typical of the behaviorist movement, and he studies only human subjects in social interaction.

Rotter's system deals with cognitive processes more extensively than Bandura's. Rotter takes the position that we always perceive ourselves as conscious beings who are capable of influencing the experiences that affect our lives. Both external stimuli and the reinforcement they provide can affect human behavior, but the nature and extent of their influence are always mediated by cognitive factors (Rotter, 1982).

Four cognitive principles have been proposed. (1) We possess a subjective expectation of the outcome or result of our behavior in terms of the amount and kind of reinforcement that is likely to follow. (2) We form estimates of the likelihood that behaving in a particular way will lead to a certain reinforcer, and we regulate or adjust our behavior accordingly. (3) We place different values or degrees of importance on different reinforcers, and we judge or assess their relative worth in different situations. (4) Because we function in different psychological environments that are unique to us as individuals, the same reinforcer can have different values for different people. Thus, our subjective expectations and experiences, which are internal cognitive states, determine the effects that different external experiences will have on us.

Rotter's social learning theory also deals with our beliefs about the source of control of our reinforcement. His research has shown that some people believe that reinforcement depends on their own behavior; they are said to have an ***internal locus of control***. Other people believe that reinforcement depends on outside forces; they are said to have an ***external locus of control***.

These two sources of control exert differing influences on human behavior. External locus-of-control persons think that their own abilities and responses make little difference in the reinforcers they receive, and so they make little attempt to improve or change their situations. Internal locus-of-control persons think they are in charge of their lives and behave accordingly.

Rotter's social learning theory has attracted a large and loyal band of followers who are primarily experimentally oriented and agree on the importance of cognitive variables in influencing behavior. His research is considered to be as rigorous and well controlled as his subject matter allows, and he has defined his concepts with a degree of precision that makes them amenable to experimental testing. Large numbers of research studies, particularly on internal/external locus of control, are supportive of his cognitive approach to behaviorism.

Comment

Although the cognitive challenge to behaviorism from within has succeeded in modifying the behaviorist movement that we have followed from Watson through Skinner, it is important to remember that Bandura, Rotter, and other neo-neobehaviorists who subscribe to the cognitive approach still consider themselves behaviorists. Behavior remains their theoretical focus and the subject of their research. It must be noted, however, that the work of the neo-neobehaviorists has changed the nature of behaviorism in American psychology today.

A loyal core of Skinnerians remain active within the radical behaviorist tradition Skinner fostered, but their popularity and influence reached a plateau by the 1980s, and the decline of the system may well be hastened by Skinner's death in 1990. In 1987 Skinner conceded that his form of behavioral psychology was losing ground and that the cognitive approach was on the ascendant (Goleman, 1987). Other contemporary scholars agree, noting that Skinnerian behaviorism has "fallen from favor among the majority of active workers in the field.... Fewer scholars at major universities now call themselves behaviorists in the traditional sense. In fact, 'behaviorism' is often referred to in the past tense" (Baars, 1986, pp. viii, 1).

The behaviorism that does remain intact and vital in today's psychology — and that is especially visible within applied psychology where behavior modification techniques are popular — is a different form than was promoted in the decades between Watson's 1913 manifesto and Skinner's recent death. As with all evolutionary movements in science and in nature, the species continues to evolve. In that sense, behaviorism survives in the spirit, if not the original letter, of its intent.

Suggested Readings

Neobehaviorists

Bergmann, G., & Spence, K. W. (1941). Operationism and theory in psychology. *Psychological Review, 48*, 1–14. Describes some of the difficulties with the use of operationism and assesses Hull's theory in the context of these problems.

Guthrie, E. R. (1952). *The Psychology of Learning* (rev. ed.). New York: Harper. Offers a behavioristic framework for the study of topics of interest to learning theorists.

Tolman, E. C. (1922). A new formula for behaviorism. *Psychological Review, 29,* 44–53. Suggests that a less physiological approach to behaviorism will allow psychologists to deal more comprehensively with such topics as motivation and emotion.

B. F. Skinner

Benjamin, L. T., Jr. (1988). A history of teaching machines. *American Psychologist, 43,* 703–712. Describes the pioneering work of Sidney Pressey in the 1920s on classroom teaching devices, three decades before B. F. Skinner developed his teaching machine. Discusses the popularity of these machines through the 1960s, and their eventual replacement by personal computers.

Elms, A. C. (1981). Skinner's dark year and *Walden Two. American Psychologist, 36,* 470–479. Suggests that Skinner experienced an identity crisis in his youth when he failed as a writer and that his novel was written as a form of self-therapy when identity issues again became paramount for him in midlife.

Skinner, B. F. (1953). *Science and Human Behavior.* New York: Free Press. Details Skinner's approach to the scientific analysis of human behavior; discusses conditioned reflexes, operant behavior, punishment, the controlling environment, and self-control as well as implications of behaviorist principles for government, religion, and education.

Skinner, B. F. (1971). *Beyond Freedom and Dignity.* New York: Knopf. Deals with broad social issues, arguing that we must work to modify our physical, social, and cultural environments if we are to achieve maximum freedom and dignity.

Skinner, B. F. (1976). *Particulars of My Life*; (1979). *The Shaping of a Behaviorist*; (1983). *A Matter of Consequences.* New York: Knopf. Skinner's lengthy and detailed autobiography in three volumes.

Skinner, B. F. (1987). *Upon Further Reflection.* Englewood Cliffs, NJ: Prentice-Hall. A collection of essays on such diverse topics as cognitive psychology, the evolution of verbal behavior, the American educational system, and self-management in old age.

Social Learning Theorists

Bandura, A. (1976). Albert Bandura. In R. I. Evans (Ed.), *The Making of Psychology: Discussions with Creative Contributors.* New York: Knopf. Interviews with Bandura about his life and work.

Bandura, A. (1986). *Social Foundations of Thought and Action: A Social Cognitive Theory.* Englewood Cliffs, NJ: Prentice-Hall. Presents Bandura's theory of human nature, emphasizing the self-regulation of behavior.

Rotter, J. B. (1982). *The Development and Applications of Social Learning Theory: Selected Papers.* New York: Praeger. Covers the development of Rotter's theory and its application to problems in clinical, personality, and social psychology; includes a brief autobiographical sketch.

Gestalt Psychology 12

Introduction

We have traced the development of psychology from the initial ideas of Wilhelm Wundt and their elaboration by E. B. Titchener, through the growth of the functionalist school of thought, to the spread of the behaviorism of Watson and Skinner and the cognitive challenge within that movement. While these ideas were forming in the United States, the Gestalt revolution was taking hold in Germany. It was yet another protest against Wundtian psychology, further testimony to the importance of Wundt's ideas as an inspiration for opposing points of view and as an effective base from which to launch new systems of psychology.

In its attack on the Wundtian establishment, the Gestalt rebellion focused primarily on one aspect of Wundt's work—his atomism or elementism. The Gestalt psychologists seized on Wundt's recognition of the fundamental status of sensory elements and made that the target of their opposition. "We had been shocked," wrote Wolfgang Köhler, a founder of Gestalt psychology, "by the thesis that all psychological facts... consist of unrelated inert atoms and that almost the only factors which combine these atoms and thus introduce action are associations" (Köhler, 1959, p. 728).

To understand the nature of the Gestalt revolution, we must go back to around 1912, the year described as a "time of troubles" for the old approach to psychology, the time when behaviorism was beginning its attack on Wundt and Titchener and on the newer functionalism. The animal research of Thorndike and Pavlov had been on the rise for a decade, Thorndike's first full statement of his position was made during that time, and the significance for psychology of Pavlov's conditioned reflex was soon to be acknowledged. Another new approach, psychoanalysis, was already more than a decade old.

The Gestalt psychologists' attack on Wundt's elementistic position was simultaneous with, although independent of, the behaviorist movement in the United States. Both schools of thought started by opposing the same ideas, but later came to oppose each other. There were clear differences between the Gestalt psychologists and the behaviorists. Gestalt psychologists accepted the value of consciousness but criticized the attempt to analyze it into elements. Behavioral psychologists refused even to acknowledge the existence of consciousness for psychology.

Gestalt psychologists referred to the Wundtian approach (as they understood it) as "brick and mortar" psychology, implying that the elements (the bricks) were held together by the mortar of the process of association. They argued that when we look out a window we see immediately the trees and the sky, not any alleged sensory elements such as brightnesses and hues that may constitute our perception of trees and sky. Further, they accused the Wundtians of claiming that our perception of objects consists merely of the accumulation or summation of elements into groups or bundles. The Gestalt psychologists maintained that when sensory elements are combined, some new pattern or configuration is formed. Put together a group of musical notes and something new—a melody or tune—emerges from the combination, something that did not exist in any of the individual elements or notes. Stated succinctly: The whole is different from the sum of its parts. It should be noted, however, that Wundt recognized this point in his doctrine of apperception.

To illustrate the difference between the Gestalt and the Wundtian approaches to perception, imagine that you are a subject in a psychology laboratory in Germany around 1915. The psychologist in charge asks you what you see on the table. You say:

"A book."

"Yes, of course, it is a book," he agrees, "but what do you really see?"

"What do you mean, 'What do I really see?' " you ask, puzzled. "I told you that I see a book. It is a small book with a red cover."

The psychologist is persistent. "What is your perception really?" he insists. "Describe it to me as precisely as you can."

"You mean it isn't a book? What is this, some kind of trick?"

There is a hint of impatience. "Yes, it is a book. There is no trickery involved. I just want you to describe to me exactly what you can see, no more and no less."

You are growing very suspicious now. "Well," you say, "from this angle the cover of the book looks like a dark red parallelogram."

"Yes," he says, pleased. "Yes, you see a patch of dark red in the shape of a parallelogram. What else?"

"There is a grayish white edge below it and another thin line of the same dark red below that. Under it I see the table —" He winces. "Around it I see a somewhat mottled brown with wavering streaks of lighter brown running roughly parallel to one another."

"Fine, fine." He thanks you for your cooperation.

As you stand there looking at the book on the table you are a little embarrassed that this persistent fellow was able to drive you to such an analysis. He made you so cautious that you were not sure any longer what you really saw and what you only thought you saw. . . . In your caution you began talking about what you saw in terms of sensations, where just a moment earlier you were quite certain that you perceived a book on a table.

Your reverie is interrupted suddenly by the appearance of a psychologist who looks vaguely like Wilhelm Wundt. "Thank you, for helping to confirm once more my theory of perception. You have proved," he says, "that the book you see is nothing but a compound of elementary sensations. When you were trying to be precise and say accurately what it was you really saw, you had to speak in terms of color patches, not objects. It is the color sensations that are primary, and every visual object is reducible to them. Your perception of the book is constructed from sensations just as a molecule is constructed from atoms."

This little speech is apparently a signal for battle to begin. "Nonsense!" shouts a voice from the opposite end of the hall. "Nonsense!

Any fool knows that the book is the primary, immediate, direct, compelling, perceptual fact!" The psychologist who charges down upon you now bears a faint resemblance to William James, but he seems to have a German accent, and his face is so flushed with anger that you cannot be sure. "This reduction of a perception into sensations that you keep talking about is nothing but an intellectual game. An object is not just a bundle of sensations. Any man who goes about seeing patches of dark redness where he ought to see books is sick!"

As the fight begins to gather momentum you close the door softly and slip away. You have what you came for, an illustration that there are two different attitudes, two different ways to talk about the information that our senses provide. (Miller, 1962, pp. 103–105)*

Gestalt psychologists believe that there is more to perception than meets the eye, that our perception somehow goes beyond the sensory elements, the basic physical data provided to the sense organs.

Antecedent Influences on Gestalt Psychology

As with all movements, the ideas of the Gestalt protest have their historical antecedents. The basis of the Gestalt position, its focus on the unity of perception, can be found in the work of the German philosopher Immanuel Kant (1724–1804). This eminent man, who never ventured more than sixty miles from his birthplace, dominated philosophical thinking for more than a generation. Although his contribution to psychology is less extensive than his contribution to philosophy, it is important nonetheless.

Kant influenced psychology through his emphasis on the unity of a perceptual act. He argued that when we perceive what we call objects, we encounter mental states that might seem to be composed of bits and pieces; these are the sensory elements the British empiricists and associationists dealt with. These elements are meaningfully organized in *a priori* fashion, however, and not through some mechanical process of association. The mind, in the process of perceiving, forms or creates a unitary experience.

According to Kant, perception is not a passive impression and combination of sensory elements, as the empiricists and associationists claimed, but an active organization of these elements into a coherent

*From pp. 103–105 in *Psychology* by George A. Miller. Copyright 1962 by George A. Miller. Reprinted by permission of Harper & Row, Publishers, Inc.

experience. Thus, the mind gives form and organization to the raw material of perception. This position is contrary to the doctrine of association. To Kant, some of the forms the mind imposes on experience are innate (such as space, time, and causality), in that they do not derive from experience but exist in the mind as intuitively knowable.

The psychologist Franz Brentano (1838–1917) at the University of Vienna opposed Wundt's focus on the elements or content of conscious experience and proposed instead that psychology study the process or act of experiencing (Chapter 4). He was thus an anticipator of the formal Gestalt movement. He considered Wundtian introspection to be artificial and favored a less rigid and more direct observation of experience as it occurs, much like the later Gestalt method.

Ernst Mach (1838–1916), a professor of physics at the University of Prague, exerted a more direct influence on the Gestalt revolution. In his book *The Analysis of Sensations* (1885), Mach wrote about sensations of space-form and time-form. He considered spatial patterns such as geometric figures and temporal patterns such as melodies to be sensations. These space-form and time-form sensations were independent of their elements. For example, the space-form of a circle might be white or black, large or small, and lose nothing of its elemental quality of circularity.

Mach argued that our visual or aural perception of an object does not change, even if we change our spatial orientation to it. A table remains a table in our perception whether we look at it from the side or from the top or from an angle. Similarly, a tune remains the same in our perception even when its time-form is changed, that is, when it is played faster or slower.

Mach's ideas were expanded by Christian von Ehrenfels (1859–1932), who worked at Vienna and Graz. He suggested that there are qualities of experience that cannot be explained in terms of combinations of sensations. He called these qualities *Gestalt qualitäten* (form qualities), perceptions based on something beyond the individual sensations. A melody, for example, is a form quality because it sounds the same even when transposed to different keys. The melody is thus independent of the particular sensations of which it is composed. To Ehrenfels, and the Austrian school of *Gestalt qualität* centered at Graz, form itself was an element (though not a sensation), a new element created by the action of the mind operating on the sensory elements. Thus, the mind creates form out of elementary sensations.

Although Mach and Ehrenfels thought along the lines that came to be known as Gestalt psychology, they deviated little from the orthodox elementist position. Rather than oppose the notion of elementism, as the Gestalt psychologists later did, they simply added form as a new element. Although they criticized the same position as the Gestalt psychologists, they offered a different solution. Still, Ehrenfels in particular had an impact on the Gestalt movement. Max Wertheimer, a founder of Gestalt psychology, studied under Ehrenfels at Prague. In Wertheimer's article reprinted in this chapter, he noted that the most important impulse for the Gestalt movement came from the work of Ehrenfels.

William James, who opposed psychological elementism, was also a precursor of Gestalt psychology. James regarded elements of consciousness as artificial abstractions, and he emphasized that we see objects as wholes, not as bundles of sensations.

Another early influence is the phenomenological movement in German philosophy and psychology. Methodologically, *phenomenology* refers to an unbiased description of immediate experience just as it occurs. It is uncorrected observation in which the experience is not analyzed into elements or otherwise artificially abstracted. It involves the almost naive experience of common sense rather than experience as reported by a trained introspector with a particular systematic orientation.

A group of phenomenological psychologists worked at G. E. Müller's laboratory at the University of Göttingen in Germany in the years 1909 to 1915, the period when the Gestalt movement was beginning to develop. These psychologists, including Erich R. Jaensch, David Katz, and Edgar Rubin, conducted extensive phenomenological research. Their work anticipated the formal Gestalt school of thought, which later adopted their approach.

Not to be neglected among the antecedent influences on Gestalt psychology is the Zeitgeist, especially the intellectual climate in physics. In the closing decades of the nineteenth century, that discipline was becoming less atomistic as physicists were coming to recognize and accept the notion of fields of force (regions or spaces crossed by lines of force, such as from an electric current or a magnet).

The classic instance of this new direction in physics is magnetism, a property or quality that seemed difficult to define or understand in traditional Galilean-Newtonian terms. For example, when iron filings are shaken onto a sheet of paper that is resting on top of a magnet, the filings become arranged in a characteristic pattern. The iron filings do not touch the magnet, yet they are obviously affected by the field of force around the magnet. Light and electricity were considered to operate similarly. These fields of force were thought to possess the properties of spatial extension and pattern or configuration. They were, in other words, believed to be new structural entities, not summations of the effects of individual elements or particles.

Thus, the notion of atomism or elementism, which had been so influential in the establishment of the new science of psychology, was being reconsidered in physics. Physicists were coming to think in terms of fields or organic wholes, a concept congruent with Gestalt psychology. The changes offered to psychology by the Gestalt psychologists reflected the changes in the physics of the day, as psychologists strove again to emulate the older, well-established natural sciences.

The impact on psychology of this changing emphasis in physics came about in a personal way. Wolfgang Köhler had a strong background in physics and had studied with Max Planck, one of the architects of modern physics. Köhler wrote that it was because of Planck's influence that he began to sense a connection between field physics and the Gestalt emphasis on wholes. He saw in physics an increasing reluctance to continue to deal with elements such as atoms and molecules and a focus instead on larger systems or fields. He wrote that "Gestalt psychology has since become a kind of application of field physics to essential parts of psychology" (Köhler, 1969, p. 77).

The founder of behaviorism, John B. Watson, in contrast, apparently had no training in the new physics, and so he continued to develop a reductionistic approach to psychology that focused on elements — the elements of behavior — a view that was compatible with the principles of the older atomistic physics.

The Founding of Gestalt Psychology

The formal movement known as Gestalt psychology grew out of a research study conducted in 1910 by Max Wertheimer. While riding on a train during his vacation, Wertheimer got an idea for an experiment about the seeing of motion when no actual motion had occurred. Promptly abandoning his vacation plans, he got off the train at Frankfurt, bought a toy stroboscope,* and verified his insight in a preliminary way in his hotel room. He later carried out more formal research at the University of Frankfurt, which provided a tachistoscope for his use. Two other young psychologists, Kurt Koffka and Wolfgang Köhler, who had been students at the University of Berlin, were also at Frankfurt, and shortly they all embarked on a joint crusade.

Wertheimer's research problem, in which Koffka and Köhler served as subjects, involved the perception of apparent movement, that is, the perception of motion when no actual physical movement has taken place.

---

*The stroboscope, invented about eighty years earlier by J. Plateau, was a forerunner of the motion picture camera. It is an instrument that rapidly projects a series of different pictures on the eye, producing apparent motion.

Wertheimer referred to it as the "impression of movement" (Seaman, 1984, p. 3). Using the tachistoscope, Wertheimer projected light through two slits, one vertical and the other 20° or 30° from the vertical. If light was shown first through one slit and then through the other, with a relatively long interval between (more than 200 milliseconds), the subjects saw what appeared to be two successive lights, first a light at one slit and then a light at the other. When the interval between the lights was shorter, the subjects saw what appeared to be two lights on continuously. With an optimal time interval (about 60 milliseconds) between the lights, the subjects saw a single line of light that appeared to move from one slit to the other and back again.

These findings may seem straightforward. Scientists had been aware of the phenomenon for years, and it may even be considered a matter of common sense. However, according to the then prevailing position in psychology, the Wundtian viewpoint, all conscious experience could be analyzed into its sensory elements. Yet how could this perception of apparent movement be explained in terms of a summation of the individual sensory elements, which were simply two stationary slits of light? Could one stationary stimulus be added to another to produce a sensation of movement? It could not, and this was precisely the point of Wertheimer's brilliantly simple demonstration: It defied explanation by the Wundtian system.

Wertheimer believed that the phenomenon he verified in his laboratory was, in its own way, as elementary as a sensation, yet it obviously differed from a sensation or even a succession of sensations. He gave the phenomenon a name befitting its unique status: the *phi phenomenon*. And how did Wertheimer explain the phi phenomenon when the traditional psychology of the day could not? His answer was as simple and ingenious as the verifying experiment: apparent movement did not need explaining. It existed as it was perceived, and it could not be reduced to anything simpler.

According to Wundt, introspection of the stimulus would produce two successive lines and nothing more, but no matter how rigorously one might introspect the two exposures of light, the experience of a single line in motion persisted. Any further attempt at analysis failed. The whole (the apparent movement of the line) was different from the sum of its parts (the two stationary lines). The traditional associationist–atomist psychology, dominant for so many years, had been challenged, and this was a challenge it could not meet. Wertheimer published the results of his research in 1912 in "Experimental Studies of the Perception of Movement," an article considered to mark the beginning of the Gestalt psychology school of thought.

With his study of
the perception
of apparent
motion, Max
Wertheimer
started the move-
ment known
as Gestalt
psychology.

Max Wertheimer (1880–1943)

Born in Prague, Max Wertheimer went to the local *Gymnasium* until he was eighteen and then studied law for a few years at the University of Prague. He switched to philosophy, attending lectures by Ehrenfels, and later went to the University of Berlin to study philosophy and psychology. He earned his doctoral degree in 1904 at the University of Würzburg under Oswald Külpe, at the height of the imageless-thought controversy. Between 1904 and 1910, Wertheimer spent his time at universities in Prague, Vienna, and Berlin before settling at the University of Frankfurt. There he did research and lectured for several years, receiving a professorship in 1929. During World War I, he conducted military research on listening devices for submarines and harbor fortifications.

Wertheimer was the oldest of the three original Gestalt psychologists and the intellectual leader of the movement. (Although Koffka and Köhler served to promote Wertheimer's prominent position, each was influential in his own right, as we shall see.) Wertheimer produced important papers on creative thinking and perceptual grouping.

In 1921, Wertheimer, Koffka, and Köhler, assisted by Kurt Goldstein and Hans Gruhle, founded the journal *Psychologische Forschung* (*Psychological Research*), which became the official organ of the Gestalt school of thought. Twenty-two volumes were published before it was suspended in 1938 by the Nazi regime; publication resumed in 1949 (Scheere, 1988).

Wertheimer was among the first group of refugee scholars to flee Nazi Germany, and he arrived in New York City in 1933. He became associated with the New School for Social Research, where he remained until his death in 1943. His years in the United States were active, but he became increasingly exhausted by the burdens of adapting to a new language and culture. His research program was informal, communicated personally to friends and colleagues at professional meetings.

During his last years in New York, Wertheimer apparently made a strong impression on a young American psychologist, Abraham Maslow. Maslow was so in awe of Wertheimer that he began to study the man's qualities and characteristics. It was from these initial observations of Wertheimer (and of the anthropologist Ruth Benedict) that Maslow developed his concept of self-actualization (Chapter 15).

Kurt Koffka (1886–1941)

Kurt Koffka was probably the most inventive of the founders of Gestalt psychology. He received his education at the University of Berlin, the city of his birth, and developed an interest in science and philosophy that was strengthened by a year at the University of Edinburgh, in Scotland. After returning to Berlin, he studied psychology with Carl Stumpf and received his Ph.D. in 1909. In 1910 Koffka began his long and fruitful association with Wertheimer and Köhler at the University of Frankfurt. In 1911 he accepted a position at the University of Giessen, only forty miles from Frankfurt, and remained there until 1924. During World War I he worked with brain-damaged and aphasic patients at the psychiatric clinic.

Kurt Koffka's writings brought the Gestalt school of psychology to the attention of American psychologists.

After the war, when psychologists in the United States were becoming aware that a new school of thought was developing in Germany, Koffka was persuaded to write an article for the American journal *Psychological Bulletin*. This article, "Perception: An Introduction to Gestalt-Theorie" (Koffka, 1922), presented the basic concepts of Gestalt psychology and the results and implications of much research. Although the article was important as the first formal exposition to American psychologists of the Gestalt revolution, it may have done a disservice to the spread of the movement. The title, "Perception," started a misunderstanding that lingers today, namely, the idea that Gestalt psychology deals exclusively with perception and therefore has no relevance for other areas of psychology.

In reality, Gestalt psychology was more broadly concerned with problems of thinking and learning.

> The main reason why the early Gestalt psychologists concentrated their systematic publications on perception was because of the Zeitgeist: Wundt's psychology, against which the Gestaltists rebelled, had obtained most of its support from studies of sensation and perception, so the Gestalt psychologists chose perception as the arena in order to attack Wundt in his own stronghold. (Michael Wertheimer, 1979, p. 134)

In 1921 Koffka published *The Growth of the Mind*, a book on developmental child psychology that became a success both in Germany and the United States. He came to America as visiting professor at Cornell University and the University of Wisconsin, and in 1927 was appointed professor at Smith College in Northampton, Massachusetts, where he remained until his death in 1941. In 1935 he published *Principles of Gestalt Psychology*, which was a difficult book to read and so did not become the definitive treatment of Gestalt psychology he had intended it to be.

Wolfgang Köhler (1887–1967)

Wolfgang Köhler, the youngest of the three, was the spokesman for the Gestalt movement. His books, written with care and precision, became the definitive works on several aspects of Gestalt psychology. Köhler's training in physics under the eminent Max Planck persuaded him that psychology must ally itself with physics. Born in Estonia, Köhler was five years old when his family moved to northern Germany. His university education was at Tübingen, Bonn, and Berlin, and he received his doctorate from Carl Stumpf at the University of Berlin in 1909. He went to the University of Frankfurt, arriving just before Wertheimer and his toy stroboscope.

In 1913, at the invitation of the Prussian Academy of Science, Köhler embarked on a voyage to Tenerife in the Canary Islands, off the northwest coast of Africa, to study chimpanzees. Six months after his arrival, World War I began, and he reported that he was unable to leave, although other German citizens did manage to return home during the war years. One psychologist has suggested, based on his interpretation of new data of

Wolfgang Köhler, trained in physics, studied learning in chimpanzees and became a prominent spokesman for the Gestalt movement.

history, that Köhler may have been a spy for Germany and that his research facility was actually a cover for his espionage activities (Ley, 1990). It is charged that on the top floor of his home he concealed a powerful radio transmitter that he used to broadcast information about allied ship movements. The evidence to support this claim is circumstantial, however, and has been challenged by historians and Gestalt psychologists.

Whether a spy or simply a scientist marooned by war, Köhler spent the next seven years studying behavior in chimpanzees. He produced the now classic volume, *The Mentality of Apes* (1917), which appeared in a second edition in 1924 and was translated into English and French.

In 1920, Köhler returned to Germany and two years later succeeded Stumpf as professor of psychology at the University of Berlin, where he remained until 1935. The apparent reason for his appointment to this coveted position was the publication of the book *Static and Stationary Physical Gestalts* (1920), which won considerable acclaim for its high level of scholarship.

The mid-1920s were difficult years in Köhler's personal life. He divorced his wife, married a young Swedish student, and after that had no contact with the four children of his first marriage. He developed a tremor in his hands, which became more noticeable when his mood darkened. As a way to gauge his temper, his laboratory assistants would observe him every morning, to see how badly his hands were shaking. He was extremely nervous whenever he lectured, and he never allowed visitors in his classroom (Ley, 1990).

In the 1925–1926 academic year, Köhler lectured at Harvard University and at Clark University, where he taught the graduate students to dance the tango. In 1929 he published, in English, *Gestalt Psychology*, a comprehensive argument for the Gestalt movement. He left Nazi Germany in 1935, because of continual conflicts with the government. After he spoke against the government in his lectures, a gang of Nazi thugs invaded his classroom. He wrote a courageous anti-Nazi letter to a Berlin newspaper, because he was incensed by the dismissal of all Jewish professors from German universities. On the evening his letter was published, he and a few friends waited quietly at his home, playing chamber music, expecting the Gestapo to arrest him. The dreaded knock on the door never came (Henle, 1978).

After Köhler emigrated to the United States, he taught at Swarthmore College in Pennsylvania, published several books, and edited the Gestalt journal *Psychological Research*. In 1956 he received the Distinguished Scientific Contribution Award from the American Psychological Association and shortly thereafter was elected its president.

The Nature of the Gestalt Revolt

The Gestalt principles were in direct opposition to much of the academic tradition of psychology in Germany. Behaviorism was less of an immediate revolt against Wundt and structuralism because functionalism had already brought about some changes in American psychology. No such tempering paved the way for the Gestalt revolt in Germany. The pronouncements of the Gestalt psychologists were nothing short of heresy to the German tradition.

The initiators of the Gestalt movement realized that they were taking on a powerful and entrenched force, striking at the foundation of psychology as it was then defined. Like most revolutionaries, the leaders of the Gestalt school of thought demanded a complete revision of the old order, almost like "intellectual missionaries, spreading a new gospel" (Sokal, 1984, p. 1257). Wolfgang Köhler wrote that "We were excited by what we found, and even more by the prospect of finding further revealing facts. Moreover, it was not only the stimulating newness of our enterprise which inspired us. There was also a great wave of relief—as though we were escaping from a prison. The prison was psychology as taught at the universities when we still were students" (Köhler, 1959, p. 285).

After the study of the perception of apparent movement, the Gestalt psychologists were quick to seize on other perceptual phenomena to support their position. The experience of *perceptual constancies* afforded ample corroboration. When we stand directly in front of a window, for example, a rectangular image is projected onto the retina of the eye, but when we stand off to one side and look at the window, the retinal image becomes a trapezoid, although we continue to perceive the window as rectangular. Our perception of the window remains constant, even though the sensory data (the images projected on the retina) have changed.

Similarly, with brightness and size constancy, the actual sensory elements may change, but our perception does not. In these cases, as with apparent movement, the perceptual experience has a quality of wholeness or completeness that is not found in any of the parts. There exists, then, a difference between the character of the actual perception and the character of the sensory stimulation. The perception cannot be explained simply as a collection of sensory elements or as the mere sum of the parts.

The perception is a whole, a Gestalt, and any attempt to analyze or reduce it to elements will destroy it.

> To begin with elements is to begin at the wrong end; for elements are products of reflection and abstraction, remotely derived from the immediate experience they are invoked to explain. *Gestalt* psychology attempts to get back to naive perception, to immediate experience . . . and it insists that it finds there not assemblages of elements, but unified wholes; not masses of sensations, but trees, clouds, and sky. And this assertion it invites anyone to verify simply by opening

his eyes and looking at the world about him in his ordinary everyday way. (Heidbreder, 1933, p. 331)

The word *Gestalt* has caused difficulty because it does not clearly indicate, as does functionalism or behaviorism, what the movement stands for. Also, it has no precise counterpart in English. Several equivalents in common use are form, shape, and configuration, and Gestalt itself has become part of the English language. In his book, *Gestalt Psychology* (1929), Köhler noted that the word is used in two ways in the German language. One usage denotes shape or form as a property of objects; in this sense, Gestalt refers to general properties that can be expressed in such terms as angular or symmetrical, and describes characteristics such as triangularity in geometric figures or tempos in a melody. The second usage denotes a whole or concrete entity that has as one of its attributes a specific shape or form; in this sense the word may refer, for example, to triangles rather than the notion of triangularity. Thus, the word *Gestalt* can be used for reference to objects as well as to their characteristic forms.

Also, the term is not restricted to the visual field or even the total sensory field. "According to the most general functional definition of the term, the processes of learning, of recall, of striving, of emotional attitude, of thinking, acting, and so forth, may have to be included" (Köhler, 1947, pp. 178–179). And it is in this larger sense of the word that the Gestalt psychologists attempted to deal with the entire province of psychology, as we see in the following lecture by Max Wertheimer.

Original Source Material on Gestalt Psychology: From *Gestalt Theory* by Max Wertheimer

The following material comes from a lecture given by Max Wertheimer to the Kant Society in Berlin, Germany, on December 17, 1924.* In a talk that encompassed psychology, philosophy, and the social sciences, Wertheimer pointed out the differences between a Gestalt or wholes approach and an approach that involves the reduction of the subject matter to elements. The specific points discussed include: (1) the basic definition of Gestalt psychology; (2) the Wundtian elementistic or atomistic approach to psychology and the attempt by Ehrenfels to add new elements; (3) examples of the Gestalt wholes approach; (4) the nature of psychological fields,

*From Max Wertheimer, "Gestalt Theory." In W. D. Ellis (Ed.), *A Source Book of Gestalt Psychology* (London: Routledge & Kegan Paul, 1938; New York: Humanities Press, 1967), pp. 1–11.

which are more than summations of sensations; and (5) the relationship between mind and body (the spiritual and material worlds) and the similarity, in Gestalt terms, between the two.

What is Gestalt theory and what does it intend? . . .

The fundamental "formula" of Gestalt theory might be expressed in this way: There are wholes, the behaviour of which is not determined by that of their individual elements, but where the part-processes are themselves determined by the intrinsic nature of the whole. It is the hope of Gestalt theory to determine the nature of such wholes.

With a formula such as this, one might close, for Gestalt theory is neither more nor less than this. It is not interested in puzzling out philosophic questions which such a formula might suggest. Gestalt theory has to do with concrete research; it is not only an *outcome* but a *device*: not only a theory *about* results but a means toward further discoveries. This is not merely the proposal of one or more problems but an attempt to *see* what is really taking place in science. This problem cannot be solved by listing possibilities for systematization, classification, and arrangement. If it is to be attacked at all, we must be guided by the spirit of the new method and by the concrete nature of the things themselves which we are studying, and set ourselves to penetrate to that which is really given by nature. . . .

About all I can hope for in so short a discussion is to suggest a few of the problems which at present occupy the attention of Gestalt theory and something of the way they are being attacked.

To repeat: the *problem* has not merely to do with scientific work — it is a fundamental problem of our times. Gestalt theory is not something suddenly and unexpectedly dropped upon us from above; it is, rather, a palpable convergence of problems ranging throughout the sciences and the various philosophic standpoints of modern times.

Let us take, for example, an event in the history of psychology. One turned from a living experience to science and asked what it had to say about this experience, and one found an assortment of elements, sensations, images, feelings, acts of will and laws governing these elements — and was told, "Take your choice, reconstruct from them the experience you had." Such procedure led to difficulties in concrete psychological research and to the emergence of problems which defied solution by the traditional analytic methods. Historically the most important impulse came from v. Ehrenfels who raised the following problem. Psychology had said that experience is a compound of elements: we hear a melody and then, upon hearing it again, memory enables us to recognize it. But what is it that enables us to recognize the melody when it is played in a new key? The sum of the elements is different, yet the melody is the same; indeed, one is often not even aware that a transposition has been made.

When in retrospect we consider the prevailing situation we are struck by two aspects of v. Ehrenfels's thesis; on the one hand one is surprised at the essentially summative character of his theory, on the other one admires his courage in propounding and defending his proposition. Strictly interpreted v. Ehrenfels's position was this: I play a familiar melody of six tones and employ six *new* tones, yet you recognize the melody despite the change. There must be a something *more* than the sum of six tones, viz. a seventh something, which is the form-quality, the *Gestaltqualität*, of the original six. It is this *seventh* factor or element which enabled you to recognize the melody despite its transposition.

However strange this view may seem, it shares with many another subsequently abandoned hypothesis the honour of having clearly seen and emphasized a fundamental problem.

But other explanations were also proposed. One maintained that in addition to the six tones there were intervals — relations — and that *these* were what remained constant. In other words we are asked to assume not only elements but "relations-between-elements" as additional components of the total complex. But this view failed to account for the phenomenon because in some cases the relation *too* may be altered without destroying the original melody.

Another type of explanation, also designed to bolster the elementaristic hypothesis, was that *to* this total of six or more tones there come certain "higher processes" which operate upon the given material to "*produce*" unity.

This was the situation until Gestalt theory raised the radical question: Is it really true that when I hear a melody I have a *sum* of individual tones (pieces) which constitute the primary foundation of my experience? Is not perhaps the reverse of this true? What I really have, what I hear of each individual note, what I experience at each place in the melody is a *part* which is itself determined by the character of the whole. What is given me by the melody does not arise (through the agency of any auxiliary factor) as a *secondary* process from the sum of the pieces as such. Instead, what takes place in each single part already depends upon what the whole is. The flesh and blood of a tone depends from the start upon its role in the melody. . . .

It belongs to the flesh and blood of the things given in experience (*Gegebenheiten*), how, in what role, in what function they are in their whole.

Let us leave the melody example and turn to another field. Take the case of threshold phenomena. It has long been held that a certain stimulus necessarily produces a certain sensation. Thus, when two stimuli are sufficiently different, the sensations also will be different. Psychology is filled with careful inquiries regarding threshold phenomena. To account for the difficulties constantly being encountered it was assumed that these phenomena must be influenced by higher mental functions, judgments, illusions, attention, etc. And this continued until the radical question was raised: Is it really true that a specific stimulus *always* gives rise to the same sensation? Perhaps the prevailing whole-conditions will themselves determine the effect of stimulation? This kind of formulation leads to experimentation, and experiments show, for example, that when I see two colours the sensations I have are determined by the whole-conditions of the entire stimulus situation. Thus, also, the same local *physical* stimulus pattern can give rise to either a unitary and homogeneous figure, or to an articulated figure with different parts, all depending upon the whole-conditions which may favour either unity or articulation. Obviously the task, then, is to investigate these "whole-conditions" and discover what influences they exert upon experience. . . .

Our next point is that my field comprises also my Ego. There is not from the beginning an Ego over-against others, but the genesis of an Ego offers one of the most fascinating problems, the solution of which seems to lie in Gestalt principles. However, once constituted, the Ego is a functional part of the total field. Proceeding as before we may therefore ask: What happens to the Ego as a part of the field? Is the resulting behaviour the piecewise sort of thing associationism, experience theory, and the like, would have us believe? Experimental results contradict this interpretation and again we often find that the laws of whole-processes operative in such a field tend toward a meaningful behaviour of its parts.

This field is not a summation of sense data and no description of it which considers such separate pieces to be *primary* will be correct. If it were, then for children, primitive peoples and animals experience would be nothing but piece-sensations. The next most developed creatures would have, in addition to independent sensations, something higher, and so on. But this whole picture is the opposite of what actual inquiry has disclosed. We have learned to recognize the "sensations" of our textbooks as products of a late culture utterly different from the experiences of more primitive stages. Who experiences the sensation of a specific red in that sense? What the man of the streets, children, or primitive men normally reach to is something coloured but at the same time exciting, gay, strong, or affecting — *not* "sensations."

The programme to treat the organism as a part in a larger field necessitates the reformulation of the problem as to the relation between organism and environment. The stimulus–sensation connection must be replaced by a connection between alteration in the field conditions, the vital situation, and the total reaction of the organism by a change in its attitude, striving, and feeling.

There is, however, another step to be considered. A man is not only a part of his field, he is also one among other men. When a group of people work together it rarely occurs, and then only under very special conditions, that they constitute a mere sum of independent Egos. Instead the common enterprise often becomes their mutual concern and each works *as* a meaningfully functioning part of the whole. Consider a group of South Sea Islanders engaged in some community occupation, or a group of children playing together. Only under very special circumstances does an "I" stand out alone. Then the balance which obtained during harmonious and systematic occupation may be upset and give way to a surrogate (under certain conditions, pathological) *new* balance. . . .

The fundamental question can be very simply stated: Are the parts of a given whole determined by the inner structure of that whole, or are the events such that, as independent, piecemeal, fortuitous and blind the total activity is a sum of the part-activities? Human beings can, of course, *devise* a kind of physics of their own — e.g., a sequence of machines — exemplifying the latter half of our question, but this does not signify that *all natural* phenomena are of this type. Here is a place where Gestalt theory is least easily understood and this because of the great number of prejudices about nature which have accumulated during the centuries. Nature is thought of as something essentially blind in its laws, where whatever takes place in the whole is purely a sum of individual occurrences. This view was the natural result of the struggle which physics has always had to purge itself of teleology. Today it can be seen that we are obliged to traverse other routes than those suggested by this kind of purposivism.

Let us proceed another step and ask: How does all this stand with regard to the problem of body and mind? What does my knowledge of another's mental experiences amount to and how do I obtain it? There are, of course, old and established dogmas on these points: The mental and physical are wholly heterogeneous: there obtains between them an absolute dichotomy. (From this point of departure philosophers have drawn an array of metaphysical deductions so as to attribute all the good qualities to mind while reserving for nature the odious.) As regards the second question, my discerning mental phenomena in others is traditionally explained as inference by analogy. Strictly interpreted the principle here is that something mental is meaninglessly coupled with something physical. I observe the physical and infer the mental from it more or less according to the following scheme: I see someone press a button on the wall and infer that he wants the light to go on. There *may be* couplings of this sort. However, many scientists have been disturbed by this dualism and have tried to save themselves by recourse to very curious hypotheses. Indeed, the ordinary person would violently refuse to believe that when he sees his companion startled, frightened, or angry he is seeing only certain physical occurrences which themselves have nothing to do (in their inner nature) with the mental, being only superficially coupled with it: you have frequently seen this and this combined . . . etc. There have been many attempts to surmount this problem. One speaks, for example, of *intuition* and says there can be no other possibility, for I *see* my companion's fear. It is not true, argue the intuitionists, that I see only the bare bodily activities meaninglessly coupled with other and invisible activities. However inadmissible it may otherwise be, an intuition theory does have at least this in its favour, it shows a suspicion that the traditional procedure might be successfully reversed. But the word intuition is at best only a *naming* of that which we must strive to lay hold of.

This and other hypotheses, apprehended as they now are, will not advance scientific pursuit, for science demands fruitful penetration, not mere cataloguing and systematization. But the question is, How does the matter really stand? Looking more closely we find a third assumption, namely that a process such as fear is a matter of consciousness. Is this true? Suppose you see a person who is kindly or benevolent. Does anyone suppose that this person is feeling mawkish? No one could possibly believe that. The characteristic feature of such behaviour has very little to do with consciousness. It has been one of the easiest contrivances of philosophy to identify a man's real behaviour and the direction of his mind with his consciousness. Parenthetically, in the opinion of many people the distinction between idealism and materialism implies that between the noble and the ignoble. Yet does one really mean by this to contrast consciousness with the blithesome budding of trees? Indeed, what is there so repugnant about the materialistic and mechanical? What is so attractive about the idealistic? Does it come from the *material* qualities of the connected pieces? Broadly speaking most psychological theories and textbooks, despite their continued emphasis upon consciousness, are far more "materialistic," arid, and spiritless than a living tree — which probably has no consciousness at all. The point is not what the material pieces are, but what *kind* of whole it is. Proceeding in terms of specific problems one soon realizes how many bodily activities there are which give no hint of a separation between body and mind. Imagine a dance, a dance full of grace and joy. What is the situation in such a dance? Do we have a summation of *physical* limb movements and a *psychical* consciousness? No. Obviously this answer does not solve the problem; we have to start anew — and it seems to me that a proper and fruitful point of attack has been discovered. One finds many processes which, in their dynamical form, are identical regardless of variations in the material character of their elements. When a man is timid, afraid or energetic, happy or sad, it can often be shown that the course of his physical processes is Gestalt-identical with the course pursued by the mental processes.

Again I can only indicate the direction of thought. I have touched on the question of body and mind merely to show that the problem we are discussing also has its philosophic aspects. . . .

This brings us to the close of an attempt to present a view of the problem as illustrated by its specific appearances in various fields. In concluding I may suggest a certain unification of these illustrations somewhat as follows. I consider the situation from the point of view of a theory of aggregates and say: How should a world be where science, concepts, inquiry, investigation, and comprehension of inner unities were impossible? The answer is obvious. This world would be a manifold of disparate pieces. Secondly, what kind of world would there have to be in which a piecewise science would apply? The answer is again quite simple, for here one needs only a system of recurrent couplings that are blind and piecewise in character, whereupon everything is available for a pursuit of the traditional piecewise methods of logic, mathematics, and science generally in so far as these presuppose this kind of world. But there is a third kind of aggregate which has been but cursorily investigated. These are the aggregates in which a manifold is not compounded from adjacently situated pieces but rather such that a term at its place in that aggregate is determined by the whole-laws of the aggregate itself.

Pictorially: suppose the world were a vast plateau upon which were many musicians. I walk about listening and watching the players. First suppose that the world is a meaningless plurality. Everyone does as he will, each for himself. What happens together when I hear ten players might be the basis for my guessing as to what they all are doing, but this is merely a matter of chance and probability much as in the kinetics of gas molecules. — A second possibility would be that each time one musician played *c*, another played *f* so and so many seconds later. I work out a theory of blind couplings but the playing as a whole remains meaningless. This is what many people think physics does, but the real work of physics belies this. — The third possibility is, say, a Beethoven symphony where it would be possible for one to select one part of the whole and work from that towards an idea of the structural principle motivating and determining the whole. Here the fundamental laws are not those of fortuitous pieces, but concern the very character of the event.

Gestalt Principles of Perceptual Organization

Wertheimer's *principles of perceptual organization* were presented in a paper in 1923. He took the position that we perceive objects in the same manner in which we perceive apparent motion, that is, as unified wholes, not as clusters of individual sensations. The principles of perceptual organization, which are described in most introductory psychology textbooks, are essentially laws or rules by which we organize or arrange our perceptual world.

A basic premise of these principles is that in perception, organization occurs instantly whenever we see or hear different shapes or patterns. Parts of the perceptual field become connected, uniting to form structures that are distinct from the background. Perceptual organization is spontaneous and inevitable whenever we look around. We do not have to learn to form patterns, as the associationists claimed, although higher-level perception, such as labeling objects by name, does depend on learning.

According to Gestalt theory, the primary brain process in visual perception is not a collection of separate activities. The visual area of the brain does not respond to separate elements of visual input, connecting these elements by some mechanical process of association. Rather, the brain is a dynamic system in which all the elements that are active at a given time interact; elements that are similar or close together tend to combine, and elements that are dissimilar or far apart do not tend to combine.

Several of the principles of perceptual organization are listed here and illustrated in Figure 12-1.

Figure 12-1

Examples of perceptual organization.

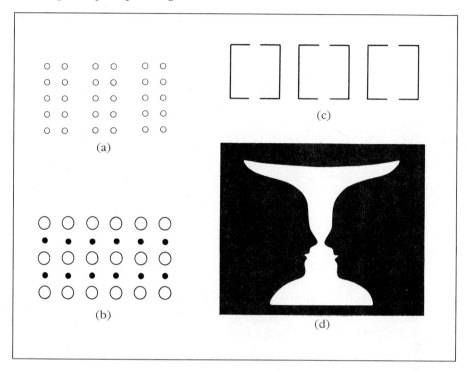

1. *Proximity*: Parts that are close together in time or space appear to belong together and tend to be perceived together. In Figure 12-1 (a) you see the circles in three double columns rather than as one large collection.

2. *Continuity*: There is a tendency in our perception to follow a direction, to connect the elements in a way that makes them seem continuous or flowing in a particular direction. In Figure 12-1 (a) you tend to follow the columns of small circles from top to bottom.

3. *Similarity*: Similar parts tend to be seen together as forming a group. In Figure 12-1 (b) the circles and the dots each appear to belong together, and you tend to perceive rows of circles and rows of dots instead of columns.

4. *Closure*: There is a tendency in our perception to complete incomplete figures, to fill in gaps. In Figure 12-1 (c) you perceive three squares even though the figures are incomplete.

5. *Simplicity*: We tend to see a figure as being as good as possible under the stimulus conditions; the Gestalt psychologists called this *prägnanz* or "good form." A good Gestalt is symmetrical, simple, and stable, and cannot be made simpler or more orderly. The squares in Figure 12-1 (c) are good Gestalts because they are clearly perceived as complete and organized.

6. *Figure/ground*: We tend to organize perceptions into the object being looked at (the figure) and the background against which it appears (the ground). The figure seems to be more substantial and to stand out from its background. In Figure 12-1 (d) the figure and the ground are reversible; you may see two faces or you may see a vase, depending on how you organize your perception.

These organizing principles do not depend on our higher mental processes or on past experiences. They are present in the stimuli themselves. Wertheimer called them peripheral factors, but he also recognized that central factors within the organism will influence perception; for example, the higher mental processes of familiarity and attitude can affect perception. In general, however, the Gestalt psychologists tended to concentrate more on the peripheral factors of organization than on the effects of learning or experience.

Gestalt Principles of Learning

We have seen that perception was an early focus of the Gestalt psychologists. They took the position that learning plays a role mainly in the higher-level perceptual processes. Some of the most significant experiments in the history of psychology are those devised by Köhler to study learning, specifically problem solving, in apes.

From the beginning, Gestalt psychologists opposed Thorndike's trial-and-error conception of learning, and, later, Watson's stimulus-response (S-R) learning. Gestalt psychologists believed that their consistent criticism of associationist and stimulus-response learning theories constituted a significant contribution to the development of psychology. The Gestalt view of learning is expressed in Köhler's research on the mentality of apes and in Wertheimer's work on productive thinking in humans.

The Mentality of Apes

We mentioned Köhler's stay on the island of Tenerife from 1913 to 1920, when he investigated the intelligence of chimpanzees as demonstrated in their ability to solve problems (Köhler, 1917). These studies were con-

A chimpanzee uses sticks of different lengths to reach a piece of fruit.

ducted in and around the animals' cages and involved simple props, such as the bars of the cages (used to block access), bananas, sticks for drawing the bananas into the cages, and boxes on which the animals could climb. Congruent with the Gestalt view of perception, Köhler interpreted the results of his animal studies in terms of the whole situation and the relationships among the various stimuli found therein. He considered problem solving to be a matter of restructuring the perceptual field.

In one study, a banana was placed outside the cage and a string that was attached to the banana led into the cage. The ape pulled the banana into the cage with little hesitation. Köhler concluded that in this situation the problem as a whole was easy for the animal to grasp. However, if several strings led from the cage in the general direction of the banana, the ape would not recognize at first which string to pull to get the banana. This indicated to Köhler that the problem could not be envisioned clearly all at once.

In another study, a piece of fruit was placed outside the cage just beyond the ape's reach. If a stick was placed near the bars of the cage in front of the fruit, the stick and the fruit would be visualized as part of the same situation, and the ape would use the stick to pull the fruit into the cage. If the stick was placed at the back of the cage, then the two objects (the stick and the fruit) would be less readily seen as parts of the same situation. In this case, a restructuring of the perceptual field would be necessary to solve the problem.

Another experiment involved positioning a banana outside the cage, beyond reach, and placing two hollow bamboo sticks inside the cage. Each stick by itself was too short to get the banana. To reach the banana, the animal had to push the two sticks together (inserting the end of one into the end of the other) to make a stick of sufficient length. Thus, to solve the problem and reach the banana, the animal had to perceive a new relationship between the sticks.

Sultan, Köhler's brightest ape, failed when initially confronted with this situation. He first tried to reach the banana with one stick. Next he pushed a stick out as far as he could, then pushed it farther with the second stick until the first stick touched the banana. He did not succeed during a one-hour trial but immediately after the experimental session was over, while playing with the sticks, Sultan solved the problem, as reported by his keeper.

> Sultan first of all squats indifferently on the box, which has been left standing a little back from the railings; then he gets up, picks up the two sticks, sits down again on the box and plays carelessly with them. While doing this, it happens that he finds himself holding one rod in either hand in such a way that they lie in a straight line; he pushes the thinner one a little way into the opening of the thicker, jumps up and is already on the run toward the railings, to which he has up to now half turned his back, and begins to draw a banana towards him with the double stick. (Köhler, 1927, p. 127)

In later trials, Sultan solved similar problems without difficulty, even when some of the sticks provided would not fit together. Köhler reported that Sultan did not even attempt to join the unsuitable sticks.

Studies such as these were interpreted by Köhler as evidence of *insight*, the apparently spontaneous and immediate apprehension or understanding of relationships. In another example of independent, simultaneous discovery, the American animal psychologist Robert Yerkes found evidence in orangutans to support the concept of insight. He called the phenomenon *ideational learning*.

In 1974, the keeper of Köhler's chimps, Manuel Gonzalez y Garcia, then 87 years old, related to an interviewer many stories about the animals, particularly Sultan, who used to help him feed the others. Gonzalez would give Sultan bunches of bananas to hold. "Then, on the oral command, 'two each,' Sultan would walk about the compound and dole out two bananas to each of the other apes" (Ley, 1990, pp. 12–13).

One day Sultan watched as the keeper painted a door. When the keeper left, Sultan picked up the paintbrush and began to imitate the behavior he had observed. On another occasion, Köhler's young son Claus sat in front of a cage, trying unsuccessfully to pull a banana out between the bars. Sultan, inside the cage and apparently not hungry, turned the banana 90° so that it would fit between the bars, whereupon Köhler told Claus that Sultan was smarter than he was.

Problem solving and insight differed dramatically from the trial-and-error learning described by Thorndike and others. Köhler was a vocal critic of Thorndike's work, arguing that its experimental arrangements were artificial and allowed only random behavior by the animal. Köhler said that the cats in Thorndike's puzzle box could not survey the entire release mechanism (all the elements pertaining to the whole), and thus could engage only in trial-and-error behavior. Similarly, an animal in a maze could not see the overall pattern or design but only each alley it encountered, and so it could do nothing but blindly try each path. In the Gestalt view, the organism must be able to see the relationships among the various parts of the problem before insight can occur.

The studies of insight lend support to the Gestalt psychologists' molar conception of behavior, as opposed to the molecular view promoted by the associationists and behaviorists. The research also reinforces the Gestalt idea that learning involves a reorganization or restructuring of the psychological environment.

Productive Thinking in Humans

Max Wertheimer's book on *productive thinking* (Wertheimer, 1945), published posthumously, applied the Gestalt principles of learning to creative thinking in humans. He suggested that such thinking is done in terms of wholes. Not only does the learner regard the situation as a whole, but the teacher must also present the situation as a whole. This approach differs from Thorndike's trial-and-error learning, in which a solution to the problem is, in a sense, hidden, and the learner is required to make errors before chancing on the correct path.

The case material in Wertheimer's book ranges from children solving geometric problems to the thought processes of the physicist Albert

Einstein that led to his theory of relativity. At different ages and at various levels of problem difficulty, Wertheimer found evidence to support the idea that the whole problem must dominate the parts. He believed that the details of a problem should be considered only in relation to the structure of the total situation, and that problem solving should proceed from the whole problem downward to the parts, not the reverse.

Wertheimer suggested that if a teacher arranged the elements of classroom exercises so that they were organized into meaningful wholes, then insight would occur. He demonstrated that once the principle of a problem's solution had been grasped, that principle could be transferred readily to other situations. He attacked the traditional educational practices of mechanical drill and rote learning, which derive from the associationist approach to learning. Repetition is rarely productive, Wertheimer argued, and he cited as evidence a student's inability to solve a variation of a problem when the solution had been learned by rote rather than insight. He did agree, however, that material such as names and dates should be learned by rote through association strengthened by repetition. He conceded that repetition was useful to a point, but he asserted that its habitual use led to mechanical performance rather than truly creative or productive thinking.

The Principle of Isomorphism

Having established that we perceive organized wholes rather than bundles of sensations, the Gestalt psychologists turned to the problem of the brain mechanisms involved in perception. They attempted to develop a theory of the underlying neurological correlates of perceived Gestalts. Gestalt psychologists view the cerebral cortex as a dynamic system, in which the elements active at a given time interact. This idea contrasts with the machine-like conception that compares neural activity to a telephone switchboard mechanically linking sensory inputs by the principles of association. In the latter view, the brain functions passively and is incapable of actively organizing or modifying the sensory elements it receives; this view also implies a direct correspondence between the perception and its neurological counterpart.

In his research on the apparent movement phenomenon, Wertheimer suggested that brain activity is a configural whole process. Because apparent and actual motion are experienced identically, the cortical processes for apparent and actual motion must be similar. On the assumption that these two kinds of motion are identical, there must then be corresponding brain processes. In other words, to account for the phi phenomenon, there must be a correspondence between the psychological or conscious experience and the underlying brain experience. This view is called *isomorphism*, an idea already widely accepted in biology and chemistry. The Gestalt psychologists likened a perception to a map, in that it is identical (*iso*) in form or shape (*morph*) to what it represents, without being a literal copy of the terrain. It does, however, serve as a reliable guide to the perceived real world.

Wertheimer's position was extended by Köhler in his book, *Static and Stationary Physical Gestalts* (1920). Köhler considered that cortical processes behave in a manner similar to fields of force, and he suggested that, like the behavior of an electromagnetic field of force around a magnet, fields of neuronal activity may be established by electromechanical processes in the brain in response to sensory impulses. He conducted extensive research on these ideas as one phase of an ambitious project to demonstrate that physics, chemistry, biology, and psychology all involve Gestalts.

The Spread of Gestalt Psychology

By the mid-1920s, the Gestalt movement was a cohesive, dominant, and forceful school of thought in Germany, centered at the Psychological Institute of the University of Berlin, where it attracted large numbers of students from many countries. Housed in a wing of the former Imperial Palace, it had one of the largest and best equipped laboratories in the world. The Gestalt journal *Psychological Research* was active, and Gestalt researchers were investigating various psychological problems.

After the Nazis came to power in Germany in 1933, their rampant anti-intellectualism and anti-Semitism and their repressive actions forced many scholars, including the leaders of Gestalt psychology, to leave the country. The movement was reduced to a minor position in the German academic system of the day, and the center of Gestalt psychology shifted to the United States. The work of the Gestalt psychologists had preceded them, so that they and their positions were well known in America by the time they arrived.

The spread of the Gestalt movement within the United States was carried out through personal contacts as well as articles and books. In the early years of the twentieth century, even before Gestalt psychology was founded, soon-to-be influential American psychologists were studying under future leaders of the Gestalt school. Herbert Langfeld of Princeton

University met Koffka in Berlin in the first decade of the century and sent his student Edward Chace Tolman to Germany, where Tolman served as a subject in Koffka's early Gestalt research. Robert Ogden of Cornell University also knew Koffka. The personality researcher Gordon Allport of Harvard University spent a year in Germany, where he declared that he was much impressed with the quality of the experimental research coming from the Gestalt school of psychology.

In the 1920s, a few books by Koffka and Köhler were translated into English and reviewed in American psychology journals. A series of articles on Gestalt psychology by the American psychologist Harry Helson, published in the *American Journal of Psychology*, also did much to spread the Gestalt viewpoint in the United States (Helson, 1925, 1926). Koffka and Köhler visited the United States to lecture at universities and conferences. Koffka gave thirty talks on Gestalt psychology in three years, and Köhler was one of the keynote speakers at the Ninth International Congress of Psychology held at Yale University in 1929. (The other keynote speaker was Ivan Pavlov, who was spat on by one of Robert Yerkes's chimps.)

Although Gestalt psychology was attracting attention in the United States, and some American psychologists considered it a useful antidote to what they saw as the extremes of behaviorism, it did not meet with overwhelming acceptance from all quarters. Its progress as a school of thought was comparatively slow for several reasons. First, behaviorism was then at the peak of its popularity in American psychology. A second problem was the language barrier. The major Gestalt publications were in German, and the need for translation delayed the full and accurate dissemination of the tenets of the Gestalt school in the United States. Third, as we noted earlier, many psychologists incorrectly believed that Gestalt psychology dealt only with perception. And fourth, Wertheimer, Koffka, and Köhler settled at American colleges that did not have graduate programs, so it was difficult for them to attract disciples who would expand and carry on the movement. Because the Gestalt psychologists did not teach at universities that granted graduate degrees, there was no new generation of disciples and researchers being trained. We might consider this to be a contextual factor that restricted the growth of Gestalt psychology in the United States.

The most important reason, however, for the relatively slow acceptance of Gestalt psychology in the United States was that American psychology had already advanced far beyond the ideas of Wundt and Titchener. Behaviorism was the second phase of American opposition. Hence, American psychology was already further removed from Wundt's elementistic position than was European psychology at that time. American psychologists believed that the Gestalt psychologists had come to the United States protesting something that was no longer an issue. This was dangerous for the Gestalt school. We have seen many times that revolutionary movements need something to oppose, something to push against, if they are to survive.

When the Gestalt psychologists became aware of the trends within American psychology, they readily perceived a new target — the reductionistic and atomistic behaviorist school of thought. The Gestalt psychologists argued that behaviorism, like the earlier Wundtian psychology, also dealt with artificial abstractions. It made little difference to them whether analysis was in terms of introspective reduction to mental elements or of objective reduction to conditioned reflexes. The result was the same: a molecular instead of a molar approach. The Gestalt psychologists also criticized the behaviorists' denial of the validity of introspection and their elimination of consciousness. Koffka argued that it was senseless to develop a psychology that lacked consciousness, as the behaviorists had done, because that reduced psychology to a collection of animal research studies and nothing more.

The battles between the Gestalt psychologists and the behavioral psychologists grew emotional and personal. On a social occasion in 1941, when Clark Hull, E. C. Tolman, Wolfgang Köhler, and several other psychologists went out to a bar for a few beers after a meeting in Philadelphia, Köhler told Hull that he had heard that Hull used the insult "those goddamned Gestalters" in his classroom lectures. Hull was embarrassed — the charge was correct — and he told Köhler that scientific matters should not be decided on the basis of some sort of warfare. Köhler said that he "was willing to discuss most things in a logical and scientific manner, but when people try to make man out to be a kind of slot machine, then he would fight." When he said the word "fight," as Hull recalled it, Köhler "brought his fist down on the table with a resounding smack, and he did not smile when he said it" (Amsel & Rashotte, 1984, p. 23).

In time, the principles of Gestalt psychology were absorbed in the areas of child psychology, applied psychology, psychiatry, education, anthropology, and sociology. In addition, some clinical psychologists combined the Gestalt approach with psychoanalysis. The general tendency in American psychology has been to consider the teachings of the Gestalt psychologists as interesting and potentially useful additions to other systems but not as the basis of an all-encompassing system. American psychologists have attempted to demonstrate that both elemental and organized responses occur, and that both are useful ways of explaining psychological processes.

For some psychologists, the Gestalt view remains vital, and it continues to stimulate research. Although it no longer boasts the combative spirit of a revolution, its adherents are working to refine its basic points. Gestalt psychology has not been totally absorbed into the mainstream of American psychology but retains an identity as a minority movement. It has exerted a visible influence on many areas of psychology, including perception, thinking, learning, personality, social psychology, and motivation.

Field Theory: Kurt Lewin (1890–1947)

The trend in late nineteenth-century science was to think in terms of field relationships and to move away from an atomistic and elementistic framework. As we have seen, Gestalt psychology reflected this trend. Field theory arose within psychology as an analogy to the concept of fields of force in physics. In psychology the term *field theory* has now come to refer almost exclusively to the work of Kurt Lewin. Lewin's work is largely Gestalt in its orientation, but his ideas extended beyond the framework of the orthodox Gestalt position. The Gestalt psychologists emphasized perception and learning and proposed physiological constructs to explain behavior; Lewin's work centered on needs and personality and dealt with social influences on behavior.

Kurt Lewin was born in Mogilno, Germany, and undertook his education at universities in Freiburg, Munich, and Berlin. In 1914, he received his Ph.D. in psychology from the University of Berlin, where he also studied mathematics and physics. During World War I Lewin served in the military and was awarded Germany's Iron Cross decoration. Afterward he returned to the University of Berlin and became such a productive and creative member of the Gestalt group that he was considered to be a colleague of the three senior Gestaltists. He conducted research on association and motivation and began to develop his field theory, which he presented to psychologists in the United States at the 1929 International Congress of Psychology at Yale.

Lewin was already well known in the United States when, in 1932, he became a visiting professor at Stanford University. The following year he decided to leave Germany permanently because of the Nazi menace. He spent two years at Cornell and in 1935 he went to the University of Iowa to conduct research on the social psychology of the child. As a result of this work he was invited to develop and head the new Research Center for Group Dynamics at the Massachusetts Institute of Technology. Although he died within a few years of accepting the position, his program was so effective that the research center, now at the University of Michigan, remains active.

Throughout his thirty years of professional activity Lewin devoted himself to the broadly defined area of human motivation. His research

The field theory of Kurt Lewin has influenced work on group dynamics and other areas of social psychology.

emphasized the study of human behavior within its total physical and social context (Lewin, 1936, 1939).

Field theory in physics led Lewin to consider that a person's psychological activities occur within a kind of psychological field, which he called the *life space*. The life space encompasses all the past, present, and future events that may possibly influence a person. From a psychological standpoint, each of these events can determine behavior in a given situation.

Thus the life space consists of the individual's needs interacting with the psychological environment.

The life space may show varying degrees of differentiation as a function of the amount and kind of experience the person has accumulated. Because an infant lacks experiences, he or she has few differentiated regions in the life space. A highly educated, sophisticated adult shows a complex and well-differentiated life space, as a function of past experiences.

Lewin wanted to use a mathematical model to represent his theoretical conception of psychological processes. Because he was interested in the single case rather than groups or averages, statistics were not useful to him. He chose, instead, a form of geometry called topology to map or diagram the life space, to show at any given moment a person's possible goals and the paths leading to them.

To represent direction, Lewin developed a form of qualitative geometry called hodological space, in which he used vectors to represent the direction of movement toward a goal. To complete the schematic representation of his system, Lewin used the notion of valences to refer to the positive or negative value of objects within the life space. Objects that are attractive to the individual or that satisfy needs have a positive valence; objects that are threatening have a negative valence.

This field theory approach, which has been called a blackboard psychology, includes complex diagrams to represent psychological phenomena. To Lewin, all forms of behavior can be represented by a diagram. A simple bit of behavior is mapped out in Figure 12-2, which illustrates a

Figure 12-2 ▬▬▬▬▬▬▬▬▬▬▬▬▬▬▬▬▬▬▬▬▬▬▬▬▬▬▬▬▬
A simplified example of a life space.

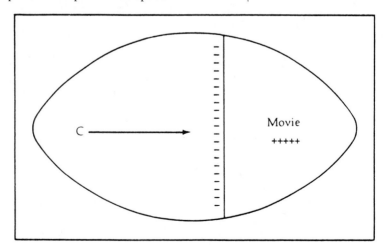

situation in which a child wants to go to the movies but is forbidden to do so by its parents. The ellipse represents the life space; C represents the child. The arrow is a vector indicating that C is motivated to achieve the goal of going to the movie, which, as indicated, has a positive valence, or value, for the child. The vertical line is the barrier to the goal, established by the parents, and it has a negative valence.

Lewin postulated a state of balance or equilibrium between the person and his or her environment. When this equilibrium is disturbed, a tension arises (Lewin's concept of motivation or need), which leads to some movement in an attempt to restore the balance. Lewin believed that human behavior involves the continual appearance of tension, locomotion, and relief. This sequence is akin to need-activity-relief. Whenever a need is felt, a state of tension exists, and the organism attempts to relieve the tension by acting to restore the equilibrium.

The first experimental attempt to test this proposition was performed under Lewin's supervision by Bluma Zeigarnik in 1927. Subjects were given a series of tasks and allowed to complete some of them, but they were interrupted before they could complete others. Lewin predicted that (1) a tension-system develops when subjects are given a task to perform, (2) when the task is completed, the tension is dissipated, and (3) when the task is not completed, the persistence of the tension results in a greater likelihood that the task will be recalled. Zeigarnik's results confirmed the predictions. The subjects remembered the uncompleted tasks more easily than they recalled the completed tasks. Much subsequent research has been performed on what is now known as the ***Zeigarnik effect***.

In the early years of his career, Lewin was chiefly concerned with theoretical issues, but by the 1930s he had become interested in social psychology. His pioneering efforts in this field alone are sufficient to justify his position in the history of psychology. Some prominent social psychologists associated with Lewin as students or colleagues at the Research Center for Group Dynamics are Dorwin Cartwright, Leon Festinger, J. P. French, Harold H. Kelley, Rensis Likert, Stanley Schachter, and Alvin Zander.

The outstanding feature of Lewin's social psychology is group dynamics, the application of concepts dealing with individual and group behavior. Just as the individual and his or her environment form a psychological field, so the group and its environment form a social field. Social behaviors occur within, and result from, simultaneously existing social entities such as subgroups, group members, barriers, and channels of communication. Thus, group behavior is a function of the total field situation at any given time.

Lewin conducted research on behavior in various social situations. A classic experiment involved authoritarian, democratic, and laissez-faire leadership styles and their effects on the productivity and behavior of groups of boys (Lewin, Lippitt, & White, 1939). Studies such as this one opened up important new areas of social research and contributed to the growth of social psychology.

In addition, Lewin emphasized the importance of social action research, the study of relevant social problems with a view to introducing change. He was concerned about racial conflicts, and he conducted community studies on the effects of integrated housing on prejudice, on equalizing employment opportunities, and on the development and prevention of prejudice in children. His social action research transformed problems such as discrimination and prejudice into controlled studies, applying the rigor of the experimental approach without the artificiality and sterility of the academic laboratory.

Lewin was also instrumental in fostering sensitivity training, which has been applied to many situations in education as well as the business world, to reduce intergroup conflicts and to develop individual potential. His sensitivity training groups (T-groups) were the beginning of the movement later popularized by encounter groups.

His experimental programs and research findings are, in general, more acceptable to psychologists than his theoretical views. His influence on social and child psychology and, to some extent, experimental psychology, is considerable. Many of his concepts and experimental techniques are widely used in the areas of personality and motivation. An International Kurt Lewin Conference was held at Temple University in Philadelphia in 1984.

Criticisms of Gestalt Psychology

Criticisms of the Gestalt position include the charge that the Gestalt psychologists were trying to solve problems by changing them into postulates. The organization of conscious perception, as in the phi phenomenon, was not treated as a problem that required solving but as a phenomenon that simply existed in its own right. Critics argued that this was tantamount to solving a problem by denying its existence. Similarly, it was argued that the Gestalt psychologists never explained the laws of their system. Many experimental psychologists asserted that the Gestalt position was vague, and that the basic concepts and terms were not defined with sufficient rigor to be scientifically meaningful. The Gestalt psychologists countered these charges by insisting that in a young science attempts at explanation and definition must necessarily be incomplete, but that being incomplete was not the same as being vague.

It was also claimed that the tenets of Gestalt psychology were not really new, and this, of course, is true. The Gestalt movement, like the others we have discussed, had its anticipators, but this point has no bearing on the relative merits of the Gestalt position.

Other critics alleged that Gestalt psychology was too occupied with theory at the expense of experimental research and empirical supporting data. The Gestalt school of thought has been theoretically oriented, but since the time of its founders it has also emphasized experimentation and has been directly and indirectly responsible for a considerable amount of research.

Related to this point is the suggestion that the experimental work of the Gestalt psychologists is inferior to that of S-R theorists, because it lacks adequate controls and because its unquantified data are not amenable to statistical analysis. The Gestalt psychologists take the position that because qualitative results take precedence, much of their research has deliberately been less quantitative than psychologists of other viewpoints consider necessary. Much Gestalt research is exploratory, investigating problems within a different framework.

Köhler's notion of insight has not gone unchallenged. Attempts to replicate Köhler's two-stick experiment with chimps have provided little support for the role of insight. These later studies suggest that the apes' solution of the problem does not occur suddenly and may depend on prior learning or experience (Windholz & Lamal, 1985).

A final criticism relates to what some psychologists consider to be poorly supported and poorly defined physiological assumptions. The Gestalt psychologists admit that their theorizing in this area is tentative, but they add that their speculations are a useful adjunct to their system. Gestalt psychology has inspired much research, and the validity of the results is not lessened by the speculative framework within which it has been conducted.

Contributions of Gestalt Psychology

The Gestalt movement has left an indelible imprint on psychology. Like other movements that challenged traditional views, it had a refreshing and stimulating effect on psychology as a whole. The Gestalt point of view has influenced the areas of perception and learning, and recent work deriving from the Gestalt school suggests that the movement still has contributions to make.

Unlike its chief temporal competitor, behaviorism, Gestalt psychology retains much of its separate identity, in that its major tenets have not been fully absorbed into the mainstream of psychological thought. It continues to foster interest in conscious experience as a legitimate problem for at least some psychologists. This focus on conscious experience is not of the Wundt/Titchener variety but centers on a modern version of phenomenology. Contemporary adherents of the Gestalt position are convinced that conscious experience does occur and must be studied. They recognize, however, that it cannot be investigated with the same precision and objectivity as overt behavior. Proponents of a phenomenological approach to psychology are numerous in Europe, and the viewpoint is gaining support in the United States. Its influence can be seen in the humanistic psychology movement. Finally, as we shall see in Chapter 15, many aspects of cognitive psychology owe their origins to the work of Wertheimer, Koffka, and Köhler, and the movement they founded more than eighty years ago.

Suggested Readings

Eng, E. (1978). Looking back on Kurt Lewin: From field theory to action research. *Journal of the History of the Behavioral Sciences, 14*, 228–232. Notes Lewin's move from Germany to the United States and describes the impact of that change on his theories and research.

Heider, F. (1970). Gestalt theory: Early history and reminiscences. *Journal of the History of the Behavioral Sciences, 6*, 131–139. Recalls such pioneers of the Gestalt movement as Ehrenfels, Wertheimer, Koffka, and Köhler.

Helson, H. (1925, 1926). The psychology of Gestalt. *American Journal of Psychology, 36*, 342–370, 494–526; *37*, 25–62, 189–223. A series of articles that did much to spread the Gestalt viewpoint in the United States.

Henle, M. (1978). One man against the Nazis — Wolfgang Köhler. *American Psychologist, 33*, 939–944. An account of Köhler's last years at the Psychological Institute of the University of Berlin, before he emigrated to the United States in 1935; describes his struggle to preserve the integrity of the institute in the face of Nazi repression.

Henle, M. (1986). *1879 and All That: Essays in the Theory and History of Psychology.* New York: Columbia University Press. A collection of critical and provocative essays on the major issues and figures in the history of psychology, especially the founders of Gestalt psychology.

Henle, M. (1987). Koffka's *Principles* after fifty years. *Journal of the History of the Behavioral Sciences, 23*, 14–21. Discusses Koffka's goals in writing his *Principles of Gestalt Psychology* and evaluates the impact of this book on psychology today.

Köhler, W. (1959). Gestalt psychology today. *American Psychologist, 14*, 727–734. Describes specific topics in Gestalt psychology and discusses how Gestalt psychologists and behavioral psychologists differ in their approaches to these problems.

O'Neil, W. M., & Landauer, A. A. (1966). The phi phenomenon: Turning point or rallying point? *Journal of the History of the Behavioral Sciences, 2*, 335–340. Discusses the term "phi phenomenon" and describes misinterpretations that have arisen since Wertheimer published his findings on this topic.

Sokal, M. M. (1984). The Gestalt psychologists in behaviorist America. *American Historical Review, 89,* 1240–1263. Analyzes the spread of the Gestalt movement in the United States and suggests that American psychology was more receptive than many historians admit.

Psychoanalysis: The Beginnings   13

Introduction

The term *psychoanalysis* and the name Sigmund Freud are recognized
the world over. Other prominent figures in the history of psychology, such
as Fechner, Wundt, and Titchener, are little known outside professional
psychology, but Freud continues to enjoy phenomenal popularity among
the general public. More than forty years after Freud's death, *Newsweek*

magazine noted that his ideas had become so pervasive that "it would be difficult to imagine twentieth-century thought without him" (November 30, 1981). Whether you agree or disagree with his theories, there is no denying the impact of his work. He is one of a small core of individuals who have been pivotal in the history of civilization by changing the way we think about ourselves.

Chronologically, psychoanalysis overlaps the other schools of thought in psychology with which we have dealt. Consider the situation in 1895, the year Freud published his first book marking the formal beginning of his new movement. In that year Wundt was sixty-three years old. Titchener, just twenty-eight, had been at Cornell University only two years and was beginning to develop his system of structural psychology. The spirit of functionalism was beginning to grow in the United States, but it had not yet been formalized into a school. Neither behaviorism nor Gestalt psychology had begun; Watson was then seventeen and Wertheimer fifteen.

Yet, by the time of Freud's death in 1939, the entire psychological world had changed. Wundtian psychology, structuralism, and functionalism were history. Gestalt psychology was being transplanted from Germany to the United States, and behaviorism had become the dominant form of American psychology. Freud had achieved international prominence, but his position was already being splintered into subschools and derivative movements.

The relationship between Freudian psychoanalysis and the other schools of thought in psychology was only temporal. There was no substantive link, either through assent or dissent, between Freud and the other founders in psychology. The other schools owed their impetus and form to Wundt, either evolving from his work, as with structuralism and functionalism, or revolting against it, as with behaviorism and Gestalt psychology. In contrast, psychoanalysis was not directly related to these evolutionary and revolutionary movements, because it did not originate within academic psychology. Freud's study of the human personality and its disturbances was far removed from the psychology of the university laboratory.

Despite their fundamental disagreements, the other systems of thought shared an academic heritage. Their basic concepts and methods had been formed and refined in laboratories, libraries, and lecture halls. Their traditional concerns were topics such as sensation, perception, and learning. They were — or strove to be — pure science. Psychoanalysis was neither a product of academe nor a pure science. Thus it was not, and still is not, a school of psychology directly comparable with the others.

Psychoanalysts do not deal with traditional areas of psychology, primarily because they are concerned with providing therapy for emotionally disturbed persons. From the beginning, psychoanalysis was separate and distinct from mainstream psychological thought in goals, subject matter, and methods. Its subject matter is abnormal behavior, which had been relatively neglected by the other schools of thought, and its primary method is clinical observation, not controlled laboratory experimentation. Also, psychoanalysis deals with the unconscious, a topic virtually ignored by the other systems of thought.

Wundt and Titchener did not admit the unconscious into their systems for one simple reason: It is impossible to introspect the unconscious. And because it cannot be introspected, it cannot be reduced to its elementary components to determine its contents. The functionalists, too, with their exclusive focus on consciousness, had no use for the unconscious. In James Rowland Angell's lengthy textbook published in 1904, he devoted no more than two pages at the end to the notion of an unconscious. Robert Woodworth's 1921 textbook had little more to say about it, covering the topic in the last few pages — like Angell, as an afterthought.

John B. Watson, of course, had no more room in his system for the unconscious than he did for consciousness. Neither entity had any validity for his natural-science approach to psychology. Between 1912 and 1920, the *Psychological Bulletin* published annual articles entitled "Consciousness and the Unconscious," which each year derided and denounced the concept of those mental states more and more vociferously, until finally the articles were stopped (Fuller, 1986).

Despite these differences, psychoanalysis shares some background characteristics with at least functionalism and behaviorism. All were influenced by the spirit of mechanism, by the work of Gustav Fechner, and by the revolutionary ideas of Charles Darwin.

Antecedent Influences on Psychoanalysis

As with all schools of thought, the psychoanalytic movement had definite intellectual and cultural antecedents. Two major sources of influence were the early philosophical speculations about the nature of unconscious psychological phenomena and the early work in psychopathology.

Theories of the Unconscious

We have seen that most of the early history of scientific psychology, until the advent of behaviorism, dealt with conscious mental experience. Similarly, the empirical philosophers, who provided a background for the new psychology, focused on conscious experience. However, not everyone who worked in these fields agreed with this orientation. Some also recognized the importance of nonconscious processes. Although interest in the influence of the unconscious can be traced to Plato, more recent thought on the topic followed the work of Descartes in the seventeenth century.

In the early eighteenth century, the German philosopher and mathematician Gottfried Wilhelm Leibnitz (1646–1716) developed a theory of *monadology*. Monads, which Leibnitz considered to be the individual elements of all reality, were not physical atoms. They were not even wholly matter, in the usual sense of the word. Each monad was an unextended psychic entity, which, although mental in nature, had some of the properties of physical matter. When enough of them were grouped together, they created an extension.

In general terms, monads can be likened to perceptions. Leibnitz believed that mental events (the activity of monads) had different degrees of clearness or consciousness, which could range from completely unconscious to the most clear or definitely conscious. Lesser degrees of consciousness were called *petites perceptions*, and the conscious actualization of these was called *apperception*. For example, the sound of waves breaking on the beach is an apperception. This apperception is composed of all the individual falling drops of water (the *petites perceptions*). The individual drops are not consciously perceived by themselves, but when enough of them collect, they summate to produce an apperception.

A century later the German philosopher and educator Johann Friedrich Herbart (1776–1841) developed Leibnitz's notion of the unconscious into the concept of the threshold or limen of consciousness. Those ideas below the threshold are unconscious. When an idea rises to a conscious level of awareness it is apperceived, in Leibnitz's terms, but Herbart went beyond this. For an idea to rise into consciousness, it must be compatible and congruent with the ideas already in consciousness. Incongruous ideas cannot exist in consciousness at the same time, and ideas that are irrelevant are forced out of consciousness to become inhibited ideas. Inhibited ideas exist below the threshold of consciousness; they are similar to Leibnitz's *petites perceptions*. According to Herbart, there is a conflict among ideas in which they struggle for conscious realization, and he proposed mathematical formulas and equations to account for the mechanics of ideas as they enter into or are pushed out of consciousness. Thus, his work shows the influence of the mechanistic spirit.

Gustav Fechner also contributed to the development of theories about the unconscious. He used the notion of limen or threshold, but it was his suggestion that the mind is like an iceberg that had a greater impact on Freud. In his iceberg analogy, Fechner speculated that a considerable

The theory of monadology proposed by Gottfried Wilhelm Leibnitz was an early attempt to explain unconscious processes.

portion of the mind is hidden below the surface, where it is influenced by unobservable forces.

It is interesting that Fechner, to whom experimental psychology owes so much, was also a precursor of psychoanalysis. Freud quoted from Fechner's book, *Elements of Psychophysics,* in several of his own, and he derived major concepts (the pleasure principle, psychic energy, the topographical concept of mind, and the importance of the destructive instinct) from Fechner's work. One of Freud's biographers noted that Fechner was "the only psychologist from whom Freud ever borrowed any idea" (Jones, 1957, p. 268).

The notion of the unconscious was very much a part of the Zeitgeist of the 1880s in Europe, the time when Freud was beginning his clinical practice. Not only was the idea of interest to professionals, but it was also considered a fashionable topic of conversation among the public. A book entitled *Philosophy of the Unconscious* (Hartmann, 1869) was so popular that it appeared in nine editions between 1869 and 1882. In the 1870s, at least a half dozen other books were published in Germany with the word *unconscious* in their titles.

Freud, therefore, was not the first to discover or even to discuss seriously the unconscious mind. He readily conceded that poets and philosophers before him had dealt extensively with the unconscious. What he discovered, he claimed, was a way to study it.

Psychopathology

We have observed that a new movement always requires something to revolt against, something to push away from in order to gain momentum. Because psychoanalysis did not develop within academic psychology, the existing order that it opposed was not Wundtian psychology or any other school of psychological thought. To uncover what Freud did oppose, we must consider the prevailing thought in the area in which he worked — the understanding and treatment of mental disorders.

The history of the treatment of the mentally ill is both fascinating and depressing and presents a striking picture of inhumanity. In the Middle Ages, disturbed individuals received no understanding and little treatment. The mind was alleged to be a free agent, responsible for its own condition. Treatment of mentally disturbed persons consisted primarily of blame and punishment, because the causes of emotional disturbance were believed to be wickedness, demonic possession, and witchcraft.

Conditions did not improve during the Renaissance.

> The great changes in the social structure at the time of the Renaissance created a general feeling of uncertainty and insecurity. . . . Insecure men, uncertain of the future, frustrated by change, stand ready to exorcise the threat of evil by an uncritical distribution of blame and punishment. . . . In the fifteenth century the Church did it for them. In 1489 Jacob Sprenger and Heinrich Kraemer, two Dominican brothers, taking advantage of the recent invention of the printing

press, published the *Malleus Maleficarum*, a title which perhaps can best be translated as the *Witch Hammer*, since the book was designed to be a tool for hammering at witches.

The *Malleus Maleficarum* is a cruel encyclopedia on witchcraft, the detection of witches and the procedures for examining them by torture and for sentencing them.... It identifies witchcraft with the mental disorders, many of whose symptoms it describes with care. For three hundred years in nineteen editions this malevolent compendium remained the authority and guide of the Inquisition. (Boring, 1950, pp. 694–695)

By the nineteenth century a more humane and rational attitude toward the mentally ill began to emerge. In Europe and America the chains were struck, literally, from the insane, as a decline in the influence of religious superstition paved the way for the scientific investigation of the causes of mental illness. The treatments offered were primitive at best and sometimes caused more suffering than the disturbances they were supposed to cure.

Consider the techniques developed by Benjamin Rush (1745–1813), the first psychiatrist to practice in the United States. He believed that some bizarre behaviors were caused by too much or too little blood, and his remedy was to drain blood out of or pump blood into the patient. He developed a rotating chair that spun the unfortunate person at high speed, a procedure that often led to fainting. In an early form of shock treatment, Rush dunked patients in a tub of water. He may also be credited with the first tranquilizing technique. Patients were strapped in a tranquilizing chair, and pressure was applied to their heads by large wooden blocks held in a vise.

Although these techniques sound cruel to us today, we must remember that Rush was trying to help the mentally ill instead of dumping them in custodial institutions where their needs would be ignored. He recognized that his patients were sick, and he established the first hospital in the United States solely for the treatment of emotional disturbances.

During the nineteenth century, there were two main schools of thought in psychiatry — the somatic and the psychic. The somatic school held that abnormal behavior had physical causes, such as brain lesions, understimulation of the nerves, or nerves that were too tight. The psychic school subscribed to mental or psychological explanations. In general, nineteenth-century psychiatry was dominated by the somatic school, a view that had received considerable support in the previous century from Immanuel Kant, who derided the view that emotions could cause mental illness. Psychoanalysis developed as one aspect of a revolt against this somatic orientation. As work with the mentally ill progressed, some scientists became convinced that emotional factors were of even greater importance than brain lesions or other possible physical causes.

Hypnosis played a role in fostering interest in the psychic causes of abnormal behavior. In the latter part of the eighteenth century, the phenomenon of hypnosis was brought to the attention of the medical profession by Franz Anton Mesmer (1734–1815), an Austrian physician, but for a century the medical establishment rejected it, equating mesmerism with quackery. (The public, however, embraced the idea of hypnotic states, making of them a sort of parlor game.) In England, James Braid (1795–1860) called the hypnotic state neurypnology, from which the term hypnosis was eventually derived. Braid's careful work and his disdain for exaggerated claims earned the phenomenon a degree of scientific respectability.

Hypnosis achieved professional acceptance with the work of the French physician Jean Martin Charcot (1825–1893), head of a neurological clinic at Salpêtrière, a Paris hospital for the insane. Charcot treated hysterical patients by means of hypnosis with some success. Most important, he described the symptoms of hysteria and his use of hypnosis in medical terms, making it more acceptable to other physicians and to the French Academy of Science, which three times had rejected the idea of mesmerism. Approval by the academy was vital, because that would open the door to the investigation of psychological aspects of mental illness.

Charcot's work was primarily neurological, however, emphasizing physical disturbances and symptoms such as paralysis. Doctors continued to ascribe hysteria to somatic causes until 1889, when Charcot's pupil, Pierre Janet (1859–1947), accepted an invitation to become director of the psychological laboratory at Salpêtrière. Janet rejected the opinion that hysteria was a physical problem and saw it instead as a mental disorder. He emphasized mental phenomena—especially memory impairments, fixed ideas, and unconscious forces—as causal factors, and he preferred hypnosis as the method of treatment. Thus, during the early years of Freud's career, the published literature on hypnosis and on psychological causes of mental illness was growing. Janet's work, in particular, anticipated many of Freud's ideas. Personally, however, Janet later expressed contempt for Freud himself (Abel, 1989).

The work of Charcot and Janet in the treatment of the mentally disturbed helped to change beliefs in psychiatry, from the somatic to the psychic or mental school of thought. Physicians began to think in terms of curing emotional disturbances by treating the mind instead of the body. By the time Freud started to publish his ideas, the term *psychotherapy* was already in widespread use.

The Influence of Darwin

In 1979, Frank J. Sulloway, a distinguished historian of science, published *Freud: Biologist of the Mind*, in which he argued that Freud had been greatly influenced by the work of Charles Darwin. Sulloway drew on new data of history; more precisely, he examined data that had existed for years but which no one else had viewed in the same way.

Sulloway examined the books in Freud's personal library and found copies of Darwin's works. Freud had read them all, made notes in their margins, and was known to have praised them. Freud acknowledged that Darwin's work, along with an essay on nature by the German poet Goethe, had influenced his choice of medicine as a profession. In addition, many similarities with Darwin's ideas can be detected in Freud's writings. Sulloway concluded that Darwin "probably did more than any other individual to pave the way for Sigmund Freud and the psychoanalytic revolution" (Sulloway, 1979, p. 238).

Darwin discussed several ideas that Freud later made central issues in psychoanalysis, including unconscious mental processes and conflicts, the significance of dreams, the hidden symbolism in bizarre symptoms of behavior, and the importance of sexual excitation. Overall, Darwin focused, as Freud did later, on nonrational aspects of thought and behavior.

Darwin's theories also influenced Freud's thinking on childhood development. We noted that Darwin gave his notes and unpublished materials to George John Romanes, who later wrote two books, based on Darwin's material, on mental evolution in humans and animals. Sulloway found copies of Romanes's books in Freud's library, also with Freud's handwritten comments in the margins. Romanes elaborated on Darwin's notion of the continuity in emotional behavior from childhood to adulthood, and on the suggestion that the sex drive appears in infants as early as seven weeks after birth. Both of these themes became central to Freudian psychoanalysis.

Darwin insisted that humans were driven by biological forces, particularly love and hunger, which he believed were the foundation of all behavior. Less than a decade later, the German psychiatrist Richard von Krafft-Ebing expressed the same view, that self-preservation and sexual gratification were the only two instincts in human physiology. Thus, respected scientists following Darwin's lead were recognizing the role of sex as a basic human motivation.

There are other points of similarity between the works of Darwin and Freud. Freud's emphasis on internal conflict is conceptually identical to Darwin's theme of the struggle for existence. Freud wrote that "the individual perishes from his internal conflicts, the species [perishes] in its struggle with the external world to which it is no longer adapted" (Freud, 1938/1941, p. 299). In both cases the struggle is to the death, be it psychological or physiological. Thus, we must count Darwin as a major precursor to Freud, who drew on many aspects of evolutionary theory to develop his revolutionary theory of psychoanalysis.

Other Sources of Influence

Several other influences on Freud deserve mention. The intellectual climate of the eighteenth and nineteenth centuries embraced the doctrine of hedonism, the proposition that humans are motivated to gain pleasure and to avoid pain. Associated primarily with the English philosopher Jeremy Bentham and his notion of utilitarianism, hedonism was also supported by some of the British associationists. Freud's concept of the pleasure principle is supported by the doctrine of hedonism.

During Freud's university training, he was exposed to the idea of mechanism, as represented by the physiologists Carl Ludwig, Emil du Bois-Reymond, Ernst Brücke, and Hermann von Helmholtz. These students of the great Johannes Müller had united to take the position that there are no forces to be found in living things that do not exist in inanimate objects. In other words, there are no forces active within the organism other than the common physical and chemical ones. As a student of Brücke's, Freud was influenced by this mechanistic orientation. He later formulated a deterministic theory of the nature of human behavior, which he called psychic determinism.

Another aspect of the Zeitgeist that both influenced and reinforced Freud's work was the attitude toward sex in Vienna in the late nineteenth century. It has been alleged that because society in Freud's day was so repressive and puritanical, he was far ahead of his time in discussing sexual matters so frankly. Although sexual inhibitions may have characterized the upper-middle-class neurotic women who were Freud's patients (as well as Freud himself), this was not typical of the culture as a whole. Turn-of-the-century Vienna was a permissive and open society, and this widespread acceptance of sensuality was not accompanied by feelings of guilt or by repression. Research suggests that even Victorian England and Puritan America were not really characterized by the excessive prudery and inhibitions usually associated with those cultures (see Gay, 1983).

Interest in sexual matters was visible in everyday Viennese life and in the scientific literature. In the years before Freud advanced his sex-based theory, a large number of studies had been published on sexual pathologies, infantile sexuality, and the suppression of sexual impulses and its effects on mental and physical health. In 1845, the German physician Adolf Patze argued that the sex drive was present in children as young as three, a point reiterated in 1867 by Henry Maudsley, a well-known British psychiatrist. In 1886 Krafft-Ebing published his sensational book *Psychopathia Sexualis*. And in 1897 a Viennese physician, Albert Moll, wrote a book about sexuality in the child and the child's love for the parent of the opposite sex (Steele, 1985a).

A colleague of Freud's in Vienna, the neurologist Moritz Benedikt, had achieved dramatic cures with hysterics by getting them to talk about problems with their sex lives. The French psychologist Alfred Binet published work on sexual perversions in the late 1880s and early 1890s. Even the word *libido*, which was to assume such importance in Freud's psychoanalysis, was already in use and had the same meaning Freud later gave it. Thus, much of the sexual component of Freud's work had been anticipated in one form or another. Because the professional and the public Zeitgeists were already receptive, Freud's ideas received a great deal of attention.

The concept of *catharsis* was also popular before Freud published any of his work. In 1880, a year before Freud received his M.D., an uncle of his future wife wrote a book about Aristotle's concept of catharsis. There ensued a "craze for the topic of catharsis. . . . For a time catharsis was one of the most discussed subjects among scholars and one of the topics of conversation in sophisticated Viennese salons" (Ellenberger, 1972, p. 272). By 1890 there were more than 140 publications in German on the topic (Sulloway, 1979).

Finally, many of Freud's ideas about dreams had been anticipated in the literature in philosophy and physiology as far back as the seventeenth century. There were many, diverse influences on Freud's thinking. No small part of his genius, and the genius of all founders, was the ability to draw on these various ideas to develop a cohesive system.

Sigmund Freud (1856–1939) and the Development of Psychoanalysis

The psychoanalytic movement that Sigmund Freud developed is intimately related to his own life and is, to a great extent, autobiographical. Consequently, knowledge of the story of his life is vital to an understanding of his system.

Freud was born on May 6, 1856, in Freiberg, Moravia (now Pribor, Czechoslovakia). In 1990, the town renamed its Stalin Square as Freud Square. Freud's father was a relatively unsuccessful wool merchant who, when his business failed in Moravia, moved the family to Leipzig and later,

The psychoanalytic movement founded by Sigmund Freud has had a profound influence on modern psychology and on many aspects of Western culture.

when Freud was four years old, to Vienna. Freud remained in Vienna for nearly eighty years.

Freud's father was twenty years older than his wife and was strict and authoritarian. As a young boy, Freud felt both fear and love toward his father. Freud's mother was protective and loving, and toward her he felt a passionate attachment. This fear of the father and sexual attraction to the mother is what Freud later called the Oedipus complex, and it seems to have derived from his boyhood experiences and recollections.

One of eight children, Freud early demonstrated great intellectual ability, which the family did everything possible to encourage. His was the only room in the house to have an oil lamp, providing better light for study than the candles used by the others. The rest of the children, toward whom Freud showed considerable resentment, were not allowed to study music, lest their practicing disturb the young scholar.

Freud entered the *Gymnasium* a year earlier than was usual, and was considered a brilliant student, graduating with distinction at the age of seventeen. He was undecided about a career; his interests included civilization, human culture, human relationships, and military history. Darwin's theory of evolution awakened in him an interest in the scientific approach to knowledge, and with some hesitation Freud decided to study medicine. He had no desire to be a practicing physician, but he hoped that a medical degree would lead to a career in scientific research.

He began his studies at the University of Vienna in 1873. Because he wanted to study several subjects not directly connected with his medical training (he took five philosophy courses from Franz Brentano, for example), he took eight years to get his degree. At first he concentrated on biology; he dissected more than four hundred male eels to determine the structure of the testes. His findings were inconclusive, but it is noteworthy that his first attempt at research concerned sex. He moved on to physiology and work on the spinal cord of the fish. Apparently he enjoyed the subject, because he worked for six years over a microscope in Ernst Brücke's physiological institute.

During his medical training Freud began experimenting with the drug cocaine. He used it himself, made it available to his fiancée, his sisters, and his friends, and was responsible for introducing it into medical practice. He was enthusiastic about the substance and found that it cured his depression and helped his almost chronic indigestion. He was convinced that in cocaine he had discovered a miracle drug that would cure everything from sciatica to seasickness and win for him the fame and recognition he craved.

But this was not to be. One of Freud's medical colleagues, after hearing Freud's casual conversation about the drug, conducted his own experiments and found that cocaine could be used to anesthetize the human eye, thus making eye surgery possible for the first time. Freud published his paper on the beneficial uses of cocaine in 1884, and this work was considered partly responsible for the epidemic of cocaine use that swept over Europe and the United States, lasting well into the 1920s.

Freud was criticized severely for advocating the use of cocaine for purposes other than eye surgery and for unleashing this scourge upon the world. For the rest of his life he deliberately tried to erase any memory of his endorsement of cocaine, even omitting references to his work in his own bibliography. For many years it was believed that Freud stopped using cocaine after his medical school days, but newly available data of history, in the form of Freud's own letters, reveal that he used the drug for at least ten years more, well into middle age (Masson, 1985).

Freud wanted to continue to pursue scientific work within an academic setting, but Brücke discouraged him because of his financial circumstances. Freud was too poor to support himself during the many years he would have had to wait to secure one of the few available university professorships. Reluctantly Freud agreed that Brücke was right, and so he decided to take his medical examinations and enter private practice. This required him to undertake additional work in clinics and hospitals, because he had neglected the clinical side of his medical education in favor of his physiological research. During his hospital training he specialized in the anatomy and organic diseases of the nervous system, in particular paralysis, aphasia, childhood brain injuries, and speech pathology.

He received his M.D. in 1881 and the following year opened a practice as a clinical neurologist. He did not find medical practice to be any more attractive than he had anticipated, but economic realities won out. He had become engaged to Martha Bernays, who also had no money, and they had postponed their marriage several times for financial reasons. Finally, after a frustrating four-year engagement, they were married, but even then, Freud had to borrow money and pawn their watches. Their situation eventually improved, but Freud never forgot those early years of poverty.

Freud's long working hours prevented him from spending a great deal of time with his wife and children (of whom there were eventually six). He took vacations alone or with his sister-in-law, because Martha could not maintain his pace of hiking and sightseeing.

During those years Freud developed an important relationship with the physician Josef Breuer (1842–1925), who had gained fame for his study of respiration and his discovery of the functioning of the semicircular canals in the ear. The successful and sophisticated Breuer offered the young Freud advice and friendship, and even loaned him money. Freud looked upon Breuer as a father-figure, and Breuer apparently viewed Freud as a precocious younger brother. "Freud's intellect is soaring at its highest," Breuer wrote to a friend. "I gaze after him as a hen at a hawk" (Hirschmuller, 1989, p. 315). They frequently discussed Breuer's patients, including Anna O., whose case became pivotal in the development of psychoanalysis.

An intelligent and attractive twenty-one-year-old woman, Anna O. showed a wide range of severe hysterical symptoms, including paralysis, memory loss, mental deterioration, nausea, and disturbances of vision and speech. The symptoms first appeared while she was nursing her dying father. Breuer began treating her by using hypnosis. He found that under hypnosis she would remember specific experiences that seemed to have given rise to certain symptoms, and that talking about the experiences while in a hypnotic state seemed to relieve the symptoms.

For example, Anna went through a period when she could not drink water, despite intense feelings of thirst. Under hypnosis she related an aversion to water in childhood and recalled seeing a dog she disliked drinking from a glass. After telling this incident to Breuer, Anna found that she could drink water again, and the symptom never recurred.

Breuer saw Anna O. every day for more than a year. During their meetings Anna would recount the disturbing incidents of the day, after which she often reported relief from her symptoms. She referred to her talks with Breuer as "chimney sweeping" and "the talking cure." As the treatment continued, Breuer realized — and described to Freud — that the incidents Anna recalled under hypnosis involved some thought or event that she found repulsive. Reliving the disturbing experience under hypnosis reduced or eliminated the symptoms.

Breuer's wife grew jealous of the close emotional relationship that developed between Breuer and Anna O., who exhibited what was later called a positive **transference** to Breuer, that is, she transferred her feelings for her father to her doctor. This transference was aided by the close physical resemblance between her father and Breuer. Breuer, too, may have experienced an emotional attachment to his patient; "her youthful attractions, her charming helplessness, and her very name . . . reawakened in Breuer his dormant Oedipal longings for his own mother" (Gay, 1988, p. 68). Breuer finally perceived the situation as a threat and told Anna that he could no longer treat her. A few hours later Anna experienced the symptoms of hysterical childbirth. Breuer terminated this event through hypnosis and, according to legend, left with his wife for a second honeymoon in Venice, at which time she became pregnant.

This tale turns out to be a myth perpetuated by several generations of psychoanalysts and historians and provides another example of the distortions that can occur with the data of history. In this case the myth persisted for almost one hundred years. Breuer and his wife may indeed have gone to Venice, but the birthdates of their children reveal that none could have been conceived during that trip (Ellenberger, 1972). Indeed, much of the story of Anna O. seems to be more fiction than fact, particularly her cure by Breuer's cathartic treatments. After Breuer stopped treating her she was institutionalized for some time and spent hours sitting beneath a portrait of her father and talking incessantly about visiting his grave. Breuer told Freud that she was "deranged" and expressed the hope that she might die so as to end her suffering. She later became a feminist and social worker in Germany. She never spoke of her experiences with Breuer and held a negative attitude toward psychoanalysis for the rest of her life (Freeman, 1972). Breuer's report of this case is important in the development of psychoanalysis, because it introduced Freud to the method of catharsis, the talking cure, that later figured so prominently in his work.

In 1885, Freud received a small postgraduate grant that enabled him to spend several months studying in Paris under Jean Martin Charcot. At a reception one evening, Freud heard Charcot assert that a particular patient's difficulties had a sexual basis. "But in this sort of case it's always a question of the genitals—always, always, always" (Freud, 1914, p. 14). To Freud, this assessment was an illuminating and exciting insight. After that he was alert to the suggestion of sexual problems in his patients.

He had an opportunity to observe Charcot's use of hypnosis in the treatment of hysteria. Charcot had shown that the traditional view of hysteria as an exclusively female malady (the word derives from the Greek *hystera*, meaning womb) was incorrect; he demonstrated the existence of hysterical symptoms in some of his male patients.

A year after his return from Paris, Freud was again reminded of the possible sexual basis of emotional disturbance. A noted gynecologist asked Freud if he would take the case of a woman patient who suffered anxiety attacks that were relieved only when she knew where her doctor was at every moment. The physician told Freud that the anxiety was caused by the woman's impotent husband; after eighteen years, their marriage had not been consummated. "The sole prescription for such a malady," the doctor told Freud, "is familiar enough to us, but we cannot order it. It runs: ℞ *Penis normalis dosim repetatur*!" (Freud, 1914).

Freud had adopted Breuer's methods of hypnosis and catharsis to treat his patients, but he gradually became dissatisfied with hypnosis. Although it was apparently successful in relieving or eliminating symptoms, it did not seem able to effect a cure. Many patients returned with complaints of a new set of symptoms. Also, Freud found that some neurotic patients could not be easily or deeply hypnotized. These and other problems led Freud to abandon hypnosis, but he retained catharsis as a treatment method and developed from it what has been called the most significant technique in the evolution of psychoanalysis: ***free association***. (We noted in Chapter 1 that Freud meant, in German, free intrusion or invasion, not free association.)

In free association, the patient lies on a couch and is encouraged to talk openly and spontaneously, giving complete expression to every idea, no matter how embarrassing, unimportant, or foolish it may seem. The aim of Freud's psychoanalysis was to bring into conscious awareness repressed memories or thoughts, which he assumed to be the source of the patient's abnormal behavior. He believed that there was nothing random about the material uncovered during free association, and that it was not subject to the patients' conscious choice. The information revealed by patients during free association was predetermined, forced or intruded on their consciousness by the nature of their conflicts.

Through the technique of free association Freud found that his patients' memories invariably went far back into childhood, and that many of the repressed experiences they recalled concerned sexual matters. Already sensitive to the possible role of sexual factors in the etiology of his patients' illnesses, and aware of the current professional literature on sexual pathology, Freud turned his attention to the sexual material revealed in his patients' narratives.

In 1895 Freud and Breuer published *Studies on Hysteria*, which is considered by many to mark the formal beginning of psychoanalysis. The book contained a joint paper that had been published previously; five case histories, including that of Anna O.; a theoretical paper by Breuer; and a chapter by Freud on psychotherapy. Although the book received some negative reviews, it also received praise in scientific and literary journals throughout Europe and was considered to be a valuable contribution to the field. It was a definite, if modest, beginning of the recognition Freud desired. Breuer, however, had been reluctant to publish the book. They argued about Freud's contention that sex was the sole cause of neurosis. Breuer agreed that sexual factors were important, but he was not persuaded that they were the only cause. He suggested that Freud did not have sufficient evidence on which to base his conclusion. The decision to publish the book anyway led to a rift in their friendship.

Freud was convinced that he was correct and that there was no need to accumulate additional data to support his position. He may have been unwilling to wait for more documentation because a delay might permit someone else to publish the idea and thus claim priority. His ambition for success and fame may have taken precedence over any scientific caution about rushing into print with insufficient evidence. Freud's dogmatic attitude about his work disturbed Breuer, and within a few years the break between them was complete. Freud became embittered toward the man who had done so much for him, telling a friend that the mere sight of Breuer made him want to leave the country. By the time of Breuer's death in 1925, however, Freud's feelings had softened. He wrote a sensitive obituary for Breuer, in which he acknowledged his mentor's accomplishments. He also sent a letter of condolence to Breuer's son, noting the "magnificent part played by your late father in the creation of our new science" (Hirschmuller, 1989, p. 321).

By the mid-1890s Freud's conviction that sex played the determining role in neurosis was firm. He observed that most of his patients reported traumatic sexual experiences in childhood, often involving members of their own families. He also came to believe that it was not possible for neurosis to develop in a person who led a normal sex life.

In a paper presented to the Viennese Society of Psychiatry and Neurology in 1896, Freud reported that his patients had revealed experiences resembling seduction in childhood, with the seducer usually being an older relative, most often the father. Today such experiences are clearly labeled child abuse. These seduction traumas, Freud believed, were the cause of neurotic behavior in adults. He further reported that his patients were hesitant about describing details of the seduction experience and that the events somehow seemed unreal. Patients spoke in a manner suggesting that they did not fully remember the experiences, almost as though they had never really happened. The paper was received with skepticism. The group's president, Krafft-Ebing, said that it sounded like "a scientific fairy tale" (Jones, 1953, p. 263). Freud retorted that his critics were asses and could all go to hell.

About a year later, Freud reversed his position, now claiming that, in most cases, the childhood seduction experiences his patients described had never actually occurred. This marks another turning point in the history of psychoanalysis. At first, the awareness that some of his patients were reporting fantasies came as a blow to Freud, because his theory of neurosis was based on his belief that his patients' childhood sexual traumas were real. On reflection, however, he concluded that the patients' fantasies were quite real to them. And, because the fantasies centered on sex, sex remained the root of their problems. Thus, Freud was able to preserve the basic thesis of sex as the cause of neurosis.

Nearly a century later, in 1984, controversy erupted when a psychoanalyst who had briefly been the director of the Freud Archives, Jeffrey Masson, charged that Freud was lying about the reality of his patients' childhood sexual experiences. Masson claimed that most of the sexual abuses reported by Freud's patients had indeed occurred, and that Freud had decided to call them fantasies only to make his system more acceptable to colleagues and to the public (Masson, 1984).

Most reputable scholars denounced Masson's claims, arguing that he did not present convincing evidence (see Gay, 1988; Krüll, 1986; Malcolm, 1984). The dispute received nationwide newspaper and magazine publicity. In an interview in the *Washington Post* (February 19, 1984), Freud scholars Paul Roazen and Peter Gay described Masson's theory as "a hoax," "a grave slander," and "a severe distortion of the history of psychoanalysis." It should be noted that Freud had never abandoned his belief that childhood sexual abuse had sometimes occurred; what he denied was his earlier view that these experiences had *always* taken place, and he stated that such widespread child abuse was hardly credible. After all, who could believe that so many fathers and uncles were sexually abusing little girls?

Yet, more recent evidence indicates that childhood sexual abuse is more common than had generally been thought, leading scholars to suggest that Freud's original conception of the seduction theory may have been the correct one. We do not know whether Freud deliberately suppressed the truth, as Masson claimed, or genuinely believed that his patients were reporting only fantasies. However, it is possible to suggest that "more of Freud's patients were telling the truth about their childhood experiences than he was ultimately prepared to believe" (Crewsdon, 1988, p. 41).

The same conclusion had been reached in the 1930s by Freud's disciple Sandor Ferenczi. On the basis of the reports of his own patients, Ferenczi decided that the Oedipus complex resulted from real acts of sexual abuse and not from fantasies. When Ferenczi presented his views at a psychoanalytic congress in 1932, Freud tried to prevent him from reading the paper. When that failed, Freud led a spirited opposition to Ferenczi's position.

It has also been suggested that Freud modified the seduction theory because he realized that if it were true, then all fathers, including his own, would stand guilty of perverse acts against their children (Krüll, 1986).

Whatever the ultimate judgment of the seduction theory, it is clear that Freud, who emphasized the role of sex in emotional life, held a negative attitude toward sex in general and experienced sexual difficulties of his own. He wrote of the dangers of sexuality, even for people who were not neurotic, and argued that we should strive to rise above that "common animal need." He considered the sex act to be degrading, arguing that it contaminated both the mind and the body. In 1897, when he was forty-one years old, Freud reported that personally he had given up sex, writing to a friend that "sexual excitation is of no more use to a person like me" (Freud, 1954, p. 227). Freud occasionally experienced impotence and had sometimes abstained from sex for various periods of time because of his expressed abhorrence of condoms and coitus interruptus, the standard methods of birth control of the day.

In the same year Freud decided to give up sex, he began the monumental task of self-analysis. He had for several years experienced a number of neurotic difficulties and diagnosed his condition as anxiety neurosis, which he attributed to the accumulation of sexual tension. This was a time of intense inner turmoil for Freud, yet it was also one of his most creative periods. He undertook the self-analysis as a means of better understanding himself and his patients, and the method he used was ***dream analysis***.

In the course of his work Freud had discovered that a patient's dreams could be a rich source of significant emotional material. Dreams often contained clues to the underlying causes of a disturbance. Because of his positivist belief that everything had a cause, he thought that events in a dream could not be completely without meaning but must result from something in the patient's unconscious.

Realizing that he could not analyze himself by the technique of free association (it being difficult to assume the roles of both patient and therapist at the same time), Freud decided to analyze his dreams instead. On awakening each morning, he wrote down his dream material from the night before and then free-associated to it. This self-analysis continued for about two years, culminating in the publication of *The Interpretation of Dreams* (1900), a book now considered Freud's major work. In it he outlined for the first time the nature of the Oedipus complex, drawing largely on his own childhood experiences. The book was not universally praised, but it drew much favorable recognition and comment. Professional journals in fields as diverse as philosophy and neuropsychiatry reviewed it, as did popular magazines and newspapers in Vienna, Berlin, and other major European cities. In Zurich, Switzerland, a young man by the name of Carl Jung read the book and quickly became a convert to the new psychoanalysis, at least for a time.

The Interpretation of Dreams was eventually so successful that it appeared in eight editions during Freud's lifetime. He incorporated dream analysis into the body of techniques he used in psychoanalysis, and thereafter devoted the last half-hour of each day to self-analysis.

In the productive years after 1900, Freud developed and expanded his ideas. In 1901 he published *The Psychopathology of Everyday Life*, which contains a description of the now famous **Freudian slip**. Freud suggested that in the everyday behavior of the normal person, as well as in neurotic symptoms, unconscious ideas are struggling for expression and are capable of modifying thought and action. What might seem to be casual slips of the tongue or acts of forgetting are actually reflections of real, although unacknowledged, motives.

Freud's next book, *Three Essays on the Theory of Sexuality*, appeared in 1905. Three years earlier some students had urged him to conduct a weekly discussion group, so that they might learn about his psychoanalysis. These disciples, including Alfred Adler and Carl Jung, later achieved fame through their opposition to Freud, who, as we saw with Breuer, would tolerate no dispute about his emphasis on the role of sexuality. Anyone who did not accept or who sought to modify this tenet was excommunicated. Freud wrote: "Psychoanalysis is my creation; for ten years I was the only person who concerned himself with it. . . . No one can know better than I do what psychoanalysis is" (Freud, 1914, p. 7).

During the first decade of the twentieth century, Freud's personal and professional situations showed considerable improvement. His private practice increased, and a growing number of people took his pronouncements seriously. In 1909, he received a sign of international recognition when he and Jung were invited by G. Stanley Hall to speak at the twentieth anniversary celebration of Clark University in Massachusetts. Freud was awarded an honorary doctorate in psychology. He found the experience deeply moving, and he met many prominent American psychologists, including William James, E. B. Titchener, and James McKeen Cattell. The five lectures he delivered at Clark were published in the *American Journal of Psychology* and were translated into several languages (Freud, 1909/1910). A few months after the ceremonies at Clark, the annual meeting of the American Psychological Association devoted a three-hour session to a discussion of Freud's work, evidence of the impact of his appearance in the United States.

Although Freud was welcomed and received with honor on his visit, he departed with an unfavorable impression of the United States, a feeling he harbored for many years. He complained of the quality of American cooking, the scarcity of bathrooms, difficulties with the language, and the informality in manners. He was offended when a tour guide at Niagara Falls referred to him as "the old fellow." He never returned and told his biographer, Ernest Jones, that "America is a mistake; a gigantic mistake, it is true, but nonetheless a mistake" (Jones, 1955, p. 60). In fairness, it should be noted that Freud also claimed to dislike Vienna, the city in which he lived for so many years.

It was not long before the official psychoanalytic family was torn by discord, dissent, and defections. The break with Alfred Adler came in 1911, and with Carl Jung—whom Freud had considered his spiritual son and the heir to the system of psychoanalysis—in 1914. Freud complained bitterly about these defections. At a family dinner party, he lamented his inability to retain the loyalty of those who had once been so faithful to him and his cause. "The trouble with you, Sigi," Freud's aunt remarked, "is that you just don't understand people" (Hilgard, 1987, p. 641).

By the onset of World War I, three rival factions existed, but Freud retained the name *psychoanalysis* for his group. The war years impeded the advancement of his system and reduced the number of his patients, and hence his income. With a wife, six children, and a sister-in-law to support, he remained concerned about financial matters. He reached the pinnacle of his fame in the years 1919–1939, and continued to write, see patients for several hours each day, and take three months of vacation every summer. By the 1920s psychoanalysis had evolved as a theoretical system for the understanding of all human motivation and personality, not simply as a method of treatment for the emotionally disturbed.

Freud, surrounded by members of the American psychological community, at Clark University in 1909. *First row, left to right*: Franz Boas, E. B. Titchener, William James, William Stern, Leo Burgerstein, G. Stanley Hall, Sigmund Freud, Carl Jung, Adolf Meyer, H. S. Jennings. *Second row*: C. E. Seashore, Joseph Jastrow, James McKeen Cattell, E. F. Buchner, E. Katzenellenbogen, Ernest Jones, A. A. Brill, William H. Burnham, A. F. Chamberlain. *Third row*: Albert Schinz, J. A. Magni, B. T. Baldwin, F. Lyman Wells, G. M. Forbes, E. A. Kirkpatrick, Sandor Ferenczi, E. C. Sanford, J. P. Porter, Sakyo Kanda, Hikoso Kakise. *Fourth row*: G. E. Dawson, S. P. Hayes, Edwin B. Holt, C. S. Berry, G. M. Whipple, Frank Drew, J. W. A. Young, L. N. Wilson, K. J. Karlson, H. H. Goddard, H. I. Klopp, S. C. Fuller.

In 1923, Freud was diagnosed as having cancer of the mouth. Over the last sixteen years of his life he suffered almost continuous pain and underwent thirty-three operations; portions of his palate and upper jaw were removed. He was given X-ray and radium treatments and also had a vasectomy, which some physicians believed would reverse the growth of the cancer. The artificial device made necessary by his mouth surgery hampered his speech, and it became increasingly difficult to understand what he was saying. Although he continued to see patients and disciples, he shunned other personal contact. He typically had smoked twenty cigars a day, and he did not stop smoking after his illness was diagnosed. (The contemporary writer Anthony Burgess described in the *New York Times* (October 7, 1984) his visit to Freud's home in Vienna, now a museum. There you can purchase a vivid reminder of Freud's last grim years. "You can buy a phonograph record in which [Freud] speaks from the dead in precise English tortured by the clicks of his prosthesis.")

After Adolf Hitler came to power in Germany in 1933, the official Nazi position on psychoanalysis was made clear — Freud's books were publicly burned in May 1933, at a rally in Berlin. As the volumes were flung onto the fire, a Nazi speaker shouted, "Against the soul-destroying overestimation of the sex life — and on behalf of the nobility of the human soul — I offer to the flames the writings of one Sigmund Freud!" (Schur, 1972, p. 446). Freud commented, "What progress we are making. In the Middle Ages they would have burnt me; nowadays they are content with burning my books" (Jones, 1957, p. 182).

By 1934, the more farsighted Jewish analysts had left Germany. The vigorous Nazi campaign to eradicate psychoanalysis in Germany was so effective that knowledge of Freud, once so widespread, was almost obliterated. A student at the Institute for Psychological Research and Psychotherapy, established by the Nazis in Berlin, recalled that "Freud's name was never mentioned, and his books were kept in a locked bookcase" (*New York Times*, July 3, 1984). Nearly fifty years after the war, many important books on psychoanalysis still cannot be found in Germany.

Against the advice of friends, Freud insisted on remaining in Vienna. In March 1938, Germany invaded Austria, and on March 15, his home was overrun by a Nazi gang. A week later his daughter Anna was arrested and detained for a day. Freud was finally convinced that he should flee. Partly through the intervention of the American ambassador to France, the Nazis agreed to let Freud go to England. Four of Freud's sisters died in Nazi concentration camps. To secure an exit visa, Freud had to sign a document attesting to his respectful and considerate treatment by the Gestapo, and noting that he had no reason to complain. He signed the form and added the sarcastic comment: "I can heartily recommend the Gestapo to anyone" (Jones, 1957, p. 226).

Although Freud was received well in England, he was unable to enjoy the last year of his life because of failing health. "It is tragic," he said, "when a man outlives his body" (*Time*, April 10, 1939). He remained mentally alert, however, and worked almost to the end. Some years before, when he selected Max Schur to be his personal physician, Freud made Schur promise that he would not let him suffer unnecessarily. On September 21, 1939, he reminded Schur of his vow. "You promised me then not to forsake me when my time comes. Now it's nothing but torture and makes no sense anymore" (Schur, 1972, p. 529). The doctor gave Freud three injections of morphine over a twenty-four-hour period, bringing Freud's many years of suffering to an end.

Psychoanalysis as a Method of Treatment

Freud found that the method of free association did not always operate freely. Sooner or later his patients reached a point in their narratives where they were unable or unwilling to continue. He believed that these ***resistances*** indicated that the patients had called into conscious awareness memories or ideas that were too horrible, shameful, or repulsive to be faced. Freud thought that resistance was a form of protection against emotional pain and that the presence of the pain indicated that the analysis was getting close to the source of the problem.

Thus he assumed that resistance indicated that the treatment was proceeding in the right direction and that the analyst must continue to probe in that area. Freud placed great emphasis on helping patients overcome these resistances. He insisted that they face the hidden experiences, no matter how disturbing, and see them in the light of reality. It was expected that, in the course of a complete analysis, resistance would be encountered and overcome a number of times.

Freud's notion of resistance led to his formulation of the fundamental psychoanalytic principle of ***repression***, which is the process of ejecting or excluding unacceptable ideas, memories, or desires from conscious awareness, leaving them to operate in the unconscious. Freud regarded repression as the only adequate explanation for the occurrence of resistances. Unpleasant ideas or impulses are pushed out of consciousness and forcefully kept out. The therapist must help patients bring this repressed material back into consciousness so that they can confront it and learn to live with it. (Some scholars suggested that Freud developed the concepts of resistance and repression from the work of the German philosopher Arthur Schopenhauer. Freud said that he had not read Schopenhauer but did acknowledge his precedence.)

Freud recognized that effective work with neurotic patients depended on the development of an intimate personal relationship between patient and therapist. We noted earlier how the transference Anna O. developed toward Breuer so disturbed Breuer that he ended her treatment. Freud viewed this transference of a patient's emotional attitudes from parent to therapist as vital and necessary to the therapeutic process. A goal of therapy was to wean patients from this childish dependence and help them assume a more adult role.

Freud in his Vienna study in 1937 surrounded by his collection of Greek, Roman, and Egyptian antiquities.

We noted Freud's recognition of the importance of dream material in his own self-analysis. He believed that dreams represent a disguised satisfaction of repressed desires and wishes and that the dream story is much more meaningful and complex than it might seem. The story is told that on a Wednesday evening, July 24, 1895, at a table in the northeast corner of the terrace of Vienna's Bellevue Restaurant, Freud realized that the essence of a dream is *wish fulfillment*. In accordance with the notion that genius often flatters itself by dating its own inspirations, Freud quipped that a tablet should be erected at that spot, noting that "Here the secret of dreams was revealed to Dr. Sigm. Freud on July 24, 1895" (Jones, 1953, p. 354).

Dreams have both a manifest and a latent content. The *manifest content* is the actual story told in recalling the events that occurred in the dream. The true significance of the dream, however, lies in the *latent content*, which is its hidden or symbolic meaning. To interpret the hidden meaning, the therapist must proceed from manifest to latent content, interpreting the symbolic meaning from the events that the patient relates in the dream story.

Dream analysis is a complex task. Freud believed that the forbidden desires in the latent dream content are expressed, in the manifest content, only in symbolic or disguised form. Although many of the symbols that appear in dreams are relevant only to the person reporting a particular dream, other symbols are common to all of us. Freud suggested, for example, that gardens, balconies, and doors signify the female body, and church spires, candles, and serpents signify the male genitals. Dreams about falling represent surrendering to erotic wishes, and dreams of flying indicate a desire for sexual achievement. Freud warned that despite the universality of these symbols, the interpretation of a particular dream required knowledge of a patient's specific conflicts.

Freud also wrote that not all dreams are caused by emotional conflicts. Some arise from mundane stimuli such as the temperature of the room, contact with one's partner, or overeating before bedtime. Not all dreams, therefore, contain hidden or symbolic material.

Freud believed that a long and intensive course of therapy was required to effect a cure. With his patients, he found that no fewer than five sessions a week for months or even years were necessary. Thus, an analyst could typically treat only a relatively few patients at a time.

He also had definite ideas about how therapists should be trained. He thought that each analyst should undergo analysis and work for at least two years under supervision before being permitted to treat patients. Further, he believed that the practice of psychoanalysis should be a profession independent of medicine. Ironically, he predicted that at some time in the future, chemical substances would be developed to treat emotional disturbances, thus rendering the practice of psychoanalysis obsolete.

Despite the growing use of psychoanalysis as a method of treatment, Freud had little interest in its potential therapeutic value. He was not primarily concerned with curing people, but rather with explaining the dynamics that underlie human behavior. He viewed himself more as a scientist than a therapist, and he considered his techniques of free association and dream analysis to be research tools for the collection of data. The fact that these techniques also had therapeutic applications was, to Freud, secondary to their scientific use.

Perhaps because of his relative lack of interest in treating patients, he has been described as impersonal, indifferent, and brisk in dealing with them. He placed his chair at the head of the psychoanalytic couch because, he said, he did not want the patients staring at him. On occasion he fell asleep during analytic sessions. "I lack that passion for helping," he admitted to a friend (Jones, 1955, p. 446). Freud's passion was his research and the analysis of the data on which he built his personality theory.

Freud's Method of Research

Freud's system differed greatly in content and methodology from the traditional experimental psychology of the time. It is difficult to reconcile some of his theories with his scientific training, especially his years of physiological research. Despite his background, Freud did not use experimental research methods. Although he was familiar with experimental psychology, he did not collect data from controlled experiments or analyze his results quantitatively. The data he collected and the ways in which he interpreted them were at odds with the methods of experimental psychology. They had to be, given the subject matter Freud chose to study.

Freud reported that he had little faith in the experimental approach. When, in the 1930s, an American psychologist sent him reprints of articles about experiments he had conducted to validate some Freudian concepts, Freud "threw the reprints across the table in a gesture of impatient rejection." He wrote to the psychologist that he could not "put much value on such confirmation" (Rosenzweig, 1985, pp. 171, 173).

Yet Freud believed that his work was scientific and that the case histories of his patients provided ample support for his conclusions. He suggested that only psychoanalysts who used his techniques were qualified to judge the scientific worth of his findings. He wrote that his system was based on an "incalculable number of observations and experiences, and only someone who has repeated those observations on himself and on others is in a position to arrive at a judgment of his own upon it" (Freud, 1940, p. 144).

His theories derived from self-observation as well as from observations of his patients undergoing psychoanalysis. He used primarily the free association and dream analysis techniques, and he found no inherent obstacles to drawing relevant and meaningful conclusions from this material.

> When I set myself the task of bringing to light what human beings keep hidden within them, not by the compelling power of hypnosis, but by observing what they say and what they show, I thought the task was a harder one than it really is. He that has eyes to see and ears to hear may convince himself that no mortal can keep a secret. If the lips are silent, he chatters with his fingertips; betrayal oozes out of

him at every pore. And thus the task of making conscious the most hidden recesses of the mind is one which it is quite possible to accomplish. (Freud, 1901/1905b, pp. 77–78)

Freud's theories were formulated, revised, and extended in terms of the evidence as he alone interpreted it. His own critical abilities were the predominant guide to his theory building. He ignored criticism from others, particularly from those who were not sympathetic to psychoanalysis; even comments from friends and colleagues had little influence on his thinking. Only rarely did he bother to respond to his critics. Psychoanalysis was his system, and his alone.

Psychoanalysis as a System of Personality

Freud's theoretical system did not encompass the topics usually included in psychology textbooks of the day. He explored areas that psychologists tended to ignore, such as unconscious motivating forces, the conflicts among those forces, and the effects of those conflicts on human behavior.

Instincts

Instincts are the propelling or motivating factors in the dynamics of personality, the biological forces that release mental energy. Although the word *instinct* has become accepted usage in English, it does not convey Freud's original meaning. He did not use the German word *Instinkt* when referring to humans, but only when describing the innate drives of animals. Freud's term when referring to humans was *Trieb*, best translated as driving force or impulse (Bettelheim, 1982). The Freudian instincts are not inherited predispositions, which is the usual meaning of instinct, but rather refer to sources of stimulation within the body. Their aim is to remove or reduce the stimulation through some activity such as eating, drinking, or sex.

Freud did not attempt to delimit the number of instincts, but he grouped them in two categories: the life instincts and the death instinct. The *life instincts* (*eros*) include hunger, thirst, and sex, and are concerned with self-preservation and the survival of the species. These are the creative forces that sustain life itself, and the form of energy through which they are manifested is called *libido*. The *death instinct* (*thanatos*) is a destructive force. It can be directed inward as in masochism or suicide, or outward as in hatred and aggression. Freud believed that we are drawn irresistibly toward death, even that the "aim of all life is death" (Freud, 1920, p. 38).

He gradually acknowledged that hostility and aggression, as well as sex, are important forces in personality. As he grew older, he became convinced that aggression could even be as powerful as sex in motivating human behavior. This is another example of the autobiographical nature of Freud's system. He did not develop the notion of a death instinct and its outward manifestation in aggression until death became a personal concern — after his cancer worsened, after he witnessed the horrors of war, and after his daughter Sophie died at the age of twenty-six, leaving two young children.

Freud was devastated by that loss and proposed the death instinct concept less than three weeks later. Freud also became aware of an aggressive tendency within himself. Colleagues have described him as a good hater, and some of his writings, as well as the sharpness and finality of his breaks with dissenters within the psychoanalytic movement, suggest a high personal level of aggressiveness.

Freud's concept of aggression as a motivating force has been better accepted than his suggestion of a death instinct. One psychoanalyst wrote that the idea of the death instinct could be "relegated to the dustbin of history" (Becker, 1973, p. 99). Another suggested that if Freud was a genius, then the positing of the death instinct was an excellent example of a genius having a bad day (Eissler, 1971).

Conscious and Unconscious Aspects of Personality

In his early work Freud expressed the belief that psychic life consists of two parts, the conscious and the unconscious. The conscious part, like the visible portion of an iceberg, is small and insignificant, representing but a superficial aspect of the total personality. The vast and powerful unconscious contains the instincts that are the driving power behind all human behavior. Freud also postulated the existence of a preconscious or foreconscious. Unlike the material in the unconscious, material in the preconscious has not been actively repressed and can easily be summoned into consciousness. For example, if your mind strayed from the words on this page and you began thinking about something you did last night, you would be summoning material from the preconscious into your conscious awareness.

Freud later revised this simple conscious/unconscious distinction and introduced the id, ego, and superego constructs. The *id*, which corresponds somewhat to Freud's earlier notion of the unconscious, is the most primitive and least accessible part of the personality. The powerful forces of the id include sexual and aggressive instincts. "We call it a chaos, a cauldron full of seething excitations," Freud wrote. And he added that the id "knows no judgments of value, no good and evil, no morality" (Freud, 1933, p. 74). The id seeks immediate satisfaction without regard for the circumstances of objective reality, and thus it operates in accordance with what Freud called the *pleasure principle*, which is concerned with reducing tension by seeking pleasure and avoiding pain. We noted in Chapter 1 that Freud's word in German for the id was *es*, meaning *it*, a term suggested by the psychoanalyst Georg Groddeck, who in 1921 sent Freud the manuscript of the first five chapters of a book he was writing entitled *The Book of It* (Isbister, 1985).

Our basic psychic energy or libido is contained in the id and is expressed through tension reduction. Increases in libidinal energy result in increased tension that we attempt to reduce to a more tolerable level. To satisfy our needs and maintain a comfortable tension level, we must interact with the real world. Persons who are hungry, for example, must find food if they are to discharge the tension induced by hunger. An appropriate liaison between the demands of the id and the circumstances of reality must therefore be effected. The *ego*, which serves as a mediating agent between the id and the external world, facilitates this interaction. The ego represents what we mean by reason or rationality, in contrast to the unthinking and insistent passions of the id. Freud called the ego *ich*, which translates into English as *I*.

The id craves blindly, unaware of reality. The ego is aware of reality, perceives and manipulates it, and regulates the id with reference to it. The ego operates in accordance with what Freud called the *reality principle*, holding in abeyance the pleasure-seeking demands of the id until an appropriate object has been found with which to satisfy the need and reduce or discharge the tension. The ego does not exist independently of the id; indeed, it derives its power from the id. The ego serves to help and not to hinder the id, and it is constantly striving to bring about id satisfaction. Freud compared the relationship of the ego and the id to a rider on a horse. The horse supplies the energy that is directed along the path the rider wants to travel. However, the power of the horse must be constantly guided or checked, or else the horse may throw the rider to the ground. Similarly, the id must be constantly guided and checked or it will overthrow the rational ego.

The third part of Freud's structure of personality, the *superego*, develops early in childhood when rules of conduct taught by parents, through a system of rewards and punishments, are assimilated. Behaviors that are wrong (that bring punishment) become part of the child's *conscience*, which is one part of the superego. Behaviors that are right (that are rewarded) become part of the child's *ego-ideal*, the other part of the superego. Thus, childhood behavior is initially governed by parental control, but once the superego has formed a pattern for conduct, behavior is determined by self-control. At that point, rewards and punishments are administered by the individual. Freud's term for the superego was a word he coined, *über-ich*, meaning, literally, *above I*.

The superego represents "every moral restriction," Freud said, and is the "advocate of a striving toward perfection — it is, in short, as much as we have been able to grasp psychologically of what is described as the higher side of human life" (Freud, 1933, p. 67). We can see that the superego is obviously in conflict with the id. Unlike the ego, the superego does not merely attempt to postpone id satisfaction, it tries to inhibit it completely.

Thus, there is a never-ending conflict within the human personality. The ego is in a difficult position, pressured on all sides by insistent and opposing forces. It must try to delay the relentless urgings of the id, perceive and manipulate reality to relieve the tensions of the id impulses, and deal with the superego's striving for perfection. One Freud scholar likened the unconscious to a maximum security prison in which the id impulses are like antisocial inmates — some of them languishing for years and others newly arrived — who must be "harshly treated and heavily guarded" by the ego and the superego. They are, however, "barely kept under control and forever attempting to escape" (Gay, 1988, p. 128). Whenever the ego is too greatly pressured, the inevitable result is anxiety.

Anxiety

Anxiety functions as a warning that the ego is being threatened. Freud described three kinds of anxiety: objective, neurotic, and moral. *Objective anxiety* arises from fear of actual dangers in the real world. The other two types derive from it.

Neurotic anxiety comes from the recognition of the potential dangers inherent in instinctual gratification. It is not fear of the instincts themselves but fear of the punishment that is likely to follow indiscriminate, id-dominated behavior. In other words, neurotic anxiety is a fear of being punished for expressing impulsive desires.

Moral anxiety arises out of a fear of one's conscience. When a person performs or even thinks of performing some act that is contrary to the conscience's set of moral values, he or she may experience guilt or shame. Moral anxiety, then, depends on how well developed one's conscience is. The less virtuous individual is less likely to experience moral anxiety.

Anxiety is a tension-inducing force in human behavior, motivating the individual to act to reduce the tension. Freud suggested that the ego develops a number of protective defenses against anxiety — the ***defense mecha-nisms*** — which are unconscious denials or distortions of reality. For example, in the mechanism of ***identification***, a person assumes the manner, dress, or speech of someone who appears admirable and less vulnerable to the conditions giving rise to the anxiety. In the defense mechanism of ***repression***, anxiety-provoking impulses or thoughts are barred from conscious awareness. ***Sublimation*** involves substituting socially acceptable goals for ones that cannot be satisfied directly, such as diverting sexual energy from sexual behaviors into artistically creative endeavors.

In ***projection***, the source of the anxiety is attributed to someone else, such as saying "He hates me" instead of "I hate him." In ***reaction formation***, a person conceals a disturbing impulse by converting it into its opposite, replacing hate with love, for example. With the mechanism of ***fixation***, a person's development becomes arrested at an early stage, because the next stage is a source of too much anxiety. The defense mechanism of ***regression*** involves behavior that indicates a reversion to an earlier developmental stage, one at which there was greater security and less anxiety. Freud believed that when an individual cannot cope adequately with anxiety it becomes traumatic, reducing the person to a state of infantile helplessness.

Psychosexual Stages of Personality Development

Freud was convinced that the neurotic disturbances manifested by his patients had originated in childhood experiences. Consequently, he became one of the first theorists to assign an important role to child development. He believed that the personality pattern of the adult was established early in life and had been almost completely formed by the age of five. In the psychoanalytic theory of development, children pass through a series of ***psychosexual stages***. During these stages children are considered to be autoerotic, that is, they derive sensual or erotic pleasure by stimulating the ***erogenous zones*** of the body or by being stimulated by parents or caregivers in their normal caretaking activities. Each stage of development tends to be localized in a specific erogenous zone.

The ***oral stage*** lasts from birth into the second year of life. During this stage, stimulation of the mouth, such as sucking, biting, and swallowing, is the primary source of erotic satisfaction. Inadequate satisfaction at this stage — either too much or too little — may produce an oral type of personality, a person who becomes preoccupied with mouth habits such as smoking, kissing, and eating. Freud believed that a wide range of adult behaviors, from excessive optimism to sarcasm and cynicism, were attributable to incidents that occurred during the oral stage of development.

In the *anal stage*, gratification shifts from the mouth to the anus, and children derive pleasure from the anal zone. During this stage, which coincides with the period of toilet training, children may expel or withhold feces, in both cases defying their parents. Conflicts during this period can produce an anal-expulsive adult, who is dirty, wasteful, and extravagant, or an anal-retentive adult, who is excessively neat, clean, and compulsive.

During the *phallic stage*, which occurs around the fourth year, erotic satisfaction shifts to the genital region. There is much fondling and exhibiting of the genitals as well as sexual fantasizing. Freud posited the development during this stage of the *Oedipus complex*, after the Greek legend in which Oedipus unknowingly kills his father and marries his mother. Freud suggested that children become sexually attracted to the parent of the opposite sex and fearful of the parent of the same sex, who is now perceived as a rival. Freud derived this notion from his own childhood experiences. "I have found love of the mother and jealousy of the father in my own case too," he wrote (Freud, 1954, p. 223).

Ordinarily, children overcome the Oedipus complex by identifying with the parent of the same sex and substituting affection for the sexual longing for the parent of the opposite sex. However, the attitudes toward the opposite sex that develop during this stage will persist and influence adult relationships with members of the opposite sex. One of the results of identifying with the parent of the same sex is the development of the superego. In taking on the mannerisms and attitudes of that parent, children also adopt the parent's superego standards.

Children who outlast the many struggles of these early stages enter a period of latency, which lasts from about the fifth to the twelfth year. Then, in Freud's view, the start of adolescence and the onset of puberty signal the beginning of the *genital stage*. Heterosexual behavior becomes evident, and the person begins to prepare for marriage and parenthood.

Original Source Material on Psychoanalysis: From *An Outline of Psychoanalysis* by Sigmund Freud

The following material deals with the development of sexual life in infants and children.* It was written some thirty years after Freud first proposed

*From Sigmund Freud, *An Outline of Psycho-Analysis*. In J. Strachey (Ed. and Trans.), *The standard edition of the complete psychological works of Sigmund Freud* (1940, Vol. 23, pp. 141–207). Chapter III: The Development of the Sexual Function. London: Hogarth Press. Original work published 1938.

the psychosexual stages of personality and represents his later thinking on issues of sexual development. In this passage Freud discusses (1) the appearance of the sex drive early in life, (2) its reappearance at the time of puberty, (3) the oral, anal, and phallic stages of psychosexual development, and (4) homosexuality, which Freud viewed as a developmental inhibition.

According to the prevailing view human sexual life consists essentially in an endeavour to bring one's own genitals into contact with those of someone of the opposite sex. With this are associated, as accessory phenomena and introductory acts, kissing this extraneous body, looking at it and touching it. This endeavour is supposed to make its appearance at puberty — that is, at the age of sexual maturity — and to serve the purposes of reproduction. Nevertheless, certain facts have always been known which do not fit into the narrow framework of this view. (1) It is a remarkable fact that there are people who are only attracted by individuals of their own sex and by their genitals. (2) It is equally remarkable that there are people whose desires behave exactly like sexual ones but who at the same time entirely disregard the sexual organs or their normal use; people of this kind are known as "perverts." (3) And lastly it is a striking thing that some children (who are on that account regarded as degenerate) take a very early interest in their genitals and show signs of excitation in them.

It may well be believed that psycho-analysis provoked astonishment and denials when, partly on the basis of these three neglected facts, it contradicted all the popular opinions on sexuality. Its principal findings are as follows:

(*a*) Sexual life does not begin only at puberty, but starts with plain manifestations soon after birth.

(*b*) It is necessary to distinguish sharply between the concepts of "sexual" and "genital." The former is the wider concept and includes many activities that have nothing to do with the genitals.

(*c*) Sexual life includes the function of obtaining pleasure from zones of the body — a function which is subsequently brought into the service of reproduction. The two functions often fail to coincide completely.

The chief interest is naturally focused on the first of these assertions, the most unexpected of all. It has been found that in early childhood there are signs of bodily activity to which only an ancient prejudice could deny the name of sexual and which are linked to psychical phenomena that we come across later in adult erotic life — such as fixation to particular objects, jealousy, and so on. It is further found, however, that these phenomena which emerge in early childhood form part of an ordered course of development, that they pass through a regular process of increase, reaching a climax towards the end of the fifth year, after which there follows a lull. During this lull progress is at a standstill and much is unlearnt and there is much recession. After the end of this period of latency, as it is called, sexual life advances once more with puberty; we might say that it has a second efflorescence. And here we come upon the fact that the onset of sexual life is *diphasic*, that it occurs in two waves — something that is unknown except in man and evidently has an important bearing on hominization. It is not a matter of indifference that the events of this early period, except for a few residues, fall a victim to *infantile amnesia*. Our views on the aetiology of the neuroses and our technique of analytic therapy are derived from these conceptions; and our tracing of the developmental processes in this early period has also provided evidence for yet other conclusions.

The first organ to emerge as an erotogenic zone and to make libidinal demands on the mind is, from the time of birth onwards, the mouth. To begin with, all psychical activity is concentrated on providing satisfaction for the needs of that zone. Primarily, of course, this satisfaction serves the purpose of self-preservation by means of nourishment; but physiology should not be confused with psychology. The baby's obstinate persistence in sucking gives evidence at an early stage of a need for satisfaction which, though it originates from and is instigated by the taking of nourishment, nevertheless strives to obtain pleasure independently of nourishment and for that reason may and should be termed *sexual*.

During this oral phase sadistic impulses already occur sporadically along with the appearance of the teeth. Their extent is far greater in the second phase, which we describe as the sadistic-anal one, because satisfaction is then sought in aggression and in the excretory function. Our justification for including aggressive urges under the libido is based on the view that sadism is an instinctual fusion of purely libidinal and purely destructive urges, a fusion which thenceforward persists uninterruptedly.*

The third phase is that known as the phallic one, which is, as it were, a forerunner of the final form taken by sexual life and already

---

*The question arises whether the satisfaction of purely destructive instinctual impulses can be felt as pleasure, whether pure destructiveness without any libidinal admixture occurs. Satisfaction of the death instinct remaining in the ego seems not to produce feelings of pleasure, though masochism represents a fusion which is entirely analogous to sadism.

much resembles it. It is to be noted that it is not the genitals of both sexes that play a part at this stage, but only the male ones (the phallus). The female genitals long remain unknown: in children's attempts to understand the sexual processes they pay homage to the venerable cloacal theory — a theory which has a genetic justification.[†]

With the phallic phase and in the course of it the sexuality of early childhood reaches its height and approaches its dissolution. Thereafter boys and girls have different histories. Both have begun to put their intellectual activity at the service of sexual researchers; both start off from the premise of the universal presence of the penis. But now the paths of the sexes diverge. The boy enters the Oedipus phase; he begins to manipulate his penis and simultaneously has phantasies of carrying out some sort of activity with it in relation to his mother, till, owing to the combined effect of a threat of castration and the sight of the absence of a penis in females, he experiences the greatest trauma of his life and this introduces the period of latency with all its consequences. The girl, after vainly attempting to do the same as the boy, comes to recognize her lack of a penis or rather the inferiority of her clitoris, with permanent effects on the development of her character; as a result of this first disappointment in rivalry, she often begins by turning away altogether from sexual life.

It would be a mistake to suppose that these three phases succeed one another in a clear-cut fashion. One may appear in addition to another; they may overlap one another, may be present alongside of one another. In the early phases the different component instincts set about their pursuit of pleasure independently of one another; in the phallic phase there are the beginnings of an organization which subordinates the other urges to the primacy of the genitals and signifies the start of a co-ordination of the general urge towards pleasure into the sexual function. The complete organization is only achieved at puberty, in a fourth, genital phase. A state of things is then established in which (1) some earlier libidinal cathexes are retained, (2) others are taken into the sexual function as preparatory, auxiliary acts, the satisfaction of which produces what is known as forepleasure, and (3) other urges are excluded from the organization, and are either suppressed altogether (repressed) or are employed in the ego in another way, forming character-traits or undergoing sublimation with a displacement of their aims.

[†]The occurrence of early vaginal excitations is often asserted. But it is most probable that what is in question are excitations in the clitoris — that is, in an organ analogous to the penis. This does not invalidate our right to describe the phase as phallic.

This process is not always performed faultlessly. Inhibitions in its development manifest themselves as the many sorts of disturbance in sexual life. When this is so, we find fixations of the libido to conditions in earlier phases, whose urge, which is independent of the normal sexual aim, is described as *perversion*. One such developmental inhibition, for instance, is homosexuality when it is manifest. Analysis shows that in every case a homosexual object-tie was present and in most cases persisted in a *latent* condition. The situation is complicated by the fact that as a rule the processes necessary for bringing about a normal outcome are not completely present or absent, but *partially* present, so that the final result remains dependent on these *quantitative* relations. In these circumstances the genital organization is, it is true, attained, but it lacks those portions of the libido which have not advanced with the rest and have remained fixated to pregenital objects and aims. This weakening shows itself in a tendency, if there is an absence of genital satisfaction or if there are difficulties in the real external world, for the libido to hark back to its earlier pregenital cathexes (*regression*).

During the study of the sexual functions we have been able to gain a first, preliminary conviction, or rather a suspicion, of two discoveries which will later be found to be important over the whole of our field. Firstly, the normal and abnormal manifestations observed by us (that is, the phenomenology of the subject) need to be described from the point of view of their dynamics and economics (in our case, from the point of view of the quantitative distribution of the libido). And secondly, the aetiology of the disorders which we study is to be looked for in the individual's developmental history — that is to say, in his early life.

Mechanism and Determinism in Freud's System

During Freud's university training, he was influenced by the mechanistic school of thought in German physiology. It might seem that the notion of mechanism, which pervades so much of experimental psychology, would be irrelevant to Freud's work on the hidden motives of behavior. The structuralists, and later the behaviorists, considered humans to be like machines in their processes and functions. First the human mind and then human behavior were reduced to their most elemental components, analyzed, and studied in positivist and materialist terms. It may appear surprising, then, to learn that Freud, too, was affected by the same mechanistic tradition. No less than the experimental psychologists, Freud believed that all mental events — even misstatements and dreams — were determined. No bit of behavior or thought could occur by chance or by free will. To Freud, there was always a cause for each action, always a conscious or unconscious motive.

But there is more to the mechanistic spirit than determinism. We noted the pledge taken by four young scientists, including Brücke (Freud's professor in medical school): No other forces than the common physical– chemical ones are active within the organism. And from early in his career Freud subscribed to this physicalism, the notion that all phenomena could be reduced to the principles of physics.

In 1895 Freud was working on a project for a scientific psychology, in which he attempted to show that psychology must have a physical basis and that purely mental phenomena exhibit many of the same characteristics and patterns as the neurophysiological processes on which they are based. Psychology, in Freud's view, must be a natural science whose aim is to "represent psychical processes as quantitatively determined states of specifiable material particles" (Freud, 1895, p. 359). This project was never completed, but we can discern in his later writings the principles with which he grappled and the terminology he adopted from physics, especially mechanics, electricity, and hydraulics. His work along these lines provides another example of data lost to history for a period of time. The work was not found until more than fifty years after he wrote it, and eleven years after his death. Until then, no one knew that Freud had even considered such an idea, much less worked so extensively on it.

Freud modified his original intention to model his psychology after physics (when he found that his subject matter was not amenable to physical and chemical techniques), but he remained true to the positivist philosophy, especially determinism, that nurtured experimental psychology. And though Freud was obviously influenced by this view, he was not constrained by it. Where he saw that it would not fit, he altered or discarded it. In the end he demonstrated how restrictive the mechanistic conception of human beings was.

Relations between Psychoanalysis and Psychology

Psychoanalysis developed outside the mainstream of academic psychology, where it remained for many years. "Academic psychology largely closed its doors to psychoanalytic doctrine. An unsigned editorial in a 1924 issue of the *Journal of Abnormal Psychology* bemoaned the endless stream of writings on the unconscious by European psychologists" (Fuller, 1986, p. 123). It dismissed those writings as essentially worthless. Following that statement, few articles on psychoanalysis were accepted for publication, a prohibition that continued for at least two decades.

The fact that both the system and its originator were outsiders also complicated and delayed their acceptance. Indeed, this was even a barrier to serious consideration of psychoanalysis for a time. Eventually, however, the barriers between the two disciplines, at first so rigid and absolute, were breached.

Several factors operated to keep psychoanalysis and academic psychology apart. The first involves the absence of a sense of continuity in Freud's work, relative to advances in psychology. There were no parallels, no overlapping efforts, because Freud's work had no precedents within the development of psychology. Psychologists could not find a meaningful way to connect his efforts with their own work or with that of their predecessors. Wilhelm Wundt, for example, was never moved to admit the unconscious into his psychology as a result of learning about Freud's work, because it did not relate to his own investigation of the nature of consciousness. Commenting on Wundt's position, Freud said, "We cannot help thinking that the old psychology has been killed by my... doctrine, but the old psychology is quite unaware of the fact, and goes on teaching as usual" (Wittels, 1924, p. 130).

A second reason for the conflicts between psychologists and psychoanalysts is that psychology, in its early attempts to be a pure science, was method centered. Psychoanalysis, in contrast, was problem centered. The application of psychoanalysis to the treatment of neuroses was at variance with psychology's aim of finding laws of human behavior through the methods of natural science. These differences in goals and subject matter necessitated different methods. Freud's concern was the more global — the total human personality, instead of specific functions such as perception and learning. Psychology had adopted the experimental method, in which each variable, each small aspect of behavior, was isolated for study for a brief time in the laboratory. Psychoanalysis dealt with the whole human being over a long period of time, gathering data on all aspects of past and present experiences.

Academic psychologists — steeped in the rigor of science, seeking precise and operational definitions of their concepts — disliked and distrusted the Freudian ideas that could not be quantified or related to concrete empirical variables. Terms such as ego, id, and repression were anathema to psychologists who sought to work only with specific stimulus-response terms.

Criticisms of Psychoanalysis

The amount of criticism directed against Freud and his theories, much of which comes from outside of psychology, is enormous, but we shall restrict our discussion to criticisms from psychologists, some of which were noted above. Particularly vulnerable to attack by experimental psychologists are Freud's methods of collecting data. He drew his insights and conclusions from his patients' responses while they were undergoing analysis. Consider some of the deficiencies of this approach, compared with the experimental method of systematically collecting objective data under controlled conditions of observation.

First, the conditions under which Freud collected his data are unsystematic and uncontrolled. He did not make a verbatim transcript of each patient's words but worked from notes he made several hours after seeing the patient. Some of the original data (the patient's words) would surely have been lost in the interim because of the vagaries of memory and the well-documented possibility of distortion and omission. Thus, the data consisted only of what Freud remembered.

Also, it is possible that in the course of recalling his patients' words, Freud reinterpreted them. His reconstruction of the data might not accurately reflect them. In drawing his inferences, Freud may have been guided by a desire to find material that supported his hypotheses. In other words, he may have remembered and recorded only what he wanted to hear. We must also consider the possibility that Freud's notes were highly accurate, but it is impossible to be certain of this because the original data have not survived.

Another criticism relates to discrepancies found between Freud's notes on his therapy sessions and the case histories he eventually published, which supposedly were based on those notes. One study compared Freud's notes and the subsequent published case history and reported several differences. Among these were a lengthening of the period of analysis, an incorrect version of the sequence of events disclosed by the patient during analysis, and an unsubstantiated claim that the patient was cured (Eagle, 1988; Mahoney, 1986). There is no way to determine if these distortions were made by Freud deliberately, to bolster his position, or if they were products of his own unconscious. We also cannot determine if similar errors characterize his other case studies, because he destroyed most of his patient files.

There is an additional criticism to make of Freud's raw data. Even if a complete and verbatim record had been kept, it would not always have been possible to determine the accuracy of what his patients reported. Freud made few attempts to verify his patients' accounts of their childhood experiences. Critics argue that he should have tried to check these by questioning relatives and friends, for example, about the events described. Thus, the first step in Freud's theory building — data collection — may be characterized as incomplete, imperfect, and inaccurate.

As for the next step — drawing inferences and generalizations from the data — we do not know exactly how this was done, because Freud never explained the process. And because his data were not amenable to quantification, there can be no determination of their reliability or statistical significance.

These are serious charges from the standpoint of scientific methodology and theory building. We are asked, in a sense, to accept on faith the validity of Freud's operations and conclusions. His observations cannot be repeated, because it is not known precisely what he did in amassing data and drawing his generalizations. The language of science is precise, leaving no room for ambiguity or distortion. It appears that Freud was not speaking that language, and it is difficult to translate from one to the other.

Another point of criticism concerns the difficulty of deriving empirically testable propositions from many of Freud's hypotheses. How, for instance, would we test for the notion of a death wish? Psychoanalysts may use the idea to explain behavior such as suicide, after the fact, but how can it be studied in the laboratory?

Freud's theories and assumptions about human behavior also have come under attack. Even Freudians agree that he often contradicted himself, and that his definitions of some key concepts — such as id, ego, and superego — are unclear. Freud recognized this and noted in his later writings the difficulties of defining some of his ideas.

Many psychologists have challenged Freud's views on women. He suggested that women have poorly developed superegos and feel inferior about their bodies, because they do not have penises. The analyst Karen Horney (Chapter 14) left Freud's psychoanalytic circle because of this issue and later developed her own system. Today, however, the widespread belief among psychologists is that the "fallacies of Freud's theory of female psychosexual development [are] nearly totally disproved and incorrect" (Schwartz, 1988, p. 502).

In Chapters 14 and 15 we examine the work of other theorists who broke with Freud and attempted to modify his position. They argued that he placed too much emphasis on biological forces, particularly sex, as the primary shapers of personality. They believed that personality was influenced more by social forces. Others challenged Freud's determinism and the denial of free will, and his focus on past behavior to the exclusion of hopes and goals for the future. Some criticized Freud for developing a personality theory based only on observations of neurotics, ignoring the characteristics of emotionally healthy persons. All of these points were used to build competing views of the human personality and quickly led to divisiveness within the psychoanalytic camp and to the formalization of several derivative schools of Freudian analysis.

The Scientific Validation of Psychoanalytic Concepts

We noted that Freud placed little faith in experimental evaluations of his theory. In the years since his death in 1939, however, many of his concepts have been submitted to experimental test. An analysis of some two thousand studies drawn from psychiatry, psychology, anthropology, and other disciplines examined the scientific credibility of some of Freud's formulations (Fisher & Greenberg, 1977). Case histories, the major research method in the psychoanalytic literature, were not included, for some of the reasons noted above. The researchers accepted only those data that had been "secured through procedures that are repeatable and involve techniques that make it possible to check on the objectivity of the reporting observer" (Fisher & Greenberg, 1977, p. 15).

Although some broader Freudian concepts (such as id, ego, superego, death wish, libido, and anxiety) resisted attempts at scientific validation, others were found to be amenable to scientific testing. Published studies provide support for some of the characteristics of the oral and anal personality types, for some causative factors of homosexuality, for the notion that dreams serve as an outlet for tension, and for aspects of the Oedipus complex in boys (rivalry with the father, sexual fantasies about the mother, and castration anxiety).

Freudian concepts that were tested but were not supported by the experimental results include the notion that dreams satisfy symbolically repressed wishes and desires; that in resolving the Oedipus complex boys identify with the father and accept his superego standards out of fear; and that women have an inferior conception of their bodies, have less severe superego standards than men, and find it more difficult to achieve an identity.

Other research has shown support for unconscious processes and their influence on thoughts and behavior, suggesting that unconscious influences may be even more pervasive than Freud claimed (Brody, 1987; Jacoby & Kelley, 1987; Silverman, 1976). In addition, experiments on the so-called Freudian slip have shown that at least some of these verbal misstatements appear to be just what Freud said they were — unconscious conflicts and anxieties revealing themselves in embarrassing ways (Motley, 1985).

As we noted, not all of the research conducted on these concepts supports psychoanalysis. For example, research on personality development does not confirm Freud's contention that personality is largely formed by age five and changes little after that. Studies show that personality continues to develop over time and can change dramatically after the age of five (Kagan, Kearsley, & Zelazo, 1978; Olweus, 1979).

The most important point about these scientific attempts to validate Freudian ideas is that they show that at least some psychoanalytic concepts can be reduced to propositions that are testable by the experimental method.

Contributions of Psychoanalysis

Why has psychoanalysis not only survived but also prospered despite the criticisms offered against it? All theories of behavior can be criticized for lacking scientific validity to some degree. Psychologists in search of a theory must sometimes select it on the basis of criteria other than formal, scientific rigidity and precision. Those who choose psychoanalysis do not do so in the absence of evidence, however. Psychoanalysis does offer evidence, although it is not the kind usually accepted by science. But if psychoanalytic evidence is not scientific in the traditional sense, that does not mean the theory is incorrect or misleading. Belief in psychoanalysis must be based instead on the intuitive grounds of the appearance of plausibility.

> Anyone who accepts or rejects the psychoanalytic theories does so by means of the same kind of reasoning that gives him the thousand and one judgments he is forced to make in everyday life on the basis of insufficient or inadequate evidence — the kind of judgments, in fact, that he is forced to live by, but which have no standing in science. Such estimates, growing out of a multitude of impressions and interpretations, guesses and insights, often result in unshakable convictions, convictions which may be right or wrong but which, from the standpoint of science, cannot be recognized as either proved or disproved. (Heidbreder, 1933, pp. 403–404)

In general, Freud's theory has had a strong impact on American academic psychology. Nearly fifty years after his death, the first in a series of annual volumes devoted to the study of psychoanalysis was published.

The editor of that initial issue wrote of a "veritable renaissance in Freud studies" (Stepansky, 1986, p. xv). Although interest in the theory remains high, interest in psychoanalysis as a therapeutic technique has declined when measured by the number of patients choosing psychoanalysis and the number of applicants in training to become analysts (see Gelman, 1988; Smith, 1986). Expensive, long-term Freudian therapy is being superseded by briefer and less expensive forms of psychotherapy (some of which derive from Freudian psychoanalysis) and by the various behavioral and cognitive therapies.

Some of Freud's concepts have gained wide acceptance and been assimilated into the mainstream of contemporary psychology. These include the role of unconscious motivation, the importance of childhood experiences in shaping adult behavior, and the operation of the defense mechanisms. Interest in these areas has generated much research that has provided support for the existence of unconscious influences on behavior. Although these investigations of the unconscious are not of the Freudian type, the recognition of the unconscious within psychology is nonetheless a legacy of Freud's work.

Freud's impact on the popular culture has, of course, been enormous. This was felt immediately after his visit to Clark University in 1909. Newspapers featured many stories about Freud, and by 1920, more than two hundred books had been published in the United States on Freudian psychoanalysis. The British press called psychoanalysis a "craze" (Rapp, 1988, p. 191). Magazines such as *Ladies Home Journal, The Nation*, and *The New Republic* carried articles about psychoanalysis. In 1935 a major movie studio, MGM, offered Freud $100,000 to collaborate on a film about love. He refused. This public enthusiasm for Freudian ideas came about much earlier than his acceptance by academic psychology.

The twentieth century has seen a gradual loosening of sexual restraint in behavior, the arts, literature, and entertainment. It is widely believed that inhibiting or repressing sexual satisfaction can be harmful. It is ironic, however, that Freud's message about sex has been subject to such misinterpretation. He was not arguing for a weakening of sexual codes of conduct or for increased sexual freedom. His consistent position was that the inhibition of the sex drive was necessary for the survival of civilization. Despite his intention, the greater sexual freedom of our times is partly a result of Freud's work. His emphasis on sex helped to popularize his views. Even in scientific journals, articles about sex have a sensational appeal.

Despite the criticisms of a lack of scientific rigor and methodological weaknesses, Freudian psychoanalysis continues to be an important force in modern psychology. The historian E. G. Boring expressed regret in the 1929 edition of his *A History of Experimental Psychology* that psychology had no truly great exponent of the stature of a Darwin or a Helmholtz. Only twenty-one years later, in the second edition of his text, Boring revised his opinion. Reflecting the development of psychology during the intervening decades, he spoke of Freud with admiration.

> Now he is seen as the greatest originator of all, the agent of the Zeitgeist who accomplished the invasion of psychology by the principle of the unconscious process. . . . It is not likely that the history of psychology can be written in the next three centuries without mention of Freud's name and still claim to be a general history of psychology. And there you have the best criterion of greatness: posthumous fame. (Boring, 1950, pp. 743, 707)

Suggested Readings

Drinka, G. F. (1984). *The Birth of Neurosis: Myth, Malady, and the Victorians*. New York: Simon and Schuster. Examines the social and cultural influences on theories of neurosis before the time of Freud.

Ellenberger, H. F. (1970). *The Discovery of the Unconscious: The History and Evolution of Dynamic Psychiatry*. New York: Basic Books. Traces the study of the unconscious from primitive times to Freudian psychoanalysis and its derivatives.

Evans, R. B., & Koelsch, W. A. (1985). Psychoanalysis arrives in America: The 1909 psychology conference at Clark University. *American Psychologist, 40,* 942–948. Describes the meeting, organized by G. Stanley Hall, that introduced Sigmund Freud, Carl Jung, and the psychoanalytic movement to an American academic audience.

Freeman, L., & Strean, H. S. (1987). *Freud and Women*. New York: Continuum. Explores Freud's relationships with his mother, sisters, wife, and daughters and with female colleagues and patients.

Freud/Jung Letters. (1974). Princeton NJ: Princeton University Press. Presents some 360 letters dating from 1906 to 1913 showing the development and dissolution of the friendship between Freud and Jung.

Gay, P. (1988). *Freud: A Life for Our Time*. New York: Norton; Sulloway, F. J. (1979). *Freud, Biologist of the Mind: Beyond the Psychoanalytic Legend*. New York: Basic Books. Two biographies of Freud: the first is an insightful work on Freud's life and career that draws on much previously unpublished material; the second places Freud's work in the context of its times and disputes the legend that Freud was a "lonely hero" working in isolation.

Krüll, M. (1986). *Freud and His Father*. New York: Norton. An examination of the lives of Sigmund Freud and his father; analyzes the influence of Freud's experiences as a son on the development of his system of psychoanalysis.

Rapp, D. (1988). The reception of Freud by the British press: General interest and literary magazines, 1920–1925. *Journal of the History of the Behavioral Sciences, 24*, 191–201. A survey of popular magazines showing that interest in psychoanalysis in England peaked around 1921 and declined thereafter, and that public hostility focused on Freud's emphasis on sexual factors.

Roazen, P. (1975). *Freud and His Followers*. New York: Knopf. A lively and well-written account of Freud's life and of the men and women who became his disciples, some of whom later broke away to form their own movements.

Psychoanalysis: Dissenters and Descendants

14

After the Founding

As was the case with Wundt and his experimental psychology, Freud did not long enjoy a monopoly on his new system of psychoanalysis. Barely twenty years after he founded the movement, it splintered into competing factions led by analysts who disagreed with him on basic points. During Freud's lifetime, these men and women developed their own approaches. While they did not completely disavow his psychoanalytic orientation, they did try to correct what they saw as serious deficiencies and inadequacies in Freud's formulations.

Freud did not react well to the dissenters. Those analysts who espoused the new positions met with disapproval and even hostility, "the sort of invective that was once heaped upon the heads of heretics" (Brown, 1963, p. 37). No matter how close they may have been to Freud, personally and professionally, once they abandoned his teachings, he cast them out and never spoke to them again.

We discuss three of the most prominent dissenters: Carl Jung, Alfred Adler, and Karen Horney. All were orthodox Freudians before they left the master's circle to promote their own views. We also deal with three descendants of the Freudian position—Gordon Allport, Henry Murray, and Erik Erikson—who developed their approaches after Freud's death. They were not dissenters, having never been orthodox Freudians; rather, they derived their ideas from those of Freud, either elaborating on or opposing his work.

The Neo-Freudians and Ego Psychology

Before proceeding to the dissenters and the descendants, we note that not all who came after Freud in the psychoanalytic tradition felt the need to radically change, abandon, or overthrow his system. There has remained a large group of neo-Freudian analysts who adhere to the central tenets and premises of psychoanalysis but who have, over the years, modified and extended certain aspects of Freud's system.

The major change these Freudian loyalists have introduced into psychoanalysis is an expanded emphasis on the ego (see Hartmann, 1964). Rather than being the servant of the id, the ego has an amplified role. The ego is believed to be more independent of the id, possessing its own energy not derived from the id, and having its own functions separate from the id. These psychoanalysts consider the ego to be capable of performing the normal functions of consciousness, such as perception, learning, and memory, free of the conflict that Freud said was produced when the id impulses pressed for satisfaction. In Freud's view, the ego was forever responsive to the id, never free of its demands. In the revised view, the ego can carry out its functions independently of the id, a significant departure from orthodox Freudian thought.

Another change introduced by the neo-Freudians is the deemphasis of biological forces as influences on personality and the favoring instead of social and psychological forces. The neo-Freudians also minimize the importance of infantile sexuality and the Oedipus complex. They suggest that personality development is determined primarily by psychosocial rather than psychosexual forces. Social interactions in childhood assume greater importance than sexual interactions, either real or imagined.

One of the leaders of the new-Freudian ego psychology movement was Freud's daughter Anna.

Anna Freud (1895–1982)

The youngest of the Freuds' six children, Anna Freud wrote that she would never have been born if any safe form of contraception had been available to her parents. Her father announced her birth, which was greeted with more resignation than happiness, in a letter to a friend, commenting that he would have sent the news by telegram if the infant had been a son (Young-Bruehl, 1988). Yet the year of Anna's birth, 1895, was perhaps symbolic—or prophetic—because it coincided with the birth of psychoanalysis and because Anna would be the only Freud child to follow her father's path and become an analyst.

That outcome was not in accordance with Freud's wishes. He expected Anna to marry and have children, and he resisted the idea that she would pursue psychoanalysis as a career. In the end, however, he relented. "What could I do?" he said. "She was my daughter" (*New York Times*, November 12, 1985). And so, at the age of fourteen, Anna Freud sat unobtrusively in a corner at the meetings of the Vienna Psychoanalytic Society, absorbing everything that was said.

At twenty-two, driven by her close emotional attachment to her father and by her own worries about what Freud called "her sexuality," Anna entered into analysis with him. Five years later she read her first scholarly paper to the Vienna Psychoanalytic Society. Entitled "Beating Fantasies and Daydreams," it was allegedly based on the case history of an anonymous patient. (It was really about her own fantasies; she had not yet begun to treat patients.) The paper described dreams of an incestuous father-daughter love relationship, a beating, and gratification through masturbation. The paper was well received by Freud and his colleagues and won her admission into the society.

Three years later Anna Freud published her first book, *Introduction to the Technique of Child Analysis* (1927), which foretold the direction of her interests. She developed an approach to psychoanalytic therapy with children that took into account their relative immaturity and the low level of their verbal skills. Her innovations include the use of play materials and the observation of the child in the home. Most of her work was carried out in London, where the Freud family settled after escaping from the Nazis in

Anna Freud revised her father's orthodox theoretical position and applied psychoanalytic therapy to children.

1938. She opened a clinic next door to the house in which her father died, and there she treated patients and established a psychoanalytic training center at which many American clinical psychologists studied. Her work was reported in annual volumes of *The Psychoanalytic Study of the Child*, which began publication in 1945.

Anna Freud also contributed substantially to the revision of her father's orthodox theoretical position, expanding the role of the ego as it functions independently of the id. In *The Ego and the Mechanisms of Defense* (1936), she elaborated on and clarified Sigmund Freud's views on the use of the defense mechanisms in protecting the ego from anxiety.

What has come to be the standard list of Freudian defense mechanisms, such as those mentioned in Chapter 13, was really the work of Anna Freud. She defined them more clearly and contributed examples from her analyses of children.

Ego psychology, as developed by Anna Freud and others, became the primary American form of psychoanalysis from the 1940s to the early 1970s. These neo-Freudians set out to make psychoanalysis "part of scientific psychology. They did so by translating, simplifying, and operationally defining Freudian notions, by encouraging the experimental investigation of psychoanalytic hypotheses, and by modifying psychoanalytic psychotherapy" (Steele, 1985b, p. 222). In the process, they fostered a rapprochement between psychoanalysis and academic experimental psychology.

Another attempt to modify Freudian psychoanalysis is object relations theory, which also developed in England. This approach focuses on the intense emotional relationship formed between infants and their mothers. It describes this bond in social and cognitive terms rather than exclusively sexual terms. The infant-mother relationship is studied by observing infants directly, rather than by asking adult patients to reconstruct their early childhood experiences in case histories.

The neo-Freudians still identify themselves, in general, as Freudians. That label cannot be applied to the dissenters and the descendants, to whom we now turn.

Carl Jung (1875–1961)

Jung, who was an expert yodeler, was for some time regarded by Freud as a surrogate son and heir apparent to the psychoanalytic movement. Freud had called him, in a letter, "my successor and crown prince" (McGuire, 1974, p. 218). After his friendship with Freud disintegrated in 1914, Jung began what he called *analytical psychology*, which was totally at odds with Freud's theory.

The Life of Jung

Carl Jung was reared in a small village in northern Switzerland, near the famous Rhine Falls. By his own account, his childhood was lonely, isolated, and unhappy (Jung, 1961). His father was a clergyman who had apparently lost his faith and was often moody and irritable. His mother suffered from

An early Freudian, Carl Jung came to disagree with Freud about the issues of the unconscious mind and the importance of sex, and developed a system he called analytical psychology.

emotional disorders. Her behavior was erratic, and she could change in an instant from a happy housewife to a bewitched demon who mumbled incoherently. The marriage was an unhappy one. Jung learned at an early age not to trust or confide in either parent and, by extension, not to trust the external world as a whole. As a result he turned inward, to the world of his dreams, visions, and fantasies, the world of his unconscious. Dreams and the unconscious—not the conscious world of reason—became his guides in childhood and remained so through his entire adult life.

At critical times in his life, Jung resolved problems and made decisions on the basis of what his unconscious told him through dreams. When he was ready to start college, the solution to the problem of what to study was revealed to him in a dream. He found himself unearthing bones of prehistoric animals and interpreted this to mean that he should study nature and science. That dream about digging beneath the earth's surface, plus a dream he recalled from age three in which he was in an underground cavern, determined the direction his future study of the human personality would take: he would deal with the unconscious forces that lie beneath the mind's surface.

Jung attended the University of Basel, in Switzerland, and graduated with a medical degree in 1900. He was interested in psychiatry, and his first professional appointment was at a mental hospital in Zurich. The director was Eugen Bleuler, a psychiatrist noted for his work on schizophrenia. In 1905 Jung was appointed lecturer in psychiatry at the University of Zurich, but after several years he resigned this position to devote his time to research, writing, and private practice.

In his work with patients, Jung declined to follow Freud's habit of asking patients to lie on a couch, saying that he had no wish to put them to bed. Instead, Jung and his patient sat in chairs facing each other. Occasionally he held therapy sessions aboard his sailboat, happily racing across the lake in a high wind. Sometimes he would sing to his patients, and at other times he was deliberately rude. "Oh no," he told one patient who appeared at the appointed time. "I can't stand the sight of another one. Just go home and cure yourself today" (Brome, 1981, p. 185).

Jung became interested in Freud's work in 1900 after reading *The Interpretation of Dreams*, which he described as a masterpiece. By 1906 the two men had begun to correspond, and a year later Jung went to Vienna to meet Freud. At their initial meeting, they talked with great animation for thirteen hours, an exciting beginning for their intimate but short-lived friendship. In 1909, Jung accompanied Freud to the United States for the Clark University ceremonies, at which they both delivered lectures.

Unlike most of Freud's disciples, Jung had already established an impressive professional reputation of his own before he began his association with Freud. He was the best known of all the early converts to psychoanalysis. As a result, he was perhaps less malleable, less suggestible, than the younger analysts who joined Freud's psychoanalytic family, many of whom were still in medical school or were graduate students, unsure of their professional identities.

Although he did, for a time, become a disciple of Freud's, Jung was never an uncritical one. Early in their affiliation, however, he tried to suppress his doubts and objections. While writing *The Psychology of the Unconscious* (Jung, 1912), he was greatly troubled, realizing that when this statement of his own position was published, it would damage his relationship with Freud, because his ideas differed in major ways from Freud's views. For months Jung was unable to proceed with the book, so disturbed was he about Freud's possible reaction. Of course he did eventually publish, and the inevitable occurred.

In 1911, at Freud's insistence, and in the face of opposition from the Viennese members, Jung became the first president of the International Psychoanalytic Association. Freud believed that anti-Semitism might impede the growth of the psychoanalytic movement if the head of the group was Jewish. The Viennese analysts, almost all of whom were Jewish, resented and distrusted the Swiss-born Jung, who was clearly Freud's favorite. They not only had seniority in the movement, but they also believed that Jung was anti-Semitic.

Shortly after Jung's election to the presidency, his friendship with Freud began to show signs of strain. In *The Psychology of the Unconscious* and in lectures at Fordham University in New York, Jung deemphasized the role of sex in his theory and proposed a different conception of libido. Friction arose over these professional differences, and by 1912 the two men agreed to terminate their personal correspondence as well. They severed relations in 1914, when Jung resigned his position and withdrew from the association.

Beginning in 1913, when Jung was thirty-eight years old, he suffered a period of intense emotional turmoil that lasted three years; Freud had experienced a similar period at the same time of life. Believing that he was going insane, Jung was unable to carry out intellectual work or even read a scientific book. (He did not stop treating patients, however.) He resolved his problem in essentially the same way Freud did, by confronting his unconscious mind. Although he did not analyze his dreams systematically, as Freud had done, Jung followed the impulses of his unconscious as they were revealed to him in dreams and fantasies. As with Freud, Jung's emotional crisis later became a time of immense creativity, and it led to the formulation of his unusual approach to personality.

In line with his interest in mythology, Jung made a number of field expeditions to Africa and the southwestern United States in the 1920s, to study the mental processes of preliterate peoples. In 1932 he was appointed professor at the Federal Polytechnical University in Zurich, a position he held until poor health forced him to resign in 1942. Two years later a chair of medical psychology was founded for him at the University of Basel, but illness prevented him from keeping that position for more than a year. He remained active in research and writing, however, for most of his eighty-six years, publishing an astonishing array of books. The night before he died, he said to a friend, "Let's have a really good wine tonight" (Wehr, 1987, p. 454). He had always lived his life with gusto.

Analytical Psychology

A major point of difference between Jung's analytical psychology and Freud's psychoanalysis concerns the nature of libido. Whereas Freud defined libido in predominantly sexual terms, Jung regarded it as a generalized life energy, of which sex was only one part. For Jung, this basic libidinal life energy expressed itself in growth and reproduction, and in other activities as well, depending on what was most important for an individual at a particular time.

Jung's refusal to regard libido as exclusively sexual left him free to give different interpretations to behavior that Freud could describe only in sexual terms. To Jung, for example, during the first three to five years of life, which he called the presexual phase, libidinal energy serves the functions of nutrition and growth and has none of the sexual overtones of Freud's conception of those early years.

Jung also rejected the Freudian Oedipus complex and explained a child's attachment to its mother in terms of a dependency need with all the satisfactions and rivalries associated with the mother's ability to provide food. As the child matures and develops sexual functioning, the nourishing functions become overlaid with sexual feelings. Jung believed that libidinal energy took a heterosexual form only after puberty. He did not deny the existence of sexual factors, but he reduced the role of sex to one of several drives that compose libido.

It is easy to see how Jung's own life experiences influenced his theory, which, like Freud's, was intensely autobiographical. We have already noted how Jung's personal immersion in his unconscious presaged his later professional interest in the topic. With regard to sex, the evidence is also highly suggestive. Jung had no use or need for an Oedipus complex in his theory because it was not relevant to his own childhood. He had described his mother as fat and unattractive, and so he could never understand Freud's insistence that every little boy had a sexual longing for his mother.

Jung developed no adult insecurities, inhibitions, or anxieties about sex, as Freud did, and he made no attempt to limit his sexual activities, as

Freud had. Indeed, Jung carried on a number of affairs with his women patients and disciples. "To Jung, who freely and frequently satisfied his sexual needs, sex played a minimal role in human motivation. To Freud, beset by frustrations and anxious about his thwarted desires, sex played the central role" (Schultz, 1990, p. 148).

The second basic difference between the work of Jung and Freud is in their views of the direction of the forces that influence the human personality. Freud viewed people as victims of childhood events; Jung believed that we are shaped by our goals, hopes, and aspirations for the future, as well as by our past. Jung proposed that human behavior is not fully determined by early life experiences but is subject to change in later years.

A third difference between Jung and Freud is that Jung placed greater emphasis on the unconscious. He tried to probe more deeply into the unconscious mind, and he added a new dimension to it — the inherited experiences of humans as a species and those of their animal ancestors (the collective unconscious).

Jung used the term *psyche* to refer to the mind, which he said consisted of three levels: the conscious, the personal unconscious, and the collective unconscious. At the center of the conscious mind is the ego, which is akin to our conception of ourselves. Consciousness includes perceptions and memories, and it is the avenue of contact with reality that enables us to adapt to our environment. Jung believed, however, that too much attention had been paid to the conscious, which he considered to be second in importance to the unconscious. He likened the conscious part of the psyche to the visible portion of an island. A larger unknown part exists beneath the small part that can be seen above the waterline, and it was on this mysterious hidden base that Jung focused his attention.

He postulated two levels of the unconscious. Just beneath the conscious is the *personal unconscious*, which belongs to the individual. It consists of all the memories, impulses, wishes, faint perceptions, and other experiences in a person's life that have been suppressed or forgotten. Incidents from the personal unconscious can easily be recalled to conscious awareness, which indicates that this level of unconsciousness is not very deep.

The experiences in the personal unconscious are grouped into *complexes*. These are patterns of emotions, memories, wishes, and the like with common themes. Complexes are manifested in the individual by a preoccupation with some idea, such as power or inferiority, that will influence behavior. Thus, a complex is essentially a smaller personality that forms within the total personality.

Below the personal unconscious is the third and deepest level of the psyche, the *collective unconscious*, which is unknown to the individual and contains the cumulative experiences of all previous generations, including our animal ancestors. The collective unconscious consists of universal evolutionary experiences, and it forms the basis of the personality. Because it directs all current behavior, it is considered to be the most powerful force within the personality. It is important to note that the evolutionary experiences within the collective unconscious are, indeed, unconscious; we are not aware of them, nor do we remember them or have images of them, as we do of the experiences in the personal unconscious. Jung believed that the universality of the collective unconscious could be accounted for by the theory of evolution, through the similarity in brain structures found in all human races.

In Jung's island analogy, a number of small islands rising above the surface of the water represent the individual conscious minds of a number of people. The land area of each island that is just beneath the water, which from time to time is exposed by the action of the tides, represents each individual's personal unconscious. The ocean floor, on which all the islands rest, is the collective unconscious.

Jung emphasized the power of the collective unconscious in contributing to the development of the psyche. Inherited tendencies within the collective unconscious—what Jung called *archetypes*—are preexisting or innate determinants of mental life that dispose a person to behave in a manner similar to that of ancestors who confronted analogous situations.

Archetypes are experienced as emotions and other mental events and are typically associated with such significant life experiences as birth and death, with particular stages such as adolescence, and with reactions to extreme danger. Jung undertook an extensive investigation of the mythical and artistic creations of various civilizations and uncovered symbols that were common to all, even in cultures so widely separated in time and place that there was no possibility of direct influence. He also found what he considered to be traces of these symbols in the dreams reported by his patients. All of this material supported his conception of the collective unconscious.

Four of the archetypes Jung described seemed to occur more frequently than the others. They were laden with high levels of emotional significance and were traceable to ancient myths of diverse origins. These principal archetypes, which Jung viewed as separate personality systems, are the persona, the anima and animus, the shadow, and the self.

The *persona*, the outermost aspect of personality, conceals the true self. It is the mask each of us wears when we come in contact with others, and it presents us as we want to appear to society. The persona may not correspond to an individual's true personality. The notion of the persona is similar to the sociological concept of role playing, in which we may act as we think other people expect us to act in different situations.

The archetypes *anima* and *animus* reflect the idea that each person of one sex exhibits some of the characteristics of the other sex. The anima refers to feminine characteristics in man; the animus denotes masculine characteristics in woman. As with the other archetypes, these arise from the primitive past of the human species, in which men and women each took on some of the behavioral and emotional tendencies of the other sex.

The *shadow* archetype, our darker self, is the most primitive, animalistic part of the personality. Jung considered it to be our racial heritage from lower forms of life. The shadow contains all immoral, passionate, and unacceptable desires and activities. Jung wrote that the shadow urges us to do those things that ordinarily we would not allow ourselves to do. Once having done such a thing, we are apt to insist that something came over us. Jung claimed that the "something" is the primitive part of our nature. The shadow also has a positive side; it is the source of spontaneity, creativity, insight, and deep emotion, all of which are necessary for full human development.

Jung considered the self to be the most important archetype in his system. Balancing all aspects of the unconscious, the self provides unity and stability to the personality. As a representation of the whole person, the self attempts to achieve integration of the personality and can be likened to a drive or urge toward self-realization or self-actualization. By self-actualization Jung meant a harmony and completeness of the personality, the fullest development of all aspects of the self.

He believed that self-actualization could not be attained until middle age, and he viewed these years (ages thirty-five to forty) as crucial to personality development, a natural time of transition when the personality undergoes necessary and beneficial changes. We see in this belief another autobiographical element of Jung's theory. Middle age was the time in his own life when he believed he had achieved the integration of his self, following the resolution of his neurotic crisis. Thus, to Jung, the most important stage in personality development was not childhood, as in Freud's life and system, but middle age, the time of his own personal crisis.

Jung's work on the attitudes of introversion and extraversion is well known. He viewed these modes of reacting to different situations as part of the conscious mind and defined them in terms of the direction of libidinal energy. The extravert directs libido outside the self to external events and people. A person of this type is strongly influenced by forces in the environment and is sociable and self-confident in a wide range of situations. The libido of the introvert is directed inward. Such a person is more contemplative, introspective, and resistant to external influences, less confident in relations with other people and with the external world, and less sociable than the extravert. Both of these opposing attitudes exist in everyone, to some degree, but one attitude is usually more pronounced than the other. No one is a complete extravert or introvert. The dominant attitude at any given moment can be influenced by the situation. For example, normally introverted persons may become sociable and outgoing in situations that capture their interest.

According to Jung's theory, personality differences are also manifested through the four functions, the ways we orient ourselves to both the external objective world and our internal subjective world. These functions are thinking, feeling, sensing, and intuiting. Thinking is a conceptual process that provides meaning and understanding. Feeling is a subjective process of weighing and valuing. Sensing is the conscious perception of physical objects. And intuiting involves perceiving in an unconscious manner.

Jung considered thinking and feeling to be rational modes of responding, because they involve reason and judgment. Sensing and intuiting are considered nonrational, because they depend on the concrete and specific stimulus world and do not involve the use of reason. Within each pair of functions, only one can be dominant at a given time. The dominant functions can be combined with the dominance of extraversion or introversion to yield eight different *psychological types*.

Jung developed the ***word association test*** as a diagnostic and therapeutic tool to uncover personality complexes in his patients. He began his research on word association after a colleague told him of Wilhelm Wundt's association experiment. In Jung's word association procedure, the analyst reads a list of words to a patient, one word at a time. The patient responds to each word with the first word that comes to mind. Jung measured the time the patient took to respond to each word, as well as changes in breathing rate and in the electrical conductivity of the skin, all thought to be evidence of emotional reactions. If a particular word produced a long response time, breathing irregularities, and a change in skin conductivity, Jung deduced the existence of an unconscious emotional problem connected with the stimulus word or with the reply.

Comment

Jung's work has had some influence on psychology and psychiatry but more on such diverse fields as religion, history, art, and literature. Many historians, theologians, and writers acknowledge him as a source of inspiration. In general, however, scientific psychology has ignored his analytical psychology. Many of his books were not translated into English until the 1960s, and his less than lucid writing style has impeded a complete understanding of his formulations. His disdain for traditional scientific methods repels many experimental psychologists, for whom Jung's ideas, with their mystical and religious basis, hold even less appeal than Freud's. Further, the criticisms we noted in Chapter 13, about the supporting evidence for Freud's theory, also apply to Jung's work. Jung, too, relied on clinical observation and interpretation rather than controlled laboratory investigation. Analytical psychology has received less searching evaluation than Freudian psychoanalysis, however, probably because Freud's stature in the field relegated Jung and others to second place in the competition for professional attention.

Jung's delineation of the eight psychological types has stimulated considerable research. Of particular importance is the Myers–Briggs Type Indicator, a personality test constructed in the 1920s by Katharine Briggs and Isabel Briggs Myers. It has become a primary tool for research and assessment. Jung's work on introversion and extraversion inspired the English psychologist Hans Eysenck to develop the Maudsley Personality Inventory, a popular test to measure those two attitudes. Research using these instruments has provided some empirical support for Jung's ideas and demonstrates that at least some of his notions are amenable to experimental testing. As with Freud's work, the larger aspects of Jung's theory (such as complexes, the archetypes, and the collective unconscious) resist attempts at scientific validation.

Jung made other contributions to psychology. The word association test has become a standard projective technique and spurred the development of the Rorschach Inkblot Test. The concept of self-actualization anticipated the work of Abraham Maslow and others who have since developed Jung's theme. Jung's suggestion that middle age is a crucial time of personality change was embraced by Maslow and Erik Erikson and has been accepted by contemporary personality theorists as a necessary developmental stage (see Levinson, 1978; Wrightsman, 1981).

Despite these contributions, the bulk of Jung's work has not been popular within psychology. His ideas enjoyed a burst of public attention in the 1970s and 1980s, apparently because of their mystical content. Formal training in Jungian analysis is offered in New York, San Francisco, and Los Angeles and at Jungian training institutes in Europe and Israel.

Social Psychological Theories in Psychoanalysis: The Zeitgeist Strikes Again

Sigmund Freud was influenced by the mechanistic and positivistic outlook that pervaded nineteenth-century science. Toward the end of the nineteenth century, however, new disciplines were offering new ways of viewing human nature, ways that went beyond the biological and physical frames of reference. Anthropology, sociology, and social psychology were presenting evidence to support the proposition that human beings are the product of the social forces and institutions that make up their environments. This evidence suggested that humans should be studied as social rather than as strictly biological beings.

As anthropologists made public their studies of different cultures, it became clear that some of the neurotic symptoms and taboos hypothesized by Freud were not universal, as he had believed. For example, taboos against incest do not exist in all societies. Further, sociologists and social psychologists had found that much human behavior seemed to stem from social conditioning, instead of from any attempt to satisfy biological needs.

The intellectual spirit of the times, the Zeitgeist, was calling for a revised conception of human nature, but Freud, to the dismay of some of his followers, clung to his emphasis on the biological determinants of personality. Younger analysts, less constrained by tradition, drifted away from the orthodox psychoanalytic position and began to reshape Freudian theory along lines more congruent with the orientation of the social sciences. Their idea that personality is more a product of environment than of biology was compatible with American culture and thought, and it presented a more optimistic image of human nature than Freud's deterministic position.

We discuss two of these dissenters who presented their own social psychological theories: Alfred Adler and Karen Horney. They and others suggested that human behavior was determined not by biological forces but by the interpersonal relationships to which the person was exposed, particularly in childhood. Just as biological forces are minimized in their theories, so is the role of libido and its manifestation in the Oedipus complex and the psychosexual stages of development. To the social psychological theorists, anxiety and other expressions of emotional disturbance do not originate in libido, instincts, or sex, but develop instead from early social relationships. Thus we are not doomed to anxiety, as in Freud's deterministic theory, because anxiety can be avoided by the proper social experiences in childhood.

According to Freud, our thoughts and behaviors are determined by biological forces. In contrast, the social psychological theorists consider behavior to be flexible and capable of being consciously changed by the individual. Social institutions as well are flexible and open to change. Although the social psychological theorists recognize that society's mores and standards can be modified only gradually and with difficulty, they nonetheless agree that people are capable of developing the kind of social system that is appropriate for their needs.

Alfred Adler, who broke with Freud in 1911, viewed human motivation as a striving for superiority and emphasized the importance of social factors in the development of personality.

Alfred Adler (1870–1937)

Adler is usually considered to be the first proponent of the social psychological form of psychoanalysis because he broke with Freud in 1911. Adler developed a theory in which social interest plays a major role, and he is the only psychologist to have a string quartet named after him.

The Life of Adler

Alfred Adler was born to wealthy parents in a suburb of Vienna, Austria. His unhappy childhood was marked by sickness, jealousy of an older brother, and feelings of being puny, unattractive, and rejected by his mother. Adler felt much closer to his father than to his mother. Perhaps he later rejected the Freudian concept of the Oedipus complex because it did not reflect his own childhood experience. As a child, Adler worked intently to become popular with his peers, and as he grew older, he achieved a sense of self-esteem and acceptance from others that he had not found within his own family.

Initially Adler was a poor student, so inept that a teacher told his father that the only job the boy was fit for was shoemaker's apprentice. Through persistence and dedication, Adler rose from the bottom to the top of his class. Both academically and socially he strove to overcome his handicaps and inferiorities; thus, he became a textbook example of his adult theory of the necessity of compensating for one's weaknesses. Inferiority feelings, which form the core of his system, are a direct reflection of his own childhood experiences. Adler acknowledged this debt, confessing that "those who are familiar with my life work will clearly see the accord existing between the facts of my childhood and the views I expressed" (Bottome, 1939, p. 9).

At the age of four, while recovering from a near-fatal bout with pneumonia, Adler decided to become a physician. He received his medical degree from the University of Vienna in 1895. After specializing in ophthalmology and practicing general medicine, he went into psychiatry. In 1902 he joined Sigmund Freud's weekly discussion group on psychoanalysis, as one of the four charter members. Although he worked closely with Freud, their relationship was not a personal one. Freud once said that Adler bored him.

Over the next several years Adler developed a theory of personality that was different from Freud's in several ways, and he openly criticized Freud's emphasis on sexual factors. In 1910 Freud named Adler president of the Vienna Psychoanalytic Society, apparently in an effort to reconcile the growing differences between them, but by 1911 their inevitable split was complete. Adler resigned the presidency and officially broke with the Freudian position. The parting was bitter. Adler described Freud as a swindler and called psychoanalysis "filth" (Roazen, 1975, p. 210). Freud referred to Adler as "abnormal" and "driven mad by ambition" (Gay, 1988, p. 223).

Adler served as a physician in the Austrian army during World War I and later organized child guidance clinics in the Vienna school system. During the 1920s his social psychological system, which he called *individ-*

ual psychology, attracted favorable comment from the professional community, and many followers came to Vienna to study with him. He lectured in several countries and in 1926 made the first of several visits to the United States. In 1934 he was appointed professor of medical psychology at the Long Island College of Medicine in New York. Three years later, while on a strenuous lecture tour, he died in Aberdeen, Scotland.

Freud, replying to a letter from a friend who expressed sadness at Adler's death, wrote, "I don't understand your sympathy for Adler. For a Jewish boy out of a Viennese suburb a death in Aberdeen is an unheard-of career in itself and a proof of how far he had got on. The world really rewarded him richly for his service in having contradicted psychoanalysis" (Scarf, 1971, p. 47).

Individual Psychology

Adler developed his system of individual psychology along social lines. He believed that human behavior is determined not by biological forces but by social forces. He suggested that we can understand personality only by investigating a person's social relationships and attitudes toward others. He proposed that this *social interest*, which can be defined as an innate potential to cooperate with others to achieve personal and societal goals, develops in infancy through learning experiences. Like Freud, Adler recognized the importance of the early formative years of childhood, but, as we said, his focus was on social, not biological, forces. He also minimized the role of sex in the shaping of personality (Adler, 1930).

Another point of difference between the theories of Adler and Freud concerns the importance of consciousness. Whereas Freud focused on unconscious determinants of behavior, Adler emphasized the conscious. He considered humans to be conscious beings, aware of their motivations.

To Freud, human behavior was determined by past experiences. In contrast, Adler believed that we are more strongly influenced by what we think the future holds. Striving for goals or anticipating future events can affect our present behavior. For example, a person who lives in fear of eternal damnation after death will behave differently from a person who does not have that expectation.

Freud divided the personality into separate parts (id, ego, and super-ego), but Adler emphasized the essential unity and consistency of the personality. He posited a single dynamic driving force that channels the various resources of the personality toward one overriding goal. This goal, to which we all strive, is superiority or perfection, and it encompasses the complete development, fulfillment, and realization of the self. In Adler's view, sex is not the dominant drive but is only one of a number of means to achieving superiority or perfection.

Adler believed that this striving for superiority, for the betterment of the self, is innate and is manifest in every aspect of the personality. It is responsible for all human progress and achievement, not only for the individual but for civilization as well.

We noted that Adler did not agree with Freud's contention that the primary basis of motivation is sex. Adler believed instead that a generalized feeling of inferiority is the determining force in behavior, as apparently it was in his own life. Initially Adler related this feeling of inferiority to defective parts of the body. The child with a hereditary organic weakness will attempt to compensate for the defect, overemphasizing the deficient function. A child who stutters may, through speech therapy, become a great orator; a child with weak limbs may, through intensive exercise, excel as an athlete or dancer.

Adler later broadened this concept to include any physical, mental, or social handicap, real or imagined. He also believed that an infant's smallness, helplessness, and total dependence on its environment produce a sense of inferiority that is experienced by everyone. Consciously aware of this inferiority and the need to overcome it, the child is also driven by the innate striving for superiority or perfection. Adler believed that this pushing and pulling process continues throughout life, impelling an individual toward ever greater accomplishments.

Feelings of inferiority also function to the advantage of both the individual and society, because they lead to continuous improvement. But if in childhood these feelings are met with excessive pampering or with rejection, the result can be abnormally expressed compensatory behaviors. Failure to compensate adequately for inferiority feelings can lead to the development of an *inferiority complex*, which renders the person incapable of coping with life's problems.

According to Adler, the overriding goal of striving for superiority is universal, but there are various behaviors by which each of us may reach that goal. We demonstrate our striving in different ways and develop a unique or characteristic mode of responding, what Adler called a style of life. This style of life involves the behaviors by which we compensate for real or imagined inferiority. In the example of the child with the weakened body, the life style includes those activities, such as exercise or practice at sports, that will result in increased physical strength and stamina. Formed at around the age of four or five, the style of life becomes fixed and difficult to change thereafter, and it provides the framework within which all later experiences are handled. Again we see that Adler recognized the importance of the early years of life, but he differed from Freud in his belief that we consciously create our own life style or self.

Adler also focused on the family as a factor in personality development. Children with disabilities may consider themselves to be failures, but through compensation and with the help of understanding parents, they can transform inferiorities into strengths. Children who are indulged by their parents may become self-centered. They are unlikely to develop social interest and will expect others to accede to their wishes. Neglected children may develop life styles that involve seeking revenge against society. Both pampering and neglect undermine our confidence in our ability to cope with life's demands.

Adler's concept of the creative power of the self is considered to be the pinnacle of his theory. He suggested that we have the capacity to determine our own personality in accordance with our unique style of life. This creative power represents an active principle of human existence that may be likened to the notion of a soul. Certain abilities and experiences come to us through our heredity and our environment, but it is the way we actively use and interpret these experiences that provides the basis for our attitude toward life. This means that we are consciously involved in shaping our own personality and destiny. Adler believed that we can determine our own fate, rather than having it determined for us by past experience.

In examining the childhoods of his patients, Adler became interested in the relationship between personality and order of birth. He found that the oldest, middle, and youngest child, because of their positions in the family, have different social experiences that result in different personalities. The oldest child receives a great deal of attention until dethroned by the birth of the second child. The first-born may then become insecure and hostile, authoritarian and conservative, with a strong interest in maintaining order. Adler suggested that criminals, neurotics, and perverts are often first-born children. (Sigmund Freud was a first-born; Adler called him a typical eldest son.)

Adler found the second child to be intensely ambitious, rebellious, and jealous, constantly striving to surpass the first-born. (Adler was a second-born and all his life had a competitive relationship with his older brother, whose name was Sigmund.) Nevertheless, Adler considered the second-born to be better adjusted than the first-born or the youngest child. He believed the youngest child to be spoiled and the one most likely to have behavior problems in both childhood and adulthood.

Comment

Adler's theories were warmly received by many people who were dissatisfied with or disgusted by Freud's picture of human beings as dominated by sexual forces and determined by childhood experiences. It is, after all, more pleasant to consider that we can consciously direct our own development. Adler presented a satisfying and optimistic image of human nature. His belief in the importance of social factors, to the relative exclusion of biological determinants, reinforced that growing trend within the social sciences. There was also the beginning of a similar reorientation within psychoanalysis, to render its principles more applicable to the diversity of human behavior.

Adler's individual psychology does not lack critics, however. Many claim that his theories are superficial and rely on common-sense observations from everyday life. Others consider his ideas to be shrewd and insightful. Freud said that Adler's system was too simple. He remarked that it can take two years to learn psychoanalysis because it is complex, but that Adler's ideas can be "learned in two weeks because with Adler there is so little to know" (Sterba, 1982, p. 156). Adler responded that that was precisely his point; it had taken him forty years to make his psychology simple.

It is also argued that Adler was not a consistent or a systematic theorist and that his position leaves many questions unanswered. What precisely is the creative force by which we direct our behavior? What prevents people from becoming reconciled to their inferiority? What are the relative roles of heredity and environment in this process? Further, the criticisms directed by the experimental psychologists toward Freud and Jung also apply to Adler.

His observations of his patients cannot be replicated and verified, nor were they conducted in controlled and systematic fashion. He did not attempt to confirm the accuracy of his patients' reports, and, like Freud and Jung, he did not explain the procedures by which he analyzed his data and reached his conclusions.

Although many of Adler's concepts resist attempts at scientific validation, his notion of birth order has been the subject of considerable research. Studies show that first-borns are high in intelligence and in the need for achievement and support his notion that they experience anxiety when dethroned by the arrival of a second child (Belmont & Marolla, 1973; Breland, 1974; Schachter, 1963). There is research support for Adler's view that dreams can help us resolve current problems, and for his idea that our earliest childhood memories can give some indication of our adult style of life (Grieser, Greenberg, & Harrison, 1972; Jackson & Sechrest, 1962).

In general, Adler's influence on post-Freudian psychoanalysis has been substantial. The work of the ego psychologists, which focuses more on conscious and rational processes than on the unconscious, follows Adler's lead. His emphasis on social forces in personality can be seen in the work of Karen Horney, and his focus on the unity of personality is reflected in the theory of Gordon Allport. The stress on the creative power of the self to shape one's life style influenced the thinking of Abraham Maslow, who commented that "Adler becomes more correct year by year" (Maslow, 1970, p. 13). Adler's influence extends into the present, as we saw in the work of the social learning theorist Julian Rotter. Some psychologists have suggested that Adler was far ahead of his time, that his emphases on social and cognitive variables are more compatible with trends in psychology today than they were with the psychology of his own day.

Adler's views remain influential among psychologists, psychiatrists, social workers, and educators. Research on his theory and therapy is reported in the quarterly journal *Individual Psychology: The Journal of Adlerian Theory, Research, and Practice*. Adlerian training institutes are in operation in New York and other American cities, and a new generation of Adlerians is extending, elaborating, and applying his work, particularly in the area of child counseling.

Karen Horney (1885–1952)

Horney, an early feminist, was trained as a Freudian psychoanalyst in Berlin. She described her work as a modification and extension of Freud's system rather than an effort to supplant it.

The Life of Horney

Karen Horney was born in Hamburg, Germany. Her father was a devout, morose ship's captain many years older than her mother, a liberal and vivacious woman. Horney's childhood was far from idyllic. Her mother rejected her in favor of an older brother (whom Karen envied for being a boy), and her father frequently belittled her appearance and intelligence, leaving her with feelings of inferiority, worthlessness, and hostility. This lack of love fostered what she later called basic anxiety, and it provides another instance of the influence of personal experiences on a theorist's view of personality development.

Beginning at the age of fourteen, Horney experienced a series of adolescent crushes as part of her increasingly frantic search for the love and acceptance she could not find at home. At seventeen she started a newspaper she called "a virginal organ for supervirgins" and took to walking the streets frequented by prostitutes. "In my imagination," she confided to her diary, "there is no spot on me that has not been kissed by a

Although Karen Horney shared Freud's emphasis on the importance of early childhood, she proposed basic anxiety, arising from the parent-child relationship, as the major force motivating people to seek safety and security.

burning mouth. In my imagination there is no depravity I have not tasted, to the dregs" (Horney, 1980, p. 64).

In spite of opposition from her father, Horney entered medical school at the University of Berlin and received her M.D. in 1913. She married, gave birth to three daughters, and endured a long period of emotional distress. She felt overwhelmingly unhappy and oppressed, suffered stomach pains, had sexual difficulties with her husband, and engaged in several affairs. She divorced her husband in 1927 and continued her restless quest for love for the rest of her life. From 1914 to 1918 she undertook orthodox psychoanalytic training at the Berlin Psychoanalytic Institute. The following year she became a faculty member at the institute and began a private practice.

Over the next fifteen years Horney wrote many journal articles, most of them concerned with problems of the female personality, in which she outlined her disagreement with certain Freudian concepts. In 1932 she came to the United States as associate director of the Chicago Institute for Psychoanalysis. She continued to see private patients and taught at the New York Psychoanalytic Institute, but a growing disaffection with orthodox Freudian theory led her to break with this group. She founded the American Institute of Psychoanalysis and remained its head until her death.

The Development of Personality

Let us first consider Horney's points of disagreement with Freud. She believed that some of his basic assumptions were influenced by the times in which he worked, and that by the 1930s and 1940s, when she was formulating her system, the Zeitgeist had changed dramatically. Cultural standards differed, and attitudes about sexual conduct and sex roles had been revised. Freud's theories were no longer consistent with the prevailing intellectual climate.

Not only were the times in which Horney worked different from Freud's, but so was the place. Horney developed her theories in the United States, which had its own popular attitudes about sex. Her American patients were unlike her earlier European patients, and the differences between them could be accounted for only in terms of social influences, not universal biological factors, as Freud claimed.

Horney did not agree with Freud that personality depends on unchangeable biological forces. She denied the preeminent position of sexual factors, challenged the validity of the Oedipal theory, and discarded the concepts of libido and the Freudian structure of personality. Opposed to Freud's belief that women are motivated by penis envy, Horney argued that men are motivated by womb envy, that they envy women for their ability to give birth. Horney believed that this womb envy and its accompanying resentment are manifested unconsciously in men through behaviors designed to disparage and belittle women, to promote and maintain their inferior status. By denying women equal rights, minimizing their opportunities to contribute to society, and downgrading their efforts to achieve, men attempt to retain an alleged natural superiority. To Horney, the fundamental reason for such masculine behavior is a sense of inferiority resulting from womb envy.

Horney and Freud also differed in their basic views of human nature. Horney wrote:

> Freud's pessimism as regards neuroses and their treatment arose from the depths of his disbelief in human goodness and human growth. Man, he postulated, is doomed to suffer or to destroy. . . . My own belief is that man has the capacity as well as the desire to develop his potentialities and become a decent human being. . . . I believe that man can change and go on changing as long as he lives. (Horney, 1945, p. 19)

Although Horney rejected much of Freud's system, she did accept the notion of unconscious motivation and the existence of emotional, nonrational motives.

The underlying concept in Horney's theory is ***basic anxiety***, which she defined as "the feeling a child has of being isolated and helpless in a potentially hostile world" (Horney, 1945, p. 41). This definition characterizes her own feelings as a child. Basic anxiety can result from various parental actions toward the child, including an attitude of dominance, lack of protection, lack of love, and erratic behavior. Anything that disturbs the secure relationship between the child and the parents is capable of producing basic anxiety. Thus, basic anxiety is not innate but results from social forces in the child's environment.

In place of Freud's instincts as major motivating forces, Horney believed that the helpless infant was seeking security in a threatening world. She proposed that the driving power for human behavior is this need for safety, security, and freedom from fear.

Horney shared with Freud a belief that personality develops in early childhood, but she also maintained that personality could change throughout life. Whereas Freud detailed psychosexual stages of development, Horney focused on the way the growing child is treated by the parents. She denied universal developmental phases, such as oral or anal stages, suggesting that if a child developed any such tendencies, they occurred as a result of parental behaviors. Nothing in a child's development was seen as universal; everything depended on cultural, social, and environmental factors. Horney attempted to show how the conflicts Freud ascribed to biological sources could be attributed instead to social forces. Thus Horney focused on early childhood experiences involving the parents' interaction with the child, because the parents can either satisfy or frustrate the child's need for safety and security. The environment the parents provide for the child, and the way the child reacts to it, will form the structure of the child's personality.

We noted that basic anxiety arises from the parent-child relationship. When this socially or environmentally produced anxiety appears, the child develops various behavioral strategies to deal with the resulting feelings of helplessness and insecurity, responding to the parents' attitudes and behaviors. If any of the child's behavioral strategies becomes a fixed part of the personality, it is called a ***neurotic need***, a mode of defense against anxiety. Horney postulated ten neurotic needs, including the needs for affection, personal achievement, and self-sufficiency.

In later writings she grouped the ten needs in three categories: (1) the compliant type (movement toward people, as in the need for love); (2) the detached type (movement away from people, as in the need for self-sufficiency); and (3) the aggressive type (movement against people, as in the need for power). Movement toward people involves acceptance of helplessness and an attempt to win the affection of others and be dependent on them; this is the only way the person can feel secure with other people. Movement away from people involves staying apart from others to avoid any situation of dependency. Movement against people involves hostility, rebellion, and aggression against others.

Horney believed that none of these needs or types is a realistic way to deal with anxiety. The needs themselves can give rise to conflicts because of their incompatibility. Once a person establishes a behavioral strategy for coping with anxiety, that behavior ceases to be flexible enough to permit alternative modes of expression. When a fixed behavior is inappropriate for a particular situation, the person is unable to change in response to the situation's demands. These entrenched behaviors intensify the individual's difficulties because they permeate the whole personality, "encompassing not only the person's relation to others but also his relation to himself and to life in general" (Horney, 1945, p. 46).

She invoked the concept of the ***idealized self-image***, which, in a sense, provides a false picture of the personality. It is an imperfect and misleading mask that prevents neurotic persons from understanding and accepting their true selves. In donning the mask, neurotics deny the existence of their inner conflicts. Neurotics see the idealized self-images as genuine, and those images enable them to believe that they are superior to the persons they truly are. Horney believed that neurotic conflicts are neither innate nor inevitable but arise from undesirable situations in childhood. They can be prevented if the child's home life is characterized by warmth, understanding, security, and love.

Comment

Horney's optimism about the possibility of avoiding neurotic conflicts was welcomed by psychologists and psychiatrists as a relief from the pessimism of Freudian theory. In addition, her contribution to psychology is noteworthy because she introduced a model of personality that is based on social factors and attributes little if anything to innate factors.

Her theory of personality may be weaker than Freud's in terms of clarity, internal consistency, and formal development. Many psychologists believe that it would have been easier to accept or reject Freudian theory than attempt to reshape it as Horney did. So radical is her departure from basic Freudian doctrine that her system is spurned by orthodox psychoanalysts. Although Freud did not comment directly on Horney's work, he once said of her, "she is able but malicious" (Blanton, 1971, p. 65).

The evidence for Horney's theory, like that of Freud, Jung, and Adler, is taken from clinical observations and thus is subject to the questions of scientific credibility noted previously. Little research has been conducted on the concepts in her system, and some consider that a major limitation of her work. However, the research cited in Chapter 13, to refute Freudian notions that women have inadequately developed superegos and inferior conceptions of their bodies, may be taken as support for some of Horney's views.

Although Horney did not have a loyal band of disciples or a journal in which to develop and disseminate her ideas, her work has had considerable impact. The Karen Horney Clinic and the Karen Horney Psychoanalytic Institute (a training center for analysts) are both active in New York City. With the feminist movement that began in the 1960s, her books have enjoyed renewed popularity. It is her writings on feminine psychology that today are considered her major contribution. "Had she written nothing else," a biographer noted, "these papers would have earned Horney a place of importance in the history of psychoanalysis" (Quinn, 1987, p. 211).

Horney was an early and ardent feminist, and many of her positions, written more than fifty years ago, have a strong contemporary ring. In 1934 she contrasted the traditional woman, who seeks her identity through marriage and motherhood, with the modern woman, who seeks her identity through a career. This conflict between love and work, as she saw it, characterized her own life. Horney focused on work, which brought her enormous satisfaction, but continued throughout her life to search for love. Her dilemma is as germane in the 1990s as it was to her in the 1930s, and she fought vigorously for women to have the right to choose, to make their own decisions in the face of strictures imposed by a male-dominated society.

The Descendants

We have seen that Freudian psychoanalytic theory did not long remain the sole approach to the understanding of the human personality. The changes introduced by the neo-Freudian loyalists, by Carl Jung, and by the social psychological theorists represent some of the alternatives developed during Freud's lifetime. The area of personality theory and research has grown immensely in the subsequent years and has splintered into many conflicting viewpoints. Contemporary textbooks on personality typically discuss some fifteen or more fully developed theories. Although these approaches differ in both specifics and generalities, they have a common heritage. All owe their origin and form, in some degree, to the founding efforts of Sigmund Freud.

Freud served the same purpose on the psychoanalytic side of the history of psychology that Wilhelm Wundt served on the experimental side, as a source of inspiration as well as a force to oppose. Every structure, actual and theoretical, depends on the soundness of its foundation, and Freud, like Wundt, provided a solid and challenging base on which to build.

As examples of the evolution in personality theory since the time of Freud, we discuss the works of three descendants: Gordon Allport, Henry Murray, and Erik Erikson.

Gordon Allport (1897–1967)

Over the course of a long and productive career at Harvard University, Gordon Allport, more than anyone else, made the study of personality an academically respectable part of psychology. The area of personality was not formally considered to be part of psychology until he published *Personality: A Psychological Interpretation* in 1937. Never psychoanalyzed or in private practice himself, Allport took the study of personality out of the clinical setting and brought it into the university.

As a child, Allport felt isolated and rejected by other children, but his home life was happy and marked by affection and trust. Unlike Freud and the early post-Freudians, Allport does not seem to have had any noteworthy childhood experiences that bear directly on his adult view of personality. Perhaps that is why he chose to approach the field from an intellectual and academic standpoint, rather than from a more personal one through psychoanalysis.

Between his undergraduate and graduate school years at Harvard, Allport took time off to travel. In Vienna he met Sigmund Freud, an event

Gordon Allport stressed the uniqueness of the individual personality and made personality theory a major part of academic psychology.

that did have an impact on his approach to personality. Ushered into the great man's office, young Allport could think of nothing to say. Freud sat still, looking at him, waiting for him to start the conversation. Finally Allport blurted out an account of an incident that had occurred on the streetcar that morning involving a boy with an obvious and extreme fear of dirt. When Allport finished the story, Freud stared in silence for a moment and then asked, "Was that little boy you?"

Freud was expressing his belief that Allport was revealing his own inner conflicts through this story (Allport, 1968, pp. 383–384). One psychologist has suggested that Freud's question to Allport was insightful and much to the point. "Allport was indeed a person who was neat, meticulous, orderly and punctual — possessing many of the characteristics associated by Freud with the compulsive personality" (Pervin, 1984, p. 267).

Allport was shaken by Freud's question. He began to suspect that psychoanalysis focused too greatly on the unconscious to the neglect of conscious motives, and he went on to fashion a view of personality that was different from Freud's. Allport minimized the role of the unconscious in normal adults, arguing that they function in more rational and conscious terms. Only neurotics, Allport said, are significantly influenced by the unconscious. He also disagreed with Freud about the impact of childhood experiences on conflicts in adult life, insisting that we are influenced much more by present experiences and by our hopes for the future than we are by the past.

Another major difference is Allport's conviction that the only way to investigate personality is to study normal adults, not neurotics. Unlike Freud, he did not believe there was a continuum between the normal and the neurotic. Allport argued that there were no similarities between normal and neurotic individuals, and thus there was no basis for comparison. He emphasized the uniqueness of each individual personality and did not believe there were universal laws that could be applied to everyone.

To Allport, the core of any personality theory is its treatment of motivation. To explain motivation in the normal adult he proposed the concept of *functional autonomy*, the idea that a motive is not functionally related to any childhood experience. Human motives are independent of the original circumstances in which they appeared. An analogy can be made with a tree, which is no longer functionally related to the seed from which it grew. The tree becomes self-determining, just as the adult human being does. For example, when we begin our careers, we work hard, motivated perhaps to attain the goals of money and job security. Years later, when we have become successful and financially secure, we may continue to work hard, but for other reasons, because our original goals have been reached. Adult motivation, in Allport's view, cannot be traced to childhood but can only be understood in terms of our present behavior and intentions.

Allport's term for the self is the *proprium*, which is used in the sense of being appropriate. The self is what belongs to or is appropriate for each of us. It includes everything that is unique, that sets us apart from all others, and it is an important and conscious aspect of the personality. The proprium develops through seven stages from infancy to adolescence. These developmental stages are not psychosexual, nor do they involve Freudian conflicts centered on erogenous zones of the body. Instead, social relationships, particularly those with the mother, are crucial in the development of the proprium.

Allport's study of personality traits, the first undertaken in the United States, began with his doctoral dissertation. He distinguished between traits, which can be shared by any number of people, and personal dispositions, which are the traits unique to each person. Both can be inferred from the observation of behavior over a period of time, looking for consistencies and regularities. Allport postulated three kinds of traits: (1) cardinal traits, which are ruling passions that dominate every aspect of life; (2) central traits, which are behavioral themes, such as aggressiveness or sentimentality; and (3) secondary traits, which are behaviors displayed less frequently and consistently than the other traits.

His theory has been more influential in psychology than the work of the early psychoanalysts. It has not inspired a great deal of research, however, because of the difficulty in translating his concepts into specific propositions that can be tested under laboratory conditions. Allport's own most notable research dealt with *expressive behavior*, the facial expressions, vocal inflections, gestures, and mannerisms that tend to reveal, to a trained observer, various facets of personality.

Critics charge that Allport's exclusive focus on the individual makes it impossible to generalize from one person to another and to formulate laws of human behavior. Nevertheless, his work on the definition and assessment of traits is considered to be a significant contribution to the study of personality. His books are clear and his concepts easily understood. He developed a psychological test, the Study of Values, to measure the values an individual holds. It has proved to be a successful assessment device for research, counseling, and personnel selection and is judged to be a useful outgrowth of his theory. Allport received the Gold Medal Award from the American Psychological Foundation and the Distinguished Scientific Contribution Award from the American Psychological Association; he was also elected president of the APA.

Henry Murray (1893–1988)

Whereas Allport's theory of personality was a complete rejection of Freudian psychoanalysis, Murray's system, which he called *personology*, was built on Freud's theory. Like Allport, Murray chose to study personality in a university setting rather than in a clinic. Although he underwent psychoanalysis himself (and said that his analyst became bored), he did not conduct a private practice. He preferred to investigate the human personality through the intensive study of normal subjects.

Murray's childhood was distinguished by rejection from his mother, a great sensitivity to the sufferings of others, and Adlerian compensation for physical defects (stuttering and ineptness at sports). After graduating from Columbia University medical school, he interned in surgery, undertook biochemical research, and earned a Ph.D. in biochemistry from Cambridge University in England — certainly one of the more circuitous routes to a career in psychology.

He had taken only one psychology course in college and reported that by the second lecture he was looking for the nearest exit. The next psychology course he attended was one he taught years later. Murray apparently came to psychology as a result of a personal crisis. He fell in love with a younger woman but did not want to leave his wife. At the urging of his lover, he went to Zurich to consult with Carl Jung.

At the time, Jung was having an affair with a younger woman, which he maintained openly while living with his wife and family. He advised Murray to do the same, and Murray did so for many years. Thus, not only did Jung resolve Murray's personal dilemma, he also steered Murray toward a career in psychology. Jung showed him that psychology, particularly the study of the unconscious, could provide the answers to life's problems. "The great floodgates of the wonder-world swung open," Murray wrote of his time with Jung. "I had experienced the unconscious" (Murray, 1940, p. 153).

In 1927 Murray joined the new Harvard Psychological Clinic, which was formed specifically to study personality. He remained at Harvard for the rest of his career, except for the years of World War II, when he established an assessment program for the Office of Strategic Services (a forerunner of the C.I.A.). That program, in which candidates were observed in stressful, real-life situations, evolved into the assessment-center approach to executive selection now widely used in business and government. It provides a striking example of the practical application of an assessment technique originally undertaken as pure research.

It is not surprising, given his training in medicine and biochemistry, that Murray chose to emphasize physiological functioning as it relates to personality. He stressed the concept of tension reduction, which he considered to be a primary law of human behavior, much as Freud did. Also in the Freudian vein, Murray noted the importance of the unconscious and the impact of childhood experiences on adult behavior. His system incorporated the id, ego, and superego, albeit with some modification of the orthodox Freudian position.

Murray divided personality into these three basic structures — id, ego, and superego (Murray, 1938). The id contains our innate, impulsive tendencies and provides the energy for the operation of the personality, a view virtually identical to Freud's. However, in addition to primitive and lustful impulses, the id in Murray's system also contains socially desirable tendencies, such as empathy, identification, and forms of love. Although parts of the id must be suppressed for normal development to occur, other parts must be allowed full expression. We can see here the influence of Jung's concept of the shadow archetype, which also contained desirable and undesirable qualities.

In Murray's system, as in the work of the ego psychologists, the ego assumes a more active role in determining behavior than it does in Freudian psychoanalysis. Murray believed that the ego is not merely the servant of the id but is also a conscious organizer of behavior. The ego acts to suppress undesirable id impulses and facilitate the expression of desirable id impulses.

Murray agreed with Freud that the superego represents the internalization of cultural values and that individuals judge their own behavior in terms of those values. He disagreed with Freud, however, about the forces that shape the superego and the period over which it is formed. Murray argued that the superego is influenced not only by the teachings of one's parents but also by one's peer group and by the literature and mythology of the society. Further, the superego is not fixed by the age of five but continues to develop throughout life.

Motivation is central to Murray's personality theory. His classification of needs to explain motivation is his most significant contribution to psychology. Needs involve a chemical force in the brain that organizes intellectual and perceptual functioning. Needs arouse tension levels within the organism, which can be reduced only by satisfying the needs. Thus, needs activate behavior, directing it in whatever ways are necessary to bring about this satisfaction and tension reduction. Murray's research identified twenty needs, such as achievement, affiliation, aggression, autonomy, and dominance.

Like Freud, Murray believed that personality develops through a series of stages in childhood. Each stage is characterized by some condition that brings pleasure, and each leaves its imprint on the personality in the form of a complex, which is a normal behavior pattern that unconsciously affects the person's later development. The pleasurable conditions of childhood and their complexes are similar to some of Freud's psychosexual stages of development: (1) the secure existence within the womb (the *claustral complex*); (2) the sensuous enjoyment of sucking nourishment while being held (the *oral complex*); (3) the pleasure resulting from defecation (the *anal complex*); (4) the pleasure accompanying urination (the *urethral complex*); and (5) genital pleasures (the *castration complex*).

Murray's proposed classification of needs was the basis of his Thematic Apperception Test (TAT), which he developed with Christiana Morgan. This projective technique is widely used in research to assess aspects of personality, and it is also used for clinical diagnosis and personnel selection. The concept of the ***projective technique*** derives from Freud's defense mechanism of projection, in which a person projects disturbing impulses onto someone else. In the TAT, the person projects those impulses onto the figures in a series of ambiguous pictures. Another popular test, the Edwards Personal Preference Schedule, is used to measure fifteen of Murray's proposed needs. The Jackson Personality Research Form measures traits drawn from Murray's list of needs.

Murray's theory has generated considerable research on specific needs and on the techniques he developed to assess personality. Much of that research supports his ideas, especially his proposed needs for affiliation and achievement. There is little scientific support for other aspects of his theory, however. In recognition of his contributions to the study of personality, Murray received the Gold Medal Award of the American Psychological Foundation and the Distinguished Scientific Contribution Award of the American Psychological Association.

Erik Erikson (1902–   )

Erik Erikson was trained in orthodox psychoanalysis by Anna Freud. He developed a popular approach to personality that retains much of Freud's system while extending it in several ways. Erikson elaborated on the stages of development, argued that personality continues to grow throughout life, and recognized the impact on personality of cultural, historical, and social forces.

Erikson is well known for his concept of the identity crisis, an idea that may have arisen from personal crises he experienced in his early years. "My best friends will insist," he wrote, "that I needed to name this crisis and see it in everybody else in order to really come to terms with it in myself" (Erikson, 1975, pp. 25–26).

The first such crisis for Erikson involved his name. For many years he believed his last name was Homburger, the name of the stepfather whom Erikson believed was his natural father. He changed his name to Erikson at age thirty-nine, when he became a United States citizen. The second crisis of identity occurred during his school years in Germany. Erikson considered himself to be German, but his classmates rejected him because he was Jewish. At the same time, his Jewish classmates shunned him because of his blond Aryan appearance.

The third crisis occurred after his high school graduation. He dropped out of society and for several years wandered about Europe seeking his identity. When he was twenty-five, he took a job teaching in a

The search for an ego identity during adolescence, drawn from his own life experiences, is the central theme in Erik Erikson's life-span theory of personality development.

small school in Vienna that had been established for the children of Sigmund Freud's patients and friends. He got married and received training in psychoanalysis, and said that he had found both a personal and a professional identity. Although he had no formal education beyond high school (he enrolled in a Ph.D. program at Harvard University, but failed his first course and did not continue), Erikson eventually taught at Harvard and became one of the most influential psychoanalysts of modern times.

His theory takes a developmental or life-span approach in that it focuses on personality growth over the life of the individual. The central theme in the development of personality is the search for an *ego identity*. Erikson divided the life span into eight *psychosocial stages* of development, each of which involves a conflict or crisis that must be resolved. These conflicts arise in each developmental stage as the environment makes new demands. The person is faced with a choice between two ways of coping with the crisis, an adaptive way or a maladaptive way. Only when the crisis at each stage has been resolved, and the personality has thus changed, does the person have sufficient strength to deal with the next stage of development.

The first four stages Erikson proposed are similar to Freud's oral, anal, and phallic stages and the latency period, although Erikson emphasizes social rather than biological and sexual factors. The last four stages of development are unique to Erikson's system and carry the individual from adolescence through old age, a period largely ignored by Freud.

Each of these stages of growth, although stressful enough to be called a crisis, can have a positive outcome if it is resolved in an adaptive way. In addition, if a person fails at any one stage and is left with a maladaptive way of responding, it can be corrected by successful adaptation at a later stage. There is, then, hope for the future at all stages of personality growth.

Erikson believed that we can consciously influence and direct our own growth at each stage. This is in contrast to Freud's view that we are the products of childhood experiences and are unable to change later in life. Although Erikson recognized that childhood influences are important and can even be harmful, he argued that events at later stages can counteract and overcome negative childhood experiences and contribute to our ultimate goal: the establishment of a positive ego identity.

The question of one's basic ego identity must be resolved during the period of adolescence (approximately ages twelve to eighteen). This is a time of consolidation, when the person must form a self-image that makes sense and provides a continuity with the past and an orientation toward the future. Erikson suggested that the process of shaping and accepting one's identity is difficult and filled with anxiety. The adolescent must experiment with different roles and ideologies to determine the best fit. Persons who achieve a strong sense of identity are equipped to deal with the problems of adulthood. Those who fail to achieve an identity are said to be experiencing an *identity crisis*. They may withdraw from the normal life sequence (education, job, marriage), as Erikson himself did for a time, and perhaps even seek a negative identity in socially unacceptable behaviors such as drug addiction or crime.

A controversial aspect of Erikson's work is his agreement with Freud that personality differences between the sexes are biologically based, arising from the possession or the lack of a penis. Erikson based his conclusion on research with children, notably a study in which boys and girls ages ten to twelve constructed scenes out of toy figures and wooden blocks (Erikson, 1968). The girls' constructions were low, static structures into which animals and male figures tried to force their way. The boys' constructions were action oriented and featured tall, towering structures. Erikson interpreted these play constructions to mean that girls and boys were symbolically expressing their genitals. He conceded, however, that the personality differences could be the result of sex-role training in which boys are taught to be more aggressive than girls.

Considerable research has been conducted on Erikson's concept of ego identity. Studies show that adolescents who developed a strong, positive identity had coped with the crises of the earlier developmental stages in an adaptive way. Adolescents who developed a weak ego identity had resolved the crises in a maladaptive way (see, for example, Waterman, Buebel, & Waterman, 1970). These findings and others are in line with Erikson's predictions. Some research, however, suggests that the identity crisis may occur later than Erikson proposed. One study showed that the identity crisis begins in late adolescence and that up to 30 percent of the subjects were still searching for an identity at age twenty-four (Archer, 1982). Additional findings indicate that those who take full-time jobs after high school graduation achieve ego identity sooner than those who attend college. Thus, going to college may delay the resolution of the identity crisis (Adams & Fitch, 1982). This confirms Erikson's notion of an identity crisis but indicates that his estimate of its resolution by age eighteen may be in error.

In general, there is considerable evidence to support the notion of ego identity but not as much for the childhood stages of development or the stage of adulthood (McAdams, Ruetzel, & Foley, 1986). Less attention has been paid to maturity, Erikson's final developmental stage, and critics charged that he had little to say about it himself. He responded to these criticisms in 1986 by writing, at age eighty-four, *Vital Involvement in Old Age* (Erikson, Erikson, & Kivnick, 1986). The book shows Erikson's own vitality during his later years in continuing to develop and apply his theory.

Erikson's work has been influential in psychoanalysis as well as in education, social work, vocational counseling, and marriage counseling. The growth in the field of life-span developmental psychology and the current interest in developmental problems of middle age and old age are direct outgrowths of Erikson's work. His books remain popular with professionals and the public at large, and his photograph has appeared on the covers of *Newsweek* and the *New York Times Magazine*, unusual recognition for a psychologist.

Comment

We have described the diversity and divisiveness that have characterized developments in the psychoanalytic tradition during and after Freud's lifetime. Some of the contemporary positions bear little resemblance to Freud's views and may be labeled psychoanalytic only by default, to distinguish them from the behavioral/experimental tradition within psychology. Although they owe their origin to Freud, in that they arose from opposition to his views, they share with orthodox psychoanalysis only a broad interest in understanding the human personality. Allport, who diverged so far from Freudian views, might more appropriately be called a humanistic psychologist. The works of Murray and Erikson bear a clearer similarity to Freud's but differ from psychoanalysis on both major and minor points.

There is considerably more fragmentation within the psychoanalytic tradition than within the behaviorist position in psychology. Despite the changes introduced by neobehaviorists and neo-neobehaviorists, all share the belief of John B. Watson that behavior, in some form, should remain a focus of study. In contrast, not all, or even most, of Freud's heirs agree that the focus of their study should be unconscious or biological forces, or that the motivators of human behavior are sex and aggression.

There are today many more subschools of psychoanalysis than of behaviorism. This greater plurality of viewpoints may be taken as a sign of strength and vitality or as a weakness and failing, but at the present time these developments are too recent to judge. They are still history in the making.

Suggested Readings

Dissenters and Descendants

Ellenberger, H. F. (1970). *The Discovery of the Unconscious: The History and Evolution of Dynamic Psychiatry*. New York: Basic Books. Traces the study of the unconscious from primitive times to Freudian psychoanalysis and its derivatives; see especially Chapter 8, "Alfred Adler and Individual Psychology," and Chapter 9, "Carl Gustav Jung and Analytical Psychology."

Roazen, P. (1975). *Freud and His Followers*. New York: Knopf. A lively and well-written account of Freud's life and of the men and women who became his disciples, some of whom later broke away to form their own movements.

Young-Bruehl, E. (1988). *Anna Freud: A Biography*. New York: Summit Books. An account of the life and work of Freud's youngest daughter, who developed a system of child analysis and served as her father's colleague and confidante.

Carl Jung

Freud/Jung Letters. (1974). Princeton NJ: Princeton University Press. Presents some 360 letters dating from 1906 to 1913 showing the development and dissolution of the friendship between Freud and Jung.

Hannah, B. (1976). *Jung: His Life and Work*. New York: Putnam's; Stern, P. J. (1976). *C. G. Jung: The Haunted Prophet*. New York: Braziller. Two biographies of Jung: the first is a memoir by a Jungian analyst who was a friend of Jung's for more than thirty years; the second is a more provocative treatment depicting Jung's life as a war against "inner demons."

Jung, C. G. (1961). *Memories, Dreams, Reflections*. New York: Vintage. Jung's recollections of his life, written at the age of eighty-one.

Alfred Adler

Orgler, H. (1963). *Alfred Adler, The Man and His Work: Triumph Over the Inferiority Complex*. New York: Liveright. Presents an overview of Adler's life and work; discusses the practical applications of his system of individual psychology to child counseling and education.

Karen Horney

Horney, K. (1937). *The Neurotic Personality of Our Time*. New York: Norton. Describes the development of conflict and anxiety within the human personality and relates neuroses to past experiences and to the general social/cultural climate.

Quinn, S. (1987). *A Mind of Her Own: The Life of Karen Horney*. New York: Summit Books. Draws on previously unpublished diaries to describe Horney's life, her work on feminine psychology, and her conflicts with the orthodox Freudian establishment.

Gordon Allport

Allport, G. (1955). *Becoming: Basic Considerations for a Psychology of Personality*. New Haven: Yale University Press. Outlines Allport's approach to the human personality, emphasizing the capacity for growth and development.

Allport, G. (1967). Autobiography. In E. G. Boring & G. Lindzey (Eds.), *A History of Psychology in Autobiography* (Vol. 5). New York: Appleton-Century-Crofts; Evans, R. I. (1971). *Gordon Allport: The Man and His Ideas*. New York: Dutton. Accounts of Allport's life and work: the first is an essay by Allport; the second is a series of interviews.

Maddi, S. R., & Costa, P. T. (1972). *Humanism in Personology: Allport, Maslow, and Murray*. New York: Aldine-Atherton. A clear presentation of the background and work of these three psychologists, explaining the similarities and differences among their theories as well as the influence of events from their early lives.

Henry Murray

Anderson, J. W. (1988). Henry A. Murray's early career: A psychobiographical exploration. *Journal of Personality, 56*(1), 139–171. An analysis of Murray's life through his early thirties, examining his decision to become a psychologist, his involvement with psychoanalysis, and the impact of his personal and academic experiences on his work.

Murray, H. A. (1967). Autobiography. In E. G. Boring & G. Lindzey (Eds.), *A History of Psychology in Autobiography* (Vol. 5). New York: Appleton-Century-Crofts. Murray's reflections on his life and work.

Erik Erikson

Erikson, E. H. (1968). *Identity: Youth and Crisis*. New York: Norton. The classic work on the identity crisis and the ways of coping with conflict at that stage of development.

Evans, R. I. (1967). *Dialogue with Erik Erikson*. New York: Harper & Row. Conversations with Erikson about his life and work.

Beyond
the Schools
of Thought:
More Recent
Developments

15

Schools of Thought in Perspective

Throughout this book we have described how the major schools of thought in psychology came into being, prospered for a time, and then (with the exception of psychoanalysis) became part of the mainstream of contemporary American psychology — or contributed to it. We have seen that each movement grew strong and vital through its opposition to the previous school. When there was no longer any need for protest, when the new school had vanquished its opposition, that school ceased to be a movement and became the established position, at least for a while.

497

Each school of thought was successful in its own way. Each made substantial contributions to the evolution of psychology. This is true even for structuralism, although it left little direct imprint on the modern psychological scene. There are no longer structuralists of the Titchenerian variety in psychology, nor have there been for decades. Yet structuralism was an enormous success in that it helped in the enterprise begun by Wilhelm Wundt: the establishment of an independent science of psychology that was finally free of philosophy. That structuralism failed to remain the dominant position in psychology for more than a short time does not detract from its revolutionary achievement as the first school of thought in a new science, and as a source of opposition for the schools that followed.

Consider the success of functionalism, which also has not endured as a separate school of thought. As an attitude or viewpoint, which is all it hoped to be, functionalism permeates contemporary American psychological thought. To the extent that American psychology today is as much profession as science and is actively applying its findings to virtually every aspect of life, the functional, utilitarian idea has changed the nature of psychology.

What of Gestalt psychology? It, too, on a more modest scale, accomplished its mission. Its opposition to elementism, its support of a molar approach, and its continuing interest in consciousness have influenced psychologists working in the areas of clinical psychology, learning, perception, social psychology, and thinking. Unlike structuralism and functionalism, Gestalt psychology retains many of the characteristics of a separate school of thought; there are psychologists today who define their research and professional identity as Gestalt. Although the Gestalt school did not transform psychology the way its founders hoped it would, it has had considerable impact and must therefore be described as a success.

As noteworthy as the accomplishments of structuralism, functionalism, and Gestalt psychology are, they take second place to the phenomenal influences of behaviorism and psychoanalysis. The effects of these movements have been pronounced, and they have maintained their identities as unique schools of thought. For decades, particularly in the United States, psychologists have declared themselves as belonging to either the behaviorist or the psychoanalytic tradition. Although relations between these two schools have improved over the years, in general they remain separate forces within psychology.

We discussed how both behaviorism and psychoanalysis splintered into various positions after the days of their founders, John B. Watson and Sigmund Freud. There is today no single form of behaviorism or of psychoanalysis that has won allegiance from all members of either school (although for many years B. F. Skinner enjoyed a prominence in behaviorism). The emergence of subschools divided both systems into competing factions, each with its own map of the true path. Despite the internal diversity of the schools, behaviorists and psychoanalysts stand firmly against each other in many of their definitions of and approaches to problems in psychology. Skinnerian behaviorists, for example, still have more in common with sociobehaviorist followers of Bandura or Rotter than they do with followers of Jungian or Eriksonian psychoanalysis.

The vitality of these two major schools of thought is evident in their continuing evolution. We have seen that Skinner's psychology is not the last stage in the development of behaviorism any more than Adler's or Horney's psychology is the final stage of psychoanalysis.

In this chapter we consider several developments that characterize American psychology in the last half of the twentieth century. Among these developments are practical matters that advance psychology as a profession, for example, the role of women and minorities, which we address in terms of some of the contextual factors noted in Chapter 1. Other developments are theoretical and advance psychology's scientific evolution. In this regard we discuss two movements — humanistic psychology and cognitive psychology — that have helped to reshape the field by returning to the study of consciousness.

Women in the History of Psychology

More than one-half of all those who receive a Ph.D. in psychology every year are women, yet the history of psychology clearly has been dominated by men. This gender imbalance is not, of course, unique to psychology. If we look at the history of any discipline, be it in the other sciences, humanities, music, arts, or literature, we find the same preponderance of male names on the pages of their written histories. In this text the works of such notable women as Margaret Floy Washburn, Mary Whiton Calkins, Mary Cover Jones, Bluma Zeigarnik, Anna Freud, and Karen Horney have been noted, but they are in the minority compared to the space necessarily devoted to the contributions of men.

There are historical reasons why the contributions of women in psychology have gone unrecognized, and they have to do with some of the contextual forces we mentioned in Chapter 1 and discussed throughout the book. One reason is that for many years women faced restrictions, discrimination, and inequities in graduate schools, not only in the United

States but in Europe as well. Recall the example of Washburn who, because she was a woman, could not be admitted to Columbia University. It was not until 1892 that Yale, the University of Chicago, and a few other institutions agreed to accept a few women in graduate programs. Thus, for almost two decades after the formal founding of psychology as a scientific discipline, it was difficult for women to become psychologists, much less to make contributions to the field.

The explanation offered for these academic restrictions, and another form of discrimination women faced at that time, was the widespread social and cultural belief in the intellectual superiority of men. Even if women were provided with educational opportunities equal to those offered to men, so this argument ran, their innate intellectual deficits would prevent them from benefiting from those opportunities. Prominent nineteenth-century scientists, including Darwin and a majority of the psychologists of the day (among them Hall, Thorndike, Cattell, and Freud), subscribed to this view. Even today this belief has not completely disappeared.

A related theory about women suggested that they would suffer physical and emotional damage from being exposed to higher education. G. Stanley Hall, among others, argued that educating women would endanger their biological imperative to motherhood by disrupting the menstrual cycle and weakening the maternal urge, leading to "race suicide." If women were to be educated at all, Hall urged, "they should be educated to motherhood" (Diehl, 1986, p. 872). In 1873, a former Harvard University medical school professor published a book cataloguing "in gruesome detail the dire effects of higher education on women's physical well-being," including "monstrous brains and puny bodies; abnormally active cerebration and abnormally weak digestion; flowing thought and constipated bowels" (Scarborough & Furumoto, 1987, p. 4). The book was so popular that it appeared in seventeen editions over the following thirteen years.

Another reason why women in the history of psychology have been insufficiently recognized lies in the nature of the jobs to which they have been largely restricted. In many fields, not only psychology, it has been difficult for women to obtain positions on university faculties, except at women's colleges. Even when women were hired, they faced discrimination in promotion and tenure, tended to be concentrated at lower faculty ranks, and received lower pay than men in comparable positions.

Because women were, in effect, locked out of many university positions, they were forced to seek employment in the applied fields, particularly in the helping professions such as clinical and counseling psychology, child guidance, and school psychology. Although they have made significant contributions in those areas — pioneering the development and use of psychological tests, for example — working in applied psychology put women at a professional disadvantage. Jobs in nonacademic settings do not provide the time, financial support, and graduate student assistance needed to conduct research and write papers and books, the primary vehicles for professional visibility. In applied settings, one's contributions rarely become known beyond the confines of the institution for which one works.

The tremendous growth of applied psychology in the United States in the twentieth century offered women employment opportunities they would otherwise not have had, but it also meant that women remained outside the mainstream of academic psychology, where the theories, research programs, and schools of thought — the themes that define the history of psychology — were being developed.

Many academic psychologists held negative views about applied work, considering it to be somehow menial and inferior. And for a time, some of the applied areas of psychology were referred to, disparagingly, as "women's work." Also, because most histories of psychology have been written by college professors, the field of applied psychology has been minimized or overlooked, and with it the contributions of the many women who worked in these areas.

Women who did secure university teaching appointments and who carried out research and published their findings and ideas faced yet another obstacle that deprived them of recognition as women psychologists. The accepted method of documentation listing authors' names in professional publications (last name and initials only) makes it impossible for readers to determine the sex of the author. Thus, awareness of the contributions of women as a group is likely to be lower than if first names were used in citations. In addition, "we will probably never know how much work was done by women but credited to men: how many footnotes of appreciation should rightfully have been coauthorship, how many times junior authorship should have been senior authorship, or how many times it was the male coauthor who should have received the footnote" (Bernstein & Russo, 1974, p. 131).

Historians of psychology are beginning to address these problems and provide greater recognition of the contributions of women. The professional literature on the role of women in psychology has been growing rapidly since the 1970s (see Furumoto, 1989; Lerner, 1979; O'Connell & Russo, 1983, 1988; and Scarborough & Furumoto, 1987). This awareness also led the American Psychological Association to establish the Task

Force on the Status of Women in 1970 and the Committee on Women in Psychology in 1973. The committee's purpose is to ensure that "women achieve equality as members of the psychological community, in order that all human resources be utilized" (*Women in the American Psychological Association*, 1986, p. 1).

Also in 1973, the Division of Psychology of Women (Division 35) was established in the APA, to promote the study of women and the appreciation of the work of women psychologists. One of their priorities is to increase the participation in psychology of ethnic minority women and to develop a multicultural approach to the psychological and social aspects of women's lives.

By the beginning of the twentieth century, some twenty women had managed to earn doctoral degrees in psychology. In the 1906 edition of Cattell's *American Men of Science*, 12 percent of those listed as psychologists were women, a high figure considering the barriers to their graduate education. These first women psychologists were actively encouraged to join the APA. At the second meeting of the organization, in 1893, two women were elected to membership; twelve years later Mary Whiton Calkins became the APA's first woman president. Some other professional societies denied women membership for many years. Women doctors were not permitted to join the American Medical Association until 1915, and women lawyers were banned from the American Bar Association until 1918 (Furumoto, 1987). By 1917 women constituted 13 percent of all APA members, a higher proportion of women than could be found in any other scientific society at the time. The number of women elected to the presidency of the APA has also increased in recent years. Although only two women became president in the seventy-eight years between 1892 and 1970, five women have been elected president since 1970.

In the 1970s and 1980s, women earned approximately half of all Ph.D.s granted in the field. There has been a marked increase in the number of women researchers and women authors of books and journal articles, even in traditionally male-dominated areas such as industrial/organizational psychology. Increasing numbers of women have served as officers in professional organizations and have received prestigious medals and awards.

Although women are no longer invisible within psychology, sex discrimination remains a problem in college teaching. In 1944, women constituted 26 percent of the faculty of psychology departments, yet forty years later that percentage was essentially unchanged. Women remain primarily in the lower, nontenured faculty ranks and continue to be paid less than men with comparable experience.

The research of Leta Stetter Hollingworth refuted widely accepted notions of female inferiority and suggested that women were constrained more by social than by biological factors.

Leta Stetter Hollingworth (1886–1939) and the Psychology of Women

In addition to advancing within psychology as a profession and a science, women psychologists have contributed to the study of the psychology of women. A pioneer in this area is Leta Stetter Hollingworth, who received her Ph.D. from Columbia University in 1916. By that time she had already published significant work on the psychology of women. She conducted extensive empirical research on the *variability hypothesis*, the idea that in terms of both physical and intellectual abilities, women were a more homogeneous group than men. Because men were said to show greater variation, and thus some were more likely to exhibit above-average and superior abilities, they obviously would benefit from diverse educational and career opportunities. Women, said to be more alike and more clustered in the average range of abilities, had little need to be educated for more than domestic duties.

Hollingworth's data refuted the variability hypothesis and other notions of female inferiority. She found that the female menstrual cycle was not related to any performance decrements in perceptual and motor skills or intellectual abilities. Her work challenged the idea that women could find satisfaction only through motherhood and that their desire to achieve in other fields was somehow abnormal and unhealthy. She suggested that social attitudes rather than biological factors kept women from becoming fully contributing members of society (Benjamin, 1975; Shields, 1975). Thus, the work of Hollingworth, who advanced these ideas in the period from 1913 into the 1930s, must be recognized as a precursor to contemporary thinking on the psychology of women.

African-Americans in the History of Psychology

We noted in Chapter 1 that African-Americans had also been largely excluded from psychology for many years. As recently as 1940, only four black colleges in the United States offered undergraduate majors in psychology. When blacks were permitted to enroll at predominantly white universities, they faced various forms of discrimination. In the 1930s and 1940s, for example, black students were not allowed to live on the campuses of many universities.

For many years, the leading university providing instruction in psychology for African-American students was Howard University in Washington, D.C. Between the years 1919 and 1938, twenty black graduate students were enrolled there. Between 1920 and 1950, only thirty-two blacks earned doctoral degrees in psychology. And from 1920 to 1966, the ten most prestigious psychology departments in the United States awarded only eight doctorates to blacks, out of a total of more than 3,700 doctoral degrees granted overall (Guthrie, 1976; Russo & Denmark, 1987). We noted earlier that G. Stanley Hall at Clark University was one of the few psychologists to encourage the enrollment of blacks in his graduate programs.

A few African-Americans went to Germany for graduate study; Gilbert Haven Jones, for example, earned his Ph.D. from the University of Göttingen in 1901. American blacks did not meet the same sort of prejudice at

European schools that they did at home, but few had the financial resources to study abroad.

Earning a Ph.D. was only the first hurdle on the path to a career as a psychologist. Finding a job was often just as difficult. Virtually no white universities would employ a black faculty member, and most of the organizations hiring applied psychologists — a major source of jobs for women psychologists — were closed to blacks. That left black colleges as the primary place of employment, but conditions at those schools rarely afforded opportunities for scholarly research that could lead to professional visibility and recognition. In 1936, a professor wrote about the plight of the black faculty member:

> Lack of money, overwork, and other unpleasant factors make it practically impossible for him to do anything outstanding in the field of pure scholarship. He cannot buy books on a large scale himself, and he cannot get them at his school libraries, because there are no really adequate libraries in the Negro schools. Probably the worst handicap of all is the lack of a scholarly atmosphere about him. There is no incentive, and, of course, no money for research in most schools. (Guthrie, 1976, p. 123)

The situation for African-American psychologists has improved in recent years in terms of both graduate degrees and employment opportunities. In 1970, Kenneth B. Clark became the first black psychologist to be elected president of the American Psychological Association. Clark received his B.S. and M.S. degrees in psychology from Howard University and his Ph.D. from Columbia in 1940. His academic and research career is distinguished. He was first affiliated with the Hampton Institute, then with City College of New York. His research on the effects of racial segregation was cited by the United States Supreme Court in its landmark 1954 ruling on civil rights, which banned racial segregation in the public schools. Clark has published many influential books and articles and has received professional honors for his contributions to psychology and to society.

Humanistic Psychology: The Third Force

In the early 1960s, more than three decades ago, a movement developed in American psychology known as *humanistic psychology* or the *third force*. It was not intended to be a revised or adapted form of any current school of thought, as was the case with some neo-Freudian and

The work of Kenneth B. Clark on the effects of racial segregation was cited by the United States Supreme Court in a 1954 decision that ended segregation in the public schools.

neo-behavioristic positions. Instead, as the term *third force* implies, humanistic psychology wanted to replace behaviorism and psychoanalysis, the two major forces in psychology.

The basic themes of humanistic psychology, like those of all movements, had been recognized and called for in earlier times. The essential points were (1) an emphasis on conscious experience, (2) a belief in the wholeness of human nature and conduct, (3) a focus on free will, spontaneity, and the creative power of the individual, and (4) the study of everything that is relevant to the human condition. Anticipations of these ideas can be found in the works of earlier psychologists.

Consider Franz Brentano (Chapter 4), an opponent of Wundt's and a precursor of Gestalt psychology. Brentano criticized the mechanistic, reductionistic, natural-science approach to psychology and favored the study of consciousness as an active molar quality rather than a passive molecular content. Oswald Külpe demonstrated that not all conscious experience could be reduced to elementary form or be explained in terms of responses to stimuli. William James argued against the mechanistic approach and urged a focus on consciousness and the whole individual.

The Gestalt psychologists believed that psychology should take a wholes approach to consciousness. In the face of the primacy of behaviorism, they continued to insist that conscious experience was a legitimate and profitable area of study for psychology. Some psychologists have argued that the similarity between Gestalt psychology and humanistic psychology is so strong that there is no reason to give the newer movement any other name. They believe that the label *Gestalt* is adequate to describe the themes encompassed by humanistic psychology (Wertheimer, 1978).

There are several antecedents of the humanistic position in psychoanalysis. Adler, Horney, Erikson, and Allport opposed Freud's view that personality is determined by biological forces and past events. They also disagreed with Freud's notion that people are ruled by unconscious forces. These dissenters from orthodox psychoanalysis believed that people are primarily conscious beings who possess spontaneity and free will and are influenced by the present and future at least as much as by the past. They credited the human personality with the creative power to shape itself.

With all movements in modern psychology, the Zeitgeist is influential in turning antecedents and trends into an effective viewpoint. Humanistic psychology appeared to be reflecting the unrest and disaffection voiced by young people in the 1960s against the mechanistic and materialistic aspects of contemporary Western culture. We have said that every new movement has used its older opponent, the establishment, as a base against which to push to gain its own momentum. In practical terms, the new movement needs to state articulately and loudly the weaknesses and failings of the current dominant view. Humanistic psychology had two such targets: behaviorism and psychoanalysis.

Humanistic psychologists believed that behaviorism was a narrow, artificial, and relatively sterile approach to human nature. The emphasis on overt behavior was, they said, dehumanizing, reducing us to animals or machines. They resisted the conception of human beings functioning in a deterministic manner, in response to childhood experiences or environmental stimulus events. Further, behaviorism did not come to grips with uniquely human characteristics, those subjective conscious qualities and capacities that set people apart from laboratory animals. A psychology based on discrete conditioned responses makes of the individual a mechanized organism responding only to the stimuli presented. The humanistic psychologists argued that human beings are much more than white rats, robots, or computers, and that we cannot be objectified, quantified, and reduced to stimulus-response units. In other words, people are not empty organisms.

The humanistic psychologists were also opposed to the deterministic tendencies found in the Freudian approach to psychology and to its minimization of the role of consciousness. The Freudians were criticized for studying only disturbed individuals — neurotics and psychotics. If psychologists focused only on mental illness, how could they learn anything about mental health, about positive human qualities and characteristics? By disregarding attributes such as joyfulness, satisfaction, contentment, ecstasy, kindness, and generosity, and concentrating on the darker side of the human personality, psychology ignored all those distinctly human strengths and virtues. Thus it was in response to the limiting form of psychology promoted by both behaviorism and psychoanalysis that the humanistic psychologists advanced their alternative as the third force in psychology.

All aspects of uniquely human experience come under the purview of humanistic psychology: love, hate, fear, hope, happiness, humor, affection, responsibility, and the meaning of life. These aspects of human existence are not dealt with in many modern psychology textbooks, because they are not amenable to operational definition, quantification, or laboratory manipulation. Critics of humanistic psychology assert that its scope seems vague, but that is the nature of the movement. It is easier to describe what humanistic psychologists are against than what they are for or how they hope to achieve their goals. The term *humanistic psychology* has come to have many meanings, and it is "unlikely that an explicit definition of it could be written that would satisfy even a small fraction of the people who call themselves 'humanistic psychologists'" (Wertheimer, 1978, p. 743).

Because humanistic psychology, unlike early psychoanalysis, focused more on psychologically healthy persons than on those who are emotionally disturbed, its approach to therapy was different. Called growth therapy, part of the human potential movement, humanistic therapies proliferated in the 1960s and 1970s when millions of people enrolled in encounter groups and sensitivity training programs in schools, businesses, churches, prisons, and private clinics. The popularity of these programs has since declined dramatically.

Derived in part from the work of Kurt Lewin (Chapter 12), growth therapies were used with people of normal or average mental health to raise their levels of consciousness, help them relate better to themselves and to others, and release hidden potentials for creativity and self-development. In other words, the programs were designed to enhance psychological health and self-actualization.

Unfortunately, the human potential movement attracted more than its share of quacks, well-intentioned but untrained practitioners, and self-styled gurus and messiahs who did more harm than good. Studies of the aftereffects of participation in encounter groups revealed psychological casualty rates ranging from less than 1 percent to almost 50 percent (Hartley, Robach, & Abramowitz, 1976). Many people believe that encounter groups represented what humanistic psychology was all about, but the movement is much more than that. It is a serious study of human nature and conduct and is perhaps best expressed in the works of Abraham Maslow and Carl Rogers.

Abraham Maslow (1908–1970)

Abraham Maslow has been called the spiritual father of humanistic psychology and probably did more than anyone else to spark the movement and confer on it some degree of academic respectability. Maslow wanted to understand the highest achievements humans are capable of reaching, and so he studied a small sample of the psychologically healthiest people he could find, to determine how they differed from those of average mental health. Out of that study he developed a personality theory that focuses on the motivation to grow, develop, and actualize the self, to fulfill our human potentials and capabilities.

Born in Brooklyn, New York, Maslow had an unhappy childhood. His father was a distant and aloof womanizer and alcoholic who disappeared for long periods of time. His mother was intensely superstitious, and she punished the young Maslow for the slightest misbehavior, openly rejecting him in favor of her two younger children. She once killed two cats he had brought home, bashing their heads against the wall in front of him. He never forgave her attitude and behavior toward him, and when she died, he refused to attend her funeral. These experiences had a lifelong effect on Maslow. "The whole thrust of my life-philosophy," he wrote, "and all my research and theorizing . . . has its roots in a hatred for and revulsion against everything she stood for" (Hoffman, 1988, p. 9).

Maslow felt a sense of inferiority in childhood, because of his scrawny physique and large nose, and he characterized his adolescence as consisting of a giant inferiority complex, for which he tried to compensate by developing athletic skills. Thus, the man who later became interested in the work of Alfred Adler was himself an example of Adler's theory of

Abraham Maslow, the spiritual father of humanistic psychology, emphasized each person's capacity for self-actualization.

inferiority feelings and compensation. Maslow failed to gain acceptance and esteem on the athletic field, and turned to books and study instead. In that arena he excelled.

He enrolled at Cornell University, where he reported that his first psychology course was "awful and bloodless and had nothing to do with people, so I shuddered and turned away from it" (Hoffman, 1988, p. 26). Ironically, Maslow's professor for that course was E. B. Titchener, who even by then (1927) was still teaching only his own narrow form of structural psychology, ignoring the other schools of thought. Maslow transferred to the University of Wisconsin and received his Ph.D. in 1934.

Initially Maslow was an ardent behaviorist, convinced that the mechanistic natural-science approach provided answers to all the world's problems. Then a series of personal experiences, ranging from the birth of his first child to the start of World War II, plus exposure to other approaches to human nature (such as philosophy, Gestalt psychology, and Freudian psychoanalysis) persuaded him that behaviorism was too limited to be relevant to enduring human issues. Maslow was also influenced by his contact with some of the European psychologists who had fled Nazi Germany and settled in the United States—Alfred Adler, Karen Horney, Kurt Koffka, and Max Wertheimer. His feelings of awe toward Wertheimer and toward the American anthropologist Ruth Benedict led to his first study of psychologically healthy self-actualizing persons. Wertheimer and Benedict were Maslow's models of the best of human nature.

Working primarily at Brandeis University in Waltham, Massachusetts, from 1951 to 1969, Maslow developed and refined his theory in a series of provocative books. He supported the sensitivity group movement and became one of the most widely known psychologists of the 1960s. He was elected president of the APA in 1967.

In Maslow's view, each person possesses an innate tendency to become self-actualizing (Maslow, 1970). This highest level of human existence involves the supreme development and use of all our qualities and capacities, the realization of all our potential. To become self-actualizing, it is necessary to satisfy the needs that stand lower in Maslow's proposed *hierarchy of needs*. These needs are innate, and each must be satisfied in turn before the next need in the hierarchy emerges to motivate us. The needs are, in the order in which they must be satisfied, (1) the physiological needs for food, water, air, sleep, and sex, (2) the safety needs for security, stability, order, protection, and freedom from fear and anxiety, (3) the belonging and love needs, (4) the needs for esteem from others and from oneself, and (5) the need for self-actualization.

The bulk of Maslow's research focused on the characteristics of persons who have satisfied the need for self-actualization and are thus considered to be psychologically healthy. Maslow said that they make up fewer than one percent of the population. Such persons are free of neuroses and psychoses and are almost always middle-aged or older. They share the following characteristics: an objective perception of reality; a full acceptance of their own natures; a commitment and dedication to some kind of work; simplicity and naturalness in their behavior; a need for autonomy, privacy, and independence; mystical or peak experiences (moments of intense ecstasy, wonder, awe, and delight); empathy with and affection for all humanity; a resistance to conformity; a democratic character structure; an attitude of creativeness; and a high degree of social interest (a concept borrowed from Alfred Adler).

In this description Maslow offered an optimistic and flattering image of human nature, a view of psychological health and fulfillment that may be seen as a welcome antidote to the sickness, prejudice, and hostility we may find in our daily lives. Many people find it reassuring to believe that at least some of us are capable of reaching a state near perfection.

Maslow's research method and data have been criticized on the grounds that his sample of some two dozen people is too small to allow for generalizations. Also, his subjects were selected according to his own subjective criteria of psychological health, and his terms are defined ambiguously and inconsistently. Maslow agreed that his studies did not meet the requirements of scientific research, but he argued that there was no other way to study self-actualization. He referred to his research program as consisting of pilot studies, and he remained convinced that his conclusions would one day be confirmed.

The self-actualization theory has only limited empirical laboratory support; most research has failed to support the theory. It has been applied in business and industry, where many executives believe that the need for self-actualization is a useful motivating force and a potential source of job satisfaction. Despite its popularity with business leaders, the theory has a low degree of scientific validity and only limited applicability to the world of work. Maslow's theory has also been applied in other areas, including psychotherapy, education, and medicine.

Carl Rogers (1902–1987)

Carl Rogers is known for a popular approach to psychotherapy called *person-centered* or *client-centered therapy*. On the basis of data derived from his therapy, Rogers developed a personality theory that focuses on a single overriding motivation that is similar to Maslow's concept of self-actualization. Rogers proposed that each person possesses an innate tendency to actualize the abilities and potentials of the self. Unlike Maslow, however, Rogers's views were not formulated from the study of healthy people, but from the treatment of emotionally disturbed individuals through person-centered therapy.

The name of his therapy suggests something of his view of the human personality. By placing the responsibility for change on the person or client rather than on the therapist, as is the case in orthodox psychoanalysis, Rogers assumed that people can consciously and rationally alter their thoughts and behaviors from undesirable to desirable ones. He did not believe that people are controlled by unconscious forces or childhood experiences. Personality is shaped by the present and by how we consciously perceive it.

Rogers's idea that personality can be understood only in terms of our subjective experiences may reflect an incident in his own life. When he was twenty-two and attending a Christian student conference in China, he began to question his parents' fundamentalist religious beliefs and to develop a more liberal philosophy of life (see Rogers, 1967). He became convinced that people must depend on their own examination and interpretation of their own experiences. He also believed that people can consciously improve themselves. These concepts became cornerstones of his theory of personality. Over the course of an active career, Rogers

The person-centered approach to psychotherapy developed by Carl Rogers places the responsibility for change on the client rather than on the therapist.

developed his theory and his approach to psychotherapy, expressing his ideas in a number of popular articles and books.

Rogers suggested that the major motivating force in personality is the actualization of the self (Rogers, 1961). Although this urge toward self-actualization is innate, it can be helped or hindered by childhood experiences and by learning. Rogers emphasized the importance of the mother-child relationship as it affects the child's growing sense of self. If the mother satisfies the infant's need for love, which Rogers called *positive regard*, then the infant will tend to become a healthy personality. If the mother makes her love for her child conditional on proper behavior (called *conditional positive regard*, then the child will internalize the mother's attitude and develop *conditions of worth*. In that situation, the child feels a sense of self-worth only under certain conditions, and thus will avoid those behaviors that bring disapproval from the mother. As a result, the child's self is not allowed to develop fully, because it cannot express all of its aspects.

The primary requisite for the development of psychological health is *unconditional positive regard* in infancy. During that period the mother must demonstrate her love and acceptance of the child, regardless of the child's behavior. The child who receives such unconditional positive regard will not develop conditions of worth and will not have to repress any portion of the emerging self. Only in this way can self-actualization be achieved.

Self-actualization is the highest level of psychological health, and it is reached through a process Rogers called fully functioning. This level of supreme development in Rogers's theory is similar in principle to Maslow's proposed state of self-actualization. The two theories differ somewhat on the characteristics of the psychologically healthy or fully functioning person. To Rogers, fully functioning persons are characterized by an openness to all experience, a tendency to live fully in every moment, an ability to be guided by one's own instincts rather than by reason or the opinions of others, a sense of freedom in thought and action, and a high degree of creativity.

Rogers's person-centered approach to psychotherapy has had a great impact on psychology and on the general public, and it is at least as popular as Freudian psychoanalysis. His theory of personality has been well received, particularly its emphasis on the importance of the self. Criticism has been directed at the lack of specificity about the innate potential for self-actualization, and at the emphasis on subjective conscious experiences to the exclusion of possible unconscious influences. Both the theory and the therapy have generated considerable supportive research and are widely used in clinical settings. Rogers was influential in the human potential movement, and his work is seen as a major part of the trend toward humanizing psychology. He was elected president of the APA in 1946 and received their Distinguished Scientific Contribution Award and Distinguished Professional Contribution Award.

The Influence of Humanistic Psychology

Humanistic psychology displayed early in its development the same characteristics we have seen in every other new movement in the history of psychology. Its members were vocal in pointing out the weaknesses of the older positions, behaviorism and psychoanalysis, which were both solid bases against which to push. Many humanistic psychologists were zealous and filled with righteousness, prepared to do battle with the evils of the establishment.

The movement became formalized with the founding of the *Journal of Humanistic Psychology* in 1961, the American Association for Humanistic Psychology in 1962, and the Division of Humanistic Psychology of the American Psychological Association in 1971. Thus the distinguishing traits of a cohesive school of thought were evident. Humanistic psychologists offered their own definition of psychology, distinct from the other two forces in the field, and described their own subject matter, methods, and terminology. Above all they possessed what every other school of thought boasted in its early days: a passionate conviction that theirs was the best path for psychology to follow.

Despite these symbols and characteristics of a school of thought, humanistic psychology did not actually become a school. That was the judgment of humanistic psychologists themselves at a 1985 meeting, nearly three decades after the movement began. "Humanistic psychology was a great experiment," one said, "but it is basically a failed experiment in that there is no humanistic school of thought in psychology, no theory that would be recognized as a philosophy of science" (Cunningham, 1985, p. 18).

Carl Rogers agreed. "Humanistic psychology has not had a significant impact on mainstream psychology," he said. "We are perceived as having relatively little importance" (Cunningham, 1985, p. 16). Rogers told his supporters that if they wanted evidence for his statement they had only to examine any introductory psychology textbook. There they would find the same topics that characterized psychology twenty-five years before, with little mention of the whole person. A review of current textbooks revealed that Rogers was correct. Fewer than one percent of the books' contents dealt with humanistic psychology. What little coverage there was focused on Maslow's hierarchy of needs and Rogers's person-centered therapy (Churchill, 1988).

Why didn't humanistic psychology become part of the mainstream of psychological thought? One reason is that most humanistic psychologists are in private clinical practice, rather than at universities. Unlike academic psychologists, humanistic psychologists have not, to the same extent, conducted research or published papers or trained new generations of graduate students to carry on their tradition.

Another reason has to do with the timing of their protest. At their peak, the 1960s and early 1970s, humanistic psychologists were attacking positions that were no longer so influential within psychology. Both

Freudian psychoanalysis and Skinnerian behaviorism had already been tempered and weakened by divisiveness within their ranks, and both were already beginning to change in the direction urged by the humanistic psychologists. Like the Gestalt psychologists when they first came to the United States, the humanistic psychologists in the 1960s were arguing against movements that were no longer dominant in their original form.

Although humanistic psychology has not transformed the field as a whole, it did reinforce the idea within psychoanalysis that we can consciously and freely choose to shape our own lives. It may have helped to strengthen the growing recognition of consciousness in academic psychology, because it was contemporaneous with the cognitive movement. Humanistic psychology fostered methods of therapy that emphasize self-actualization, personal responsibility, and freedom of choice, and the consideration of the person within the context of the family, work, and social environments. Humanistic psychology helped to expand and ratify changes already taking place, and from that standpoint, the movement may be called successful.

The Cognitive Movement in Psychology

"Psychology," wrote John B. Watson in his behaviorist manifesto of 1913, "must discard all reference to consciousness." The psychologists who followed Watson's dictates eliminated all references to the mind and conscious processes, and banished mentalistic terms. Banned were will, feeling, image, mind, and consciousness, never to be uttered except in tones of derision. And so B. F. Skinner could talk about an empty organism and build an influential system of psychology that never attempted to investigate what might be going on inside. For decades introductory textbooks in psychology did not discuss any conception of the human mind. It appeared that psychology had "lost consciousness" forever.

Suddenly, or so it seemed, although it had been building for some time, psychology began to regain its consciousness. The once taboo words were being uttered aloud in meetings and conferences and appearing in print in the professional journals. In 1979 the *American Psychologist* published an article entitled "Behaviorism and the Mind: A (Limited) Call for a Return to Introspection" (Lieberman, 1979), invoking not only mind but also the suspect technique of introspection. A few months earlier the same journal had published an article with the simple title "Consciousness," blatantly and openly displayed. "After decades of deliberate neglect," its author wrote, "consciousness is again coming under scientific scrutiny, with discussions of the topic appearing at entirely respectable locations in psychology's literature" (Natsoulas, 1978, p. 906). The president of the American Psychological Association, delivering his annual address, told the assembled audience that the conception of psychology was changing and that the change involved a return to consciousness. As a result, psychology's image of human nature was becoming "human rather than mechanical" (McKeachie, 1976, p. 831).

When an officer of the APA and a prestigious journal discuss consciousness so optimistically, we might suspect that a new movement, another revolution, is under way. Revisions in introductory textbooks followed, defining psychology as the science of "behavior and mental processes" instead of just behavior, and as the science that "systematically studies and attempts to explain observable behavior and its relationship to the unseen mental processes that go on inside the organism" (Hilgard, Atkinson, & Atkinson, 1975, p. 12; Kagan & Havemann, 1972, p. 9). These definitions show us how far contemporary psychology has moved beyond the desires and the designs of Watson and Skinner.

Antecedent Influences on Cognitive Psychology

Like all movements in psychology, the cognitive revolution did not spring up overnight. Many of its basic features had been anticipated by the work of others. Indeed, it has been suggested that "cognitive psychology is both the newest and the oldest strand in the history of the subject" (Hearnshaw, 1987, p. 272). What this means is that interest in consciousness was shown in the earliest days of psychology, even before it became a formal science. The writings of Plato and Aristotle deal with cognitive faculties and processes, as do the theories of the British empiricists and associationists.

Even when psychology became a separate scientific discipline, the focus remained on consciousness. Wilhelm Wundt has been called a forerunner of cognitive psychology because of his emphasis on the constructive or creative activity of the mind. Structuralism and functionalism dealt with consciousness, focusing on its elements in one case and its functions in the other. Behaviorism brought about a fundamental change, banishing consciousness from the field for nearly fifty years.

The return to consciousness, the beginnings of cognitive psychology, can be traced to the 1950s, although signs of the resurgence of the mind were noticed as early as the 1930s. One of the earliest proponents was E. R. Guthrie (Chapter 11), who for most of his career was an ardent behaviorist. Toward the end of his life, however, he came to deplore the mechanistic model and argued that stimuli cannot always be reduced to physical terms. We must describe the stimuli with which psychology deals in perceptual or cognitive terms, he suggested, so that they will be meaningful for the responding organism. Psychologists cannot deal with meaning solely in behaviorist terms, because it is a mentalistic or conscious process.

The purposive behaviorism of E. C. Tolman (which is a molar approach) was another precursor of the cognitive movement. His form of behaviorism recognized the importance of cognitive variables and contributed to the decline of the stimulus-response approach. Tolman proposed the notion of cognitive maps, attributed purpose to animals, and emphasized intervening variables as a way of operationally defining internal, unobservable states.

Rudolf Carnap, a positivist philosopher, called for a return to introspection. In 1956 Carnap noted that "a person's awareness of his own state of imagining, feeling, et cetera, must be recognized as a kind of observation, in principle not different from external observation, and therefore as a legitimate source of knowledge" (Koch, 1964, p. 22). Even P. W. Bridgman, the physicist who gave psychology the notion of operational definitions that was so compatible with behaviorism, later renounced behaviorism. Bridgman insisted that introspective reports from individual subjects be invoked to give meaning to operational analyses.

Some psychologists see Gestalt psychology as an influence on the cognitive movement. The "emphasis on organization, structure, relationships, the active role of the subject, and the important part played by perception in learning and memory — reflects the influence of its Gestalt antecedents" (Hearst, 1979, p. 32). Gestalt psychology helped keep alive at least a peripheral interest in consciousness during the years when behaviorism was dominant.

Another antecedent of the cognitive movement is the Swiss psychologist Jean Piaget (1896–1980), who produced important work on the development of the child, not in terms of psychosexual or psychosocial stages (as proposed by Freud and Erikson), but in terms of cognitive stages. Piaget's initial formulations, published in the 1920s and 1930s, were highly influential in Europe, although less so in the United States, where they were not compatible with the dominant behaviorist position. However, Piaget's emphasis on cognitive factors was welcomed by early proponents of the cognitive movement. As the ideas of the cognitive psychologists took hold in the United States, the relevance of Piaget's work became more apparent; in 1969 Piaget became the first European psychologist to receive the APA's Distinguished Scientific Contribution Award. Because his work focused on the development of the child, it helped broaden the range of behavior to which the growing cognitive psychology could be applied.

The Swiss psychologist Jean Piaget proposed a theory of child development that focused on cognitive processes.

When we find a major shift in the evolution of a science, we know that it is reflecting changes already under way in the Zeitgeist in which it functions. As we have seen, a science, like a living species, adapts to new demands and conditions in its environment. What was the intellectual climate that led to the cognitive movement, that dictated a tempering of behaviorism by the readmission of consciousness? We may look to the Zeitgeist in physics, often a role model for psychology, which has influenced the field of psychology since its beginnings as a science.

Early in the twentieth century a new viewpoint was developing in physics as a result of the work of Albert Einstein, Neils Bohr, Werner Heisenberg, and others. Their approach rejected the Galilean-Newtonian mechanistic model of the universe, the model from which psychology drew its mechanistic, reductionistic, lawful, and predictable view of human nature expounded by psychologists from Wundt to Skinner. The new look in physics discarded the classical world of total objectivity and the complete separation of the external world from the observer. This new model had important implications for psychology.

Physicists came to recognize that we cannot observe the course of nature without disturbing it. The artificial gap between the observer and the observed, the inner world and the outer world, the world of conscious experience and the world of matter, was thus bridged. The focus of scientific investigation shifted from an independent and objectively knowable universe to our observation of that universe. Modern scientists, no longer detached from the focus of their observation, would become participant-observers.

The ideal of a totally objective reality was seen as unattainable. Today physics is characterized by the belief that what we call objective knowledge is actually subjective, that is, it is dependent on the observer. This position that all knowledge is personal sounds suspiciously like what George Berkeley proposed some two hundred years ago—that all knowledge is subjective because it depends on the nature of the person perceiving it (Chapter 2). One writer described that situation in these terms: our picture of the world, "far from being a genuine photographic reproduction of an independent reality 'out there,' [is] rather more on the order of a painting: a subjective creation of the mind which can convey a likeness but can never produce a replica" (Matson, 1964, p. 137).

The physicists' rejection of an objective, machine-like subject matter and their recognition of subjectivity restored the vital role of conscious experience in obtaining our knowledge of the world. This revolution in physics was an effective argument for the acceptance of consciousness as a legitimate part of the subject matter of psychology. Although scientific psychology resisted the new physics for a half-century, clinging to an outdated model by defining itself as an objective science of behavior, it eventually responded to the Zeitgeist and modified its form to readmit the role of consciousness.

The Founding of Cognitive Psychology

A retrospective look at the cognitive movement gives the impression of a logical and rapid transition, something on the order of a revolution, that shook the foundations of the psychological world in only a few short years. At the time, of course, that was not at all apparent. This dramatic change in psychology emerged slowly and quietly, with no beating drums and no fanfare. Indeed, "no one announced its existence until long after the fact" (Baars, 1986, p. 141). The progression of history is often clear only after the event. We noted that the founding of cognitive psychology did not take place overnight, nor could it be attributed to the force and persuasiveness of a single founder who, like John B. Watson, changed the field almost singlehandedly. Like functional psychology, the cognitive psychology movement can lay no claim to a solitary founder, perhaps, in part (again, like functionalism), because none of those working in the area had the personal ambition to lead a new movement. They were simply interested in getting on with the work of redefining psychology.

However, two people can be identified who, while not founders in the formal sense of the term, did contribute seminal work in the form of an important research center and a major book, considered to be milestones in the development of the new cognitive psychology. They are George Miller and Ulric Neisser, and their stories illustrate some of the personal factors involved in shaping new movements.

George Miller (1920–   )

George Miller began his career by majoring in English and speech at the University of Alabama; he received his M.A. in speech in 1941. While a student at Alabama, he expressed an interest in psychology. He was given an instructorship to teach sixteen sections of introductory psychology, having never taken a course in the field. He said that after teaching the same material sixteen times each week, he began to believe it himself.

Miller went on to Harvard University, where he worked on problems in vocal communication at the psychoacoustic laboratory, and in 1946 he received his Ph.D. He embarked on the study of psycholinguistics, publishing *Language and Communication* in 1951. Miller accepted the dominant behaviorist position, noting that he had little choice because behaviorists held all the leadership positions in the major universities and professional organizations. "The power," he wrote, "the honors, the authority, the textbooks, the money, everything in psychology was owned by the behavior-

George Miller established a research center at Harvard University to investigate cognitive issues such as language, perception, and concept formation.

istic school. . . . those of us who wanted to be scientific psychologists couldn't really oppose it. You just wouldn't get a job" (Baars, 1986, p. 203).

By the mid-1950s, after delving into statistical learning theory, information theory, and early attempts to simulate the human mind with computers, Miller reached the conclusion that behaviorism was not, as he put it, "going to work out." The similarities between the operations of computers and the human mind impressed him, and his interests began to shift to a more cognitively oriented psychology. At the same time, an allergy to animal hair and dander meant that he could not conduct research with laboratory rats. He had to work only with human subjects, a disadvantage in a world dominated by behaviorists.

In addition, Miller's move toward a cognitive psychology was helped by his rebellious spirit, which he said typified many of his generation of psychologists. He and a growing number of others were ready to rebel against the kind of psychology then being taught and practiced and to offer a new approach, one that would focus on cognitive rather than behavioral factors.

Together with a colleague, Jerome Bruner (1915-   ), who had studied with William McDougall, Miller decided to establish a research center for the investigation of the human mind. They asked the president of Harvard for space, and in 1960 they were given a house in which William James had once lived, an appropriate location because James had dealt so exquisitely with the nature of mental life.

The choice of a name for the new enterprise was not a trivial matter. Being at Harvard, it would have the potential for exerting an enormous impact on psychology, indeed, for defining a new psychology. Miller and Bruner chose the word *cognition* to denote their subject matter, and they called the new facility the Center for Cognitive Studies. Miller said:

> In using the word "cognition" we were setting ourselves off from behaviorism. We wanted something that was *mental* — but "mental psychology" seemed terribly redundant. "Common-sense psychology" would have suggested some sort of anthropological investigation, and "folk psychology" would have suggested Wundt's social psychology. What word do you use to label this set of views? We chose cognition. (Baars, 1986, p. 210)

Two of the early students at the center recalled that no one there could tell them what the word *cognition* really meant or what they were supposed to be in favor of. The center, they said, "was not set up to be for anything in particular; it was set up to be against things. What was important was what it was not" (Norman & Levelt, 1988, p. 101).

It was not behaviorism. It was not the ruling authority, the establishment, the psychology of the present. In defining the Center, its founders were demonstrating how sharply they differed from behaviorism. And as we have seen with every new movement, proclaiming how their position or attitude differs from the ongoing school of thought is a necessary preliminary stage to later defining what they are all about and how they propose to change the field.

Despite the revolutionary nature and ardor, Miller did not believe that cognitive psychology was a true revolution. He called it an "accretion," that is, an increase or change by growth or accumulation. He saw the movement as more evolutionary than revolutionary and believed that it was a return to a common-sense psychology, one that recognizes and affirms that psychology must deal with mental life as well as behavior.

A wide range of topics were investigated at the Center, including language, memory, perception, concept formation, thinking, and developmental psychology, most of which were taboo in the lexicon of the behaviorists. Miller later established the program for cognitive sciences and the laboratory of cognitive sciences at Princeton University, where he continues to work.

In recognition of his efforts, Miller became president of the American Psychological Association in 1969 and received their Distinguished Scientific Contribution Award and the Gold Medal Award for Life Achievement in the Application of Psychology. Perhaps the greater acknowledgment of his work can be found in the number of laboratories and institutes of cognitive psychology that followed his and in the rapid development of the approach to psychology that he did so much to define.

Ulric Neisser (1928–   )

Born in Kiel, Germany, Ulric Neisser was brought to the United States by his parents at the age of three. He began his college studies at Harvard, majoring in physics. Impressed with a young professor by the name of George Miller, Neisser decided that physics did not "sing" to him and switched to psychology. He took an honors course with Miller dealing with the psychology of communications, and was introduced to information theory and other aspects of the early cognitive approach. He was also influenced by Kurt Koffka's book *Principles of Gestalt Psychology*.

After receiving his B.A. from Harvard in 1950, Neisser took his master's degree at Swarthmore College, studying under Wolfgang Köhler. He returned to Harvard for his Ph.D., which he received in 1956. Despite his growing interest in cognitive factors, he saw no escape from the grip of behaviorism on an academic career. "It was what you had to learn," he said. "That was the age when it was supposed that no psychological phenomenon was real unless you could demonstrate it in a rat. To establish whether there was such a thing as thinking, for example, one attempted to show that rats thought. A very peculiar enterprise, it seemed to me" (Baars, 1986, p. 275).

Ulric Neisser, whose 1967 book on cognitive psychology helped launch the new movement, later came to criticize the field for its narrowness and artificiality.

Neisser found behaviorism not only peculiar but "crazy" as well, and it was fortunate that his first academic job was at Brandeis University, where the head of the psychology department was Abraham Maslow. At the time, Maslow was beginning to move away from his own behaviorist training and develop a humanistic approach to the field. Maslow was not successful in turning Neisser into a humanistic psychologist, or in turning humanistic psychology into psychology's third force — Neisser later contended that cognitive psychology was the third force — but he did provide an opportunity for Neisser to pursue his interests in cognitive matters.

In 1967 Neisser published *Cognitive Psychology*, a book that "established and christened the field" (Goleman, 1983, p. 54). He reported that the book was a personal one, really an attempt to define himself, that is, the kind of psychologist he was and wanted to be. The book also helped to define a new psychology. It became extremely popular, and Neisser was embarrassed to find himself introduced as the "father" of cognitive psychology. He had no desire to found a school of thought, but his book nevertheless helped to push psychology away from behaviorism and toward cognition.

Neisser defined cognition in reference to those processes "by which the sensory input is transformed, reduced, elaborated, stored, recovered, and used.... cognition is involved in everything a human being might possibly do" (Neisser, 1967, p. 4). Thus, cognitive psychology is concerned with sensation, perception, imaging, retention, recall, problem solving, thinking, and all other mental activities.

Nine years after writing the book that launched the field, Neisser published *Cognition and Reality* (1976), in which he expressed his dissatisfaction with what he saw as the narrowing of the cognitive position and its tendency to stress artificial laboratory situations instead of the real world. He became disillusioned, concluding that the cognitive psychology movement as then constituted had little to do with providing an understanding of how human beings deal with reality. And so Neisser, one of the most important figures in the founding of cognitive psychology, became its vocal critic, challenging it as he had earlier challenged behaviorism. He currently teaches at Emory University in Atlanta, Georgia, after spending seventeen years at Cornell, where his office was not far from the pickled brain of E. B. Titchener.

The Role of the Computer in Cognitive Psychology

Clocks and automata served in the seventeenth century as metaphors for the mechanical view of the universe and, by extension, for the human mind (see Chapter 2). Those machines were readily available and easily understood models of the way in which the mind was said to operate. Today, the mechanical model of the universe and the behavioral psychology that derived from it have been superseded by other viewpoints, namely, the new look in physics and the cognitive movement in psychology.

It is apparent that the clock is no longer a useful example for the twentieth-century view of the mind. A new metaphor is required, and a twentieth-century machine, the computer, has emerged to serve as the model. The computer is increasingly being used as a way of explaining cognitive phenomena. Computers are said to display artificial intelligence, and their functioning is often described in human terms. The storage capacity of a computer, for example, is its memory, programming codes are called languages, and newer generations of computers are said to be evolving (Campbell, 1988; Roszak, 1986).

Computer programs — essentially sets of instructions for dealing with symbols — may be said to operate similarly to the human mind. Both the computer and the mind receive and digest large amounts of information (stimuli) from the environment. They process this information, manipulating, storing, and retrieving it, and acting on it in various ways. Thus, computer programming is the pattern for the cognitive view of human information processing, reasoning, and problem solving. It is the program, not the computer itself (the software, not the hardware), that serves as the explanation for mental operations. Cognitive psychologists are interested not in any physiological correlates of mental processes but in the sequence of symbol manipulation that underlies thought. Their goal is to discover that "library of programs the human has stored away in memory — programs that enabled the person to understand and produce sentences, to commit certain experiences and rules to memory, and to solve novel problems" (Howard, 1983, p. 11).

This information-processing view of the human mind underlies cognitive psychology. In the more than one hundred years of its history, psychology has moved from clocks to computers as models for its subject matter, but it is significant that both are machines. This demonstrates the historical continuity in the evolution of psychology between older and newer views. "For psychologists, always looking for reassurances that their theories refer to some physically possible reality, the lure of machine metaphors is well-nigh irresistible" (Baars, 1986, p. 154). We are left to wonder whether the expression, "the more things change, the more they remain the same," contains a lesson about history for those who try to learn from it.

The Nature of Cognitive Psychology

We described how the introduction of cognitive factors in the social learning theories of Albert Bandura and Julian Rotter tempered the nature of American behaviorism (Chapter 11). But it is not only in behavioral psychology that the cognitive movement has had an impact. Cognitive factors are being considered in virtually every other area of the field: attribution theory in social psychology, cognitive dissonance theory, motivation and emotion, personality, learning, memory, perception, and, as we noted, the information-processing approach to decision making and problem solving. In applied areas such as clinical, community, industrial/organizational, and school psychology, there is also an emphasis on cognitive factors.

Cognitive psychology differs from behaviorism on several issues. First, cognitive psychologists focus on the process of knowing, rather than simply responding to stimuli. The emphasis is on mental processes and events, not stimulus-response connections, on the mind rather than on behavior. This does not mean that cognitive psychologists ignore behavior. What it does mean is that behavioral responses are not the sole objects of research. Responses are used as sources for inference about the mental processes that accompany them.

Second, cognitive psychologists are interested in how the mind structures or organizes experience. The Gestalt psychologists, as well as Jean Piaget, argued that the tendency to organize conscious experience (sensations and perceptions) into meaningful wholes and patterns is innate. The mind gives form and coherence to mental experience, and it is this process of organizing that is the subject matter of cognitive psychology. The British empiricists and associationists, and their twentieth-century derivatives the Skinnerian behaviorists, held that the mind possesses no such inherent organizational abilities.

Third, in the cognitive view the individual is actively and creatively arranging the stimuli received from the environment. We are capable of participating in the acquisition and use of knowledge, deliberately attending to some aspects of experience and choosing to commit them to memory. We are not passive responders to external forces or blank slates on which sensory experience will write. You will recognize the latter idea as the behaviorist position derived from the empiricists and associationists.

We noted above the many research areas influenced by the cognitive movement. In one of these areas, sleep and dreaming, experimental studies have identified REM (rapid eye movement) sleep as the stage at which most dreaming occurs; this work provides an excellent example of the combination of objective physiological data with subjective conscious data. Dreams are conscious products, and their demonstrated relationship to underlying physiological processes makes such subjective data more acceptable within psychology today. These consciously recalled experiences would not have been admitted within the strict behaviorist framework.

Cognitive researchers investigating information processing during sleep are dealing with such phenomena as the transferral to sleep of conditioned responses acquired while awake, the effect of verbal suggestions made during sleep, and the attempt to improve performance through learning that occurs during sleep (Bootzin, Kihlstrom, & Schacter, 1990). These, too, are cognitive experiences that could not have been discussed, much less seriously studied, under behaviorism.

Psychologists are also studying the effects of drugs on behavior in terms of changes in both physiological responses and reported conscious experiences — on what individuals do under the influence of drugs as well as what they say they feel. These data were also inadmissible to the behaviorists. Even such nonconscious processes as biofeedback, in which persons learn to control physiological functions such as heart rate, muscle tension, and body temperature, may rely more on cognitive processes than was previously supposed. Therapists using biofeedback are paying closer attention to the role of patients' goals and expectations in bringing about the desired physiological changes.

As the study of conscious mental processes has returned to psychology, that has fostered interest in unconscious mental processes, another area banned by the behaviorists. Research on such topics as selective attention, hypnosis, subliminal perception, and visual phenomena involving perceptual processing suggests that the first stage of cognition in response to stimulation is unconscious (Kihlstrom, 1987; Shevrin & Dickman, 1980).

Under the impact of the cognitive movement, consciousness is once again being attributed to animals. Research on animal cognition infers evidence of animal consciousness from observations of behavior, particularly behavior that shows adaptability to changing environmental conditions (Domjan, 1987; Pearce, 1987). This work focuses on the ability of animals to think about specific objects and events, even when those objects and events are not present, and to initiate some action. Other work has demonstrated that mental processes — such as coding and organizing symbols — exist in animal memory, as does the ability to form basic abstractions about space, time, and number (Gallistel, 1989; Roitblat, Bever, & Terrace, 1984).

With the cognitive influence in experimental psychology and the emphasis on consciousness in humanistic psychology and post-Freudian psychoanalysis, we can see that consciousness has reclaimed the central position in psychology that it held one hundred years ago. It has made a substantial and vigorous comeback.

Comment

The cognitive movement has obviously been a success. By the early 1970s, the field had attracted so many followers that it needed its own journals.

Within a decade six new journals were established: *Cognitive Psychology* (1970), *Cognition* (1971), *Memory and Cognition* (1983), *Journal of Mental Imagery* (1977), *Cognitive Therapy and Research* (1977), and *Cognitive Science* (1977).

Jerome Bruner has described cognitive psychology as "a revolution whose limits we still cannot fathom" (Bruner, 1983, p. 274). Its impact has extended to most areas of psychology and has moved beyond the United States to influence psychological thought in Europe and the Soviet Union. It has also moved beyond psychology itself. "Perhaps the most exciting recent development growing out of the cognitive revolution is a new trend toward integrating all the major disciplines concerned with studying the nature of knowledge" (Baars, 1986, p. 180).

This proposed new perspective, dubbed "cognitive science," is an amalgamation of cognitive psychology, linguistics, anthropology, philosophy, computer sciences, artificial intelligence, and the neurosciences. Although George Miller has questioned how unified such disparate fields of study can become, suggesting that they be spoken of in the plural as cognitive sciences, there is no denying the growth of this multidisciplinary approach. Laboratories and institutes of cognitive science have been established at universities throughout the United States, and some psychology departments have been renamed cognitive science departments. All this suggests that, by whatever name, the study of mental phenomena and processes may dominate not only psychology, but other disciplines as well, through the 1990s and into the twenty-first century.

No revolution, however successful, is without its critics. Most Skinnerian behaviorists oppose the cognitive movement (Skinner, 1987b, 1989), and even those who support it have pointed out weaknesses and limitations. They argue that there are few concepts on which the majority of cognitive psychologists agree, or even consider important, and that there is considerable confusion about terminology and definitions. Another criticism relates to what some see as an overemphasis on cognition at the expense of other influences on thought and behavior, such as motivation and emotion. The number of professional books and articles on motivation and emotion has declined sharply over the past two decades, while the literature on cognition has increased (Pervin, 1985). The result, as Ulric Neisser suggested, is a narrowing and a sterility of the field. Neisser commented that "human thinking is passionate and emotional, people operate from complex motives. A computer program, by contrast . . . has no emotion and is monomaniacal in its singlemindedness" (Goleman, 1983, p. 57). There is the danger that cognitive psychology is becoming too one-sided, focusing only on thought to the same extent that the previous school focused only on behavior.

Other critics charge that the progress of cognitive psychology is more illusory than real, because many psychologists have simply adopted the words *cognitive* or *cognition* without making any fundamental changes in the way they approach their research problems. B. F. Skinner noted that it had become "fashionable to insert the word 'cognitive' wherever possible" (Skinner, 1983b, p. 194). George Miller agrees:

> What seems to have happened is that many experimental psychologists who were studying human learning, perception, or thinking began to call themselves cognitive psychologists without changing in any obvious way what they had always been thinking and doing — as if they suddenly discovered they had been speaking cognitive psychology all their lives. So our victory may have been more modest than the written record would have led you to believe. (Bruner, 1983, p. 126)

Cognitive psychology is not yet complete; it is not yet history. The movement is still forming, growing, and developing, still history in the making. It is too soon to judge its ultimate impact and contribution. But cognitive psychology does have the trappings and characteristics that define each of the earlier schools of thought. Cognitive psychology has its own journals, laboratories, meetings, jargon, and convictions, as well as the zeal of the righteous. We now speak of cogniti*vism*, as we do of functionalism and behaviorism. Cognitive psychology has become what other schools of thought became in their time, part of the mainstream of psychology. And that, as we have seen, is the natural progression of revolutions and movements when they become successful.

A Final Note

If the history of psychology as portrayed in these chapters tells us anything at all, it is that when a movement becomes formalized into a school, it gains a momentum that can be stopped only by its own success in overthrowing the established position. When that happens, the unobstructed arteries of the once vigorous and youthful movement begin to harden. Flexibility turns to rigidity, revolutionary passion to protection of position, and eyes and minds begin to close to new ideas. And in this way a new establishment is born. So it is in the progress of any science, an evolutionary building to ever-higher levels of development. There is no culmination — no finish, no end — but a never-ending process of growth, as newer species evolve from older ones and attempt to adapt to a continually changing environment.

Suggested Readings

Women in the History of Psychology

Hollingworth, H. L. (1990). *Leta Stetter Hollingworth: A Biography*. Bolton MA: Anker Publishing. A reprint of Harry Hollingworth's biography of Leta Stetter Hollingworth, recounting her life and her pioneering work on the psychology of women.

O'Connell, A. N., & Russo, N. F. (1983). *Models of Achievement: Reflections of Eminent Women in Psychology*. New York: Columbia University Press. (1988). *Models of Achievement: Reflections of Eminent Women in Psychology* (Vol. 2). Hillsdale NJ: Erlbaum. Contains autobiographical sketches of women who have made significant contributions to psychology. Presents data on patterns of achievement and analyzes the impact of such factors as birthplace, family characteristics, marital status and children, graduate education, employment opportunities, mentors, and social networks.

Scarborough, E., & Furumoto, L. (1987). *Untold Lives: The First Generation of American Women Psychologists*. New York: Columbia University Press. Examines the barriers to careers in psychology for women, such as limited opportunities for graduate education and for jobs, demands of family and marriage, and discrimination by male colleagues; discusses the experiences of Mary Whiton Calkins, Margaret Floy Washburn, and Christine Ladd-Franklin, among others.

African-Americans in the History of Psychology

Guthrie, R. V. (1976). *Even the Rat Was White: A Historical View of Psychology*. New York: Harper & Row. Documents the history of American psychology from a black perspective. Covers the contributions of black psychologists and various psychological theories about the abilities of blacks.

Urban, W. J. (1989). The black scholar and intelligence testing: The case of Horace Mann Bond. *Journal of the History of the Behavioral Sciences, 25*, 323–334. Considers the problem of racism in intelligence testing and the role of Horace Mann Bond in the debate about the interpretation of IQ scores of blacks and whites.

Abraham Maslow

Hoffman, E. (1988). *The Right to Be Human: A Biography of Abraham Maslow*. Los Angeles: Tarcher. A major biography based on published and unpublished works (including diaries, correspondence, and extensive interviews), describing Maslow's difficult childhood and tracing his career from his early work with primates to his involvement with the human-potential movement.

Maddi, S. R., & Costa, P. T. (1972). *Humanism in Personology: Allport, Maslow, and Murray*. New York: Aldine-Atherton. A clear presentation of the background and work of these three psychologists, explaining the similarities and differences among their theories as well as the influence of events from their early lives.

Maslow, A. H. (1968). *Toward a Psychology of Being* (2nd ed.). New York: Van Nostrand Reinhold. States Maslow's view that humans can be loving, noble, and creative as well as capable of pursuing the highest values and aspirations.

Carl Rogers

Evans, R. I. (1975). *Carl Rogers: The Man and His Ideas.* New York: Dutton. Presents interviews with Rogers covering the evolution of the self, techniques of person-centered therapy, and applications of his humanistic psychology to education.

Kirschenbaum, H. (1979). *On Becoming Carl Rogers.* New York: Delacorte. A biographical sketch of Rogers and an account of his contributions to humanistic psychology.

Rogers, C. R. (1967). Autobiography. In E. G. Boring & G. Lindzey (Eds.), *A History of Psychology in Autobiography* (Vol. 5). New York: Appleton-Century-Crofts. Presents Rogers's assessment of his work and the influence of his early experiences.

The Cognitive Movement in Psychology

Baars, B. J. (1986). *The Cognitive Revolution in Psychology.* New York: Guilford Press. Discusses the historical/philosophical background of behaviorism and the transition from post-Watsonian behaviorism to cognitive psychology. Includes transcripts of interviews with George Miller, Ulric Neisser, and others influential in the cognitive revolution.

Kihlstrom, J. F. (1987, September 18). The cognitive unconscious. *Science, 237,* 1445–1452. Describes the information-processing model of cognitive functioning and considers research on subliminal perception, implicit memory, and hypnosis.

Rachlin, H. (1989). *Judgment, Decision, and Choice: A Cognitive/Behavioral Synthesis.* New York: Freeman. A readable and scholarly attempt to reconcile the behavioral and cognitive approaches to psychology, focusing on problems in learning, problem solving, and decision making.

Skinner, B. F. (1987). Whatever happened to psychology as the science of behavior? *American Psychologist, 42,* 780–786. Presents Skinner's view that humanistic psychology, psychotherapy, and cognitive psychology are "obstacles" standing in the way of psychology's acceptance of his program for the experimental analysis of behavior.

References

Abel, T. M. (1989). Some famous psychologists I have known. *History of Psychology Newsletter, 21*(2), 53–55.

Adams, G. (1928, December). The decline of psychology in America. *American Mercury*, pp. 450–454.

Adams, G. R., & Fitch, S. A. (1982). Ego stage and identity status development: A cross-sequential analysis. *Journal of Personality and Social Psychology, 43*, 574–583.

Adler, A. (1930). Individual psychology. In C. Murchison (Ed.), *Psychologies of 1930* (pp. 395–405). Worcester MA: Clark University Press.

Allen, G. W. (1967). *William James*. New York: Viking Press.

Allport, G. W. (1937). *Personality: A psychological interpretation*. New York: Holt.

Allport, G. W. (1968). *The person in psychology*. Boston: Beacon Press.

Altman, I. (1987). Centripetal and centrifugal trends in psychology. *American Psychologist, 42*, 1058–1069.

Amsel, A., & Rashotte, M. E. (Eds.). (1984). *Mechanisms of adaptive behavior: Clark L. Hull's theoretical papers with commentary*. New York: Columbia University Press.

Anderson, R. J. (1980). Wundt's prominence and popularity in his later years. *Psychological Research, 42*, 87–101.

Angell, J. R. (1904). *Psychology*. New York: Holt.

Angell, J. R. (1907). The province of functional psychology. *Psychological Review, 14*, 61–91.

Archer, S. L. (1982). The lower age boundaries of identity development. *Child Development, 53*, 1551–1556.

Ash, M. G. (1987). Psychology and politics in interwar Vienna: The Vienna Psychological Institute, 1922–1942. In M. G. Ash & W. R. Woodward (Eds.), *Psychology in twentieth-century thought and society* (pp. 143–164). Cambridge, England: Cambridge University Press.

Averill, L. A. (1990). Recollections of Clark's G. Stanley Hall. *Journal of the History of the Behavioral Sciences, 26*, 125–130.

Baars, B. J. (1986). *The cognitive revolution in psychology*. New York: Guilford Press.

Balance, W. D. G., & Bringmann, W. G. (1987). Fechner's mysterious malady. *History of Psychology Newsletter, 19*(1,2), 36–47.

Baldwin, B. T. (Ed.). (1980). In memory of Wilhelm Wundt. In W. G. Bringmann & R. D. Tweney (Eds.), *Wundt studies: A centennial collection* (pp. 280–308). Toronto: C. J. Hogrefe. (Original work published 1921.)

Bandura, A. (1986). *Social foundations of thought and action: A social cognitive theory*. Englewood Cliffs NJ: Prentice-Hall.

Becker, E. (1973). *The denial of death*. New York: Free Press.

Beers, C. (1908). *A mind that found itself*. London: Longmans, Green.

Bekhterev, V. M. (1932). *General principles of human reflexology*. New York: International Publishers.

Belmont, L., & Marolla, F. A. (1973). Birth order, family size and intelligence. *Science, 182*, 1096–1101.

Ben-David, J., & Collins, R. (1966). Social factors in the origin of a new science: The case of psychology. *American Sociological Review, 31*, 451–465.

Benjamin, L. T., Jr. (1975). The pioneering work of Leta Hollingworth in the psychology of women. *Nebraska History, 56*, 493–505.

Benjamin, L. T., Jr. (1986). Why don't they understand us? A history of psychology's public image. *American Psychologist, 41*, 941–946.

Benjamin, L. T., Jr. (1987). Knee jerks, Twitmyer, and the Eastern Psychological Association. *American Psychologist, 42*, 1118–1120.

Benjamin, L. T., Jr. (1988a). E. B. Titchener and structuralism. In L. T. Benjamin, Jr. (Ed.), *A history of psychology: Original sources and contemporary research* (pp. 208–211). New York: McGraw-Hill.

Benjamin, L. T., Jr. (1988b). A history of teaching machines. *American Psychologist, 43*, 703–712.

Benjamin, L. T., Jr. (1991). A history of the New York branch of the American Psychological Association: 1903–1935. *American Psychologist, 46*, 1003–1011.

Benjamin, L. T., Jr., Acord, J., Durkin, M., Link, M., & Vestal, M. (1992). Wundt's American doctorates. *American Psychologist, 47*, in press.

Benjamin, L. T., Jr., Rogers, A. M., & Rosenbaum, A. (1991). Coca-Cola, caffeine, and mental deficiency: Harry Hollingworth and the Chattanooga trial of 1911. *Journal of the History of the Behavioral Sciences, 27*, 42–55.

Berkeley, G. (1957). An essay towards a new theory of vision. In M. W. Calkins (Ed.), *Berkeley: Essay, principles, dialogues* (pp. 1–98). New York: Scribners. (Original work published 1709).

Berkeley, G. (1957). A treatise concerning the principles of human knowledge. In M. W. Calkins (Ed.), *Berkeley: Essay, principles, dialogues* (pp. 99–216). New York: Scribners. (Original work published 1710).

Berman, L. (1927). *The religion called Behaviorism*. New York: Boni & Liveright.

Bernstein, M. D., & Russo, N. F. (1974). The history of psychology revisited: Or, up with our foremothers. *American Psychologist, 29*, 130–134.

Bettelheim, B. (1982). *Freud and man's soul*. New York: Alfred A. Knopf.

Binet, A. (1971). *The psychic life of micro-organisms*. West Orange NJ: Saifer. (Original work published 1889.)

Bjork, D. W. (1983). *The compromised scientist: William James in the development of American psychology*. New York: Columbia University Press.

Blanton, S. (1971). *Diary of my analysis with Sigmund Freud*. New York: Hawthorn Books.

Blumenthal, A. L. (1975). A reappraisal of Wilhelm Wundt. *American Psychologist, 30*, 1081–1088.

Blumenthal, A. L. (1977). Wilhelm Wundt and early American psychology: A clash of two cultures. *Annals of the New York Academy of Sciences, 291*, 13–20.

Blumenthal, A. L. (1979). Wilhelm Wundt: The founding father we never knew [Book review]. *Contemporary Psychology, 24*, 547–550.

Blumenthal, A. L. (1985). Wilhelm Wundt: Psychology as the propaedeutic science. In C. E. Buxton (Ed.), *Points of view in the modern history of psychology* (pp. 19–50). Orlando FL: Academic Press.

Boakes, R. (1984). *From Darwin to behaviourism: Psychology and the minds of animals*. Cambridge, England: Cambridge University Press.

Boas, M. (1961). *The scientific renaissance: 1450–1630*. London: Collins.

Boorstin, D. J. (1983). *The discoverers*. New York: Random House.

Bootzin, R. R., Kihlstrom, J. F., & Schacter, D. L. (Eds.) (1990). *Sleep and cognition: Information processing outside of awareness*. Washington DC: American Psychological Association.

Boring, E. G. (1929). *A history of experimental psychology*. New York: Appleton.

Boring, E. G. (1950). *A history of experimental psychology* (2nd ed.). New York: Appleton-Century-Crofts.

Boring, E. G. (1967). Titchener's Experimentalists. *Journal of the History of the Behavioral Sciences, 3*, 315–325.

Bottome, P. (1939). *Alfred Adler*. New York: Putnam.

Breland, H. M. (1974). Birth order, family configuration and verbal achievement. *Child Development, 45*, 1011–1019.

Breland, K., & Breland, M. (1961). The misbehavior of organisms. *American Psychologist, 16*, 681–684.

Brentano, F. (1874). *Psychology from an empirical standpoint*. Leipzig: Duncker & Humblot.

Breuer, J., & Freud, S. (1895). Studies on hysteria. In *Standard edition* (vol. 2). London: Hogarth Press.

Bridgman, P. W. (1927). *The logic of modern physics*. New York: Macmillan.

Bridgman, P. W. (1954). Remarks on the present state of operationism. *Scientific Monthly, 79*, 224–226.

Broad, W., & Wade, N. (1982). *Betrayers of the truth: Fraud and deceit in the halls of science*. New York: Simon & Schuster.

Brody, N. (1987). Introduction: Some thoughts on the unconscious. *Personality and Social Psychology Bulletin, 13*, 293–298.

Brome, V. (1981). *Jung: Man and myth*. New York: Atheneum.

Brown, J. A. C. (1963). *Freud and the post-Freudians*. London: Cassell.

Brožek, J. (1980). The echoes of Wundt's work in the United States, 1887–1977: A quantitative citation analysis. *Psychological Research, 42*, 103–107.

Bruner, J. S. (1982, May). Psychology has been responding to the so-called post-industrial revolution. *Psychology Today*, pp. 42–43.

Bruner, J. S. (1983). *In search of mind: Essays in autobiography*. New York: Harper & Row.

Buckley, K. W. (1982). The selling of a psychologist: John Broadus Watson and the application of behavioral techniques to advertising. *Journal of the History of the Behavioral Sciences, 18*, 207–221.

Buckley, K. W. (1989). *Mechanical man: John Broadus Watson and the beginnings of behaviorism*. New York: Guilford Press.

Burnham, J. (1968). On the origins of behaviorism. *Journal of the History of the Behavioral Sciences, 4*, 143–151.

Burt, C. (1962). The concept of consciousness. *British Journal of Psychology, 53*, 229–242.

Cadwallader, T. C. (1984). Neglected aspects of the evolution of American comparative and animal psychology. In G. Greenberg & E. Tobach (Eds.), *Behavioral evolution and integrative levels* (pp. 15–48). Hillsdale NJ: Erlbaum.

Cadwallader, T. C. (1987). Early zoological input to comparative and animal psychology at the University of Chicago. In E. Tobach (Ed.), *Historical perspectives and the international status of comparative psychology* (pp. 37–59). Hillsdale NJ: Erlbaum.

Campbell, J. (1988). *The improbable machine: What the upheavals in artificial intelligence research reveal about how the mind really works.* New York: Simon & Schuster.

Carr, H. A. (1925). *Psychology.* New York: Longmans, Green.

Carr, H. A. (1930). Functionalism. In C. Murchison (Ed.), *Psychologies of 1930* (pp. 59–78). Worcester MA: Clark University Press.

Cattell, J. McK. (1890). Mental tests and measurements. *Mind, 15,* 373–381.

Cattell, J. McK. (1896). Address of the president before the American Psychological Association, 1895. *Psychological Review, 3,* 134–148.

Cattell, J. McK. (1904). The conceptions and methods of psychology. *Popular Science Monthly, 66,* 176–186.

Cattell, J. McK. (1928). Early psychological laboratories. *Science, 67,* 543–548.

Chomsky, N. (1959). Review of *Verbal Behavior* by B. F. Skinner. *Language, 35,* 26–58.

Chomsky, N. (1972). *Language and mind.* New York: Harcourt Brace Jovanovich.

Churchill, S. D. (1988, August). Humanistic psychology and introductory psychology textbooks: Wizards and straw men. Paper presented at the meeting of the American Psychological Association, Atlanta GA.

Comte, A. (1896). *The positive philosophy of Comte.* London: Bell. (Original work published 1830).

Coon, D. J. (1982). Eponymy, obscurity, Twitmyer, and Pavlov. *Journal of the History of the Behavioral Sciences, 18,* 255–262.

Cranston, A. (1986). Psychology in the Veterans Administration. *American Psychologist, 41,* 990–995.

Crewsdon, J. (1988). *By silence betrayed: Sexual abuse of children in America.* Boston: Little, Brown.

Cunningham, S. (1985, May). Humanists celebrate gains, goals. *APA Monitor,* pp. 16, 18.

Cuny, H. (1965). *Ivan Pavlov: The man and his theories.* New York: Eriksson.

Dallenbach, K. (1967). Autobiography. In E. G. Boring & G. Lindzey (Eds.), *A history of psychology in autobiography* (vol. 5, pp. 57–93). New York: Appleton-Century-Crofts.

Danziger, K. (1987). Social context and investigative practice in early twentieth-century psychology. In M. G. Ash & W. R. Woodward (Eds.), *Psychology in twentieth-century thought and society* (pp. 13–33). Cambridge, England: Cambridge University Press.

Danziger, K. (1988). A question of identity: Who participated in psychological experiments? In J. G. Morawski (Ed.), *The rise of experimentation in American psychology* (pp. 35–52). New Haven CT: Yale University Press.

Darwin, C. (1859). *On the origin of species by means of natural selection.* London: Murray.

Darwin, C. (1871). *The descent of man.* London: Murray.

Darwin, C. (1872). *The expression of the emotions in man and animals.* London: Murray.

Darwin, C. (1877). A biographical sketch of an infant. *Mind, 2*, 285–294.

Demarest, J. (1987). Two comparative psychologies. In E. Tobach (Ed.), *Historical perspectives and the international status of comparative psychology* (pp. 127–155). Hillsdale NJ: Erlbaum.

Dennis, P. M. (1984). The Edison questionnaire. *Journal of the History of the Behavioral Sciences, 20*, 23–37.

Descartes, R. (1912). *A discourse on method*. London: Dent. (Original work published 1637.)

Dewey, J. (1886). *Psychology*. New York: Harper.

Dewey, J. (1896). The reflex arc concept in psychology. *Psychological Review, 3*, 357–370.

Dewey, J. (1900). Psychology and social practice. *Psychological Review, 7*, 105–124.

Diamond, S. (1980). A plea for historical accuracy [Letter to the editor]. *Contemporary Psychology, 25*, 84–85.

Diehl, L. A. (1986). The paradox of G. Stanley Hall: Foe of coeducation and educator of women. *American Psychologist, 41*, 868–878.

Domjan, M. (1987). Animal learning comes of age. *American Psychologist, 42*, 556–564.

Duke, C., Fried, S., Pliley, W., & Walker, D. (1989). Contributions to the history of psychology: LIX. Rosalie Rayner Watson: The mother of a behaviorist's sons. *Psychological Reports, 65*, 163–169.

Eagle, M. N. (1988). How accurate were Freud's case histories? [Book review of *Freud and the Rat Man*]. *Contemporary Psychology, 33*, 205–206.

Ebbinghaus, H. (1885). *On memory*. Leipzig: Duncker & Humblot.

Ebbinghaus, H. (1902). *The principles of psychology*. Leipzig: Veit.

Ebbinghaus, H. (1908). *A summary of psychology*. Leipzig: Veit.

Eissler, K. R. (1971). *Talent and genius: The fictitious case of Tausk contra Freud*. New York: Quadrangle.

Ellenberger, H. F. (1970). *The discovery of the unconscious: The history and evolution of dynamic psychiatry*. New York: Basic Books.

Ellenberger, H. F. (1972). The story of "Anna O": A critical review with new data. *Journal of the History of the Behavioral Sciences, 8*, 267–279.

Erikson, E. H. (1968). *Identity: Youth and crisis*. New York: Norton.

Erikson, E. H. (1975). *Life history and the historical moment*. New York: Norton.

Erikson, E. H., Erikson, J. M., & Kivnick, H. Q. (1986). *Vital involvement in old age*. New York: Norton.

Evans, R. B. (1972). E. B. Titchener and his lost system. *Journal of the History of the Behavioral Sciences, 8*, 168–180.

Evans, R. B., & Scott, F. J. D. (1978). The 1913 International Congress of Psychology: The American congress that wasn't. *American Psychologist, 33*, 711–723.

Evans, R. I. (1968). *B. F. Skinner: The man and his ideas*. New York: Dutton.

Evans, R. I. (1989). *Albert Bandura: The man and his ideas*. New York: Praeger.

Fechner, G. (1966). *Elements of psychophysics*. New York: Holt, Rinehart and Winston. (Original work published 1860).

Fernald, D. (1984). *The Hans legacy: A story of science*. Hillsdale NJ: Erlbaum.

Ferster, C. B., & Skinner, B. F. (1957). *Schedules of reinforcement*. New York: Appleton-Century-Crofts.

Fisher, S., & Greenberg, R. P. (1977). *The scientific credibility of Freud's theories and therapy*. New York: Basic Books.

Fowler, R. D. (1990). In memorium: Burrhus Frederick Skinner, 1904–1990. *American Psychologist, 45*, 1203.

Freeman, L. (1972). *The story of Anna O*. New York: Walker.

Freud, A. (1936). *The ego and the mechanisms of defense*. London: Hogarth Press.

Freud, A. (1966). Introduction to the technique of child analysis. In *The writings of Anna Freud* (vol. I, pp. 3–69). New York: International Universities Press. (Original work published as "Four lectures on child analysis," 1927).

Freud, S. (1895). On the origins of psychoanalysis. In J. Strachey (Ed. & Trans.), *The standard edition of the complete psychological works of Sigmund Freud* (vol. 1). London: Hogarth Press.

Freud, S. (1896). Heredity and the etiology of the neuroses. In *Standard edition* (vol. 3, pp. 142–156). London: Hogarth Press.

Freud, S. (1900). The interpretation of dreams. In *Standard edition* (vols. 4, 5). London: Hogarth Press.

Freud, S. (1901). The psychopathology of everyday life. In *Standard edition* (vol. 6). London: Hogarth Press.

Freud, S. (1905a). Three essays on the theory of sexuality. In *Standard edition* (vol. 7, pp. 125–243). London: Hogarth Press.

Freud, S. (1905b). Fragment of an analysis of a case of hysteria. In *Standard edition* (vol. 7, pp. 3–122). London: Hogarth Press. (Original work published 1901).

Freud, S. (1910). Five lectures on psychoanalysis. In *Standard edition* (vol. 11, pp. 3–55). London: Hogarth Press. (Original work published 1909.)

Freud, S. (1914). On the history of the psychoanalytic movement. In *Standard edition* (vol. 14, pp. 3–66). London: Hogarth Press.

Freud, S. (1920). Beyond the pleasure principle. In *Standard edition* (vol. 18, pp. 3–64). London: Hogarth Press.

Freud, S. (1933). New introductory lectures on psychoanalysis. In *Standard edition* (vol. 22, pp. 3–182). London: Hogarth Press.

Freud, S. (1940). An outline of psychoanalysis. In *Standard edition* (vol. 23, pp. 141–207). London: Hogarth Press.

Freud, S. (1941). Findings, ideas, problems. In *Standard edition* (vol. 23, pp. 299–300). London: Hogarth Press. (Original work published 1938.)

Freud, S. (1954). *The origins of psychoanalysis: Letters to Wilhelm Fliess, drafts and notes: 1887–1902*. New York: Basic Books.

Freud, S. (1964). *The letters of Sigmund Freud*. New York: McGraw-Hill.

Fuller, R. C. (1986). *Americans and the unconscious*. New York: Oxford University Press.

Furumoto, L. (1987). On the margins: Women and the professionalization of psychology in the United States, 1890–1940. In M. G. Ash & W. R. Woodward (Eds.), *Psychology in twentieth-century thought and society* (pp. 93–113). Cambridge, England: Cambridge University Press.

Furumoto, L. (1988). Shared knowledge: The Experimentalists, 1904–1929. In J. G. Morawski (Ed.), *The rise of experimentation in American psychology* (pp. 94–113). New Haven CT: Yale University Press.

Furumoto, L. (1989). The new history of psychology. In I. S. Cohen (Ed.), *The G. Stanley Hall lecture series* (vol. 9, pp. 5–34). Washington DC: American Psychological Association.

Gallistel, C. R. (1989). Animal cognition: The representation of space, time, and number. *Annual Review of Psychology, 40*, 155–189.

Galton, F. (1869). *Hereditary genius*. London: Macmillan.

Galton, F. (1874). *English men of science: Their nature and nurture*. London: Macmillan.

Galton, F. (1889). *Natural inheritance*. London: Macmillan.

Gantt, W. H. (1941). Introduction. In I. P. Pavlov, *Lectures on conditioned reflexes*. New York: International Publishers.

Gantt, W. H. (1979, February). Interview with Professor Emeritus W. Horsley Gantt. *Johns Hopkins Magazine*, pp. 26–32.

Gay, P. (1983). *The bourgeois experience: Victoria to Freud: Vol. 1. Education of the senses*. New York: Oxford University Press.

Gay, P. (1988). *Freud: A life for our time*. New York: Norton.

Gazzaniga, M. S. (1988). Life with George: The birth of the Cognitive Neuroscience Institute. In W. Hirst (Ed.), *The making of cognitive science: Essays in honor of George A. Miller* (pp. 230–241). Cambridge, England: Cambridge University Press.

Gelman, D. (1988, June 27). Where are the patients? *Newsweek*.

Gengerelli, J. A. (1976). Graduate school reminiscences: Hull and Koffka. *American Psychologist, 31*, 685–688.

Gerow, J. R. (1986). Psychology through *Time:* The first ten years. Paper presented at the meeting of the Southeastern Psychological Association.

Geuter, U. (1987). German psychology during the Nazi period. In M. G. Ash & W. R. Woodward (Eds.), *Psychology in twentieth-century thought and society* (pp. 165–187). Cambridge, England: Cambridge University Press.

Gilgen, A. R. (1982). *American psychology since World War II: A profile of the discipline*. Westport CT: Greenwood Press.

Goleman, D. (1983, May). A conversation with Ulric Neisser. *Psychology Today*, pp. 54–62.

Goleman, D. (1987, August 30). B. F. Skinner: On his best behavior. *New York Times*.

Goodstein, L. D. (1988). The growth of the American Psychological Association. *American Psychologist, 43*, 491–498.

Gould, S. J. (1976). Darwin and the captain. *Natural History, 85*(1), 32–34.

Gould, S. J. (1986). Knight takes bishop? *Natural History, 95*(5), 18–33.

Grieser, C., Greenberg, R., & Harrison, R. H. (1972). The adaptive function of sleep: The differential effects of sleep and dreaming on recall. *Journal of Abnormal Psychology, 80*, 280–286.

Gruber, C. (1972). Academic freedom at Columbia University, 1917–1918: The case of James McKeen Cattell. *American Association of University Professors Bulletin, 58*(3), 297–305.

Gundlach, H. U. K. (1986). Ebbinghaus, nonsense syllables, and three-letter words [Book review]. *Contemporary Psychology, 31*, 469–470.

Guthrie, E. R. (1935). *The psychology of learning*. New York: Harper.

Guthrie, E. R. (1959). Association by contiguity. In S. Koch (Ed.), *Psychology: A study of a science* (vol. 2, pp. 158–195). New York: McGraw-Hill.

Guthrie, R. V. (1976). *Even the rat was white: A historical view of psychology*. New York: Harper & Row.

Hale, M., Jr. (1980). *Human science and social order: Hugo Münsterberg and the origins of applied psychology*. Philadelphia: Temple University Press.

Hall, G. S. (1904). *Adolescence*. New York: Appleton.

Hall, G. S. (1912). *Founders of modern psychology*. New York: Appleton.

Hall, G. S. (1917). *Jesus, the Christ, in the light of psychology*. Garden City NY: Doubleday.

Hall, G. S. (1919). Some possible effects of the war on American psychology. *Psychological Bulletin, 16*, 48–49.

Hall, G. S. (1920). *Recreations of a psychologist*. New York: Appleton.

Hall, G. S. (1922). *Senescence*. New York: Appleton.

Hall, G. S. (1923). *The life and confessions of a psychologist*. New York: Appleton.

Hannush, M. J. (1987). John B. Watson remembered: An interview with James B. Watson. *Journal of the History of the Behavioral Sciences, 23*, 137–152.

Harris, B. (1979). Whatever happened to little Albert? *American Psychologist, 34*, 151–160.

Harrison, R. (1963). Functionalism and its historical significance. *Genetic Psychology Monographs, 68*, 387–423.

Hartley, D. (1749). *Observations on man, his frame, his duty, and his expectations*. London: Leake & Frederick.

Hartley, D., Robach, H. B., & Abramowitz, S. I. (1976). Deterioration effects in encounter groups. *American Psychologist, 31*, 247–255.

Hartmann, E. (1884). *Philosophy of the unconscious*. London: Trübner. (Original work published 1869).

Hartmann, H. (1964). *Essays on ego psychology*. New York: International Universities Press.

Hearnshaw, L. S. (1987). *The shaping of modern psychology*. London: Routledge & Kegan Paul.

Hearst, E. (Ed.). (1979). *The first century of experimental psychology*. Hillsdale NJ: Erlbaum.

Heidbreder, E. (1933). *Seven psychologies*. New York: Appleton.

Helmholtz, H. (1856–1866). *Physiological optics*. Leipzig: Voss.

Helmholtz, H. (1954). *On the sensations of tone*. New York: Dover. (Original work published 1863).

Helson, H. (1925, 1926). The psychology of Gestalt. *American Journal of Psychology, 36*, 342–370, 494–526; *37*, 25–62, 189–223.

Henle, M. (1974). E. B. Titchener and the case of the missing element. *Journal of the History of the Behavioral Sciences, 10*, 227–237.

Henle, M. (1978). One man against the Nazis — Wolfgang Köhler. *American Psychologist, 33*, 939–944.

Hilgard, E. R. (1956). *Theories of learning* (2nd ed.). New York: Appleton-Century-Crofts.

Hilgard, E. R. (1987). *Psychology in America: A historical survey*. San Diego CA: Harcourt Brace Jovanovich.

Hilgard, E. R. , Atkinson, R., & Atkinson, R. (1975). *Introduction to psychology* (6th ed.). New York: Harcourt Brace Jovanovich.

Hilgard, E. R., Leary, D. E., & McGuire, G. R. (1991). The history of psychology: A survey and critical assessment. *Annual Review of Psychology, 42*, 79–107.

Hirschmuller, A. (1989). *The life and work of Josef Breuer: Physiology and psychoanalysis*. New York: New York University Press.

Hoffman, E. (1988). *The right to be human: A biography of Abraham Maslow*. Los Angeles: Tarcher.

Holder, A. (1988). Reservations about the *Standard Edition*. In E. Timms & N. Segal (Eds.), *Freud in exile: Psychoanalysis and its vicissitudes* (pp. 210–214). New Haven CT: Yale University Press.

Horney, K. (1945). *Our inner conflicts*. New York: Norton.

Horney, K. (1980). *The adolescent diaries of Karen Horney, 1899–1911*. New York: Basic Books.

Howard, D. V. (1983). *Cognitive psychology: Memory, language and thought*. New York: Macmillan.

Hull, C. L. (1928). *Aptitude testing*. Yonkers NY: World.

Hull, C. L. (1933). *Hypnosis and suggestibility*. New York: Appleton.

Hull, C. L. (1943). *Principles of behavior*. New York: Appleton.

Hull, C. L. (1951). *Essentials of behavior*. New Haven CT: Yale University Press.

Hull, C. L. (1952). *A behavior system*. New Haven CT: Yale University Press.

Hull, C. L., Hovland, C. L., Ross, R. T., Hall, M., Perkins, D. T., & Fitch, F. G. (1940). *Mathematico-deductive theory of rote learning: A study in scientific methodology*. New Haven CT: Yale University Press.

Hume, D. (1739). *A treatise of human nature*. London: Noon.

Isbister, J. N. (1985). *Freud: An introduction to his life and work*. Cambridge, England: Polity Press.

Jackson, M., & Sechrest, L. (1962). Early recollections in four neurotic diagnostic categories. *Journal of Individual Psychology, 18*, 52–56.

Jacobson, J. Z. (1951). *Scott of Northwestern: The life story of a pioneer in psychology and education*. Chicago: Mariano.

Jacoby, L. L., & Kelley, C. M. (1987). Unconscious influences of memory for a prior event. *Personality and Social Psychology Bulletin, 13*, 314–336.

James, W. (1890). *The principles of psychology*. New York: Holt.

James, W. (1899). *Talks to teachers*. New York: Holt.

James, W. (1902). *The varieties of religious experience*. New York: Longmans, Green.

James, W. (1907). *Pragmatism*. New York: Longmans, Green.

Jaynes, J. (1970). The problem of animate motion in the seventeenth century. *Journal of the History of Ideas, 31*, 219–234.

Johnson, R. C., McClearn, G. E., Yuen, S., Nagoshi, C. T., Ahern, F. M., & Cole, R. E. (1985). Galton's data a century later. *American Psychologist, 40*, 875–892.

Jonçich, G. (1968). *The sane positivist: A biography of Edward L. Thorndike*. Middletown CT: Wesleyan University Press.

Jones, E. (1953, 1955, 1957). *The life and work of Sigmund Freud* (3 vols.). New York: Basic Books.

Jones, M. C. (1924). A laboratory study of fear: The case of Peter. *Pedagogical Seminary, 31,* 308–315.

Jones, M. C. (1974). Albert, Peter, and John B. Watson. *American Psychologist, 29,* 581–583.

Jones, R. A. (1987). Psychology, history, and the press: The case of William McDougall and the *New York Times. American Psychologist, 42,* 931–940.

Jung, C. G. (1912). *The psychology of the unconscious.* Leipzig: Franz Deuticke.

Jung, C. G. (1961). *Memories, dreams, reflections.* New York: Random House.

Kagan, J., & Havemann, E. (1972). *Psychology: An introduction* (2nd ed.). New York: Harcourt Brace Jovanovich.

Kagan, J., Kearsley, R., & Zelazo, P. (1978). *Infancy.* Cambridge MA: Harvard University Press.

Kihlstrom, J. F. (1987). The cognitive unconscious. *Science, 237,* 1445–1452.

Koch, S. (1964). Psychology and emerging conceptions of knowledge as unitary. In T. Wann (Ed.), *Behaviorism and phenomenology* (pp. 1–41). Chicago: University of Chicago Press.

Koelsch, W. A. (1970). Freud discovers America. *Virginia Quarterly Review, 46,* 115–132.

Koelsch, W. A. (1987). *Clark University: 1887–1987.* Worcester MA: Clark University Press.

Koenigsberger, L. (1965). *Hermann von Helmholtz.* New York: Dover.

Koffka, K. (1921). *The growth of the mind.* New York: Harcourt.

Koffka, K. (1922). Perception: An introduction to Gestalt-theorie. *Psychological Bulletin, 19,* 531–585.

Koffka, K. (1935). *Principles of Gestalt psychology.* New York: Harcourt.

Köhler, W. (1917, 1924, 1927). *The mentality of apes.* Berlin: Royal Academy of Sciences; New York: Harcourt Brace.

Köhler, W. (1920). *Static and stationary physical Gestalts.* Braunschweig: Vieweg.

Köhler, W. (1929). *Gestalt psychology.* New York: Liveright.

Köhler, W. (1947). *Gestalt psychology: An introduction to new concepts in modern psychology.* New York: Liveright.

Köhler, W. (1959). Gestalt psychology today. *American Psychologist, 14,* 727–734.

Köhler, W. (1969). Gestalt psychology. In D. Krantz (Ed.), *Schools of psychology* (pp. 69–85). New York: Appleton-Century-Crofts.

Konorski, J. (1974). Autobiography. In G. Lindzey (Ed.), *A history of psychology in autobiography* (vol. 6, pp. 183–217). Englewood Cliffs NJ: Prentice-Hall.

Krüll, M. (1986). *Freud and his father.* New York: Norton.

Kuhn, T. S. (1970). *The structure of scientific revolutions* (2nd ed.). Chicago: University of Chicago Press.

Külpe, O. (1893). *Outline of psychology.* Leipzig: Engelmann.

Kuna, D. P. (1976). The concept of suggestion in the early history of advertising psychology. *Journal of the History of the Behavioral Sciences, 12,* 347–353.

Larson, C. (1979, May). Highlights of Dr. John B. Watson's career in advertising. *The Industrial-Organizational Psychologist,* pp. 3–5.

Larson, C., & Sullivan, J. J. (1965). Watson's relation to Titchener. *Journal of the History of the Behavioral Sciences, 1*, 338–354.

Lashley, K. (1929). *Brain mechanisms and intelligence*. Chicago: University of Chicago Press.

Leahey, T. H. (1981). The mistaken mirror: On Wundt's and Titchener's psychologies. *Journal of the History of the Behavioral Sciences, 17*, 273–282.

Leary, D. E. (1987). Telling likely stories: The rhetoric of the new psychology, 1880–1920. *Journal of the History of the Behavioral Sciences, 23*, 315–331.

Leonard, G. (1983, December). Abraham Maslow and the new self. *Esquire*, pp. 326–336.

Lerner, G. (1979). *The majority finds its past: Placing women in history*. New York: Oxford University Press.

Levinson, D. J. (1978). *The seasons of a man's life*. New York: Knopf.

Lewin, K. (1936). *Principles of topological psychology*. New York: McGraw-Hill.

Lewin, K. (1939). Field theory and experiment in social psychology: Concept and methods. *American Journal of Sociology, 44*, 868–896.

Lewin, K., Lippitt, R., & White, R. (1939). Patterns of aggressive behavior in experimentally created social climates. *Journal of Social Psychology, 10*, 271–299.

Ley, R. (1990). *A whisper of espionage: Wolfgang Köhler and the apes of Tenerife*. Garden City Park NY: Avery.

Lieberman, D. A. (1979). Behaviorism and the mind: A (limited) call for a return to introspection. *American Psychologist, 34*, 319–333.

Locke, J. (1959). *An essay concerning human understanding*. New York: Dover. (Original work published 1690.)

Loeb, J. (1918). *Forced movements, tropisms, and animal conduct*. Philadelphia: Lippincott.

Loevinger, J. (1987). *Paradigms of personality*. New York: Freeman.

Loftus, E. (1979). *Eyewitness testimony*. Cambridge MA: Harvard University Press.

Loftus, E., & Monahan, J. (1980). Trial by data: Psychological research as legal evidence. *American Psychologist, 35*, 270–283.

Logue, A. W. (1978). Behaviorist John B. Watson and the continuity of the species. *Behaviorism, 6*(1), 71–79.

Logue, A. W. (1985a). The origins of behaviorism: Antecedents and proclamation. In C. E. Buxton (Ed.), *Points of view in the modern history of psychology* (pp. 141–167). Orlando FL: Academic Press.

Logue, A. W. (1985b). The growth of behaviorism: Controversy and diversity. In C. E. Buxton (Ed.), *Points of view in the modern history of psychology* (pp. 169–196). Orlando FL: Academic Press.

Lowry, R. (1982). *The evolution of psychological theory: A critical history of concepts and presuppositions* (2nd ed.). Hawthorne NY: Aldine.

Lubek, I., & Apfelbaum, E. (1987). Neobehaviorism and the Garcia effect: A social psychology of science approach to the history of a paradigm clash. In M. G. Ash & W. R. Woodward (Eds.), *Psychology in twentieth-century thought and society* (pp. 59–91). Cambridge, England: Cambridge University Press.

Mach, E. (1914). *The analysis of sensations*. Chicago: Open Court. (Original work published 1885.)

Mackenzie, B. (1977). *Behaviourism and the limits of scientific method*. Atlantic Highlands NJ: Humanities Press.

MacLeod, R. B. (1959). Review of *Cumulative record* by B. F. Skinner. *Science, 130*, 34–35.

MacLeod, R. B. (Ed.). (1969). *William James: Unfinished business*. Washington DC: American Psychological Association.

Mahoney, P. J. (1986). *Freud and the Rat Man*. New Haven CT: Yale University Press.

Malcolm, J. (1984). *In the Freud archives*. New York: Knopf.

Malthus, T. (1914). *Essay on the principle of population*. New York: Dutton. (Original work published 1789.)

Marx, M., & Hillix, W. A. (1979). *Systems and theories in psychology* (3rd ed.). New York: McGraw-Hill.

Maslow, A. H. (1970). *Motivation and personality* (2nd ed.). New York: Harper & Row.

Masson, J. M. (1984). *The assault on truth: Freud's suppression of the seduction theory*. New York: Farrar Straus Giroux.

Masson, J. M. (Ed.). (1985). *The complete letters of Sigmund Freud to Wilhelm Fliess, 1887–1904*. Cambridge MA: Harvard University Press.

Matarazzo, J. D. (1987). There is only one psychology: No specialties, but many applications. *American Psychologist, 42*, 893–903.

Matson, F. W. (1964). *The broken image*. New York: Braziller.

Maurice, K., & Mayr, O. (Eds.). (1980). *The clockwork universe: German clocks and automata, 1550–1650*. New York: Neale Watson.

May, W. W. (1978). A psychologist of many hats: A tribute to Mark Arthur May. *American Psychologist, 33*, 653–663.

McAdams, D. P., Ruetzel, K., & Foley, J. M. (1986). Complexity and generativity at midlife: Relations among social motives, ego development, and adults' plans for the future. *Journal of Personality and Social Psychology, 50*, 800–807.

McDougall, W. (1908). *Introduction to social psychology*. London: Methuen.

McDougall, W. (1912). *Psychology: The study of behavior*. London: Oxford University Press.

McGovern, T. V. (1990, July). Goals for major in psychology outlined. *APA Monitor*, p. 50.

McGraw, M. B. (1990). Memories, deliberate recall, and speculations. *American Psychologist, 45*, 934–937.

McGuire, W. (Ed.). (1974). *The Freud/Jung letters*. Princeton NJ: Princeton University Press.

McKeachie, W. J. (1976). Psychology in America's bicentennial year. *American Psychologist, 31*, 819–833.

McKinney, F. (1978). Functionalism at Chicago: Memories of a graduate student, 1929–1931. *Journal of the History of the Behavioral Sciences, 14*, 142–148.

McReynolds, P. (1987). Lightner Witmer: Little-known founder of clinical psychology. *American Psychologist, 42*, 849–858.

Merton, R. (1957). Priorities in scientific discovery. *American Sociological Review, 22*, 635–659.

Meyer, M. (1911). *The fundamental laws of human behavior*. Boston: Badger.

Mill, J. (1829). *Analysis of the phenomena of the human mind*. London: Baldwin & Cradock.

Miller, G. A. (1951). *Language and communication*. New York: McGraw-Hill.

Miller, G. A. (1962). *Psychology: The science of mental life*. New York: Harper & Row.

Miller, G. A. (1985). The constitutive problem of psychology. In S. Koch & D. Leary (Eds.), *A century of psychology as science* (pp. 40–45). New York: McGraw-Hill.

Miller, G. A., & Buckhout, R. (1973). *Psychology: The science of mental life* (2nd ed.). New York: Harper & Row.

Misceo, G., & Samelson, F. (1983). History of psychology: XXXIII. On textbook lessons from history, or how the conditioned reflex discovered Twitmyer. *Psychological Reports, 52*, 447–454.

Moses, S. (1991, March). APA calls for recast psychology major. *APA Monitor*, p. 37.

Motley, M. T. (1985). Slips of the tongue. *Scientific American, 253*, 116–127.

Mueller, C. G., & Schoenfeld, W. N. (1954). Edwin R. Guthrie. In W. Estes et al. (Eds.), *Modern learning theory* (pp. 345–379). New York: Appleton-Century-Crofts.

Münsterberg, H. (1909). *Psychotherapy* . New York: Moffat Yard.

Münsterberg, H. (1913). *Psychology and industrial efficiency*. Boston: Houghton Mifflin.

Münsterberg, M. (1922). *Hugo Münsterberg: His life and work*. New York: Appleton.

Murray, H. A. (1938). *Explorations in personality*. New York: Oxford University Press.

Murray, H. A. (1940). What should psychologists do about psychoanalysis? *Journal of Abnormal and Social Psychology, 35*, 150–175.

Myers, G. E. (1986). *William James: His life and thought*. New Haven CT: Yale University Press.

Natsoulas, T. (1978). Consciousness. *American Psychologist, 33*, 904–916.

Neisser, U. (1967). *Cognitive psychology*. New York: Appleton-Century-Crofts.

Neisser, U. (1976). *Cognition and reality*. San Francisco: W. H. Freeman.

Norman, D. A., & Levelt, W. J. M. (1988). Life at the Center. In W. Hirst (Ed.), *The making of cognitive science: Essays in honor of George A. Miller* (pp. 100–109). Cambridge, England: Cambridge University Press.

O'Connell, A. N., & Russo, N. F. (1983). *Models of achievement: Reflections of eminent women in psychology*. New York: Columbia University Press.

O'Connell, A. N., & Russo, N. F. (1988). *Models of achievement: Reflections of eminent women in psychology* (vol. 2). Hillsdale NJ: Erlbaum.

O'Donnell, J. M. (1979). The crisis of experimentalism in the 1920s: E. G. Boring and his uses of history. *American Psychologist, 34*, 289–295.

O'Donnell, J. M. (1985). *The origins of behaviorism: American psychology, 1870–1920*. New York: New York University Press.

Olweus, D. (1979). The stability of aggressive reaction patterns in human males: A review. *Psychological Bulletin, 86*, 852–875.

Paskauskas, R. A. (1988). The Jones-Freud era, 1908–1939. In E. Timms & N. Segal (Eds.), *Freud in exile: Psychoanalysis and its vicissitudes* (pp. 109–123). New Haven CT: Yale University Press.

Pauly, P. J. (1979, December). Psychology at Hopkins: Its rise and fall and rise and fall and. . . . *Johns Hopkins Magazine*, pp. 36–41.

Pauly, P. J. (1986). G. Stanley Hall and his successors: A history of the first half-century of psychology at Johns Hopkins. In S. H. Hulse & B. F. Green, Jr. (Eds.), *One hundred years of psychological research in America: G. Stanley Hall and the Johns Hopkins tradition* (pp. 21–51). Baltimore MD: Johns Hopkins University Press.

Pavlov, I. P. (1927). *Conditioned reflexes.* Oxford, England: Oxford University Press.

Pavlov, I. P. (1955). *Selected works.* Moscow: Foreign Languages Publishing House.

Pearce, J. M. (1987). *An introduction to animal cognition.* Hillsdale NJ: Erlbaum.

Pervin, L. (1984). *Personality: Theory and research* (4th ed.). New York: Wiley.

Pervin, L. (1985). Personality: Current controversies, issues and directions. *Annual Review of Psychology, 36,* 83–114.

Pickering, G. (1974). *Creative malady.* New York: Oxford University Press.

Pillsbury, W. (1911). *Essentials of psychology.* New York: Macmillan.

Planck, M. (1949). *Scientific autobiography.* New York: Philosophical Library.

Quinn, S. (1987). *A mind of her own: The life of Karen Horney.* New York: Summit Books.

Rapp, D. (1988). The reception of Freud by the British press: General interest and literary magazines, 1920–1925. *Journal of the History of the Behavioral Sciences, 24,* 191–201.

Reed, J. (1987a). Robert M. Yerkes and the mental testing movement. In M. M. Sokal (Ed.), *Psychological testing and American society, 1890–1930* (pp. 75–94). New Brunswick NJ: Rutgers University Press.

Reed, J. (1987b). Robert M. Yerkes and the comparative method. In E. Tobach (Ed.), *Historical perspectives and the international status of comparative psychology* (pp. 91–101). Hillsdale NJ: Erlbaum.

Rice, B. (1968, March 17). Skinner agrees he is the most important influence in psychology. *New York Times Magazine,* pp. 27ff.

Richards, R. J. (1980). Wundt's early theories of unconscious inference and cognitive evolution in their relation to Darwinian biopsychology. In W. G. Bringmann & R. D. Tweney (Eds.), *Wundt studies: A centennial collection* (pp. 42–70). Toronto: Hogrefe.

Richards, R. J. (1987). *Darwin and the emergence of evolutionary theories of mind and behavior.* Chicago: University of Chicago Press.

Roazen, P. (1975). *Freud and his followers.* New York: Knopf.

Roback, A. A. (1952). *History of American psychology.* New York: Library Publishers.

Robinson, D. N. (1981). *An intellectual history of psychology* (rev. ed.). New York: Macmillan.

Roethlisberger, F. J., & Dickson, W. J. (1939). *Management and the worker: An account of a research program conducted by the Western Electric Company, Chicago.* Cambridge MA: Harvard University Press.

Rogers, C. R. (1961). *On becoming a person.* Boston: Houghton Mifflin.

Rogers, C. R. (1967). Autobiography. In E. G. Boring & G. Lindzey (Eds.), *A history of psychology in autobiography* (vol. 5, pp. 341–384). New York: Appleton-Century-Crofts.

Roitblat, H. L., Bever, T. G., & Terrace, H. S. (Eds.). (1984). *Animal cognition.* Hillsdale NJ: Erlbaum.

Romanes, G. J. (1883). *Animal intelligence.* London: Routledge & Kegan Paul.

Rose, P. (1983). *Parallel lives: Five Victorian marriages.* New York: Knopf.

Rosenzweig, S. (1985). Freud and experimental psychology: The emergence of idiodynamics. In S. Koch & D. Leary (Eds.), *A century of psychology as science* (pp. 135–207). New York: McGraw-Hill.

Ross, D. (1972). *Granville Stanley Hall: The psychologist as prophet.* Chicago: University of Chicago Press.

Roszak, T. (1986). *The cult of information: The folklore of computers and the true art of thinking.* New York: Pantheon.

Rotter, J. B. (1982). *The development and applications of social learning theory: Selected papers.* New York: Praeger.

Ruckmick, C. A. (1913). The use of the term "function" in English textbooks of psychology. *American Journal of Psychology, 24,* 99–123.

Russo, N. F., & Denmark, F. L. (1987). Contributions of women to psychology. *Annual Review of Psychology, 38,* 279–298.

Samelson, F. (1980). J. B. Watson's little Albert, Cyril Burt's twins, and the need for a critical science. *American Psychologist, 35,* 619–625.

Samelson, F. (1981). Struggle for scientific authority: The reception of Watson's behaviorism, 1913–1920. *Journal of the History of the Behavioral Sciences, 17,* 399–425.

Sarton, G. (1936). *The study of the history of science.* New York: Dover.

Scarborough, E., & Furumoto, L. (1987). *Untold lives: The first generation of American women psychologists.* New York: Columbia University Press.

Scarf, M. (1971, February 28). The man who gave us "inferiority complex," "compensation," "aggressive drive" and "style of life." *New York Times Magazine,* pp. 10ff.

Scarr, S. (1987, May). Twenty years of growing up. *Psychology Today,* pp. 24–28.

Schachter, S. (1963). Birth order, eminence, and higher education. *American Sociological Review, 28,* 757–767.

Scheere, E. (1988). Fifty volumes of *Psychological Research/Psychologische Forschung:* The history and present status of the journal. *Psychological Research, 50,* 71–82.

Scheibe, K. E. (1988). Metamorphoses in the psychologist's advantage. In J. G. Morawski (Ed.), *The rise of experimentation in American psychology* (pp. 53–71). New Haven CT: Yale University Press.

Schultz, D. (1990). *Intimate friends, dangerous rivals: The turbulent relationship between Freud and Jung.* Los Angeles: Tarcher.

Schur, M. (1972). *Freud: Living and dying.* New York: International Universities Press.

Schwartz, A. E. (1988). Freud and the feminine fallacy [Book review of *A mote in

Freud's eye: From psychoanalysis to the psychology of women]. *Contemporary Psychology, 33,* 501–502.

Scott, W. D. (1903). *The theory and practice of advertising: A simple exposition of the principles of psychology in their relation to successful advertising.* Boston: Small, Maynard.

Seaman, J. D. (1984). On phi-phenomena. *Journal of the History of the Behavioral Sciences, 20,* 3–8.

Shevrin, H., & Dickman, S. (1980). The psychological unconscious: A necessary assumption for all psychological theory? *American Psychologist, 35,* 421–434.

Shields, S. (1975). Ms. Pilgrim's progress: The contributions of Leta Stetter Hollingworth to the psychology of women. *American Psychologist, 30,* 852–857.

Siegel, A. W., & White, S. H. (1982). The child study movement. In H. W. Reese (Ed.), *Advances in child development and behavior* (vol. 17, pp. 233–285). New York: Academic Press.

Silverman, L. H. (1976). Psychoanalytic theory: "The reports of my death are greatly exaggerated." *American Psychologist, 31,* 621–637.

Skinner, B. F. (1938). *The behavior of organisms.* New York: Appleton.

Skinner, B. F. (1945a, October). Baby in a box. *Ladies Home Journal,* pp. 30ff.

Skinner, B. F. (1945b). The operational analysis of psychological terms: Rejoinders and second thoughts. *Psychological Review, 52,* 291–294.

Skinner, B. F. (1948). *Walden Two.* New York: Macmillan.

Skinner, B. F. (1953). *Science and human behavior.* New York: Macmillan.

Skinner, B. F. (1956). A case history of scientific method. *American Psychologist, 11,* 221–233.

Skinner, B. F. (1957). *Verbal behavior.* New York: Appleton.

Skinner, B. F. (1963). Behaviorism at fifty. *Science, 140,* 951–958.

Skinner, B. F. (1967). Autobiography. In E. G. Boring & G. Lindzey (Eds.), *A history of psychology in autobiography* (vol. 5, pp. 387–413). New York: Appleton-Century-Crofts.

Skinner, B. F. (1968). *The technology of teaching.* New York: Appleton-Century-Crofts.

Skinner, B. F. (1969). *Contingencies of reinforcement.* New York: Appleton-Century-Crofts.

Skinner, B. F. (1971). *Beyond freedom and dignity.* New York: Knopf.

Skinner, B. F. (1976). *Particulars of my life.* New York: Knopf.

Skinner, B. F. (1979). *The shaping of a behaviorist.* New York: Knopf.

Skinner, B. F. (1983a). Intellectual self-management in old age. *American Psychologist, 38,* 239–244.

Skinner, B. F. (1983b). *A matter of consequences.* New York: Knopf.

Skinner, B. F. (1986). What is wrong with daily life in the Western world? *American Psychologist, 41,* 568–574.

Skinner, B. F. (1987a). *Upon further reflection.* Englewood Cliffs NJ: Prentice-Hall.

Skinner, B. F. (1987b). Whatever happened to psychology as the science of behavior? *American Psychologist, 42,* 780–786.

Skinner, B. F. (1989). The origin of cognitive thought. *American Psychologist, 44,* 13–18.

Skinner, B. F. (1990). Can psychology be a science of mind? *American Psychologist, 45*, 1206–1210.

Smith, C. (1987). David Hartley's Newtonian neuropsychology. *Journal of the History of the Behavioral Sciences, 23*, 123–136.

Smith, D. (1986, March 31). What would Freud think? The uproar in the shrine of psychoanalysis. *New York,* pp. 38–45.

Smith, M. B. (1989). Comment on "The case of William McDougall." *American Psychologist, 44*, 446.

Sokal, M. M. (1971). The unpublished autobiography of James McKeen Cattell. *American Psychologist, 26*, 626–635.

Sokal, M. M. (1981a). *An education in psychology: James McKeen Cattell's journal and letters from Germany and England, 1880–1888.* Cambridge MA: MIT Press.

Sokal, M. M. (1981b). The origins of the Psychological Corporation. *Journal of the History of the Behavioral Sciences, 17*, 54–67.

Sokal, M. M. (1984). The Gestalt psychologists in behaviorist America. *American Historical Review, 89*, 1240–1263.

Sokal, M. M. (1987). James McKeen Cattell and mental anthropometry: Nineteenth-century science and reform and the origins of psychological testing. In M. M. Sokal (Ed.), *Psychological testing and American society, 1890–1930* (pp. 21–45). New Brunswick NJ: Rutgers University Press.

Sokal, M. M. (1990). G. Stanley Hall and the institutional character of psychology at Clark, 1889–1920. *Journal of the History of the Behavioral Sciences, 26*, 114–124.

Spence, K. W. (1952). Clark Leonard Hull: 1884–1952. *American Journal of Psychology, 65*, 639–646.

Spencer, H. (1855). *The principles of psychology.* London: Smith & Elder.

Steele, R. S. (1985a). Paradigm found: A deconstruction of the history of the psychoanalytic movement. In C. E. Buxton (Ed.), *Points of view in the modern history of psychology* (pp. 197–219). Orlando FL: Academic Press.

Steele, R. S. (1985b). Paradigm lost: Psychoanalysis after Freud. In C. E. Buxton (Ed.), *Points of view in the modern history of psychology* (pp. 221–257). Orlando FL: Academic Press.

Stepansky, P. E. (Ed.). (1986). *Freud: Appraisals and reappraisals.* New York: Analytic Press.

Sterba, R. F. (1982). *Reminiscences of a Viennese psychoanalyst.* Detroit MI: Wayne State University Press.

Stumpf, C. (1883, 1890). *Psychology of tone.* Leipzig: Hirzel.

Sulloway, F. J. (1979). *Freud: Biologist of the mind.* New York: Basic Books.

Thompson, T. (1988). Benedictus behavior analysis: B. F. Skinner's magnum opus at fifty [Book review of *The behavior of organisms: An experimental analysis*]. *Contemporary Psychology, 33*, 397–402.

Thorndike, E. L. (1898). Animal intelligence: An experimental study of the associative processes in animals (monograph supplement no. 8). *Psychological Review, 5*, 68–72.

Thorndike, E. L. (1905). *The elements of psychology.* New York: Seiler.

Thorndike, E. L. (1931). *Human learning.* New York: Appleton.

Titchener, E. B. (1896). *An outline of psychology.* New York: Macmillan.

Titchener, E. B. (1898a). The postulates of a structural psychology. *Philosophical Review, 7,* 449–465.

Titchener, E. B. (1898b). *Primer of psychology.* New York: Macmillan.

Titchener, E. B. (1901–1905). *Experimental psychology.* New York: Macmillan.

Titchener, E. B. (1909). *A textbook of psychology.* New York: Macmillan.

Titchener, E. B. (1912a). Prolegomena to a study of introspection. *American Journal of Psychology, 23,* 427–448.

Titchener, E. B. (1912b). The schema of introspection. *American Journal of Psychology, 23,* 485–508.

Titchener, E. B. (1921). Wilhelm Wundt. *American Journal of Psychology, 32,* 161–178.

Tolman, E. C. (1932). *Purposive behavior in animals and men.* New York: Appleton.

Tolman, E. C. (1945). A stimulus-expectancy need-cathexis psychology. *Science, 101,* 160–166.

Tolman, E. C. (1952). Autobiography. In E. G. Boring, H. S. Langfeld, H. Werner, & R. Yerkes (Eds.), *A history of psychology in autobiography* (vol. 4, pp. 323–339). Worcester MA: Clark University Press.

Turner, C. H. (1906). A preliminary note on ant behavior. *Biological Bulletin, 12,* 31–36.

Turner, F. J. (1947). *The significance of the frontier in American history.* New York: Holt.

Turner, M. (1967). *Philosophy and the science of behavior.* New York: Appleton-Century-Crofts.

Turner, R. S. (1982). Helmholtz, sensory physiology, and the disciplinary development of German psychology. In W. R. Woodward & M. G. Ash (Eds.), *The problematic science: Psychology in nineteenth-century thought* (pp. 147–166). New York: Praeger.

Tweney, R. D. (1987). Programmatic research in experimental psychology: E. B. Titchener's laboratory investigations, 1891–1927. In M. G. Ash & W. R. Woodward (Eds.), *Psychology in twentieth-century thought and society* (pp. 35–57). Cambridge, England: Cambridge University Press.

Twitmyer, E. B. (1905). Knee-jerks without stimulation of the patellar tendon. *Psychological Bulletin, 2,* 43–44.

Urban, W. J. (1989). The black scholar and intelligence testing: The case of Horace Mann Bond. *Journal of the History of the Behavioral Sciences, 25,* 323–334.

Von Mayrhauser, R. T. (1989). Making intelligence functional: Walter Dill Scott and applied psychological testing in World War I. *Journal of the History of the Behavioral Sciences, 25,* 60–72.

Washburn, M. F. (1908). *The animal mind: A textbook of comparative psychology.* New York: Macmillan.

Washburn, M. F. (1932). Autobiography. In C. Murchison (Ed.), *A history of psychology in autobiography* (vol. 2, pp. 333–358). Worcester MA: Clark University Press.

Waterman, C. K., Buebel, M. E., & Waterman, A. S. (1970). Relationship between resolution of the identity crisis and outcomes of previous psychosocial crises.

Proceedings of the Annual Convention of the American Psychological Association, 5, 467–468.

Watson, J. B. (1903). *Animal education.* Chicago: University of Chicago.

Watson, J. B. (1907). Review of C. H. Turner, "A preliminary note on ant behavior." *Psychological Bulletin, 4*, 296–297.

Watson, J. B. (1908). Review of Pfungst's *Das Pferd des Herrn Von Osten. Journal of Comparative Neurology and Psychology, 18*, 329–331.

Watson, J. B. (1913). Psychology as the behaviorist views it. *Psychological Review, 20*, 158–177.

Watson, J. B. (1914). *Behavior: An introduction to comparative psychology.* New York: Holt.

Watson, J. B. (1916). The place of the conditioned reflex in psychology. *Psychological Review, 23*, 89–116.

Watson, J. B. (1919). *Psychology from the standpoint of a behaviorist.* Philadelphia: Lippincott.

Watson, J. B. (1925). *Behaviorism.* New York: Norton.

Watson, J. B. (1928). *Psychological care of the infant and child.* New York: Norton.

Watson, J. B. (1929). Behaviorism. *Encyclopedia Britannica* (vol. 3, pp. 327–329).

Watson, J. B. (1930). *Behaviorism* (rev. ed.). New York: Norton.

Watson, J. B. (1936). Autobiography. In C. Murchison (Ed.), *A history of psychology in autobiography* (vol. 3, pp. 271–281). Worcester MA: Clark University Press.

Watson, J. B., & McDougall, W. (1929). *The battle of behaviorism.* New York: Norton.

Watson, J. B., & Morgan, J. J. B. (1917). Emotional reactions and psychological experimentation. *American Journal of Psychology, 28*, 163–174.

Watson, J. B., & Rayner, R. (1920). Conditioned emotional reactions. *Journal of Experimental Psychology, 3*, 1–14.

Watson, R. (1978). *The great psychologists* (4th ed.). Philadelphia: Lippincott.

Wehr, G. (1987). *Jung: A biography.* Boston: Shambhala.

Wertheimer, Max (1912). Experimental studies of the perception of movement. *Zeitschrift für Psychologie, 61*, 161–265.

Wertheimer, Max (1938). Gestalt theory. In W. D. Ellis (Ed.), *A source book of Gestalt psychology* (pp. 1–11). London: Routledge & Kegan Paul.

Wertheimer, Max (1945). *Productive thinking.* New York: Harper.

Wertheimer, Michael (1978). Humanistic psychology and the humane but tough-minded psychologist. *American Psychologist, 33*, 739–745.

Wertheimer, Michael (1979). *A brief history of psychology* (2nd ed.). New York: Holt, Rinehart and Winston.

White, A. D. (1965). *A history of the warfare of science with theology in Christendom.* New York: Free Press. (Original work published 1896).

White, S. H. (1990). Child study at Clark University, 1894–1904. *Journal of the History of the Behavioral Sciences, 26*, 131–150.

Windholz, G. (1986). A comparative analysis of the conditional reflex discoveries of Pavlov and Twitmyer, and the birth of a paradigm. *Pavlovian Journal of Biological Science, 21*, 141–147.

Windholz, G. (1990). Pavlov and the Pavlovians in the laboratory. *Journal of the History of the Behavioral Sciences, 25*, 64–74.

Windholz, G., & Lamal, P. A. (1985). Köhler's insight revisited. *Teaching of Psychology, 12*, 165–167.

Witmer, L. (1896). Practical work in psychology. *Pediatrics, 2*, 462–471.

Wittels, F. (1924). *Sigmund Freud*. New York: Dodd, Mead.

Women in the American Psychological Association. (1986). Washington DC: Committee on Women in Psychology, American Psychological Association.

Woodworth, R. S. (1918). *Dynamic psychology*. New York: Columbia University Press.

Woodworth, R. S. (1921). *Psychology*. New York: Holt.

Woodworth, R. S. (1930). Dynamic psychology. In C. Murchison (Ed.), *Psychologies of 1930* (pp. 327–336). Worcester MA: Clark University Press.

Woodworth, R. S. (1938, 1954). *Experimental psychology*. New York: Holt.

Woodworth, R. S. (1943). The adolescence of American psychology. *Psychological Review, 50*, 10–32.

Woodworth, R. S. (1948). *Contemporary schools of psychology* (2nd ed.). New York: Ronald Press.

Woodworth, R. S. (1958). *Dynamics of behavior*. New York: Holt.

Wrightsman, L. S. (1981). Personal documents as data in conceptualizing adult personality development. *Personality and Social Psychology Bulletin, 7*, 367–385.

Wundt, W. (1858–1862). *Contributions to the theory of sensory perception*. Leipzig: Winter.

Wundt, W. (1863). *Lectures on the minds of men and animals*. Leipzig: Voss.

Wundt, W. (1873–1874). *Principles of physiological psychology*. Leipzig: Engelmann.

Wundt, W. (1888). Zur Erinnerung an Gustav Theodor Fechner. *Philosophische Studien, 4*, 471–478.

Wundt, W. (1896). *Outline of psychology*. Leipzig: Engelmann.

Wundt, W. (1900–1920). *Cultural psychology*. Leipzig: Engelmann.

Yerkes, R. M., & Morgulis, S. (1909). The method of Pavlov in animal psychology. *Psychological Bulletin, 6*, 257–273.

Young-Bruehl, E. (1988). *Anna Freud: A biography*. New York: Summit Books.

Zeigarnik, B. (1938). On finished and unfinished tasks. In W. D. Ellis (Ed.), *A source book of Gestalt psychology* (pp. 300–314). London: Routledge & Kegan Paul. (Original work published 1927.)

Index